Cornerstone on the Planning Court

Dedicated to our sorely missed friend and colleague

Peter Miller
1961–2013

Cornerstone on the Planning Court

Second Edition

General Editor
Michael Bedford, QC, Barrister

Contributors
Wayne Beglan BA (Hons), Barrister
Dr Ashley Bowes DPhil (Law), Barrister
Josef Cannon LLB (Hons), Barrister
Rowan Clapp BA (Hons) LLM (Dist), Barrister
Estelle Dehon BA (Hons) LLB (Wits) BCL MPhil (Oxon), Barrister
Edward Grant MA (Oxon), Barrister
Matt Hutchings QC, Barrister
James Findlay QC MA (Cantab), Barrister
John Fitzsimons LLB (Ling Franc), BCL (Oxon), Barrister
Dr Sam Fowles MA (Hons) DPhil (Law), Barrister
Robin Green LLB (Hons), Barrister
Emmaline Lambert LLB (Hons), Barrister
Matt Lewin BA (Hons), Barrister
Mark Lowe QC, Barrister
Jack Parker BA (Hons) MSt, Barrister
Clare Parry BA (Oxon), Barrister
Ruchi Parekh LLB (Hons) LLM (Harvard), Barrister
Paul Shadarevian QC, Barrister
Dr Alex Williams BA (Hons), MA (Cantab), MJur DPhil (Law), Barrister
Robert Williams LLB (Hons), Barrister

All members of Cornerstone Barristers, London.

Bloomsbury Professional

LONDON • DUBLIN • EDINBURGH • NEW YORK • NEW DELHI • SYDNEY

BLOOMSBURY PROFESSIONAL
Bloomsbury Publishing Plc
50 Bedford Square, London, WC1B 3DP, UK
1385 Broadway, New York, NY 10018, USA
29 Earlsfort Terrace, Dublin 2, Ireland

BLOOMSBURY and the Diana logo are trademarks of Bloomsbury Publishing Plc

Cover image courtesy of Charles Jones
fulfordtapestry.info
fulfordbattle.com
Cover image: a scene from the Fulford Tapestry. Fulford was the site of the first battle of the fateful autumn of 1066 that would spell the end of the Anglo-Saxon rule in England. The first hearing in the Planning Court was a judicial review of English Heritage's decision not to designate land at Germany Beck, York on the Battlefields Register as the site of the 1066 Battle of Fulford.

British Library Cataloguing-in-Publication Data

A catalogue record for this book is available from the British Library.

ISBN: PB: 978-1-52651-672-5
ePDF: 978-1-52651-675-6
ePub: 978-1-52651-673-2

Typeset by Evolution Design & Digital Ltd (Kent)

To find out more about our authors and books visit www.bloomsburyprofessional.com. Here you will find extracts, author information, details of forthcoming events and the option to sign up for our newsletters

Foreword

By
The Honourable Mr Justice Holgate

The Planning Court was established in 2014 by section II of Part 54 of the Civil Procedure Rules to handle planning claims for judicial review or statutory challenges in a 'specialist list'. The first edition of this work was published in 2015. Much has happened since then and the appearance of this new edition is both timely and welcome.

The Court's cases cover a wide compass: developments ranging from nationally important infrastructure projects to dwelling extensions, enforcement, environmental law, climate change, commons and village greens, highways and traffic regulation, and compulsory purchase. They give rise to issues which are often important and controversial. They may affect many parties: landowners, developers, neighbours, local communities, local authorities and public agencies. The public interest is engaged, sometimes at a national or international level.

Decision-making procedures determine the merits of the competing arguments in each case. The Court exists to deal solely with any public law issues that arise from those decisions and to do so as efficiently as possible, avoiding unnecessary delay.

Many of our key principles of public law were laid down in planning cases well before the Planning Court was created. Even with the considerable expansion of public law in other areas, that has continued to be the case. There is a healthy cross-fertilisation between these areas. Planning law should never be seen as an isolated subject. It is rooted in general principles of public law.

For example, much of the litigation in the Court has been concerned with either the interpretation of, or the application of, policies which are central to decision-making. On interpretation of policy, a matter ultimately for the Court, the seminal decision in *Tesco Stores v Dundee City Council*[1] flowed from *R (Raissi) v Secretary of State for the Home Department*,[2] a case on a compensation scheme for wrongful convictions.

On the other hand, application of policy generally involves the use of judgment. That is a matter for the decision-maker as part of his or her overall assessment of the planning merits of the case and subject to challenge in the Court only on *Wednesbury* grounds (a case on the licensing of films in cinemas on Sundays). This area of the law has recently been revisited by the Supreme Court in *R (Samuel Smith Old Brewery (Tadcaster) v North Yorkshire County Council*[3] and *R (Friends of the Earth Limited) v Heathrow Airport Limited*.[4]

1 [2012] UKSC 13.
2 [2008] EWCA Civ 72.
3 [2020] UKSC 3.
4 [2020] UKSC 52.

At the heart of this discussion, as in so many areas of public law, lie two of the fundamental foundations of our constitution: the rule of law and the separation of power between the courts, the legislature and the executive. These govern the Planning Court just as much as any other part of our legal system.

The interface between interpretation and application of policy illustrates the importance of these points very well. As Lord Justice Lindblom recently said in *R (Asda Stores Limited) v Leeds City Council*,[5] often the Court will be entitled to say that a policy 'simply means what it says' and requires no elaboration from a judge. It is a matter for the decision-maker to apply the language used in the policy with realism and good sense in the circumstances of each case. It is a matter of planning judgment.

In *Hopkins*[6] Lord Carnwath JSC had already highlighted the responsibility borne by parties and, by the same token, practitioners. He said: '... the judges are entitled to look to applicants, seeking to rely on matters of planning policy in applications to quash planning decisions (at local or appellate level), to distinguish clearly between issues of interpretation of policy, appropriate for judicial analysis, and issues of judgment in the application of that policy; and not to elide the two.'

The authors of this book are planning and public law specialists with an excellent understanding of these issues. They have a breadth and depth of experience which has enabled them to provide a clear and detailed analysis of the legal principles applied in the Planning Court, as well as its practice and procedure. They provide an invaluable reference source for all users of the Court to whom I commend it.

The Honourable Mr Justice Holgate

5 [2021] EWCA Civ 32.
6 [2017] UKSC 37.

Preface

The purpose of 'Cornerstone on the Planning Court' was succinctly described by Tom Cosgrove QC in his Preface to the first edition: '*a work... that could bring relevant material relating to the Planning Court together in a single book in a practical and useable way [so as] to provide a procedural and tactical guide to planning judicial review and related statutory challenges in the Planning Court.*'

That remains the purpose of this second edition. It is intended as a textbook that will prove useful to all potential users of the Planning Court, whether bringing, resisting, or otherwise participating in claims. It is also aimed at those who simply wish to understand the law and practice which is applied in a field which, because of the nature of the Planning Court's work, can have profound implications for individuals, communities, businesses, land owners, local authorities, statutory bodies, and other organisations.

In the six years since the publication of the first edition there has been a large volume of new case law (including several significant planning cases in the Supreme Court), as well as changes to primary and secondary legislation on both matters of procedure and matters of substance. It therefore seemed to me that an updated version of the original work was warranted in order to keep it relevant and up to date.

Tom Cosgrove QC, the general editor of the first edition, has taken up the challenge of becoming Joint Head of Chambers at Cornerstone Barristers, and so I took it upon myself to step into his previous shoes and marshal my colleagues within our Planning Team[1] to produce a second edition. I am very grateful to each of my co-contributors for all the hard work they put into that task, not least because they were doing so whilst coping with the rigours of professional and domestic life during the coronavirus pandemic and maintaining and adapting their practices to cope with our new ways of remote working. It is no cliché to say that without them this book would not exist.

The detailed editing of the results of their labours by the team at Bloomsbury Professional (assisted by the close proof reading by my younger son, Edward) makes my own role as general editor something of a misnomer. However, I am very happy to take credit for all errors and omissions in the final text. Whilst the bulk of the text was written during the summer of 2020 we have attempted to bring the work generally up to date to January 2021, notwithstanding the best efforts of the Court of Appeal to overwhelm us with new decisions.

At times during the gestation of the second edition it seemed as if the prospect of a 'hard' Brexit would require wholesale changes to those many aspects of the text influenced by European Directives or jurisprudence. Whatever the merits of such a 'clean break' in policy terms, at the more prosaic level of legal continuity it

1 Mark Lowe QC, who co-authored Chapter 1, retired from Chambers in the summer of 2020 after a distinguished 48 year career at the Bar, including involvement in many of the largest Inquiries and leading Planning cases.

has been reassuring to find that the post-Brexit legal landscape looks pretty much like the pre-Brexit legal landscape. The same is also true of the 'fundamental' reforms of the Planning White Paper (at least at the time of writing). However, even if the architecture within which planning decisions are to be made is subject to major reform, and even if the opportunities for legal challenge to those decisions are reduced consequent upon the Faulks review, there will remain a need to understand the business of the Planning Court and for its users to engage effectively with its procedural requirements and practices. This book is intended to assist in that task.

Lastly, I am very grateful that Mr Justice Holgate, as the Planning Liaison Judge, has kindly provided a new foreword for the second edition. The powerful points he makes there about the proper role of the Planning Court in relation to planning and environmental disputes will no doubt register with all potential users of the Court.

Michael Bedford QC
Cornerstone Barristers
2-3 Gray's Inn
London
February 2021

Contents

Foreword *v*
Preface *vii*
Table of Statutes *xv*
Table of Statutory Instruments *xix*
Table of Cases *xxiii*

1 LIFE BEFORE THE PLANNING COURT: A HISTORY OF THE COURT'S ROLE IN THE PLANNING SPHERE

A Introduction 1

B A historical overview of town and country planning to 1990 4

C The framework of the current scheme and its evolution 6
Forward planning 7
Decision making 10
Enforcement 14
Environmental regulation, human rights and conservation 14

D The demise of Planning 'exceptionalism'? 17

E The role of the Court 20

2 JURISDICTION AND PROCEDURES OF THE PLANNING COURT

A Introduction 25

B Jurisdiction 26
Planning Court claims 26
Judges of the Planning Court 29

C Planning Court procedures 30
Procedural rules 30
Significant Planning Court claims 31
Timetabling 32
Case management 34

D Venues 35

3 PREPARING AND PURSUING CLAIMS

A Introduction 38

B Pre-action conduct and the judicial review protocol 40
Pre-action conduct generally 40
Judicial review pre-action protocol 42
Pre-action disclosure 45

C	Preparing and issuing the claim	46
	Standing in judicial review planning challenges	46
	Local action groups	47
	Individuals as claimants	50
	Standing in statutory challenges	54
D	The provision of information about financial resources and Aarhus Convention claims	58
	Financial resources	58
	Aarhus Convention claims	59
E	Time limits, promptness and delay	62
	Calculating time for the purposes of issuing a claim	62
	Extending time	64
F	Issuing the claim	66
	Judicial review claims	67
	Statutory challenges	68
	Category of claim – 'significant' claims	71
G	Responding to an acknowledgment of service	72
H	Seeking permission to proceed	73
	Judicial review claims	73
	Statutory challenges	75
	The permission hearing	75
	Appealing the refusal of permission	76
I	Applications for interim relief	76
	Interim relief in judicial review claims	77
	Interim relief in statutory challenges	80
J	Case management	81
K	Settlement	83
L	The substantive hearing	83
	Case preparation	83
	The hearing	85
	Relief	85
	Costs	86
	Permission to appeal	86
	Appeals in the Court of Appeal and Supreme Court	87
4	**RESISTING CLAIMS**	
A	Introduction	88
B	Pre-action responses	89
C	Judicial review	92
	Practice Directions 54A, 54D, 54E	92
	Summary Grounds of Defence	92
	Interim orders: interim relief, striking out, disclosure	96
	Detailed grounds	99
	Evidence	100
	Substantive hearing	101

D Planning Statutory Reviews 101
Practice Directions 8C, 54D and 54E 102
AoS and Summary Grounds 104
Interim orders planning statutory reviews: interim relief, striking out, disclosure 105
The statutory six-week time period 107
Matters specific to challenges to development plans and other relevant documents (PCPA 2004, s 113) 109
Matters specific to challenges to the grant or refusal of planning permission and listed building consent (TCPA 1990, s 288 and P(LBCA)A 1990, s 63) 112

E Planning Statutory Appeals 115
Practice Directions 52D and 54D 115
Overlap between s288 and s289 TCPA 1990 117
Permission 118

F Compromise, consenting to judgment, redetermination 120

G Resisting claims in the Court of Appeal and Supreme Court 122

5 POWERS OF THE PLANNING COURT

A Planning Court Jurisdiction 125

B General Powers Of Case Management 126
The overriding objective 127
General powers relating to orders 127
Relief from sanctions 128
Remedying errors of procedure 128
Amendment of claim and substitution of parties 129
Striking out a statement of case 129
Protective costs orders 130
Transfer 131
Control of evidence 131
Inherent jurisdiction 132

C Case Management Of Judicial Review Claims 132
Permission to proceed 133
Delay 134
Urgent claims 136
Rolled up hearings 136
Disclosure 137

D Case Management Of Statutory Challenges 139
Applications to the High Court 139

E Interim Relief 142
Judicial review proceedings 142
Statutory challenges 146

F Final Relief 147
Judicial review claims 147
Statutory challenges 150

G Other Powers 150
Declarations of incompatibility 150

References to Europe 150
Contempt 151

6 COSTS

A Introduction 153

B General Principles Relating To Costs 153
Court's discretion and the general rule 153
Method of assessing the amount of costs 154
Basis of assessment 155
Relevance of conduct 155
Costs against non-parties 156
Partial success 158
Special methods of funding 158

C Judicial Reviews In The Planning Court – Costs At The Permission Stage 159
Where permission is granted 159
Where permission is refused 159

D Statutory Challenges In The Planning Court – Costs At The Permission Stage 161

E Costs Following Discontinuance/Consent To Relief 163
Discontinuance 163
Settled or withdrawn claims 163

F Costs Upon Final Determination 166
Exercise of discretion in judicial review/planning appeals 166
Multiple defendants and interested parties 167
Part 36 offers in judicial reviews 168
Interveners 168

G Protective Costs Orders And Cost Capping 169
Summary 169
Background and Corner House 169
Aarhus Convention: overview of relevant provisions 171
Aarhus Convention: application 172
The meaning of 'not prohibitively expensive' 173
Problems with using PCOs to achieve compliance with the Aarhus Convention: Commission v UK 174
Fixed costs regime under CPR Part 45 175
Problems with the fixed costs regime 177
Criminal Justice and Courts Act 2015: non-environmental cases 179
Criminal Justice and Courts Act 2015: environmental cases 182

H Conclusion 182

7 KEY LEGAL PRINCIPLES IN PLANNING COURT CLAIMS

A Introduction 185

B Grounds of challenge 186
Misinterpretation of policy 186
NPPF 188

	Material and immaterial considerations and s 70 Town and Country Planning Act 1990	194
	Reasons	195
	Procedural regularity	197
	Consistency of decisions	198
	Error of law	199
	Error of fact	200
	Rationality	201
	Legitimate expectation	202
	Procedural fairness	203
	Bias	205
	Duty to make inquiries	206
	Fettering discretion	207
C.	Approach taken by Court in challenges	208
	Challenges not reflecting way case put to Inspector/Council	208
	Council decision making	208
	Approach to Inspectors' decision letters	212
	Secretary of State's approach to Inspector's recommendations	214
	Improper purposes	214
D	Relief/discretion to quash	215
	Examples of refusal to quash	215
	Examples of refusing to exercise the discretion not to quash	216
	In European cases	217
E	Substantive issues	217
	Conditions	218
	Interpretation	218
	Condition/limitation distinction	219
	Grampian conditions	219
	Whitley conditions	219
	Section 106 agreements	219
	Community Infrastructure Levy	220
	Planning permissions	220
	Fallback	221
	General Permitted Development Order ('GPDO')	222
	Meeting full objectively assessed need	222
	Enforcement	222
	Green belt	222
	Heritage	224
	NPPF	225
	Alternative sites/schemes	226
	Consultee requests	227
	Reservoirs	227
	Village greens	227
	Commons	228
	Relationship with other regulatory regimes	228
	Local plans/neighbourhood plans	228
F	Human rights/equality	230
	Human Rights Act 1998	230
	Best interests of children	231
	Equality Act 2010	232

G	European legislation	232
	EIA	232
	Habitats Regulations	234
	Strategic Environmental Assessment/Sustainability Appraisal	236
H	Litigation procedure	237
	Statements of common ground	237
	Mitchell principles	237
	Time limits	238
	Pre-action letters	239
	Striking out	239
	Failure properly to complete claim form	239
	What can be challenged under s 288 or 289	240
	Judicially reviewing development plans in progress	240
	Cross examination	240
	Disclosure and the duty of candour	241
	Issue estoppel	241
	Totally without merit claims	242
	Alternative remedy	242
	Procedural exclusivity	243
I	Information	243
	Availability of relevant documents	243
	Viability assessments/confidential information	244
	Right to see draft s 106 agreements	244

Appendices

A	CPR Provisions	245
B	Practice Directions and Protocols	331
C	Forms	419

Index **453**

Table of Statutes

[References are to paragraph numbers]

Access to Justice Act 1999
s 51(1) 3.171
Acquisition of Land Act 1981
s 23 .... 3.54; 5.36, 5.43
(4) 3.80
24(1) 5.59
Administration of Justice Act 1969
s 12, 13, 15 .... 3.170
Business and Planning Act 2020 .... 1.12
Commons Registration Act 1965 .... 7.171
Constitutional Reform Act 2005
s 40(2), (6) 3.173
Contempt of Court Act 1981
s 14(1) 5.74
Criminal Justice and Courts Act
2015 .... 3.73, 3.167; 5.16, 5.66; 6.14, 6.28, 6.49, 6.69, 6.85, 6.99, 6.101
Pt 4 (ss 84–92) 3.66
s 85 .... 3.66
(1) 3.66; 5.23; 6.14
(2) 3.66; 6.14
86 .... 3.66
(1), (2) 3.66; 6.15
(3) 6.15
87 .... 6.47, 6.48
(5)–(8) 6.48
88 .... 3.69, 3.73; 5.16; 6.85, 6.87, 6.91
(2) 6.85
(3) 5.16; 6.88
(4) 3.69
(6) 5.16; 6.89, 6.91
(7) 6.90
(a) 6.93
(8) 6.92, 6.93
(9) 6.92
(12) 6.86
89 .... 3.69, 3.73; 5.16; 6.85, 6.87, 6.94, 6.100
(2) 6.95
90 .... 3.73; 5.16; 6.85, 6.87, 6.100, 6.101
91 .... 2.32, 2.33; 5.44
92(4) 4.17
(a)(ii) 4.47
Sch 16 .... 2.32; 5.44
para 8 .... 4.70
Enterprise and Regulatory Reform
Act 2013 .... 1.42
Equality Act 2010 .... 7.187
s 19(1) 7.188
European Union (Withdrawal) Act 2018
s 6(1)(b) 1.34, 5.73
Freedom of Information Act
2000 .... 3.18, 3.22; 4.36; 5.32
Green Belt (London and Home
Counties) Act 1938 .... 1.9
Growth and Infrastructure Act 2013 .... 1.12
Highways Act 1980
s 105D 3.54; 5.36, 5.43
(1) 3.80
Sch 2
para 2 .... 3.54, 3.80; 5.36, 5.43
Human Rights Act 1998 .... 1.12, 1.40; 7.178
s 4 .... 5.72
Interpretation Act 1978
Sch 1 .... 3.37, 3.63
Land Compensation Act 1973
s 33(2) 7.180
Local Government Act 1972 .... 7.246
s 100B 7.244
100D(5) 7.58
Localism Act 2011 .... 1.12
Minister of Town and Country
Planning Act 1943 .... 1.10
Planning Act 2008 .... 1.12; 4.17
s 13 .... 3.82
(1) 7.222
118 .... 3.82; 4.47
(1) 4.17
(b) 4.17
Planning and Compensation Act
1991 .... 1.12; 3.74
Planning and Compulsory Purchase
Act 2004 .... 1.12, 1.17, 1.20, 1.57; 3.74, 3.142
s 18, 19 .... 1.22
20(5) 1.22
33A 7.176
38(6) 1.16, 1.17, 1.29, 1.30, 1.31
37(3) 1.21
38(3) 1.21
(3A) 1.21
(6) 1.27; 7.15, 7.39, 7.40, 7.41, 7.122
113 .... 1.52, 1.59; 2.9, 2.33; 3.3, 3.54, 3.61, 3.97, 3.143; 4.48, 4.51, 4.58, 4.60, 4.61, 4.68, 4.69, 4.73, 4.74, 4.75; 5.36, 5.43, 5.44; 6.18, 6.28; 7.226

Planning and Compulsory Purchase Act 2004 – *contd*
s 113(1) 4.68
(3) 1.52
(3A) 4.70
(3B) 3.76; 4.63
(4) 4.70
(5) 3.142; 4.58; 5.59
(6) 4.75
(8) 3.142
(11) 4.70
Planning (Consequential Provisions) Act 1990 .... 5.26
Planning (Hazardous Substances) Act 1990 .... 1.12; 3.74, 3.145; 5.26
s 22 .... 2.33; 3.54, 3.97; 5.36, 5.43, 5.44
(2B) 3.76
(3)(a) 3.145
Planning (Listed Buildings and Conservation Areas) Act 1990 .... 1.12, 1.41; 3.74, 3.145; 4.17; 5.26
s 12 .... 7.124
39(3) 5.60
62(1) 4.76
(c) 4.76
63 .... 2.33; 3.54, 3.97; 4.48, 4.51, 4.76, 4.81, 4.82, 4.83; 5.36, 5.43, 5.44
(1) 4.76
(1A) 4.76
(3A) 3.76; 4.63
(4) 4.83
(a) 3.145
65 .... 2.34; 3.81, 3.105, 3.116, 3.124, 3.126, 3.127, 3.129; 4.110; 5.40, 5.44, 5.60
(3A) 5.60
(5) 4.85
66 .... 1.41; 7.162
(1) 7.160
72 .... 7.163
Public Health Act 1875 .... 1.9
Public Health Act 1936 .... 1.9
s 301 .... 3.59
Reservoirs Act 1975 .... 7.168
Restriction of Ribbon Development Act 1935 .... 1.9
Roads (Scotland) Act 1984 .... 3.56
Sch 2
para 2–4 .... 3.55
Road Traffic Regulation Act 1984
Sch 9
para 35 .... 3.80; 5.36
36(1)(a) 5.59
Senior Courts Act 1981
Pt II (ss 15–52) 5.1
s 19(2)(b) 5.21
Senior Courts Act 1981 – *contd*
s 29 .... 5.61
31 .... 3.167; 4.19; 5.24
(2) 5.46, 5.61
(2A) 3.167; 4.39; 5.64, 5.66
(2B) 3.167; 4.39; 5.66
(2C) 5.66
(3) 1.57; 3.27; 5.23; 6.14
(a) 5.23
(b) 3.66, 3.117; 5.23
(3A) 3.66; 6.14
(3B) 3.66; 6.14
(3C) 3.90, 3.110, 3.118, 3.123, 3.124; 4.18; 5.24
(3D), (3E) 3.90, 3.118, 3.123, 3.124; 5.24
(3F) 5.24
(4) 5.62, 5.66
(5), (5A) 5.63
(6) 3.166; 5.26, 5.27, 5.64, 5.65
33(2) 3.23; 5.35
37(1) 5.61
51 .... 6.13
(1) 6.5
Town and Country Planning Act 1947 .... 1.1, 1.8, 1.10, 1.11, 1.24, 1.30, 1.52
Town and Country Planning Act 1990 .... 1.1, 1.11, 1.12, 1.33, 1.44, 1.57; 3.74; 4.17; 5.26
s 28 .... 2.21
54A 1.16
55(1) 1.24
(2) 1.25
57 .... 1.24
(3) 1.25
61E 1.21
61N 3.82; 4.47
70 .... 7.43
(2) 1.16, 1.27
72 .... 1.42
73 .... 1.48
74 .... 1.42
77 .... 7.124
78 .... 2.9; 3.144; 7.55
79 .... 7.242
106 .... 1.30; 7.141, 7.142, 7.247
106C 3.82
Pt VII (ss 171A–196D) 1.33
s 171B 1.33, 1.50
(2) 1.51
171BA–171BC 1.51
174 .... 4.86, 4.87
(2)(a) 4.94, 4.96
175(4) 4.99; 5.60
177 .... 4.96
(1) 4.94

Town and Country Planning Act
1990 – *contd*
s 179(2) 2.9
187B 2.9
191 .... 1.33
284 .... 1.52, 1.59; 4.68
(1)(f) 3.106
(g) 4.76
(2) 3.144
(3) 3.144; 4.76
(e) 3.106; 4.94
(4) 4.76
285 .... 1.52, 1.59
286 .... 1.52
287 .... 1.52, 1.59; 2.33; 3.54, 3.97, 3.140; 4.48; 5.36, 5.39, 5.43, 5.44
(2) 1.52
(3) 3.140
(2B) 3.76
(3C) 3.140
288 .... 1.2, 1.52, 1.59; 2.9, 2.18, 2.24, 2.32, 2.33; 3.3, 3.10, 3.35, 3.54, 3.71, 3.88, 3.97, 3.106, 3.144; 4.48, 4.51, 4.61, 4.76, 4.77, 4.81, 4.82, 4.83, 4.84, 4.88, 4.89, 4.94, 4.95, 4.96; 5.36, 5.39, 5.43, 5.44; 6.18, 6.28, 6.70; 7.3, 7.101, 7.221, 7.222, 7.225, 8.242
(1) 3.106, 3.144
(1A) 4.48, 4.76
(4) 3.106, 3.144; 4.76, 4.94, 4.96

Town and Country Planning Act
1990 – *contd*
s 288(4B) 3.76; 4.63
(5) 4.83
(a) 3.144; 5.59
(6) 3.144
289 .... 1.2, 1.59; 2.9, 2.18, 2.24, 2.34; 3.81, 3.105, 3.106, 3.108, 3.116, 3.124, 3.126, 3.127, 3.129, 3.171; 4.84, 4.85, 4.86, 4.87, 4.90, 4.92, 4.94, 4.95, 4.96, 4.98, 4.99, 4.102, 4.103, 4.104, 4.105, 4.106, 4.110; 5.40, 5.44, 5.60; 6.18, 6.29, 6.30; 7.182, 7.225, 7.228
(1) 3.106; 4.87
(4A) 4.99; 5.60
(5A) 4.110
(6) 3.171; 4.110
336 .... 4.17; 5.26
(1) 5.26
Sch 4B 1.21
Transport and Works Act 1992 .... 1.12; 2.3; 3.97; 5.1
s 22 .... 3.54; 5.36, 5.43
(1) 3.79
(2)(a) 5.59
Wildlife and Countryside Act 1981
Sch 11
para 7 .... 3.54; 5.36, 5.43
(2) 3.80
Sch 15
para 12 .... 3.54; 5.36, 5.43
(1) 3.80

Table of Statutory Instruments

[*References are to paragraph numbers*]

Act of Sederunt (Rules of the Court of Session 1994) 1994, SI 1994/1443
r 58.8(2) 3.49
Act of Sederunt (Rules of the Court of Session Amendment No 5) (Public Interest Intervention in Judicial Review) 2000, SI 2000/317 .... 3.49
Civil Procedure (Amendment No 3) Rules 2019, SI 2019/1118 .... 3.72
Civil Procedure (Amendment) Rules 2017, SI 2017/95 .... 3.72
Civil Procedure Rules 1998, SI 1998/3132 .... 1.59; 2.8, 2.18; 3.20, 3.71, 3.72, 3.81, 3.105, 3.113, 3.150, 3.161; 4.2, 4.95, 4.97; 5.1, 5.3, 5.6, 5.7, 5.9, 5.14, 5.21; 6.14, 6.30, 6.33, 6.41, 6.49, 6.84
r 1.1(1), (2) 5.6
1.2 .... 5.7
1.4(1) 5.7
2.8(2), (3) 3.81
Pt 3 (rr 3.1–3.21) 4.66; 5.4, 5.21
3.1(1) 5.21
(2) 5.4
(a) 3.84, 3.105; 5.28, 5.40
(3) 5.8
(5), (6), (6A) 5.8
(7) 5.9
3.3(1) 5.5
3.4 .... 7.222
(2) 5.13
(a) 4.30
(3), (6), (7) 5.13
3.9(1) 5.10
3.10 .... 5.11, 5.40
PD 3A 5.13
PD 3C 5.13
r 7.1A 2.38
7.1B 2.38
Pt 8 (rr 8.1–8.9) 2.9, 2.18; 3.97, 3.98, 3.146; 4.2, 4.46, 4.48, 4.62, 4.70; 5.4, 5.13, 5.36, 5.37, 5.38, 5.59
r 8.1(6) 5.4, 5.36
8.2 .... 3.98; 5.37
(b)(ii) 3.146
8.3 .... 3.115; 4.54
(3) 4.54
8.4 .... 4.54
8.5 .... 4.62

Civil Procedure Rules 1998, SI 1998/3132 – *contd*
r 8.5(3), (4) 4.74
8.6 .... 4.62, 4.80
(1) 4.32
(2), (3) 5.20
PD 8A 2.35; 3.86, 3.97, 3.98, 3.101, 3.103, 3.115; 4.48; 5.4, 5.11
PD 8C 2.8, 2.18, 2.33; 3.97, 3.98, 3.100, 3.103, 3.114, 3.123, 3.123, 3.126; 4.48, 4.49, 4.50, 4.51, 4.54, 4.55, 4.62, 4.63, 4.72, 4.74; 5.36, 5.37, 5.39; 6.28
r 10.5 .... 4.54
Pt 17 (rr 17.1–17.4) 3.88, 3.150; 5.12
r 17.1(2) 4.94
Pt 19 (rr 19.1–19.15) 3.87; 5.12
r 19.4A 5.72
Pt 23 (rr 23.1–23.12) 3.130; 5.46
r 23.6 .... 3.146
23.12 .... 4.24, 4.31; 5.13, 5.25
Pt 24 (rr 24.1–24.6) 4.30
Pt 25 (rr 25.1–25.15) 3.130
r 25.1 .... 5.45
(1)(i) 3.23
25.2 .... 5.46
25.3 .... 5.46
PD 25A 5.46, 5.52
30.5(2) 2.11; 5.17
(3) 5.17
Pt 31 (rr 31.1–31.23) 4.62
r 31.1(2) 5.39
31.5 .... 5.39
31.12 .... 3.151; 5.33, 5.39
31.16 .... 3.23; 5.35, 5.39
32.1 .... 5.18
32.6 .... 3.146
(1) 3.146
Pt 36 (rr 36.1–36.30) 6.45
Pt 38 (rr 38.1–38.8) 6.32, 6.33
r 38.6 .... 6.32
39.2(3)(c) 6.76
Pt 44 (rr 44.1–44.18) 3.17; 6.4, 6.72
r 44.2 .... 6.16, 6.96
(1) 3.169; 6.5
(2) 3.169
(a) 6.6
(4) 6.5
(a) 6.10

Civil Procedure Rules 1998, SI 1998/3132 – *contd*
r 44.2(4)(b) ... 6.16
(6) ... 6.5
(a), (b) ... 6.6
44.4(1)(a), (b) ... 6.9
(3)(a)(i) ... 6.21
44.10(2)(a), (b) ... 6.19
PD 44 ... 6.7
Pt 45 (rr 45.1–45.47) ... 3.17; 6.49, 6.60, 6.61, 6.64, 6.65, 6.68, 6.69, 6.70, 6.77, 6.82, 6.83, 6.87, 6.99, 6.100
r 45.41 ... 3.68, 3.71, 3.72; 5.15
(2) ... 4.7; 6.83
(a) ... 3.72; 5.14; 6.70, 6.84
45.42 ... 3.68
(1) ... 3.73; 6.78
(a) ... 3.73
(2) ... 3.73
45.43 ... 3.68, 3.73; 4.7
(1) ... 5.14; 6.71
(2), (3) ... 6.71
(4) ... 6.74
45.44 ... 3.68, 3.73
(1) ... 6.75
(2)(a), (b) ... 6.75
(3)(b) ... 6.75
(5)–(7) ... 6.76
45.45 ... 3.68
(1) ... 6.78
(2) ... 3.73; 6.78
(3)(a), (b) ... 6.79
(5), (6) ... 6.76
PD 45 ... 5.14
Pt 46 (rr 46.1–46.15) ... 3.17
r 46.15 ... 6.48
46.17(1) ... 6.97
(iv) ... 6.98
(2), (3) ... 6.97
46.18 ... 6.98
46.19(1), (3) ... 6.99
PD 46 ... 6.97
Pt 47 (rr 47.1–47.17) ... 3.17; 6.7
Pt 48 (rr 48.1–48.6A) ... 3.17
PD 51Y ... 3.16
Pt 52 (rr 52.1–52.21) ... 2.18; 3.105; 4.46, 4.111; 5.4, 5.40
r 52.1(4) ... 4.110
52.3 ... 3.170
(2) ... 3.170
52.5 ... 4.111
52.6 ... 3.170
52.7 ... 3.171
52.8 ... 3.121, 3.128, 3.150; 5.12
(2) ... 3.92
(3), (5), (6) ... 3.128

Civil Procedure Rules 1998, SI 1998/3132 – *contd*
r 52.10 ... 3.123, 3.128
(5), (6) ... 5.13
52.13 ... 5.40
(2)(b) ... 5.40
52.20 ... 5.4
52.21(1), (3) ... 3.172
52.25 ... 5.41
52.28 ... 4.85
(1), (3) ... 4.85
52.30 ... 3.128
PD 52A ... 3.154, 3.161, 3.170; 4.111
PD 52C ... 4.111
PD 52D ... 2.18, 2.34, 2.35; 3.81, 3.86, 3.105, 3.116, 3.124, 3.126, 3.127; 4.57, 4.85, 4.88, 4.90, 4.91, 4.92, 4.93, 4.105, 4.111; 5.4, 5.40, 5.41, 5.42, 5.70; 6.29
PD 52E ... 2.15
Pt 54 (rr 54.1–54.36) ... 2.8, 2.18; 3.94; 4.13, 4.48; 5.4; 6.20
r 54.5 ... 3.77, 3.94; 5.22, 5.26
(A1) ... 3.74; 4.17
(1) ... 3.74, 3.92, 3.121
(b) ... 5.27, 5.28
(2) ... 3.84, 3.92, 3.121
(4) ... 3.74
(5) ... 3.74; 4.5, 4.17; 5.28
54.6(1)(c) ... 3.134, 3.146
(2) ... 3.94
54.7 ... 3.94; 5.22
(1)(b) ... 3.138
54.8 ... 5.22; 6.11, 6.24
(1) ... 3.110
(2) ... 3.110; 4.31
(a) ... 3.113, 3.138; 4.16
(4)(a) ... 4.16
(i) ... 3.110
(ia) ... 3.110; 4.18
(ii) ... 3.110; 4.22
(b) ... 3.110; 4.22
54.9 ... 4.22
(1)(a) ... 6.11
(2) ... 6.11
54.10 ... 5.22
(2) ... 3.92
(a) ... 3.137; 5.54
54.11 ... 5.22
54.11A ... 3.119; 5.24
54.12 ... 3.120; 5.22
(3) ... 4.24
(4) ... 3.120
(7) ... 3.92, 3.121; 4.24, 4.31; 5.25
54.13 ... 4.37
54.14 ... 2.24; 3.108, 3.155, 3.156; 5.22
(1) ... 4.38, 4.40

Civil Procedure Rules 1998, SI 1998/3132 – *contd*
r 54.15 .... 3.112, 3.150; 5.12
54.16(1) 4.32
54.19 .... 5.63
Pt 54 Pt II (rr 54.21–54.24) 2.2, 2.3, 2.8, 2.18
r 54.21 .... 2.8; 5.17
(1) 2.7
(2) 1.12; 2.3, 2.8; 5.1
(a) 2.5, 2.8
(i) 2.6, 2.10
(ii)–(viii) 2.6
(ix) 2.11
(b) 2.5, 2.6
54.22(1) 2.4; 5.17
(2) 2.3, 2.4
(3) 2.15, 2.16
54.23 .... 2.18; 5.3
PD 54A 3.94, 3.112, 3.117, 3.126, 3.150, 3.152, 3.159, 3.160; 4.13, 4.14, 4.24, 4.26, 4.44, 4.108; 5.12, 5.22, 5.28, 5.29; 6.23, 6.24
PD 54D 2.6, 2.35, 2.36, 2.37; 4.13, 4.14, 4.45, 4.48, 4.50, 4.88, 4.92
PD 54E 2.2, 2.6, 2.18, 2.19, 2.20, 2.22, 2.24, 2.28, 2.31, 2.34; 3.94, 3.108, 3.109, 3.115, 3.116, 3.133, 3.138; 4.13, 4.15, 4.23, 4.48, 4.50; 5.3, 5.22, 5.38, 5.40
Pt 68 (rr 68.1–68.5) 5.73
PD 68 .... 5.73
Pt 81 (rr 81.1–81.38) 5.74
PD 81 .... 5.74
Community Infrastructure Levy Regulations 2010, SI 2010/948 4.11
reg 40(7) 7.143
122 .... 4.11
Conservation of Habitats and Species Regulations 2017, SI 2017/1012 .... 1.12
Criminal Justice and Courts Act 2015 (Disapplication of Sections 88 and 89) Regulations 2017, SI 2017/100 3.69
reg 2 .... 6.87, 6.100
Environmental Assessment of Plans and Programmes Regulations 2004, SI 2004/1633 .... 1.12
Environmental Information Regulations 2004, SI 2004/3391 .... 3.18, 3.22; 4.36; 5.32; 7.237
Rules of the Supreme Court 1965, SI 1965/1776
Order 53 .... 3.27, 3.28
Supreme Court Rules 2009, SI 2009/1603 .... 4.112
PD 3 .... 4.112
Town and Country Planning (Consultation) (England) Direction 2009 .... 4.17
Town and Country Planning (Development Management Procedure) (England) Order 2015, SI 2015/595 .... 1.12
Town and Country Planning (Development Management Procedure) (Wales) Order 2012, SI 2012/801 .... 1.12
Town and Country Planning (Environmental Impact Assessment) Regulations 2017, SI 2017/571 .... 1.12, 1.35
Sch 1 .... 1.35
Sch 2 .... 1.35
Town and Country Planning (General Permitted Development) Order 1995, SI 1995/418 .... 1.12
Town and Country Planning (General Permitted Development) (England) Order 2015, SI 2015/596 .... 1.12; 3.74
Sch 2 .... 1.25
Town and Country Planning (Local Planning) (England) Regulations 2012, SI 2012/767
reg 2 .... 1.21
5 .... 1.21
Town and Country Planning (Use Classes) Order 1987, SI 1987/764 .... 1.12, 1.26

Table of Cases

[*References are to paragraph numbers*]

A

A4 Metal Recycling v Secretary of State for Communities & Local Government [2014] EWHC 2524 (Admin) 7.101, 7.117, 7.149
AXA General Insurance Ltd v HM Advocate; AXA General Insurance, Petrs [2011] UKSC 46, [2012] 1 AC 868, [2011] 3 WLR 871 .... 3.49, 3.50, 3.51
Abramovich v Hoffman [2019] EWHC 509 (Ch), [2019] 2 WLUK 621 .... 3.92
Agecrest v Gwynedd CC [1998] JPL 325, [1996] NPC 106 1.46
Aireborough Neighbourhood Development Forum v Leeds City Council [2020] EWHC 45 (Admin), [2020] 1 WLR 2355, [2020] 1 WLUK 32 ... 3.37, 3.63; 6.84
Aireborough Neighbourhood Development Forum v Leeds City Council [2020] EWHC 1461 (Admin), [2020] 6 WLUK 81 .... 7.55
Aldergate Properties Ltd v Mansfield DC [2016] EWHC 1670 (Admin), [2016] 7 WLUK 178 .... 7.23
Alfred McAlpine Homes (Yorkshire) Ltd v Kirklees Metropolitan Council (2000) 79 P & CR 352 .... 4.58, 4.59
Allan v City of London Corpn *see* R v City of London Corpn, ex p Allan (1981) JPL 685, 79 LGR 223
Al-Rawi v Security Service [2011] UKSC 34, [2012] 1 AC 531, [2011] 3 WLR 388.. 5.21
Alwoodly Golf Club v Leeds CC *see* R (on the application of Alwoodly Golf Club) v Leeds CC
American Cyanamid Co v Ethicon Ltd (No 1) [1975] AC 396, [1975] 2 WLR 316, [1975] 1 All ER 504 .... 3.135; 4.28; 5.46, 5.57
Arora Management Services Ltd v Hillingdon LBC [2019] EWHC 1945 (Ch), [2019] 7 WLUK 628, [2019] 5 CMLR 24 .... 2.6, 2.16
Arsenal FC v Secretary of State for Communities & Local Government [2014] EWHC 2620 (Admin) 7.119
Arsenal FC Ltd v Smith (Valuation Officer) [1979] AC 1, [1977] 2 WLR 974, [1977] 2 All ER 267 .... 3.58
Arun District Council v Secretary of State for Communities & Local Government [2013] EWHC 190 (Admin), [2013] JPL 1011 .... 4.84
Asda Stores v Leeds City Council *see* R (on the application of Asda Stores Ltd) v Leeds CC
Ashbridge Investments Ltd v Minister of Housing & Local Government [1965] 1 WLR 1320, [1965] 3 All ER 371, (1965) 129 JP 580 .... 3.2
Ashdown Forest Economic Development LLP v Secretary of State for Communities & Local Government [2014] EWHC 406 (Admin), [2014] 2 WLUK 714, [2015] Env LR D1; rev'sd [2015] EWCA Civ 681, [2016] PTSR 78, [2015] 7 WLUK 310 .... 7.199, 7.202
Associated Provincial Picture Houses Ltd v Wednesbury Corpn [1948] 1 KB 223, [1947] 2 All ER 680, (1947) 63 TLR 623 .... 1.31; 3.2; 7.95, 7.196, 7.204
Austin v Miller Argent (South Wales) Ltd [2014] EWCA Civ 1012, [2015] 1 WLR 62, [2015] 2 All ER 524 .... 6.51, 6.61

B

BDW Trading Ltd (t/a Barratt Homes) v Cheshire West & Chester BC [2014] EWHC 1470 (Admin) 7.175
BDW Trading Ltd (t/a David Wilson Homes (Central Mercia & West Midlands)) v Secretary of State for Communities & Local Government [2016] EWCA Civ 493, [2017] PTSR 1337, [2016] 5 WLUK 659 .... 7.42
Barker v Hambleton DC [2012] EWCA Civ 610, [2013] PTSR 41, [2013] 1 P & CR 1 .... 3.79, 3.86; 4.70; 5.11

Barker Mill Estates v Test Valley BC & Secretary of State for Housing, Communities & Local Government [2016] EWHC 3028 (Admin), [2017] PTSR 408, [2016] 11 WLUK 666........ 2.26; 4.108; 7.10, 7.234
Barlow (on behalf of Harthill Against Fracking) v Secretary of State for Housing, Communities & Local Government [2019] EWHC 146 (QB), [2019] 1 WLUK 348, [2019] JPL 707........ 7.83
Baroness Cumberlege v Secretary of State for Housing, Communities & Local Government *see* DLA Delivery Ltd v Baroness Cumberlege of Newick
Barwood Strategic II LLP v East Staffordshire BC; East Staffordshire BC v Secretary of State for Communities & Local Government [2017] EWCA Civ 893, [2018] PTSR 88, [2017] 6 WLUK 670........ 7.3
Bates v Maldon DC *see* R (on the application of Bates) v Maldon DC
Beg v Luton BC [2017] EWHC 3435 (Admin), [2017] 12 WLUK 86, [2018] CTLC 75........ 2.9
Begum v Tower Hamlets London BC [2003] UKHL 5, [2003] 2 AC 430, [2003] 2 WLR 388........ 3.2; 5.2
Behrman v Secretary of State for the Environment [1979] JPL 677........ 4.80
Belize Alliance of Conservation Non-Governmental Organisations v Department of Environment (Interim Injunction) [2003] UKPC 63, [2003] 1 WLR 2839, [2004] Env LR 16........ 3.135, 3.136; 5.32, 5.49, 5.52, 5.53
Belize Alliance of Conservation Non-Governmental Organisations v Department of the Environment [2004] UKPC 6, [2004] Env LR 38........ 4.33
Belmont Riding Centre v Secretary of State for the Environment, Transport & the Regions [2001] PLCR 12, [2001] JPL 734 (Note), (2000) 97 (41) LSG 41...... 4.62; 5.39
Benson (Juliet) v Secretary of State for Housing, Communities & Local Government [2018] EWHC 2354 (Admin), [2018] 9 WLUK 186........ 7.228
Berkeley v Secretary of State for the Environment, Transport & the Regions (No 1) [2001] 2 AC 603, [2000] 3 WLR 420, [2000] 3 All ER 897.......... 1.38; 3.166; 4.83; 5.64
Berkeley v Secretary of State for the Environment [2000] UKHL 36........ 1.57
Binning Property Corpn Ltd v Secretary of State for Housing, Communities & Local Government [2019] EWCA Civ 250, [2019] 2 WLUK 472, [2019] JPL 844........ 3.129; 4.98; 7.182
Bland v Chief Supplementary Benefit Officer [1983] 1 WLR 262, [1983] 1 All ER 537, (1983) 127 SJ 53........ 4.98
Bloor Homes East Midlands Limited v Secretary of State for Communities & Local Government, Hinckley and Bosworth Borough Council [2014] EWHC 754 (Admin)........ 1.28; 3.2; 7.3
Bolton MDC v Secretary of State for the Environment (Costs) [1995] 1 WLR 1176, [1996] 1 All ER 184, (1995) 71 P & CR 309........ 4.52, 4.93; 6.42
Bond v Vale of White Horse DC *see* R (on the application of Bond) v Vale of the White Horse DC
Botton v Secretary of State for the Environment (1991) 3 Admin LR 848, [1992] 1 PLR 1, [1992] JPL 941........ 4.86
Bovale Ltd v Secretary of State for Communities & Local Government [2008] EWHC 2143 (Admin), [2009] CP Rep 6, [2009] ACD 30........ 2.32
Bovale Ltd v Secretary of State for Communities & Local Government [2009] EWCA Civ 171, [2009] 1 WLR 2274, [2009] 3 All ER 340........ 5.21, 5.37
Bown v Secretary of State [2003] EWCA Civ 1170, [2004] Env LR 26, [2004] 2 P & CR 7........ 1.57; 4.83, 4.101
Bramshill v Secretary of State for Housing, Communities & Local Government [2019] EWHC 3437 (Admin)........ 7.162
Brent LBC v Secretary of State for Housing, Communities & Local Government [2019] EWHC 1399 (Admin), [2019] 6 WLUK 107, [2019] JPL 1473........ 7.67
Brien v Secretary of State for the Environment & Bromley London BC [1995] JPL 523........ 5.39
Brightwell v Secretary of State for the Environment (1997) 73 P & CR 418, [1997] 2 PLR 38, [1996] EG 170........ 5.12

Brink's-MAT Ltd v Elcombe [1988] 1 WLR 1350, [1988] 3 All ER 188, [1989] 1 FSR 211 .... 3.131; 5.58
British Gas Trading Ltd v Oak Cash & Carry Ltd [2016] EWCA Civ 153, [2016] 1 WLR 4530, [2016] 4 All ER 129 .... 5.10
British Union for the Abolition of Vivisection (BUAV) v Secretary of State for the Home Department [2014] EWHC 43 (Admin), [2014] ACD 69 .... 3.23; 5.21, 5.35
Britannia Assets (UK) Ltd v Secretary of State for Communities & Local Government [2011] EWHC 1908 (Admin) 4.87
Britaniacrest Recyling Ltd v Secretary of State for Communities & Local Government [2015] EWHC 1019 (Admin) 7.117
Button v Jenkins [1975] 3 All ER 585, 74 LGR 48, (1975) 119 SJ 697 .... 4.86

C

Cala Homes (South) Ltd v Chichester DC (Time Limits) [2000] CP Rep 28, (2000) 79 P & CR 430, [1999] 4 PLR 77 .... 4.61, 4.66
Cala Homes (South) Ltd v SOSCLG [2010] EWHC 3278 (Admin), [2011] JPL 553, [2011] 1 EG 65 .... 3.132, 3.137; 5.54
Campaign to Protect Rural England v Herefordshire Council *see* R (on the application of Campaign to Protect Rural England) v Herefordshire Council
Campaign to Protect Rural England – Kent Branch v Secretary of State for Housing, Communities & Local Government [2019] EWCA Civ 1230, [2020] 1 WLR 352, [2019] 7 WLUK 206 .... 4.51, 4.52; 6.20, 6.22, 6.28, 6.41, 6.71, 6.73
Campaign to Protect Rural England Surrey v Waverley BC [2018] EWHC 2969 (Admin), [2018] 11 WLUK 30, [2019] JPL 379; aff'd [2019] EWCA Civ 1826, [2019] 10 WLUK 467, [2020] JPL 505 .... 6.76; 7.55, 7.91
Canterbury City Council v Secretary of State for Communities & Local Government *see* Gladman Developments Ltd v Canterbury CC
Capel Parish Council v Surrey County Council [2009] EWHC 350 (Admin), [2009] JPL 1302, [2009] All ER (D) 48 (Mar) 4.75
Cash v Secretary of State for Communities & Local Government [2012] EWHC 2908 (Admin), [2012] 10 WLUK 634, [2013] JPL 420 .... 3.124; 7.182
Cash v Secretary of State for Communities & Local Government [2015] EWHC 2357 (Admin), [2015] 8 WLUK 28 .... 7.186
Cash v Wokingham BC [2014] EWHC 3748 (Admin), [2014] 10 WLUK 789 .... 7.197, 7.241
Caswell v Dairy Produce Quota Tribunal for England & Wales *see* R v Dairy Produce Quota Tribunal for England & Wales, ex p Caswell [1990] 2 AC 738, [1990] 2 WLR 1320, [1990] 2 All ER 434
Catesby Estates Ltd v Secretary of State for Housing, Communities & Local Government [2018] EWCA Civ 1697 .... 7.159
Cheshire East Council v Secretary of State for Communities & Local Government [2014] EWHC 3536 (Admin), [2015] Env LR 10 .... 7.200, 7.219
Chichester DC v Secretary of State for the Environment & Hall Aggregates (South Coast) [1981] JPL 591 .... 4.81
City & Council Bramshill Ltd v Secretary of State for Housing, Communities & Local Government [2019] EWHC 3819 (Admin), [2019] 12 WLUK 636 .... 7.14, 7.22
Clarke v Secretary of State for the Environment (1993) 65 P & CR 85, [1992] 3 PLR 146, [1992] 42 EG 100 .... 4.102
Coates v Secretary of State for Communities & Local Government [2017] EWCA Civ 940, [2017] 7 WLUK 115 .... 4.61; 5.13; 7.222
Commercial Estates Group Ltd v Secretary of State for Communities & Local Government [2014] EWHC 3089 (Admin) 7.236
Commercial Land Ltd v Secretary of State for Transport, Local Government & the Regions [2002] EWHC 1264 (Admin), [2002] 5 WLUK 853, [2003] JPL 358 .... 1.49
Commission v Germany (Case C-137/14) 4.19
Commission of the European Communities v Ireland (Case C-427/07) [2009] ECR I-6277, [2011] 3 CMLR 46, 2010] Env LR 8 .... 6.59

Compton Parish Council v Guildford BC [2019] EWHC 3242 (Admin), [2019] 12 WLUK 59, [2020] JPL 661 .... 1.58; 7.27, 7.33, 7.55
Connolly v Havering LBC *see* R (on the application of Connolly) v Havering LBC
Connors v Secretary of State for Communities & Local Government [2014] EWHC 2358 (Admin), [2015] JPL 196 .... 7.157, 7.180, 7.184, 7.186, 7.242
Cook v Southend-on-Sea BC [1990] 2 QB 1, [1990] 2 WLR 61, [1990] 1 All ER 243 3.59
Cooper Estates Strategic Land Ltd v Royal Tonbridge Wells BC [2017] EWHC 224 (Admin), [2017] 2 WLUK 368 .... 7.55
Copas v Secretary of State for Communities & Local Government [2014] EWHC 2634 (Admin), [2015] JPL 83 .... 7.117
Corus UK Ltd v Erewash BC [2006] EWCA Civ 1175, [2006] CP Rep 41, [2007] 1 P & CR 22 .... 5.40
Cotswold Grange Country Park LLP v Secretary of State for Communities & Local Government [2014] EWHC 1138 (Admin), [2014] JPL 981 .... 7.136
Covent Garden Community Association Ltd v Greater London Council (1981) JPL 183 .... 3.28
Coyle v Secretary of State for Communities & Local Government [2008] EWHC 2466 (Admin) 4.61
Cran v Camden LBC; R v Camden LBC, ex p Cran [1995] RTR 346, 94 LGR 8 .. 3.149; 5.20
Crane v Secretary of State for Communities & Local Government [2015] EWHC 425 (Admin) 7.177
Croke v Secretary of State for Communities & Local Government [2019] EWCA Civ 54, [2019] PTSR 1406, [2019] 2 WLUK 11 .... 3.83, 3.86; 4.17, 4.65; 7.215
Crondall Parish Council v Secretary of State for Housing Communities & Local Government; Canterbury City Council v Secretary of State for Housing, Communities & Local Government [2019] EWHC 1211 (Admin), [2019] 5 WLUK 225, [2019] JPL 1321 .... 3.73; 6.83; 7.67

D

DB Symmetry Ltd v Swindon BC [2020] EWCA Civ 1331, [2020] 10 WLUK 164 .... 7.135
DLA Delivery Ltd v Baroness Cumberlege of Newick [2018] EWCA Civ 1305 (Admin), [2018] PTSR 2063, [2018] 6 WLUK 129 .... 7.60, 7.69, 7.94
DW Trading Ltd v Secretary of State for Housing, Communities & Local Government [2016] EWCA Civ 493 .... 1.29
Dacorum BC v Purcell [2009] EWHC 742 (QB) 4.61
Dartford BC v Secretary of State for Communities & Local Government *see* Walsall MBC v Secretary of State for Communities & Local Government [2013] EWCA Civ 370, [2013] JPL 1183 .... 4.98
Daventry DC v Secretary of State for Communities & Local Government [2016] EWCA Civ 1146, [2016] 11 WLUK 616, [2017] JPL 402 .... 7.18
Davey v Aylesbury Vale DC [2007] EWCA Civ 1166, [2008] 1 WLR 878, [2008] 2 All ER 178 .... 6.20, 6.40
Davies v Hammersmith & Fulham LBC (1981) JPL 682 .... 3.28
Day (Peter) v Shropshire Council *see* R (on the application of Day) v Shropshire Council
Dear v Secretary of State for Communities & Local Government [2015] EWHC 29 (Admin) 7.128, 7.186
Denton v TH White Ltd [2014] EWCA Civ 906, [2014] 1 WLR 3926, [2015] 1 All ER 880 .... 5.10
Deutsche Bank AG v Sebastian Holdings Inc [2016] EWCA Civ 23, [2016] 4 WLR 17, [2016] 1 WLUK 376 .... 6.13
Dignity Funerals v Breckland DC [2017] EWHC 1492 (Admin), [2017] 6 WLUK 503 .... 1.29; 6.41
Dill v Secretary of State for Housing, Communities & Local Government [2020] UKSC 20, [2020] 1 WLR 2206, [2020] 4 All ER 631 .... 7.159
Dinedor Hill Action Association v County of Herefordshire DC [2008] EWHC 1741 (Admin), [2009] 1 P & CR 4, [2008] NPC 90 .... 5.39

Djurberg v Secretary of State for Housing, Communities & Local Government [2014] EWHC 4137 (Admin), [2014] 12 WLUK 493 .... 7.147
Dover DC v Campaign to Protect Rural England (Kent) [2017] UKSC 79, [2018] 1 WLR 108, [2018] 2 All ER 121 .... 7.48, 7.50, 7.89
Dulgheriu v Ealing LBC [2018] EWHC 1302 (Admin), [2018] 5 WLUK 472, [2018] ACD 73 .... 6.51
Dymocks Franchise Systems (NSW) Pty Ltd v Todd (Costs) [2004] UKPC 39, [2004] 1 WLR 2807, [2005] 4 All ER 195 .... 6.13

E

E v Secretary of State for the Home Department [2004] EWCA Civ 49, [2004] QB 1044, [2004] 2 WLR 1351 .... 7.68
EC Commission v UK (Case C-530/11) [2014] QB 988, [2014] 3 WLR 853, [2014] 3 CMLR 6 .... 3.136; 6.65
Earl Shilton Action Group v Hinckley & Bosworth BC [2014] EWHC 1764 (Admin) 7.103
East Dunbartonshire Council v Secretary of State for Scotland 1999 SLT 1088, 1999 SCLR 396, [1999] 1 PLR 53 .... 1.46
East Hertfordshire DC v Doherty [2019] EWHC 2292 (QB), [2019] 9 WLUK 76 .... 2.9
East Northamptonshire DC v Secretary of State for Communities & Local Government [2014] EWCA Civ 137, [2015] 1 WLR 45, [2014] 1 P & CR 22 .... 1.41
Eco-Energy (GB) Ltd v First Secretary of State [2004] EWCA Civ 1566, [2005] 2 P & CR 5, [2005] 2 PLR 33 .... 3.86, 3.87, 3.88; 4.61, 4.67; 5.11, 5.12
Ecotricity v Secretary of State for Communities & Local Government [2015] EWHC 801 (Admin) 7.70, 7.125, 7.129
Elghanian v Secretary of State for Housing, Communities & Local Government [2018] EWHC 4073 (Admin), [2018] 4 WLUK 728 .... 4.85, 4.93
Elghanian v Secretary of State for Housing, Communities & Local Government (unreported, 18 April 2018) 6.28, 6.30
Ensign Group Ltd v First Secretary of State [2006] EWHC 255 (Admin), [2006] 2 P & CR 19 .... 4.75
Equiom (Isle of Man) Ltd v London Borough of Croydon [2014] EWHC 3660 (Admin) 7.246
Evans v First Secretary of State [2003] EWCA Civ 1523, [2004] Env LR 17, (2003) 147 SJLB 1306 .... 4.30
Evans v Secretary of State for Communities & Local Government [2014] EWHC 4111 (Admin), [2015] JPL 589 .... 7.151
Eweida v British Airways plc [2009] EWCA Civ 1025, [2010] CP Rep 6, [2010] 1 Costs LR 43 .... 6.51

F

FCC Environment v (1) Secretary of State for Communities & Local Government (2) East Riding of Yorkshire Council [2014] EWHC 2035 (Admin) 7.117, 7.138
FG Whitley & Sons v Secretary of State for Wales (1992) 64 P & CR 296, [1992] 3 PLR 72, [1992] JPL 856 .... 1.47
F Hoffman La Roche & Co AG v Secretary of State for Trade & Industry [1975] AC 295, [1974] 3 WLR 104, [1974] 2 All ER 1128 .... 4.84
Fidler v First Secretary of State [2004] EWCA Civ 1295, [2005] 1 P & CR 12, [2005] JPL 510 .... 1.26
Finn-Kelcey v Milton Keynes BC [2008] EWCA Civ 1067, [2009] Env LR 17, [2009] JPL 493 .... 3.1, 3.84; 5.28
Flattery v Secretary of State for Communities & Local Government [2010] EWHC 2868 (Admin) 3.149; 4.80; 5.20
Flaxby Park Ltd v Harrogate BC [2020] EWHC 3204 (Admin), [2020] 11 WLUK 373 .... 3.95; 4.78
Flynn v Southwark LBC [2019] EWHC 3575 (Admin), [2019] 12 WLUK 416 .... 7.69
Forest of Dean Friends of the Earth v Forest of Dean District Council [2014] EWHC 1353 (Admin) 7.195

Forge Field Society v Sevenoaks DC *see* R (on the application of Forge Field Society) v Sevenoaks DC
Fuller v Secretary of State for Communities & Local Government [2015] EWHC 142 (Admin) 7.118, 7.121
Freemont (Denbigh) Ltd v Welsh Ministers [2016] EWHC 482 (Admin) 4.31
Friends of the Earth Ltd v Secretary of State for Housing, Communities & Local Government *see* R (on the application of Friends of the Earth Ltd) v Secretary of State for Housing, Communities & Local Government

G

Gallagher Homes Ltd v Solihull MBC [2014] EWHC 1283 (Admin), [2014] JPL 1117 .... 7.156
Gare v Babergh DC [2019] EWHC 2041 (Admin) 7.40, 7.51, 7.57
Geogas SA v Trammo Gas Ltd (The Baleares) [1991] 1 WLR 776, [1991] 3 All ER 554, [1991] 2 Lloyd's Rep 318 .... 4.98
George v Secretary of State for the Environment (1979) 77 LGR 689, (1979) 38 P & CR 609, (1979) 250 EG 339 .... 4.80
Gerber v Wiltshire Council *see* R (on the application of Gerber) v Wiltshire Council
Gerber v Wiltshire Council [2015] EWHC 524 (Admin), [2015] 3 WLUK 162, [2015] Env LR 33 .... 7.160
Gill v Secretary of State for the Environment & North Warwickshire DC [1985] JPL 710 .... 3.106
Gill v Secretary of State for Communities and Local Government [2015] EWHC 2660 (Admin), [2015] 9 WLUK 489, [2016] JPL 262 .... 1.29
Gladman Developments Ltd v Canterbury CC [2019] EWCA Civ 669, [2019] PTSR 1714, [2019] 4 WLUK 346 .... 7.6, 7.42
Gladman Developments Ltd v Secretary of State for Housing, Communities & Local Government [2019] EWHC 127 (Admin), [2019] PTSR 1302, [2019] 1 WLUK 248 .... 7.18
Gladman Developments Ltd v Daventry DC *see* Daventry DC v Secretary of State for Communities & Local Government
Gladman Developments Ltd v Secretary of State for Communities & Local Government [2019] EWCA Civ 1543, [2020] PTSR 128, [2019] 9 WLUK 330 .... 7.34, 7.82
Gladman Developments Ltd v Secretary of State for Housing, Communities & Local Government [2020] EWHC 518 (Admin), [2020] PTSR 993, [2020] 3 WLUK 99 [2021] EWCA Civ 104 .... 3.93; 4.27; 7.10, 7.19
Gladman Developments Ltd v Secretary of State for Housing, Communities & Local Government [2019] EWHC 2001 (Admin), [2019] 7 WLUK 376, [2020] Env LR 7 .... 1.39; 7.194
Gladman Development Ltd v Wokingham BC [2014] EWHC 2320 (Admin), [2014] PTSR D24 .... 7.175
Glover v Secretary of State for the Environment (1982) 44 P & CR 359, [1981] JPL 110 .... 4.81
Goodson v HM Coroner for Bedfordshire & Luton [2006] C Rep 6, [2005] EWCA Civ 1172, [2006] CP Rep 6, [2005] Inquest LR 175 .... 6.51
Grand Union Investments Ltd v Dacorum BC [2014] EWHC 1894 (Admin) 7.175, 7.202, 7.204
Greater London Council v Secretary of State for the Environment, ex p Harrow LBC [1985] JPL 868 .... 3.59
Great Hadham Country Club Ltd v Secretary of State for Housing, Communities & Local Government [2019] EWHC 1203 (Admin), [2019] 4 WLUK 222, [2019] JPL 1075 .... 4.107, 4.108
Greaves v Boston BC [2014] EWHC 3590 (Admin), [2014] All ER (D) 03 (Dec) 3.149; 5.20, 5.23; 7.135, 7.228
Gregory v Turner [2003] EWCA Civ 183, [2003] 1 WLR 1149, [2003] 2 All ER 1114 .... 3.92

Griffiths v Secretary of State for the Environment [1983] 2 AC 51, [1983] 2 WLR 172, [1983] 1 All ER 439 .... 3.78, 3.81; 4.64
Guinness v Secretary of State for Communities & Local Government [2014] EWHC 4114 (Admin) 7.121

H

HJ Banks & Co Ltd v Secretary of State for Housing, Communities & Local Government [2018] EWHC 3141 (Admin), [2019] PTSR 668, [2018] 11 WLUK 388 .... 7.63
Hall v City of Bradford MDC *see* R (on the application of James Hall & Co Ltd) v City of Bradford MDC
Hamilton v Secretary of State for Scotland 1972 SC 72, 1972 SLT 233 .... 4.65
Hanily v Minister of Local Government & Planning [1951] 2 KB 917, [1951] 2 All ER 749, (1951) 115 JP 547 .... 5.12
Harrogate BC v Secretary of State for Communities & Local Government [2014] EWHC 1506 (Admin) 3.10, 3.11; 5.11, 5.40; 7.213, 7.218, 7.221
Havering LBC v Stokes [2019] EWHC 3006 (QB), [2019] 9 WLUK 131 .... 2.9
Heard v Broadland District Council [2012] EWHC 344, [2012] Env LR 23, [2012] PTSR D25 .... 7.201
Heathrow Hub Ltd, Runway Innovations Ltd v Secretary of State for Transport *see* R (on the application of Heathrow Hub Ltd) v Secretary of State for Transport
Hertfordshire CC v Secretary of State for Communities & Local Government [2012] EWCA Civ 1473, [2013] JPL 560 .... 1.26
Hillside Parks Ltd v Snowdonia National Park Authority [2020] EWCA Civ 1440, [2020] 11 WLUK 8 .... 7.145
Hinde v Rugby BC [2011] EWHC 3684 (Admin), [2012] JPL 816 .... 4.61, 4.70
Hollis v Secretary of State for the Environment (1984) 47 P & CR 351, (1983) 265 EG 476, [1983] JPL 164 .... 4.81
Hook v Secretary of State for Housing, Communities & Local Government [2020] EWCA Civ 486, [2020] 4 WLUK 49, [2020] JPL 1260 .... 7.82
Hopkins Developments Ltd v Secretary of State for Housing, Communities & Local Government [2014] EWCA Civ 470, [2014] PTSR 1145, [2014] 4 WLUK 586 .... 7.79
Hopkins Homes Ltd v Secretary of State for Communities & Local Government [2017] UKSC 37 .... 7.42
Horsham District Council v Secretary of State for Communities & Local Government [2015] EWHC 109 (Admin), [2015] PTSR D16 .... 7.165
Hossain v Secretary of State for the Home Department *see* R (on the application of W) v Secretary of State for the Home Department
Howard v Wigan MBC [2014] EWHC 4296 (Admin), [2015] Env LR D5 .... 7.190
Howell v Secretary of State for Communities & Local Government [2014] EWHC 3627 (Admin) 7.117, 7.133, 7.147
Hunt v North Somerset Council [2015] UKSC 51, [2015] 1 WLR 3575, [2016] 1 All ER 95 .... 3.166

I

IRC v National Federation of Self-Employed & Small Businesses Ltd [1981] AC 617 .... 3.27, 3.28; 5.23
Ikram v Secretary of State for Housing, Communities & Local Government [2019] EWHC 1869 (Admin), [2019] 7 WLUK 266 .... 7.69
I'm Your Man Ltd v Secretary of State for the Environment, Transport & the Regions (1999) 77 P & CR 251, [1998] 4 PLR 107, [1999] PLCR 109 .... 7.136
Ioannou v Secretary of State for Communities & Local Government [2014] EWCA Civ 1432, [2015] 1 P & CR 10 .... 4.79; 5.19
Islam v Secretary of State for Communities & Local Government [2012] EWHC 1314 (Admin) [2012] JPL 1378 .... 3.106; 5.11
Islington LBC v Secretary of State for Housing, Communities & Local Government [2019] EWHC 2691 (Admin), [2019] 10 WLUK 263, [2020] JPL 532 .... 2.9; 7.67

J

JB Trustees Ltd v Secretary of State for Communities & Local Government [2013] EWHC 3555 (Admin), [2014] JPL 656, [2013] 48 EG 124 (CS).............. 5.43
Jackson v Secretary of State for Communities & Local Government [2015] EWHC 20 (Admin), [2015] 2 P & CR 8, [2015] JPL 830.................... 1.33; 7.153
Jackson v Secretary of State for Communities & Local Government [2015] EWCA Civ 1246, [2016] QB 811, [2016] 2 WLR 1407............................ 1.51
Jarmain v Secretary of State for the Environment, Transport & the Regions (No 2) [2001] EWHC Admin 1140, [2002] 1 PLR 105, [2002] 3 EG 124 (CS).. 4.95, 4.96; 5.11
Jayes v Flintshire CC [2018] EWCA Civ 1089, [2018] 5 WLUK 246, [2018] ELR 416 .... 7.92, 7.186
Johnson v Windsor & Maidenhead RBC [2019] EWHC 160 (Admin), [2019] 2 WLUK 5.......... 2.9; 7.69
Jones v Secretary of State for Wales (1995) 70 P & CR 211, [1995] 2 PLR 26, (1995) 159 LG Rev 689 .... 3.149; 4.80; 5.20
Jones v Welsh Assembly Government [2008] EWHC 3515 (Admin).......................... 5.69
Jopling v Richmond-Upon-Thames LBC [2019] EWHC 190 (Admin), [2019] 2 WLUK 93, [2019] JPL 830.......... 7.59

K

Kaur v S Russell & Sons Ltd [1973] 1 QB 336.......... 4.65
Keep Bourne End Green v Buckinghamshire Council (formerly Wycombe DC) [2020] EWHC 1984 (Admin), [2020] 7 WLUK 372, [2021] JPL 181.............. 7.20, 7.57
Kemball v Secretary of State for Communities & Local Government *see* R (on the application of Kemball) v Secretary of State for Communities & Local Government
Kendall v Rochford DC [2014] EWHC 3866 (Admin), [2015] Env LR 21........... 3.166; 5.64; 7.131, 7.208
Kensington & Chelsea RLBC v Secretary of State for the Environment [1992] 2 PLR 116, [1993] JPL 139 .... 3.124; 4.56, 4.97
Kent CC v Secretary of State for the Environment & Burmah-Total Refineries Trust (1977) 33 P & CR 70, 75 LGR 452, [1976] JPL 755 .... 4.83
Kenyon v Secretary of State for Housing, Communities & Local Government [2020] EWCA Civ 302, [2020] 3 WLUK 47, [2021] Env LR 8.......... 7.190
Kerry v Secretary of State for Housing, Communities & Local Government [2020] EWHC 908 (Admin), [2020] 3 WLUK 541.......... 7.82
Khan v Secretary of State for the Home Department [2018] EWCA Civ 1684, [2018] 7 WLUK 360, [2019] Imm AR 54.......... 6.36
Kingswood DC v Secretary of State for the Environment [1987] 7 WLUK 181, (1989) 57 P & CR 153, [1988] JPL 248 .... 4.84
Kirklees MBC v Wickes Building Supplies Ltd [1993] AC 227, [1992] 3 WLR 170, [1992] 3 All ER 717.......... 5.52
Kuznetsov v Secretary of State for Housing, Communities & Local Government [2017] EWHC 2713 (Admin), [2017] 9 WLUK 398.......... 7.88

L

Lambeth LBC v Secretary of State for Housing, Communities & Local Government [2019] UKSC 33, [2019] 1 WLR 4317, [2019] 4 All ER 981 .... 1.48
Lane v Esdaile [1891] AC 210.......... 4.98
Lark Energy Ltd v Secretary of State for Communities & Local Government [2014] EWHC 2006 (Admin) 7.119, 7.120, 7.149
Law v Essex County Council [2015] EWHC 329 (Admin), [2015] 2 WLUK 533....... 7.103, 7.128
Law Society of England & Wales v Legal Services Commission [2010] EWHC 2550 (Admin), [2010] 9 WLUK 523, [2011] Costs LR Online 57.......... 3.85
Lawrence v Fen Tigers Ltd; Coventry (t/a RDC Promotions) v Lawrence [2014] UKSC 13, [2014] AC 822, [2014] 2 WLR 433.......... 5.48
Leach, Re [2001] EWHC Admin 445, [2001] CP Rep 97, [2001] 4 PLR 28 .... 6.20

Lenlyn Ltd v Secretary of State for the Environment (1984) 50 P & CR 129, [1985] JPL 482, (1985) 82 LSG 358 .... 4.87
Lesoochranárske Zoskupenie VLK v Ministerio Životného Prostresia Slovenskei Republicky (Case C-240/09) [2012] QB 606, [2012] 3 WLR 278, [2012] PTSR 822 .... 6.61
Lisle-Mainwaring v Kensington & Chelsea RBC [2015] EWHC 1814 (Admin), [2015] 4 WLUK 459 .... 3.143; 4.28
Lochailort Investments Ltd v Mendip DC *see* R (on the application of Lochailort Investments Ltd) v Mendip DC
Lochailort Investments Ltd v Secretary of State for Communities & Local Government [2014] EWHC 3358 (Admin) 5.46
London & Henley (Middle Brook Street) Ltd v Secretary of State for Communities & Local Government [2013] EWHC 4207 (Admin) 2.26
London Parachuting Ltd v Secretary of State for the Environment [1986] JPL 428 .... 4.103
Lough v First Secretary of State [2004] EWCA Civ 905, [2004] 1 WLR 2557, [2005] 1 P & CR 5, [2004] 1 WLR 2557 .... 1.40
Lovejoy v Secretary of State for the Environment, Transport & the Regions (1999) 78 P & CR 1, [1999] JPL 441 .... 4.102

M

McLennan v Medway Council *see* R (on the application of McLennan) v Medway Council
Main v Swansea City Council [1984] 7 WLUK 289, (1985) 49 P & CR 26, [1985] JPL 558 .... 3.28
Mansell (Michael) v Tonbridge & Malling BC [2017] EWCA Civ 1314, [2019] PTSR 1452, [2017] 9 WLUK 111 .... 7.66, 7.103
Manydown Co Ltd v Basingstoke & Deane BC [2012] EWHC 977 (Admin), [2012] JPL 1188, [2012] 17 EG 111 (CS) 1.59; 4.68
Marshall v Deputy Governor of Bermuda [2010] UKPC 9 .... 5.32
Martin v Folkestone & Hythe DC *see* R (on the application of Martin) v Folkestone & Hythe DC
Masri v Consolidated Contractors International Co SAL [2011] EWHC 1024 (Comm), [2011] 5 WLUK 98 .... 5.74
Mass Energy Ltd v Birmingham City Council [1994] Env LR 298 .... 5.23
Matthews v Secretary of State for the Environment, Transport & the Regions [2001] EWHC Admin 815, [2002] 2 P & CR 34, [2002] JPL 716 .... 4.65
Maugham v Uber London Ltd [2019] EWHC 391 (Ch), [2020] STC 496, [2019] 2 WLUK 620 .... 6.51
Mawbey v Lewisham LBC *see* R (on the application of Mawbey) v Lewisham LBC
Mayor of London v Secretary of State for Housing, Communities & Local Government [2020] EWHC 1176 (Admin), [2020] 5 WLUK 109, [2020] JPL 1387 .... 1.4; 7.80
Memory Corpn plc v Sidhu (No 2) [2000] 1 WLR 1443, [2000] CPLR 171, [2000] FSR 921 .... 3.131; 5.58
Mendip DC v Secretary of State for the Environment & Castle Housing Society [1993] JPL 434, [1993] COD 274, [1992] EG 156 (CS) 4.66
Miaris v Secretary of State for Communities & Local Government [2015] EWHC 2094 (Admin), [2015] 1 WLR 4333, [2015] 7 WLUK 604 .... 3.17; 4.110
Miller v Weymouth & Melcombe Regis Corpn (1974) 27 P & CR 468, (1974) 118 SJ 421 .... 4.83
Mills v Secretary of State for Housing, Communities & Local Government [2019] EWHC 3476 (Admin), [2019] 12 WLUK 247 .... 7.5, 7.9, 7.62
Mitchell v News Group Newspapers Ltd [2013] EWCA Civ 1537, [2014] 1 WLR 795, [2014] 2 All ER 430 .... 5.10
Monkhill Ltd v Secretary of State for Housing, Communities & Local Government [2019] EWHC 1993 (Admin), [2021] EWCA Civ 74, [2020] PTSR 416, [2019] 7 WLUK 371 .... 7.15, 7.33

Moore v Secretary of State for Communities & Local Government [2016] EWHC 2736 (Admin), [2016] 11 WLUK 65, [2016] ACD 135 (Admin) . 7.98
Moore v Secretary of State for Communities & Local Government [2015] EWHC 44 (Admin), [2015] JPL 762, [2015] PTSR D14 .... 7.182, 7.188
Moore v Secretary of State for Communities & Local Government [2014] EWHC 3592 (Admin), [2015] ACD 44 .... 7.123
Mordue v Secretary of State for Communities & Local Government [2015] EWHC 539 (Admin) 7.160, 7.162
Morgan v Hinton Organics (Wessex) Ltd [2009] EWCA Civ 107, [2009] CP Rep 26, [2009] Env LR 30 .... 5.15; 6.59, 6.61
Morge v Hampshire CC [2010] EWCA Civ 150, [2010] Env LR 31 .... 3.132
Mulvenna v Secretary of State for Communities & Local Government [2015] EWHC 3494 (Admin), [2015] 12 WLUK 176, [2016] JPL 487 .... 1.59

N

NWL Ltd v Woods (The Nawala) (No 2) [1979] 1 WLR 1294, [1979] 3 All ER 614, [1980] 1 Lloyd's Rep 1 .... 5.49
National Commercial Bank Jamaica Ltd v Olint Corpn Ltd [2009] UKPC 16, [2009] 1 WLR 1405, [2009] Bus LR 1110 .... 5.51, 5.53
Naylor v Essex County Council [2014] EWHC 2560 (Admin), [2015] JPL 217 .... 7.170
Newbury DC v Secretary of State for the Environment [1981] AC 578, [1980] 2 WLR 379, [1980] 1 All ER 731 .... 1.30
Newbury DC v Secretary of State for the Environment (1988) 55 P & CR 100, [1988] JPL 460, [1988] JPL 185 .... 4.106
No Adastral New Town Ltd v Suffolk Coastal DC [2015] EWCA Civ 88, [2015] 2 WLUK 532, [2015] Env LR 28 .... 7.202
Norman v Secretary of State for Housing Communities & Local Government [2019] EWHC 2910 (Admin), [2018] 11 WLUK 7, [2019] Env LR 14 .... 3.61
North Cote Farms Ltd v Secretary of State for Communities & Local Government [2015] EWHC 292 (Admin) 7.122
North Norfolk DC v Secretary of State for Housing, Communities & Local Government [2018] EWHC 2076 (Admin), [2018] 8 WLUK 18, [2019] JPL 87 . 4.84
Nottingham City Council v Calverton Parish Council [2015] EWHC 503 (Admin), [2015] All ER (D) 44 (Mar) 4.17, 4.61, 4.70; 5.11; 7.217

O

O'Connor v Secretary of State for Communities & Local Government [2014] EWHC 3821 (Admin) 7.125
Okolo v Secretary of State for the Environment [1997] 4 All ER 242, [1997] JPL 1009, [1998] COD 8 .... 3.80; 4.64
O'Reilly v Mackman [1983] 2 AC 237, [1982] 3 WLR 1096, [1982] 3 All ER 1124 .... 3.1, 3.149; 5.20
Oxford City Council v Secretary of State for Communities & Local Government [2007] EWHC 769 (Admin), [2007] 2 P & CR 29, [2007] LLR 403 .... 4.94
Oxfordshire County Council v Secretary of State for Communities & Local Government [2015] EWHC 186 (Admin), [2015] JPL 846, [2015] PTSR D24 ... 7.142

P

Pagham Parish Council v Arun DC [2019] EWHC 1721 (Admin), [2019] 7 WLUK 39 .... 7.57, 7.159
Palmer v Herefordshire Council *see* R (on the application of Palmer) v Herefordshire Council
Paul Newman Homes v Secretary of State for Housing, Communities & Local Government [2019] EWHC 2367 (Admin), [2020] PTSR 434, [2019] 9 WLUK 73, [2021] EWCA Civ 15 .... 7.12, 7.16, 7.17
Peak Park Joint Planning Board v Secretary of State for the Environment (1979) 39 P & CR 361, [1980] JPL 114 .... 4.83

Peel Investments (North) v Secretary of State for Housing, Communities & Local Government [2019] EWHC 2143 (Admin), [2020] PTSR 503, [2019] 8 WLUK 7 .... 7.17, 7.21
People Over Wind v Coillte Teoranta (Case C-323/17) [2018] PTSR 1668, [2018] 4 WLUK 111, [2018] Env LR 31 .... 1.39
Persimmon Homes (Thames Valley) Ltd v Stevenage BC [2005] EWCA Civ 1365, [2006] 1 WLR 334, [2006] 1 P & CR 31 .... 4.72
Petter (James) v EMC Europe Ltd [2015] EWCA Civ 480, [2015] 4 WLUK 178 .... 3.147
Pioneer Aggregates (UK) Ltd v Secretary of State for the Environment [1985] AC 132, [1984] 3 WLR 32, [1984] 2 All ER 358 .... 1.45
Plant v Lambeth LBC *see* R (on the application of Plant) v Lambeth LBC
Porter v McGill [2001] UKHL 67, [2002] 2 AC 357, [2002] 2 WLR 37 .... 7.85, 7.87
Prashar v Secretary of State for the Environment, Transport & the Regions [2001] EWCA Civ 1231, [2001] 3 PLR 116 .... 3.129
Pugh v Secretary of State for Communities & Local Government [2015] EWHC 3 (Admin) 7.121

R

R v Board of Visitor of Hull Prison, ex p St Germain (No 2) [1979] 1 WLR 1401, [1979] 3 All ER 545, [1979] Crim LR 726 .... 3.149; 5.20
R v Chichester DC, ex p Kirdford Conservation Society [1998] 4 WLUK 356, [1999] JPL 374 .... 1.59
R v Chief Constable of Merseyside Police, ex p Calveley [1986] QB 424, [1986] 2 WLR 144, [1986] 1 All ER 257 .... 5.23
R v City of London Corpn, ex p Allan (1981) JPL 685, 79 LGR 223 .... 3.28
R v Cornwall CC, ex p Huntingdon [1992] 3 All ER 566, [1992] COD 223, (1992) 142 NLJ 348 .... 4.65
R v Cotswold DC, ex p Barrington Parish Council (1998) 75 P & CR 515, [1997] EG 66 (CS), [1997] NPC 70 .... 5.23
R v Criminal Injuries Compensation Board, ex p A [1999] 2 AC 330, [1999] 2 WLR 974, [1999] COD 244 .... 5.31
R v Dairy Produce Quota Tribunal for England & Wales, ex p Caswell; Caswell v Dairy Produce Quota Tribunal for England & Wales [1990] 2 AC 738, [1990] 2 WLR 1320, [1990] 2 All ER 434 .... 5.26, 5.65
R v Darlington BC, ex p Association of Darlington Taxi Owners; Belize Alliance of Conservation Non-Governmental Organisations v Department of the Environment of Belize [1994] COD 424 .... 3.136; 5.52, 5.56
R v Derbyshire County Council, ex p Woods [1997] 2 WLUK 148, [1998] Env LR 277, [1997] JPL 958 .... 1.44; 5.23
R v F, S, G & W [2013] EWCA Crim 84, [2013] 2 WLUK 278 .... 3.92
R v Secretary of State for Foreign & Commonwealth Affairs, ex p World Movement Ltd [1995] 1 WLR 386, [1995] 1 All ER 611, [1994] 11 WLUK 148 .... 3.45; 5.23
R v Hammersmith & Fulham LBC, ex p People Before Profit Ltd (1983) 45 P & CR 364, 80 LGR 322, [1981] JPL 869 .... 3.28, 3.29
R v Inspectorate of Pollution, ex p Greenpeace (No 1) [1994] 1 WLR 570, [1994] 4 All ER 329, [1993] 9 WLUK 15 .... 1.57; 3.136, 3.137; 5.56
R v Lancashire CC, ex p Huddleston [1986] 2 All ER 941, (1986) 136 NLJ 562 .... 4.32
R v Leicestershire CC, ex p Blackfordby & Boothorpe Action Group [2001] Env LR 2, [2000] EHLR 215, [2000] JPL 1266 .... 3.33, 3.36
R v London Docklands Development Corpn, ex p Frost (1997) 73 P & CR 199 .... 3.85
R v Lord Chancellor, ex p Child Poverty Action Group [1999] 1 WLR 347, [1998] 2 All ER 755, [1998] COD 267 .... 6.50
R v North Hertfordshire DC, ex p Sullivan [1981] JPL 752 .... 3.28
R v North Somerset DC & Pioneer Aggregates UK Ltd, ex p Garnett & Pierrsenne [1998] Env LR 91, [1997] JPL 1015 .... 3.39, 3.41
R v Secretary of State for the Home Department, ex p Ruddock [1987] 1 WLR 1482, [1987] 2 All ER 518, (1987) 113 SJ 1550 .... 3.85

R v Secretary of State for Education & Science, ex p Avon County Council (No 2) [1991] 1 QB 558, [1991] 2 WLR 702, [1991] 1 All ER 282 .... 3.137; 5.54
R v Secretary of State for the Environment, Transport & the Regions, ex p National Farmers' Union (unreported, 24 November 1999).. 5.11
R v Secretary of State for the Environment, ex p Kent (1989) 57 P & CR 431, [1988] 3 PLR 17, [1988] JPL 706 .... 3.86
R v Secretary of State for the Environment, ex p Kirkstall Valley Campaign Ltd [1996] 3 All ER 304, [1997] 1 PLR 8, [1996] JPL 1042.................................. 3.32, 3.62
R v Secretary of State for the Environment, ex p Ostler [1977] QB 122, [1976] 3 WLR 288, [1976] 3 All ER 90 .... 3.86; 4.65; 5.11
R v Secretary of State for the Environment, ex p Rose Theatre Trust Co [1990] 1 QB 504, [1990] 2 WLR 186, [1990] 1 All ER 754............. 1.57; 3.30, 3.31, 3.32, 3.34
R v Secretary of State for the Environment, ex p The Royal Society for the Protection of Birds (RSPB) [1997] Env LR 431, (1995) 7 Admin LR 434, (1995) 139 SJLB 86.. 5.57
R v Secretary of State for the Environment, Transport & the Regions, ex p Alconbury Developments Ltd *see* R (on the application of Alconbury Developments Ltd) v Secretary of State for the Environment, Transport & the Regions
R v Secretary of State for the Home Department, ex p Muboyayi [1992] QB 244, [1991] 3 WLR 442, [1991] 4 All ER 72 .... 3.137; 5.54
R v Secretary of State for Trade & Industry, ex p Eastaway *see* R (on the application of Eastaway) v Secretary of State for Trade & Industry
R v Secretary of State for Transport, ex p Factortame Ltd (No 2) [1991] 1 AC 603, [1990] 3 WLR 818, [1991] 1 All ER 70 .... 4.29; 5.46, 5.53
R v Secretary of State for Trade & Industry, ex p Trades Union Congress [2001] 1 CMLR 8 .... 5.57
R v Secretary of State for Wales, ex p Rozhon [1994] COD 111, 91 LGR 667, [1993] NPC 72... 3.126; 4.93; 6.29, 6.30
R v Servite Houses, ex p Goldsmith (interim relief) (2000) [2000] 5 WLUK 415, (2000) 3 CCL Rep 354.. 5.52
R v Somerset CC, ex p Dixon [1998] Env LR 111, (1998) 75 P & CR 175, [1997] JPL 1030... 1.57; 3.40, 3.46; 5.23
R v Stroud DC, ex p Goodenough, Usborne & Tomlin (1980) 43 P & CR 59, [1982] JPL 246.. 3.28
R v Westminster City Council, ex p Ermakov [1996] 2 All ER 302, [1996] 2 FCR 208, (1996) 28 HLR 819 .... 5.19
Residents against Waste Site Ltd v Lancashire CC [2007] EWHC 2558 (Admin) [2008] Env LR 27, [2008] JPL 644.. 3.35
River Thames Society v First Secretary of State [2006] EWHC 2829 (Admin), [2007] JPL 782, (2006) 150 SJLB 1253 .... 3.59, 3.88; 4.67; 5.12
R (on the application of A) v Secretary of State for Communities & Local Government [2011] EWCA Civ 1253, [2012] JPL 579........................... 5.11, 5.13, 5.37
R (on the application of Advearse) v Dorset Council [2020] EWHC 807 (Admin), [2020] 4 WLUK 78 .... 5.67
R (on the application of Alconbury Developments Ltd) v Secretary of State for the Environment, Transport & the Regions [2001] UKHL 23, [2003] 2 AC 295, [2001] 2 WLR 1389 .... 1.57; 3.2; 5.2
R (on the application of Al-Sweady) v Secretary of State for Defence [2009] EWHC 2387 (Admin), [2010] HRLR 2, [2010] UKHRR 300 ... 3.149; 4.32; 5.20
R (on the application of Alwoodly Golf Club) v Leeds CC [1995] 9 WLUK 94, [1995] NPC 149 .... 3.37
R (on the application of Archway Sheet Metal Works) Ltd v Secretary of State for Communities & Local Government [2014] EWHC 4450 (Admin)...................... 5.39
R (on the application of Asda Stores Ltd) v Leeds CC [2019] EWHC 3578 (Admin), [2020] PTSR 874, [2019] 12 WLUK 421 .... 7.24
R (on the application of Ash Parish Council) v Guildford BC [2014] EWHC 3864 (Admin)... 7.103, 7.128

R (on the application of Association of British Civilian Internees (Far East Region)) v Secretary of State for Defence [2003] EWCA Civ 473, [2003] QB 1397, [2003] 3 WLR 80 ..... 3.37
R (on the application of Bahta) v Secretary of State for the Home Department [2011] EWCA Civ 895, [2011] CP Rep 43, [2011] 5 Costs LR 857 ..... 6.35
R (on the application of Bancoult) v Secretary of State for Foreign & Commonwealth Affairs [2012] EWHC 2115 (Admin) 4.45
R (on the application of Bates) v Maldon DC [2018] EWHC 3421 (Admin), [2018] 11 WLUK 110; aff'd [2019] EWCA Civ 1272, [2019] 7 WLUK 334 ..... 7.36, 7.57, 7.64
R (on the application of Beety) v Nursing & Midifery Council [2017] EWHC 3579 (Admin), [2017] 6 WLUK 235 ..... 6.90, 6.92, 6.93, 6.94
R (on the application of Ben Hoare Bell Solicitors) v Lord Chancellor [2015] EWHC 523 (Admin) 4.26
R (on the application of Berky) v Newport City Council [2012] EWCA Civ 378, [2012] 2 CMLR 44, [2012] Env LR 35 ..... 1.57; 3.80; 5.26, 5.27, 5.28
R (on the application of Bertoncini) v Hammersmith & Fulham LBC (unreported, 2 June 2020) 6.77
R (on the application of Bishop's Stortford Civic Federation) v East Hertfordshire DC [2014] EWHC 348 (Admin), [2014] PTSR 1035, [2014] BLGR 161 ..... 1.57
R (on the application of Blue Green London Plan) v Secretary of State for the Environment, Food & Rural Affairs [2015] EWHC 495 (Admin) 3.79; 4.17, 4.47
R (on the application of Bond) v Vale of the White Horse DC [2019] EWHC 3080 (Admin), [2020] PTSR 724, [2019] 11 WLUK 244 ..... 7.77
R (on the application of Boxall) v Waltham Forest LBC (2000) 4 CCL Rep 258, [2010] LLR 1 ..... 6.35
R (on the application of British Union for the Abolition of Vivisection) v Secretary of State for the Home Department [2006] EWHC 250 (Admin), [2007] ACD 4 .. 6.51
R (on the application of Brown) v Carlisle City Council [2010] EWCA Civ 523, [2011] Env LR 5, [2010] JPL 1571 ..... 4.11
R (on the application of Buckinghamshire CC) v Secretary of State for Transport [2014] UKSC 3, [2014] 1 WLR 324, [2014] 2 All ER 109 ..... 7.207
R (on the application of Buglife: The Invertebrate Conservation Trust) v Thurrock Thames Gateway Development Corpn [2009] EWCA Civ 29, [2009] 2 P & CR 8, [2009] JPL 1060 ..... 6.51
R (on the application of Bullmore) v West Hertfordshire Hospitals NHS Trust [2007] EWHC 1350 (Admin) 6.51
R (on the application of Burkett) v Hammersmith & Fulham LBC (No 1) [2002] UKHL 23, [2002] 1 WLR 1593, [2002] 3 All ER 97 ..... 1.57; 3.24, 3.77; 4.17; 5.26
R (on the application of Butler) v East Dorset DC [2016] EWHC 1527 (Admin), [2016] 6 WLUK 682 ..... 1.29
R (on the application of CBRE Lionbrook (General Partners) Ltd) v Rugby BC [2014] EWHC 646 (Admin), [2014] Env LR D3 ..... 3.166; 5.64
R (on the application of CK Properties (Theydon Bois) Ltd) v Epping Forest DC [2018] EWHC 1649 (Admin), [2019] PTSR 183, [2018] 6 WLUK 655 ..... 1.59; 4.68; 7.226
R (on the application of CPRE Kent) v Dover DC *see* Dover DC v Campaign to Protect Rural England (Kent)
R (on the application of Cairns) v Hertfordshire Council [2018] EWHC 2050 (Admin), [2018] 8 WLUK 2, [2019] Env LR 6 ..... 7.190
R (on the application of Campaign to Protect Rural England) v Herefordshire Council [2019] EWHC 3458 (Admin), [2019] 12 WLUK 296 ..... 7.32, 7.58, 7.78
R (on the application of Capel Parish Council) v Surrey CC [2008] EWHC 2364 (Admin) 3.143
R (on the application of Carnegie (on behalf of the Oaks Action Group)) v Ealing LBC [2014] EWHC 3087 (Admin) 7.103, 7.111, 7.159, 7.224

R (on the application of Cash) v Secretary of State for Housing, Communities & Local Government *see* Cash v Secretary of State for Communities & Local Government
R (on the application of Catt) v Brighton & Hove City Council [2007] EWCA Civ 298, [2007] Env LR 32, [2007] BLGR 331 .... 3.77; 4.17
R (on the application of Champion) v North Norfolk DC [2013] EWCA Civ 1657, [2014] Env LR 23, [2015] 1 WLR 3710 .... 3.77; 4.17, 4.19, 4.111
R (on the application of Champion) v North Norfolk DC [2015] UKSC 52, [2015] 1 WLR 3710, [2015] 4 All ER 169 .... 1.38, 1.39; 7.190, 7.192
R (on the application of Cherkley Campaign Ltd) v Mole Valley District Council [2014] EWHC 567 (Admin), [2014] 2 EGLR 98, [2014] PTSR D14 .... 3.33
R (on the application of Cherkley Campaign Ltd) v Mole Valley District Council [2014] EWHC 3663 (Admin), ... 7.192
R (on the application of Cherkley Campaign Ltd) v Mole Valley District Council [2014] EWCA Civ 567, [2014] EWHC 3291 (Admin), [2014] 5 WLUK 192 .... 7.213, 7.214, 7.233
R (on the application of Cheshire East Council) v Secretary of State for Communities & Local Government [2015] EWHC 410 (Admin) 7.129
R (on the application of Cheshire East Council) v Secretary of State for Communities & Local Government [2014] EWHC 2824 (Admin), [2015] JPL 185 .... 7.222
R (on the application of Chilton Parish Council) v Baberg DC [2019] EWHC 280 (Admin), [2019] 1 WLUK 249 .... 4.5
R (on the application of Citizens UK) v Secretary of State for the Home Department [2018] EWCA Civ 1812, [2018] 4 WLR 123, [2019] 1 All ER 416 .... 4.32
R (on the application of ClientEarth) v Secretary of State for Business, Energy & Industrial Strategy [2020] EWHC 1303 (Admin), [2020] PTSR 1709, [2020] 5 WLUK 330, [2021] EWCA Civ 43 .... 1.4, 1.28; 7.4, 7.7, 7.8, 7.44, 7.53, 7.72, 7.100
R (on the application of Coleman) v Barnet LBC [2012] EWHC 3725 (Admin), [2013] Eq LR 223 .... 4.107
R (on the application of Compton) v Wiltshire Primary Care Trust (Practice Note), [2008] EWCA Civ 749, [2009] 1 WLR 1436, [2009] 1 All ER 978 .... 6.51, 6.92
R (on the application of Connolly) v Havering LBC [2009] EWCA Civ 1059, [2009] 10 WLUK 390, [2010] 2 P & CR 1 .... 4.102
R (on the application of Cooper) v Ashford BC [2016] EWHC 1525 (Admin), [2016] PTSR 1455, [2016] 6 WLUK 622 .... 7.61
R (on the application of Corbett) v Cornwall Council [2020] EWCA Civ 508, [2020] 4 WLUK 127, [2020] JPL 1277 .... 1.29; 7.40, 7.42
R (on the application of Corner House Research) v Secretary of State for Trade & Industry [2005] EWCA Civ 192, [2005] 1 WLR 2600, [2005] 4 All ER 1 .... 3.69, 3.73; 5.15; 6.49, 6.51, 6.52, 6.59, 6.60, 6.61, 6.65, 6.67, 6.68, 6.85, 6.90, 6.91, 6.92
R (on the application of Corrie) v Suffolk CC [2014] EWHC 2490 (Admin), [2015] Env LR 5 .... 7.103, 7.190
R (on the application of Corus UK Ltd (t/a Orb Electrical Steels) v Newport City Council; Tata Steel UK Ltd v Newport City Council [2010] EWCA Civ 1626 .... 3.166; 5.64
R (on the application of Couves) v Gravesham BC [2015] EWHC 504 (Admin) 4.11; 7.113, 7.115
R (on the application of Coventry Gliding Club Ltd) v Harborough DC [2019] EWHC 3059 (Admin), [2019] 11 WLUK 245 .... 3.74; 7.45
R (on the application of Davey) v Aylesbury Vale District Council *see* Davey v Aylesbury Vale DC
R (on the application of Davies) v Carmarthenshire County Council [2015] EWHC 230 (Admin) 4.11; 7.131
R (on the application of Davison) v Elmbridge BC [2019] EWHC 1409 (Admin), [2019] 5 WLUK 504, [2020] 1 P & CR 1 .... 7.65
R (on the application of Day) v Shropshire Council [2019] EWHC 3539 (Admin), [2019] 12 WLUK 366 .... 7.28, 7.50, 7.90

R (on the application of Dowley) v Secretary of State for Communities & Local Government [2016] EWHC 2618 (Admin), [2016] 10 WLUK 428, [2016] ACD 129 .... 6.57
R (on the application of Eastaway) v Secretary of State for Trade & Industry [2000] 1 WLR 2222, [2001] 1 All ER 27, [2001] CP Rep 67 .... 4.112
R (on the application of East Meon Forge & Cricket Ground Protection Association) v East, Hampshire DC [2014] EWHC 3543 (Admin), [2015] ACD 45....... 4.107, 4.109; 7.103, 7.165, 7.167
R (on the application of Edwards) v Environment Agency [2004] EWHC 736 (Admin), [2004] 3 All ER 21, [2004] Env LR 43 .... 1.57; 3.46
R (on the application of Edwards) v Environment Agency (No 2) [2008] UKHL 22, [2008] 1 WLR 1587, [2009] 1 All ER 57 .... 3.166; 4.83; 5.64
R (on the application of Edwards) v Environment Agency [2014] 1 WLR 55, [2013] UKSC 78, [2014] 1 WLR 55, [2014] 1 All ER 760 .... 6.62
R (on the application of Edwards) v Environment Agency (No 2) (Case C-260/11) [2013] 1 WLR 2914, [2013] 3 CMLR 18, [2014] All ER (EC) 207........ 6.63, 6.64
R (on the application of Elan-Cane) v Secretary of State for the Home Department [2020] EWCA Civ 363, [2020] QB 929, [2020] 3 WLR 386 .... 6.96
R (on the application of Essex CC) v Secretary of State for Communities & Local Government [2012] EWHC 1460 (Admin), [2012] ELR 383, [2012] ACD 93..... 6.16
R (on the application of Feakins) v Secretary of State for the Environment, Food & Rural Affairs [2003] EWCA Civ 1546, [2004] 1 WLR 1761, [2004] Eu LR 275. 5.23
R (on the application of Finch) v Surrey County Council [2020] EWHC 3566 (Admin), [2021] EWHC 170 (QB) 5.74
R (on the application of Forge Field Society) v Sevenoaks DC [2014] EWHC 1895 (Admin), [2014] 6 WLUK 385, [2015] JPL 22 .... 7.159, 7.165
R (on the application of Frack Free Balcombe Residents Association) v West Sussex County Council [2014] EWHC 4108 (Admin) 7.173
R (on the application of Friends of the Earth Ltd) v Secretary of State for Transport [2021] EWCA Civ 13, [2021] 1 WLUK 51 .... 6.71
R (on the application of Friends of the Earth England, Wales & Northern Ireland) v Welsh Ministers [2015] EWHC 776 (Admin), [2015] PTSR D28 .... 7.202
R (on the application of Friends of the Earth Ltd) v Secretary of State for Housing, Communities & Local Government [2019] EWHC 518 (Admin), [2019] PTSR 1540, [2019] 3 WLUK 58 .... 7.207
R (on the application of Friends of the Earth) v Secretary of State for Transport & Heathrow Airport Ltd *see* R (on the application of Plan B Earth) v Secretary of State for Transport
R (on the application of G) v Ealing LBC (No 2) [2001] EWHC 250 (Admin), [2002] MHLR 140, [2002] ACD 48 .... 3.149; 5.20
R (on the application of GRA Acquisition Ltd) v Oxford City Council [2015] EWHC 76 (Admin), [2015] PTSR 751 .... 7.126, 7.163
R (on the application of GSTS Pathology LLP) v R & C Comrs [2013] EWHC 1801 (Admin), [2013] STC 2017, [2013] STI 2566 .... 5.49
R (on the application of Gardner) v Harrogate BC [2008] EWHC 2942 (Admin), [2009] JPL 872 .... 3.166; 5.64
R (on the application of Garner) v Elmbridge BC [2010] EWCA Civ 1006, [2011] 3 All ER 418, [2012] PTSR 250 .... 5.15; 6.59, 6.67
R (on the application of Gavin) v Haringey LBC [2003] EWHC 2591 (Admin), [2004] 2 P & CR 13, [2004] 1 PLR 61 .... 3.166; 5.64, 5.65
R (on the application of Gerber) v Wiltshire Council; Gerber v Wiltshire Council [2016] EWCA Civ 84, [2016] 1 WLR 2593, [2016] 2 WLUK 609 .... 3.85
R (on the application of Gladman Developments Ltd) v Aylesbury Vale DC [2014] EWHC 4323 (Admin), [2015] JPL 656, [2021] EWCA Civ 104........ 7.177
R (on the application of Gleeson Developments Ltd) v Secretary of State for Communities & Local Government [2014] EWCA Civ 1118, [2014] PTSR 1226, [2014] JPL 1386 .... 6.10

R (on the application of Gottlieb) v Winchester City Council [2015] EWHC 231 (Admin), [2015] ACD 74 .... 7.129
R (on the application of Grace) v Secretary of State for the Home Department [2014] EWCA Civ 1091, [2014] 1 WLR 3432, [2015] Imm AR 10 .... 4.31
R (on the application of Guiney) v Greenwich LBC [2008] EWHC 2012 (Admin), [2009] JPL 211 .... 3.166; 5.64
R (on the application of H) v Ashworth Special Hospital Authority [2002] EWCA Civ 923, [2003] 1 WLR 127, (2002) 5 CCL Rep 390 .... 3.137; 5.54
R (on the application of HS2 Action Alliance Ltd) v Secretary of State for Transport [2015] EWCA Civ 203, [2015] 2 Costs LR 411 .... 3.73; 5.14; 6.83
R (on the application of HS2 Action Alliance Ltd) v Secretary of State for Transport *see* R (on the application of Buckinghamshire CC) v Secretary of State for Transport
R (on the application of Hammerton) v London Underground Ltd [2002] EWHC 2307 (Admin), [2003] JPL 984, [2002] 47 EG 148 (CS) 3.45, 3.46
R (on the application of Harrier Developments Ltd) v Fenland DC CO/1489/2014 .... 4.31
R (on the application of Hart DC) v Secretary of State for Communities & Local Government [2008] EWHC 1204 (Admin), [2008] 5 WLUK 7, [2008] 2 P & CR 16 .... 1.39
R (on the application of Hart Aggregates Ltd) v Hartlepool BC [2005] EWHC 840 (Admin), [2005] 2 P & CR 31, [2005] JPL 1602 .... 1.47; 7.139
R (on the application of Harvey) v Leighton Linslade Town Council [2019] EWHC 760 (Admin), [2019] 2 WLUK 241, [2019] LLR 564 .... 6.97
R (on the application of Hawking) v Secretary of State for Health & Social Care [2018] EWHC 989 (Admin), [2018] 2 WLUK 524, [2018] ACD 41 .... 6.90
R (on the application of Hayes) v Wychavon District Council [2014] EWHC 1987 (Admin), [2015] JPL 62 .... 7.103
R (on the application of Heath & Hampstead Society) v City of London [2014] EWHC 3868 (Admin), [2015] Env LR 11, [2015] ACD 47 .... 7.168
R (on the application of Heathrow Hub Ltd) v Secretary of State for Transport [2020] EWCA Civ 213, [2020] 2 WLUK 347, [2020] 4 CMLR 17 .... 5.67; 7.76
R (on the application of Hemming t/a Simply Pleasure Ltd)) v Westminster City Council [2013] EWCA Civ 591, [2013] PTSR 1377, [2013] 6 Costs LO 780 .... 6.45
R (on the application of Hereford Waste Watchers Ltd) v Herefordshire Council [2005] EWHC 191 (Admin), [2005] Env LR 29, [2005] JPL 1469 .... 3.31
R (on the application of Hillingdon LBC) v Secretary of State for Transport [2017] EWHC 121 (Admin), [2017] 1 WLR 2166, [2017] 1 WLUK 598 .... 3.82; 7.222
R (on the application of Hinds) v Blackpool Council [2011] EWHC 591 (Admin), [2011] NPC 32 .... 3.112; 5.12
R (on the application of Holborn Studios Ltd) v London Borough of Hackney v GHL (Eagle Wharf Road) Ltd [2017] EWHC 2823 (Admin), [2018] PTSR 997, [2017] 11 WLUK 241 .... 7.35
R (on the application of Holder) v Gelding BC [2014] EWCA Civ 599, [2014] JPL 1087 .... 1.16
R (on the application of Horeau) v Secretary of State for Foreign & Commonwealth Affairs [2018] EWHC 1508 (Admin), [2018] 5 WLUK 312, [2018] ACD 91 .. 4.32; 5.32
R (on the application of Hourhope Ltd) v Shropshire Council [2015] EWHC 518 (Admin) 7.143
R (on the application of Hudson) v Legoland Windsor Ltd [2019] EWHC 3505 (Admin), [2019] 12 WLUK 364, [2020] JPL 779 .... 7.196
R (on the application of Hughes) v South Lakeland District Council [2014] EWHC 3979 (Admin) 7.131, 7.160
R (on the application of Hunt) v North Somerset Council *see* Hunt v North Somerset Council
R (on the application of Hysaj) v Secretary of State for the Home Department [2014] EWCA Civ 1633, [2015] 1 WLR 2472, [2015] CP Rep 17 .... 5.10, 5.40
R (on the application of IM Properties Development Ltd) v Lichfield District Council [2014] EWHC 2440 (Admin), [2014] PTSR 1484 .... 4.69; 7.156, 7.226

R (on the application of IXPL Ltd) v Harlow Council [2014] EWHC 3860 (Admin), [2014] 11 WLUK 567 .... 7.135
R (on the application of Isherwood Carter) v Swansea City & County Council [2015] EWHC 75 (Admin) 7.133
R (on the application of Island Farm Development Ltd) v Bridgend County BC [2006] EWHC 2189 (Admin), [2007] BLGR 60, [2007] LLR 230 .... 1.57
R (on the application of Ismail) v Secretary of State for the Home Department [2019] EWHC 3192 (Admin), [2019] 11 WLUK 508, [2020] ACD 18 .... 4.32
R (on the application of JD Wetherspoon plc) v Guildford BC [2006] EWHC 815 (Admin), [2007] 1 All ER 400, [2006] BLGR 767 .... 5.23
R (on the application of James Hall & Co Ltd) v Bradford MBC [2019] EWHC 2899 (Admin), [2019] 11 WLUK 110 .... 7.67, 7.159
R (on the application of Jedwell) v Denbighshire CC [2015] EWCA Civ 1232, [2016] PTSR 715, [2015] 12 WLUK 71 .... 4.45; 7.228
R (on the application of Johnson) v Windsor & Maidenhead RBC *see* Johnson v Windsor & Maidenhead RBC
R (on the application of Joicey) v Northumberland CC [2014] EWHC 3657 (Admin), [2015] PTSR 622, [2015] BLGR 1 .... 7.129, 7.133, 7.244
R (on the application of Kemball) v Secretary of State for Communities & Local Government [2015] EWHC 3338 (Admin), [2015] 10 WLUK 415, [2016] JPL 359 .... 4.108; 7.234
R (on the application of Khan) v London Borough of Sutton [2014] EWHC 3663 (Admin) 7.103, 7.191
R (on the application of Khodari) v Royal Borough of Kensington & Chelsea [2017] EWCA Civ 333, [2018] 1 WLR 584, [2017] 5 WLUK 277 .... 1.44
R (on the application of Kides) v South Cambridgeshire DC [2002] EWCA Civ 1370, [2003] 1 P & CR 19, [2003] JPL 431 .... 1.53, 1.57; 3.42, 3.45, 3.46; 4.5; 7.112, 7.113
R (on the application of Lady Hart of Chilton) v Babergh DC [2014] EWHC 3261 (Admin), [2015] JPL 491 .... 3.166; 5.64; 7.107, 7.128, 7.142, 7.159, 7.244
R (on the application of Lancashire CC) v Secretary of State for the Environment, Food & Rural Affairs; R (NHS Property Services Ltd) v Surrey CC [2019] UKSC 58, [2020] 2 WLR 1, [2020] 2 All ER 925 .... 7.170
R (on the application of Langton) v Secretary of State for Environment, Food & Rural Affairs [2018] EWHC 2190 (Admin), [2018] 8 WLUK 146, [2019] Env LR 9 .... 7.194
R (on the application of Lanner Parish Council) v Cornwall Council [2013] EWCA Civ 1290 .... 4.111; 5.19
R (on the application of Larkfleet Homes Ltd) v Rutland County Council [2014] EWHC 4095 (Admin), [2015] PTSR 589, [2015] JPL 697 .... 7.177
R (on the application of Larkfleet) v South Kestevan DC [2015] EWCA Civ 887, [2015] 8 WLUK 53, [2016] Env LR 4 .... 7.191, 7.232
R (on the application of Leeds City Council) v Secretary of State for the Home Department [2004] EWHC 2477 (Admin) 4.103
R (on the application of Lee Valley Regional Park Authority) v Broxbourne BC [2015] EWHC 185 (Admin) 7.74
R (on the application of Legard) v Royal Borough of Kensington & Chelsea [2018] EWHC 32 (Admin), [2018] PTSR 1415, [2018] 1 WLUK 100 .... 7.230
R (on the application of Lewis) v Redcar & Cleveland BC [2008] EWCA Civ 746, [2009] 1 WLR 83, [2008] BLGR 781 .... 1.57
R (on the application of Leyton Orient FC) v London Legacy Development Corpn [2013] EWHC 3653 (Admin) 5.33
R (on the application of Lichfield Securities Ltd) v Lichfield DC [2001] EWCA Civ 304, (2001) 3 LGLR 35, [2001] 3 PLR 3 .... 5.31
R (on the application of Littlejohns) v Devon County Council [2015] EWHC 730 (Admin), [2015] 2 P & CR DG6 .... 7.171

R (on the application of Litvinenko) v Secretary of State for the Home Department [2013] EWHC 3135 (Admin), [2014] ACD 25 ..... 6.51
R (on the application of Liverpool Open & Green Spaces Community Interest Co) v Liverpool City Council [2020] EWCA Civ 861, [2020] 7 WLUK 142, [2021] 1 P & CR 10 ..... 7.159
R (on the application of Loader) v Rother DC [2016] EWCA Civ 795, [2016] 7 WLUK 734, [2017] JPL 25 ..... 7.159
R (on the application of Longacre Properties Ltd) v Winchester City Council [2014] EWHC 3373 (Admin) 4.45; 7.115, 7.128, 7.228
R (on the application of Luton BC) v Central Bedfordshire Council [2014] EWHC 4325 (Admin) 7.101, 7.155, 7.165, 7.246
R (on the application of Luton BC) v Secretary of State for Education [2011] EWHC 556 (Admin) 6.16
R (on the application of M) v Croydon LBC [2012] EWCA Civ 595, [2012] 1 WLR 2607, [2012] 3 All ER 1237 ..... 6.35, 6.36
R (on the application of McClellan) v Lambeth LBC [2014] EWHC 1964 (Admin) 7.129, 7.163
R (on the application of McLennan) v Medway Council [2019] EWHC 1738 (Admin), [2019] PTSR 2025, [2019] 7 WLUK 104 ..... 7.74
R (on the application of Mahoney) v Secretary of State for Communities & Local Government [2015] EWHC 589 (Admin), [2015] RVR 237 ..... 7.180
R (on the application of Martin) v Folkestone & Hythe DC [2020] EWHC 1614 (Admin), [2020] 6 WLUK 297 ..... 7.41
R (on the application of Mawbey) v Lewisham LBC [2019] EWCA Civ 1016, [2020] PTSR 164, [2019] 6 WLUK 249 ..... 7.67
R (on the application of Medical Justice) v Secretary of State for the Home Department [2010] EWHC 1425 (Admin), [2010] 5 WLUK 569, [2010] ACD 70 ..... 5.46, 5.47
R (on the application of Lochailort Investments Ltd) v Mendip DC [2020] EWHC 1146 (Admin), [2020] 5 WLUK 89; rev'sd [2020] EWCA Civ 1259, [2020] 10 WLUK 2 ..... 7.29, 7.56
R (on the application of Menston Action Group) v Bradford Metropolitan DC [2015] EWHC 184 (Admin) 7.135
R (on the application of Midcounties Co-operative) Ltd v Forest of Dean DC [2015] EWHC 1251 (Admin), [2015] PTSR D32 ..... 4.32; 7.231
R (on the application of Midcounties Co-operative) Ltd v Forest of Dean DC [2014] EWHC 3059 (Admin), [2015] JPL 288 ..... 7.129, 7.142
R (on the application of Midcounties Co-operative) Ltd v Wyre Forest DC [2009] EWHC 964 (Admin) 3.166; 5.64
R (on the application of Midlands Co-operative Society Ltd) v Birmingham City Council [2012] EWHC 620 (Admin), [2012] 3 WLUK 541, [2012] Eu LR 640 .. 5.31
R (on the application of Morge) v Hampshire CC [2011] UKSC 2, [2011] 1 WLR 268, [2011] 1 All ER 744 ..... 1.57; 4.83
R (on the application of Mount Cook Land Ltd) v Westminster City Council [2003] EWCA Civ 1346, [2004] CP Rep 12, [2004] 2 Costs LR 211 ..... 6.20, 6.21, 6.24, 6.25, 6.28, 6.30
R (on the application of Naing) v Immigration Appeal Tribunal [2003] EWHC 771 (Admin) 3.92
R (on the application of Nash) v LB Barnet [2013] EWCA Civ 1004, [2013] PTSR 1457 ..... 5.26
R (on the application of Nasserj) v Secretary of State for the Home Department [2009] UKHL 23, [2010] 1 AC 1, [2009] 2 WLR 1190 ..... 5.72
R (on the application of National Association of Probation Officers) v Secretary of State for Justice [2014] EWHC 4349 (Admin), [2014] 11 WLUK 740 ..... 3.23
R (on the application of Network Rail Infrastructure Ltd) v Secretary of State for the Environment, Food & Rural Affairs [2017] EWHC 2259 (Admin), [2017] PTSR 1662, [2017] 9 WLUK 107 ..... 1.3; 3.92, 3.93

R (on the application of Newsmith Stainless Ltd) v Secretary of State for the Environment, Transport & the Regions [2001] EWHC Admin 74, [2017] PTSR 1126 .... 3.2, 3.93, 3.149; 5.20
R (on the application of Organisation for Promotion of Environmental Needs) v London Borough of Hackney [2014] EWHC 4272 (Admin) 7.163
R (on the application of Ortona Ltd) v Secretary of State for Communities & Local Government [2009] EWCA Civ 863, [2010] 1 P & CR 15, [2010] JPL 361 .... 4.81
R (on the application of Oxted Residential Ltd) v Secretary of State for Communities & Local Government [2015] EWHC 793 (Admin) 4.27
R (on the application of Oyston Estates Ltd) v Fylde BC [2019] EWCA Civ 1152, [2019] 1 WLR 5484, [2019] WLUK 68 .... 3.82; 4.45
R (on the application of Palmer) v Herefordshire Council [2016] EWCA Civ 1061, [2017] 1 WLR 411, [2016] 11 WLUK 107 .... 7.162
R (on the application of Parveen) v Redbridge LBC [2020] EWCA Civ 194, [2020] 4 WLR 53, [2020] 3 WLUK 163 .... 6.36, 6.37
R (on the application of Pascoe) v Liverpool City Council [2007] EWHC 1024 (Admin) 3.136, 3.138
R (on the application of Pearl) v Maldon DC & Brown [2018] EWHC 212 (Admin), [2018] 2 WLUK 229 .... 7.229
R (on the application of Pemberton International Ltd) v Lambeth LBC [2014] EWHC 1998, [2015] JPL 42 .... 7.115, 7.129
R (on the application of Perrett) v SSLCG [2009] EWCA Civ 1365, [2010] 2 All ER 578 [2010] JPL 999 .... 4.106; 5.70
R (on the application of Perry) v London Borough of Hackney [2014] EWHC 3499 (Admin), [2015] JPL 454, [2014] PTSR D30 .... 3.166; 5.64; 7.109, 7.238, 7.246
R (on the application of Perry) v London Borough of Hackney [2014] EWHC 1721 (Admin), [2014] JPL 1329 .... 5.32, 5.33
R (on the application of Piffs ELM Ltd) v Tewkesbury BC [2016] EWHC 3248 (Admin), [2016] 11 WLUK 146 .... 7.239
R (on the application of Plan B Earth) v Secretary of State for Transport; R (on the application of Friends of the Earth) Ltd) v Secretary of State for Transport [2020] EWCA (Civ) 214, [2020] UKSC 52, [2020] PTSR 1446, [2020] 2 WLUK 372 .... 1.4; 4.18, 4.19, 4.39; 5.67; 7.190
R (on the application of Plant) v Lambeth LBC [2016] EWHC 3324 (Admin), [2017] PTSR 453, [2016] 12 WLUK 642 .... 7.93, 7.246
R (on the application of Police & Crime Comr for Leicestershire) v Hallam Land Management [2014] EWHC 1719 (Admin) 7.113, 7.247
R (on the application of Public & Commercial Services Union) v Minister for the Cabinet Office [2017] EWHC 1787 (Admin), [2018] 1 All ER 142, [2018] ICR 269 .... 4.18
R (on the application of Quark Fishing Ltd) v Secretary of State for Foreign & Commonwealth Affairs (No 1) [2002] EWCA Civ 1409 .... 4.32
R (on the application of R) v Chief Constable of Greater Manchester Police [2018] UKSC 47, [2018] 1 WLR 4079, [2019] 1 All ER 391 .... 3.172
R (on the application of Redditch BC) v FSOS [2003] EWHC 650 (Admin), [2003] 1 WLUK 578, [2003] 2 P & CR 25 .... 3.59
R (on the application of Reprotech (Pebsham) Ltd) v East Sussex CC [2002] UKHL 8, [2003] 1 WLR 348, [2002] 4 All ER 58 .... 1.45
R (on the application of Richards) v Pembrokeshire County Council [2004] EWCA Civ 1000, [2005] BLGR 105 .... 5.19
R (on the application of River Thames Society) v First Secretary of State *see* River Thames Society v First Secretary of State
R (on the application of Robert Hitchins Ltd) v Worcestershire County Council [2014] EWHC 3809 (Admin), [2015] PTSR D5 .... 7.129
R (on the application of Rockware Glass Ltd) v Chester CC [2005] EWHC 2250 (Admin), [2006] Env LR 30, [2006] JPL 699 .... 5.23

R (on the application of Roszowski) v Secretary of State for the Home Department [2017] EWCA Civ 412, [2017] 3 WLUK 19 .... 6.51
R (on the application of Royal Society for the Protection of Birds) v Secretary of State for Justice [2017] EWHC 2309 (Admin), [2017] 9 WLUK 240, [2017] 5 Costs LO 691 .... 6.75
R (on the application of SDR) v Bristol City Council [2012] EWHC 859 (Admin) 5.12
R (on the application of Samuel Smith Old Brewery (Tadcaster) v North Yorkshire County Council [2020] UKSC 3, [2020] 3 All ER 527, [2020] PTSR 221 .... 1.58; 7.4, 7.25, 7.44, 7.157
R (on the application of Save Britain's Heritage) v Liverpool CC [2016] EWHC 48 (Admin), [2016] 1 WLUK 213 .... 7.228
R (on the application of Save Britain's Heritage) v Secretary of State for Communities & Local Government [2010] EWCA Civ 1500 .... 3.132
R (on the application of Save Britain's Heritage) v Secretary of State for Communities & Local Government [2018] EWCA Civ 2137, [2019] 1 WLR 929, [2019] 1 All ER 1117 .... 7.48, 7.49, 7.75
R (on the application of Scarisbrick) v Secretary of State for Housing, Communities & Local Government v Whitemoss Landfill Ltd [2017] EWCA Civ 787, [2017] 6 WLUK 494 .... 7.10
R (on the application of Scott) v Hackney LBC [2009] EWCA Civ 217, [2009] LLR 775 .... 6.35
R (on the application of Sharma) v Secretary of State for Housing, Communities & Local Government *see* Sharma v Secretary of State for Housing, Communities & Local Government
R (on the application of Shave) v Maidstone BC [2020] EWHC 1895 (Admin), [2020] 7 WLUK 216 .... 6.72; 7.67
R (on the application of Silus Investments SA) v London Borough of Hounslow [2015] EWHC 358 (Admin) 7.129, 7.163
R (on the application of Smech Properties Ltd) v Runnymede BC [2015] EWHC 823 (Admin) 4.5; 7.128
R (on the application of Smith) v North East Derbyshire Primary Care Trust [2006] EWCA Civ 1291, [2006] 1 WLR 3315, (2006) 9 CCL Rep 663 .... 5.64
R (on the application of Spurrier) v Secretary of State for Transport [2019] EWHC 1070 (Admin), [2020] PTSR 240, [2019] 4 WLUK 424 .... 7.71
R (on the application of Squire) v Shropshire Council [2019] EWCA Civ 888, [2019] 5 WLUK 424, [2020] 1 CMLR 2 .... 7.191
R (on the application of Stephenson) v Secretary of State for Housing, Communities & Local Government [2019] EWHC 519 (Admin), [2019] PTSR 2209, [2019] 3 WLUK 60 .... 7.47
R (on the application of Stroud) v North West Leicestershire DC [2018] EWHC 2886 (Admin), [2018] 11 WLUK 132 .... 7.188
R (on the application of Swire) v Secretary of State for Housing, Communities & Local Government [2020] EWHC 1298 (Admin), [2020] 5 WLUK 329, [2020] Env LR 29 .... 7.190
R (on the application of Technoprint plc) v Leeds City Council [2010] EWHC 581 (Admin), [2010] JPL 1244, [2011] Env LR D5 .... 4.11
R (on the application of Tesco Stores Ltd) v Forest of Dean District Council [2014] EWHC 3348 (Admin) 7.105, 7.142, 7.211
R (on the application of Tewkesbury BC v Secretary of State for Communities, Housing & Local Government [2019] EWHC 1775 (Admin), [2019] PTSR 2144, [2019] 7 WLUK 375 .... 4.77; 5.23
R (on the application of Thornton Hall Hotel Ltd) v Wirral MBC [2019] EWCA Civ 737, [2019] PTSR 1794, [2019] 4 WLUK 422 .... 3.1, 3.85; 5.65; 7.216
R (on the application of Thornton Hall Hotel Ltd) v Wirral MBC [2018] EWHC 560 (Admin), [2018] PTSR 954, [2018] 3 WLUK 582 .... 6.10

R (on the application of Trago Mills Ltd) v Secretary of State for Housing, Communities & Local Government [2016] EWHC 1792 (Admin), [2016] 7 WLUK 527 .... 7.220
R (on the application of United Trade Action Group Ltd) v Transport for London [2021] EWHC 73 (Admin), [2021] 1 WLUK 155 .... 3.95; 4.78
R (on the application of W) v Secretary of State for the Home Department [2016] EWCA Civ 82, [2016] 1 WLR 2793, [2016] 2 WLUK 247 .... 4.31
R (on the application of WJ (China)) v Secretary of State for the Home Department [2010] EWHC 776 (Admin), [2010] All ER (D) 97 (Apr) 5.31
R (on the application of Wandsworth LBC) v Secretary of State for Transport, Local Government & the Regions [2003] EWHC 622 (Admin), [2004] 1 P & CR 32, [2004] , JPL 291 .... 1.59; 3.81, 3.106; 4.94; 5.11, 5.40
R (on the application of Warley) v Wealden DC [2011] EWHC 2083 (Admin), [2012] Env LR 4 .... 4.11
R (on the application of Watt) v Hackney [2016] EWHC 1978 (Admin), [2016] 9 WLUK 161, [2017] JPL 192 .... 7.68
R (on the application of We Love Hackney Ltd) v Hackney LBC [2019] EWHC 1007 (Admin), [2019] 4 WLUK 318, [2019] Costs LR 463 6.92
R (on the application of Welwyn Hatfield BC) v Secretary of State [2011] UKSC 15, [2011] 2 AC 304, [2011] 2 WLR 905 .... 1.33, 1.51; 7.153
R (on the application of West Berkshire DC) v Secretary of State for Communities & Local Government [2016] EWCA Civ 441, [2016] 1 WLR 3923, [2016] PTSR 982 .... 1.18; 7.98, 7.188
R (on the application of Westerleigh Group Ltd) v Aylesbury Vale District Council [2015] EWHC 885 (Admin) 7.131, 7.165, 7.200
R (on the application of Westminster Council) v Secretary of State for Communities & Local Government [2014] EWHC 1248 (Admin) 3.81; 5.40
R (on the application of Williams) v Caerphilly CBC [2019] EWHC 1618 (Admin), [2019] 6 WLUK 352, [2020] LLR 204 .... 7.188
R (on the application of Williams) v Cardiff City Council CO/4255/2014 .... 4.31
R (on the application of Williams) v Powys CC [2017] EWCA Civ 427, [2018] 1 WLR 439, [2017] 6 WLUK 137 .... 7.162
R (on the application of Williams) v Secretary of State for Energy & Climate Change [2015] EWHC 1202 (Admin), [2015] 4 WLUK 650, [2015] JPL 1257 .... 3.86; 4.17
R (on the application of Wilson) v Prime Minister [2019] EWCA Civ 304, [2019] 1 WLR 4174, [2019] 3 All ER 230 .... 6.41
R (on the application of Wilson) v Wychavon DC [2007] EWCA Civ 52, [2007] QB 801, [2007] 2 WLR 798 .... 7.184
R (on the application of Wiltshire Council) v Secretary of State for Housing, Communities & Local Government *see* Wiltshire Council, Secretary of State for Housing, Communities & Local Government
R (on the application of Wingfield) v Canterbury City Council [2019] EWHC 1975 (Admin), [2019] 7 WLUK 373, [2020] JPL 154 aff'd [2020] EWCA Civ 1588, [2020] 11 WLUK 404 .... 3.128; 5.67
R (on the application of Wright) v Resilient Energy Severndale Ltd [2019] UKSC 53, [2019] 1 WLR 6562, [2020] 2 All ER 1 .... 1.16, 1.30; 7.44
R (on the application of Wyn-Williams) v Secretary of State for Communities & Local Government [2014] EWHC 3374 (Admin) 7.101, 7.149
R (on the application of XSWFX) v Ealing LBC [2020] EWHC 1485 (Admin), [2020] 4 WLUK 37, [2020] Env LR D1 .... 4.19; 7.192
R (on the application of Young) v Oxford City Council [2012] EWCA Civ 46 .... 6.51
Rainbird v Tower Hamlets LBC [2018] EWHC 657 (Admin), [2018] 3 WLUK 718... 7.38
Raja v Van Hoogstraten (No 9) [2008] EWCA Civ 1444, [2009] 1 WLR 1143, [2009] CP Rep 18 .... 5.21
Redhill Aerodrome Ltd v Secretary of State for Communities & Local Government [2014] EWCA Civ 1386, [2015] PTSR 274, [2015] 1 P & CR 3 .... 4.111; 7.155

Renew Land Developments Ltd v Welsh Ministers [2020] EWCA Civ 143, [2020] 2 WLUK 137, [2021] 1 P & CR 1 .... 7.73, 7.96
Rhymney Valley DC v Secretary of State for Wales [1985] JPL 27 .... 4.87
Richborough Estates v Secretary of State for Housing, Communities & Local Government [2018] EWHC 33 (Admin), [2018] PTSR 1168, [2018] 1 WLUK 83 .... 7.69
Risby v East Hertfordshire DC [2019] EWHC 3474 (Admin), [2019] 12 WLUK 245 7.62
Routh v Reading Corpn (1970) 217 EG 1337 .... 4.65
Royal Borough of Kensington & Chelsea v Secretary of State for Communities & Local Government [2012] EWHC 1785 (Admin), [2012] 28 EG 81 (CS), (2012) 162 NLJ 963 .... 4.52
Rozhon v Secretary of State for Wales *see* R v Secretary of State for Wales, ex p Rozhon

S

St Albans City & District Council v Secretary of State for Communities & Local Government [2015] EWHC 655 (Admin), [2015] 3 WLUK 410 .... 7.99
St Albans City & District Council v Secretary of State for Communities & Local Government [2009] EWHC 1280 (Admin), [2010] JPL 70 .... 4.75
St Modwen Developments Ltd v Secretary of State for Communities & Local Government [2017] EWCA Civ 1643, [2018] PTSR 746, [2017] 10 WLUK 496 1.28
Sabey (H) & Co Ltd v Secretary of State for the Environment [1978] 1 All ER 586, (1977) 245 EG 397, [1977] JPL 661 .... 4.81
Safe Rottingdean Ltd v Brighton & Hove City Council [2019] EWHC 2632 (Admin) 7.39, 7.162
Sage v Secretary of State for the Environment, Transport & the Regions [2003] UKHL 22, [2003] 1 WLR 983, [2003] 2 All ER 689 .... 1.49
Sahota v Singh [2018] EWHC 1685 (Ch), [2018] 6 WLUK 133 .... 5.40
Salford Estates (No 2) Ltd v Altomart Ltd (Practice Note) [2014] EWCA Civ 1408, [2015] 1 WLR 1825, [2016] 2 All ER 328 .... 5.40
Samuel Smith Old Brewery (Tadcaster) v North Yorkshire County Council *see* R (on the application of Samuel Smith Old Brewery) v North Yorkshire CC
Samuel Smith Old Brewery (Tadcaster) v Selby District Council [2014] EWHC 3441 (Admin), [2015] PTSR 719, [2015] JPL 427 .... 7.176, 7.205
San Vicente v Secretary of State for Communities & Local Government [2013] EWCA Civ 817, [2014] 1 WLR 966, [2014] 1 P & CR 7 .... 3.88; 5.12; 7.219
Sarodia v Redbridge LBC [2017] EWHC 2347 (Admin), [2017] 9 WLUK 207 .... 2.9
Satnam Millenium Ltd v Secretary of State for Housing, Communities & Local Government [2019] EWHC 2631 (Admin), [2019] 10 WLUK 125 .... 7.31, 7.46, 7.74, 7.87
Satnam Millenium Ltd v Warrington BC [2015] EWHC 370 (Admin), [2015] 2 WLUK 639, [2015] Env LR 30 .... 7.152
Save Britain's Heritage v Secretary of State for Housing, Communities & Local Government *see* R (on the application of Save Britain's Heritage) v Secretary of State for Communities & Local Government
Save Guana Cay Reef Association v R [2009] UKPC 44 .... 5.32
Save Historic Newmarket Ltd v Forest Heath DC [2010] EWHC 3268 (Admin)..... 4.29, 4.72
Secretary of State for Education & Science v Tameside MBC [1977] AC 1014, [1976] 3 WLR 641, [1976] 3 All ER 665 .... 7.94
Seddon Properties Ltd v Secretary of State for the Environment [1981] 42 P & CR 26, (1978) 248 EG 951, [1978] JPL 835 .... 1.52
Sevenoaks DC v First Secretary of State [2004] EWHC 771 (Admin), [2004] 3 WLUK 605, [2005] 1 P & CR 13 .... 1.48
Sevenoaks DC v Secretary of State for Housing, Communities & Local Government [2020] EWHC 3054 (Admin), [2020] 11 WLUK 157 .... 7.176
Sharma v Secretary of State for Housing, Communities & Local Government [2018] EWHC 2355 (Admin), [2018] 9 WLUK 111 .... 2.9

Shortt v Secretary of State for Communities & Local Government [2014] EWHC 2480 (Admin), [2015] JPL 75 .... 7.122
Silver v Secretary of State for Communities & Local Government [2014] EWHC 2729 (Admin), [2015] JPL 154 .... 7.140, 7.145, 7.153
Simplex GE (Holdings) Ltd v Secretary of State for the Environment (1989) 57 P & CR 306, [1988] 3 PLR 25, [1988] JPL 809 .... 3.166; 4.18, 4.39; 5.64, 5.66, 5.67
Sky Blue Sports & Leisure Ltd v Coventry City Council [2013] EWHC 3366 (Admin), [2014] BLGR 34, [2014] ACD 48 .... 5.33
Smith v East Elloe Rural DC [1956] AC 736, [1956] 2 WLR 888, [1956] 1 All ER 855 .... 3.86; 4.65; 5.11
Smith v Secretary of State for the Environment (The Times, 6 July 1987) 3.81; 4.88
Smyth v Secretary of State for Housing, Communities & Local Government [2015] EWCA Civ 174, [2015] PTSR 1417, [2015] 3 WLUK 169 .... 7.196
South Buckinghamshire DC v Porter (No 1) [2003] UKHL 26, [2003] 2 AC 558, [2003] 2 WLR 1547 .... 1.40; 5.48
South Buckinghamshire DC v Porter (No 2) [2004] UKHL 33, [2004] 1 WLR 1953, [2005] 1 P & CR 6 .... 7.50, 7.55, 7.56, 7.57
South Derbyshire DC v Secretary of State for Housing, Communities & Local Government [2020] EWHC 872 (Admin), [2020] PTSR 1120, [2020] 4 WLUK 130 .... 3.20; 7.218
South Northamptonshire DC v Charles Church Developments Ltd [2000] PLCR 46 .... 4.75
South Gloucestershire Council v Secretary of State for Communities & Local Government [2014] EWHC 4555 (Admin), [2014] 11 WLUK 715; rev'sd [2016] EWCA Civ 74, [2016] 2 WLUK 192, [2016] JPL 798 .... 4.18; 7.129
South Oxfordshire DC v Secretary of State for the Environment, Transport & the Regions [2000] 2 All ER 667, [2000] PLCR 315, (2000) 97 (2) LSG 32 .... 4.81
Spackman v Secretary of State for the Environment [1977] 1 All ER 257, (1977) 3 P & CR 430, [1977] JPL 174 .... 1.46
Spitfire Bespoke Homes Ltd v Secretary of State for Housing, Communities & Local Government [2020] EWHC 958 (Admin), [2020] 4 WLUK 186 .... 7.81
Spurrier v Secretary of State for Transport *see* R (on the application of Spurrier) v Secretary of State for Transport
Starbones Ltd v Secretary of State for Housing, Communities & Local Government [2020] EWHC 526 (Admin), [2020] 3 WLUK 111 .... 7.52, 7.54
Staffordshire Moorlands DC v Secretary of State for Communities & Local Government [2008] EWHC 3619 (Admin) 3.80
Stainer v Secretary of State for the Environment (1993) 65 P & CR 310, [1994] JPL 44, [1992] EG 130 (CS) 4.64, 4.70
Stephenson v Secretary of State for Housing, Communities & Local Government *see* R (on the application of Stephenson) v Secretary of State for Housing, Communities & Local Government
Stevenson, ex p (1892) 1 QB 609 .... 4.98
Stringer v Minister of Housing & Local Government [1970] 1 WLR 1281, [1971] 1 All ER 65, [1970] 7 WLUK 15 .... 1.30
Suffolk Coastal DC v Hopkins Homes [2017] UKSC 37, [2017] 1 WLR 1865, [2017] 4 All ER 938 .... 1.18; 7.4, 7.6, 7.10, 7.13
Summers v Fairclough Homes Ltd [2012] UKSC 26, [2012] 1 WLR 2004, [2012] 4 All ER 317 .... 5.13
Sustainable Shetland v Scottish Ministers [2015] UKSC 4, [2015] 2 All ER 545, 2015 SC (UKSC) 51 .... 1.38
Sykes v Cheshire West & Chester BC [2018] EWHC 3655 (Admin), [2017] 12 WLUK 518 .... 7.84
Symphony Group plc v Hodgson [1994] QB 179, [1993] 3 WLR 830, [1993] 4 All ER 143 .... 6.13

T

TA Miller Ltd v Minister of Housing & Local Government [1968] 1 WLR 992, [1968] 2 All ER 633, (1968) 19 P & CR 263.. 5.39
Tata Steel UK Ltd v Newport City Council *see* R (on the application of Corus UK Ltd (t/a Orb Electrical Steels) v Newport City Council
Taylor Wimpey West London v Secretary of State for Communities & Local Government [2014] EWHC 2082 (Admin) 7.117
Telford & Wrekin BC v Secretary of State for Housing, Communities & Local Government [2016] EWHC 3073 (Admin), [2016] 12 WLUK 24........................ 7.18
Terry Adams Ltd v Bolton MBC (1997) 73 P & CR 446 .... 3.141; 4.58, 4.60
Tesco Stores Ltd v Dundee CC [2012] UKSC 13, [2012] PTSR 983, [2012] 2 P & CR 9 .... 1.16, 1.32, 1.44, 1.58; 7.4, 7.37
Tesco Stores Ltd v Secretary of State for the Environment [1995] 1 WLR 759, [1995] 2 All ER 636, 93 LGR 403.. 1.1
Tewkesbury BC v Secretary of State for Communities, Housing & Local Government *see* R (on the application of Tewkesbury BC v Secretary of State for Communities, Housing & Local Government
Thorpe Hall Leisure Ltd v Secretary of State for Housing, Communities & Local Government [2020] EWHC 44 (Admin), [2020] 1 WLUK 40............................. 7.30
Thurrock BC v Secretary of State for the Environment, Transport & the Regions [2000] 12 WLUK 328, [2001] CP Rep 55, [2001] 1 PLR 94........................ 3.106; 5.11
Thurrock BC v Secretary of State for the Environment, Transport & the Regions [2001] EWHC Admin 128, [2001] 2 WLUK 608, [2001] JPL 1388.................... 1.50
Thurrock BC v Secretary of State for the Environment, Transport & the Regions [2001] CP Rep 55, [2001] 1 PLR 94, [2001] 3 EG 132 (CS)............................... 4.94
Times Investments Ltd v Secretary of State for the Environment (1991) 61 P & CR 98, [1990] 3 PLR 111, [1991] JPL 67 .... 3.58, 3.59
Tombstone Ltd v Raja *see* Raja v Van Hoogstraten
Tower Hamlets LBC v Secretary of State for Housing, Communities & Local Government [2019] EWHC 2219 (Admin), [2020] 2 All ER 909, [2020] PTSR 111 .... 7.54
Trail Riders Fellowship v Secretary of State for the Environment, Food & Rural Affairs [2015] EWHC 85 (Admin) 7.121
Transport for London v Griffin [2012] EWHC 1105 (QB).. 5.57
Turner v Secretary of State for Communities & Local Government [2015] EWHC 375, [2015] 2 WLUK 821, [2015] JPL 936; aff'd [2015] EWCA Civ 582, [2015] 6 WLUK 330, [2015] CP Rep 38................. 7.86, 7.246
Turner v Secretary of State for the Environment (1974) 28 P & CR 123, 72 LGR 380, (1973) 228 EG 335... 3.58
Tweed v Parades Commission for Northern Ireland [2006] UKHL 53, [2007] 1 AC 650, [2007] 2 WLR 1 .... 3.18, 3.151; 5.32, 5.33

U

USB Waste Essex Ltd v Essex County Council [2019] EWHC 1924 (Admin), [2019] 7 WLUK 314.. 7.67
Uniplex (UK) Ltd v NHS Business Services Authority (Case C-406/08) [2010] PTSR 1377, [2010] 2 CMLR 47 .... 5.26, 5.27
United Trade Action Group Ltd v Transport for London *see* R (on the application of United Trade Action Group Ltd) v Transport for London

V

Valentino Plus Ltd v Secretary of State for Housing, Communities & Local Government [2015] EWHC 19 (Admin), [2015] 1 WLUK 119, [2015] JPL 707. 7.151
Vallis v Secretary of State for Communities & Local Government [2012] EWHC 578 (Admin)... 4.84
Various Claimants v Giambrone & Law (a firm) [2019] EWHC 34 (QB), [2019] 4 WLR 7, [2019] 1 All ER (Comm) 1104.. 6.13

Venn v Secretary of State for Communities & Local Government [2014] EWCA Civ 1539, [2015] 1 WLR 2328, [2015] CP Rep 12 .... 3.71; 5.14; 6.57, 6.61
Venn v Secretary of State for Communities & Local Government [2015] EWHC 1186 (Admin) 7.128
Veolia ES (UK) Ltd v Secretary of State for Communities & Local Government [2015] EWHC 91 (Admin) 7.74, 7.128

W

WSPA v Welsh Ministers [2014] EWHC 1896 (Admin)... 7.73, 7.159
Walsall MBC v Secretary of State for Communities & Local Government; Dartford BC v Secretary of State for Communities & Local Government [2013] EWCA Civ 370, [2013] JPL 1183...3.129; 5.44
Walsham Chalet Park Ltd (t/a Dream Lodge Group) v Tallington Lakes Ltd [2014] EWCA Civ 1607, [2014] 12 WLUK 443, [2015] CP Rep 15.................... 5.13
Walton v Scottish Ministers [2012] UKSC 44, [2013] PTSR 51, [2013] Env LR 16 ... 1.38; 3.2, 3.28, 3.47, 3.53, 3.55, 3.59, 3.60, 3.61, 3.62, 3.102, 3.166; 5.2, 5.23, 5.43, 5.64, 5.68, 5.69; 7.130
Warners Retail (Moreton) Ltd v Cotswold District Council [2014] EWHC 2504 (Admin).. 7.103
Watt v Hackney *see* R (on the application of Watt) v Hackney
Wavendon Properties Ltd v Secretary of State for Housing, Communities & Local Government [2019] EWHC 1524 (Admin), [2019] PTSR 2077, [2019] 6 WLUK 198.. 1.27
Wealdon DC v Secretary of State for Housing, Communities & Local Government [2017] EWHC 351 (Admin), [2017] 3 WLUK 476, [2017] Env LR 31............... 7.194
Wealdon DC v Secretary of State for Housing, Communities & Local Government [2016] EWHC 247 (Admin), [2016] 2 WLUK 454, [2016] Env LR 19............... 7.199
Wells v United Kingdom (Admissibility) (Application No 37794/05) [2007] 1 WLUK 231, (2007) 44 EHRR SE20... 7.184
Welwyn Hatfield Council v Beesley *see* R (on the application of Welwyn Hatfield Borough Council) v Secretary of State for Communities & Local Government
Wendy Fair Markets Ltd v Secretary of State for the Environment [1996] JPL 649, (1995) 159 LG Rev 769, (1995) 139 SJLB 93....................................... 3.129; 4.98; 5.44
Wenman v Secretary of State for the Environment [1995] JPL 1040........................ 4.90; 5.40
Westminster City Council v Secretary of State for Housing, Communities & Local Government [2020] EWHC 1472 (Admin), [2020] 3 WLUK 649, [2020] JPL 1162, [2020] ACD 66.................................. 2.26; 3.112; 4.108; 7.229, 7.234
Westminster City Council v Secretary of State for Communities & Local Government [2014] EWHC 1234 (Admin) 7.118
Western Fish Products Ltd v Penwith DC [1981] 2 All ER 204, 77 LGR 185, (1979) 38 P & CR 7.. 1.45
Whitworth v Secretary of State for the Environment, Food & Rural Affairs [2010] EWCA Civ 1468 .... 5.2, 5.69
Williams v Devon CC [2015] EWHC 568 (Admin)... 3.63
Williams v Secretary of State for Communities & Local Government [2009] EWHC 475 (Admin) 3.126; 4.93; 6.29, 6.30
Wilson v Secretary of State for the Environment [1973] 1 WLR 1083........................ 3.58
Wiltshire Council, Secretary of State for Housing, Communities & Local Government [2020] EWHC 954 (Admin), [2020] PTSR 1409, [2020] 4 WLUK 235.. 1.58; 7.5, 7.8, 7.9, 7.26
Wiltshire CC v Secretary of State for Communities & Local Government [2010] EWHC 1009 (Admin) 4.30
Wind Prospect Developments Ltd v Secretary of State for Communities & Local Government [2014] EWHC 4041 (Admin) 7.125
Winters v Secretary of State for Housing, Communities & Local Government [2017] EWHC 357 (Admin), [2017] PSTR 568, [2017] 2 WLUK 660................ 7.95

Wokingham BC v Secretary of State for Housing, Communities & Local Government [2017] EWHC 1863 (Admin), [2018] PTSR 303, [2017] 7 WLUK 446 .... 7.69

X

XYZ v Travellers Insurance Co Ltd [2019] UKSC 48 .... 6.13

Y

Yadly Marketing Co Ltd v Secretary of State for the Home Department [2016] EWCA Civ 1143, [2017] 1 WLR 1041, [2016] 11 WLUK 607 .... 4.65
Ynys Mon BC v Secretary of State for Wales [1992] 3 PLR 1, [1992] COD 410..... 3.81; 4.88

Z

Zurich Assurance Ltd v Winchester City Council [2014] EWHC 758 (Admin) 3.61

CHAPTER 1

Life before the Planning Court: a history of the Court's role in the planning sphere

Mark Lowe QC
Jack Parker

Despite all the land left free
For the first time I feel somehow
That it isn't going to last
That before I snuff it, the whole
Boiling will be bricked in…
And that will be England gone
The shadows, the meadows, the lanes,
The guildhalls, the carved choirs

Extract from *Going, Going* by Philip Larkin[1]

A	Introduction	1.1
B	A historical overview of town and country planning to 1990	1.8
C	The framework of the current scheme and its evolution	1.12
	Forward planning	1.15
	Decision making	1.23
	Enforcement	1.33
	Environmental regulation, human rights and conservation	1.34
D	The demise of Planning exceptionalism?	1.44
E	The role of the court	1.52

A INTRODUCTION

1.1 When we wrote the introductory chapters to the first edition of *Cornerstone on the Planning Court* in 2014, the Court was in its infancy. Now

1 As recited by Lord Hoffmann in *Tesco Stores Ltd v Secretary of State for the Environment* [1995] 1 WLR 759 at 777.

it is a fixed feature in the planning firmament and practitioners are beginning to take the advantages of a specialist list for granted. This is a true measure of its success. Also, we write after the third decade of life under the Town and Country Planning Act 1990, and the longer we live with it the more we can admire its enduring nature and its quality as a codifying statute. Many of its features would have been recognisable by the town planners, surveyors, and lawyers practising in 1948, when the then new planning system enshrined in the Town and Country Planning Act 1947 first took effect. The question is whether, in the latest drive to update the planning system to make it more responsive to the perceived needs of the day, we will lose more in terms of coherence than any gains in terms of delivering growth. First indications are of apparently radical change but underneath the headlines there remains continued use of many familiar concepts and certainly a continued need for the Planning Court to adjudicate where environmental disputes go beyond the realm of planning merits and enter the world of lawful administrative decision-making by public bodies.

1.2 The Courts Service website states that the Planning Court:

> '... was created because of the clear need to deal more swiftly with planning cases, large and small, in the interests of justice for everyone involved in the planning process. As a result new time limits, tighter than before and tighter than those for other cases within the Administrative Court, are now applied to planning cases. In addition, the Planning Liaison Judge has responsibility for identifying which cases might be considered to be particularly substantial or difficult and these cases are then usually allocated to a judge with a significant expertise of the issues at hand. The definition of a 'significant' case will be applied broadly but can be thought of as those applications involving a development with a substantial economic impact at a local, regional or national level or a case which seems to be particularly complex.
>
> The new timetables are rigorous. In essence:
>
> - applications for permission to apply for judicial review are to be determined within three weeks of the expiry of the time limit for filing of the acknowledgment of service;
> - oral renewals of applications for permission to apply for judicial review are to be heard within one month of receipt of request for renewal;
> - applications for permission under section 289 of the Town and Country Planning Act 1990 are to be determined within one month of issue;
> - substantive statutory applications, including applications under section 288 of the Town and Country Planning Act 1990, are to be heard within six months of issue; and
> - judicial reviews are to be heard within ten weeks of the expiry of the period for the submission of detailed grounds by the defendant or any other party as provided in Rule 54.14.

The Planning Court can sit in any of the regional Administrative Courts (Birmingham, Cardiff, Manchester, Leeds and Bristol). Hearing cases at court centres outside of London is particularly important given the inherent local nature of cases involving land disputes.'

1.3 In 2014 we warmly welcomed the development of the Planning Court, created largely to avoid the multifarious pressures on the courts administering judicial review. It is headed by the Planning Liaison Judge. The first to hold this position was Mr Justice (now Lord Justice) Lindblom who, having been the lead judge of the Court since its foundation, was appointed to the Court of Appeal in November 2015 and is now Senior President of Tribunals. Mr Justice Lindblom was succeeded as Planning Liaison judge by the late Mrs Justice Patterson DBE until her tragic premature death. Mr Justice Holgate has been the holder of that office from 13 February 2017 and is another distinguished former planning practitioner. Holgate J has been in the vanguard of judges to urge litigants to increased efficiency in their use of court time and particularly in matters such as the preparation of bundles,[2] and now their e-equivalents, and the citation of authority. On the latter point he has found an ally in the approved use of citation from the ICLR's Leading Planning Cases (1st edition 2019), that should save several forests from early demise. He has championed proactive case management, limiting grounds to those that are truly arguable at the permission stage, delivering short and direct skeleton arguments and directing the use of core bundles etc when they are needed.

1.4 The Planning Court continues to find itself examining the lawfulness (but conspicuously not the merits) of some of the most controversial and topical cases of the day. Recently it has been the forum for a number of highly political challenges to major infrastructure projects from the Third Runway at Heathrow,[3] the HS2 project and most recently the ClientEarth litigation challenging the grant of a DCO for the construction of a new gas-fired plant at the Drax Power Station[4] and has not been found wanting. The Planning Court led the way in the use of virtual hearings from the outset of the Court system's response to the Covid-19 pandemic. On 12 May 2020, after such a two-day virtual hearing in April 2020, Holgate J handed down a judgment dismissing the Mayor of London's challenge to the decision of the Secretary of State, given on 31 October 2019 to allow the appeal of Harrow School for permission to erect new sports and science buildings.[5] The passage of less than six months from the decision to challenge to judgment is precisely what the Planning Court was intended to do and is an excellent advertisement for the effectiveness of its practices.

2 *Network Rail Infrastructure Ltd, R v The Secretary of State for the Environment, Food and Rural Affairs* [2017] EWHC 2259 at 10 where he observed that a core bundle of 250 pages should be the normal maximum to allow the parties legal arguments to be made.

3 *R (Friends of the Earth) v Secretary of State for Transport and Heathrow Airport Ltd* [2020] EWCA Civ 214, [2020] UKSC 52.

4 *R (ClientEarth) v Secretary of State for Business, Energy and Industrial Strategy etc* [2020] EWHC 1303 (Admin), [2021] EWCA Civ 43.

5 *The Mayor of London v SSHCLG etc* [2020] EWHC 1176 (Admin).

1.5 One only needs a passing knowledge of the area to understand how welcome this development is. The framework of regulatory control of land use in England is complex and is not contained in any single statute or code. In the years following the Second World War it grew like the proverbial 'Topsy'. For example, in 1982 Sir Malcolm Grant published his seminal work, *Urban Planning Law,* which, the fruit of four years' labour, provided an authoritative and up to date guide to the law of planning covering some 15 chapters in just less than 800 pages. At the same time the *Encylopedia of Planning Law* was beginning to spread beyond the confines of three loose-leaf volumes. In the 38 years that have since passed no-one has been able to repeat Professor Grant's great achievement and the *Encyclopedia* now spreads into no fewer than seven volumes. Yet despite the enormous growth in both the complexity of planning law and the volume of planning cases in the High Court, these cases had, necessarily, to take second place in the work of the Administrative Court as they rarely involved the liberty of the subject. As a result long delays were experienced in getting planning cases heard as they languished in the list behind that other major growth area, immigration challenges. At a stroke these problems have been resolved by the creation of this specialist court which has adopted a welcome and business-like efficiency to the despatch of its business.

1.6 The law of town and country planning provides a framework within which the various demands of land use policy, many of them conflicting, are played out. The responsibility for controlling land use lies with the politician and the bureaucrat and the court stands aside from the debate of the merits of the individual decision. The law may however be invoked, according to context, either by way of judicial review or through the framework of statutory challenges to decision making, to ensure that decisions are taken in accordance with the statutory process and are sound by reference to familiar public law tests, many of which were established or developed in planning cases.

1.7 This chapter seeks to set the scene for what follows by the provision of a brief and necessarily partial overview of the development of the law and practice of planning to equip the reader with an understanding of the basic planning landscape within which the disputes arise that provide the Planning Court with its case work.

B A HISTORICAL OVERVIEW OF TOWN AND COUNTRY PLANNING TO 1990

1.8 The control of land use in the public interest is the creation of statute, largely within the second half of the 20th century. The post-war Labour administration, undertaking a widespread centralising role in the public sphere, was ideally placed to bring this about and the first comprehensive[6] set of controls was brought into force in the Town and Country Planning Act 1947. The

6 There had been piecemeal provision prior to this date (the first 'Planning' Act was enacted in 1909).

framework established by the 1947 Act has endured and is readily identifiable as the basis of the current regime despite being, as described by Mr Lewis Silkin MP who introduced the original Bill to Parliament, 'long, technical and complex, and naturally, in some respects, controversial'.[7] How apt are these words to describe the torrent of subsequent planning legislation reaching down the last 73 years!

1.9 By the time of the first statutory planning controls, there was a clear need for the intervention of Parliament. We are a relatively small island land mass with a burgeoning economy and an expanding population. As a result, principally, of the industrial revolution, that population was increasingly drawn to the new and existing urban centres which led to intense pressure on the use of land in built up areas. In addition, there was, and remains still, a strongly perceived need to protect the countryside from becoming overdeveloped through industry and housing. The growth of the motor car as an affordable means of mass movement brought many rural areas in reach of commuters looking to match an idyllic home life with earning a living in the towns and cities. Even in the 1930s there were calls to regulate the unchecked expansion of towns along the corridors of their arterial roads, leading to the passing of the Restriction of Ribbon Development Act 1935 and the Green Belt (London and Home Counties) Act 1938, but these were piecemeal measures to address particular problems rather than a comprehensive scheme of control. The common law, which had developed incrementally over the centuries, was, despite its inherent flexibility, failing to protect the interests of the public in how land was being used. The law of nuisance and the developing use of restrictive covenants in built up areas provided some protection by reference to the private interests of the occupier or owner of land, and public health legislation (including the Public Health Acts of 1875 and 1936) sought to protect the health and safety of the public, but there was no general statutory control over the use the Englishman made of his land and home; these truly remained his castle and his keep.

1.10 The 1947 Act repealed all previous legislation[8] and, with effect from 1 July 1948, set up a system of centralised control, entrusting significant powers to the Minister of Town and Country Planning and requiring the local planning authority (usually the county council or county borough council) to carry out a survey of its area and prepare a development plan based on physical, social and economic attributes. Areas were earmarked for comprehensive development and no development was henceforth to take place without planning permission. Special provision was made in respect of buildings of architectural or historic interest, trees and outdoor advertisements.

1.11 In the years that followed the 1947 Act, constant legislative activity saw the system evolve by amendment, alongside significant consolidation in the Town and Country Planning Acts of 1962 and 1971, before the enactment

7 *Hansard* HC Deb. Vol.432 col 1137.

8 Other than the Minister of Town and Country Planning Act 1943. The Green Belt Act 1938 also continues as a separate system of control outside of the planning regime, more akin to restrictive covenants on land.

of the 1990 Act which remains in force today. Two of the most significant considerations underlying this post-1947 evolution were the recognition that the country's population would not, as had previously been thought to be the case, become static but would instead continue to expand, and the need to address the consequences of the dramatic increase in the use of the motor car.

C THE FRAMEWORK OF THE CURRENT SCHEME AND ITS EVOLUTION

1.12 The main elements of the present planning regime are to be found by tripping through the glades and struggling through the thickets of the Town and Country Planning Act 1990 (as amended by the Planning and Compensation Act 1991), the Planning (Listed Buildings and Conservation Areas) Act 1990 and the Planning (Hazardous Substances) Act 1990. Further change has been implemented by the Planning and Compulsory Purchase Act 2004, the Planning Act 2008, the Localism Act 2011, the Growth and Infrastructure Act 2013 and, most recently, the Business and Planning Act 2020. However the aspiring planner's education only just begins at this point, as we would add the need to know one's way around the Human Rights Act 1998, a few key European Directives and their English/Welsh regulatory counterparts, such as the Habitats Directive[9] and equivalent 2017 Regulations,[10] the EIA Directive[11] and 2017 Regulations[12] and the SEA Directive[13] and 2004 Regulations[14] conjoined, in a heady mix, with other key elements of delegated legislation such as the Town and Country Planning (General Permitted Development) (England) Order 2015 (and its 1995 predecessor[15]), the Town and Country Planning (Use Classes) Order 1987 and the Town and Country Planning (Development Management Procedure) (England) Order 2015.[16] With this in their knapsack the aspirant planning lawyer would have a reasonable grasp of the main parameters of the subject but far more reading would be required before it could be said that they were in any position to grapple with the intricacies of plan making or decision taking. They would have yet more to read if the proposal was for a nationally significant infrastructure project (NSIP), as such proposals have a separate statutory regime in the Planning Act 2008. To be prepared for whatever the weather might throw at them, however, our hardy rambler would need to bring with them on their journey knowledge of the Transport and Works Act 1992, the law relating to wayleaves,

9 Directive 92/43/EEC on the conservation of natural habitats and of wild fauna and flora.

10 The Conservation of Habitats and Species Regulations 2017, SI 2017/1012.

11 Directive 2011/92/EU on the assessment of the effects of certain public and private projects on the environment, as amended by Directive 2014/52/EU.

12 The Town and Country Planning (Environmental Impact Assessment) Regulations 2017, SI 2017/571.

13 Directive 2001/42/EC on the assessment of the effects of certain plans and programmes on the environment.

14 The Environmental Assessment of Plans and Programmes Regulations 2004, SI 2004/1633.

15 Which, as amended, remains in force in Wales.

16 In Wales, the Town and Country Planning (Development Management Procedure) (Wales) Order 2012, SI 2012/801.

highways and other rights of way, compulsory purchase and compensation and village greens.[17]

1.13 The full range of Planning Court matters is dealt with in the chapters that follow, but we shall stick in this introduction to the well-trodden paths of town and country planning as traditionally understood.

1.14 Although the scheme has dirigiste origins, it is, as we shall see, an exemplar of the spirit of English compromise in its structure. Planning decisions can be divided into two categories: (i) forward planning, which involves the setting of policies to guide the development and use of land, whether by specific land allocations or by general criteria for different types of development; and (ii) decision making on individual applications as assessed against those policies, principally in the determination of applications for planning permission. To ensure compliance with the statutory regime, there are also detailed enforcement provisions.

Forward planning

1.15 The plan making or forward planning aspect of the regime is devolved to the democratic process. A key notion in this respect is that of the 'development plan'.

1.16 By s 38(6) of the 2004 Act, the determination of a planning application must be made in accordance with the development plan unless material considerations indicate otherwise.[18] This provision enshrines a key tenet of national policy for some decades; namely, that planning decisions should be 'plan led'. That primacy is not absolute as is apparent from the language of the section. The decision maker must first identify and construe as a matter of law[19] the true meaning of the relevant policy or policies in the development plan and then strike the balance between the result of that application and the identified material considerations. The latter is a broad concept incapable of any hard edged definition.[20] Whilst one can be reasonably confident that matters relating to land use will fall within its grasp, the decision in point may require consideration of

17 The full list of matters dealt by the planning court is contained in CPR 54.21(2).

18 Successor to s 54A of the 1990 Act. Note that TCPA 1990, s 70(2) similarly requires the decision maker to have regard to the provisions of the development plan, so far as material to the application and to any material considerations.

19 *Tesco Stores Ltd v Dundee CC* [2012] 2 P&CR 9.

20 Although the Supreme Court in *R (Wright) v Resilient Energy Severndale Ltd* [2019] UKSC 53 has equated the scope of material considerations properly relevant to an individual planning application to the tests that must be satisfied for the lawful imposition of a planning condition. The Supreme Court rejected a plea on behalf of the Secretary of State that those tests were in need of updating or, if they were, that it was the role of the courts to undertake such a task. This decision may help to rein in an expansionist approach to non-land use social or community factors being treated as material considerations.

economic and social matters falling outside the conventional framework of land use considerations, particularly where policy requires it to do so.[21]

1.17 The highest level of policy is that made by central government. This does not form part of the development plan and although it is 'merely' a material consideration for the purpose of s 38(6) of the 2004 Act, significant weight is accorded to it. Land use is naturally an area for public controversy and political debate. The government from time to time will have priorities in this field that it will wish to promote in its perception of the public interest. Conventionally this was set out in Circular advice. These were aggrandised and became Planning Policy Guidance Notes, which, as part of the 'regionalisation' of planning policy under the 2004 Act, were then consolidated into a bundle of about 20 individual Planning Policy Statements. These, together with the extant Circular advice, ran to over 1,000 pages. The 2010 coalition administration carried out a root and branch review of this material and, in March 2012, distilled national guidance into the 100 or so pages of the National Planning Policy Framework (NPPF) which it supplemented with a new on-line, practical guidance resource, known as the National Planning Practice Guidance (NPPG). The latest iteration of the NPPF is the streamlined version published in February 2019 that runs to a mere 64 pages. Its claimed purpose was to replace nearly 1,000 pages of planning policy with around 50 'allowing people and communities back into planning'.[22] Significant topics in relation to which the government has consistently set national policies include housing, transport, communications, design, the environment, green belt policy and the historic environment. In earlier manifestations there was 'a presumption in favour of sustainable development, which should be seen as a golden thread running through both plan-making and decision-taking.'[23] That poetic language is missing from the streamlined version of 2019 but the sentiment (and its presumption in favour) persists.

1.18 Since its publication, the NPPF has in practice become the first port of call for many when considering an application for planning permission, notwithstanding its recognition (in paragraph 12) of the development plan as the 'starting point'. Its legal parentage was first said to be 'an exercise of the Crown's common law powers conferred by royal prerogative' but was later identified as being derived, expressly or by implication, from the planning Acts which give the Secretary of State overall responsibility for the oversight of the planning

21 Eg, economic considerations are frequently invoked in the context of enabling development or viability and social and economic considerations lie at the heart of policy concerning the provision of affordable housing. For a recent discussion see *R (on the application of CJ Holder) v Geldling BC* [2014] EWCA Civ 599. However, that which is immaterial in law cannot be made material by the mere statement of policy, whether at national or local levels: per Lord Sales in *Wright* at 42 and 43. The Supreme Court was clear that the way in which land was occupied by particular individuals or groups (whether by an agricultural worker or as affordable rather than general market housing) was a land use matter, notwithstanding that any external manifestations of the use may be no different from other forms of occupation. This seems to move some distance from the view that land use matters are concerned with the character of the use of the land (rather than the purposes of the individual occupier).

22 Foreword to first publication.

23 Paragraph 14 of the NPPF.

system.[24] The document itself acknowledges its limitations. It does not change the statutory status of the development plan and it is no more than guidance (however persuasive) for local planning authorities and decision-takers both in drawing up plans and as a material consideration in determining planning applications.[25] Later chapters will explore what has been described as the over-legalisation of the planning process as a consequence of persistent litigation concerning the application of the former paragraph 49 (now 73) in particular and the requirement for a minimum five year land supply for the development plan to be up to date for the purposes of the application of the tilted balance under paragraph 11 (former 14).

1.19 Governments have, over the last few decades, used primary legislation supported by various 'carrot and stick' policies to encourage early and up to date plan making at the local level. By these means they seek to ensure that local communities are responsible for their own decision making subject to the many requirements of central government policy. However, the processes are slow and can be cumbersome. As a result there has been a succession of tinkerings with the legislative scheme undertaken by successive administrations. The Planning White Paper of summer 2020 heralds further reform and sets out an ambition for all development plans to be adopted within a 30-month period. It remains to be seen whether this will deliver the comprehensive geographic completion of the 'plan-led' system, which has been a work in progress since 1948.[26]

1.20 The tripartite system of structure plans, (old) local plans and unitary development plans was replaced in England in 2004[27] by a new three-tier system, which interposed a new level of policy between central government policy and local policy in the form of regional spatial strategies. The country was divided into eight regions (London was later added as a ninth), administered by Regional Development Agencies which aimed to stimulate economic development. As part of this reform, the regional spatial strategies, produced by regional planning bodies, were intended to go beyond traditional land use planning to integrate land use policies with other regional strategies, simplify the plan hierarchy and enable shorter, better focused plans at the local level which could be adopted and revised more quickly. This scheme lasted only a few years. The Regional Development Agencies were abolished in 2012, and the Regional Spatial Strategies progressively revoked from 2010 at a time of widespread government cuts and as part of the 2010 coalition administration's localism agenda, which sought to achieve greater participation at a local level in planning matters and remove what by then was stigmatised as 'top-down planning'.

24 Laws LJ in *R (West Berkshire DC) v SSETR* [2016] 1 WLR 3923 at 12 cited with disapproval by Lord Carnwath in *Suffolk Coastal DC & ors v Hopkins Homes* [2017] UKSC 37 at 19.

25 Lord Carnwath above at 21: 'It cannot, and does not purport to, displace the primacy given by the statute and policy to the statutory development plan. It must be exercised consistently with, and so as not to displace or distort, the statutory scheme.'

26 The City of York still has no adopted local plan to set the detailed boundaries of its Green Belt, despite the concept of that Green Belt first emerging in the 1950s.

27 The Planning and Compulsory Purchase Act 2004 (PCPA 2004).

1.21 As matters currently stand, the development plan is defined to include local development documents which are specified by the authority to be a development plan document[28] (called a local plan[29]) and which specify various matters, including the development and use of land which the local planning authority wish to encourage during any specified period, the allocation of sites for a particular type of development or use, and development management and site allocation policies, which are intended to guide the determination of planning applications.[30] Neighbourhood Plans, prepared by neighbourhood bodies (such as parish councils or neighbourhood forums) and subject to local referenda after passing scrutiny by an examiner looking at compliance with specified basic conditions rather than detailed matters, also take their place as part of the development plan, once 'made' by the local planning authority.[31]

1.22 The public has a role in plan making via the necessary stages of public consultation. The planning authority must provide a 'statement of community involvement', setting out the authority's policy as to the involvement in the process of persons who appear to the authority to have an interest in matters relating to development in their area.[32] The interest of the public is also maintained via the public scrutiny of the 'soundness' of local plans undertaken by independent planning inspectors appointed by PINS.[33] Central government remains the plan maker of last resort via reserve powers to call-in plans for the determination of the Secretary of State. These reserve powers are rarely invoked but nevertheless the threat of their use can provide a useful constraint on a rogue planning authority.[34]

Decision making

1.23 We now turn to the scheme for decision making or 'development management' as it is termed in the trade, formerly known as development control. These are the decisions taken at a site-specific level on applications for individual planning permission (which must be determined in accordance with the development plan, unless material considerations indicate otherwise, as set

28 See PCPA 2004, ss 37(3) and 38(3).

29 Town and Country Planning (Local Planning) (England) Regulations 2012, SI 2012/767, reg 2.

30 Town and Country Planning (Local Planning) (England) Regulations 2012, SI 2012/767, reg 5.

31 See TCPA 1990, s 61E and Schedule 4B, together with PCPA 2004, s 38(3A) in relation to neighbourhood plans (in England) which have been endorsed by a referendum but not yet 'made' by the local planning authority.

32 See PCPA 2004, ss 18 and 19.

33 An independent agency funded by central government. See PCPA 2004, s 20(5).

34 In March 2020, the Secretary of State did intervene in the South Oxfordshire local plan, which the council had wanted to withdraw (after a change of political control). The Secretary of State required the local plan examination to continue with an accelerated timetable. The Examining Inspector recommended in favour of some seven strategic greenfield development areas and a limited consultation on the Inspector's modifications is unlikely to lead to an overall change in direction. The Secretary of State may compel adoption of the local plan. Intervention was also threatened in Wirral, Thanet, and Castle Point but in these cases the threat was sufficient to encourage progress on the local plans to continue, albeit only Thanet achieved an adopted plan in 2020.

out above), listed building consent, conservation area consent and the like. In the first instance this activity is reserved to the local planning authority. Appeals may be made to the Secretary of State against the refusal of planning permission or the failure to determine an application in the due time. Appeals are permitted from decisions to refuse these applications to the Secretary of State. The Minister may take the decision or it may be devolved to PINS and, thus, the inspector who determines the appeal. The Secretary of State has a reserve power to 'call in' or reserve/recover the decision for his determination at any time prior to a permission being issued on the application by the planning authority or, in the case of an appeal, the issue of the decision of the inspector.

1.24 A key element of the statutory regime since the introduction of the 1947 Act, is the requirement that 'development' may not be carried out without the benefit of planning permission.[35] Development is defined, by s 55(1) of the 1990 Act as: 'the carrying out of building, engineering, mining, or other operations in, on, over or under land[36] or the making of a material change in the use of any buildings or other land'.

1.25 The first category is known collectively as 'operational development'. Section 55(2) provides that limited categories of operational development are nevertheless excluded from control, such as works of internal maintenance and improvement not altering the external appearance of a building and development by certain statutory bodies. Certain categories of development have the benefit of a deemed planning permission by operation of s 57(3) of the 1990 Act, as set out in Sch 2 to the Town and Country Planning (General Permitted Development) Order 2015.[37]

1.26 The concept of making a material change in use is not further defined by statute although s 55 exempts the use of any land for the purposes of agriculture or forestry and the use of any buildings or other land within the curtilage of a dwellinghouse for any purpose incidental to the enjoyment of the dwellinghouse as such from these controls. The process of determination whether a material change of use has occurred is a fact sensitive exercise requiring knowledge of the classification of the existing use and the extent to which a material change in that use has taken place by reference to the relevant planning unit in which the use takes place. Whilst the cases accept the proposition that a material change can take place through the intensification of an existing use that will only occur if the result is to take the activity in question into a different category of use. These cases will be very rare with no example as yet in the law reports.[38] Knowledge is also required of the concepts of predominant and ancillary uses, composite uses, dual uses, recurrent or seasonal uses, existing and established uses. These concepts are beyond the bounds of this introductory chapter. Certain changes of use, either within the defined Use Classes or from one Use Class to another,

35 TCPA 1990, s 57.
36 By amendment defined for the avoidance of doubt to include the demolition of buildings.
37 SI 2015/596.
38 *Fidler v The First Secretary of State* [2004] EWCA Civ 1295. See *also Hertfordshire CC v Secretary of State for Communities and Local Government* [2012] EWCA Civ 1473.

are also excluded from the definition of development, as set out in the Town and Country Planning (Use Classes) Order 1987 (as amended).[39]

1.27 Section 38(6) of the Planning and Compulsory Purchase Act 2004 requires the decision maker to determine matters before him in accordance with the development plan unless material considerations indicate otherwise. In the same exercise s 70(2) of the 1990 Act requires regard to be had to the development plan and 'any other material consideration.' That precedence to the development plan accorded by statute cannot be removed by policy, even that made at a national level. As observed above, the NPPF is a material consideration to be weighed in the balance in making the decision, not a substitute for the development plan policy in point. The focus is thus drawn to the identification of the development plan for these purposes, the proper interpretation of the policy as a matter of law and whether its 'most important' policies are, collectively, to be regarded as up to date for the purposes of the application of the tilted balance in the NPPF,[40] what are the material considerations in play and whether the balance struck by the decision maker between the policy and the material considerations was undertaken soundly as a matter of law.

1.28 Before turning to those issues, if one is seeking to challenge a decision before the court, it must be appreciated that the court strongly deprecates excessive legal analysis and dissection of decisions which have been entrusted by Parliament to non-lawyers, be they councillors, planning officers, inspectors or, ultimately, the Secretary of State. The current authoritative guide to the approach taken by the court to such a challenge is set out in the judgments of the Court of Appeal in *St Modwen Developments Ltd v SSCLG* [2017] EWCA Civ 1643 and that of Lindblom LJ in principle where he restated the seven relevant principles already familiar from his judgment in *Bloor Homes East Midlands Ltd v SSCLG* [2014] EWHC 754 (Admin) given in the Planning Court. As an extension of that principle it has been established that no higher standard of scrutiny should be utilised when scrutinising a decision of the Secretary of State where he is differing from the advice given by the Panel in determining a Development Consent Order: per Holgate J in *R (ClientEarth) vSSHCLG* [2020] EWHC 1303 (Admin).

1.29 The starting point to the consideration of whether the decision-maker has exercised the duty under s 38(6) is the case of *DW Trading Ltd v SSCLG* [2016] EWCA Civ 493, which is another example of Lindblom LJ's helpful practice of setting out the relevant general propositions of law in the decisions of the Court of Appeal in planning cases. The fourth proposition endorsed by the Court was that 'the duty can only be properly performed if the decision-maker, in the course of making the decision, establishes whether or not the proposal accords with the development plan as a whole'. This test can easily lead to an overly legalistic analysis of a decision letter written to the parties to a public inquiry as Lindblom LJ found in that case. It may be sufficient to

39 SI 1987/764.

40 *Wavendon Properties Ltd v SSHCLG* [2019] EWHC 1524 (Admin).

reduce that question to a single issue without making reference to the plan as a whole where appropriate. Moreover, where the plan's policies pull in different directions, it will be a matter of planning judgment for the decision-maker whether the proposal in question can be said to comply with the development plan as a whole so as to take advantage of the statutory presumption: *R (Corbett) v Cornwall Council* [2020] EWCA Civ. The court is always ready to uphold the decision if it is implicit from the decision that the decision-maker has considered the relevant development plan policies: *Gill v Secretary of State for Communities and Local Government* [2015] EWHC 2660 (Admin) at §22 – §24 and *R (Butler) v East Dorset DC* [2016] EWHC 1527 (Admin) at §32 5 [2015] 1 WLR 2367 at §37 – §43. Further, the courts are ready to recognise that in applying the statutory test it is legitimate and necessary for the decision-maker to make the relevant judgment 'bearing in mind such factors as the *importance* of the policies that are complied with or infringed and the *extent* of that compliance or breach'.[41]

1.30 The material consideration is a concept which has been with the planning system since the dawn of time, which in this case is the 1947 Act. We are brought up with *Stringer v Minister of Housing and Local Government* [1970] 1 WLR 1281 and *Newbury District Council v Secretary of State for the Environment* [1981] AC 578 to regard this as a broad concept to be assessed contextually with regard to its relationship with the character of the use of the land without over distinction between public and private law attributes. However, clear boundaries remain. In *R (Wright) v Resilient Energy Severndale Ltd etc* [2019] UKSC 53 the Court rejected an intriguing submission to the effect that government policy that encouraged developers of certain 'green energy' projects to make contributions to local community projects as part of the s 106 package associated with the grant of new permissions could be taken into account as a material consideration in favour of the proposal under s 38(6) etc. It remains a fundamental proposition of planning law that planning permissions cannot be bought or sold.

1.31 Once it is established that the decision-maker has properly identified and construed the relevant policies of the development plan and the material considerations relevant to the striking of the balance under s 38(6) the task of the court is complete. The court will always refuse to be drawn into the arena of striking the balance, which is a matter exclusively for the expert judgment of the decision maker, unless the decision can otherwise be found to be defective in public law terms ie *Wednesbury* principles of rationality etc.

1.32 It is not enough to identify an error of law in the decision in question. The court will not quash the decision unless the claimant has discharged the burden of demonstrating that had the error not been made there was a real rather than a forensic possibility that the decision would be different: *Tesco v Dundee* (above).

41 Per Sullivan J in *Rochdale*, recently applied by Holgate J in *Dignity Funerals v Breckland District Council* [2017] EWHC 1492 (Admin).

Enforcement

1.33 In this imperfect world, development is from time to time undertaken without the benefit of planning permission; whether deliberately or through inadvertence. The code (set out principally in Part VII of the 1990 Act) provides an enforcement regime permitting the local planning authority to intervene to correct such irregularities where it is expedient to do so. There is an enforcement notice procedure buttressed by provisions enabling the grant of injunctions, stop notices, and powers to permit the authority to undertake the necessary corrective work itself. The law also provides immunity from enforcement, since the 1990 Act provides that development, which is by definition unlawful, will become lawful as a result of the passage of time.[42] Operational development becomes immune from enforcement after the end of four years beginning when the operations were substantially complete, except where development has been concealed from the planning authority.[43] In the case of a material change in the use of land, no action may be taken after the end of the period of ten years beginning with the date of the breach. That time period is reduced to four years in the case of making a change of use to a single dwellinghouse.

Environmental regulation, human rights and conservation

1.34 This has been an increasing area of focus of activity in recent years in terms of legislation, both European and domestic, and in terms of challenges by interested parties and groups to the planning decisions of local and national government. Parliament has also been busy in this field in its supervisory capacity with the select committees of both Houses considering the petitions against the HS2 legislation. The EIA Directive and SEA Directive and equivalent domestic regulations ensure that the environmental impacts of development are assessed and taken into account before the grant of planning permission or the adoption or submission of a plan or programme. The final departure of the United Kingdom from the European Union on 31 December 2020 has not led to any immediate cutting loose of the ties of European law. By virtue of sections 2 to 6 of the European Union (Withdrawal) Act 2018 (as amended by the European Union (Withdrawal Agreement) Act 2020), the existing body of EU law and its associated jurisprudence is incorporated into domestic law, save to the extent that the Supreme Court or a relevant court (as defined by the European Union (Withdrawal) Act 2018 (Relevant Court) (Retained EU Case Law) Regulations 2020, SI 2020/1525) concludes it should not be bound by that jurisprudence.

1.35 In the case of a planning application, the EIA Regulations provide that an 'environmental impact assessment' will be necessary for certain types of development invariably,[44] or in certain other types of development,[45] either

42 See TCPA 1990, s 171B and s 191.

43 *R (Welwyn Hatfield BC) v Secretary of State* [2011] UKSC 15; *Jackson v Secretary of State* [2015] EWHC 20 (Admin).

44 As set out in SI 2017/571, Sch 1.

45 As set out in SI 2017/571, Sch 2.

where the development exceeds certain thresholds (mostly in relation to its size) or is located in an environmentally sensitive area and is likely to have to have significant effects on the environment by virtue of factors such as its nature, size or location.
Similar provisions apply to high level plans and programmes by virtue of the SEA Directive.

1.36 The Habitats Directive and equivalent domestic regulations provide for the designation and protection of sites which are important for various habitats or species[46] and provide that plans or projects which are likely to have significant effects on such a site must be subject to an appropriate assessment of the implications for that site in view of that site's conservation objectives and ensures that they do not adversely affect the integrity of those sites.

1.37 An example of the potential potency of this ground of objection is provided by the litigation concerning the decision of the government to authorise the Third Runway at Heathrow. In February 2020, the Court of Appeal found the decision to be unlawful on the basis that the government had not taken into account its own commitments to climate change entered into by way of international treaty obligations and in May 2020 the Supreme Court gave permission to appeal. This is an instructive case on the power of environmental issues to disrupt infrastructure decision making. The need for and the consequent policy to support the runway was set out in the Airports National Policy Statement issued by the government which was the foundation of its policy case. This challenge was taken as an opportunity to challenge the lawfulness of that policy on the basis that there was an inadequate explanation of how, if at all, in making this policy the government had taken into account its commitments to climate change targets entered into by the ratification of the Paris Accord in November 2016. In so concluding the Court of Appeal[47] differed from the decision of the Planning Court[48] which had preferred to leave the implications of this international treaty to reduce global carbon emissions as a matter of high policy for the government with which it would not interfere. The Supreme Court in December 2020 ([2020] UKSC 52) reversed the decision of the Court of Appeal and found that the Airports National Policy Statement did not need to have regard to the Paris Accord, which was not yet translated into any formal statement of government policy. Ministerial statements were not formal expressions of government policy.

1.38 Consistent with the reluctance of the common law to endorse arid technicalities there has been a consistent line of decision making to the effect that claims of breach of European environmental directives should be considered in a pragmatic way. In *R (Champion) v North Norfolk District Council* [2015] UKSC 52 the Supreme Court found that the application in point should have been the subject of an EIA assessment so that the planning permission

46 As listed in Annexes I and II of the Habitats Directive.

47 Lord Justices Linblom, Singh and Haddon-Cave.

48 Hickinbottom and Holgate JJ. Despite their judgment being described by the court as 'a tour de force'.

was granted unlawfully. Despite this error the Court followed the practice it had adopted in *Walton v Scottish Ministers* [2012] UKSC 44 and refused to grant relief on the basis that there had been no substantial prejudice. Likewise, in *Sustainable Shetland* [2015] UKSC 4 the breach of the Birds Directive met a robust pragmatic response from the Court led by Lord Carnwath (as in *Walton* and *Champion*). The Court has moved a long way since the far more restrictive approach to the refusal of discretionary relief was voiced in *Berkeley v SSETR* [2001] 2 AC 603.

1.39 The European Court could be said to have hit back in *People Over Wind v Coille Teoranta* (Case C-323/17) (2018) where the ECJ found it to be a breach of the Appropriate Assessment procedure under the Habitats Directive to take account of proposed mitigation measures when judging the implications of the proposal for the significance of the habitat in question and that the test was whether there was the removal of all reasonable scientific doubt as to the effects of the proposed works on the protected site. This decision was contrary to English experience and it caused many authorities to delay their emerging plans because of the likely failure of their screening decisions against this test. It overthrew the existing domestic position established by the decision of Sullivan J in *R (Hart) v SSCLG* [2008] 2 P&CR 16. The ECJ has taken a similar approach to the taking into account of mitigating measures in the context of Appropriate Assessments in the *Dutch Nitrogen* cases.[49] The Planning Court has held that the ECJ approach is now *acte clair* and to be followed[50] but the Court nevertheless applied the *Champion* principle and dismissed the claim as it had not been demonstrated that the decision was not likely to be different had the proper procedure been followed.

1.40 The incorporation of the European Convention of Human Rights into the domestic law of the UK by way of the Human Rights Act 1998 has had a significant impact on planning law. Enforcement proceedings taken against the development of a new house or the siting of a new caravan, for example, may raise issues by reference the Article 8 right to family and private life and local planning authorities must now be alive in such cases to the need to ensure that enforcement action is proportionate.[51] Whilst various aspects of the procedure (and particularly the Secretary of State's involvement in the process) have been challenged as being incompatible with the Article 6 right to a fair trial, the scheme as drafted has broadly been upheld as being in conformity with the Convention, particularly in light of the availability of judicial review as a remedy for those disaffected by the decisions taken by central and local government.[52]

1.41 Listed building consent is required under the Planning (Listed Buildings and Conservation Areas) Act 1990 for the demolition, alteration or extension of a building which is entered on the list of special architectural or historic interest

49 Cooperative Mobilisation for the Environment and Vereniging and Leefmilieu Case C-293/17.

50 *Canterbury CC & Gladman v SSHCLG* [2019] EWHC 2001 (Admin) per Dove J.

51 See, eg, *South Buckinghamshire District Council v Porter* [2003] UKHL 26.

52 See *R v Secretary of State for the Environment, Transport and the Regions, ex p Alconbury Developments Ltd* [2001] UKHL 23 and *Lough v First Secretary of State* [2004] 1 WLR 2557.

maintained by English Heritage. Section 66 of this Act imposes a particular duty on decision makers when considering whether or not to grant planning permission for development which affects a listed building or its setting or any features of special architectural or historical interest which it possesses. The Court of Appeal has recently reminded us that this establishes a need to give particular weight to this objective.[53]

1.42 Section 74 of the 1990 Act provides that Conservation Area consent is required to demolish any building in a conservation area.[54] Section 72 imposes a general duty that in the exercise of any planning functions with respect to any buildings or land within a conservation area requires the paying of special attention to the desirability of preserving or enhancing the character or appearance of that area.

1.43 Other controls exist over trees protected by the Tree Preservation Orders and trees within conservation areas and there is a separate statutory code regulating advertising and caravan development.

D THE DEMISE OF PLANNING 'EXCEPTIONALISM'?

1.44 Any casual reader of the structure of the 1990 Act and associated statutes would be likely to assume that Parliament had legislated for a complete statutory regime governing land use planning without the need to refer to concepts or principles of law outside the regime. Certainly, there was a time when the courts saw the planning system as a comprehensive and complete regulatory code and the case law on that regime seemed at times to develop its own jurisprudence, outside of the mainstream of wider principles of administrative law.[55] More recently, the trend has been to see planning as a facet of public body or local authority decision making, and so subject to the same broad principles of law, both as regards the interpretation of statutory provisions, policies or other guidance, and as regards their deployment when making individual decisions.[56]

1.45 Lord Scarman in *Pioneer Aggregates (UK) Ltd v Secretary of State for the Environment*[57] was among the first to describe the statutes and orders making up the planning system as a 'comprehensive code'. This led him to reject the idea that a planning permission could be 'abandoned' after a prolonged period of non-use on the basis that no reference was made to abandonment in the statutory

53 *East Northamptonshire DC v Secretary of State for Communities and Local Government* [2014] EWCA Civ 137.

54 Now required only in Wales. The Enterprise and Regulatory Reform Act 2013 implemented the Penfold Review recommendation to reduce 'red tape' by removing the need to obtain both planning permission and conservation area consent.

55 See, eg, *R v Derbyshire County Council ex parte Woods* [1997] JPL 958 at 967 on the interpretation of policy statements in government guidance.

56 See per Lord Reed in *Tesco v Dundee City Council* [2012] UKSC at 18 to 20; per Lewison LJ in *R (Khodari) v Royal Borough of Kensington & Chelsea* [2017] EWCA Civ 333 at 38.

57 [1985] AC 132.

scheme. This has led to the reduction in the use of judge-made 'fixes' to fill the gaps, existing or perceived, in the code. Lord Hoffmann accelerated that process in *R (on the application of Reprotech (Pebsham) Ltd) v East Sussex County Council*[58] declaring that it was 'unhelpful to introduce private law concepts of estoppel into planning law' and that the time had come for planning law 'to stand upon its own two feet' unaided in this way.

1.46 In the early days of the development of planning law attention was frequently paid to the underlying purpose of actions to see if they were genuine or merely 'colourable'; that is, undertaken for technical advantage only without intention of completion. This common law ornament to the statute has, in a similar spirit, been swept away.[59]

1.47 One area of judicial creation to supplement the statute that survives arises in the determination of whether a planning permission has been lawfully implemented in accordance with its conditions. In such cases the courts have found it necessary to consider whether or not conditions can be said to 'go to the heart' of the permission and thus require compliance before the permission can be said to be implemented or, alternatively, are ones that may be breached without putting the permission itself at risk. Here the court is engaged in taking value judgments which are not recognised in any way by the legislative scheme but which have been accepted by the Court of Appeal as necessary in order to address the underlying reality of the situation.[60]

1.48 Another judicial supplement to the framework of the Act is the concept of implying conditions into planning permissions where it is appropriate to do so. The received wisdom was that the need for certainty in public documents ruled out such a process: Sullivan J in *Sevenoaks District Council v The First Secretary of State* [2005] 1 P&CR 186. The Supreme Court has considered this process in two recent decisions. In *Trump International Golf Club Scotland Ltd v The Scottish Ministers* [2015] UKSC 74 the Court was prepared to include within a statutory consent requirements derived from the application not made explicit in the consent in question and in his judgment Lord Carnwath foreshadowed his approach to the issue in planning cases. His opportunity to explore the issue expressly in the context of the implication of conditions to a planning permission arose in *London Borough of Lambeth v SSHCLG* [2019] UKSC 33. This concerned the failure of the planning authority to repeat conditions from an earlier permission to another permission granted under s 73 of the 1990 Act. Here the intention of the s 73 application was to relax a condition imposed on the permission under which development had already commenced. The Court was

58 [2003] 1 WLR 348 where the Court rejected the claim that a local planning authority was bound by the erroneous advice given by a planning officer that a particular development would not require planning permission. In so doing he brushed away the decision of the majority in the Court of Appeal in *Western Fish Products Ltd v Penwith DC* [1981] 2 All ER 204.

59 See *East Dunbartonshire Council v Secretary of State for Scotland* [1999] 1 PLR 53 in contrast to, eg *Spackman v SOSE* [1977] 1 ALL ER 257 and *Agecrest v Gwynedd CC* [1998] JPL 325.

60 See Woolf LJ in *Whitley & Sons v Secretary of State for Wales* [1992] 3 PLR 72 and *R (on the application of Hart Aggregates Ltd) v Hartlepool BC* [2005] 2 P&CR 31.

ready to imply the inclusion of those conditions that remained unchanged in the first permission into that granted under s 73 as a matter of necessary implication as in *Trump*. The Court also held, obiter, that in any event the development would remain subject to those conditions as the first permission had been implemented despite subsequent implementation of the later s 73 permission since the two permissions remained compatible with one another.

1.49 A number of potentially problematic judicial supplements to the code arises in the field of enforcement against breaches of planning control. For example, in deciding whether works of operational development have been 'substantially completed' so as to trigger the commencement of the four-year period required for immunity from enforcement, the court has determined that a 'holistic approach' is required, comparing the completed development with what was permitted. A holistic test is also used to consider whether a development as a whole is unlawful because of a failure to obtain planning permission for part of the works in question. The concept of a 'holistic approach' was first used by Lord Hobhouse in *Sage v SSE* and was considered by Ouseley J in *Commercial Land v SSTLG &R* [2003] JPL 358. In the author's experience the test is widely relied on the context of a breach of condition attached to a planning permission to promote the argument that as a matter of principle the entire development undertaken in reliance on that permission is unlawful. Context is probably the most important touchstone here as the court would not, for example, be likely to find a development as a whole unlawful because the wrong materials were used in its construction or there was some minor departure from the approved plans. In that context one would hope that the court would find that an adequate remedy already exists in the enforcement framework to remedy a breach of condition as such. Perhaps the answer lies in an analogy with Lord Hodge's judgment in *Trump* to the effect that an invalid condition attached to a consent could not render that consent invalid unless it was 'a fundamental condition which determines the scope and nature of a development'.

1.50 In cases involving a change in use, the court's intervention has also been necessary by way of clarification of the relevant provisions. For example, when deciding whether a change in use has arisen, the proper approach is to compare the present use with the previous use and assess whether there has been any material change of use: see *Thurrock BC v Secretary of State for the Environment, Transport and the Regions*.[61] A use will only be immune from enforcement by reference to s 171B of the 1990 Act if the local planning authority could have taken enforcement action during the entirety of the relevant period. Whilst short periods of inactivity would not necessarily amount to a cessation of the unlawful activity, longer periods could and cessation of the unlawful use merely constituted compliance with the law, in which case the clock would be reset. While enforcement action may be taken during the applicable time period even if at the precise moment of taking enforcement action the use objected to is not actually occurring, the land would need to be properly described as being used for the objectionable activity.

61 [2001] JPL 1388.

1.51 Particular issues have been thrown up in cases involving a change in use to a single dwelling house. Where it is claimed that there has been a change in use of any building to use as a single dwelling house by reference to s 171B(2) of the 1990 Act, it was established in *Welwyn Hatfield Borough Council v Secretary of State for Communities and Local Government*[62] (reversing the Court of Appeal on this point) that the building in question must have been in some active use prior to the change in that use to a single dwelling house, in order for the four-year period required for immunity to be triggered. The Supreme Court in *Welwyn Hatfield* also confirmed (following judicial authority suggesting otherwise) that a change in use to a single dwelling house may take place even before any 'actual use' for such purposes (and it has been suggested, for example, that a change of use might take place when the necessary physical alterations had been made to enable such use to take place). The issue was required to be approached 'in the round' and the question asked of what use the building has or of what use it is. Finally, the Court in *Welwyn Hatfield* also made clear that the planning regime was subject to the general principle that law should serve the public interest and that a person should not be able to take advantage of the law to benefit from his own wrong. The relevant parts of the Act were required to be interpreted in such a way that a person like Mr Beesley (who had deliberately constructed a house to look like a barn so as to evade enforcement action) should not be entitled to invoke the benefits of immunity from enforcement action afforded by s 171B(2) of the 1990 Act. In the Court's view, Mr Beesley had engaged in positive deception in matters integral to the planning process (applying for and obtaining planning permission) which was directly intended to and did undermine the regular operation of that process and such a person should not be permitted to profit directly from this deception. Such issues of 'concealment' were the subject of swift legislative action in the form of ss 171BA-BC of the 1990 Act (albeit that the principles in *Welwyn Hatfield* stand: see *Jackson v Secretary of State for Communities and Local Government*).[63]

E THE ROLE OF THE COURT

1.52 The legislation has, since the advent of the 1947 Act, granted a supervisory role to the High Court in respect of the full range of decisions made under the regime, including development control, forward planning decisions and enforcement.[64] The right to challenge, consistent with the court's supervisory as opposed to appellate role, has been consistently restricted to errors of law in decision making and actionable procedural failures. The relevant statutory provisions limit the scope of challenges to decision making in the planning sphere by reference to the strict time period for challenge, the identity of the person who may make the challenge[65] and, in some situations, the grounds on

62 [2011] 2 AC 304.
63 [2016] QB 811.
64 See TCPA 1990, ss 284–288 of the 1990 Act and PCPA 2004, s 113.
65 To a 'person aggrieved', TCPA 1990, s 287(2) and PCPA 2004, s 113(3).

which the challenge may be made.[66] The errors of law required to support a claim are otherwise similar to those established as grounds of judicial review.[67] No summary of those tests can be comprehensive but the main features are that the decision follows the appropriate statutory framework; a fair procedure has been adopted; rational reasons have been given for making decisions; that the decision maker has considered the relevant material considerations and discounted the irrelevant. These tests are applied pragmatically, conscious of the context in which the decisions fall to be made, and the court will act to quash decisions only where it is appropriate to do so.

1.53 There is one area in the field of validity where the statutory code is incomplete. The anomaly is the absence of a statutory challenge to the grant of planning permission by the local planning authority. In this instance the remedy is an application for judicial review. Here the class of persons with sufficient standing to commence proceedings is anyone with a real and genuine interest in obtaining the relief sought.[68] The requirement for permission to make such a challenge applies, as to all judicial review applications, in the normal way.

1.54 The confluence of the planning regime and judicial review streams (including statutory challenges to planning decisions) has been an immensely productive one for both disciplines. From the trickle of early planning and judicial review cases prior to the codification of the procedure for challenging the decision of an administrative body in 1977,[69] both streams have become raging torrents and some of the most important public law cases have arisen out of planning decisions and vice versa.

1.55 The reasons for this level of activity are manifold. First, as discussed earlier in this chapter we are a small island with a large population. There is a great amount of pressure on the use to which we put our land. There is very often a tension between the use to which the owner would wish to put to his land (whether a multinational development company wishing to build 2,000 homes or the humble occupier of a bungalow wishing to build an extension) and the views of surrounding residents who would wish to preserve the status quo. The views of those involved are, more often than not, extremely strongly held. Add to that the political imperative behind certain types of development and the sometimes eye-watering commercial reward that the grant of planning permission for a particular development may bring (particularly where new homes are involved) and you have the perfect recipe for many a planning court claim.

66 For example, a challenge to the validity of development plan documents adopted under the 2004 Act may only be challenged on the grounds that the document is not within the appropriate power or that a procedural requirement has not been complied with (PCPA 2004, s 113(3)).

67 See, eg, in relation to appeals under s 288 of the 1990 Act, *Seddon Properties Ltd v Secretary of State for the Environment* [1981] 42 P & CR 26.

68 *R (Kides) v South Cambridgeshire District Council* [2003] JPL 431 CA.

69 With the amendment of the Rules of the Supreme Court.

1.56 Secondly much of the activity derives from the complex and technical nature of the issues involved in making a planning decision. These have been discussed above and can be wide ranging. They can involve the provisions of one or more of the many statutes, the application of relevant policy tests which may be required to be met in the individual case (for example in relation to the Green Belt or where heritage assets are involved), and they may be procedural such as environmental assessment or the obligation to involve the public in decision making by way of consultation (and otherwise). The scrutiny on planning decisions is intense and the corresponding scope for error would be large were it not for the self-denying ordinance of the court. The court is scrupulous to leave the planning judgments to the decision maker and will only intervene where a clear error of law can be established.

1.57 Planning has given rise to some of the most important judicial review cases and led to the development of important public law concepts. For example, a string of planning cases shaped the meaning and limits of the requirement that an applicant must have a 'sufficient interest'[70] in the matter to which the claim relates; the court on the one hand preventing a group of theatre enthusiasts from challenging the decision by the Secretary of State not to schedule the Rose Theatre in London as a listed building[71] while on the other permitting Greenpeace to challenge a decision to licence a new method of treating radioactive waste.[72] The concept of bias as a ground for challenging decisions was developed in a series of planning judicial reviews[73] while *R (Burkett) v Hammersmith and Fulham LB*[74] was a seminal case on the three-month time period for bringing judicial review proceedings. In *R (Alconbury Developments Ltd) v Secretary of State*[75] the court

70 See Senior Courts Act 1981, s 31(3). The sufficient interest requirement must be distinguished from the need to be a 'person aggrieved' in order to bring a statutory challenge to a planning decision under the 1990 and 2004 Acts, which is a narrower concept.

71 On the basis that mere weight of numbers did not mean that a group of persons had a sufficient interest (*R v Secretary of State, ex parte Rose Theatre Trust* [1990] 1 QB 504).

72 On the basis that 2,500 members lived near the site and that Greenpeace was a long-established body with great expertise in area which could assist the court better than any one individual (*R v Inspectorate of Pollution ex parte Greenpeace* [1994] 4 All ER 329). See also *R v Somerset County Council, ex parte Dixon* [1998] Env L 111; *R (Kides) v South Cambridgeshire District Council* [2002] EWCA Civ 1370 and *R (Edwards) v Environment Agency* [2004] EWHC 736.

73 See in particular *R (Island Farm Development Ltd) v Bridgend County Borough Council* [2006] EWHC 2189 (Admin); *R (Lewis) v Redcar and Cleveland Borough Council* [2008] EWCA Civ 746; *R (Berky) v Newport City Council* [2012] EWCA Civ 378 and *R (Bishop's Stortford Civic Federation) v East Hertfordshire District Council* [2014] EWHC 348 (Admin).

74 [2002] UKHL 23 where the applicant sought to challenge a resolution to grant planning permission seven months after the decision, although the court held that the time period runs from the actual grant of the permission, rather than the resolution so that there was no delay in the circumstances. The application of the principles regarding delay will in any event now be limited by the requirement to challenge any decision made by the Secretary of State or local planning authority under the planning acts within six weeks (CPR 54.5(5)).

75 [2001] UKHL 23. In particular, whether the Secretary of State's power to 'call in' and determine for himself planning applications and appeals where he would inevitably have regard to his own policies was Article 6 compliant, the Court finding that although the Secretary of State was not independent or impartial, the planning system as a whole together with judicial review was compliant. The case is also notable for its consideration of a decision maker's failure to take into account relevant considerations and the taking into account of irrelevant considerations.

examined in detail the scope of the Article 6 ECHR right to an independent and impartial tribunal by reference to the planning regime while the proposition that a breach of EU law was fatal to an administrative decision made on these shores was established by *Berkeley v Secretary of State.*[76]

1.58 An ever-present tension in planning law is the divide between law and policy. In the former the court is the ultimate authority: *Tesco v Dundee* firmly identified the court as the ultimate arbiter on the meaning of planning policy albeit with a nod to its character as a formulation of land use policy rather than law. The application of policy has been equally firmly identified as a matter for the exclusive judgment of the decision maker, whether that is the planning authority or the Secretary of State and his inspectorate on appeal. The bright line distinction is clear but it tends to blur at the margins. A recent decision of the Supreme Court provides an instructive example. In *R (Samuel Smith Old Brewery (Tadcaster) v North Yorkshire County Council* [2020] UKSC 3 the Court had to apply its mind to the meaning of the concept of 'openness' as found in Green Belt policy set out in the NPPF in general and the question of whether 'visual impact', to use the clumsy jargon essential to the process, was a necessary part of the assessment of the effect of the proposal on openness. The Supreme Court (judgment of the Court given by Lord Carnwath whose signal contribution to the development of planning law could be the subject of a separate chapter), overriding the Court of Appeal, decided that the concept of 'openness' was 'a good example' of a policy expressed in broad terms that does not require or lend itself to an intense form of legal analysis. Whilst the visual effects of the proposed development could be a relevant consideration to the decision of whether the proposal adversely affected the openness of the Green Belt at the relevant location, it was, on the facts of the case, not an error of law to conclude it was not material. Hereafter the court will need to distinguish between those factors which in law are material considerations of such significance that they must be considered if a decision is to be lawful and those which may as a matter of planning judgment be discounted as necessary to the decision in hand. Similar robust handling of legal challenges to what are at core planning judgments in the application of Green Belt policy is found in *Compton Parish Council & ors v Guildford Borough Council* [2019] EWHC 3242 (Admin) where Ouseley J found that the NPPF 'exceptional circumstances' test applicable to plan made releases of Green Belt land as another area in danger of 'being judicially over-analysed'. The test is met in 'an accumulation or combination of circumstances, of varying natures, which entitle the decision-maker, in the rational exercise of planning judgment, to say that the circumstances are sufficiently exceptional to warrant altering the Green Belt boundary'. But where the issue of policy interpretation is capable of an objective answer the court will not hesitate to intervene: *R (Wiltshire Council) v SSHCLG* [2020] EWHC 954 (Admin) Lieven J on the meaning of 'dwelling' in NPPF 79.

76 [2000] UKHL 36 where there had been a complete failure to produce an Environmental Statement for the purpose of the EIA Directive. Although it should be noted that the courts have since sought to limit the application of the principle in *Berkeley* (see *Bown v Secretary of State* [2003] EWCA Civ 1170 and *R (Edwards) v Environment Agency* [2008] UKHL 22). See also *R (Morge) v Hampshire County Council* [2011] UKSC 2 in relation to the compatibility of a planning permission with the Habitats Directive.

1.59 One area where the courts have subjected the statutory regime to close scrutiny is in the field of 'ouster clauses' which seek to limit the circumstances in which or the time within which legal challenges can be brought to planning decisions. Sections 284 and 285 of the Act provide a prescriptive means of challenging decisions made by the Secretary of State on planning appeals (s 288)[77] and enforcement appeals (s 289).[78] Section 113 of the Planning and Compulsory Purchase Act 2004 sets out restrictions on challenging development plans. [79]

77 Strictly applied in *Mulvenna v SSCLG* [2015] EWHC 3494 (Admin) to prevent challenge to an appeal decision which had only come before the Secretary of State by reason of an admitted unlawful recovery of jurisdiction. However, if a claim is made within time, it is not a bar that service takes place outside of the applicable time limit: *South Derbyshire District Council v SSHCLG* [2020] EWHC 872 (Admin).

78 Since the relevant time limit in enforcement appeals appears in the Civil Procedure Rules rather than in the statute, the courts have been able to exercise a discretion to allow late challenges to proceed in appropriate cases: *Wandsworth London Borough Council v SSTLR* [2003] EWHC 622 (Admin).

79 Narrowly construed in *Manydown Co Ltd v Basingstoke & Deane Borough Council* [2012] EWHC 977 (Admin) and *R (CK Properties) v Epping Forest District Council* [2018] EWHC 1649 (Admin) so as to not preclude challenges to draft local plans; cf *R v Chichester District Council ex parte Kirdford Conservation Society* [1999] JLP 374, where an attempt to challenge a draft plan *prior* to its adoption was rejected as being impermissible under the differently worded provisions of TCPA 1990, ss 284, 287.

CHAPTER 2

Jurisdiction and procedures of the Planning Court

Paul Shadarevian QC,
Robert Williams,
and Rowan Clapp

A	Introduction	2.1
B	Jurisdiction	2.3
	Planning Court claims	2.3
	Judges of the Planning Court	2.12
C	Planning Court procedures	2.18
	Procedural rules	2.18
	Significant Planning Court claims	2.19
	Timetabling	2.24
	Case management	2.31
D	Venues	2.35

A INTRODUCTION

2.1 This chapter discusses, by way of overview, rules and procedures of particular importance in the context of the Planning Court. Subsequent Chapters – in particular Chapter 3 (Preparing and Pursuing Claims), Chapter 4 (Resisting Claims) and Chapter 5 (Powers of the Planning Court) – provide a more detailed discussion on the particular application of various statutory tests, procedures and case law in the context of making and defending claims, as well as highlighting particular powers at the disposal of the Planning Court.

2.2 The primary jurisdictional and procedural provisions relating specifically to the Planning Court are found in Civil Procedures Rules (CPR) Pt 54 Pt II, comprising rr 54.21 to 54.24, and a Practice Direction 54E 'Planning Court Claims'. Copies of CPR Parts 54.21-24 and PD54E, along with key statutory provisions, are provided in the Appendices.

B JURISDICTION

Planning Court claims

2.3 Despite being the epithet given to Part II of CPR 54, the Civil Procedure Rules do not attempt to define the concept of the 'Planning Court'. Instead, CPR 54.21(2) establishes the jurisdiction of the Planning Court by defining what is meant by a 'Planning Court claim'. This means:

> '…a judicial review or statutory challenge which
>
> (a) involves any of the following matters —
>
> (i) planning permission, other development consents, the enforcement of planning control and the enforcement of other statutory schemes;
>
> (ii) applications under the Transport and Works Act 1992;
>
> (iii) wayleaves;
>
> (iv) highways and other rights of way;
>
> (v) compulsory purchase orders;
>
> (vi) village greens;
>
> (vii) European Union environmental legislation and domestic transpositions, including assessments for development consents, habitats, waste and pollution control;
>
> (viii) national, regional or other planning policy documents, statutory or otherwise; or
>
> (ix) any other matter the judge appointed under rule 54.22(2) considers appropriate; and
>
> (b) has been issued or transferred to the Planning Court'.

2.4 Planning Court claims form a specialist list comprising judicial reviews and statutory challenges in planning-related matters.[1] A Planning Liaison Judge, nominated by the President of the Queen's Bench Division, is in charge of the list.[2] Currently, Mr Justice Holgate is the resident Planning Liaison Judge. His appointment has been effective since 13 February 2017. The first Planning Liaison Judge was the then Mr Justice Lindblom, who was succeeded by the late Mrs Justice Patterson DBE.

2.5 As can be seen, a wide range of cases have the potential to be classified as 'Planning Court claims' and thus fall within the jurisdiction of the Planning

1 CPR 54.22(1). The Royal Court of Justice Cause List (www.justice.gov.uk/courts/court-lists/list-cause-rcj) identifies the Planning Court as a separate list within the Administrative Court.

2 CPR 54.22(2).

Court. However, it might be noted that, technically at least, the mere fact that a claim falls within the categories established by CPR 54.21(2)(a) does not mean that a claim is so designated. Such claims must also be issued in, or transferred to, the Planning Court as required by the use of the word 'and' separating the list at r 54.21(2)(a) from r 54.21(2)(b).

2.6 It follows that the Planning Court does not have exclusive jurisdiction over judicial reviews or statutory challenges involving, for example, the grant of planning permission: in theory these cases can still be dealt with by the Administrative Court, Queen's Bench Division, as they had been historically. Whilst neither the CPR nor the Practice Direction expressly require that cases falling within the definition at CPR 54.21(2)(a)(i)-(viii) must be issued in the Planning Court, it is, however, a requirement of Practice Direction 54E that 'Planning Court claims' must be issued or lodged in the Administrative Office of the High Court and marked the 'Planning Court'.[3] As such it is expected that the vast majority of such claims[4] will ultimately be heard in the Planning Court.[5] It is unsurprising, therefore, that the Administrative Court website refers to the Planning Court as that 'which handles judicial reviews of decisions about planning permission and other challenges to planning decisions' without qualification.[6]

2.7 The principal areas of work of the Planning Court include challenges (either statutory or by way of judicial review) to decisions involving the grant of planning permission, challenges to planning policy documents, and those based on rights derived from EU environmental legislation.[7]

2.8 The breadth of cases potentially falling within the jurisdiction of the Planning Court and the scope of CPR 54.21(2) does throw up some anomalies. In particular, the restriction to judicial reviews and statutory challenges potentially constrains the jurisdiction of the court to some extent. Whilst the concept of a judicial review is readily understandable (and a 'claim for judicial review' is

3 Practice Direction 54E, paras 2.1 & 2.2.

4 As Master Clark stated in *Arora Management Services Ltd v Hillingdon LBC* [2019] EWHC 1945 (Ch) (at [71]), 'those judges who regularly sit in the Planning Court have expertise in planning law, albeit in the context of the public law issues arising in that Court. Whilst there was no evidence as to the listing practices of the Queen's Bench Division, I consider it likely that a case requiring planning law expertise would be listed, if practicable, before a judge with that expertise.'

5 Although it is to be noted that the interrelationship between CPR 54.21 and Practice Direction 54E, paras 2.1 and 2.2 is somewhat circular. 'Planning Court claims' must be issued or lodged in the Administrative Court Office of the High Court in accordance with Practice Direction 54D and the form marked 'Planning Court' (PD54E, paras 2.1 & 2.2), yet a claim is only a 'Planning Court claim' if, inter alia, it 'has been issued or transferred to the Planning Court' (CPR 54.21(2)(b)).

6 See under 'What the Administrative Court does' (www.gov.uk/courts-tribunals/administrative-court).

7 CPR 54.21.1.

defined in the CPR[8]) the concept of a 'statutory challenge'[9] is not defined within Part II of CPR 54.[10]

2.9 The paradigm statutory challenge, and one which is likely to be most frequently invoked, is an application under s 288 of the Town and Country Planning Act 1990 (TCPA 1990) challenging the validity of certain orders, actions and decisions made under the 1990 Act.[11] It would also appear that statutory appeals against enforcement notice appeal decisions pursuant to s 289 of TCPA 1990 also fall within the concept of a statutory challenge.[12] So too do challenges to development plan documents, by way of an application under s 113 of the Planning and Compulsory Planning Act 2004 (PCPA 2004).[13] The jurisdiction of the Planning Court has also extended to statutory challenges brought by way of case stated, although there has been some inconsistency as to the appropriate venue for such appeals.[14] In contrast, applications for planning injunctions pursuant to section 187B of TCPA 1990 do not automatically fall within the jurisdiction of the Planning Court, notwithstanding that they are one of the most effective mechanisms for 'the enforcement of planning control', as these applications are not readily describable as a 'statutory challenge'.[15]

2.10 Similarly, the description of the matters which, if they are the subject of judicial review or statutory challenge, fall within the definition of a Planning

8 By virtue of CPR 54.1(2)(a) a 'claim for judicial review' means a claim to review the lawfulness of –(i) an enactment; or (ii) a decision, action or failure to act in relation to the exercise of a public function.

9 CPR 54 is headed 'Judicial Review and Statutory Review' but the latter term is not expressly defined and CPR 54.21 refers to 'statutory challenges' also without defining that term.

10 Although note that PD8C sets out the procedure for the 'planning statutory reviews', all of which undoubtedly fall within the ambit of a 'statutory challenge'.

11 Section 288, TCPA 1990 encompasses a wide range of potential challenges to decisions, orders and actions made under the 1990 Act, most notably any decision on a s 78 appeal.

12 See para 29 of the Listing Policy in Annex 4 of The Administrative Court: Judicial Review Guide 2020 (July 2020), in which the 'three broad categories' of cases within the Planning Court are listed (including appeals brought under s 289, TCPA 1990). For recent examples of statutory appeals brought under s 289, TCPA 1990 within the Planning Court see *London Borough of Islington v Secretary of State for Housing, Communities and Local Government* [2019] EWHC 2691 (Admin); *R (Johnson) v Royal Borough of Windsor and Maidenhead* [2019] EWHC 160 (Admin); and *R (Sharma) v Secretary of State for Housing, Communities and Local Government* [2018] EWHC 2355 (Admin).

13 Curiously, the PCPA 2004 is not included in the definition of 'the planning acts' in CPR 54.5 so that challenges to decisions in the course of plan-making are not subject to its stricter time limits (unless they fall within the statutory time limit in PCPA 2004, s 113).

14 See, eg, the decision in *Beg v Luton BC* [2017] EWHC 3435 (Admin) in which Holgate J sitting in the Planning Court heard an appeal by way of case stated regarding the decision of the Magistrates' Court that an enforcement notice was valid for the purposes of a prosecution under s 179(2), TCPA 1990. But see also the case of *Sarodia v London Borough of Redbridge* [2017] EWHC 2347 (Admin) in which Jay J dealt with a similar issue sitting in the Administrative Court.

15 Such claims are generally heard in the Queen's Bench Division and not in the Administrative Court, which may reflect the fact that frequently there may be disputed matters of fact involved so that the Part 8 procedure is not appropriate. See, eg, *London Borough of Havering v Stokes* [2019] EWHC 3006 (QB); *East Hertfordshire District Council v Doherty* [2019] EWHC 2292 (QB).

Court claim leaves open a number of questions about the precise extent of the Planning Court's jurisdiction. For instance, the reference to 'enforcement of other statutory schemes' in CPR 54.21(2)(a)(i) is a potentially extremely wide catch-all provision.

2.11 However, it is perhaps unsurprising that in the six years since the inception of the Planning Court the precise boundaries of the Planning Court's jurisdiction have not been tested in litigation. There is no obvious benefit in claimants or defendants raising disputing the jurisdiction of the Planning Court. Even if its jurisdiction were raised as a preliminary issue, it is at least arguably open to the Planning Liaison Judge to order that the particular matter be treated as a Planning Court claim.[16]

Judges of the Planning Court

2.12 One of the objectives promoted by the government when promoting the introduction of a specialist Planning Court was for the Court to be staffed primarily by specialist judges. Before the Planning Court was established there had been a concern amongst practitioners that planning cases were, at least sometimes, being determined by judges with little experience of planning law or practice.

2.13 This was, it should be remembered, at a time when strenuous efforts were being made to reduce the backlog in the Administrative Court generally, with a special emphasis on planning cases. At that time there were only a handful of High Court judges and a smaller number of deputy High Court judges with real planning expertise from their former legal practices.

2.14 The position has now changed significantly. As a result of a series of High Court appointments which have supplemented the pool of planning expertise available to the existing judiciary, the Planning Court now has a real depth of judicial experience in the planning arena. But it would be a mistake to assume that all judges in the Planning Court are exclusively 'planning specialists'. As we have stressed, the Planning Court is 'a court within a court'. Judges who sit in the Planning Court are cross deployed across the Administrative court and hear a real mix of cases.

2.15 The combined effect of CPR 54.22(3) and Practice Direction 52E is that where a Planning Court claim has been categorised as 'significant' (in relation to which, see below), it will be dealt with by a 'specialist' planning judge nominated by the President of the Queen's Bench Division. To that end there now exists a list of 'specialist planning judges' who deal with claims that are 'significant' in London, Wales and the regions.[17]

16 Pursuant to CPR 54.21(2)(a)(ix). It is also arguable that the Court would have the power to order the transfer of any case to and from the Planning Court claims list pursuant to CPR 30.5(2).

17 The list of nominated judges is not, however, published by HMCTS.

2.16 The President also has the responsibility for nominating 'other' judges to deal with other Planning Court claims.[18] Therefore, although in theory a non-specialist High Court judge can sit in the Planning Court, the likelihood of a judge with little or no planning experience determining a Planning Court claim is minimal.[19]

2.17 Whilst there are clear advantages of ensuring that planning cases are determined by judges who are familiar not only with planning law, but also who have practical experience of the planning system, in our view it would not be healthy if the Planning Court were to be a forum in which planning cases were only being heard by specialist judges and where those same judges were only ever sitting on planning cases. Experience of the operation of the Planning Court to date suggests that such concerns are unfounded. In practice even the nominated 'specialist' judges undertake a full range of Administrative Court work.[20] The practice of ensuring that judges sitting in the Planning Court are also exposed to different areas of work is entirely in accordance with the comments on judicial specialism made extra-judicially by, Lord Neuberger, then President of the Supreme Court:

> 'The days when it was thought that a judge could try a case on any subject have not quite gone, but with ticketing in crime, with specialist civil courts, and with the tribunals being brought into the judiciary, we are, I think, moving in that direction. It is a difficult question where we go from here on judicial specialisation, but I hope it is not too far. The law is already at risk of developing in silos, and a not-too-specialist judiciary has a great deal to offer in ensuring that there is cross-fertilisation between the silos – a highly desirable exercise in the legal world … .'[21]

C PLANNING COURT PROCEDURES

Procedural rules

2.18 The procedures of the Planning Court itself are governed primarily by Part II of CPR 54 ('The Planning Court') and Practice Direction 54E ('Planning Court Claims'). Save where these provisions provide otherwise, the remainder of the CPR and their practice directions continue to apply to Planning Court claims.[22] This is of some significance, as the applicable procedural rules will

18 CPR 54.22 (3).

19 Indeed, the current website for the Planning Court states, in no uncertain terms, that Planning Court cases will be listed separately within the Administrative Court cause list, and will be heard by judges with planning expertise. See also the comments of Master Clark in *Arora Management Services Ltd* (above) at [71].

20 For example, the current Planning Liaison Judge, Holgate J is also President of the Upper Tribunal (Lands Chamber) and has sat on cases dealing with a broad range of issues.

21 'Some thoughts on the post-LASPO civil judge's role before and during trial: Address to the Manchester Law Society and Northern Circuit Commercial Bar Association' 22 January 2015 (available at www.supremecourt.uk/docs/speech-150122.pdf).

22 CPR 54.23.

depend on the type of claim in question, and are found beyond the confines of Part II of CPR 54 (for instance, a judicial review challenge to a grant of planning permission by a local planning authority continues to be governed by Parts 8 and 54 of the CPR; a statutory review pursuant to s 288 of the TCPA 288 is governed by Part 8 and PD8C, whereas an an appeal pursuant to s 289 of the TCPA 1990 would be governed by Part 52, and PD52D, para 26.1).

Significant Planning Court claims

2.19 The Planning Liaison Judge is able to categorise Planning Court claims as 'significant'.[23] It is understood that the current practice is for a court lawyer, under the supervision of the Planning Liaison Judge, to assess on a case by case basis whether they justify categorisation as significant.

2.20 Significant claims may include, but are not limited to, Planning Court claims which:

(a) relate to commercial, residential, or other developments which have significant economic impact either at a local level or beyond their immediate locality;

(b) raise important points of law;

(c) generate significant public interest; or

(d) by virtue of the volume or nature of technical material, are best dealt with by judges with significant experience of handling such matters.[24]

2.21 Since the start of the Planning Court in April 2014, in the first year or so, 39% of cases (some 217 cases) before the Court were categorised as being 'significant'.[25]

2.22 Parties wishing to make representations in respect of the categorisation of a Planning Court claim are required to do so in writing, on issuing the claim or lodging an acknowledgment of service, as appropriate.[26] As it currently stands, neither the judicial review claim form (Planning Court)[27] nor the Planning Court judicial review acknowledgment of service Acknowledgment of Service form (Planning Court)[28] specifically invite parties to identify whether they consider the

23 PD54E, para 3.1.
24 Ibid, para 3.2.
25 Figures received from the court as at 15 May 2015. Some 341 (61%) were accordingly not significant. Of the 182 claims made pursuant to TCPA 1990, s 28, some 66 were categorised as significant. Of the 49 s 289 appeals, only six were categorised as significant. Of the 303 judicial reviews, 133 were significant. Unfortunately, there is no systematic publication of more recent data on the nature of the case load of the Planning Court.
26 PD54E, para 3.3.
27 N461PC (9 April 2018).
28 N462PC (9 April 2018).

claim to be significant, so this is something that will need to be done by the party concerned unprompted.

2.23 Whilst there is currently no formal procedure for the notification of parties as to whether their claim has been designated as significant, the Court indicated[29] that this was a matter under review.

Timetabling

2.24 The ramifications of a claim being categorised as significant are two-fold. Firstly, as noted above, the case will be heard by a specialist planning judge. Secondly, there are target timescales for the hearing of significant Planning Court claims 'which the parties should be prepared to meet…subject to the overriding objective of the interests of justice.'[30] The target timescales are as follows:

(a) applications for permission to apply for judicial review are to be determined within three weeks of the expiry of the time limit for filing of the acknowledgment of service;

(b) oral renewals of applications for permission to apply for judicial review are to be heard within one month of receipt of request for renewal;

(c) applications for permission under s 289 of TCPA 1990 are to be determined within one month of issue;

(d) substantive statutory applications, including applications under s 288 of TCPA 1990, are to be heard within six months of issue; and

(e) judicial reviews are to be heard within ten weeks of the expiry of the period for the submission of detailed grounds by the defendant or any other party as provided in Rule 54.14.

2.25 The Planning Liaison Judge has the power to direct expedition of any Planning Court claim (significant or otherwise) if he considers it to be necessary to deal with the case justly. In particularly pressing cases, parties can apply for urgent consideration of the claim.[31]

2.26 Whilst inevitably there are the occasional exceptions, it would appear that these timescales are being met in the vast majority of cases. Target timescales within the Planning Court are enforced with rigour[32] and there is a clear emphasis on ensuring that the Court's resources are used economically. This approach is

29 Response to the authors from the Planning Court on 15.5.15. No more recent information is in the public domain.

30 PD54E, para 3.4.

31 A claimant in the Planning Court should indicate that they are 'claiming exceptional urgency' by marking the appropriate box within Section 4 of Form N461PC, enclosing Form N463PC (Application for urgent consideration) as instructed.

32 As was anticipated prior to the introduction of the current target timescales (see the remarks of Lindblom J in *London & Henley (Middle Brook Street) Ltd v Secretary of State for Communities and Local Government* [2013] EWHC 4207 (Admin) (at [16]).

underscored by the Court's recent criticism of a claimant who failed to provide sufficient notice to the court of their intention to discontinue proceedings. Holgate J required the parties to attend the substantive hearing date in any event to explain the reasons for late settlement, noting that:

> 'Every time a party behaves in this way, the court's resources are wasted, and other litigants have to wait longer for their cases to be heard, and judgment given than would otherwise be the case. Plainly this is not in the public interest and it is contrary to the ethos of the Planning Court and its objective of delivering justice within efficient timescales.' [33]

2.27 The listing policy of the court regarding substantive hearings is that:

> 'once the Court fee to continue the proceedings has been paid, the list office emails a window of suitable dates to the parties and encourages them to agree a mutually convenient date. The appointment to fix procedure is used only when necessary.'[34]

2.28 In respect of the listing of substantive hearings for 'significant' planning cases, the listing policy is 'necessarily stricter' due to the limited availability of judges authorised to hear 'significant' cases:

> '"Significant" cases are listed primarily by reference to the availability of a judge authorised to hear such cases. They are listed for hearings between Tuesdays to Thursdays only of any sitting week. The Court will offer the parties 3 dates within the timescales set by PD 54E. If parties are unable to agree one of those 3 dates, the case is listed without further consultation.'[35]

2.29

> Permission hearings will usually be fixed at the Court's convenience without taking the availability of counsel into account. Unless the parties notify the Administrative Court Office otherwise and the court agrees hearings of renewed applications for permission are listed for 30 minutes (including time for judgment). The fixing letter in respect of permission hearings requires that the parties state in writing prior to the hearing that they require a hearing of longer than 30 minutes, or else confirm the existing time estimate, and further states that:

33 See *Westminster City Council v SSHCLG* [2020] EWHC 1472 (Admin) per Holgate J at [39]. Elsewhere, Holgate J has also noted the importance of decision makers articulating their reasons for agreeing to a decision being quashed as 'It is also necessary that such reasons are given for the proper management of the finite resources of the Planning Court and the efficient listing and resolution of cases in general' (in *Barker Mill Estates v Test Valley Borough Council & SSCLG* [2016] EWHC 3028 (Admin) at [112]).

34 The Administrative Court: Judicial Review Guide (07.20), para 34 of the Listing Policy in Annex 4. The Guide states that this is the policy of the Planning Court in London, but records at para 36 of the Listing Policy that the regional offices generally adopt the same policy.

35 The Administrative Court: Judicial Review Guide (07.20), Listing Policy, para 35. The Guide states that this is the policy of the Planning Court in London, but records at para 36 that the regional offices generally adopt the same policy.

> 'This is a mandatory requirement. If it becomes necessary to adjourn because of a late increased time estimate, quite apart from any costs sanction, the solicitors and counsel involved may be required to appear before the Court to explain the failure to comply with the instruction above. Furthermore, the case will be re-listed for the earliest possible opportunity in accordance with the availability of a Judge and not the availability of counsel.' [36]

2.30 As set out above, relevant timetabling constraints are a key feature of litigation within the Planning Court, reflecting the public interest in having an expeditious planning system. Notably, in our experience is that the court will rarely, if ever, accept the non-availability of counsel as a good reason for significant delays to the timetabling.

Case management

2.31 The Planning Court has at its disposal the same case management powers as other courts within the Queen's Bench Division, most notably the extensive powers under Part 3 of the CPR. These powers are addressed more fully in Chapter 5. However, of particular note is the provision, almost hidden away, in Practice Direction 54E, para 3.5 which provides that:

> 'The Planning Court may make case management directions, including a direction to any party intending to contest the claim to file and serve a summary of his grounds for doing so.'

2.32 Until s 91 of the Criminal Justice and Courts Act 2015 (CJCA 2015) came into force on 26 October 2015,[37] there was no permission stage in statutory applications (such as those under s 288 of TCPA 1990) and therefore no incentive on defendants to file grounds identifying any defence. This had scope to promote inefficiency as defendants in such cases would not prepare defences until shortly before the substantive hearing.[38]

2.33 PD8C, which came into force on the same date as s 91 of the CJCA 2015, comprises 'General Provisions Applicable to Statutory Review' under ss 287 and 288 of the TCPA 1990, s 63 of the Planning (Listed Buildings and Conservation Areas) Act 1990, s 22 of the Planning (Hazardous Substances) Act 1990 and s 113 of the Planning and Compulsory Purchase Act 2004. In particular, PD8C states that any person served with a claim form wishing to take part in the

36 The Administrative Court: Judicial Review Guide (07.20), Listing Policy, para 38.

37 See Criminal Justice and Courts Act 2015, s 91, Sch 16 which impose a requirement of leave for a range of planning related challenges.

38 See the remarks of Collins J in *Bovale Ltd v Secretary of State for Communities and Local Government* [2008] EWHC 2143 (Admin) at [11].
'all too often it is not until the last minute, usually when the claim has a hearing date, that the defendant gets round to preparing a defence… That creates problems, not only for the court but also for claimants and other interested parties, and is certainly not an efficient way of managing the court's business.'

planning statutory review must file an acknowledgment of service[39] and that the acknowledgment of service must, in the event the person filing it intends to contest the claim, include a summary of his grounds for doing so.[40]

2.34 In contrast, the rules regarding appeals under s 289 TCPA 1990 and s 65 of the Planning (Listed Buildings and Conservation Areas) Act 1990 do not contain the same mandatory requirement for persons served with the application to provide acknowledgment of service or to file any other pleading. Instead, such matters proceed directly to an oral permission hearing.[41] In an appropriate case it would be open the court to exercise its power under Practice Direction 54E, para 3.5 to require summary grounds to be filed prior to the permission hearing. In practice, this is rarely necessary as parties responding to such appeals tend to file summary grounds of resistance or a skeleton argument of their own volition ahead of the oral permission hearing.

D VENUES

2.35 The provisions of CPR 54D – Administrative Court (Venue) – apply to judicial review claims, statutory applications and section 289 appeals.[42] This permits claims to be issued at the Administrative Court Office of the High Court either at the Royal Courts of Justice or (save in certain excepted classes of claim[43]) at the District Registry of the High Court at Birmingham, Cardiff, Leeds, or Manchester.[44] There is an Administrative Court Office at each of the four regional centres.[45] There are restrictions on where cases challenging the decisions of Welsh public bodies can be issued and heard.[46]

2.36 There is a general expectation that proceedings will be administered and determined in the region with which the claimant has the closest connection, subject to the following considerations, as applicable:

(1) any reason expressed by any party for preferring a particular venue;

(2) the region in which the defendant, or any relevant office or department of the defendant, is based;

(3) the region in which the claimant's legal representatives are based;

39 PD8C, para 5.2.
40 PD8C, para 5.5(a)(i).
41 PD52D, para 26.1(5)
42 Judicial Review Claims – PD54E, para 2.1; Section 288 applications – PD8A, para 22.3; Section 289 appeals – PD52D, para 26.1(6).
43 These are specified in PD54D, para 3.1 and include, for instance, proceedings relating to terrorism or alleged terrorists. It is unlikely that any of the matters which fall within the jurisdiction of the Planning Court would fall within the excepted classes of claim, although this should be checked if it is proposed to issue outside London.
44 PD54D, para 2.1.
45 The addresses and contact details for each ACO can be found in Annex 1 of the Administrative Court: Judicial Review Guide (07.20).
46 See para 2.39 below.

(4) the ease and cost of travel to a hearing;

(5) the availability and suitability of alternative means of attending a hearing (for example, by videolink);

(6) the extent and nature of media interest in the proceedings in any particular locality;

(7) the time within which it is appropriate for the proceedings to be determined;

(8) whether it is desirable to administer or determine the claim in another region in the light of the volume of claims issued at, and the capacity, resources and workload of, the court at which it is issued;

(9) whether the claim raises issues sufficiently similar to those in another outstanding claim to make it desirable that it should be determined together with, or immediately following, that other claim; and

(10) whether the claim raises devolution issues and for that reason whether it should more appropriately be determined in London or Cardiff.[47]

2.37 The court may, on an application by a party or of its own initiative, and taking into account the considerations outlined above, direct that the claim be determined in a region other than that of the venue in which the claim is currently assigned.[48] Cases where the claimant has the closest connection to the area covered by Western Circuit (which includes Devon and Cornwall as well as Dorset, Somerset, and Wiltshire) are to be issued in Cardiff and will be administered from the Cardiff ACO, albeit that any hearings will generally take place at a court on the Western Circuit (principally Bristol).[49]

2.38 CPR 7.1A requires that any claim against Welsh public bodies which challenge the lawfulness of their decisions, must be issued and heard in Wales.[50] If a claim falling within the scope of r 7.1A is issued in England a court officer must refer it to the Administrative Court Office in Cardiff or to another appropriate court office in Wales.[51] If a claim (whether against a Welsh public body or not) is filed at the Administrative Court Office in Cardiff, it may be filed in either English or Welsh languages.[52]

47 PD54D, para 5.2.
48 PD54D, para 5.4.
49 Administrative Court: Judicial Review Guide (07.20), para 6.6.2.
50 CPR 7.1A as introduced in July 2020.
51 CPR 7.1B.
52 Administrative Court: Judicial Review Guide (07.20), para 6.2.3.

CHAPTER 3

Preparing and pursuing claims

Matt Hutchings QC, Robin Green and John Fitzsimons

A	Introduction	3.1
B	Pre-action conduct and the judicial review protocol	3.6
	– Pre-action conduct generally	3.6
	– Judicial review pre-action protocol	3.15
	– Pre-action disclosure	3.22
C	Preparing and issuing the claim	3.24
	– Standing in judicial review planning challenges	3.27
	– Local action groups	3.29
	– Individuals as claimants	3.38
	– Standing in statutory challenges	3.54
D	The provision of information about financial resources and Aarhus convention claims	3.65
	– Financial resources	3.65
	– Aarhus Convention claims	3.68
E	Time limits, promptness, and delay	3.74
	– Calculating time for the purposes of issuing a claim	3.77
	– Extending time	3.84
F	Issuing the claim	3.89
	– Judicial review claims	3.94
	– Statutory challenges	3.97
	– Category of claim – 'significant' claims	3.107
G	Responding to an acknowledgment of service	3.110
H	Seeking permission to proceed	3.117
	– Judicial review claims	3.117
	– Statutory challenges	3.123
	– The permission hearing	3.124
	– Appealing the refusal of permission	3.128
I	Applications for interim relief	3.130
	– Interim relief in judicial review claims	3.132

	– Interim relief in statutory challenges	3.139
J	Case management	3.147
K	Settlement	3.152
L	The substantive hearing	3.155
	– Case preparation	3.155
	– The hearing	3.164
	– Relief	3.166
	– Costs	3.169
	– Permission to appeal	3.170
	– Appeals in the Court of Appeal and Supreme Court	3.172

A INTRODUCTION

3.1 Broadly speaking, Planning Court claims involve challenges to the decisions of public bodies in four main areas: the development of land; the expropriation of land; the grant of rights over land; and the regulation of the public's use of land. In most claims the decision under challenge will affect not only the landowner and public authority, but also third parties and the wider public. It has long been recognised that there is accordingly a public interest in the prompt commencement of proceedings challenging these decisions: 'The public interest in good administration requires that public authorities and third parties should not be kept in suspense as to the legal validity of a decision the authority has reached in purported exercise of decision-making powers for any longer period than is absolutely necessary in fairness to the person affected by the decision.'[1] Prospective claimants will need to bear this well in mind.

3.2 They will also need to bear in mind the limits of the court's jurisdiction. The Planning Court does not sit in judgment on the merits of the decision before it. It exercises a supervisory jurisdiction, concerned with whether the decision is a lawful decision, not whether it is the right decision. The grounds on which a judicial review claim or statutory challenge may be brought are extensive, including legal misdirection; failure to have regard to a material consideration; taking into account an immaterial consideration; misunderstanding an established and relevant fact; procedural impropriety; disproportionality; unfairness; bias;

1 Per Lord Diplock in *O'Reilly v Mackman* [1983] 2 AC 237, 280H–281A. See also *Finn-Kelcey v Milton Keynes Borough Council* [2008] EWCA Civ 1067, [2009] Env LR 17, paras 21, 22; *R (Thornton Hall Hotel Ltd) v Wirral MBC* [2019] PTSR 1794, para 21(1).

irrationality; and bad faith,[2] but the court will be 'astute to ensure that such challenges are not used as a cloak for what is, in truth, a rerun of the arguments on the ... merits.'[3]

3.3 There is a broad range of claims that may be brought in the Planning Court, and there will be a wide variety of claimants with differing objectives. A local resident aggrieved by a local authority's decision to grant planning permission for a nearby housing scheme might hope to preserve the land's open character in the short term by contesting the grant of planning permission in judicial review proceedings, and in the long term by seeking to challenge the authority's allocation of the land for development in its newly adopted local plan under s 113 of the Planning and Compulsory Purchase Act 2004 (PCPA 2004). A national supermarket operator might seek under s 288 of the Town and Country Planning Act 1990 (TCPA 1990) to overturn the grant by an Inspector of planning permission to a rival supermarket operator with the aim of delaying the development of the application site, whilst its own site nearby is developed and it consolidates its market share. A landowner might seek to challenge a compulsory purchase order authorising the acquisition of his house because he is not satisfied that the order is justified and he wishes to keep his property. A shopkeeper might wish to argue that a highway stopping up order should be quashed, with the aim of averting the loss of passing custom. Although the circumstances of individual claimants will vary widely, in all cases the court will expect promptness in the pursuit of claims and a focus on what is unlawful about the decision under challenge.

3.4 It is not possible within the confines of this work to explore the full array of legal arguments that might be raised in a claim brought in the Planning Court.[4] So much will depend on the particular features of the statutory scheme in issue and the factual matrix within which the impugned decision was taken. Rather, the purpose of this chapter is to draw out the procedural and practical issues which claimants may encounter as they prepare their claims and pursue them to conclusion.

3.5 Throughout this chapter we have referred to the party bringing proceedings in the Planning Court as the 'claimant', although under the Civil Procedure Rules that party may be described as an 'applicant' or 'appellant'.

2 See, eg, *Associated Provincial Picture Houses Ltd v Wednesbury Corporation* [1948] 1 KB 223, 228–9; *Ashbridge Investments Ltd v Minister of Housing* [1965] 1 WLR 1320, 1326G–H; *Regina (Alconbury Developments Ltd and Others) v Secretary of State for the Environment, Transport and the Regions* [2001] UKHL 23, [2003] 2 AC 295, paras 19–20, 49, 53, 157, 169; *Runa Begum v Tower Hamlets London Borough Council* [2003] UKHL 5, [2003] 2 AC 430, paras 7, 99; *Walton v Scottish Ministers* [2012] UKSC 44, [2013] Env LR 16, paras 108–112; *Bloor Homes East Midlands Limited v Secretary of State for Communities & Local Government, Hinckley and Bosworth Borough Council* [2014] EWHC 754 (Admin), para 19, in relation to legal principles governing statutory planning challenges.

3 Per Sullivan J in *R (Newsmith Stainless Ltd) v Secretary of State for the Environment, Transport and the Regions* [2001] EWHC Admin 74, [2017] PTSR 1126, para 6.

4 Chapter 7 provides an overview of the jurisprudence on the main strands of legal error that commonly form the basis of legal challenges in the Planning Court.

B PRE-ACTION CONDUCT AND THE JUDICIAL REVIEW PROTOCOL

Pre-action conduct generally

3.6 A potential claimant considering the issue of judicial review proceedings in the Planning Court should be aware of the Pre-Action Protocol for Judicial Review,[5] which is dealt with later in this section. Other potential claimants should consider the Practice Direction on Pre-Action Conduct,[6] which applies in those cases where no specific pre-action protocol exists.

3.7 The Practice Direction on Pre-Action Conduct sets out what the court considers to be good practice in the period before proceedings are issued. Its objectives are that the parties should have exchanged sufficient information to: (a) understand each other's position; (b) make decisions about how to proceed; (c) try to settle the issues without proceedings; (d) consider a form of Alternative Dispute Resolution (ADR) to assist with settlement; (e) support the efficient management of those proceedings; and (f) reduce the costs of resolving the dispute.[7]

3.8 Complying with these objectives will usually involve (a) a letter from the claimant giving concise details of his claim, which should include the basis for the claim, a summary of the facts, and what relief is sought; (b) a response from the defendant within a reasonable time, which should include confirmation as to whether the claim is accepted and, if it is not accepted, the reasons why, together with an explanation as to which facts and parts of the claim are disputed; and (c) disclosure of key documents relevant to the dispute.[8] Proportionality is written into the Practice Direction. The parties must not use the Practice Direction as a tactical device to secure an unfair advantage over another party; only reasonable and proportionate steps should be taken by the parties to identify, narrow and resolve the legal and factual issues; and the costs incurred in complying with the Practice Direction should be proportionate (disproportionate costs will not be recoverable).[9]

3.9 Where a party fails to comply with the substance of the Practice Direction (or an applicable pre-action protocol), the court will take that factor into account when giving directions for the management of proceedings and making orders for costs.[10]

3.10 What pre-action steps are reasonable and proportionate will depend on the circumstances of each case. In the Planning Court many of the decisions under challenge will have been taken following a well-documented and public

5 See Appendix B. Issued on 6 April 2015 and last updated on 17 September 2019
6 See Appendix B. Last updated on 1 October 2020.
7 See Practice Direction on Pre-Action Conduct, para 3.
8 Ibid, para 6.
9 Ibid, paras 4 and 5.
10 See ibid, paras 13–16.

decision-making process, leading to an order, permission or plan that cannot be set aside without the intervention of the court. In these circumstances there may be little that can be achieved by the parties through pre-action correspondence and perhaps no meaningful disclosure to give. This was recognised in *Harrogate BC v SOSCLG, Zammitt*,[11] involving an application for an extension of time for service of the claim form in a challenge to a planning inspector's decision under s 288 of the TCPA 1990. The application was resisted by the defendant on a number of grounds, including that the claimant had not complied with an earlier version of the Practice Direction on Pre-Action Conduct. After referring to the Practice Direction and relevant provisions in the Pre-Action Protocol for Judicial Review in force at the time, the court held, at paragraph 45:

> 'I agree with [counsel for the claimant] that there is an analogy between these proceedings and an application for judicial review. In particular this is a case where there is no legal power in the Secretary of State or [the defendant] to alter the decision. Thus it is not a case where the parties can settle the matter without legal proceedings. The parties are fully informed about each other's case. The only question is whether the Inspector's decision is wrong in law. In my view therefore this is not a case within the aims of the PD; it is not a normal case within paragraph 2 of the PD and circumstances do make it inappropriate within paragraph 6.1 of the PD for there to be an exchange of information prior to the commencement of the proceedings.'

3.11 Since *Zammitt* was decided the Practice Direction has been amended and there is now no express recognition within it that it may not be appropriate in certain circumstances. Nonetheless, the Practice Direction requires that only 'reasonable and proportionate steps should be taken by the parties to identify, narrow and resolve the legal, factual or expert issues',[12] which inevitably brings into consideration both the factual and legal context of the prospective challenge.

3.12 Although in many Planning Court cases there will be no scope for settlement without legal proceedings, there are two respects in which pre-action correspondence and disclosure may be of practical benefit to a prospective claimant. The first is that it may give the claimant early notice of the defendant's case, and in particular of weaknesses in the proposed challenge, permitting a better assessment of the merits and an opportunity to revise (or abandon) the claim before it is issued.

3.13 The second potential benefit to a claimant comes from pre-action correspondence, not with the defendant but with interested parties: that of minimising the risk that third party prejudice will derail an otherwise valid challenge. Where, for instance, a challenge is brought to the grant of planning permission, the recipient of the permission might seek to argue that, having taken steps in reliance on the permission, he would suffer prejudice if the

11 [2014] EWHC 1506 (Admin).
12 Practice Direction on Pre-Action Conduct, para 4.

permission were quashed. Although third party prejudice is not usually decisive of the outcome of a planning challenge, it is undoubtedly a factor, and may be compelling where the defect alleged is technical or insubstantial. By alerting interested parties to the possibility of a challenge at an early stage, the claimant will have a better chance of defeating an argument that third party prejudice should affect the claim.

3.14 Although compliance with the Practice Direction (insofar as reasonable and proportionate) is expected, claimants must keep in mind that it does not affect the time limits applying to the commencement of proceedings. Paragraph 17 of the Practice Direction explicitly addresses this where it states:

> 'This Practice Direction and the pre-action protocols do not alter the statutory time limits for starting court proceedings. If a claim is issued after the relevant limitation period has expired, the defendant will be entitled to use that as a defence to the claim. If proceedings are started to comply with the statutory time limit before the parties have followed the procedures in this Practice Direction or the relevant pre-action protocol, the parties should apply to the court for a stay of the proceedings while they so comply.'

The last suggestion in this paragraph that proceedings should be stayed to allow compliance with the Practice Direction or a pre-action protocol is unlikely to be necessary or appropriate in the vast majority of cases before the Planning Court.

Judicial review pre-action protocol[13]

3.15 The Pre-Action Protocol for Judicial Review (as issued on 6 April 2015 and updated on 17 September 2019) applies to judicial review proceedings in England and Wales. As is the case with the Practice Direction on Pre-Action Conduct, the protocol does not affect the time limits applicable to the commencement of proceedings, in particular the shorter six-week time limit which applies to judicial review claims brought in respect of decisions under the planning acts (CPR 54.5(5)).[14] Broadly speaking, the protocol requires the prospective claimant to send a letter before claim to the intended defendant, with the aim of identifying the issues in dispute and establishing whether litigation can be avoided. The defendant should then send a letter in response.

3.16 Paragraph 6 of the protocol recognises that it will not be appropriate in very urgent cases and that in those cases a claim should be made immediately.[15] Even in very urgent cases, however, it is said to be good practice to alert the defendant by telephone, and to send an email or fax of the draft claim form. Paragraph 7 goes on to require claimants to satisfy themselves whether they should follow the protocol, depending upon the circumstances of the case. Where

13 See Appendix B.

14 See para 1 of the Protocol.

15 The examples of very urgent cases given are immigration cases where directions have been set for the claimant's removal from the UK and homelessness cases where a local housing authority fails to secure interim accommodation for a homeless claimant.

the use of the protocol is appropriate, the court will normally expect all parties to have complied with it in good time before proceedings are issued. Compliance or non-compliance will be taken into account when giving directions for case management of proceedings or when making orders for costs.

3.17 Given the nature of the decisions likely to be challenged in the Planning Court, there will rarely be scope to argue that a case is sufficiently urgent such that the protocol does not have to be followed. Compliance with the protocol is clearly envisaged wherever practicable. It is also the safer course given the possibility of costs sanctions for non-compliance.[16]

3.18 The purpose of the letter before claim is to identify the issues in dispute and to establish whether they can be narrowed or litigation can be avoided.[17] A suggested standard format for the letter is contained in Annex A to the protocol. Work done in providing a full letter before claim following the standard format should save some time later when the claim form is completed. The following parts of the standard format letter before action merit further comment:

- The details of any interested parties (part 6):

  This will often include details of any developer and landowner in planning-related cases. As explained above in the context of pre-action conduct generally,[18] prompt notification of the proposed claim to a developer or landowner at the pre-action stage minimises the risk that they will act on the decision under challenge and may reduce the weight to be given to the argument that they would suffer prejudice if the decision is quashed.

- The issue (part 7):

  The standard form letter states that (inter alia) a brief summary of facts should be included. In cases before the Planning Court the relevant background facts can be relatively extensive. Where a fuller account of the background facts is provided at this stage, this may help the parties reach agreement on the relevant facts, which can then be presented to the court as agreed facts if a claim is subsequently issued.

- The details of information sought and of any documents that are considered relevant and necessary (parts 10 and 11):

  There is no automatic disclosure obligation in judicial review proceedings. The test applied to applications for specific or standard disclosure (namely, whether disclosure of the document is necessary in order to deal fairly and justly with the case taking account of all the facts and circumstances of the particular case[19]) will not be met in many judicial review cases where the

16 See CPR 44–48.
17 See para 14 of the Protocol.
18 See para **4.13** above.
19 See *Tweed v Parades Commission for Northern Ireland* [2007] 1 AC 650.

facts are not contentious and the claim raises issues of law only. Having said that, the protocol clearly envisages that reasonable requests for necessary information and documents will be made at this stage. It would therefore be sensible to remind the defendant of the duty of candour, applicable to all public authorities, to lay before the court all the relevant facts and reasoning underlying the decision under challenge.[20] On the other hand, requests which are merely 'fishing expeditions' (seeking disclosure in the hope that something might emerge which may form the basis for a claim) are unlikely to be entertained and, if pursued by way of an application to the court, will not be allowed.[21] Where information and/or documents are sought, reference should be made (where appropriate) to the Freedom of Information Act 2000 and/or the Environmental Information Regulations 2004[22] which impose on public bodies certain obligations of disclosure, although it should be made clear that the claimant expects the information and documents requested to be disclosed in accordance with the timescale envisaged by the protocol.[23]

- Proposed reply date (part 13):

  The notes to the standard format letter state that 14 days is a reasonable time to allow for a response in most circumstances, but envisage that a shorter (or longer) period may be appropriate in a particular case. A shorter period might be appropriate where the existence of a statutory time limit for bringing the claim gives the claimant very little opportunity to assimilate the defendant's reply.[24]

3.19 Section 2 of Annex A notes that public bodies have requested that, for certain types of cases, in order to ensure a prompt response, letters before claim should be sent to specific addresses. Where the claim concerns a decision by a local authority, the address on the relevant decision letter *and* the address for the local authority's legal department should be used (ie copies of the letter should be sent to both addresses).

20 Ibid, at [54].
21 Ibid, at [56].
22 SI 2004/3391.
23 While requests for information under the Environmental Information Regulations 2004 and/or Freedom of Information Act 2000 are beneficial when seeking disclosure of documents as they involve no relevance test, can be made to non-parties, and no restriction is made on the subsequent use of disclosed documents, the practical realities of the short six-week timeline to bring a challenge in the Planning Court mean that it may often be difficult to get disclosure under information law prior to the issue of a claim.
24 On the other hand, it may be possible to send a letter before claim before a decision having legal effect is taken or issued. For instance, it is not uncommon for an objector to the grant of planning permission to send what is in effect a letter before claim to the local planning authority following a committee's resolution to grant permission but before the formal issue of the notice of permission.

3.20 Where the claim concerns a decision by a department or body for whom the Treasury Solicitor[25] acts *and the Treasury Solicitor has already been involved in the case*, a copy of the letter before claim should be sent to the address on the letter notifying the decision and, quoting the Treasury Solicitor's reference, to: The Treasury Solicitor, (currently) 102 Petty France, Westminster, London, SW1H 9GL.[26]

3.21 As we have explained, there can be advantages to following the pre-action protocol for judicial review or (as the case may be) seeking to comply with the pre-action conduct Practice Direction. In any event, as long as it is remembered that the use of the protocol or Practice Direction does not affect the strict time limits applying to the issue of proceedings it will ordinarily be prudent to comply where time permits.

Pre-action disclosure

3.22 Prospective claimants who wish to have sight of documents held by the defendant before proceedings are issued should invite voluntary disclosure of them, supplemented as necessary by reference to the Freedom of Information Act 2000 and/or the Environmental Information Regulations 2004.

3.23 In the event voluntary disclosure is refused, a prospective claimant can apply to the court for an order for disclosure before the commencement of proceedings[27], but this would constitute a significant departure from the normal procedures for judicial review (and similar statutory challenges) and is unlikely to be appropriate except in a most exceptional case[28]. The way in which pre-action disclosure might be approached through the pre-action protocol is considered above.

25 The office of Treasury Solicitor continues to exist but on 1 April 2015 the Treasury Solicitor's Department became the Government Legal Department, albeit that references to the Treasury Solicitor remain in parts of the CPR and its practice directions and protocols.

26 It should not be assumed that the Government Legal Department's address will remain constant: see *South Derbyshire District Council v SSHCLG* [2020] EWHC 872 (Admin) where a claim (rather than a pre-action letter) was served on a previous address of the GLD and the Court had to consider whether it was brought in time. On the particular facts (two months after the change of address and at a time when mail was still being forwarded) the Court concluded that the claim was in time.

27 Senior Courts Act 1981, s 33(2); CPR 25.1(1)(i) and 31.16; *British Union for the Abolition of Vivisection (BUAV) v Secretary of State for the Home Department* [2014] EWHC 43 (Admin), [2014] ACD 69, at [32]–[33].

28 *British Union for the Abolition of Vivisection (BUAV) v Secretary of State for the Home Department* [2014] EWHC 43 (Admin), paras 54–57. It is worth noting that such an exceptional case arose in *R (National Association of Probation Officers) v Secretary of State for Justice* [2014] EWHC 4349 (Admin) were pre-action disclosure was granted in respect of a proposed judicial review of a plan to restructure probation services.

C PREPARING AND ISSUING THE CLAIM

3.24 In *R (Burkett) v Hammersmith and Fulham LBC*[29] Lord Steyn observed (at para 50):

> '... the preparation of a judicial review application, particularly in a town planning matter, is a burdensome task. There is a duty of full and frank disclosure on the applicant ... The applicant must present to the court a detailed statement of his grounds, his evidence, his supporting documents in a paginated and indexed bundle, a list of essential reading with relevant passages side-lined, and his legislative sources in a paginated indexed bundle. This is a heavy burden on individuals ...'.

Although *Burkett* was decided in 2002, in 2020 the burden in judicial review claims is no lighter. For other statutory challenges the procedural obligations are perhaps a little less onerous, but the most difficult task – formulating concise and compelling grounds of claim – is the same.

3.25 In this section, the key practical and procedural issues that relate to claims in the planning court are considered. Procedural guidance can be found on the Ministry of Justice website, which hosts the Administrative Court judicial review guide.[30]

3.26 In preparing to issue a judicial review claim or statutory challenge in the Planning Court, one issue which a proposed claimant may have to address is whether the court will consider that they have a sufficient interest in the matter ('standing') to bring the claim. It is in the planning sphere, where objectors may seek to contest the grant of planning permission and related consents, that this issue is most likely to arise.

Standing in judicial review planning challenges

3.27 The starting point is the statutory requirement that the court shall not grant leave to make an application for judicial review unless it considers that the applicant has 'a sufficient interest in the matter to which the application relates' (s 31(3) of the Senior Courts Act 1981). In the *Fleet Street Casuals* case,[31] the House of Lords stated that the question of sufficient interest should not be considered in the abstract, but must be taken together with the legal and factual context. It was necessary to consider the powers or duties of the public body which were at issue, the applicant's position in relation to those powers or duties, and the breach said to have been committed (per Lord Diplock at 630C–D). The practical effect is that the court will need to consider as a matter of fact

29 [2002] 1 WLR 1593.

30 At www.gov.uk/government/publications/administrative-court-judicial-review-guide, last updated in July 2020.

31 *Inland Revenue Commissioners v National Federation of Self-Employed and Small Businesses Ltd* [1981] AC 617 which considered similar wording under the former RSC Order 53.

and degree whether a claimant has sufficient interest in light of the facts of any given case.

3.28 The question of standing in planning cases has mainly arisen in relation to third party objectors and is discussed below by reference to local action groups and individuals. By way of general context however it is notable that the courts have not adopted an entirely consistent approach to the issue in recent years. Several cases in the 1980s (we discuss some below) demonstrated a liberality of approach, in which the courts accepted that sufficient standing to challenge a planning decision might be found in individuals or groups of residents likely to be affected by the matter, though without property rights at stake,[32] and by a neighbour in respect of a decision relating to development which would intrude upon her privacy and to which she had objected.[33] In other cases, a more restrictive line was taken. In the *Fleet Street Casuals* case, the House of Lords accepted that in gauging the sufficiency of an interest under the then extant RSC Ord 53, regard should be had both to the nature of the relevant function and its implications for the applicant. That approach was adopted in relation to a challenge to the validity of planning permission in *Main v Swansea City Council*[34] where the Court of Appeal accepted that there might be cases where a user of the highway adjoining the application site would have locus standi to challenge the permission if there had been a breach of the requirement to notify the Secretary of State for the application because of its highways implications. In general, as we discuss below, since the Supreme Court's judgment in *Walton v Scottish Ministers*,[35] a generally broader, liberal approach to standing has been adopted by the Planning Court.

Local action groups

3.29 A liberal approach to standing and community action groups was taken in *R v Hammersmith & Fulham LBC ex p. People Before Profit*[36] in which the applicant action group, who had appeared as an unincorporated association objecting at a public inquiry into a local plan, formed into a limited company to seek judicial review. The court rejected an argument that the company had no standing to bring the claim. Although the company was an entity separate from the unincorporated association which had appeared at the inquiry that did not deprive it of standing. The court should look at the realities of the matter. The company was made up of the same people who had objected. They were bona fide, with a legitimate interest in the matter (pp 371–372).

32 *Covent Garden Community Association Ltd v Greater London Council* (1981) JPL 183; *R v Stroud DC ex p Goodenough* (1980) 43 P & CR 59; *R v Hammersmith and Fulham BC Ltd ex p People Before Profit* (1981) JPL 869.

33 *R v North Hertfordshire DC ex p Sullivan* [1981] JPL 752 and cf *Allen v City of London Corp* [1981] JPL 685 and *Davies v London Borough of Hammersmith and Fulham* [1981] JPL 682, where no consideration of the locus standi of the applicants appears to have been undertaken, although both applications were in the event dismissed on other grounds.

34 (1984) 49 P&CR 26.

35 [2013] Env LR 16.

36 (1983) 45 P&CR 364.

3.30 A more restrictive approach to standing was taken in the *Rose Theatre* case[37] in which the court gave the view (obiter) that the applicant company, which was made up of archaeologists and others and had been formed to preserve the site of Shakespeare's Rose Theatre, did not have sufficient interest in the decision not to schedule the site as an ancient monument. It was not enough that the company had written to the Secretary of State and received a reply detailing his reasons for not scheduling the site (p 273).

3.31 Several decisions since the *Rose Theatre* case suggest that the more liberal approach to standing and community action groups has been preferred by the courts.[38]

3.32 In *R v SOSE ex p. Kirkstall Valley Campaign Ltd*,[39] neither respondent had taken any point on the standing of the applicant. The court nevertheless commented (obiter) that it had no doubt that its capacity as a community action group concerned with the interests of local residents in the development of Kirkstall valley gave it sufficient interest in the subject matter of the application. It had been incorporated several years before the claim had been made and the company had not been formed for the purposes of litigating. The issue which had arisen in the *Rose Theatre* case was that a company had been formed purely for the purpose of litigation. This was described as 'colourable incorporation': incorporation for the sole apparent purpose of escaping the impact of a costs order (p 12A–D). The court noted that the issue had been met in *Rose Theatre* by the substitution of its individual members as applicants.

3.33 In *R v Leicestershire CC ex p. Blackfordby and Boothorpe Action Group*[40] the respondents directly raised the issue that the company had been formed for the purposes of litigation and avoidance of costs. It was argued that, as a matter of public policy, standing should not be accorded in those circumstances. The court rejected any inference that the company was incorporated for those purposes and noted the unchallenged evidence that the decision to incorporate was made, firstly, to achieve a proper and formal legal structure to administer the action group's funds and manage its affairs quickly and easily, and secondly, to enable the group to represent the community in a democratic manner ([35]).

3.34 The court held that the incorporation of a local action group ought not to be a bar to bringing an application for judicial review. Whilst technically it did not have a relevant interest of its own, in substance it represented the interests of local residents, many of whom had a relevant interest. One advantage of incorporation was the avoidance of substantial personal liability of members for the costs if the application was unsuccessful. However, that should not preclude the use of a corporate vehicle, at least where incorporation was not the sole purpose of escaping the direct impact of an adverse costs order (and possibly even where

37 *R v SoSE ex p Rose Theatre Trust Co* (1990) 59 P&CR 257.

38 See also *R (Hereford Waste Watchers Ltd) v Herefordshire Council* [2005] Env LR 29.

39 [1997] 1 PLR 8.

40 [2000] Env LR 2. See also the first instance decision in *R (Cherkley Campaign Ltd) v Mole Valley DC* [2014] 1 P&CR 12, at [32]–[36] (overturned on appeal but not on this issue).

it was for that purpose). The costs position could be dealt with adequately by requiring the provision of security for costs in a realistically large sum ([37]). It was noted that the increasingly liberal approach of the courts towards standing of interest groups since the *Rose Theatre* case told against the adoption of a restrictive approach even if the company represented the private interests of local residents rather than the wider community interest ([38]).

3.35 In *Residents against Waste Site Ltd v Lancashire CC*,[41] the court held that the claimant company, which had been incorporated two days before the claim was issued, had standing. The respondent noted that the company could not have been an interested party during the course of the application for planning permission under challenge. No clear explanation had been put forward by the claimant for formation of the company and the action group's website was quoted which stated that liability could be limited by the formation of a company. Finally, the respondent argued that the person aggrieved formula from s 288 proceedings[42] should be applied as a matter of consistency and fairness.

3.36 The court held that the situation under s 288 and in judicial review was not the same. The person aggrieved test was designed to afford rights to individuals whose private interests were affected and which very often did not turn on any suggested public wrong by a public body ([17]). The proper approach was that set out in *Blackfordby*. If the true objection to the grant of standing to a company was the costs protection afforded, then the proper approach must be to address the costs problem, rather than to seek to undermine the standing of the company. In that case security for costs had been negotiated and agreed ([19]–[20]).

3.37 For Local Action Groups that do not have corporate status, a more cautious approach has traditionally been required. In some judicial review claims, the fact that unincorporated associations generally lack the legal capacity to sue or be sued in their own name has acted as a bar to permission being granted.[43] At the same time, some unincorporated associations have successfully brought judicial review proceedings.[44]

The Administrative Court Guide[45] explains the position at §2.2.1:

> 'The Court may allow unincorporated associations (which do not have legal personality) to bring judicial review proceedings in their own name. But it is sensible, and the Court may require, that proceedings are brought in the name of one or more individuals, such as an office-holder or member of the association, or by a private limited company formed by individuals.

41 [2008] Env LR 27.

42 TCPA 1990, s 288.

43 For example: *Alwoodly Golf Club v Leeds CC* [1995] NPC 149.

44 For example: *R (on the application of Association of British Civilian Internees (Far East Region)) v Secretary of State for Defence* [2003] EWCA Civ 473; [2003] QB 1397.

45 Last updated in July 2020.

> A costs order may be, and often is, made against the party or parties named as claimant(s).'

The most recent judicial position, albeit taken in the context of a statutory challenge rather than a judicial review, came in *Aireborough Neighbourhood Development Forum v Leeds City Council.*[46] In that case, Lieven J confirmed that an unincorporated neighbourhood forum was a 'person aggrieved', relying on the definition of a 'person' as including 'a body of persons corporate or incorporate' in Schedule 1 to the Interpretation Act 1978. The Judge also observed that:

> '… groups of residents or interested people, may choose to group together to make representations, or attend inquiries, on a matter of interest and importance to them. This is particularly the case in matters concerning planning or the local environment, where the nature of the impact may often fall most directly on a group of people living in a particular area. It would be unfortunate if the law prevented them challenging the decision which they had participated in, in the same grouping as they had made the representations. I accept that the Aarhus Convention is not an overwhelming factor, because challenges can still be brought by individuals, but it and the general policy position would support a finding that a claim can be brought by an unincorporated association.'[47]

There is no obvious reason why this decision, taken in the context of a statutory challenge, should not apply with equal force when it comes to the 'sufficient interest' test in the context of judicial review.

Individuals as claimants

3.38 As with the decisions on standing relating to local action groups, there have been apparently conflicting decisions in relation to individuals and standing in planning cases. A more liberal approach to standing has emerged in more recent years.

3.39 In *R v North Somerset DC and Pioneer Aggregates (UK) Limited ex p. Garnett and Pierrsenne*,[48] the court refused permission to challenge the Council's decision to grant planning permission for an extension to an existing quarry within a large public park on the outskirts of Bristol. The applicants were both Bristol residents and environmentalists. Both frequently used the park and had been part of a campaign group which objected to the proposed development. The respondent argued that the applicants were not owners and had no rights over the land, they were not neighbours, nor objectors themselves to the application. They had no commercial interest, no statutory rights of consultation, and were in the same category as any other ordinary members of the public. The court stated that it had to undertake a balancing act between various factors and exercise its

46 [2020] EWHC 45 (Admin).
47 Ibid, at [31].
48 [1998] Env LR 91.

discretion as to whether the applicants had shown sufficient interest. Sufficient interest had not been made out (pp 103–104).

3.40 In the same year, the court in *R v Somerset CC and ARC Southern Ltd ex p Dixon*[49] took a much more liberal view towards standing in a similar case. The Council had resolved to grant planning permission for the extension of a limestone operations at a quarry in Somerset which the applicant sought to challenge. The applicant was a local resident, parish councillor, and a member of more than one body concerned with the environment. The respondent argued that he had no interest as a landowner or as the possessor of a personal right or interest threatened by the proposed quarrying and therefore had no sufficient interest to bring the challenge.

3.41 Having reviewed the authorities on standing, including the decision in *Garnett*, the court held that to elevate the question of standing at the leave stage above the elementary level of excluding busybodies and troublemakers, and to demand something akin to a special private interest in the subject matter, was entirely misconceived. The applicant was plainly neither a busybody nor a mere troublemaker. The courts had always been alive to the fact that a person or organisation with no particular stake in an issue or the outcome may, without in any sense being a mere meddler, wish and be well placed to call the attention of the court to an apparent misuse of public power, which was the basis of public law. If an arguable case were made out at the leave stage, the court's only concern would be that it was not being done for an ill motive. If the substantive case were made out, everything relevant to the applicant's standing would be weighed up whether with regard to the grant of the application or the form of relief (p 121).

3.42 The more liberal approach to standing was followed by the Court of Appeal in *R (Kides) South Cambridgeshire DC*[50] where the applicant was a local resident and parish councillor who sought to challenge the grant of planning permission for residential development on grounds that, in the long period between the resolution to grant planning permission and the issue of permission, there had been a number of material changes in circumstances including the introduction of a new government circular on affordable housing. The developer had argued successfully in the High Court that the applicant had no standing to bring the proceedings since she relied inter alia on the absence of any provision in the original application for affordable housing, which was not a matter of any real concern to her.

3.43 The Court of Appeal disagreed with the lower court's decision on standing. There was an important distinction between to be drawn between, on the one hand, a person who brings proceedings having no real or genuine interest in obtaining the relief sought, and on the other hand a person who, whilst legitimately and perhaps passionately interested in obtaining the relief sought, relies as grounds for seeking that relief on matters in which he has no personal

49 [1998] Env LR 111.
50 [2003] 1 P&CR 19.

interest. It was not just to debar a litigant who has a real and genuine interest in obtaining the relief sought from relying on grounds (which may be good grounds) on which he had no interest. A litigant with such a real and genuine interest in challenging an administrative decision must be entitled to present his challenge on all available grounds ([132]–[134]).

3.44 Two further cases illustrate how the liberal approach has been applied to standing in cases involving individuals and planning and environmental cases.

3.45 In *R (Hammerton) v London Underground Ltd*[51] the claimant sought to challenge the refusal by London Underground to give an undertaking that it would not demolish Bishopsgate Goods Yard which was an area of considerable historic interest and importance. The claimant was the Honorary Secretary of the London Railway Heritage Society and sought declarations that a relevant planning permission and listed building consent had lapsed, and that the construction of the East London Line Extension would be unlawful. The court held that it was not necessary for the claimant to show that there was no one else who could bring the proceedings. The availability of other bodies or people to bring proceedings was not a determining factor but it was a relevant factor in standing.[52] Further, having considered the court's decision in *Kides* any concern that the claimant had no personal interest in the grounds for seeking relief was dispelled. The litigant with a real and genuine interest included the public interest litigant here ([200]–[209]).

3.46 The approach in *Dixon*, *Kides*, and *Hammerton* also accords with the very wide approach to standing taken in the environmental case of *R (Edwards) v Environment Agency, SoS*.[53] The claimant sought to challenge the grant of an environmental permit to allow cement works at a factory near to Rugby. It was noted that the claim form said little about the claimant's standing. He was a resident of Rugby said to be affected by the operations now permitted. Although he had lived at a number of addresses in Rugby, he was currently homeless. The respondent's argument that he did not have sufficient standing to bring the claim was rejected. The claimant was entitled to leave it to other actions groups to be active in opposition to the permit on behalf of the local people. He could still have an interest in the outcome even if he had not been active in the campaign against it. He should not be debarred from subsequently challenging the decision on the ground of inadequate consultation simply because he chose not to participate in the consultation exercise, provided he was affected by its outcome. The claimant had a sufficient interest because he was an inhabitant of Rugby and would be affected by the adverse effect on the environment which the operations may have ([16]).

51 [2003] JPL 984.

52 Applying *R v Foreign Secretary ex p World Movement Ltd* [1995] 1 WLR 386.

53 [2004] Env LR 43.

3.47 Finally, the question of standing has been considered in detail by the Supreme Court. Although the case of *Walton v Scottish Ministers*,[54] which is considered below, concerned the scope of the 'person aggrieved' formula, the court took the opportunity to comment on standing to bring judicial review proceedings, in response to the lower court's comment that the applicant in that case would have lacked standing even if that test were the same ([82]).

3.48 The court referred to its decision in *AXA General Insurance Ltd and others v HM Advocate and others*[55] in which it clarified the approach which should be adopted. Lord Reed stated that in so doing the Court had intended to put an end to an unduly restrictive approach which had too often obstructed the proper administration of justice: namely, an approach which presupposed that the only function of the court's supervisory jurisdiction was to redress individual grievances, and ignored the constitutional function of maintaining the rule of law ([90]).

3.49 Lord Reed referred first to Lord Hope's judgment in *AXA* in which he did not risk a definition of what constituted standing, but held that the words 'directly affected'[56] captured the essence of what was to be looked for. There was a distinction between a mere busybody and the interest of a person affected by or having a reasonable concern in the matter to which the application related. The word 'directly' provided the necessary qualification to the word 'affected' to enable the court to draw that distinction. A personal interest need not be shown if the individual was acting in the public interest and could genuinely say that the issue directly affected the section of the public that he sought to represent ([91]).

3.50 Lord Reed proceeded to explain that a busybody was someone who interfered in something with which he had no legitimate concern. The circumstances which justified that a person was affected by a matter to which the application related, or had a reasonable concern in it, or on the other hand was interfering in a matter with which he had no legitimate concern would plainly differ from one case to another, depending on the particular context and grounds of the application ([92]).

3.51 Lord Reed then referred to his own judgment in *AXA* in which he stated that the requirement that an applicant demonstrate an interest would not operate satisfactorily if it applied in the same way in all contexts. In some contexts, it would be appropriate to require the applicant to demonstrate that he had a particular interest in the matter complained of depending on the particular context. In other situations such as where the excess or misuse of power affected the public generally, insistence on a particular interest could prevent the matter being brought before the court, and that in turn might disable the court from performing its function to protect the rule of law [(93]).

54 [2013] Env LR 16.

55 [2012] 1 AC 868.

56 These were the words used in Rule 58.8(2) of the Act of Sederunt (Rules of the Court of Session 1994) 1994, SI 1994/1443, as amended by the Act of Sederunt (Rules of the Court of Session Amendment No 5) (Public Interest Intervention in Judicial Review) 2000, SI 2000/317.

3.52 Lord Reed proceeded to explain that there may be cases in which any individual, simply as a citizen, would have sufficient interest to bring a public authority's violation of the law to the attention of the court, without having to demonstrate any greater impact upon himself than upon members of the public. The rule of law would not be maintained if, because everyone was equally affected by an unlawful act, no-one was able to bring proceedings to challenge it [94]). Finally, he noted that the interest of a particular applicant was not merely a threshold issue which ceased to be material once the requirement of standing had been satisfied, but it may also bear on the court's exercise of its discretion as to the remedy, if any, which it should grant in the event that the challenge was well-founded[57] ([95]).

3.53 The more liberal approach to standing, as derived from the comments in *Walton*, can be summarised by the following points:

(1) A claimant must have an interest which is sufficient to bring the claim before the court.

(2) A distinction must be drawn between a mere busybody and a person affected by or having a reasonable concern in the matter. The claimant must be 'directly affected'.

(3) What constitutes sufficient interest has to be considered in the context of the issues raised.

(4) In many contexts, a particular interest will need to be shown. But there may be cases where an individual, simply as a citizen, will have a sufficient interest.

(5) The interest of the claimant is not only relevant to standing, but can also bear upon the court's exercise of its discretion as to remedy.

Standing in statutory challenges

3.54 Many of the statutory challenges that come before the Planning Court provide for a claim to be brought by a 'person aggrieved' by the relevant decision.[58]

3.55 In *Walton v Scottish Ministers* (see above), the question of standing and the 'persons aggrieved' formula received full consideration by the Supreme Court.[59]

57 Referring to Lord Carnwath's judgment at [103].

58 See, eg, TCPA 1990, ss 287 and 288; Planning (Listed Buildings and Conservation Areas) Act 1990, s 63; Planning (Hazardous Substances) Act 1990, s 22; PCPA 2004, s 113; Transport and Works Act 1992, s 22; Highways Act 1980, s 105D, Sch 2, para 2; Wildlife and Countryside Act 1981, Sch 11, para 7, Sch 15, para 12; Acquisition of Land Act 1981, s 23.

59 The court was considering Roads (Scotland) Act 1984, Sch 2, paras 2–4.

3.56 The applicant in that case sought to challenge the validity of schemes and orders to allow the construction of a road network bypassing Aberdeen made by the respondents under the Roads (Scotland) Act 1984. The applicant was the chairman of a local organisation opposing the proposals, whose members lived along the proposed route. He had also taken part in the local inquiry process to consider the proposals. The applicant himself resided in the vicinity of part of the proposed route.

3.57 The respondents had not disputed the applicant's entitlement to bring the application. However, the lower court had made observations on the issue to the effect that the applicant was not a person aggrieved.

3.58 Lord Reed, who gave the leading judgment of the court, reviewed the authorities both north and south of the border and held that the applicant was indubitably a person aggrieved within the meaning of the legislation. The following relevant principles are taken from his judgment:

(1) The meaning attributed to the phrase 'person aggrieved' will vary according to the context in which it is found. It is necessary to have regard to the particular legislation involved and the nature of the grounds[60] [84].

(2) Persons will ordinarily be regarded as aggrieved if they made objections or representations as part of the procedure which preceded the decision challenged, and their complaint is that the decision was not properly made[61] [86].

(3) There are circumstances in which a person who has not participated in the process may nonetheless be 'aggrieved': where for example an inadequate description of the development in the application and advertisement could have misled him so that he did not object or take part in the inquiry[62] [87].

(4) Ordinarily, however, it will be relevant to consider whether the applicant stated his objection at the appropriate stage of the statutory procedure, since that procedure is designed to allow objections to be made and a decision then to be reached within a reasonable time, as intended by Parliament [87].

3.59 The principles to be applied when considering whether an applicant is a person aggrieved can therefore be derived from *Walton*. However, certain previous decisions of the lower courts will remain of relevance and applicable to particular circumstances. They can be summarised as follows:

60 Referring to *Arsenal FC Ltd v Smith (Valuation Officer)* [1979] AC 1 at [32].

61 Referring to *Turner v SOSE* (1974) 28 P&CR 123 endorsed by the CA in *Times Investments Ltd v SOSE* (1991) 61 P&CR 98.

62 Referring to *Wilson v SOSE* [1973] 1 WLR 1083.

- Successors in title may be persons aggrieved for the purposes of challenging a planning permission made subject to planning conditions which continue to bind their land (*Times Investment Ltd v SOSE, LB Tower Hamlets*[63]).[64]
- A party in whose favour an appeal is allowed by an Inspector, but who seeks to challenge the reasoning of the Inspector, is not a person aggrieved. In those circumstances, an application for judicial review can be made (*Greater London Council v SOSE, Harrow LBC*[65]).
- The normal position is that a public authority which has an adverse decision made against it in an area where it is required to perform public duties, is entitled to be treated as a 'person aggrieved'. There is no need for a legal burden to be placed on a party to proceedings to give a right of appeal. The Interpretation Act 1978 will normally be decisive to determine that a local authority is a 'person' (*Cook v Southend-on-Sea BC*[66]).[67]

3.60 In the light of the more liberal approach which the courts have adopted towards standing both in judicial review proceedings and in statutory challenges, it may be thought that the question of standing will rarely arise. However, the Supreme Court in *Walton* held that the meaning of 'persons aggrieved' would vary according to context and declined to give a definitive meaning to the phrase.

3.61 There have thus been cases since *Walton* that have found some claimants not to be 'persons aggrieved.' One such recent example is *Norman v Secretary of State for Housing Communities and Local Government*[68] where the claimant was an elected Councillor and member of the Planning Committee of Herefordshire Council. She was also the Chair of the North Herefordshire Green Party. She lived 10 miles away from the development site and did not have a private interest that would be affected by the proposal. She had not participated in the appeal before an Inspector. Justine Thornton QC sitting as a Deputy High Court Judge (as she then was) held that: 'whilst the Claimant may feel aggrieved about the inspector's decision, that does not make her a person aggrieved under the 1990 Act.'[69] This decision can be contrasted with *Zurich Assurance Ltd v Winchester City Council*[70] where the claimant landowner, which had not overtly participated in a local plan examination, was found to have sufficient interest in the outcome

63 (1991) 61 P&CR 98.

64 See also *River Thames Society v First Secretary of State* [2007] JPL 782 where substitution was allowed so that the vice chairman of the applicant Society could continue s 288 proceedings from which the Society sought to withdraw.

65 [1985] JPL 868, although this case was distinguished in *R (Redditch BC) v FSOS* [2003] 2 P&CR 25 at [21].

66 [1990] 1 All ER 243.

67 Although this case concerned hackney carriage licences and the appeal provisions under Public Health Act 1936, s 301, the court took the opportunity to give its view given the many statutory situations where the 'persons aggrieved' question was in issue.

68 [2019] Env LR 14.

69 Ibid at [62].

70 [2014] EWHC 758 (Admin), per Sales J at [86]–[91].

to be 'a person aggrieved' so as to be entitled to challenge the adoption of the local plan under s 113 Planning & Compulsory Purchase Act 2004.

3.62 Where the proposed claimant is an individual or local action group, the tactical question will be whether to deal with standing in the evidence supporting the claim or to wait and respond to any point which is taken. Cases such as the *Kirkstall Valley Campaign* and *Walton* show that the courts have been prepared to raise the issue without prompting. Given that the interest of the particular applicant will not only be relevant to standing but may also be relevant to the court's exercise of discretion as to remedy, it may well be prudent to include such information in the evidence supporting the claim.

3.63 At the time proceedings are issued, the claimant must be a 'person' in law, which can include an unincorporated association.[71] This position was reiterated in *Aireborough Neighbourhood Development Forum v Leeds City Council*[72] as discussed at **3.37** above.

3.64 Whilst the issue of standing will often be uncontroversial, in those cases where the relevant statutory framework does not confer an express right of challenge on the claimant it should not be assumed. Where there is some doubt the authorities on standing will provide the surest guide, but the following checklist of considerations may also be helpful:

(1) Is the claimant a local resident, a member of a campaign group, or some other body? How proximate to the claimant is the development or scheme sought to be challenged?

(2) Did the claimant involve themselves in the procedure (if any) which preceded the decision challenged? If not, is there a reason why there was no involvement?

(3) In what way will the decision affect the claimant?

(4) If the claimant is a local campaign group, to what extent is it representative of the public's views?

(5) If the claimant is an individual, to what extent was or is the claimant involved in local environmental organisations or organisations which have sought to object to the development?

(6) Where the claimant is a company formed by a local campaign group, what were the reasons for this (were they other than, or in addition to, minimising costs liability in the event that the challenge is unsuccessful)?[73]

(7) Where the claimant cannot demonstrate a personal interest in challenging the decision, what is the claimant's real and genuine interest in challenging the decision?

71 Interpretation Act 1978, Sch 1; *Williams v Devon CC* [2015] EWHC 568 (Admin).
72 [2020] EWHC 45 (Admin).
73 See also the provision of financial information requirements discussed below.

(8) Where the claimant cannot demonstrate a personal interest in challenging the decision, are there any other bodies or people who can be expected to bring proceedings in place of the claimant?

(9) In any case involving a group of individuals, consideration should be given to whether the claim should be brought by one individual in a representative capacity, or by the group as an unincorporated association or through a company.

D THE PROVISION OF INFORMATION ABOUT FINANCIAL RESOURCES AND AARHUS CONVENTION CLAIMS

Financial resources

3.65 Costs in the Planning Court are considered in Chapter 6 and reference should be made to that chapter for full discussion of the costs provisions affecting Planning Court claims. The following points are therefore provided as summary guidance for claimants in planning and environmental cases.

3.66 The amendments made to judicial review under Part 4 of the Criminal Justice and Courts Act 2015 include detailed requirements for claimants concerning the provision of financial resources.[74] The clear thrust of those amendments is to force claimants to provide greater transparency as to the financial backing behind their claims so that where a claim fails, the court is in a position to make a costs award against the claimant and/or anyone else providing substantial financial support. The key provisions can be summarised as follows:

(1) The requirement for leave to be obtained is made contingent on, inter alia, the provision to the court of any information about the financing of the application that is specified in rules of court (SCA 1981, s 31(3)(b)[75]).

(2) The information may include:

   (a) information about the source, nature and extent of financial resources available, or likely to be available, to the applicant, to meet liabilities arising in connection with the application; and

   (b) if the applicant is a body corporate that is unable to demonstrate that it is likely to have financial resources available to meet such liabilities, information about its members and about their ability to provide financial support for the purposes of the application, though only a person whose financial support (whether direct or indirect) exceeds a level set out in the rules has to be identified (SCA 1981, s 31(3A), (3B)[76]).

74 CJCA 2015, ss 85–86 (despite it being some five years since the commencement of the majority of the Act, these sections are still not in force).

75 Amendment made by CJCA 2015, s 85(1). The section and the rules of court referred to are not yet in force.

76 Amendment made by CJCA 2015, s 85(2) (not yet in force).

(3) In determining the liability and quantum of costs in judicial review proceedings (at the leave, substantive, or appeal stage), provision has been made for the High Court and Court of Appeal to have regard to the information about the financing of the proceedings referred to in (2) above (CJCA 2015, (s 86(1), (2) [77]).

(4) The court must also consider whether to order costs to be paid by a person identified in (2)(b) above.

3.67 Among other things, these provisions are designed to ensure that individuals who have formed a company for the purposes of litigation are not easily able to avoid the costs consequences of unsuccessful challenges. There will clearly be much for individual objector and local actions group claimants to do to satisfy these requirements and given that the granting of leave will be contingent on the provision of this information, the information will ordinarily have to be obtained before issuing the claim.

Aarhus Convention claims

3.68 At the same time, where claimants are able to bring themselves within the wide scope of the Aarhus Convention, which is applicable to environmental matters, they will benefit from a degree of costs protection. The position for both judicial review and statutory challenge claimants is governed by CPR 45.41–45.45.

3.69 Although the vast majority of planning cases are likely to come within the scope of the Aarhus Convention, where the claimant in judicial review or statutory challenge proceedings cannot come within its terms, a Protective Costs Order in statutory challenges can be sought under the principles in *R (Corner House Research) v SOSTI*,[78] which include that the issues raised are of general public importance and that the public interest requires that those issues should be resolved. The costs capping orders under ss 88 and 89 of the CJCA 2015 in the context of a judicial review can only be sought once leave has been granted (s 88(4)).[79] The test for making a costs capping order is similar, though more detailed, than that established under the *Corner House* principles.[80]

3.70 For claimants bringing statutory challenges, the costs protection regime was previously more restricted than for judicial review claims. A claimant bringing a claim which did not involve the EIA or IPPCA directives could not benefit from the costs protection given to judicial review claims engaging the

77 Not yet in force.

78 [2005] 1 WLR 2600.

79 CJCA 2015, ss 88 and 89do not apply to the Aarhus Convention following the introduction of The Criminal Justice and Courts Act 2015 (Disapplication of Sections 88 and 89) Regulations 2017.

80 The full procedure for applying for a 'Judicial Review Costs Capping Order' (JRCCO) is set out in detail at §24.2–24.3 of the Administrative Court Guide (last updated July 2019).

Aarhus Convention despite the fact that such claims were likely to fall within its broad scope.

3.71 This was because the CPR rules relating to Aarhus Convention claims were specified to apply to claims for judicial review only (CPR 45.41). In *Venn v SOSCLG*[81] the claimant sought to quash an Inspector's grant of planning permission for a single storey dwelling in her neighbour's side garden through s 288 of the TCPA 1990 proceedings. It was agreed that the claim did not involve the EU environmental directives. The claimant sought a Protective Costs Order on the basis that her claim came within the ambit of CPR 45.41, alternatively that the court should exercise its inherent jurisdiction to make a PCO on the basis that it was an environmental challenge falling within Article 9 of the Convention. The court noted that the arguments were finely balanced and found that the section 288 application came within Article 9(3) of the Aarhus Convention. However, whilst the court had the power to grant costs protection in Aarhus Convention cases falling outside CPR 45.41, that discretion had to be exercised in accordance with the CPR and established principles. That discretion would not be exercised here where the exclusion of statutory appeals and applications from CPR 45.41 was a deliberate expression of legislative intent. The court therefore reluctantly refused to grant the PCO.

3.72 The court commented that insofar as the costs protection regime introduced by CPR 45.41 excluded statutory appeals and applications, it was not compliant with the Aarhus Convention. The court referred to a review of costs in environmental cases which was being undertaken at the time and stated that the review would be able to take its decision into account in the formulation of those rules. The rules were thus amended with effect from February 2017[82] by extending the scope of them to include statutory challenges and by making provision for the variation of the costs limit. However, this amendment failed to address the fact that a review under statute could only fall within the Aarhus rules if it concerned a decision within the scope of Article 9(1) or 9(2) of the Aarhus Convention, whereas a judicial review challenge could also engage Article 9(3) of the Convention in order to benefit from costs protection. Accordingly, a further amendment to the CPR was made on 1 October 2019 to bring statutory challenges within the scope of Article 9(3) as well.[83]

3.73 Claimants might thus approach the position when bringing judicial reviews or statutory challenges in the following order:

(1) Does the claim come within the scope of the Aarhus Convention? If so, the following is required:

81 [2015] 1 WLR 2328.
82 Civil Procedure (Amendment) Rules 2017 (SI 2017/95)
83 Civil Procedure (Amendment No.3) Rules 2019 (SI 2019/1118) and see r 45.41(2)(a).

a. State in the claim form that the claim is an Aarhus Convention claim[84] and explain whether the claimant seeks to vary the default Aarhus Convention costs limits and if so, why.

b. Alongside the claim form, the claimant must also file and serve a schedule of the claimant's financial resources with details of the claimant's significant assets, liabilities, income and expenditure and in relation to any financial support which any person has provided or is likely to provide to the claimant, the aggregate amount which has been provided and which is likely to be provided.[85]

c. The schedule should be verified by a statement of truth.[86]

(2) In an Aarhus Convention claim prescribed maximum levels of costs apply under CPR r45.43[87] unless the issue is contested by the defendant in its acknowledgment of service when it will be determined by the court at the earliest opportunity.[88]

(3) If the claim is for judicial review and does not fall within the scope of the Aarhus Convention, the claimant should consider whether the test for judicial review cost capping order under s 88 of the CJCA 2015 is met. This is modelled on the *Corner House* principles, but is more detailed.[89] The costs capping order can only be obtained after leave has been granted. An application for such an order should be included in ss 7 and 8 of the claim form and supported by evidence.

(4) If the claim is a review under statute and does not fall within the scope of the Aarhus Convention, the claimant should consider whether the *Corner House* principles are met, including whether the issues are of general public importance and the public interest requires that those issues should be resolved. If so, a PCO can be applied for within the Claim form, together with a Part 23 application and supporting evidence.[90]

84 CPR 45.42(1)(a).

85 CPR 45.42(1)-(2).

86 Ibid.

87 An unsuccessful individual claimant (not acting as or on behalf of a business or other legal person) can be ordered to pay up to £5,000. In all other cases the cap on the claimant's liability for costs is £10,000. An unsuccessful defendant can be ordered to pay up to £35,000. A local authority claimant in an Aarhus Convention claim is entitled to costs protection under these provisions: *R (HS2 Action Alliance) v Secretary of State for Transport* [2015] EWCA Civ 203. Similarly, a Parish Council will also fall within the scope of costs protection: *Crondall Parish Council v Secretary of State for Housing Communities and Local Government* [2019] EWHC 1211 (Admin). The cap may be varied in accordance with the provisions in CPR 45.44.

88 CPR 45.45(2).

89 See §§24.2-24.3 of the Administrative Court Guide (updated July 2019).

90 The position in respect of reviews under statute is not changed by the CJCA as ss 88, 89 and 90 apply only to judicial review claims.

E TIME LIMITS, PROMPTNESS AND DELAY

3.74 In judicial review proceedings, CPR 54.5(1) requires that the claim form must be filed at court promptly, and in any event not later than three months after the grounds to make the claim first arose. However, for claims involving Secretary of State or local authority decisions under the planning acts[91] a stricter time limit for the filing of the claim form applies. In these claims the claim form must be filed not later than six weeks after the grounds to make the claim first arose (CPR 54.5(4),(5)). There is no separate requirement that the claim must be brought promptly.

3.75 In the light of the pre-action considerations and requirements for provision of financial information referred to above, prospective claimants might wish (and need) to use much of the six-week period allowed to prepare and evidence their case fully. The time taken to issue the claim will not be a consideration for the court in the proceedings as long as the claim is issued within the six-week period.

3.76 The time limits for issuing judicial review proceedings in respect of decisions under the planning acts mirrors the time limit applicable to most statutory planning challenges, in which an absolute six week period for challenging a decision has long applied.[92] Again, there is no consideration of promptness within those provisions.

Calculating time for the purposes of issuing a claim

3.77 In judicial review claims under the planning Acts, the claim form must be filed not later than six weeks after the grounds to make the claim first arose. Where planning permission is granted by a local planning authority the formal notice of permission will in some cases be preceded by a resolution to grant permission, raising the question whether the grounds to make a claim challenging the grant of permission arise when the decision notice is issued or the resolution to grant is made. The position has been settled for some time by a decision of the House of Lords (*R (Burkett) v Hammersmith and Fulham LBC*[93]). When considering the identical form of wording for the 'promptly and in any event three-month' time limit before the amendment to CPR r 54.5, the House of Lords held that time does not start to run when the resolution to grant is made, but only after the

91 The 'planning acts' are TCPA 1990, P(LBCA)A 1990, P(HS)A 1990, and P(CP)A 1990 (see CPR 54.5(A1) and TCPA 1990, s 336). A decision by a local planning authority to grant prior approval for development within the Town and Country Planning (General Permitted Development) (England) Order 2015 is a decision under the planning acts: *R (Coventry Gliding Club Ltd) v Harborough DC* [2019] EWHC 3059 (Admin). However, a decision on local plan preparatory stages would not fall within CPR 54.5(5) because the enabling legislation for plan-making is the PCPA 2004, which is not one of the defined 'planning Acts'.

92 TCPA 1990, ss 287(2B), 288(4B); P(LBCA)A 1990, s 63(3A); P(HS)A 1990, s 22(2B); PCPA 2004, s 113(3B).

93 [2002] 1 WLR 1593.

formal issue of planning permission. This was because the resolution itself did not create any legal rights and it was only upon the formal grant of permission that the rights and obligations between the local planning authority, developer and affected individuals come into existence. Challenges to the grant of planning permission based on deficiencies in EIA screening opinions and other EIA decisions come within the same principle (*R (Catt) v Brighton and Hove CC*[94]). At the same time, it was confirmed in *Burkett* that there was no restriction on the claimant's right to challenge a local planning authority's resolution at the time it is passed, without having to wait for the final grant of planning permission; likewise in *Catt* the court held that it is possible and may be appropriate to bring a challenge to a screening opinion before planning permission has been granted.

3.78 Where in a statutory challenge the relevant application must be made to the High Court within six weeks of the date on which an order is confirmed, the date of confirmation is taken as the date of the Secretary of State's decision letter, not the date of receipt of the letter (*Griffiths v SSE*[95]).

3.79 Where an application must be made not later than the end of the period of six weeks 'starting with' or 'beginning with' the relevant date[96] (be it the confirmation of an order or the taking of some other action), the six-week period runs from (i.e. begins with) the relevant date, not the day after: *Barker v Hambleton DC;*[97] *R (Blue Green London Plan) v SSEFRA.*[98]

3.80 Where an application must be made within the period of six weeks 'from' or 'after' the relevant date[99], the six week period runs from (ie begins with) the day after the relevant date: *Okolo v SOSE*[100]; *Staffordshire Moorlands DC v SSCLG;*[101] *R (Berky) v Newport City Council.*[102]

3.81 For enforcement notice challenges under s 289 of the TCPA 1990 and listed building enforcement notice challenges under s 65 of the P(LBCA) A 1990, CPR PD52D para 26.1(1) requires that the application for permission to appeal must be made 'within 28 days after notice of the decision is given to the applicant'. Notice of the decision is given to the applicant when it is received by

94 [2007] Env LR 32. In *R (Champion) v North Norfolk DC* [2015] 1 WLR 3710, at [63], Lord Carnwath expressed reservations about this decision and indicated that delay in challenging a screening opinion might be taken into account at the permission stage or in relation to the grant of relief.

95 [1983] 2 AC 51.

96 As is currently the case under, inter alia, s 22(1) of the Transport and Works Act 1992.

97 [2013] 1 P&CR 1.

98 [2015] EWHC 495 (Admin); and see [2015] EWCA Civ 876.

99 As is the case under, inter alia, the Acquisition of Land Act 1981, s 23(4); Highways Act 1980, s 105D(1), Sch 2, para 2; Road Traffic Regulation Act 1984, Sch 9, para 35; Wildlife and Countryside Act 1981, Sch 11, para 7(2), Sch 15, para 12(1).

100 [1997] All ER 242.

101 [2008] EWHC 3691 (Admin).

102 [2012] 2 P&CR 12.

him.[103] The first day of the 28-day period is the day after notice of the decision is given.[104] Unlike a statutory time limit, the 28-period fixed by the CPR may be extended by the court.

3.82 In relation to certain planning challenges brought under ss 61N[105] and 106C[106] of the TCPA 1990 and ss 13[107] and 118[108] of the Planning Act 2008 the start date of the period within which a challenge may be brought is the day after the day on which the relevant event has occurred in each case.

3.83 Where the time period for filing a claim has begun, it continues to run over a weekend or bank holiday (Stainer v Secretary of State for the Environment (1992) 65 P & CR 310), but if the last day falls on a weekend or bank holiday, time is extended to the next day on which the court office is open: Calverton Parish Council v Nottingham City Council [2015] PTSR 1130; *Croke v Secretary of State for Communities and Local Government* [2019] PTSR 1406.

Extending time

3.84 The six-week period within which the claim form must be filed in judicial review planning claims cannot be extended by agreement between the parties (CPR 54.5(2)). However, provided there is no statutory time limit for bringing the claim the court may grant an extension of time under CPR 3.1(2)(a). The matters which the court is likely to explore when considering whether to extend time include:

(1) the strength and importance of the claim,

(2) the extent of the delay and whether there was a good reason or adequate explanation for it, and

(3) whether extending the time limit would be likely to cause substantial hardship or substantial prejudice, or be detrimental to good administration.[109]

3.85 The courts have repeatedly stressed the importance of promptness in planning challenges.[110] Although (absent a statutory time limit) there is power

103 *Griffiths v SSE* [1983] 2 AC 51; *Smith v SSE* (22 June 1987), The Times, 6 July 1987; *Ynys Mon BC v SSW* [1992] 3 PLR 1.

104 *R (Westminster Council) v SSCLG* [2014] EWHC 1248 (Admin); CPR 2.8(2), (3).
88A As happened in *Wandsworth LBC v SSTLGR* [2004] 1 P&CR 32.

105 Neighbourhood development orders. See *R (Oyston Estates Ltd) v Fylde BC* [2019] 1 WLR 5484.

106 Development consent obligations.

107 National Policy Statements. See *R (Hillingdon LBC) v Secretary of State for Transport* [2017] 1 WLR 2166.

108 Applications for orders granting development consent.

109 See *Finn-Kelcey v Milton Keynes Borough Council* [2009] Env LR 17; *Law Society of England and Wales v Legal Services Commission* [2010] EWHC 2550 (Admin); *R (Gerber) v Wiltshire Council* [2016] 1 WLR 2593; *R (Thornton Hall Hotel Ltd) v Wirral MBC* [2019] PTSR 1794.

110 See, eg, the authorities cited in *R (Thornton Hall Hotel Ltd) v Wirral MBC* at [21(1)].

to permit a claim to be brought out of time, the court will not generally exercise its discretion to extend time on the basis of legal advice that the claimant might or should have received.[111] Depending on the circumstances, ignorance of the decision could be a good reason provided the application was then made expeditiously;[112] and the fact the claim raises issues of general public importance may also be a reason for extending the time limit.[113] The applicant's conduct after making the application for leave is also relevant (*R v London Docklands Development Corp ex p Sister Christine Frost*[114]). Reference should also be made to the Pre-Action Protocol for Judicial Review, which provides (in footnote 1) that compliance with the protocol, whilst not in itself justifying an extension of time, may be a relevant factor. A court will also take account of a party's agreement 'not to take a time point' so far as concerns delay while they were responding to a letter before claim.

3.86 In contrast, the six-week time limit for bringing statutory challenges is absolute and cannot be extended by the court.[115] This is so even if the applicant was unaware of the decision and could not reasonably have known about it within the six-week period (*R v SSE ex p Kent* [116]).

3.87 There are two cases on substitution and extension of time limits in this area, with different results. In *Eco-Energy (GB) Ltd v FSOS*[117] the court refused to allow an application under CPR 19 to extend the period to allow a new party to continue the proceedings. Once the statutory six-week period of challenge had expired, the court took the view that its jurisdiction had also expired.

3.88 In *River Thames Society v FSOS*,[118] the applicant was allowed to be substituted as the claimant in s 288 proceedings. She was the vice-chairman of the original claimant, the RTS. The court exercised its inherent power of substitution. The policy of s 288 would not be undermined by the substitution and it was reasonable to assume that if the RTS had not issued the claim, the vice-chairman would have done.[119]

111 *R (Gerber) v Wiltshire Council.*

112 *R v SOSHD ex p Ruddock* [1987] 1 WLR 1482, but ignorance where proper notice of an application for planning permission had been given is unlikely to suffice: *R (Gerber) v Wiltshire Council*; *R (Thornton Hall Hotel Ltd) v Wirral MBC.*

113 *Law Society of England and Wales v Legal Services Commission.*

114 (1997) 73 P&CR 199.

115 *Smith v East Elloe Rural DC* [1956] AC 736; *R v Secretary of State for the Environment, ex p Ostler* [1977] QB 122; *Eco-Energy (GB) Ltd v First Secretary of State* [2004] EWCA Civ 1566, [2005] 2 P&CR 5; *Barker v Hambleton DC* [2012] EWCA Civ 610, [2013] 1 P&CR 1; *R (Williams) v Secretary of State for Energy and Climate Change* [2015] EWHC 1202 (Admin); *Croke v Secretary of State for Communities and Local Government* [2019] PTSR 1406. See also CPR PD 8A para 22.3; PD 52D para 3.5.

116 [1988] 3 PLR 17; and see *Croke v Secretary of State for Communities and Local Government* [2019] PTSR 1406.

117 [2004] EWCA Civ 1566.

118 [2007] JPL 782.

119 In *San Vicente v SSCLG* [2014] 1 WLR 966, the Court of Appeal considered the reasoning in both *Eco-Energy* and *River Thames Society*, albeit in the context of an application to amend the grounds of challenge under CPR Part 17.

F ISSUING THE CLAIM

3.89 The mechanics of issuing judicial review claim forms and statutory challenges are set out in Chapter 2 on the Jurisdiction and Procedures of the Planning Court. The main procedural elements are considered below.

3.90 In cases where permission to proceed is required, the initial objective on issuing the claim will be to obtain permission on the papers. To achieve this it will be necessary to show that one or more of the grounds of claim are arguable. In judicial review claims, it may also be necessary for the claimant to show some likelihood that the outcome for the claimant would have been substantially different if the conduct complained of had not occurred, or that even if this is not the case there is an exceptional public interest in the claim proceeding.[120]

3.91 Two further observations of general application can be made with regard to planning cases.

3.92 First, use of the pre-action protocol process should have allowed the claimant to identify the grounds of challenge with greatest merit. In any event, the statement of facts and grounds should focus attention on the most meritorious grounds. There are numerous judicial dicta where the courts have highlighted the dangers of overloading a case with hopeless points with the result that the arguable points are devalued and court time is wasted.[121] A poorly pleaded claim could result in the court refusing permission on the papers on the basis that the application is 'totally without merit'. In those circumstances, no reconsideration at an oral hearing could be requested (CPR 54.12(7)).[122]

3.93 Secondly, a claimant should give careful consideration to the evidence to be filed, ensuring that only material necessary for the court to determine the claim is included. In *R (Newsmith Stainless Ltd) v Secretary of State for the Environment, Transport and the Regions* [2001] EWHC Admin 74, [2017] PTSR 1126, at para 9, Sullivan J said of a challenge to an inspector's decision: 'There will seldom be a need for anything beyond purely formal evidence to produce the decision letter and the material before the inspector relevant to the grounds of challenge in section 288 applications. In exceptional cases … it may be necessary to produce additional evidence, for example to show that 'some matter of real importance has been wholly omitted from the inspector›s report'. But such cases will be rare, and even in those cases applicants should firmly resist the temptation for their evidence to stray into

120 See SCA 1981, s 31(3C)–(3E).

121 See, eg, *Gregory v Turner* [2003] 1 WLR 1149, para 81; *R (Naing) v Immigration Appeal Tribunal* [2003] EWHC 771 (Admin), para 59; *R v F, S, G and W* [2013] EWCA Crim 84, para 60; *R (Network Rail Infrastructure Ltd) v Secretary of State for the Environment, Food and Rural Affairs* [2017] PTSR 1662, paras 11, 12; *Abramovich v Hoffman* [2019] EWHC 509 (Ch), para 58.

122 Though an appeal could be made to the Court of Appeal against the refusal of permission where the application will be determined (usually) on paper without an oral hearing (CPR 52.5(1), (2); 52.8(2); 52.10(2)).

a discussion of the planning merits.' Similar observations have been made in the Planning Court on several occasions[123] and a claimant that does not confine their evidence to that which is essential risks both an adverse judicial reaction and a penalty in costs.

Judicial review claims

3.94 The procedure for judicial review claims is governed by CPR Part 54.[124] Proceedings are begun by the filing of a claim form (form N461PC) and supporting documents[125] and service of the claim form.[126] Within the claim form (or attached as a separate document) the claimant must provide a detailed statement of the grounds for bringing the claim, a statement of the facts relied upon, any application to extend the time limit for filing the claim form and any application for directions. The claim form must be accompanied by the following documents contained in a paginated and indexed bundle:

(1) any written evidence in support of the claim or application to extend time

(2) a copy of any order that the claimant seeks to have quashed

(3) where the claim relates to a decision of a court or tribunal, an approved copy of the reasons for reaching that decision

(4) copies of any documents on which the claimant proposes to rely

(5) copies of any relevant statutory material

(6) a list of essential documents for advance reading by the court (with page references to the passages relied on).

Where it is not possible to file all the above documents, the claimant must indicate which documents have not been filed and the reasons why they are not currently available [CPR 54.6(2), and 54APD paras 5.6–5.9].

3.95 The bundle should satisfy all of the requirements set out above (whilst providing no more than is necessary for the court) with the documents following a logical order. Although the Practice Direction allows for documents which the claimant has not been able to obtain to be provided after filing of the claim form, the objective should be to produce a complete bundle with a statement of facts and grounds that cross refers to the relevant documents in the bundle. The Planning Court has stressed the limited role of witness statements in judicial review or statutory challenges and has given detailed guidance on what matters it is appropriate to address and (more particularly) what matters it is inappropriate

123 See, eg, *R (Network Rail Infrastructure Ltd) v Secretary of State for the Environment, Food and Rural Affairs*, paras 8–12; *Gladman Developments Ltd v Secretary of State for Housing, Communities and Local Government* [2020] EWHC 518 (Admin), paras 67–70.

124 For further guidance see *The Administrative Court Judicial Review Guide (July 2020)* at: www.gov.uk/government/publications/administrative-court-judicial-review-guide.

125 See CPR 54.5, PD 54A paras 5.1–5.10, PD 54E paras 2.1 and 2.2.

126 See CPR 54.7, PD 54A paras 6.1 and 6.2.

to address, including commentaries on the documentary material or illegitimate ex post facto rationalisation of the challenged decision. [127]

3.96 Where urgent consideration of the claim is required, form N463PC should also be completed.

Statutory challenges

3.97 The procedure for statutory challenges under ss 287 and 288 TCPA 1990, s 63 P(LBCA)A 1990, s 22 P(HS)A 1990, and s 113 PCPA 2004 (described compendiously as claims for planning statutory review) is regulated by CPR Part 8 and PD 8C, for which the relevant claim form is N208PC.[128] A residual body of statutory challenges is dealt with under PD 8A, paras 22.1-22.11,[129] for which the standard Part 8 claim form, N208, is appropriate.

3.98 CPR 8.2 lists various matters that the claim form must state:

(1) that Part 8 applies;

(2) the question which the claimant wants the court to decide; or

(3) the remedy which the claimant is seeking and the legal basis for the claim to that remedy;

(4) if the claim is being made under an enactment, what that enactment is;

(5) if the claimant is claiming in a representative capacity, what that capacity is; and

(6) if the defendant is sued in a representative capacity, what that capacity is.

In addition, for planning statutory reviews CPR PD 8C para 2.2 requires the claimant to state or provide:

(7) the name and address of any person that the claimant considers must be served in accordance with para 4.1 of the Practice Direction;

(8) that the claimant is requesting permission to proceed with a claim for planning statutory review;

(9) a detailed statement of the claimant's grounds for bringing the claim for planning statutory review;

(10) a statement of the facts relied on;

(11) any application for directions; and

127 See *Flaxby Park Ltd v Harrogate Borough Council* [2020] EWHC 3204 (Admin) per Holgate J; *United Trade Action Group Ltd v Transport for London* [2021] EWHC 73 (Admin) per Lang J.

128 For further guidance see *Claims for Planning Statutory Review Notes for Guidance for Court Users* (August 2016) at: www.gov.uk/government/publications/claims-for-planning-statutory-review-ac017.

129 Including challenges to compulsory purchase orders and highway orders and schemes, and applications under the Transport and Works Act 1992.

(12) the remedy being claimed (including any interim remedy).

In the case of statutory challenges falling within CPR PD 8A the requirements are less onerous. The only matters that need be stated in the claim form are those set out in CPR 8.2. In practice, the details of claim in a statutory challenge would be similar to the detailed statement of grounds and statement of facts provided in a judicial review or planning statutory review

3.99 In planning statutory reviews the claimant must file with the claim form:

(1) any written evidence in support of the claim;

(2) a copy of any decision, order, relevant document or action that the claimant seeks to have quashed;

(3) copies of any documents on which the claimant proposes to rely;

(4) copies of any relevant statutory material; and

(5) a list of essential documents for advance reading by the court (with page references to the passages relied on).

3.100 Where it is not possible to file all the above documents, the claimant must indicate which documents have not been filed and the reasons why they are not currently available [CPR PD 8C paras 2.3, 2.4].

3.101 In other statutory challenges CPR PD8A para 22.8 requires the claimant to file a witness statement in support of the application in the Administrative Court within 14 days after service of the claim form, and serve a copy of the witness statement and of any exhibit on the respondent at the time of filing. The witness statement would be expected to exhibit the documents deemed necessary to determine the claim.

3.102 Most statutory challenges involve an allegation that the order, plan, permission or other instrument in question was not within the power of the relevant Act or that any relevant requirement has not been complied with. These are broadly equivalent to the principal grounds on which judicial review proceedings may be brought,[130] and it is evident that the procedure for planning statutory reviews, including the documents constituting the claim, is now largely the same.

3.103 CPR PD 8A and PD 8C make special provisions as to service depending on the order, scheme, plan, or decision which is under challenge.

3.104 Once a rule-compliant claim form and supporting documents have been filed, there is no requirement to provide any further documentation to the court for the purposes of a permission or other hearing. However, it is not uncommon for claimants to lodge responses to acknowledgements of service,

130 See *Walton v Scottish Ministers* [2013] Env LR 16, at [108–12].

or skeleton arguments responding to the court's reasons for refusing permission. Oral permission hearings are usually listed for 30 minutes, and the advantage of written advocacy will be obvious in such cases.

3.105 Certain statutory challenges in the Planning Court are brought by way of an appeal, principally appeals under s 289 of the TCPA 1990 and s 65 of the P(LBCA)A 1990. For these appeals the procedure in CPR Part 52 as modified by PD 52D para 26.1 is to be followed.[131] In summary, this requires that proceedings are begun by the service and filing[132] of an application for permission to appeal, together with a draft appellant's notice (form N161) and supporting witness evidence, within 28 days after notice of the decision appealed against is given to the applicant.[133] The application must be in writing and must set out the reasons why permission should be granted; and if the time for applying has expired, must include an application to extend the time for applying, and must set out the reasons why the application was not made within that time.[134] The application must be filed with a copy of the decision being appealed, a draft appellant's notice, a witness statement or affidavit verifying any facts relied on, and a witness statement or affidavit giving the name and address of, and the place and date of service on, each person who has been served with the application. If any person who ought to be served has not been served, the witness statement or affidavit must state that fact and the reason why the person was not served.[135] Where the court grants permission, the appellant's notice must be served and filed within seven days of the grant.[136]

3.106 One complication to note is that where planning permission is *granted* by the Secretary of State in an appeal against an enforcement notice, the grant of planning permission (but not a quashing of the notice) may be challenged by way of application under s 288 of the TCPA 1990, as well as in an appeal under s 289.[137] Uncertainty about the correct route to follow has led the court to suggest that where a challenge is to be brought against an enforcement notice appeal decision granting planning permission and quashing the enforcement notice, the prudent course is to bring proceedings under both ss 288 and 289.[138]

131 See also *Appeals under section 289 of the Town & Country Planning Act 1990: Notes for guidance for court users* (August 2016) at www.gov.uk/government/publications/appeals-under-the-town-country-planning-act-1990-ac016.
132 Under CPR PD 52D para 26.1(3) and (4) service should precede filing.
133 See CPR PD 52D para 26.1(1)–(4), (12). The 28-day period is fixed by the CPR and may be extended by the court under CPR 3.1(2)(a), although as in judicial review proceedings the claimant would need to show good reason for an extension of time.
134 CPR PD 52D para 26.1(2).
135 CPR PD 52D para 26.1(4).
136 CPR PD 52D para 26.1(11)(c). As to the persons to be served, see CPR PD 52D para 26.1(12).
137 See TCPA 1990, ss 284(1)(f), (3)(e), 288(1), (4) and 289(1); *Gill v SSE* [1985] JPL 710; *Thurrock BC v SSETR* [2001] 1 PLR 94, [34]-[35]. Where in an enforcement notice appeal planning permission is refused, the only avenue of challenge is by way of appeal under TCPA 1990, s 289: *Islam v SSCLG* [2012] JPL 1378.
138 *R (Wandsworth BC) v SSTLGR* [2004] 1 P&CR 32, at [9].

Category of claim – 'significant' claims

3.107 In the Planning Court, the speed with which a claim proceeds to a hearing will depend in part on whether it is categorised as 'significant'. Practice Direction 54E provides that Planning Court claims may be categorised as 'significant' by the Planning Liaison Judge, and for this purpose significant claims include claims which:

(a) relate to commercial, residential, or other developments which have significant economic impact either at a local level or beyond their immediate locality;

(b) raise important points of law;

(c) generate significant public interest; or

(d) by virtue of the volume or nature of technical material, are best dealt with by judges with significant experience of handling such matters.

3.108 For significant Planning Court claims, the Practice Direction sets the following target timescales which the parties should prepare to meet:

(a) applications for permission to apply for judicial review are to be determined within three weeks of the expiry of the time limit for filing of the acknowledgment of service;

(b) oral renewals of applications for permission to apply for judicial review or planning statutory review are to be heard within one month of receipt of request for renewal;

(c) applications for permission under s 289 of the TCPA 1990 are to be determined within one month of issue;

(d) planning statutory reviews are to be heard within six months of issue; and

(e) judicial reviews are to be heard within ten weeks of the expiry of the period for the submission of detailed grounds by the defendant or any other party as provided in Rule 54.14.

A claimant who considers that it would be helpful for the claim to be categorised as significant (because, for example, the development to which it relates has begun) and can point to features of the claim that would justify that categorisation should make appropriate written representations on issuing the claim.[139]

3.109 Whether or not a claim is categorised as significant, the Planning Liaison Judge may direct the expedition of any Planning Court claim if he considers it necessary to deal with the case justly,[140] and in urgent cases the claimant should not hesitate to make clear in the claim form and supporting grounds that an order for expedition is sought, giving the reasons why expedition is necessary.

139 CPR PD 54E, para 3.3.
140 CPR PD 54E, para 3.6.

G RESPONDING TO AN ACKNOWLEDGMENT OF SERVICE

3.110 In judicial review claims any person served with the claim form who wishes to take part in the judicial review must file and serve an acknowledgment of service within 21 days.[141] Where the person filing it intends to contest the claim, the acknowledgment must set out a summary of his grounds for doing so.[142] Where he intends to contest the application for permission on the basis that it is highly likely that the outcome for the claimant would not have been substantially different if the conduct complained of had not occurred, he must also set out a summary of the grounds for doing so.[143] The acknowledgement of service must also state the name and address of any person the person filing it considers to be an interested party;[144] and may include or be accompanied by an application for directions.[145]

3.111 From the acknowledgment of service and summary grounds, the claimant will know if his claim is contested on substantial grounds and, if it is, by whom. Crucially, the summary grounds should set out the main elements of the case the claimant has to meet, including whether any claim to or application for costs protection or interim relief is contested.

3.112 The claimant will need to give careful consideration to any summary grounds for contesting the claim that are filed to determine whether:

- any part of the claim should be abandoned;[146]
- amended, additional or alternative grounds of claim should be advanced;[147]
- the documents filed with the claim are sufficient;
- an application for disclosure is warranted;
- an order for cross-examination of a witness is likely to be needed;[148]
- interim relief should be sought, or an application for interim relief abandoned.

3.113 A claimant should bear in mind that a defendant (or interested party) seeking to knock out a claim at the permission stage might file more detailed grounds for contesting the claim than is required by the CPR. Evidence might

141 CPR 54.8(1), (2).

142 CPR 54.8(4)(a)(i).

143 CPR 54.8(4)(a)(ia). SCA 1981, s 31(3C) requires the court, where it is asked to do so by the defendant, to consider whether the outcome for the claimant would have been substantially different if the conduct complained of had not occurred.

144 CPR 54.8(4)(a)(ii).

145 CPR 54.8(4)(b).

146 A claimant that has decided not to pursue its claim must notify the court promptly: *Westminster City Council v Secretary of State for Housing, Communities and Local Government* [2020] EWHC 1472 (Admin).

147 See CPR 54.15, PD 54A para 11.1. Where a claimant changes his case, it is important that the pleaded grounds of challenge are amended promptly: *R (Hinds) v Blackpool Council* [2011] EWHC 591 (Admin), at [42].

148 See para **3.149** below.

also be filed. Depending on the circumstances, a claimant may choose to provide a response to the defendant's grounds, although there is nothing in the rules providing for this.

3.114 For planning statutory reviews under CPR PD 8C, the requirements for an acknowledgment of service are the same.[149]

3.115 The procedure for other statutory challenges brought under CPR PD 8A is less helpful to the claimant (and the court) than for judicial review claims because although defendants are required to file and serve an acknowledgment of service, it is a much more cursory affair. CPR 8.3 requires that the acknowledgment of service must be in the relevant practice form (N210) and must state: (a) whether the defendant contests the claim; and (b) if the defendant seeks a different remedy from that set out in the claim form, what that remedy is. There is no general requirement that a defendant to a statutory challenge must say why he opposes the claim. While in some cases this may not be problematic (not least because a defendant who intends to contest the grant of permission to proceed will almost invariably serve a skeleton argument before the permission hearing), the Planning Court has power under CPR PD 54E para 3.5 to direct that any party intending to contest the claim must file and serve a summary of his grounds for doing so. In most statutory challenges brought under CPR PD 8A it would be sensible for the claimant to include in his claim a request that such an order be made.

3.116 In the case of statutory appeals under s 289 of the TCPA 1990 or s 65 of the P(LBCA)A 1990, the respondent is required to file and serve any evidence on which he intends to rely at the permission hearing at least two clear days before the hearing,[150] but again there is no obligation to file a document before permission is granted setting out the grounds on which the appeal is opposed. It would be prudent therefore to ask the court to make an order under CPR PD 54E para 3.5 at an early stage.

H SEEKING PERMISSION TO PROCEED

Judicial review claims

3.117 Applications for permission to proceed with a judicial review claim are usually considered in the first instance by a judge looking at the papers filed by the parties.[151] The principal test is whether the claim is arguable, and permission may be granted on some grounds of claim and not others. The claimant will in future also need to provide the court with any information about the financing of the application that is specified in rules of court for this purpose.[152]

149 CPR PD 8C paras 5.1–5.5, 6.1.
150 CPR PD 52D para 26.1(8).
151 CPR PD 54A, para 8.4.
152 See SCA 1981, s 31(3)(b) (not yet in force).

3.118 When considering whether to grant permission to proceed, the court may of its own motion consider whether the outcome for the claimant would have been substantially different if the conduct complained of had not occurred, and must consider that question if the defendant asks it to do so.[153] If, on considering that question, it appears to the court to be highly likely that the outcome for the applicant would not have been substantially different, the court *must* refuse to grant permission.[154] However, the court may disregard this requirement if it considers that it is appropriate to do so for reasons of exceptional public interest.[155]

3.119 Following consideration of the papers the court may therefore wish to hear submissions on whether it is highly likely that the outcome for the claimant would not have been substantially different if the conduct complained of had not occurred, and if so whether there are reasons of exceptional public interest which make it nevertheless appropriate to give permission. If so, it will direct a hearing to determine whether to give permission. The claimant, defendant or any other person who has filed an acknowledgment of service will be given at least two days' notice of the hearing date. The court may give directions requiring the proceedings to be heard by a Divisional Court. At the conclusion of the hearing the court will give its reasons for giving or refusing permission. If the court grants permission for reasons of exceptional public interest, it will certify that fact.[156]

3.120 If permission is refused on the papers, or granted to a more limited extent than had been sought, the claimant may renew his application at an oral hearing.[157] The request for a hearing must be filed within seven days after service of the court's reasons for its decision.[158]

3.121 Where, however, the court refuses permission to proceed and records the fact that the application is totally without merit, the claimant may not request that decision to be reconsidered at a hearing.[159] Instead, the claimant may apply to the Court of Appeal for permission to appeal, and that application will ordinarily be determined on paper without an oral hearing.[160]

3.122 On occasions, the court may order a 'rolled-up' hearing, where both permission and substantive hearings are listed on the same day, with the substantive hearing following immediately after the permission hearing. In theory, the court could deal with the issue of permission first, proceeding to the substantive hearing only if permission is granted. In practice, the court will usually hear the case as though it were a substantive hearing, ruling on permission and (if the claim is arguable) the merits and relief at the end. This procedure may

153 See SCA, s 31(3C).
154 SCA 1981, s 31(3D).
155 SCA 1981, s 31(3E).
156 See CPR 54.11A.
157 CPR 54.12.
158 CPR 54.12(4).
159 CPR 54.12(7).
160 CPR 52.5(1), (2), 52.8.

be adopted where the case is urgent; where the court wishes to leave open the issue of delay; or where there is some other reason why it would be inappropriate to determine the issue of permission without full argument. Where the court has directed a rolled-up hearing, the claimant should prepare the case as for a substantive hearing (see further below).

Statutory challenges

3.123 In the case of a planning statutory review under CPR PD 8C, the permission process is essentially the same as for judicial review claims (see above),[161] although the provisions of s 31(3C)–(3E) of the Senior Courts Act 1981 (which may require the court to refuse permission to proceed where it is highly likely that the decision under challenge would have been the same even if no error had been made) do not apply.

3.124 In the case of an appeal against a decision under s 289 of the TCPA 1990 or s 65 of the P(LBCA)A 1990, a permission hearing will be fixed[162] (unless perhaps the defendant concedes in advance that permission should be granted). As in judicial review proceedings, the test at the permission hearing is one of arguability.[163] Again, however, the provisions of s 31(3C)–(3E) of the Senior Courts Act 1981 do not apply.

The permission hearing

3.125 Permission hearings are ordinarily listed to be dealt with in 30 minutes, although the parties may request a longer hearing. Save where the court is considering whether it is highly likely that the outcome for the claimant would not have been substantially different if the conduct complained of had not occurred, the primary question is whether the claim is arguable. The court should not need to consider the claim in the same detail as it would at a substantive hearing, although that is not invariably the case.

3.126 Neither the defendant nor any other interested party is required to attend a permission hearing unless the court directs otherwise.[164] Where the defendant or an interested party in a judicial review or planning statutory review does attend a hearing, the court will not generally make an order for costs against the claimant in respect of their attendance.[165] The position is different where an application

161 See CPR PD 8C paras 7.1–7.8; CPR 52.10.
162 CPR PD 52D para 26.1(5).
163 *Kensington and Chelsea RLBC v Secretary of State for the Environment* [1992] 2 PLR 116; *Cash v Secretary of State for Communities and Local Government* [2013] JPL 420.
164 CPR PD 8C para 8.1; PD 54A, para 8.5. CPR PD 52D para 26.1(7) merely states that any person served with the application is entitled to appear and be heard.
165 CPR PD 8C para 8.2; PD 54A para 8.6. See also Chapter 7.

for permission is made under s 289 of the TCPA 1990 (or s 65 of the P(LBCA)A 1990): the general rule in these cases is that costs follow the event.[166]

3.127 Where permission is granted in an appeal under s 289 of the TCPA 1990 or s 65 of the P(LBCA)A 1990, the claimant must serve the appellant's notice within seven days of grant on those persons identified in CPR PD 52D para 26.1(12).

Appealing the refusal of permission

3.128 Where permission to apply for judicial review has been refused at a hearing in the Planning Court, the claimant may apply to the Court of Appeal for permission to appeal.[167] The application must be made within seven days of the decision of the Planning Court.[168] The Court of Appeal may, instead of giving permission to appeal, give permission to apply for judicial review, in which case the claim will proceed in the Planning Court unless the Court of Appeal orders otherwise.[169] There is a similar right of appeal where permission has been refused at a hearing in a planning statutory review.[170] If the Court of Appeal refuses permission to appeal then only in exceptional circumstances of an 'egregious' error will the Court of Appeal allow that refusal to be re-opened under CPR 52.30. [171]

3.129 Where permission to proceed is refused by the Planning Court in a claim brought under s 289 of the TCPA 1990 (and presumably under s 65 of the P(LBCA)A 1990), there is no right of appeal to the Court of Appeal.[172]

I APPLICATIONS FOR INTERIM RELIEF[173]

3.130 To ensure that a legal challenge is not overtaken by events, such as the commencement or continuation of development, a claimant may seek interim relief in the form of an injunction or stay with the object of protecting the interests of the claimant or wider public until the substantive hearing of the claim. An application for interim relief may be made at any stage of the proceedings but it should be made promptly, and most applications are included within the

166 *R v The Secretary of State for Wales ex parte Rozhon 91* LGR 667; *Williams v Secretary of State for Communities and Local Government* [2009] EWHC 475 (Admin).
167 CPR 52.8.
168 CPR 52.8(3).
169 CPR 52.8(5), (6).
170 CPR 52.10.
171 *R (Wingfield) v Canterbury City Council* [2020] EWCA Civ 1588.
172 *Wendy Fair Markets Ltd v Secretary of State for the Environment* [1996] JPL 649; *Prashar v SSETR* [2001] 3 PLR 116; *Walsall MBC v Secretary of State for Communities and Local Government* [2013] JPL 1183; *Binning Property Corp Ltd v Secretary of State for Housing, Communities and Local Government* [2019] JPL 844.
173 The court's powers to grant interim relief are considered further in Chapter 5.

claim form. Where a separate application is required, application form PCPF244 should be used. CPR Parts 23 and 25 prescribe the procedural rules for interim applications and the grant of interim relief.

3.131 Sometimes the urgency of the matter prevents a claimant from giving effective notice to the defendant and any other party who might be affected by the grant of interim relief. A claimant who applies for interim relief without notice to the opposing party must make full and fair disclosure of all the facts material for the court to know in determining the application.[174] Not only must all material facts be disclosed, the claimant must also draw the court's attention to the significant factual, legal and procedural aspects of the case.[175] A failure to observe this duty may lead to an order for interim relief being set aside.[176]

Interim relief in judicial review claims

3.132 The principal interim relief likely to be sought in planning cases is an injunction. Three examples illustrate the varied circumstances in which this form of interim remedy has been considered:

(1) Where the claimant sought to challenge the grant of planning permission to demolish 118 terraced houses in circumstances where demolition was imminent and would effectively render the judicial review proceedings academic: *R (Save Britain's Heritage) v SOSCLG, Gateshead MBC.*[177]

(2) Where, in the context of judicial review proceedings concerning the failure properly to assess impacts on bats and badgers when granting permission for a bus rapid transit route, the developer sought to undertake preparatory works implementing the planning permission on the basis that there was a serious risk of losing substantial funding because of funding deadlines: *Morge v Hampshire CC.*[178]

(3) Where the Secretary of State sought to lift a stay of the effect of the Secretary of State's statement (repeated in the Chief Planner's letter) that decision makers should consider as a material consideration his intention to enact primary legislation to abolish Regional Strategies, which was under challenge: *Cala Homes (South Ltd) v SOSCLG.*[179]

3.133 Under CPR 54.8(2)(a) an acknowledgement of service must be filed not more than 21 days after service of the claim form. Consideration of permission on the papers can often take several weeks after that. Even where a Planning Court claim is categorised as significant, the target timescale for the determination of

174 See *Brink's MAT Ltd v Elcombe* [1988] 1 WLR 1350, 1356F–1357B, 1358B–C, 1359B.
175 *Memory Corporation Plc v Sidhu (No 2)* [2000] 1 WLR 1443, 1454D–H, 1459H-1460B.
176 *Brink's MAT Ltd v Elcombe* [1988] 1 WLR 1350; *Memory Corporation Plc v Sidhu (No 2)* [2000] 1 WLR 1443.
177 [2010] EWCA Civ 1500.
178 [2010] Env LR 31.
179 [2011] JPL 553.

an application for permission to apply for judicial review is within three weeks after the 21-day period for the acknowledgement of service: PD54E, 3.4(a). That is normally the first consideration of the claim by the court; any claimant who wishes to have interim relief determined before that will have to make the appropriate application.

3.134 The Planning Court claim form (N461PC) requires details to be provided of any remedy being sought, including any interim remedy,[180] and of any other applications (sections 7 and 8). Where exceptional urgency is being claimed and the application needs to be determined within a certain time scale, an application for urgent consideration will also need to be completed and signed by the claimant's advocate (N463PC). The first version of this form was issued under Practice Statement (Administrative Courts: Listing and Urgent Cases).[181] The Practice Statement provides that it is the duty of advocates to comply with its terms.[182] The form requires, inter alia, that reasons for urgency and a proposed timetable are supplied, and a draft order of the interim relief sought is attached. Details of service on the defendant(s) and interested parties must also be provided.

3.135 The test applied by the court to applications for interim relief is that set out by the House of Lords in *American Cyanamid Co v Ethicon Ltd* [1975] AC 396 with modifications appropriate to the public law context: *BACONGO v Department of Environment of Belize.*[183] In summary, the American Cyanamid principles require the court to consider whether there is a serious issue to be tried, whether the disadvantage to each party would be adequately compensated by damages in the event of their succeeding at trial, and where the balance of convenience (the lesser risk of injustice) lies. In *BACONGO*, the Board stated that the public law context is one of the 'special factors' to be taken into account referred to in *American Cyanamid.* It was stated that because the range of public law cases is so wide, the court has a wide discretion to take the course which seems most likely to minimise the risk of an unjust result: para 39.

3.136 The Board in *BACONGO* recognised that, in the absence of special circumstances, a cross-undertaking undertaking in damages should be given by the party seeking the injunction: para 38;[184] nevertheless, the grant of interim relief without a cross-undertaking in damages was a possible outcome. However, the Board stated that, since the grant of the injunction would cause the respondents significant financial loss, the strength of the claimant's case was a particularly important factor: paras 39–40. In *R (Pascoe) v Liverpool CC, the Urban Regeneration Agency,*[185] the claimant sought an interim injunction to prevent demolition of certain properties in advance of a comprehensive

180 This in turn is a requirement under CPR 54.6(1)(c).

181 [2002] 1 WLR 810.

182 Where a manifestly inappropriate application is made, consideration will be given to a wasted costs order: para 6.

183 [2003] 1 WLR 2839 at [35–39].

184 See also *R v Inspectorate of Pollution ex p Greenpeace Ltd*, 577B–C; *R v Darlington BC ex p Darlington Taxi Owners* [1994] C.O.D. 424.

185 [2007] EWHC 1024 (Admin).

regeneration scheme to be delivered by a compulsory purchase order which was not yet in force. The court held that the case was sufficiently strongly arguable to warrant interim injunctive relief to maintain the status quo until the substantive hearing, which was expedited. It was noted that the claimant was not in a position to give any cross-undertaking but neither the defendant nor interested party had identified any particular harm that would arise if an interim injunction were granted: paras 35-36. In Aarhus Convention claims the court must have particular regard to the need for the terms of the order overall (including any undertaking in damages) not to render continuing with the claim prohibitively expensive for the applicant and make such directions as are necessary to ensure that the case is heard promptly.[186]

3.137 As an alternative to an injunction, where permission to proceed is given the court may direct that there be a stay of the proceedings to which the claim relates.[187] This power extends to administrative decisions and the processes by which they are reached.[188] The effect of a stay of proceedings is to suspend them until the determination of the challenge. If a third party who is not a party to the judicial review proceedings would be detrimentally affected by the grant of a stay, the court will apply the principles applicable to the grant of an interim injunction.[189]

3.138 It is worth noting that early determination of the substantive hearing has been considered by the courts to be a relevant factor in assessing whether interim relief should be granted pending that hearing (eg *Pascoe* at [25]). Where a Planning Court claim is categorised as significant, the target timescale for the substantive hearing could be as long as just over six months from the date of issue.[190] In those circumstances, given that expedition can be sought regardless of categorisation of the claim as significant (CPR PD54E, 3.6), there might well be merit in applying for expedition of the claim alongside any application for interim relief, as this would have the effect of minimising any prejudice to a defendant or interested party.

186 See CPR PD 25A para 5.3; see also *European Commission v UK* Case C-530/11, [2014] QB 988, paras 64–68.

187 CPR 54.10(2)(a).

188 *R v Secretary of State for Education and Science, Ex p Avon County Council (No 2)* [1991] 1 QB 558; *R v Secretary of State for the Home Department x p Muboyayi* [1992] QB 244; *R (H) v Ashworth Special Hospital Authority* [2002] EWCA Civ 923, [2003] 1 WLR 127; *Cala Homes (South) Ltd v Secretary of State for Communities and Local Government* [2010] EWHC 3278 (Admin), [2011] JPL 553.

189 *R v Inspectorate of Pollution ex p Greenpeace Ltd* [1994] 1 WLR 570, 573D-G, 576F–H.

190 Service of the claim form within 7 days of issue (CPR 54.7(1)(b)); acknowledgement of service not more than 21 days after service (CPR 54.8(2)(a)); permission refused on the papers within three weeks of the acknowledgment of service (PD 54E, 3.4(a)); oral renewal sought within seven days (CPR 54.12(4)); oral renewal heard within one month of request for renewal (PD 54E, 3.4(b)); submission of detailed grounds by defendant etc. 35 days (CPR 54.14(1)); substantive hearing within 10 weeks of detailed grounds (PD 54E, 3.4(e)).

Interim relief in statutory challenges

3.139 In many of the statutory challenges brought in the Planning Court there will be an express statutory power conferred on the court to make an interim order suspending the operation of the order or decision under challenge. The considerations which the court is likely take into account are very similar to those involved in dealing with applications for interim relief in judicial review claims. However, the following specific points can be made.

3.140 Section 287 of the TCPA 1990 covers challenges to old style development plans, simplified planning zones, and other orders. Where a challenge has been made, the High Court may make an interim order suspending the operation of the relevant document: (a) wholly or in part; and (b) generally or as it affects the property of the applicant (s 287(3)). If granted, an interim order will take effect until the proceedings are finally determined (s 287(3C)).

3.141 In *Terry Adams Ltd v Bolton MBC*,[191] the court refused to grant an interim order under this section suspending a policy of a UDP to which the applicant had objected. The court summarised the principles to be applied which were essentially the same as those to be applied on judicial review: whether the applicant had an arguable case (ie whether there was some real prospect that the respondent had acted outside its statutory powers or that the applicant's interests had been substantially prejudiced by some failure on the part of the respondent to comply with statutory requirements); if so, where the balance of convenience lay. Factors to be taken into account would include the court's view about the likely outcome of the case, since it is undesirable to perpetuate, or to bring about by interim order, a state of affairs which does not accord with the eventual judgment of the court. The court would also want to consider the extent to which the applicant would be likely to be disadvantaged if interim relief were withheld. Also relevant was the fact that the decision under challenge was in the field of public law, made by a local authority in the exercise of its public function. The policy under challenge was of interest to the general public as well as other authorities whose decisions might be influenced by the policy (p 451).

3.142 An identically worded power to make an interim order suspending the operation of the various plans and documents introduced by the Planning and Compulsory Purchase Act 2004 is provided in s 113(5) and (8).

3.143 In *R (Capel PC) v Surrey CC*,[192] a parish council sought to challenge a Development Plan under s 113 of the PCPA 2004 as it related to proposals for a particular site. Interim relief was sought to suspend the operation of the relevant

191 (1997) 73 P&CR 446.

192 [2008] EWHC 2364 (Admin). An interim injunction to suspend the operation of policies on basement developments in a core strategy until a substantive challenge under s 113 PCPA 2004 was rejected in *Lisle-Mainwaring v Royal Borough of Kensington & Chelsea* [2015] EWHC 1814 (Admin), with Coulson J finding that the public interest in the policy of an adopted plan being applied, pending any finding that it was unlawful, should outweigh any disbenefits this would cause to individual developments or developers.

provisions of the plan. There was an extant planning application which at least in principle accorded with the policies of the plan. If the interim order were granted, the determination of that application would have to await the outcome of the s 113 application. The parish council highlighted its lack of financial resources and argued that it should not be exposed to the possibility of additional costs if interim relief were not granted and the parish council were forced to challenge any grant of planning permission. The court held that the spectre of additional costs was not a reason for granting interim relief, but a reason for making an order which would ensure that if there were a challenge to any decision taken on the planning application, that challenge could be heard together with the s 113 challenge. That way, there would be a saving in costs and time for the parties (para 13]). Refusing to grant interim relief would not cause prejudice to the parish council at all (para 16).

3.144 Section 288 of the TCPA 1990 covers challenges to a range of orders, decisions, and directions including decisions by the Secretary of State on appeal under s 78 of the same Act (s 288(4), s 284(2) and (3)). Under s 288(5)(a) the High Court may by interim order suspend the operation of the order or action which is being challenged until the final determination of the proceedings.[193]

3.145 An identically worded power to make an interim order suspending the operation of orders or decisions under the P(LBCA)A 1990 is provided under s 63(4)(a). The power to make an interim order against decisions under the Planning (Hazardous Substances) Act 1990 is also identically worded (s 22(3 (a)).

3.146 Statutory challenges (save for certain statutory appeals) must be brought using the CPR Part 8 procedure. Unlike in judicial review proceedings, where the claim form must state any remedy 'including any interim remedy' which is sought (CPR 54.6(1)(c)), the Part 8 procedure requires only that the claim form (N208) must state the final remedy and the legal basis for the claim to that remedy (CPR 8.2(b)(ii)). An application for interim relief within a statutory challenge will therefore need to be made by completing an application notice (PCPF244) together with supporting witness evidence (CPR 23.6),[194] although if the claimant is content for the issue of interim relief to be considered at the permission hearing, it may be possible to include a claim for interim relief in the claim form and indicate that relief will be sought at the same time as the issue of permission is determined.

J CASE MANAGEMENT

3.147 The question of expedition will usually be considered at the beginning of a claim, but if for some reason it becomes clear that the claim is more urgent

193 This power does not apply to applications questioning the validity of tree preservation orders (s 288(5)(a), (6)).

194 Since the hearing of an application is a hearing 'other than a trial' within CPR 32.6, the general rule applies which is that evidence will be by witness statement (CPR 32.6(1)).

than was first thought, it may be possible to apply to the court for an earlier listing than was originally given. Real, objectively viewed, urgency will need to be shown in order to obtain an order for expedition.[195]

3.148 Throughout the course of a case, the claimant must keep in mind that at the substantive hearing it will be for him to prove his pleaded claim. Where the defendant has filed evidence, the claimant should consider whether it raises a dispute of fact requiring resolution by the court. He will also need to consider whether the claim as set out in the pleadings requires amendment, perhaps because one or more grounds of claim have been shown to be unarguable, or because a new ground of challenge has revealed itself.

3.149 Where there is a conflict of evidence, or some other reason why the defendant's evidence should be tested, the claimant may seek an order requiring a witness to attend the substantive hearing for cross-examination.[196] This is an exceptional course and a claimant will need to show that cross-examination is truly necessary in the interests of justice.[197] If the defendant's evidence is not challenged in this way, any conflict in the evidence will usually be resolved in the defendant's favour.[198]

3.150 If a claimant wishes to amend his pleaded case, he should do so at the earliest opportunity, in accordance with the relevant provisions in the CPR.[199]

3.151 Finally, a claimant may become aware of gaps in the documentary evidence. If a defendant is unwilling to disclose relevant documents in his possession, an application for specific disclosure may be appropriate.[200] Since a challenge to an administrative decision by way of judicial review raises predominately legal issues, and the defendant's duty of candour requires it to produce documentation on which it relied to reach the challenged decision, an order for disclosure is not ordinarily necessary for fairly disposing of the matters in issue. However, if it can be shown that disclosure is necessary for the fair disposal of the claim, disclosure should be ordered.[201]

195 *James Petter v EMC Europe Ltd* [2015] EWCA Civ 480, paras 16–17.

196 ??????

197 See *O'Reilly v Mackman* [1983] 2 AC 237, 282D-283A; *Jones v Secretary of State for Wales* (1995) 70 P&CR 211, 215–216, 220–221; *R (Newsmith Stainless Ltd) v Secretary of State for the Environment, Transport and the Regions* [2001] EWHC 74 (Admin), paras 5–8, 10; *R (PG) v Ealing LBC* [2001] EWHC 250, [2002] MHLR 140, paras 14, 20, 30; *Greaves v Boston Borough Council* [2014] EWHC 3950 (Admin), [2014] All ER (D) 03 (Dec), paras 20-23.

198 *R v Board of Visitors of Hull Prison ex p St Germain (No 2)* [1979] 1 WLR 1401, 1410; *Cran v Camden LBC* [1995] RTR 346, 353H; *R (Al-Sweady) v Secretary of State for Defence* [2009] EWHC 2387 (Admin), [2010] HRLR 2, para 17; *Flattery v Secretary of State for Communities and Local Government* [2010] EWHC 2868 (Admin), para 56.

199 See CPR 17; CPR 52.8; CPR 54.15 and CPR PD 54A para 11.1.

200 Pursuant to CPR 31.12.

201 *Tweed v Parades Commission for Northern Ireland* [2007] 1 AC 650.

K SETTLEMENT

3.152 In the event the parties agree to settle the claim before a substantive hearing, a draft order will need to be produced disposing of the claim and consequential matters (such as costs and the discharge of any interim injunction or stay). CPR PD 54A, paras 17.1–17.4 set out the procedure that should be followed for the disposal of a judicial review claim following settlement:

(1) If the parties agree about the final order to be made, the claimant must file at the court a document (with two copies) signed by all the parties setting out the terms of the proposed agreed order together with a short statement of the matters relied on as justifying the proposed agreed order and copies of any authorities or statutory provisions relied on.

(2) The court will consider the documents referred to in paragraph (1) and will make the order if satisfied that the order should be made.

(3) If the court is not satisfied that the order should be made, a hearing date will be set.

(4) Where the agreement relates to an order for costs only, the parties need only file a document signed by all the parties setting out the terms of the proposed order.

3.153 If the parties reach agreement on the substantive claim but cannot agree on the issue of costs, they should follow the approach in Guidance as to how the parties should assist the Court when applications for costs are made following settlement of claims for judicial review – April 2016.[202]

3.154 For the disposal of statutory appeals by consent, see CPR PD52A section VI. For other statutory challenges, there are no equivalent rules of court or guidance documents, but there is no reason why the procedure for the settlement of judicial review claims should not be followed in those cases.

L THE SUBSTANTIVE HEARING

Case preparation

3.155 In judicial review proceedings the grant of permission to proceed will trigger CPR 54.14, which provides that a defendant and any other person served with the claim form who wishes to contest the claim or support it on additional grounds must file and serve: (a) detailed grounds for contesting the claim or supporting it on additional grounds; and (b) any written evidence, within 35 days after service of the order giving permission (unless the court directs otherwise).

202 At https://assets.publishing.service.gov.uk/government/uploads/system/uploads/attachment_data/file/716591/ac013-eng.pdf.

3.156 On receipt of any detailed grounds and/or evidence filed pursuant to CPR 54.14, the claimant should review the merits of the claim, paying attention to the points listed in para **3.110** above.

3.157 Likewise, in a statutory challenge the claimant will need to keep the claim under review, taking on board the content of any respondent's notice or further evidence filed by the defendant, and should pay particular regard to any judicial observations made in the course of a permission hearing.

3.158 Once a case is deemed ready to be heard, it enters the Administrative Court 'warned list'. When that happens, a letter is sent out to the parties notifying them that the case has entered the warned list and that a hearing date will soon be fixed. The parties are required to provide the court with their time estimates for the hearing of the case. There is also a 'short warned list', for cases that may be heard at relatively short notice. Again, the parties will be notified by letter if their case is in the short warned list.

3.159 Although different directions may be made in individual cases, in a judicial review claim CPR PD 54A, paras 15.1 and 15.2 provide:

(1) The claimant must file and serve a skeleton argument not less than 21 working days before the date of the hearing of the judicial review (or the warned date).

(2) The defendant and any other party wishing to make representations at the hearing of the judicial review must file and serve a skeleton argument not less than 14 working days before the date of the hearing of the judicial review (or the warned date).

Para 15.3 of the Practice Direction lists what must be included in a skeleton argument.

3.160 The claimant will ordinarily be responsible for compiling the bundle(s) of documents to be used at the hearing. CPR PD 54A, paras 16.1 and 16.2 provide:

(1) The claimant must file a paginated and indexed bundle of all relevant documents required for the hearing of the judicial review when he files his skeleton argument.

(2) The bundle must also include those documents required by the defendant and any other party who is to make representations at the hearing.

3.161 For statutory appeals, similar provisions apply to the contents of skeleton arguments (see section V of CPR PD52A). Where the CPR are silent as to the filing of skeleton arguments and the lodging of bundles, it will usually be sensible to observe the same requirements as apply to judicial review claims (unless the court directs otherwise).

3.162 In addition to the hearing bundle(s), the parties' advocates will be expected to produce copies of the authorities relied upon, ideally in an agreed bundle of authorities. As the applicable legal principles are often undisputed, it will usually be sensible for the advocates to seek to produce an agreed list of relevant propositions of law, to which reference can be made in their skeleton arguments.

3.163 For virtual hearings during the Covid-19 pandemic, the Protocol regarding remote hearings 26 March 2020 advises at para 24 that an indexed and paginated electronic bundle should be provided to the judge's clerk, court official or judge directly (if no official is available), and all other representatives and parties, well in advance of the hearing.[203] PD 51Y at para 2 provides that the court may direct that a virtual hearing take place in private, where it is not practicable for the hearing to be broadcast in a court building.

The hearing

3.164 In most cases the claimant will go first, although the order of proceedings is ultimately a matter for the court. The parties will address the judge on the issues, referring to relevant documents and authorities. The claimant will have an opportunity to respond to the defendant's, and any interested party's submissions.

3.165 The judge may give judgment at the end of the hearing, or reserve judgment to another day.

Relief

3.166 Even if the claimant is successful, the grant of relief is in the discretion of the court.[204] Although the starting point is that an unlawful decision will ordinarily be quashed,[205] relief may be refused (or limited relief granted) where the court considers that that would best serve the interests of justice. Thus relief has been denied where, inter alia, there is a lack of prejudice to the claimant,[206] where the error complained of made no difference to the decision under challenge,[207] where

203 www.judiciary.uk/wp-content/uploads/2020/03/Remote-hearings.Protocol.Civil_.GenerallyApplicableVersion.f-amend-26_03_20-1.pdf.

204 *R (Edwards) v Environment Agency* [2008] UKHL 22, [2008] Env LR 34, at [63].

205 *Berkeley v Secretary of State for the Environment* [2001] 2 AC 603, 616F; *R (Edwards) v Environment Agency*, para 63; *R (Gardner) v Harrogate Borough Council* [2008] EWHC 2942 (Admin), [2009] JPL 872, para 40; *Tata Steel UK Ltd v Newport City Council* [2010] EWCA Civ 1626, paras 7, 8, 15.

206 See *Walton v Scottish Ministers* [2012] UKSC 44, [2013] PTSR 51, paras 111, 112, 138, 139; and see, for example, *R (Midcounties Co-operative Ltd) v Wyre Forest DC* [2009] EWHC 964 (Admin); *R (CBRE Lionbrook (General Partners) Limited) v Rugby Borough Council* [2014] EWHC 646 (Admin); *R (Perry) v London Borough of Hackney* [2014] EWHC 3499 (Admin).

207 *Simplex v Secretary of State for the Environment* (1989) 57 P&CR 306, 326–327, 329; *R (Smith) v North East Derbyshire Primary Care Trust* [2006] EWCA Civ 1291, [2006] 1 WLR 3315, para 10; and now see SCA 1981, s 31(2A).

the grant of relief would be pointless,[208] there has been undue delay[209] or the grant of relief would cause substantial prejudice to the public interest or a third party.[210] Where it is not appropriate to make a mandatory, prohibitory or quashing order, it will usually be appropriate to make some form of declaratory order to reflect the court's finding of unlawfulness.[211]

3.167 The court's discretion to refuse relief where the error complained of made no difference to the decision under challenge has been expanded by amendments made to s 31 of the SCA 1981 by the CJCA 2015. Section 31(2A) of the SCA 1981 provides that the court *must* refuse to grant relief on an application for judicial review (and may not make a monetary award on such an application) if it appears to the court to be highly likely that the outcome for the applicant would not have been substantially different if the conduct complained of had not occurred. The court may disregard these restrictions if it considers that it is appropriate to do so for reasons of exceptional public interest (s 31(2B)).

3.168 Unless the decision under challenge was obviously finely balanced, a prospective claimant should consider in advance how he can meet the argument that it is highly likely that essentially the same decision would have been reached notwithstanding the legal errors alleged.

Costs

3.169 Costs are in the discretion of the court.[212] If the court decides to make an order about costs the general rule is that the unsuccessful party will be ordered to pay the costs of the successful party, but the court may make a different order.[213] The issue of costs is considered further in Chapter 6.

Permission to appeal

3.170 An appeal lies from the Planning Court to the Court of Appeal (or, in certain limited circumstances, to the Supreme Court[214]). Permission to appeal is required.[215] Where the Planning Court determines a claim for judicial review or

208 See, for example, *R (Edwards) v Environment Agency*. The court may defer consideration of the issue of relief so that the real effect of an established error may be investigated: see, for example, *R (Lady Hart of Chilton) v Babergh DC* [2014] EWHC 3261 (Admin), at [104–105].

209 SCA 1981, s 31(6).

210 See *Walton v Scottish Ministers* at [103], [105], [114], [128], [131], [155], [156]; and see, eg, *R (Gavin) v Haringey LBC* [2003] EWHC 2591 (Admin), [2004] 2 P&CR 13; *R (Guiney) v Greenwich LBC* [2008] EWHC 2012 (Admin), [2009] JPL 211; *Kendall v Rochford DC* [2014] EWHC 3866 (Admin), at [122–126].

211 *R(Hunt) v North Somerset Council* [2015] UKSC 51; [2015] 1 WLR 3575, at [12].

212 CPR 44.2(1).

213 CPR 44.2(2).

214 Administration of Justice Act 1969, ss 12, 13, 15.

215 CPR 52.3. In the case of appeals directly to the Supreme Court, see the Administration of Justice Act 1969, s 13.

a statutory challenge in the form of an application to the High Court, permission to appeal may be sought from the Planning Court or the Court of Appeal.[216] Permission to appeal may be granted only where the court considers that the appeal would have a real prospect of success, or there is some other compelling reason why the appeal should be heard.[217]

3.171 Where the Planning Court determines an appeal, a further appeal to the Court of Appeal would constitute a second appeal. In most cases a second appeal can proceed only with the permission of the Court of Appeal. The Court of Appeal will not grant such permission unless it considers that the appeal would raise an important point of principle or practice, or there is some other compelling reason for the Court of Appeal to hear it.[218] However, in *Miaris v SOSCLG* it was held that s 289(6) of the TCPA 1990 continued to empower the High Court to grant permission to appeal to the Court of Appeal from its determination of an appeal under s 289.[219]

Appeals in the Court of Appeal and Supreme Court

3.172 Hearings before the Court of Appeal are normally limited to a review of the decision of the lower court and the appeal court will (only) allow the appeal where the decision of the lower court was (a) wrong, or (b) unjust because of a serious procedural or other irregularity in the proceedings in the lower court.[220] If the appellant is appealing against the lower court's findings of fact, exercise of discretion or exercise of evaluative judgement on the basis that this was "wrong", the decision below must be shown to contain an error of principle or some other flaw in reasoning which renders the decision wrong; and it is not enough that the appeal court might have arrived at a different conclusion.[221]

3.173 An appeal from an order or judgment of the Court of Appeal in a civil matter lies to the Supreme Court, and requires permission to appeal granted by the Court of Appeal or the Supreme Court.[222] The Supreme Court will only grant permission to appeal if, in the opinion of the Appeal Panel, it raises an arguable point of law of general public importance which ought to be considered by the Supreme Court at that time, bearing in mind that the matter will already have been the subject of judicial decision and may have already been reviewed on appeal.[223] In practice, the Court of Appeal applies a similar test, and grants permission to appeal to the Supreme Court very sparingly.

216 CPR 52.3(2); PD 52A, para 4.1.
217 CPR 52.6.
218 Access to Justice Act 1999, s.51(1); CPR 52.7
219 [2015] 1 WLR 4333.
220 CPR 52.21(1) and (3).
221 See *R(R) v Chief Constable of Greater Manchester Police* [2018] UKSC 47; [2018] 1 WLR 4079, paras 64-65.
222 Constitutional Reform Act 2005, s 40(2) and (6).
223 Supreme Court PD3, para 3.3.3.

CHAPTER 4

Resisting claims

Wayne Beglan, Estelle Dehon and Ruchi Parekh

A	Introduction	4.1
B	Pre-action responses	4.2
C	Judicial review 4.13	
	– Practice Directions 54A, 54D, 54E	4.13
	– Summary grounds of Defence 4.16	
	– Interim orders: interim relief, striking out, disclosure	4.28
	– Detailed grounds	4.37
	– Evidence	4.40
	– Substantive hearing	4.44
D	Planning Statutory Reviews	4.46
	– Practice Directions 8C, 54D, 54E	4.48
	– AoS and Summary Grounds	4.54
	– Interim orders planning statutory reviews: interim relief, striking out, disclosure	4.58
	– The statutory six-week time period	4.63
	– Matters specific to challenges to development plans and other relevant documents (PCPA 2004, s 113)	4.68
	– Matters specific to challenges to the grant or refusal of planning permission and listed building consent (TCPA 1990, s 288 and P(LBCA)A 1990, s 63)	4.76
E	Planning Statutory Appeals	4.85
	– Practice Directions 52D and 54D	4.88
	– Overlap between s 288 and s 289 TCPA 1990	4.94
F	Compromise, consenting to judgment, redetermination	4.107
G	Resisting claims in the Court of Appeal and Supreme Court	4.110

A INTRODUCTION

4.1 This chapter considers the steps that a defendant or proposed defendant should take when faced with a legal challenge to a planning decision it has made. It looks first at responding to challenges in the Planning Court by way of judicial review and then at responding to statutory challenges. The chapter then considers what happens if the claim is not to be resisted (or is successful) and the appropriate actions to be taken in the case of appeals against decisions of the Planning Court.

B PRE-ACTION RESPONSES

4.2 The first indication of a potential judicial review claim or a planning statutory review[1] could be a letter by or on behalf of a prospective claimant which may or may not describe itself as a formal pre-action protocol letter before claim under the Civil Procedure Rules (CPR) Pre-Action Protocol for Judicial Review[2] and may or may not set a deadline for a response. There is a strong expectation that prospective judicial review will engage in pre-action correspondence and comply with the Judicial Review Pre-Action Protocol.[3] The same is not true for planning statutory reviews,[4] although they are subject to the general practice direction on Pre-Action Conduct, meaning that the court should expect the parties to have exchanged sufficient pre-action information to understand each other's position and make decisions about how to proceed.[5]

4.3 The purpose of a letter before claim is to identify the issues in dispute and establish whether they can be narrowed or litigation avoided.[6] It is a strategically important stage for a prospective defendant. A well-drafted pre-action response may dissuade a prospective claimant from bringing the claim, whereas a poorly drafted response may cause a defendant difficulties if the claim proceeds. This is particularly so if the basis on which the claim is defended shifts significantly and if factual errors are made in the response. The pre-action stage also gives the prospective defendant the opportunity to consider whether all or some of the claim should be conceded, which will allow a defendant to limit costs liability where a decision is recognised to be legally flawed.

4.4 A pre-action letter may be sent to a local authority's legal department, to its planning department, or to the chief executive. Where a local authority operates a cabinet system and a delegated decision is made by a portfolio holder, the letter may be sent direct to the portfolio holder rather than to officers. However, regulatory decisions (such as the determination of planning applications) are not matters for cabinet, and most planning decisions that may

1 These are defined in Practice Direction 8C (see **4.48** below) and include challenges to a grant or refusal of planning permission by a planning inspector.
2 Pre-Action Protocol for Judicial Review, updated 17 September 2019.
3 Section 4 of the Judicial Review Claim Form obliges the Claimant to indicate whether there has been compliance with the pre-action protocol and requires an explanation to be given for non-compliance.
4 The Part 8 Claim Form does not address pre-action correspondence.
5 Practice Direction on Pre-Action Conduct and Protocols, para 3 and para 6.
6 Para 14 of the Pre-Action Protocol (17 September 2019); see also para 3 for the aims of the Pre-Action Protocol.

be the subject of challenge will be made by committees or by officers. Letters may be sent by both post and/or by email, although the latter is most common. Administrative arrangements need to be in place to ensure that all such letters reach an appropriate officer within the legal department swiftly so that work can commence on providing a response in good time.

4.5 The Pre-Action Protocol applies even where the decision maker has no legal power to change the decision under challenge.[7] Where a planning permission has been issued, the decision maker has no power to alter or review that decision or to substitute an alternative decision. However, where there is a resolution to grant planning permission subject to the execution of a deed setting out planning obligations or subject to conditions which have not yet been finalised, the decision maker can be asked to revisit the decision.[8] The Pre-Action Protocol continues to apply notwithstanding the shorter time limits applicable in planning cases under CPR 54.5(5).[9] The onus is put on claimants to satisfy themselves that the use of the Pre-Action Protocol is appropriate.[10] The Pre-Action Protocol is therefore unclear as to whether a letter before claim is appropriate once a planning permission has been issued. Whilst such a letter before claim may not be able to avoid the need for proceedings altogether, it could serve a purpose in narrowing the issues in dispute even where a planning permission has been issued. However, unless a defendant can identify how such a letter would have avoided the need for proceedings or materially narrowed the disputed issues, it is unlikely that the omission to send a letter before claim where the challenged decision cannot be altered by the decision maker, would have material consequences for the outcome of the claim or the costs liabilities.

4.6 A letter before claim may be accompanied by a request for information or documentation relating to the challenged decision. The defendant is expected to comply with such requests where the information or documentation sought is properly necessary for the potential claimant to understand the reasons for the challenged decision or to be able to present the claim in a way which properly identifies the issues. A failure to supply such information or documentation without good reason may result in costs sanctions being imposed if a challenge is subsequently made.[11]

4.7 A letter before claim should also set out whether the prospective claimant considers the claim to be an Aarhus Convention claim under CPR 45.41(2) and what costs limit should apply. It is important for prospective defendants to address

7 Compare paras 6 and 7 of the current Pre-Action Protocol (17 September 2019) with para 6 of the version updated on 4 August 2014, which advised that the Pre-Action Protocol was not appropriate where the decision maker had no legal power to change the challenged decision.

8 See, eg, *R (Kides) v South Cambridgeshire DC* [2002] EWCA Civ 1370; *R (Smech Properties Ltd) v Runnymede BC* [2015] EWHC 823 (Admin); *R (Chilton Parish Council) v Babergh DC* [2019] EWHC 280 (Admin).

9 Compare para 1 and fn 1 of the current Pre-Action Protocol (17 September 2019) with para 6 of the version updated on 4 August 2014, which advised differently.

10 Para 7 of the Pre-Action Protocol (17 September 2019).

11 Para 13 of the Pre-Action Protocol (17 September 2019).

this in the pre-action response and carefully to consider whether in principle the claim falls within the Aarhus Convention costs provisions. At pre-action stage it may not be possible for prospective defendants to assess whether the limits in CPR 45.43 should apply or should be varied, as evidence of the prospective claimant's financial resources may not have been provided, so it may be prudent to flag the issue or reserve the position in the pre-action response.

4.8 The Pre-Action Protocol recommends that a defendant should normally respond within 14 days.[12] Failure to do so will be taken into account and sanctions may be imposed unless there are good reasons.

4.9 The Pre-Action Protocol recognises that it will not always be possible to provide a response within the requested time and suggests that in such cases an interim response should be provided, giving a reasonable date by which a full response will be available.[13] Where an extension is sought, reasons should be given and, if required, additional information can be requested. Any delay in providing a response will not alter or extend the time limits for making a challenge.

4.10 The Pre-Action Protocol sets out a model structure for a response, which it expects should be normally used.[14] Sanctions may be imposed if the model response is not used without good reason. This model response may not be appropriate if the letter before claim does not follow the model format in Annex A of the Pre-Action Protocol and respondents may need to adapt the letter of response accordingly. Where the potential claimant is a litigation in person, it is expected that the response will be accompanied by a copy of the Pre-Action Protocol. Before any response is provided it is important that the relevant officers accurately establish the facts which relate to the decision. A response which is factually incorrect can cause problems in due course, and will have to be explained if a challenge is subsequently made.

4.11 It will also be important at this early stage to consider the decision-making process 'in the round' to see whether there may be defects not so far identified by the potential claimant which could become apparent if the decision was then subject to legal challenge. An obvious point to check in any challenge to the grant of planning permission is the adequacy of the documentation in relation to screening under the Environmental Impact Assessment and Appropriate Assessment regimes.[15] If the decision under challenge is a delegated decision, consideration should be given to the local authority's scheme of arrangement to ensure that the decision has been properly authorised.[16] If a planning

12 Para 20 of the Pre-Action Protocol (17 September 2019).

13 Para 21 of the Pre-Action Protocol (17 September 2019).

14 Para 20 and Annex B of the Pre-Action Protocol (17 September 2019).

15 See, eg, *R (Brown) v Carlisle City Council* [2010] EWCA Civ 523; *R (Warley) v Wealden DC* [2011] EWHC 2083 (Admin); *R (Davies) v Carmarthenshire County Council* [2015] EWHC 230 (Admin).

16 See, eg, *R (Technoprint plc) v Leeds City Council* [2010] EWHC 581 (Admin); *R (Couves) v Gravesham BC* [2015] EWHC 504 (Admin).

permission has been granted and that planning permission has been supported by an instrument setting out planning obligations, it will be important to check that all of the planning obligations satisfy the limitations on the use of planning obligations set out in the Community Infrastructure Levy Regulations 2010.[17] It may be appropriate to instruct counsel to advise on the response to a letter before claim.

4.12 The response should be sent to all interested parties identified by the proposed claimant and contain details of any other persons who the defendant considers are interested parties.[18]

C JUDICIAL REVIEW

Practice Directions 54A, 54D, 54E

4.13 CPR Part 54 is supplemented by four Practice Directions, of which three will need to be considered in the context of planning judicial reviews: PD 54A, PD 54D and PD 54E.

4.14 PD 54A deals with supplemental procedural issues such as attendance at permission hearings, evidence and preparation for the substantive hearing. PD 54D concerns the place in which a judicial claim should be started and the venue at which it will be determined. Where relevant to defendants, the requirements of these Practice Directions have been set out below.

4.15 PD 54E deals exclusively with the Planning Court. Of particular importance is the ability under this Practice Direction for a claim to be categorised as 'significant'.[19] The effect of such designation is that the claim will be dealt with on a prioritised basis.[20]

Summary Grounds of Defence

4.16 If a claim is made for judicial review of the relevant decision or decisions, the defendant will need to file an Acknowledgement of Service (AoS) within 21 days of service of the claim (CPR 54.8(2)(a)) and, if the claim is to be resisted, include within the AoS (or as an annexed document) the Summary Grounds of Defence (CPR 54.8(4)(a)). The purpose of the Summary Grounds is to identify the arguments that show that the claim is not properly arguable and therefore should not be granted permission to proceed. If this cannot be achieved in relation to all grounds of challenge, it may still be possible to show in the Summary Grounds why permission should be limited to particular grounds.

17 SI 2010/948, reg 122.
18 Para 24 of the Pre-Action Protocol (17 September 2019).
19 PD 54E, para 3.1. See para 3.2 for the types of claims which may be categorised as significant.
20 See PD 54E, para 3.3, which sets out the target timescales for the hearing of significant Planning Court claims.

Confining the claim in this way should help to limit the scope of evidence that will then need to be prepared to respond to the claim.

4.17 When considering the AoS, the first point to review is whether the claim has been made within the relevant time limit. For decisions made under the Planning Acts[21] which can be challenged by way of judicial review that period will be six weeks from when the grounds of challenge first arose (CPR 54.5(5)). In most cases involving the grant of a planning permission, this will be the date of the grant of planning permission[22] but there may be cases where the substantive decision being challenged occurred at a prior stage of the process and that the grounds of challenge first arose at that point.[23] This may be the case, for example, where the only ground of challenge is that the decision maker should have referred the planning application to the Secretary of State under the Consultation Direction.[24] That decision may have been made well before the grant of planning permission. In calculating the six week period, the date of the decision itself is not counted and if the six weeks end on a day when the court office is closed (weekends and bank holidays), the period is treated as ending on the next working day when the court office is open.[25] For decisions made under the Planning Act 2008 (challenges to Development Consent Orders) the six week period is prescribed by s 118(1) of the Planning Act 2008 by reference to the date when the decision is first published or, if later, the date when the statement of reasons for the decision is first published[26] but also does not include that day itself within the six-week period.[27]

4.18 If the claim was made within time, the next point to consider is whether, having regard to the identity of the claimant, the case is one where it can be said

21 This term does not include the Planning Act 2008 but it does include the Town & Country Planning Act 1990 and the Planning (Listed Buildings and Conservation Areas) Act 1990: TCPA 1990, s 336. See also CPR 54.5(A1).

22 *R (Burkett) v LB Hammersmith & Fulham (No 1)* [2002] UKHL 23; *R (Catt) v Brighton & Hove City Council* [2007] EWCA Civ 298 (although see also *R (Champion) v North Norfolk DC* [2015] 1 WLR 3710, at [63]).

23 *R (Nash) v LB Barnet* [2013] EWCA Civ 1004.

24 The Town & Country Planning (Consultation) (England) Direction 2009 annexed to the former Circular 02/09.

25 *Nottingham City Council v Calverton Parish Council* [2015] PTSR 1130. This case concerned a statutory challenge under Planning & Compulsory Purchase Act 2004, s 113 but the same principle should apply to judicial review challenges which also require action by the court before a claim can be validly issued. See also its application in *Croke v Secretary of State for Communities and Local Government* [2019] PTSR 1406, involving a challenge under s 288 TCPA 1990.

26 PA 2008, s 118(1)(b) (as amended by Criminal Justice and Courts Act 2015, s 92(4) with effect from 13 April 2015. Publication can be later than the date on the decision notice itself but runs from the date of first publication (see *R (Williams) v Secretary of State for Energy and Climate Change* [2015] EWHC 1202 (Admin) which remains good law on this point despite the amendment to s 118(1)(b). An example of the date of first publication being later that the date on the decision can be seen in the case of the Whitemoss Landfill Western Extension where the decision was dated 20 May 2015 but was first published on 21 May 2015.

27 The amendment of PA 2008, s 118(1)(b) by CJCA 2015, s 92(4) has overtaken the effect of the procedural aspects of the decisions in *R (Blue Green London Plan) v Secretary of State for Environment Food and Rural Affairs* [2015] EWHC 495 (Admin) and *Williams*.

that it is highly likely that the outcome for the claimant would not have been substantially different if the alleged deficiencies in the decision-making process had not occurred.[28] If so, this is a point that must be taken in the AoS.[29] This test sets out a lower standard than that applied by the courts when refusing relief after a substantive hearing[30] and is to be applied at the permission stage of judicial review, when the court will have less information about the detailed merits of the claim. To deploy this ground for resisting a claim successfully, the defendant is likely to need to show that the flaws are procedural rather than substantive and such as to cause no real prejudice or disadvantage to the particular claimant because the end result is highly likely to remain the same. Where the substantive decision has proceeded on the basis of an error of law (eg a misinterpretation of the legislative or policy framework, or the disregard of a material consideration of significance to the judgments made), it will be very difficult to show that there would be no substantial effect on the outcome of the decision.[31] The phraseology of 'highly likely' implies something more onerous than 'on a balance of probability' or simply 'more likely than not', and the threshold still remains a high one to meet.[32] Because the test looks at the prospects of an alternative 'outcome' to the decision under challenge, the courts may be more willing to look at post-decision events and explanations. This may be particularly so where the challenge is to the adequacy of the reasons given for a decision. Similarly, if the deficiency is a failure to consult a statutory consultee but it is subsequently clear that the consultee had no objections to the decision, it should be possible to show that the defect would not have altered the outcome of the decision.

4.19 It is notable that, where the alleged unlawfulness concerns a breach of EU law (for example, concerning environmental impact assessment), it is unclear whether the section 31 test prevails over the residual discretion of the court to refuse relief.[33] The burden of proof is on the defendant to show that the decision would not have been different without the procedural defect, and the court must have regard to all the evidence on the court file in making that assessment.[34]

4.20 The AoS is an important document, not least because the Summary Grounds provide the defendant with the opportunity to explain to the court why

28 See Senior Courts Act 1981, s 31(3C).

29 CPR 54.8(4)(a)(ia).

30 See, eg, *Simplex GE (Holdings) Ltd v Secretary of State for the Environment* (1989) 57 P & CR 306; [2017] PTSR 1041; and *South Gloucestershire Council v Secretary of State for Communities and Local Government* [2016] EWCA Civ 74, at [25], where the test was: 'must be satisfied that the decision-maker would necessarily have reached the same decision'. See also *R (Plan B Earth) v Secretary of State for Transport* [2020] EWCA (Civ) 214, at [272], where the court considered how the statutory test modifies the traditional *Simplex* test in three ways.

31 *R (Plan B Earth) v Secretary of State for Transport* [2020] EWCA (Civ) 214, at [272]-[273].

32 See eg *R (Public and Commercial Services Union) v Minister for the Cabinet Office* [2017] EWHC 1787 (Admin); [2018] ICR 269, at [89].

33 *R (XSWFX) v London Borough of Ealing* [2020] EWCA (Civ) 214 at [17]. Lang J noted that the *Plan B Earth* case concerned the application of section 31 in the context of breached of domestic law, the EU points having failed in that case.

34 *R (Champion) v north Norfolk District Council* [2015] 1 WLR 3710 (SC) at [57]-[58] and *Commission v Germany* KC 137/14 at [60]. These cases remain authoritative despite the departure of the UK from the EU.

the challenge is misconceived and so should not proceed. If the claim can be convincingly answered, it should be possible to set this out in short order. The more detailed and involved the explanation in the AoS, the more likely it is that the court will conclude that the grounds of challenge are at least arguable. However, there will be cases where the claim obfuscates the real issues, misinterprets or omits relevant statutory provisions or case law, or misrepresents the factual context in which the decision was made, and in such cases a clear and full narrative of the true position is necessary to show that the claim is lacking in substance.

4.21 Whilst there is no requirement for the AoS to be accompanied by the defendant's evidence, there may be cases where it is beneficial to provide some or all of the defendant's evidence at the permission stage in order to best ensure that permission is not granted. Generally, this will only be so where the challenge proceeds on a mistaken factual basis and there is clear evidence available to demonstrate the true position. If evidence is to be provided, it will generally need to be in the form of a witness statement with relevant exhibits (unless the evidence in question is a short pre-existing document that needs no further explanation, and so can simply be annexed to the Summary Grounds).

4.22 The AoS may include or be accompanied by any application for directions that the defendant intends to seek (including any application for an interim order).[35] The AoS should include the details of any party that the defendant considers should be made an Interested Party (such as the recipient of the planning permission) if that party has not been included by the claimant.[36] Where a defendant fails to file an AoS, it will not be permitted to take part in the hearing to decide whether permission should be given unless the court expressly so rules.[37]

4.23 At the time of filing the AoS the defendant will also need to consider, if not already addressed by the claimant, whether the claim is 'significant' for the purposes of CPR PD 54E.[38] If the defendant wishes the court to categorise the claim as significant, it will need to make its representations in writing at the same time as lodging its AoS.[39] In practice, it is often possible for all sides to agree on the categorisation of a claim as significant, and for the parties to make representations to the court on an agreed basis.

4.24 Where the defendant's AoS and Summary Grounds have been sufficient to persuade the court that the claim is not arguable on the papers so that permission is refused then, unless the claim is certified to be totally without merit,[40] the claimant can request that the question of permission is reconsidered at an oral

35 CPR 54.8(4)(b).
36 CPR 54.8(4)(a)(ii).
37 CPR 54.9.
38 See PD 54E, para 3.2 for the types of claims which may be categorised as significant.
39 PD 54E, para 3.3.
40 CPR 23.12 and 54.12(7).

hearing.[41] The Judicial Review Practice Direction advises that a defendant need not attend an oral renewal hearing (unless the court so orders) and that if the defendant elects to do so, it would not normally expect to be awarded its costs if permission is refused.[42]

4.25 Whether a defendant should attend the oral renewal hearing will depend on a variety of factors including the strength of the reasoning given by the Judge refusing permission on the papers, whether the claimant has sought to introduce any additional arguments or facts to counter that reasoning, and the importance of the case to the defendant. If participation by the defendant secures the refusal of permission, the costs incurred are likely to be justified even if they cannot be recovered.

4.26 Whilst the expectation is that the initial permission stage normally will be dealt with on the papers without a hearing,[43] there may be cases in which this is not appropriate. For example, where a claim may appear to be arguable but there is a clear issue of delay a 'rolled up' hearing may be ordered.[44] A 'rolled up' hearing may also be ordered in cases of expedition to minimise delay in dealing with the claim. The defendant is unlikely to be asked in advance before a 'rolled up' hearing is ordered (although the defendant may expressly request this option if it considers an otherwise arguable claim should fail on the ground of delay). An order for a 'rolled up' hearing should include directions for the filing of evidence and skeleton arguments in advance of the hearing.

4.27 Where a 'rolled up' hearing takes place, the court will consider both the question of permission and the substantive merits of the claim at the same time. Effectively, this avoids time being spent on whether the claim is arguable but does have a tendency to bypass the permission stage as a filter to weed out unmeritorious cases.[45]

Interim orders: interim relief, striking out, disclosure

4.28 The claim form may include an application for interim relief and if so the defendant will need to consider what response should be made. The question of protective costs is addressed in Chapter 6. Other forms of interim relief may be to seek an injunction to prevent the decision-maker from determining subordinate applications in relation to the challenged decision (eg reserved matters applications or applications for the discharge of conditions under a challenged planning permission). Occasionally a claimant may seek to prevent the decision

41 CPR 54.12(3).

42 PD 54A, paras 8.5 and 8.6.

43 PD 54A, para 84.

44 See *R (Ben Hoare Bell Solicitors) v Lord Chancellor* [2015] EWHC 523 (Admin) for a general discussion by the Divisional Court of the use of *'rolled up'* hearings in judicial review claims.

45 See, eg. *Gladman Developments Ltd v Secretary of State for Housing, Communities and Local Government* [2020] EWHC 518 (Admin); [2020] PTSR 993; *R (Oxted Residential Ltd) v Tandridge DC* [2015] EWHC 793 (Admin).

maker from determining other planning applications. Applications for interim injunctions are assessed on the *American Cyanamid* principles but the balance of convenience is adapted to reflect the public law nature of the challenge.[46]

4.29 Conceding an application for an interim injunction whilst opposing the application for permission to apply for judicial review might imply that the challenge has some substance. Also, other parties may be affected if the defendant agrees to suspend its ordinary decision-making processes. In many cases a more appropriate response by the defendant would be to offer an undertaking not to make any subsequent decisions without notice to the claimant, so that both the claimant and other affected parties have the opportunity to take further action if it becomes necessary. However, there may be cases where the claim is at least arguable and the application for interim relief is soundly based. This may be so where the subsequent decision is imminent and implementation would have significant effects (eg the demolition of a building of value or the alteration of an area of ecological importance). Whilst in civil proceedings, interim injunctions are frequently accompanied by a cross-undertaking in damages, this is not generally appropriate where the defendant is a public body because damages would not be an adequate remedy.[47]

4.30 If the defendant considers that the claim is devoid of all merit and has no realistic prospects of success and that the uncertainty it represents until finally disposed of is prejudicial in some tangible respect (eg to the implementation of a large scale regeneration or infrastructure project), the defendant can consider making an application to strike out the claim.[48] The reduction in delay as a result of the introduction of the Planning Court and related reforms makes this a less attractive option than previously but in cases of real urgency it may still make sense. The application would need to be supported by a witness statement setting out the basis for the application and identifying the prejudice caused by the uncertainty. The application would not be dealt with without a hearing (unless the claimant chose not to resist the application).

4.31 An alternative (and less expensive) option would be to identify the fundamental weaknesses of the claim in the AoS and invite the Planning Court at the permission stage not only to refuse permission but also to certify that the claim is totally without merit.[49] This would prevent an oral renewal of the application for permission. The test of 'totally without merit' means no more and no less than

46 *Lisle-Mainwaring v Royal Borough of Kensington & Chelsea* [2015] EWHC 1814 (Admin) per Cranston J. The case concerned a statutory challenge to a development plan but the same principles would apply to judicial review of a planning decision.

47 See, eg, *R v Secretary of State for Transport ex parte Factortame Ltd (No 2)* [1991] 1 AC 603; *Save Historic Newmarket Ltd v Forest Heath DC* [2010] EWHC 3268 (Admin).

48 CPR 3.4(2)(a); *Evans v First Secretary of State* [2003] EWCA Civ 1523 (albeit this case involved the summary judgment procedure under CPR Part 24); *Wiltshire CC v Secretary of State for Communities & Local Government* [2010] EWHC 1009 (Admin).

49 CPR 54.12(7); CPR 23.12; *Freemont (Denbigh) Ltd v Welsh Ministers* [2016] EWHC 482 (Admin). See also *Hossain v Secretary of State for the Home Department* [2016] EWCA Civ 82 for general guidance on CPR 54.12(7).

that the claim is bound to fail.[50] A challenge to a decision which seeks to re-argue the planning merits of the decision or which attacks the weight given by the decision maker to different material considerations rather than identifying any error of law could fall into the category of being totally without merit.[51] However, the criteria for refusing permission and that for certifying applications as totally without merit remain different, and the latter is not an automatic consequence of the former.[52] Where a judicial review application has been certified as totally without merit, the claimant can make an application within 7 days to the Court of Appeal for permission to appeal but this too will be considered on the papers without an oral hearing.[53]

4.32 Judicial review claims are not routinely subject to a process of disclosure.[54] However, the defendant is subject to a 'duty of candour',[55] which arises as part of the defendant's duty to assist the court with a full and accurate explanation of what actions or decisions it has taken and why.[56] Failure to comply with the duty of candour may lead to a punitive costs order against the defendant.[57]

4.33 The duty of candour extends to interested parties in certain circumstances, including where the interested party is an independent contractor undertaking a public works project on behalf of the government.[58]

4.34 The duty of candour has been recognised by the Government Legal Department, which issued *Guidance on Discharging the Duty of Candour and Disclosure in Judicial Review Proceedings* (2010).[59] The Guidance suggests that the obligation of candour is the reason that judicial review claims are not subject to the standard disclosure rules, and emphasises that the duty imposes a weighty responsibility on government departments and agencies to be open and honest in disclosing the facts and information needed for the fair determination of the

50 *R (Grace) v Secretary of State for the Home Department* at [13].

51 See eg *R (Harrier Developments Ltd) v Fenland DC* CO/1489/2014, Mitting J, 27 May 2014 (unreported); but cf *R (Williams) v Cardiff City Council* CO/4266/2014, Dove J, 4 November 2014 (unreported).

52 *Hossain v Secretary of State for the Home Department* [2016] EWCA Civ 82 at [17].

53 CPR 52.8(2).

54 CPR 54.16(1) disapplying CPR 8.6(1).

55 See, eg, *R (Citizens UK) v Secretary of State for the Home Department* [2018] EWCA Civ 1812. See also *R (Hoareau) v Secretary of State for Foreign and Commonwealth Affairs* [2018] EWHC 1508 (Admin) for a review of the relationship between disclosure and the duty of candour; and Chapter 14 of *The Administrative Court Judicial Review Guide 2019*.

56 *R v Lancashire County Council ex p Huddleston* [1986] 2 All ER 941 per Sir John Donaldson MR, who commented: 'It is not discreditable to get it wrong. What is discreditable is a reluctance to explain fully what has occurred and why.' See also *Secretary of State for Commonwealth Affairs v Quark Fishing Ltd* [2002] EWCA Civ 1409 at [50] per Laws LJ; *R (MidCounties Co-operative Ltd) v Forest of Dean District Council* [2015] EWHC 1251 (Admin) per Singh J at [148]–[151]; and *R (Shirko Ismail) v Secretary of State for the Home Department* [2019] EWHC 3192 (Admin) at [8].

57 *R (Al-Sweady) v Secretary of State for Defence* [2009] EWHC 2387 (Admin).

58 *Belize Alliance of Conservation Non-Governmental Organisations v Department of the Environment* [2004] UKPC 6.

59 Available at https://www.gov.uk/government/uploads/system/uploads/attachment_data/file/285368/Tsol_discharging_1_.pdf.

issues.[60] The duty is said explicitly to extend to documents or information which will assist the claimant's case and/or give rise to additional and otherwise unknown grounds of challenge.[61] The duty applies to every stage of the proceedings, including the pre-action stage and the summary grounds of resistance.[62]

4.35 Whilst the Guidance is not directed to local planning authorities, which make most of the planning decisions which are susceptible to challenge by way of judicial review (rather than by statutory applications and appeals), there is no reason why a local planning authority as a public body should expect to be less accountable to the court than central government. Local planning authorities would therefore be well advised to have the Guidance, as well as *The Administrative Court Judicial Review Guide*,[63] in mind when dealing with judicial review claims.

4.36 The defendant will therefore need to consider the relevant documentation in relation to the decision-making process carefully to ensure that when its evidence is filed it does not omit material documentation and as a result run the risk of misleading the court. In parallel with a judicial review claim the defendant may find that it is subject to requests for information under the Freedom of Information Act 2000 or the Environmental Information Regulations 2004[64] and so be obliged to provide material in response to such requests.

Detailed grounds

4.37 If permission to bring the claim for judicial review is granted, the defendant will need to prepare for the substantive hearing. The defendant is not permitted to apply to set aside the order giving permission.[65]

4.38 The key document at this stage in the litigation is the preparation of the Detailed Grounds of Defence. The defendant must file and serve its Detailed Grounds within 35 days of service of the order giving permission, unless a shorter or longer period was set by that order.[66] The Detailed Grounds may be no more than a refresh of the Summary Grounds but the arguments will need to be reviewed in light of the grant of permission and the fact that the substantive hearing will not be concerned with whether the challenge is arguable. More detailed arguments will therefore usually be required, and if evidence is to be filed the Detailed Grounds should refer to it and explain its relevance to the arguments being advanced.

4.39 In some cases it will be worth revisiting in the Detailed Grounds the question of whether it is highly likely that the outcome for the claimant would

60 Section 1.2 page 3.
61 Section 1.2 page 3.
62 Section 1.2 page 4.
63 *The Administrative Court Judicial Review Guide 2019* (July 2020), Chapter 14.
64 SI 2004/3391.
65 CPR 54.13.
66 CPR 54.14(1).

not have been sufficiently different if the alleged unlawful conduct had not occurred.[67] If such a case can be made out, the court must refuse to grant relief, unless it considers it inappropriate to do so for reasons of exceptional public interest.[68] As noted above in respect of the permission stage, this statutory test modifies the traditional *Simplex* test[69] and imposes a lower threshold than that previously applied.[70]

Evidence

4.40 In preparation for the substantive hearing, the defendant must also file any evidence to be relied upon along with its Detailed Grounds within 35 days of service of the order giving permission.[71]

4.41 What evidence will be needed to defend the claim will require careful consideration, having regard to the grounds of challenge and the evidence already provided by the claimant. The defendant will want to ensure that not only is the court provided with accurate and complete factual information, but also that it is presented in an intelligible and accessible manner, so that the points arising from it can be easily followed. The claimant's evidence may present a confused or incomplete picture of events and the defendant will want to take the opportunity to provide the court with a clear narrative of events. Where the decision under challenge is the grant of planning permission, a review of the planning application file should be undertaken to identify all material relevant to the grounds of challenge. Where the challenge relates to the interpretation of policies, the full text of the relevant policy documents will need to be considered to identify the material that is relevant to a proper interpretation of the policies in question. If the challenge includes reliance on remarks made by officers or councillors during the decision maker's consideration of a planning application (for example at a committee meeting), it may be necessary to prepare a transcript of the relevant parts of the discussion so that the proper context of the remarks can be seen.

4.42 Once the documentary material has been assembled, consideration should be given to how best to present this to the court. Generally, a witness statement will be needed to produce the relevant documents and to explain their role in the decision making process. A witness statement may also need to address factual matters that are in dispute.

4.43 Where witness statements have to be prepared, it will be important to ensure that the relevant personnel are available to provide those witness statements and to attend to any queries that may arise during their preparation.

67 Senior Courts Act 1981, s 31(2A).

68 Senior Courts Act 1981, s 31(2B).

69 *Simplex GE (Holdings) Ltd v Secretary of State for the Environment* (1989) 57 P & CR 306.

70 See *R (Plan B Earth) v Secretary of State for Transport* [2020] EWCA (Civ) 214, at [272], where the court considered how the statutory test modifies the traditional *Simplex* test in three ways.

71 CPR 54.14(1).

The time required for this task should not be under-estimated. The final assembly of the documentation, especially where pagination is required, can be very time-consuming and allowance will need to be made for this within the overall 35-day deadline.

Substantive hearing

4.44 It is the claimant's responsibility to prepare the bundle(s) for the substantive hearing[72] but the defendant will need to be closely involved in this process.[73] The defendant will want to ensure that the bundle(s) contain all of the necessary documentation to support the matters raised in its defence. The defendant will need a paginated copy of the final bundle(s) in good time to allow for the preparation of its skeleton argument, which will need to cross-refer to material in the bundle(s). The defendant's skeleton argument must be filed at least 14 working days (not 14 calendar days) before the substantive hearing.[74] The defendant would therefore be well-advised to initiate discussion on the content and pagination of the bundle(s) shortly after the completion of the submission of evidence rather than leave this exercise to the run up to the substantive hearing.

4.45 A substantive hearing in the Planning Court may take place at the Royal Courts of Justice in London or the case may have been initiated in or transferred to one of the regional centres of the Administrative Court (Birmingham, Cardiff, Leeds, or Manchester).[75] Cases dealt with by one of the regional centres may be heard at any court within that region.[76] It is not necessary for persons who have made witness statements in the case to attend the substantive hearing because oral evidence is not required in judicial review cases, save exceptionally where cross-examination is ordered.[77] However, someone familiar with the facts of the case should generally attend the hearing in addition to legal representatives in order to give any necessary instructions.

D PLANNING STATUTORY REVIEWS

4.46 There are, generally, two categories of planning statutory challenge: planning statutory reviews, brought under Part 8 of the CPR, and planning statutory appeals, brought under Part 52 of the CPR. This section deals with planning statutory reviews and the next section deals with planning statutory appeals.

72 PD 54A, paras 16.1 and 16.2
73 PD 54A, para 16.2.
74 PD 54A, para 15.2.
75 PD 54D, para 2.1.
76 PD 54D para 2.2.
77 See, eg, *R (Jedwell) v Denbighshire County Council* [2015] EWCA Civ 1232; *R (Longacre Properties Ltd) v Winchester City Council* [2014] EWHC 3373 (Admin); and *R (Bancoult) v Secretary of State for Foreign & Commonwealth Affairs* [2012] EWHC 2115 (Admin).

4.47 There are also challenges which are required by statute to be brought by way of judicial review, but within a statutory six week time limit: s 61N of the TCPA concerns challenges in relation to specific steps in making neighbourhood development orders and neighbourhood development plans[78] and s 118 PA 2008 concerns challenges relating specific steps in making development consent orders.[79]

Practice Directions 8C, 54D and 54E

4.48 Practice Direction 8C defines the following as 'planning statutory reviews': challenges under s 113 of the PCPA 2004 to development plans and documents; challenges under s 288 of the TCPA 1990 to grants or refusals of planning permission on appeal to an Inspector; challenges under s 288(1A) of the TCPA 1990 to costs decisions associated with decisions challengeable under s 288 TCPA 1990; challenges under s 63 of the P(LBCA)A 1990 to decisions to approve or reject listed building consent on appeal and challenges under s 287 TCPA 1990 to simplified planning zone schemes, highways orders and directions concerning statutory undertakers. Planning statutory reviews must be brought through application to the High Court using the Part 8 claim form,[80] but following a procedure which has been modified by Practice Direction 8C to adopt the procedural steps applied in a judicial review.[81]

4.49 In summary, any person served with the claim form who wishes to take part in the planning statutory review must file an acknowledgement of service (AoS) not more than 21 days after service of the claim form.[82] This must set out whether the claim is contested and, if so, provide the summary grounds for doing so.[83] The planning statutory review is then subject to a permission stage and, if permission is granted, the defendant is required to file detailed grounds.

4.50 Practice Direction 54D, dealing with administrative court venues, and 54E, dealing with starting and categorising planning court claims, are applied to planning statutory reviews by paras 1.5 and 1.6 of Practice Direction 8C. If an application is issued in a particular region which is not convenient for the defendant, the defendant may apply for the matter to be transferred to another region, taking into account the matters set out in Practice Direction 54D para 5.2.

78 In *R (Oyston Estates Ltd) v Fylde BC* [2019] EWCA Civ 1152, the Court of Appeal held that section 61N creates a bespoke and complete scheme for such legal challenges, which prevents a challenge to an earlier stage in the process being put off to a later stage.

79 S 118 was amended by s 92(4)(a)(ii) of the Criminal Justice and Courts Act 2015 so that the six week time period runs from the day after the day on which the order is published, effectively reversing *R (Blue Green London Plan and Southwark LBC) v Secretary of State for the Environment, Food and Rural Affairs* [2015] EWHC 495 (Admin).

80 Part 8 claim form (Form N208) should be used.

81 PD 8C para 1.5 disapplies PD 8A, which sets out the usual procedure for claims under Part 8. Instead, PD 8C echoes the essential procedural steps and time limits of Part 54.

82 PD 8C, paras 5.2 and 5.3(a).

83 PD 8C, para 5.5.

4.51 The first defendant in challenges under s 63 of the P(LBCA)A 1990 and s 288 of the TCPA 1990 is the Secretary of State, represented by the Government Legal Department. With challenges under s 113 of the PCPA 2004 the first defendant is more often the local planning authority which adopted the plan in question, with the Secretary of State joined as the second defendant,[84] although the Court of Appeal has refused to lay down any hard and fast rules as to who the correct first defendant should be and has left that choice to the claimant in the circumstances of any particular case.[85] In either case, the second defendant may elect not to take any active part in resisting the challenges, or may elect to participate and effectively give the response to the claim two bites at the cherry. It is irrelevant whether the claimant describes parties other than the first defendant as defendants or interested parties, since any 'person' on whom the claim form is served is entitled to take part in the planning statutory review in order to object to the claim.[86]

4.52 The general costs practice in planning statutory reviews (as with judicial reviews) dissuades full participation by multiple defendants. All defendants are likely to recover the reasonable and proportionate costs of filing an acknowledgement of service (which is required), and it is not necessary for additional defendants or interested parties to show 'exceptional' or 'special' circumstances in order, in principle, to recover these costs.[87] However, where there is an obvious lead defendant and where a court is not assisted by the AoS or summary grounds of an additional defendant or interested party then the costs may not be reasonable and so will not be recoverable.[88] It is also only in a narrow set of circumstances that a defendant other than the lead defendant is entitled to costs beyond those of the AoS and summary grounds if the claim fails. These circumstances arise:

(a) where there is a separate issue, not covered by counsel for the lead defendant, on which the second defendant or interested party was entitled to be heard;[89]

(b) where the second defendant or interested party has contributed something over and above what the lead defendant would contribute or did contribute in any event,[90] particularly in relation to clarifying the issues.[91]

84 CPR PD 8C para 4.1.

85 *CPRE Kent v Secretary of State for Housing, Communities and Local Government* [2019] EWCA Civ 1230, [2020] 1 WLR 352 at [39–40].

86 PD 8C para 5.2, as discussed by the Court of Appeal in *CPRE Kent v Secretary of State for Housing, Communities and Local Government* [2019] EWCA Civ 1230, [2020] 1 WLR 352 at [35].

87 *CPRE Kent v Secretary of State for Housing, Communities and Local Government* [2019] EWCA Civ 1230, [2020] 1 WLR 352 at [37]. Those costs will include a reasonable allowance of time for reading the claimant's case, assessing the merits of the claim, and taking an initial decision whether to accept or to contest the claimant's claim: *Royal Borough of Kensington and Chelsea v Secretary of State for Communities and Local Government* [2012] EWHC 1785 (Admin) at [11].

88 *CPRE Kent v Secretary of State for Housing, Communities and Local Government* [2019] EWCA Civ 1230, [2020] 1 WLR 352 at [37(c)].

89 *Bolton MDC v Secretary of State for the Environment (Costs)* [1995] 1 WLR 1176 at [1179]; (1995) 71 P & CR 309 (HL).

90 *Royal Borough of Kensington and Chelsea v Secretary of State for Communities and Local Government* [2012] at [18].

91 *Bolton MDC v Secretary of State for the Environment*, see n 90 above.

4.53 It is, nevertheless, sensible for a second defendant to preserve its position by filing an acknowledgement of service, in case the lead defendant decides not to defend the decision. Where that happens, any other defendant may continue to defend the claim and would, if successful, be likely to recover their costs.

AoS and Summary Grounds

4.54 It is necessary for a defendant to file an AoS,[92] which indicate whether the defendant intends to contest all or part of the claim (along with summary grounds if the claim is contested) or does not intend to contest the claim.[93] The AoS must be signed by the defendant or the defendant's legal representative and must include the defendant's address for service.[94] Failure to file an AoS in accordance with PD 8C paras 5.1–5.7 results in a person being barred from participation in a hearing to decide whether permission should be given unless the court allows such participation.[95] In practice, unless the claimant would be prejudiced, the court will usually permit the defendant to participate in the hearing, given that it is likely to be helpful to the court and in the interests of justice to hear the defendant. Where permission is granted, a person who failed to file an AoS may nevertheless file and serve detailed grounds for contesting the claim or supporting it on additional grounds and any written evidence, in line with PD 8C paras 12.1–12.3 and any other directions of the court and may thereafter take part in the hearing of the planning statutory review.[96]

4.55 Section D of the AoS allows the defendant to give details of any orders or directions sought from the court. The time limit for filing the AoS and summary grounds cannot be extended by agreement between the parties.[97] Accordingly, a defendant wishing to file an AoS outside of the 21 days after service of the claim form will need to ask for an order extending the time for service, giving the reasons for the requested extension.

4.56 The test for permission in planning statutory reviews is essentially the same as in judicial review,[98] namely the appellant must satisfy the court that there is an arguable error of law. In light of this test, the defendant's approach to the Summary Grounds and the matters to be canvassed therein are addressed in detail in section C above. This includes the defendant's position on whether the claim is an Aarhus Convention claim, which is required to be addressed in Section E of the AoS.

92 CPR PD 8C para 5.2. Form N210PC should be used.
93 CPR PD 8C, para 5.5.
94 CPR 10.5, applied by 8.3(3) – the only part of r 8,3 not disapplied by PD 8C para 5.1.
95 CPR PD 8C, para 6.1(a).
96 CPR PD 8C, para 6.1(b). Note that CPR 8.4 is specifically disapplied by PD 8C para 6 and replaced by its provisions.
97 CPR PD 8C, para 5.4.
98 *Kensington and Chelsea RLBC v Secretary of State for the Environment* [1992] 2 PLR 116; [1993] JPL 139.

4.57 Where the court grants permission, it may impose terms as to costs and as to giving security, and it may give directions.[99]

Interim orders planning statutory reviews: interim relief, striking out, disclosure

4.58 Under s 113(5) of the PCPA 2004, the High Court may make an interim order suspending the operation of the relevant document, either wholly or in part, or generally as it affects the property of the applicant. A claimant may well seek such an order where, for example, a very large planning permission for development is about to be issued, based on a part of a plan under challenge. The principles governing a decision to grant interim relief were set out by the court in *Terry Adams Ltd v Bolton MBC*:[100]

(a) the grant of interim relief is discretionary (ie a matter for the judgment of the court);

(b) the first question is whether the claimant has an arguable case (ie whether there is 'some real prospect' that the court will be persuaded that the challenge under s 113 will be successful;

(c) the court must also consider whether there is a real prospect that the relief sought by the claimant will be granted;

(d) should requirements (b) and (c) be met, then the court will have to consider the balance of convenience, taking into account the likely consequences of both grant and refusal of interim relief (including any likely disadvantage to the claimant if interim relief is withheld) and comparing them in order to determine which would be better in all the circumstances;

(e) it is also relevant that the decision under challenge is in the field of public law, and so the public interest should be considered.

The defendant will wish to address these matters in submissions if the grant of interim relief is opposed, and may consider adducing evidence as to any likely detrimental consequences of interim relief being granted.

4.59 Where a grant or refusal of interim relief will very likely result in a grant of planning permission before the challenge comes to trial, this will weigh significantly in the balance of convenience, as the likelihood of planning permission being revoked if the challenge were unsuccessful is slim given the exposure of the local planning authority to compensation payable upon revocation of planning permission.[101]

4.60 The principles elucidated in *Terry Adams Ltd v Bolton MBC* are relevant to any interim relief sought in other statutory challenges. An example of an

99 CPR PD 52D, para 26.1(11).

100 (1997) 73 P&CR 446 at 451. See *Alfred McAlpine Homes (Yorkshire) Limited v Kirklees Metropolitan Council* (2000) 79 P&CR 352 as an example of the application of these principles.

101 *Alfred McAlpine Homes (Yorkshire) Limited* at [356].

unsuccessful attempt to secure an interim injunction to suspend the operation of a development plan policy pending the hearing of a substantive challenge under s 113 of the PCPA 2004 can be seen in *Lisle-Mainwaring v Royal Borough of Kensington and Chelsea.*[102]

4.61 Applications to strike out statutory challenges have been made on a number of grounds, with various degrees of success:

(a) An application to strike out a claim under the predecessor to s 113 of the PCPA 2004 on the basis the proceedings were begun in the wrong court office and using the wrong claim form did not succeed;[103]

(b) An application to strike out a claim under s 113 of the PCPA 2004 on the basis that it had been made out of time succeeded, even though the application was only one day late;[104] however a similar application failed where the period for filing the claim expired on a day when the court office was closed and the application had been made the following day;[105]

(c) Claims under s 288 of the TCPA 1990 may be struck out as disclosing no reasonable grounds for success: see, eg, a claim by an extended gypsy family against a decision to refuse to grant them planning permission to change the use of their land, which was within the vicinity of a large raised reservoir, which was struck out as disclosing no reasonable grounds for success[106] and a claim by a resident of a 'park home' challenging refusal of planning permission for full-time residential use of holiday homes was struck out as disclosing no reasonable grounds for success, with the court refusing to grant an adjournment to produce amended grounds given that the proposed amendments had no real prospect of success.[107]

(d) A claim under s 288 of the TCPA 1990 by a gypsy against a refusal of planning permission to site his caravan on green belt land was partially struck out.[108] A ground relating to arguments not advanced at the inquiry was struck out, but a ground alleging unlawful failure to refer to the educational needs of the children was not struck out. Mr Justice Mitting commented:

> '[I]f I had been hearing this application as a section 288 appeal, it would have required prolonged and skilful argument to persuade me to allow the appeal on that ground. I do not believe that an appeal on that basis (which is the only basis now left) is likely to succeed. But that is not the test. The test is whether there are reasonable grounds for bringing the claim on that ground, or, to use any of the other synonyms, whether

102 [2015] EWHC 1814 (Admin) per Cranston J

103 *Cala Homes (South) Limited v Chichester District Council* (2000) 79 P&CR 430.

104 *Hinde v Rugby BC* [2011] EWHC 3684 (Admin); [2012] JPL 816.

105 *Nottingham CC v Calverton Parish Council* [2015] EWHC 503 (Admin); [2015] All ER (D) 44 (Mar).

106 *Dacorum BC v Purcell* [2009] EWHC 742 (QB).

107 *Coates v SSCLG* [2017] EWCA Civ 940.

108 *Coyle v Secretary of State for Communities and Local Government* [2008] EWHC 2466 (Admin).

it is arguable, whether it would be doomed to failure, whether it would be bound to be rejected. In my judgment, this argument does not quite fall below that very high hurdle and although I reach the conclusion that I must dismiss this application with some regret, I do so because I am persuaded that that argument can reasonably be advanced and that it would be wrong to shut out the claimants from advancing it at a full hearing of their claim.'[109]

(e) A claim under s 288 of the TCPA 1990 was struck out on the basis that the 'person aggrieved' in relation to the decision could not assign that grievance to another person, so that other person had no standing to make the challenge.[110]

4.62 Turning to disclosure, statutory planning reviews are not subject to the standard disclosure regime or to specific disclosure under CPR r 31 because the pre-hearing procedure is regulated by the Part 8C Practice Direction, which provides that disclosure is not required unless the court orders otherwise.[111] Given the similarity between judicial review proceedings and planning statutory reviews, it is arguable that the same duty of candour[112] arises and defendants and interested parties would therefore be well advised to have the GLD Guidance,[113] as well as *The Administrative Court Judicial Review Guide*,[114] in mind when dealing with statutory planning reviews. A claimant may make an application requesting that the court order disclosure, but it is highly unlikely that an Inspector will be ordered to produce the notes made during the inquiry.[115]

The statutory six-week time period

4.63 Applications for permission to bring planning statutory review claims must be made within six weeks beginning with the day after the relevant date on which the decision-maker takes action[116] The claim form must be served, within the six-week period, on the appropriate minister or government department and/ or on the local authority or, if the local authority is appealing, on every person who would be entitled to apply to the High Court were she to be aggrieved by the decision.[117]

109 At [16].
110 *Eco-Energy (GB) Ltd v First Secretary of State* [2004] EWCA Civ 1566; [2005] 2 P&CR 5.
111 CPR 8, 8.5 and 8.6; CPR PD 8C, para 14.3. Curiously CPR Part 31 makes no mention of its non-application to Part 8 claims.
112 See the discussion in section C above.
113 Available at www.gov.uk/government/uploads/system/uploads/attachment_data/file/285368/Tsol_discharging_1_.pdf.
114 *The Administrative Court Judicial Review Guide 2020* (July 2020), Chapter 14.
115 *Belmont Riding Centre v Secretary of State for the Environment, Transport and the Regions* [2001] PLCR 12 per Sullivan J (the inspector was obliged to conduct the inquiry fairly, but this did not require him to make notes of the proceedings which would be usable, if necessary, by persons other than himself. The inspector had to keep such notes as he felt necessary for his own use, but they were not, and were not intended to form part of the public record).
116 S 113(3B) PCCA 2004; s 288(4B) TCPA 1990; s 63(3A) P(LBCA)A 1990.
117 CPR PD 8C, para 4.1.

4.64 Time is calculated to run from the date on which the decision letter is signed and date stamped, since that is the date when the action is taken by the Secretary of State, not from the date on which that decision was received by the claimant. The day when the decision is dated is not within the six-week period because it runs 'from' that date:[118] a position now made clear by amendments to the relevant sections. It includes bank holidays.[119] The end of the six-week period was assessed by the Court of Appeal as follows:

> 'The point in relation to the six weeks is very simple and, to my mind, one of first impression. In my judgment, if the notice is published on a Monday and you are given six weeks to challenge it, six weeks will have ended by midnight of the Monday in six weeks' time. I equiparate six weeks with six times seven days.'[120]

4.65 As the time period within which the application must be made is stipulated by statute rather than by the civil procedure rules, it is absolute, and the effect of the time limit is to render unimpeachable any decision not challenged within the time, even if the order is unjust or so flawed as to be a nullity.[121] The Court of Appeal in *Croke v Secretary of State for Communities and Local Government*,[122] however, identified two[123] exceptions to that immutable rule:

(a) Where, on the 42nd day, the court office is closed (due to it being a non-working day), the deadline expires on the next working day.[124] However, that exception does not apply where a party simply attends court late on a day when the court office was open for business but has closed, even if that lateness was not entirely the party's fault (for example, the court security staff preventing access before the official closing time);[125] and

(b) Where, in exceptional circumstances, the time limit should be extended on human rights grounds because the strict imposition of the statutory time limit

118 *Griffiths v Secretary of State for the Environment* [1983] 2 AC 51 (HL).

119 *Stainer v Secretary of State for the Environment* [1994] JPL 44, including the Christmas bank holidays.

120 *Okolo v Secretary of State for the Environment* [1997] JPL 1009; [1997] 4 All ER 242 at [247] per Schiemann J.

121 *Matthews v Secretary of State for the Environment, Transport and the Regions* [2001] EWHC Admin 815; [2002] 2 P&CR 34. See also *Smith v East Elloe Rural DC* [1956] AC 736; *Routh v Reading Corp* (1970) 217 EG 1337; *Hamilton v Secretary of State for Scotland* 1972 SLT 233; *R v Secretary of State for the Environment ex p Ostler* [1977] QB 122; *R v Cornwall CC ex p Huntingdon* [1992] 3 All ER 566.

122 [2019] EWCA Civ 54.

123 The Court of Appeal did, however, discuss, obiter, a third possible exception: where an applicant attends the court office within the six-week limit but the court office wrongly refuses to permit the application to be lodged, resulting in the applicant having to make the application outside the six-week period [58]. This might happen, for example, if the court office mistakenly considered the application was required to be made on a particular form when that was not the case.

124 Described as the 'principle' in *Kaur v S Russell and Sons Ltd* [1973] 1 QB 336. See §§14-18 of *Croke*.

125 *Croke* at [29]–[30].

would impair the very essence of the right of appeal, contrary to Article 6(1) of the European Convention on Human Rights.[126]

4.66 The court has the power to extend time for service of the claim form on the defendants.[127] It also has the power to approach other formal requirements by taking into account the overriding objective and considerations of expedition and fairness, so the issuing of proceedings in the wrong office or using the wrong form can be cured, as long as proceedings were issued within the six-week period.[128]

4.67 Once the court has lost jurisdiction because of the preclusive effect of the time limit, it cannot give further consideration to the proceedings, and this cannot be avoided by parties being substituted after the end of the limitation period.[129] It is, however, possible for an applicant to be substituted where the claim is brought within the six-week period and where to do so would not undermine the intended preclusive effect of that period.[130]

Matters specific to challenges to development plans and other relevant documents (PCPA 2004, s 113)

4.68 A development plan or other relevant document can only be questioned by way of proceedings under s 113 of the PCPA 2004. However, the High Court is not precluded from considering a challenge by way of judicial review to the decision to agree and publish a draft local plan.[131] Nor is a challenge to the lawfulness of a pre-submission draft document precluded, as this is not a 'relevant document' under s 113(1), even though such documents can affect the parameters of the process which will culminate in the adoption of the development plan or other relevant document.[132] This partially addresses one of the key difficulties that arises under s 113 – the challenge must be brought within six weeks of the date on which the document is adopted by the local authority or approved by the Secretary of State.[133] Given that the adoption process for a development plan document can take many years, the requirement to challenge only once the document is adopted may present significant evidential difficulties, requiring a paper chase through a number of years of documents.

126 *Croke* at [40]. See *Yadly Marketing Co Ltd v SSHD* [2017] 1 WLR 1041.

127 CPR Part 3, *Mendip DC v Secretary of State for the Environment and Castle Housing Society* [1993] JPL 434.

128 *Cala Homes (South) Limited v Chichester District Council* (2000) 79 P&CR 430.

129 *Eco-Energy (GB) Ltd v First Secretary of State* [2004] EWCA Civ 1566; [2005] 2 P&CR 5.

130 *River Thames Society v First Secretary of State* [2007] JPL 782.

131 *R (CK Properties (Theydon Bois) Ltd) v Eppin Forest DC* [2018] EWHC 1649 (Admin) at [29]–[53].

132 *Manydown Co Ltd v Basingstoke and Deane BC* [2012] EWHC 977 (Admin); [2012] JPL 1188.

133 The drafting of s 113 is very unclear on this point. The previous incarnation of the right of statutory challenge – s 284 of the TCPA 1990 – made it clear that plans could not be challenged before or after adoption by other means, but s 113 does not replicate that wording. In *Manydown* at [83], the court recognised that the wording of s 113 meant that a development plan document could only be questioned upon its adoption.

4.69 Once a document becomes a 'relevant document' under s 113, it cannot be challenged by way of judicial review. Accordingly, a decision concerning endorsement of main modifications to a draft local plan (made while the examination in public was suspended in order for defects identified by the Inspector to be addressed), could not be subject to judicial review, as the draft local plan became a 'development plan document' within the meaning of s 113 when it was submitted for examination and the consideration of main modifications was an integral part of the examination process.[134]

4.70 Section 113(4) of the PCPA 2004 requires the application to be made not later than the end of the period of six weeks, starting with the 'relevant date', which is defined in s 113(11) in relation to a development plan document or its revision to be the date when it is adopted by the local planning authority or approved by the Secretary of State. This period starts on the date of the plan's adoption, not the next day.[135] Although the challenge must be brought by way of a claim form under Part 8, CPR 2.8 cannot be invoked to modify the time limit expressed in the primary legislation, the meaning of which is clear and unambiguous.[136] The inclusion of the day of adoption in the calculation of the six week period will remain the case until s 113(3A) of the PCPA 2004 is brought into force which will result in the six-week period starting on the day after the day of adoption (and will also introduce a requirement for permission).[137]The six week period includes any bank holiday.[138] However, if the six-week period expires on a day when the court office is closed, then the period is treated as ending on the next working day.[139] The courts take a strict approach to compliance with the statutory time limit.

4.71 Standing to bring a statutory challenge is addressed in Chapter 3. It is notable that the courts take a generous approach to standing in s 113 challenges – since its enactment, there has not been a finding that a claimant lacked standing to bring a challenge.[140] So long as there is some basis to the challenge, it is very unlikely that a court will find against a claimant on the basis that they lack standing.

134 *IM Properties Development Ltd v Lichfield District Council* [2014] EWHC 2440 (Admin) at [60–62].

135 *Barker v Hambleton DC* [2012] EWCA Civ 610; [2013] 1 P&CR 1 at [12–15]. The use of 'starting with' requires inclusion of the day on which the document is adopted; whereas 'six weeks from' a relevant date begins on the day after the relevant action

136 *Hinde v Rugby BC* [2011] EWHC 3684 (Admin); [2012] JPL 816 at [17].

137 As inserted by the Criminal Justice and Courts Act 2015, Sch 16, para 8 from a date to be appointed.

138 *Stainer v Secretary of State for the Environment* [1994] JPL 44.

139 *Nottingham CC v Calverton Parish Council* [2015] EWHC 503 (Admin); [2015] All ER (D) 44 (Mar) per Lewis J, where the period within which to apply to quash a development plan expired on a Sunday, the last day of the six-week period was treated as expiring on the next day when the court office had been open (Monday).

140 See, eg, *Zurich Assurance Ltd v Winchester City Council* [2014] EWHC 758 (Admin) where a claim challenging the adoption of a local plan brought by a landowner who did not overtly participate in the local plan examination was allowed to proceed (albeit the substantive challenge failed).

4.72 The scope of a challenge under s 113 is limited to two grounds (which may overlap):

(a) The document has been adopted beyond the appropriate powers of the local planning authority (ie it has acted ultra vires); or

(b) Procedural requirements set out in the regulations have not been complied with and the claimant can show substantial prejudice arising from the failure.[141]

The courts have held that this results in a statutory form of judicial review;[142] a position now reflected in its inclusion in PD 8C.

4.73 An exposition of the substantive grounds on which a statutory challenge under s 113 of the PCPA 2004 may be brought and defended is beyond the scope of this work. Chapter 7 discusses the jurisprudence on the principal grounds of legal error which are commonly raised in legal challenges in the Planning Court, including in relation to development plans.

4.74 Evidence by the defendant in a challenge under s 113 will need careful consideration, particularly because the plan-making process is lengthy and there is likely to be a wealth of documentation which is potentially relevant. This information will need to be reviewed to identify the critical material that should be produced to the court. A witness statement will be required which can produce the documents or relevant extracts annexed as exhibits. The witness statement is also likely to need to provide a narrative of events so that the court can readily make sense of the sequence of events and the relevance of the different strands of evidence. The timescale for the assembly of this material should not be underestimated. If evidence is to be provided with the summary grounds, the defendant has only 21 days after the service of the claimant's evidence;[143] a period which cannot be extended by the agreement of the parties.[144] If evidence is to be served with the detailed grounds, the defendant has 35 days after service of the order giving permission.[145] It may be necessary to agree an extension of time with the claimant for service of detailed grounds and evidence and arrangements for this should be put in hand at an early stage so that any necessary applications can be made to the court if agreement cannot be reached.

4.75 Turning to relief, s 113(6) enables the court to quash the relevant document wholly or in part, and generally or as it affects the property of the applicant, if the court is satisfied that the relevant document is to any extent outside the appropriate power or that the interests of the applicant have been

141 *Save Historic Newmarket,* above.

142 *Persimmon Homes v Stevenage Borough Council* [2005] EWCA Civ 1365.

143 CPR PD 8C, para 5.3.

144 CPR PD 8C, para 5.4. Note that PD 8C does not actually make provision for the service of evidence with the AoS and summary grounds, as para 12.3 disapplies rules 8.5(3) and (4). Defendants are not precluded from serving evidence and it is common for defendants to lodge important documents bearing on the claim at this stage if the claimant has omitted to provide them.

145 CPR PD 8C, para 12.1.

substantially prejudiced by a failure to comply with a procedural requirement.[146] An anomaly arises as a result of this – the fact that the challenge under s 113 must be made when the plan is adopted may mean that an error at a far earlier stage, which could have been corrected by earlier proceedings, might at the end of the whole process lead to the quashing of the plan and to the need to start all over again.[147] This may be avoidable where only a few policies in the plan need to be quashed, and a defendant should indicate to the court as early as possible in the proceedings if only part of the plan or particular policies should be considered.

Matters specific to challenges to the grant or refusal of planning permission and listed building consent (TCPA 1990, s 288 and P(LBCA)A 1990, s 63)

4.76 Applications under s 288 of the TCPA 1990 can challenge a number of orders and decisions, set out in s 284(3) and (4) of the TCPA 1990,[148] and applications under s 63 of the P(LBCA)A 1990 can challenge the orders and decisions set out in s 62(1) of the P(LBCA)A 1990.[149] These sections are also be able to be used to challenge a relevant costs order made in connection with any such orders or decisions.[150]

4.77 A party who succeeds in a planning appeal cannot be 'aggrieved' by the decision on appeal and so cannot bring a planning statutory review under s 288 TCPA 1990. Nor can they bring a judicial review of the decision on an issue with which they disagree, having lost that issue but succeeded in relation to the outcome of the appeal.[151]

4.78 Turning to evidence, there is seldom a need for a defendant to provide a significant amount of evidence (unless there is an issue such as mistake of fact[152]). Defendants should, however, be astute to ensure that the court has been provided with the material that was before the decision-maker relevant to the grounds of challenge, particularly where the matter was determined by way of written representations. The Planning Court has stressed the limited role of witness statements in judicial review or statutory challenges and has given detailed guidance on what matters it is appropriate to address and (more particularly) what matters it is inappropriate to address, including commentaries

146 As to the exercise of the power to quash part of a development plan document see eg *Capel Parish Council v Surrey County Council* [2009] EWHC 350 (Admin), [2009] All ER (D) 48 (Mar); as to the exercise of the power to quash part of a strategy document see eg *Ensign Group Ltd v First Secretary of State* [2006] EWHC 255 (Admin), [2006] 2 P&CR 333 and *St Albans City and District Council v Secretary of State for Communities and Local Government* [2009] EWHC 1280 (Admin), [2009] All ER (D) 130 (Jul).

147 *South Northamptonshire DC v Charles Church Ltd* [2000] PLCR 46.

148 Section 288(4).

149 Section 63(1).

150 TCPA 1990, ss 284(1)(g), 288(1A) and P(LBCA)A 1990, ss 62(1)(c), 63(1A).

151 *Tewkesbury BC v SSHCLG* [2019] EWHC 1775 (Admin).

152 In these circumstances, the court will need evidence concerning the four criteria set out in *Connolly v Havering LBC* [2010] 2 P&CR 1 (CA) at [37] per Rix LJ.

on the documentary material or illegitimate ex post facto rationalisation of the challenged decision.[153]

4.79 A practice, which had developed on the part of the first defendant, to provide a witness statement from the Inspector elucidating the reasoning in the decision letter, was strongly deprecated by the Court of Appeal.[154] The obligation is for the Inspector to give reasons in the decision letter, and not by a 'backdoor decision letter' in the form of a witness statement. It may, however, be necessary and proper for an Inspector to produce a witness statement in order to give evidence of fact about what happened before him, where a challenge is based on mistake of fact, or on an allegation that the Inspector overlooked material considerations put before the inquiry, or on an allegation that the Inspector wrongly took into account matters not before the inquiry.[155]

4.80 The court has the power, on application from one of the parties or on its own motion, to require a witness to attend court for cross-examination.[156] The power is rarely exercised, and the Court of Appeal has sought to restrict it to exceptional cases.[157] In the absence of an application for cross-examination, and where there is a straight conflict of written evidence as between the claimant and the defendant which cannot be resolved, the evidence of the defendant is to be preferred.[158]

4.81 There is no absolute rule in s 288 or s 63 cases that a new point cannot be argued in the High Court which was not raised before the Inspector.[159] However, the courts are reluctant to allow admission of new evidence or evidence which was not before the Inspector,[160] and will do so in limited circumstances.[161] However, the Secretary of State was granted permission to

153 See *Flaxby Park Ltd v Harrogate Borough Council* [2020] EWHC 3204 (Admin) per Holgate J; *United Trade Action Group Ltd v Transport for London* [2021] EWHC 73 (Admin) per Lang J.
154 *Ioannou v Secretary of State for Communities and Local Government* [2014] EWCA Civ 1432; [2015] 1 P&CR 10 at [41], endorsing the finding of Ouseley J at [51] of [2013] EWHC 3945 (Admin); [2014] JPL 608 (while overturning his decision on other issues).
155 *Ioannou* [2013] EWHC 3945 (Admin) at [53].
156 CPR 8.6. As to cross-examination of the Inspector, see *Behrman v Secretary of State for the Environment* [1979] JPL 677 (it is undesirable for persons carrying out a quasi-judicial function to be cross-examined) and *Jones v Secretary of State for Wales* (1995) 70 P&CR 211 (CA) (cross-examination of an Inspector should have been allowed where there was evidence before the court which, unless satisfactorily explained, could lead to an inference of improper behaviour on that Inspector's behalf).
157 *George v Secretary of State for the Environment* (1979) 77 LGR 689.
158 *Flattery v SSCLG* [2010] EWHC 2868 (Admin) at [56] per Lindblom J.
159 *South Oxfordshire DC v Secretary of State for the Environment, Transport and the Regions* [2000] 2 All ER 667.
160 See, eg, *Glover v Secretary of State for the Environment* [1981] JPL 110.
161 *Chichester DC v Secretary of State for the Environment* [1981] JPL 591 (the Inspector completely misunderstood a matter of real importance); *Sabey (H) & Co Ltd v Secretary of State for the Environment* [1978] 1 All ER 586 (there was no evidence before the Inspector upon which he could properly have come to the conclusion he reached); or Hollis *v Secretary of State for the Environment* [1983] JPL 164 (there was material within the possession of, and thus within the knowledge of, the Secretary of State which clearly showed that what had been put before the Inspector was wrong).

rely on new evidence relating to the selection of Inspectors where there was an allegation of apparent bias.[162]

4.82 An exposition of the substantive grounds on which a statutory challenge under s 288 of the TCPA 1990 or s 63 of the P(LBCA)A 1990 may be brought and defended is beyond the scope of this work. Chapter 7 discusses the jurisprudence on the principal grounds of legal error that are commonly raised in challenges in the Planning Court.

4.83 The relief available under s 288 and s 63 is quashing of the impugned decision.[163] However, the court retains a residual discretion not to quash a decision, even if satisfied that the grounds of challenge have been made out.[164] The general rule remains, however, that the decision should be quashed unless the point is purely technical or there is no possible detriment to the claimant,[165] and the court will almost always quash if satisfied that there has been a breach of EU law.[166]

4.84 Decisions which have been quashed are usually remitted to the Secretary of State for redetermination. The effect of a decision having been quashed is that it is treated as if it has not been made and is incapable of ever having had any legal effect.[167] The role of the new Inspector is, therefore, to re-determine the case, and not to review the previous appeal decision. The decision establishing the method of re-determination (ie by written representations or re-opening a public inquiry) is susceptible to judicial review and should be made by applying the criteria in the relevant Procedural Guide.[168]

162 *Secretary of State for Communities and Local Government v Ortona Ltd* [2009] EWCA Civ 863; [2010] 1 P&CR 15.

163 TCPA 1990, s 288(5) and P(LBCA)A 1990, s 63(4).

164 Miller *v Weymouth and Melcombe Regis Corp* (1974) 27 P & CR 468 (court declined to quash discontinuance order where a clerical error in the decision letter had caused the applicants no prejudice); *Kent CC v Secretary of State for the Environment* (1976) 33 P & CR 70; [1976] JPL 755 (amendment made by Secretary of State to meet one of the applicant's major objections, and therefore not prejudicial to them).

165 *Peak Park Joint Planning Board v Secretary of State for the Environment* (1979) 39 P&CR 361 at [385]; [1980] JPL 114.

166 *Berkeley v Secretary of State for the Environment, Transport and the Regions (No1)* [2001] 2 AC 603 (HL); [2000] 3 WLR 420. As noted in Chapter 1, the courts have since sought to limit the application of the principle in *Berkeley* (see *Bown v Secretary of State* [2003] EWCA Civ 1170 and *R (Edwards) v Environment Agency* [2008] UKHL 22). See also *R (Morge) v Hampshire County Council* [2011] UKSC 2 in relation to the compatibility of a planning permission with the Habitats Directive.

167 *Kingswood District Council v Secretary of State for the Environment* (1989) 57 P&CR 152; *Hoffman La Roche & Co AG v Secretary of State for Trade and Industry* [1975] AC 295, confirmed in *Arun District Council v Secretary of State for Communities and Local Government* [2013] EWHC 190. However, a contrary position was taken in *Vallis v Secretary of State for Communities and Local Government* [2012] EWHC 578, which concerned a conjoined appeal under the TCPA 1990, ss 288, 289.

168 *North Norfolk DC v SSHCLG* [2018] EWHC 2076 (Admin).

E PLANNING STATUTORY APPEALS

4.85 Section 289 of the TCPA 1990 and 65(5) of the P(LBCA)A 1990 are 'separate and distinct from judicial reviews and [statutory planning reviews]'.[169] Proceedings under these sections are appeals and are governed by CPR 52.28 and Practice Direction 52D. These provide that the appellant, the local planning authority or any other person having an interest in the land to which the enforcement notice or listed building enforcement notice in question relates may appeal on a point of law to the High Court against the decision of the Secretary of State in an enforcement notice appeal.[170] Proceedings are commenced in the Planning Court.[171]

4.86 Challenges under s 289 of the TCPA 1990 can be brought in relation to a final decision on an appeal under s 174 of the TCPA 1990, and also in relation to decisions made by the Secretary of State in the course of such proceedings, including:

(a) a ruling rejecting an appeal for failure to supply the necessary facts or to specify the grounds of appeal;[172] and

(b) an order for costs.[173]

4.87 A decision by the Secretary of State not to entertain an appeal at all is, however, outside the language of s 289(1) and can only be challenged by way of judicial review.[174] Similarly, a decision by an Inspector to set an enforcement notice aside as a nullity is challengeable only by way of judicial review,[175] but a decision to refuse to set a notice aside can be challenged by way of s 289.[176]

Practice Directions 52D and 54D

4.88 An application for permission to appeal must be made within 28 days after notice of the decision is given to the applicant.[177] Unlike in s 288 cases, the court does have the power to extend time, as the time limit is imposed by the CPR rather than by statute. The key requirement is that there be a sufficient

169 *Elghanian v SSHCLG* CO/928/2018 (18 April 2018) at [8].

170 CPR 52.28(1) and 52.28(3).

171 A standard Appellant's Notice N161 is usually used, to which the grounds of appeal and supporting evidence are attached.

172 *Button v Jenkins* [1975] 3 All ER 585.

173 *Botton v Secretary of State for the Environment* [1992] 1 PLR 1.

174 *Lenlyn Ltd Secretary of State for the Environment* (1984) 50 P&CR 129; [1985] JPL 482.

175 *Rhymney Valley DC v Secretary of State for Wales* [1985] JPL 27.

176 *Britannia Assets (UK) Ltd v Secretary of State for Communities and Local Government* [2011] EWHC 1908 (Admin) at [33], where Wyn Williams J held that, once an Inspector determines that a notice is not a nullity (if that point is raised), his jurisdiction thereafter is governed by the terms of section 174 TCPA 1990.

177 CPR PD 52D, para 26.1(1).

explanation of the delay, and respondents can oppose an extension of time where such an explanation is lacking.[178]

4.89 Time is calculated to run from the date on which that decision is received by the appellant, which may be later than the date of the decision letter itself.[179] This contrasts with the position under s 288 of the TCPA 1990 although in practice most decision letters are sent out (and received) electronically on the same day they are dated so only rarely will this procedural quirk make much difference.

4.90 The application for permission to appeal under s 289 must be in writing and must set out the reasons why permission should be granted.[180] If time has expired, the application must include an application to extend time, which must set out the reasons why the application was not made in time.[181] In order to be a proper application, it must include the matters and documents required by the rules.[182]

4.91 The application must be served on the Secretary of State; the local planning authority who served the notice or, if the authority is appealing, the appellant in the proceedings under appeal; and any other person having an interest in the land to which the notice relates.[183] Any person served with the application is entitled to appear and to be heard.[184] There is no requirement for the respondents to provide a substantive response prior to the permission hearing, but the respondents are able to serve a witness statement or affidavit for use at the permission hearing.[185] Such evidence must be served as soon as practicable and in any event, unless the court otherwise allows, at least two days before the permission hearing. Respondents may also serve a skeleton argument setting out why permission should be refused.

4.92 CPR PD 54D, which contains the rules relating to venue for issue of judicial review proceedings, is applied to applications under s 289.[186]

178 *Smith v Secretary of State for the Environment* (CA) *The Times*, 6 July 1987 (it is not sufficient merely to set out the chronology of events which had resulted in delay without giving any reasons which would tend to excuse it); *Ynys Mon BC v Secretary of State for Wales* [1992] 3 PLR 1 (a legal adviser's mis-appreciation of the time limit was not a reason why time should be extended).

179 *Smith v Secretary of State for the Environment (CA); Ynys Mon BC v Secretary of State for Wales* per Rose J at 3C (an enforcement notice decision was dated 25 October and sent out on that day (a Friday) but not received by the local planning authority until the following Monday (28 October) because its offices were closed over the weekend although some other recipients received the decision letter in the post on 26 October (a Saturday). Rose J held that he was bound by *Smith* to find that the 28-day period began to run from the date of actual receipt by the local planning authority.).

180 CPR PD 52D, para 26.1(2)(a).

181 Ibid, 26.1(2)(b).

182 *Wenman v Secretary of State for the Environment* [1995] JPL 1040.

183 CPR PD 52D, para 26.1(12).

184 Ibid, 26.1(7).

185 Ibid, 26.1(8).

186 Ibid, 26.1(6).

Accordingly, if an application is issued in a particular region which is not convenient for the defendant, the defendant may apply for the matter to be transferred to another region, taking into account the matters set out in CPR PD 54D 5.2.

4.93 The application is heard by a single judge, and, unless the court orders otherwise, not less than 21 days after the application was filed with the court.[187] If permission is refused, the Secretary of State is usually entitled to costs,[188] but any other respondent who attends is unlikely to recover costs, unless the circumstances set out in 4.53 above pertain.[189] If permission is granted, but the appeal eventually fails, the Secretary of State is usually entitled to costs without any deduction in relation to the permission stage (the appellant is therefore not entitled to the costs of the successful permission stage).[190] As any person served with the application is entitled to appear and be heard (rather than being obliged to serve an AoS), a second respondent will generally not be entitled to any costs.[191]

Overlap between s288 and s289 TCPA 1990

4.94 There has been significant confusion about the overlap between appeals under s 288 and s 289 where the Secretary of State grants planning permission under s 177(1) following an appeal under s 174(2)(a) for a matter enforced against under a notice and upholds the appeal against the notice. A decision to grant planning permission is challengeable under s 288,[192] so if a local planning authority wishes to challenge such a grant of planning permission, it must do so via the s 288 procedure. However, if the local authority wishes to challenge the quashing of the enforcement notice, it must do so under s 289. The prudent route is to bring such a challenge under both sections.[193] The court has, however, taken a pragmatic approach and held that:

(a) an application solely under s 288 is not an abuse of process and late appeal under s 289 is permitted;[194]

187 CPR PD 52D, para 26.1(5).

188 *Rozhon v Secretary of State for Wales* (1993) 91 LGR 667 (CA) per Rose LJ (with whom Neill and Steyn LJJ agreed).

189 *Bolton MDC v Secretary of State for the Environment (Costs)* [1995] 1 WLR 1176.

190 *Williams v Secretary of State for Communities and Local Government* [2009] EWHC 475 (Admin). Although Hickinbottom J expressly stated that full argument had not been heard on this issue and that he was not authoritatively deciding the matter ([97–98]), this decision remains the only authority on the question

191 *Elghanian v SSHCLG* CO/928/2018 (18 April 2018) at [9]–[20].

192 Section 288(4), read with s 284(3)(e).

193 *R (Wandsworth LBC) v Secretary of State for Transport, Local Government and the Regions* [2003] EWHC 622 (Admin) per Sullivan J.

194 *Oxford City Council v Secretary of State for Communities and Local Government* [2007] EWHC 769 (Admin); [2007] 2 P&CR 29 at [16].

(b) an application solely under s 289 can, with the permission of the court,[195] be amended to include a claim under s 288, so long as the application was issued within six weeks of the Inspector's decision.[196]

4.95 The overriding objective of the Civil Procedure Rules is to enable the court to deal with cases justly, and the courts have recognised that to refuse amendment in circumstances of confusion around whether s 288 or 289 should be used would likely prevent an important aspect of the case being dealt with and would not be in the interests of justice, particularly where no prejudice is suffered by the defendant.[197] The courts will, however, be vigilant to prevent the appeal procedure under s 288 being used simply to prolong the process of planning enforcement or as an abuse of process.[198]

4.96 Appeal against a refusal to grant planning permission under s 177 of the TCPA 1990 following an appeal under s 174(2)(a) may not be brought under s 288, and should therefore be brought only under s 289.[199] If an appeal against refusal of planning permission is erroneously brought under s 288, the court can grant permission to amend the application for it to be brought under s 289 where it is in the interests of justice to do so.[200]

Permission

4.97 The CPR does not set out any criteria for the exercise of the court's discretion in granting or refusing permission to appeal, but plainly the intention is to filter out unmeritorious cases and the court may refuse permission where there is no arguable case.[201]

4.98 One of the oddities of section 289 is that, unlike in judicial review cases and planning statutory reviews, no appeal lies to the Court of Appeal if permission is refused because it is categorised as a 'second appeal'.[202] A decision refusing permission in these circumstances is categorised as being of a type that

195 Under CPR 17.1(2).

196 *Thurrock Borough Council v Secretary of State for the Environment, Transport & the Regions* [2001] CP Rep 55 (CA) at [27–30] per Brooke LJ.

197 *Jarmain v Secretary of State for the Environment, Transport & the Regions* [2001] EWHC Admin 1140 per Gibbs J.

198 These matters should be simplified significantly when both ss 288 and 289 are subject to a permission stage, as procedural issues will be able to be dealt with as preliminary point to the grant of permission, rather than potentially being raised at the substantive hearing to which claimants currently have a right under s 288.

199 *Jarmain v Secretary of State for the Environment, Transport & the Regions* at para 29(a), as s 288(4) refers only to the 'grant' of planning permission.

200 *Jarmain v Secretary of State for the Environment, Transport & the Regions* at [29(b)–(g)].

201 *Kensington and Chelsea Royal LBC v Secretary of State for the Environment* [1992] 2 PLR 116.

202 *Dartford BC v Secretary of State for Communities and Local Government* [2013] EWCA Civ 370; [2013] JPL 1183, applying *Wendy Fair Markets Ltd v Secretary of State for the Environment* [1996] JPL 649.

does not constitute a 'judgment',[203] and important policy reasons have been held to exist which are necessary to prevent abuse of the High Court process to gain an extension of time during which the effect of the enforcement notice is suspended. This was confirmed by the Court of Appeal yet again in *Binning Property Corp Ltd v SSHCLG*.[204]

Interim orders

4.99 The submission of a valid application for permission to appeal under s 289 of the TCPA 1990 suspends the effect of the enforcement notice until the appeal is finally decided or withdrawn.[205] Importantly, s 289(4A) of the TCPA 1990 enables the High Court or the Court of Appeal to order that an enforcement notice shall have effect, either wholly or partly, until the proceedings are finally decided and any re-determination by the Secretary of State issued.

4.100 If the court makes such an order, it can also impose such terms as it thinks fit, including a requirement that the local planning authority give an undertaking as to damages which may result from bringing the enforcement notice into effect, or such other undertaking as the court may require. It may be that the potential exposure to damages explains the reluctance on the part of respondents to use what is, on the face of it, an extremely useful and important power, designed to prevent abuse of the appellate process to extend the suspension of a notice on unmeritorious grounds.

4.101 The power appears to have been subject to one reported determination: *Bown v Secretary of State for the Environment and Harborough DC*,[206] where the notice was ordered to take effect. The court noted that the appellant had commenced his activities without previously seeking a planning permission and in the face of clear warnings from the Council; that considerable harm in terms of safety and damage to the environment was likely to be caused by continuation of the activity; that only one arguable point appeared to warrant the grant of leave for the appeal to proceed, and that the outcome might nonetheless be the same in any event.[207]

Evidence

4.102 In *Clarke v Secretary of State for the Environment*,[208] the Court of Appeal stressed that the court should not itself receive evidence on an appeal under s 289, unless in the context of an argument that the inspector had not properly summarised the evidence or had disregarded evidence.[209] An appeal

203 In *Wendy Fair Markets*, the Court of Appeal cited the following line of authority for that proposition: *Lane v Esdaile* (1891) AC 210; *Ex p Stevenson* (1892) 1 QB 609; *Bland v Chief Supplementary Benefit Officer* [1983] 1 WLR 262 and perhaps *Geogas SA v Trammo Gas Ltd* [1991] 1 WLR 776.

204 [2019] EWCA Civ 250.

205 TCPA 1990, s 175(4).

206 [1996] JPL B130.

207 See *Encyclopedia of Planning Law* (Sweet & Maxwell) § 4-1450.

208 (1993) 65 P&CR 85.

209 Above at 90–91.

under s 289 is an appeal on issues of law. Evidence which was not before the Inspector relating to facts not sought to be proved before the Inspector will not be admitted,[210] except where that evidence relates to mistake of fact.[211]

4.103 The rule as to new points is more absolute in s 289 cases than in relation to planning statutory reviews and judicial reviews. A point neither put to nor determined by an Inspector cannot be raised in a s 289 appeal,[212] except where there has been a mistake of fact.[213]

4.104 An exposition of the substantive grounds on which a statutory challenge under s 289 of the TCPA 1990 may be brought and defended is beyond the scope of this work. Chapter 7 discussed the jurisprudence on the principal grounds of legal error that are commonly raised in challenges in the Planning Court.

Powers of the Court

4.105 The court has no power under s 289 to quash an enforcement notice, even if the appeal succeeds. The court's power is limited to remitting the matter to the Secretary of State with the opinion of the court and any further information in connection with the matter as the court may direct, for re-hearing and re-determination.[214]

4.106 Even where a s 289 appeal has succeeded and the matter is remitted to the Secretary of State, the decision-maker (such as a newly-appointed Inspector) is not obliged to approach the appeal de novo or to allow a party to open up grounds not raised in the appeal to the court.[215]

F COMPROMISE, CONSENTING TO JUDGMENT, REDETERMINATION

4.107 A defendant or potential defendant should always be prepared to consider that one or more of the grounds of challenge may be well-founded. Where the potential defendant becomes aware of a proposed challenge before a final decision has been made or issued, a tactical option could be to review the decision-making process, and to reconsider the decision, taking into account

210 *Lovejoy v Secretary of State for the Environment, Transport & the Regions* (1999) 78 P&CR 1; [1999] JPL 441.

211 *Connolly v Havering LBC* [2010] 2 P&CR 1 (CA) at [35] per Rix LJ; see also [37] where the court lays down four criteria to be met in order to establish unfairness arising out of a mistake of fact.

212 *London Parachuting Limited v Secretary of State for the Environment* [1986] JPL 428 at [429] per Mann J.

213 *Leeds City Council v Secretary of State for the Home Department* [2004] EWHC 2477 (Admin), where an Inspector (and, indeed, the local planning authority in issuing the notice) had proceeded on the basis of an erroneous calculation of the extent of permitted development rights; the section 289 appeal was successful and the matter remitted on the undertaking of the local planning authority that the notice would be withdrawn.

214 CPR PD 52D, para 26.1(14).

215 *R (Perrett) v SSCLG* [2009] EWCA Civ 1365; [2010] JPL 999 at [18–19], per Richards LJ, applying *Newbury DC v Secretary of State for the Environment* [1988] JPL 185.

the suggested grounds of challenge. This could enable the decision maker to address those grounds in a way which puts the lawfulness of the decision beyond reproach and so avoid the challenge. In cases where a final decision has already been taken, but the challenge appears to be at least arguable on one or more grounds, the decision maker may conclude that conceding the challenge and an early redetermination will be a more expeditious means of achieving an unassailable decision than resisting the claim. Whilst such action might not avoid a challenge altogether, a decision maker may find it easier to defend a decision taken in the knowledge of the likely grounds of challenge than the initial decision.[216] Any offers of settlement should be clearly worded and narrowly confined to the scope of the intended concession. Otherwise difficulties can arise if decision makers are required to argue at a hearing that any concession was narrower than it appears.[217]

4.108 Where a decision is quashed by consent, the draft consent order should include a short statement setting out the basis on which the parties accept that the decision is unlawful, and identifying any relevant statutory provisions or authorities.[218] The Planning Court will consider the statement when deciding whether it is appropriate to make the agreed order.[219] Such orders are not, therefore, simply contractual as other settlements may be. The court is the final arbiter of whether a decision should be quashed.[220] Where the parties cannot agree on all grounds it will be sufficient to identify those grounds where the decision is agreed to be defective, and to leave open the merits of the other disputed grounds. The statement of reasons should be precise and unambiguous, first so that the correct basis for any redetermination is clear, and second so that if another court hearing a later challenge has to interpret the extent of the previous compromise, it can do so with relative certainty.[221] Similarly, where a defendant concedes during or prior to a hearing that a decision is erroneous or will not be defended, the public body should set out its precise reasons for taking that view, because there is a public interest in what the reasons are, and they may also influence the approach other parties take to the proceedings.[222] In proceedings where settlement appears in prospect, the parties should endeavour to conclude any settlement in good time so that court resources are not wasted.[223]

4.109 Where a decision is quashed (either by consent or by a decision of the court after a contested hearing), the subject matter of the decision will fall to be re-determined. The redetermination will need to be based on an up to date assessment of material considerations. Careful consideration will need to be

216 See, eg, *R (Coleman) v Barnet LBC* [2012] EWHC 3725 (Admin); but cf *R (East Meon Forge & Cricket Ground Protection Association) v East Hampshire DC* [2014] EWHC 3543 (Admin).
217 *Great Hadham Country Club Ltd v SSHCLG* [2019] EWHC 1203 (Admin).
218 PD 54A, para 17.1.
219 PD 54A, para 17.2.
220 *Great Hadham Country Club Ltd* (above)..
221 See, eg, *Kemball v SSCLG* [2015] EWHC 3338 (Admin); *Westminster City Council v SSHCLG* [2020] ACD 66
222 *Trustees of the Barker Mill Estates v Test Valley Borough Council* [2016] EWHC 3028 (Admin); [2017] PTSR 408.
223 *Westminster City Council v SSHCLG* [2020] ACD 66.

given as to the extent to which it is necessary in any subsequent officer report to analyse the previous litigation. It has been noted that in some circumstances it will not be necessary and may be confusing to set out for the decision maker the details as to why the initial decision was quashed.[224] Equally, there may be other cases where the basis of the previous decision means that certain material planning considerations have to be approached in a particular way or on a particular basis. In such cases, the committee will need sufficient information relating to the previous litigation to enable the defendant to make a lawful fresh decision.

G RESISTING CLAIMS IN THE COURT OF APPEAL AND SUPREME COURT

4.110 Substantive decisions of the Planning Court can be subject to appeal. Permission is, however, required, either from the Planning Court or from the Court of Appeal. Although decisions on enforcement notice appeals under s 289 of the TCPA 1990 and on listed building enforcement notices under s 65 of the Listed Buildings Act 1990 are second appeals, specific statutory provision is made for the Planning Court to determine whether permission should be granted to appeal to the Court of Appeal, and this power is unrestricted by CPR 52.1.4.[225]

4.111 The procedures regulating appeals to the Court of Appeal are set out in CPR 52 and its associated Practice Directions.[226] Where the defendant has been successful in the Planning Court, one issue that will require careful consideration is whether there is any need to serve a Respondent's Notice[227] setting out grounds for supporting the decision which differ from or are additional to those given in the first instance judgment. Service of a Respondent's Notice could imply some deficiencies in the adequacy of the reasoning in the first instance judgment. To minimise any such risk, the drafting should make clear which grounds are truly additional and separate to those in the judgment, which grounds serve to supplement it, and where (which may be much less likely) the point is mutually exclusive of part of the approach taken by the judge below. A Respondent's Notice will normally remain a sensible precaution where the first instance decision does not fully resolve all of the issues that were raised in the original challenge.[228]

4.112 Decisions of the Court of Appeal may be appealed to the Supreme Court where the grounds of appeal raise an arguable point of law of general public

224 *R (East Meon Forge & Cricket Ground Protection Association)* at [35].

225 See, eg, s 289(6) TCPA 1990 and cf s 289(5A); *Miaris v SSCLG* [2015] 1 WLR 4333.

226 PD 52A, PD 52C, and PD 52D.

227 CPR 52.5.

228 See, eg, *R (Champion) v North Norfolk DC* [2013] EWCA Civ 1657; *R (Lanner Parish Council) v Cornwall Council* [2013] EWCA Civ 1290 but cf *Redhill Aerodrome Ltd v SSCLG* [2014] EWCA *Civ 1386.*

importance that ought to be considered by the Supreme Court.[229] Otherwise, permission to appeal will be refused.[230] The procedures for appeals to the Supreme Court are beyond the scope of this work but are governed by the Rules of the Supreme Court 2009 and the associated Practice Directions issued by the President of the Supreme Court.

4.113 In the next chapter, the powers of the Planning Court are considered in detail.

229 *R v Secretary of State for Trade & Industry ex p Eastaway [2000] 1 WLR 2222; Uprichard* v Scottish Ministers [2013] UKSC 21.
230 UKSC PD 3, para 3.3.3.

CHAPTER 5

Powers of the Planning Court

Edward Grant, Emmaline Lambert and Matthew Lewin

A	Planning Court jurisdiction	5.1
B	General powers of case management	5.3
	– The overriding objective	5.6
	– General powers relating to orders	5.8
	– Relief from sanctions	5.10
	– Remedying errors of procedure	5.11
	– Amendment of claim and substitution of parties	5.12
	– Striking out a statement of case	5.13
	– Protective costs order	5.14
	– Transfer	5.17
	– Control of evidence	5.18
	– Inherent jurisdiction	5.21
C	Case management of judicial review claims	5.22
	– Permission to proceed	5.23
	– Delay	5.26
	– Urgent claims	5.30
	– Rolled up hearings	5.31
	– Disclosure	5.32
D	Case management of statutory challenges	5.36
	– Applications to the High Court	5.37
E	Interim relief	5.45
	– Judicial review proceedings	5.45
	– Statutory challenges	5.57
F	Final relief	5.61
	– Judicial review claims	5.61
	– Statutory challenges	5.67
G	Other Powers	5.71
	– Declarations of incompatibility	5.71

– References to Europe	5.72
– Contempt	5.74

A PLANNING COURT JURISDICTION

5.1 This chapter is concerned with the powers of the Planning Court to control proceedings before it and to grant interim and final relief.
As has been explained in Chapter 2,[1] the Planning Court forms part of the Administrative Court, itself a specialist court within the Queen's Bench Division of the High Court.[2] A Planning Court claim is defined by the Civil Procedure Rules[3] (CPR) as a judicial review or statutory challenge issued in or transferred to the Planning Court involving any of the following matters:

(1) planning permission, other development consents, the enforcement of planning control and the enforcement of other statutory schemes;

(2) applications under the Transport and Works Act 1992;

(3) wayleaves;

(4) highways and other rights of way;

(5) compulsory purchase orders;

(6) village greens;

(7) European Union environmental legislation and domestic transpositions, including assessments for development consents, habitats, waste and pollution control;

(8) national, regional or other planning policy documents, statutory or otherwise;

(9) any other matter the Planning Liaison Judge considers appropriate.

5.2 Although the substantive principles of law applied by the court in judicial review and allied statutory challenges are essentially the same,[4] there are procedural differences between them. The court's powers of disposal also tend to be more limited in the case of statutory challenges. For these reasons it will be necessary at certain points in this chapter to give separate consideration to judicial review claims on the one hand and statutory challenges on the other.

1 Jurisdiction and Procedures of the Planning Court

2 For the High Court's general and particular fields of jurisdiction see Part II of the Senior Courts Act 1981.

3 Rule 54.21(2).

4 See, eg, *Regina (Alconbury Developments Ltd and Others) v Secretary of State for the Environment, Transport and the Regions* [2001] UKHL 23, [2003] 2 AC 295, paras 19-20, 49, 157; *Runa Begum v Tower Hamlets London Borough Council* [2003] UKHL 5, [2003] 2 AC 430, para 7; *Whitworth v Secretary of State for Environment, Food and Rural Affairs* [2010] EWCA Civ 1468, at [13]; *Walton v Scottish Ministers* [2012] UKSC 44, [2013] Env LR 16, at [108–112].

B GENERAL POWERS OF CASE MANAGEMENT

5.3 In dealing with a judicial review or statutory challenge the Planning Court has the same case management powers as other courts within the Queen's Bench Division, although the CPR may be disapplied in relation to Planning Court claims.[5]

5.4 The main rules governing judicial review proceedings are to be found in Part 54 of the CPR. Statutory challenges are dealt with under Part 8[6] (if made by way of application to the High Court) or Part 52[7] (if made by way of appeal). None of these Parts provides a comprehensive code for every procedural exigency. Instead, the court has extensive case management powers under Part 3 of the CPR, which provides in r 3.1(2) a non-exhaustive list of measures that may be taken by the court (save where the Rules provide otherwise). Thus the court may:

(a) extend or shorten the time for compliance with any rule, practice direction or court order (even if an application for extension is made after the time for compliance has expired);

(b) adjourn or bring forward a hearing;

(c) require a party or a party's legal representative to attend the court;

(d) hold a hearing and receive evidence by telephone or by using any other method of direct oral communication;

(e) direct that part of any proceedings (such as a counterclaim) be dealt with as separate proceedings;

(f) stay the whole or part of any proceedings or judgment either generally or until a specified date or event;

(g) consolidate proceedings;

(h) try two or more claims on the same occasion;

(i) direct a separate trial of any issue;

(j) decide the order in which issues are to be tried;

(k) exclude an issue from consideration;

(l) dismiss or give judgment on a claim after a decision on a preliminary issue;

(ll) order any party to file and exchange a costs budget;

(m) take any other step or make any other order for the purpose of managing the case and furthering the overriding objective.

5 CPR 54.23. Practice Direction 54E, para 3.5, states that the Planning Court may make case management directions, including a direction to any party intending to contest the claim to file and serve a summary of his grounds for doing so.

6 See CPR 8.1(6); CPR PD 8A, paras 3.2, 9.1, table Section B.

7 See CPR 52.20; CPR PD 52D, para 26.1.

5.5 Except where a rule or some other enactment provides otherwise, the court may exercise its powers on an application or of its own initiative.[8]

The overriding objective

5.6 The CPR have the overriding objective of enabling the court to deal with cases justly and at proportionate cost.[9] This includes, so far as is practicable:

(a) ensuring that the parties are on an equal footing;

(b) saving expense;

(c) dealing with the case in ways which are proportionate:

 (i) to the amount of money involved;

 (ii) to the importance of the case;

 (iii) to the complexity of the issues; and

 (iv) to the financial position of each party;

(d) ensuring that it is dealt with expeditiously and fairly;

(e) allotting to it an appropriate share of the court's resources, while taking into account the need to allot resources to other cases; and

(f) enforcing compliance with rules, practice directions and orders.[10]

5.7 The court is required to give effect to the overriding objective in exercising any power given to it by the CPR and in interpreting the CPR (subject to certain exceptions).[11] It is required to further the overriding objective by actively managing cases.[12]

The court's main case management powers (principally, but not exclusively, in Part 3 of the CPR) are considered further below.

General powers relating to orders

5.8 When the court makes an order, it may make it subject to conditions, including a condition to pay a sum of money into court, and may specify the consequence of failure to comply with the order or a condition.[13] The court may order a party to pay a sum of money into court if that party has, without good reason, failed to comply with a rule, practice direction or a relevant pre-action protocol.[14]

8 CPR 3.3(1).
9 Ibid, 1.1(1).
10 Ibid, 1.1(2).
11 Ibid, 1.2.
12 Ibid, 1.4(1).
13 Ibid, 3.1(3).
14 Ibid, 3.1(5). See also r 3.1(6) and (6A).

5.9 A power of the court under the CPR to make an order includes a power to vary or revoke the order.[15]

Relief from sanctions

5.10 The court may grant relief from a sanction imposed for failure to comply with a rule, practice direction or court order. In determining whether relief should be granted, the court will consider all the circumstances of the case, so as to enable it to deal justly with the application, including the need: (a) for litigation to be conducted efficiently and at proportionate cost; and (b) to enforce compliance with rules, practice directions and orders.[16]

Remedying errors of procedure

5.11 Where there has been an error of procedure such as a failure to comply with a rule or practice direction, CPR 3.10 provides that: (a) the error does not invalidate any step taken in the proceedings unless the court so orders; and (b) the court may make an order to remedy the error. Where a challenge is brought in the wrong form or by reference to the wrong statutory provision, the court may (depending on the nature and extent of the error and the effect on other parties) correct the error and allow the proceedings to continue.[17] The court has no power, however, to hear a case brought outside an unqualified statutory time limit.[18]

15 Ibid, 3.1(7).

16 Ibid, 3.9(1). As to the approach to be adopted by the court, see *Mitchell v News Group Newspapers Ltd* [2013] EWCA Civ 1537, [2014] 1 WLR 795; *Denton v TH White Ltd* [2014] EWCA Civ 906, [2014] 1 WLR 3926; *R (Hysaj) v Secretary of State for the Home Department* [2014] EWCA Civ 1633, [2015] 1 WLR 2472 (in which the Court of Appeal rejected the argument that public law claims should be treated differently). A lack of promptness in applying for relief has been treated as a critical factor in considering all the circumstances of the case, see *British Gas Trading Ltd v Oak Cash and Carry Ltd* [2016] EWCA Civ 153.

17 See, eg, *R v Secretary of State for the Environment, Transport and the Regions, ex p National Farmers' Union* (unreported, 24 November 1999); *Thurrock BC v Secretary of State for the Environment, Transport and the Regions* [2001] 1 PLR 94; *Jarmain v Secretary of State for the Environment, Transport and the Regions* [2001] EWHC Admin 1140, [2002] 1 PLR 105; *R (Wandsworth LBC) v Secretary of State for Transport, Local Government and the Regions* [2003] EWHC 622 Admin, [2004] 1 P&CR 32; compare *R (A) v Secretary of State for Communities and Local Government* [2011] EWCA Civ 1253, [2012] JPL 579; *Islam v Secretary of State for Communities and Local Government* [2012] EWHC 1314 (Admin), [2012] JPL 1378.

18 *Smith v East Elloe Rural DC* [1956] AC 736; *R v Secretary of State for the Environment, ex p Ostler* [1977] QB 122; *Eco-Energy (GB) Ltd v First Secretary of State* [2004] EWCA Civ 1566, [2005] 2 P&CR 5; *Barker v Hambleton DC* [2012] EWCA Civ 610, [2013] 1 P&CR 1; *R (Williams) v Secretary of State for Energy and Climate Change* [2015] EWHC 1202 (Admin). See also CPR PD 8A para 22.3; PD 52D para 3.5. Where a statutory time limit would expire on a day when the court office is closed, the time limit is to be treated as ending on the next working day: *Nottingham City Council v Calverton Parish Council* [2015] EWHC 503 (Admin). Service of the claim form at the recipient's business address rather than last-known address was validated by the court where the service had nonetheless come to the recipient's attention: *Harrogate Borough Council v Secretary of State for Communities and Local Government* [2014] EWHC 1506 (Admin).

Amendment of claim and substitution of parties

5.12 The court may permit claims to be amended and parties substituted, either pursuant to CPR Parts 17 and 19 or under its inherent jurisdiction.[19] Further provision is made for amendments in the case of judicial review claims[20] and statutory appeals.[21]

Striking out a statement of case

5.13 The court may strike out part or all of a statement of case if it appears to the court:

(a) that the statement of case discloses no reasonable grounds for bringing or defending the claim;[22]

(b) that the statement of case is an abuse of the court's process[23] or is otherwise likely to obstruct the just disposal of the proceedings; or

(c) that there has been a failure to comply with a rule, practice direction or court order.[24]

When the court strikes out a statement of case it may make any consequential order it considers appropriate.[25] If the court strikes out a claimant's statement of case and it considers that the claim is totally without merit the court's order must record that fact and the court must at the same time consider whether it is appropriate to make a civil restraint order.[26]

19 See, eg, *Hanily v Minister of Local Government and Planning* [1951] KB 917; *Brightwell v Secretary of State for the Environment* (1997) 73 P&CR 418; *R (River Thames Society) v First Secretary of State* [2006] EWHC 2829 (Admin), [2007] JPL 782; *R (SDR) v Bristol City Council v Vence LLP, Ashton Vale Project LLP* [2012] EWHC 859 (Admin); *San Vicente v Secretary of State for Communities and Local Government* [2013] EWCA Civ 817, [2014] 1 WLR 966; compare *Eco-Energy (GB) Ltd v First Secretary of State* [2004] EWCA Civ 1566, [2005] P&CR 5.

20 See CPR 54.15 and CPR PD 54A para 11.1. See also the observations of Langstaff J on the importance of making amendments promptly in *R (Hinds) v Blackpool Council* [2011] EWHC 591 (Admin), at [42].

21 See CPR 52.8.

22 A statutory challenge brought under Part 8 of the CPR that fails to identify a legal basis for the challenge within the ambit of the relevant enactment is liable to be struck out: *R (A) v Secretary of State for Communities and Local Government* [2011] EWCA Civ 1253, [2012] JPL 579, at [63–66].

23 The power to strike out on the ground of abuse of process is a broad power, capable of exercise even at the end of a trial, but it must be exercised in accordance with the overriding objective. The test is whether striking out is just and proportionate: *Summers v Fairclough Homes Ltd* [2012] UKSC 26, [2012] 1 WLR 2004, at [33–36], [40–44], [49], [61–62]. As to proportionality, see *Walsham Chalet Park Ltd v Tallington Lakes Ltd* [2014] EWCA Civ 1607.

24 CPR 3.4(2); CPR PD 3A. In the case of statutory appeals see CPR 52.9.

25 CPR 3.4(3).

26 CPR 3.4(6). See also CPR 3.3(7), 23.12, 52.10(5), (6). As to civil restraint orders see CPR PD 3C.

It was not unfair for the court to refuse to allow an adjournment of the hearing of the Council's application to strike out in order to give the claimant more time to amend the claim form and introduce properly arguable grounds.[27]

Protective costs orders

5.14 Special provision is made in the CPR[28] limiting the costs that may be recovered by parties to an Aarhus Convention claim, meaning a claim for judicial review or statutory review of a decision, act or omission all or part of which is subject to the provisions of the UN ECE Convention on Access to Information, Public Participation in Decision-Making and Access to Justice in Environmental Matters done at Aarhus, Denmark on 25 June 1998 ('the Aarhus Convention'),[29] including a claim which proceeds on the basis that the decision, act or omission, or part of it, is so subject.

5.15 Where a claim does not qualify as an 'Aarhus Convention claim' within CPR 45.41, the court may limit a party's potential exposure to costs by way of a protective costs order (PCO). The principles to be applied in determining whether a PCO should be granted are the 'Corner House' principles,[30] considered further in Chapter 6.

5.16 Sections 88 and 89[31] of the Criminal Justice and Courts Act 2015 (CJCA 2015) prospectively regulate 'costs capping orders' – orders limiting or removing the liability of a party to judicial review proceedings to pay another party's costs in connection with any stage of the proceedings. Once those sections are brought into force the court will be able to make a costs capping order only if leave to apply for judicial review has been granted[32] and it is satisfied that: (a) the proceedings are public interest proceedings; (b) in the absence of the order, the applicant for judicial review would withdraw the application for judicial review or cease to participate in the proceedings; and (c) it would be reasonable for the applicant for judicial review to do so.[33] These provisions may, however, be disapplied in relation to environmental cases.[34] The effect of the CJCA 2015 on costs in the Planning Court is considered in Chapter 6.

27 *Coates v Secretary of State for Communities and Local Government* [2017] EWCA Civ 940.

28 In CPR 45.43(1) and CPR PD 45, para 5.1. A local authority claimant in an Aarhus Convention claim is entitled to costs protection under these provisions: *R (HS2 Action Alliance) v Secretary of State for Transport* [2015] EWCA Civ 203.

29 As to the matters within the scope of the Aarhus Convention, see generally *Venn v Secretary of State for Communities and Local Government* [2014] EWCA Civ 1539, [2015] 1 WLR 2328, at [10–18]; but noting that under CPR 45.41(2)(a) an 'Aarhus Convention claim' can include a claim for review under statute as well as judicial review.

30 See *R (Corner House Research) v Secretary of State for Trade and Industry* [2005] EWCA Civ 192, [2005] 1 WLR 2600; *Morgan v Hinton Organics (Wessex) Ltd* [2009] EWCA Civ 107, [2009] Env LR 30; *R (Garner) v Elmbridge BC* [2010] EWCA Civ 1006, [2011] 3 All ER 418.

31 At the time of writing these provisions have not yet been brought into force.

32 Criminal Justice and Courts Act 2015, s 88(3).

33 Ibid, s 88(6).

34 Ibid, s 90.

Transfer

5.17 Planning Court claims form a specialist list,[35] and a judge dealing with Planning Court claims may order proceedings to be transferred to or from that list.[36] An application for a transfer of proceedings to or from a specialist list can also be made to the judge dealing with the specialist list.[37]

Control of evidence

5.18 CPR Part 32.1 states:

'(1) The court may control the evidence by giving directions as to:

(a) the issues on which it requires evidence;

(b) the nature of the evidence which it requires to decide those issues; and

(c) the way in which the evidence is to be placed before the court.

(2) The court may use its power under this rule to exclude evidence that would otherwise be admissible.

(3) The court may limit cross-examination.'

5.19 Where the defendant to a judicial review or statutory challenge seeks to put in evidence at variance with the record of the decision in issue, this is unlikely to be permitted.[38]

5.20 In general, Planning Court claims will be determined on the written evidence filed by the parties. The court may require or permit a party to give oral evidence, and may require a witness who has given written evidence to attend for cross-examination,[39] but in very few cases in the Planning Court is this likely to be necessary or appropriate.[40] Exceptional cases where cross-examination has been ordered (including cross-examination of an Inspector) are discussed in

35 CPR 54.22(1).

36 Ibid, 54.21, 30.5(2).

37 Ibid, 30.5 (3).

38 *R v Westminster City Council, ex p Ermakov* [1996] 2 All ER 302, 315h–316d; *R (Richards) v Pembrokeshire County Council* [2004] EWCA Civ 1000, [2005] LGR 105, at [54–58]; *R (Lanner Parish Council) v Cornwall Council* [2013] EWCA Civ 1290, at [57–64]; *Ioannou v Secretary of State for Communities and Local Government* [2014] EWCA Civ 1432, [2015] 1 P&CR 10, at [41].

39 CPR 8.6(2), (3).

40 *O'Reilly v Mackman* [1983] 2 AC 237, 282D–283A; *Jones v Secretary of State for Wales* (1995) 70 P&CR 211, 215–216, 220–221; *R (Newsmith Stainless Ltd) v Secretary of State for the Environment, Transport and the Regions* [2001] EWHC 74 (Admin), at [5–8], [10]; *R (PG) v Ealing LBC* [2001] EWHC 250, [2002] MHLR 140, at [14], [20], [30]; *Greaves v Boston Borough Council* [2014] EWHC 3950 (Admin), [2014] All ER (D) 03 (Dec), at [20–23].

Chapter 7. Where evidence is not tested by cross-examination, disputes of fact will usually be resolved in favour of the defendant.[41]

Inherent jurisdiction

5.21 Notwithstanding the broad reach of the CPR, the court retains an inherent jurisdiction to regulate civil proceedings before it.[42] By this jurisdiction it may supplement the provisions of the CPR but may not act inconsistently with them. The exercise of this jurisdiction is also subject to '[t]he basic rule … that (subject to certain established and limited exceptions) the court cannot exercise its power to regulate its own procedures in such a way as will deny parties their fundamental common law right to participate in the proceedings in accordance with the common law principles of natural justice and open justice'.[43]

It is pointless for the court to exercise its inherent jurisdiction if it would mean adopting the same approach and lead to the same result as an application of the rules[44].

C CASE MANAGEMENT OF JUDICIAL REVIEW CLAIMS

5.22 Broadly speaking, the main procedural steps in a 'standard' claim for judicial review in the Planning Court comprise:

- the filing of a claim form and supporting documents;[45]
- service of the claim form;[46]
- the filing of an acknowledgment of service by any person wishing to take part in the judicial review;[47]
- the grant or refusal of permission to proceed on the papers;[48]
- if the claimant requests reconsideration of a refusal or limited grant of permission,[49] or if interim relief is contested, an oral hearing;

41 *R v Board of Visitors of Hull Prison Ex p St Germain (No.2)* [1979] 1 WLR 1401, 1410; *Cran v Camden LBC* [1995] RTR 346, 353H; *R (Al-Sweady) v Secretary of State for Defence* [2009] EWHC 2387 (Admin), [2010] HRLR 2, at [17]; *Flattery v Secretary of State for Communities and Local Government* [2010] EWHC 2868 (Admin), at [56].

42 Senior Courts Act, s 19(2)(b); CPR Part 3, r 3.1(1); *Raja v Van Hoogstraten (No 9)* [2008] EWCA Civ 1444, [2009] 1 WLR 1143, at [74–78]; *Bovale Ltd v Secretary of State for Communities and Local Government* [2009] EWCA Civ 171, [2009] 1 WLR 2274, at [41–44], [69]; *Al Rawi v Security Service* [2011] UKSC 34, [2012] 1 AC 531, at [18–22]; and see the observations of Ouseley J in *British Union for the Abolition of Vivisection (BUAV) v Secretary of State for the Home Department* [2014] EWHC 43 (Admin), [2014] ACD 69, at [38–42].

43 Per Lord Dyson JSC in *Al Rawi v Security Service*, at [22].

44 *Tombstone v Raja* [2008] EWCA Civ 1444.

45 See CPR 54.5, PD54A paras 5.1–5.10, PD54E paras 2.1 and 2.2.

46 Ibid, 54.7, PD54A paras 6.1 and 6.2.

47 Ibid, 54.8.

48 Ibid, 54.10–54.12, PD 54A para 8.4.

49 Ibid, 54.12, PD 54A paras 8.5, 8.6.

- if permission is granted, the filing by the defendant of detailed grounds for contesting the claim and written evidence;[50]
- a substantive hearing.

The court's general case management powers are dealt with above but there are four procedural aspects of judicial review claims that merit further consideration: permission to proceed; delay; urgency; and disclosure.

Permission to proceed

5.23 The court will not grant permission to proceed with a judicial review claim unless:

- the claimant has a sufficient interest[51] in the matter to which the claim relates;[52]
- [the applicant has provided the court with any information about the financing of the application that is specified in rules of court for this purpose;][53] and
- the claim is arguable.[54]

Even where these criteria are met the court retains a discretion to refuse permission where, inter alia, there is an adequate alternative remedy[55] or the claim has become academic.[56]

50 Ibid, 54.14 and PD54A, para 10.1.

51 As to which see *R v Inland Revenue Commissioners, Ex p National Federation of Self-Employed and Small Businesses Ltd* [1982] AC 617, 631C–G, 645H–646D, 653B–H, 659A–B, 662E, G; *R v Secretary of State for Foreign and Commonwealth Affairs, Ex p World Development Movement Ltd* [1995] 1 WLR 386, 395E–396B; *R v Somerset CC, ex p Dixon* (1998) 75 P&CR 175, at [179–184]; *R (Feakins) v Secretary of State for the Environment, Food and Rural Affairs* [2003] EWCA Civ 1546, [2004] 1 WLR 1761, at [21–24]; *R (Rockware Glass Ltd) v Chester CC* [2005] EWHC 2250 (Admin), [2006] Env LR 30, at [165–170], [174]; *Walton v Scottish Ministers* [2012] UKSC 44, [2013] Env LR 16, at [90–96], [102]; *Greaves v Boston BC* [2014] EWHC 3950 (Admin), [2014] All ER (D) 03 (Dec), at [47–55] (loss of sufficient interest during course of proceedings).

52 Senior Courts Act 1981, s 31(3) (prospectively amended to become s 31(3)(a) by s 85(1) of the Criminal Justice and Courts Act 2015).

53 Senior Courts Act 1981, s 31(3)(b) as prospectively inserted by s 85(1) of the Criminal Justice and Courts Act 2015.

54 *R v Inland Revenue Commissioners, Ex p National Federation of Self-Employed and Small Businesses Ltd*, 644A–B. Where the court at an oral permission hearing has heard full argument and considered substantially the same evidence as would be considered at a final hearing it may be appropriate to apply a higher threshold, granting permission only if the claim is strong (ie likely to succeed): *Mass Energy Ltd v Birmingham City Council* [1994] Env LR 298, 307–308, 311, 318; *R v Cotswold DC, ex p Barrington PC* (1998) 75 P&CR 515, 530–531; compare *R v Derbyshire County Council, ex p Woods* [1998] Env LR 277, 280–281.

55 *R v Chief Constable of Merseyside Police, ex p Calveley* [1986] QB 424, 433A–434B, 435F–437D, 440D–E; *R v Birmingham City Council, ex p Ferrero* [1993] 1 All ER 530, 536b–537c; *R (JD Wetherspoon plc) v Guildford BC* [2007] 1 All ER 400, at [87–91].

56 See the discussion of relevant principles in *Tewkesbury Borough Council v SSHCLG* [2019] EWHC 1775 (Admin) where Dove J refused to allow a challenge by a local planning authority to an appeal decision in which the Secretary of State had dismissed an appeal seeking permission for residential development but the Inspector had made adverse comments about the authority's then housing land supply in his report.

5.24 Section 31 of the Senior Courts Act 1981 (SCA 1981) (as amended) contains a further potential hurdle to the grant of permission to proceed. Subsections (3C) to (3F) state:

> '(3C) When considering whether to grant leave to make an application for judicial review, the High Court—
>
> (a) may of its own motion consider whether the outcome for the applicant would have been substantially different if the conduct complained of had not occurred, and
>
> (b) must consider that question if the defendant asks it to do so.
>
> (3D) If, on considering that question, it appears to the High Court to be highly likely that the outcome for the applicant would not have been substantially different, the court must refuse to grant leave.
>
> (3E) The court may disregard the requirement in subsection (3D) if it considers that it is appropriate to do so for reasons of exceptional public interest.
>
> (3F) If the court grants leave in reliance on subsection (3E), the court must certify that the condition in subsection (3E) is satisfied.'

As defendants will have nothing to lose, and potentially much to gain, by asking the court to consider whether the outcome for the applicant would have been substantially different if the conduct complained of had not occurred, these requests have become routine. The court may also direct a hearing to hear specific submissions on the issue.[57]

5.25 Where the court refuses permission to proceed and records the fact that the application is totally without merit in accordance with CPR 23.12,[58] the claimant may not request that decision to be reconsidered at a hearing.[59]

Delay

5.26 There are two legislative provisions requiring claimants in judicial review proceedings to have brought their claims without delay: s 31(6) of the SCA 1981 and CPR 54.5. Section 31(6) states:

> 'Where the High Court considers that there has been undue delay in making an application for judicial review, the court may refuse to grant—
>
> (a) leave for the making of the application; or

57 See CPR 54.11A.

58 CPR 23.12 states: 'If the court dismisses an application (including an application for permission to appeal or for permission to apply for judicial review) and it considers that the application is totally without merit –

(a) the court's order must record that fact; and

(b) the court must at the same time consider whether it is appropriate to make a civil restraint order.'

59 CPR 54.12(7).

(b) any relief sought on the application,

if it considers that the granting of the relief sought would be likely to cause substantial hardship to, or substantially prejudice the rights of, any person or would be detrimental to good administration'.

CPR r 54.5 (so far as relevant to Planning Court claims) states:

'(A1) In this rule—

'the planning acts' has the same meaning as in section 336 of the Town and Country Planning Act 1990;[60]

(1) The claim form must be filed—

(a) promptly; and

(b) in any event not later than 3 months after the grounds to make the claim first arose.[61]

(2) The time limits in this rule may not be extended by agreement between the parties.

(3) This rule does not apply when any other enactment specifies a shorter time limit for making the claim for judicial review.

(4) Paragraph (1) does not apply in the cases specified in paragraphs (5) and (6).

(5) Where the application for judicial review relates to a decision made by the Secretary of State or local planning authority under the planning acts, the claim form must be filed not later than six weeks after the grounds to make the claim first arose.

(6) …'

In *Caswell v Dairy Produce Quota Tribunal for England and Wales,*[62] Lord Goff summarised the effect of the time limits in judicial review proceedings in this way:

'It follows that, when an application for leave to apply is not made promptly and in any event within three months, the court may refuse leave on the ground of delay unless it considers that there is good reason for extending the period; but, even if it considers that there is such good reason, it may still

60 In s 336(1) of the Town and Country Planning Act 1990 'the planning Acts' means the Town and Country Planning Act 1990, the Planning (Listed Buildings and Conservation Areas) Act 1990, the Planning (Hazardous Substances) Act 1990 and the Planning (Consequential Provisions) Act 1990.

61 As to when grounds for making a claim first arise, see *R (Burkett) v Hammersmith and Fulham LBC (No 1)* [2002] UKHL 23, [2002] 1 WLR 1593 (grant of planning permission); compare *R (Nash) Barnet LBC* [2013] EWCA Civ 1004, [2013] PTSR 1457. Where the claim concerns a breach of European Union law, grounds will not arise until the claimant knew or ought to have known of the infringement: *Uniplex (UK) Ltd v NHS Business Services Authority* C-406/08 [2010] 2 CMLR 47; *R (Berky) v Newport City Council* [2012] EWCA Civ 378, [2012] 2 P&CR 12.

62 [1990] 2 AC 738.

> refuse leave (or, where leave has been granted, substantive relief) if in its opinion the granting of the relief sought would be likely to cause hardship or prejudice (as specified in section 31(6)) or would be detrimental to good administration. …'[63]

5.27 To the extent that a judicial review claim is based on a breach of European Union legislation, the obligation to act promptly (as distinct from the obligation to file a claim within the specific period of three months in CPR 54.5(1)(b)) is disapplied.[64] The majority of the Court of Appeal in *R (Berky) v Newport City Council*[65] also expressed the view (obiter) that in those circumstances it was not open to the court to exercise its discretion under s 31(6) of the SCA 1981 to refuse relief on the grounds of undue delay where the claim had been brought within the three-month period.

5.28 The Planning Court may extend the time limits in CPR 54.5(1)(b) and (5) for filing a claim for judicial review,[66] but given the well-recognised need for promptness and finality in challenges to planning decisions[67] it is unlikely to do so unless there are particular features of the case that warrant it. Relevant considerations are likely to include the reason for the failure to file the claim in time, the extent of the delay, the conduct of the claimant, the nature and extent of any prejudice that may be suffered by the defendant, interested parties or the public generally, and the merits of the challenge.

5.29 As stated earlier,[68] the Planning Court has no power to extend a statutory time limit (unless the statute provides otherwise).

Urgent claims

5.30 In urgent cases the court may abridge time for the service of the defendant's acknowledgment of service, detailed grounds for contesting the claim or evidence; direct an early oral hearing to consider the grant of permission and interim relief; and expedite the substantive hearing.

Rolled up hearings

5.31 It is fairly common for the court to direct a 'rolled-up' hearing, at which the issue of permission is considered first and, if permission is granted, the

63 747B–C.

64 *Uniplex (UK) Ltd v NHS Business Services Authority*; *R (U & Partners (East Anglia) Ltd) v Broads Authority* [2011] EWHC 1824 (Admin), [2012] Env LR 5; *R (Berky) v Newport City Council*.

65 [2012] EWCA Civ 378, [2012] 2 P&CR 12.

66 See CPR 3.1(2)(a); PD 54A paras 5.6(3), 5.7(1).

67 See, eg, *Finn-Kelcey v Milton Keynes BC* [2008] EWCA Civ 1067, [2009] Env LR 17; *R (Berky) v Newport City Council*. See too the discussion on this in Chapter 4

68 See para .5.11 above and the cases cited at footnote 18.

substantive hearing follows immediately afterwards[69]. Rolled-up hearings '... may be justified where there is an issue of delay which, if permission is granted, cannot be raised at the substantive hearing.[70] They may also be justified where there is an issue that has to be determined urgently, its arguability is not clear on the material before the court, but the relevant evidence has either been adduced by the time the papers are considered by the court or it can be adduced within a shortened timescale'.[71]

Disclosure

5.32 CPR PD 54A para 12.1 states that disclosure is not required unless the court orders otherwise. For a number of reasons, an order for disclosure in judicial review proceedings is exceptional:[72]

- a judicial review challenge involves focused scrutiny of those aspects of a decision that are said to be unlawful, rather than a broader inquiry into the merits of the decision;
- generally, the court is not required (or well placed) to resolve disputed issues of fact;
- many of the decisions that are challenged (particularly in the Planning Court) will have been arrived at by way of a well-documented, publicly accessible process;
- local authorities routinely make available for public inspection most of the reports and background material on which they base their decisions;
- the Freedom of Information Act 2000 and the Environmental Information Regulations 2004[73] provide statutory rights to information;
- public authorities who wish to persuade the court at the permission stage that a claim is not arguable will need to put forward sufficient material justifying that conclusion;

69 See *R (Midlands Co-operative Society Ltd) v Birmingham City Council* [2012] EWHC 620 (Admin).

70 See *R v Criminal Injuries Compensation Board, ex p A* [1999] 2 AC 330, 341A–F, 347E–H. In *R v Lichfield Borough Council, ex p Lichfield Securities Ltd* [2001] EWCA Civ 304, the Court of Appeal held, at para 34, that the respondent to judicial review proceedings 'should be permitted to recanvass, by way of undue delay, an issue of promptness which has been decided at the leave stage in the applicant's favour only: (i) if the judge hearing the initial application has expressly so indicated; (ii) if new and relevant material is introduced on the substantive hearing; (iii) if, exceptionally, the issues as they have developed at the full hearing put a different aspect on the question of promptness; or (iv) if the first judge has plainly overlooked some relevant matter or otherwise reached a decision per incuriam.'

71 Per Beatson J in *R (WJ (China)) v Secretary of State for the Home Department* [2010] EWHC 776 (Admin), [2010] All ER (D) 97 (Apr), at [18].

72 *Tweed v Parades Commission for Northern Ireland* [2006] UKHL 53, [2007] 1 AC 650, paras 3, 32, 56; *Save Guana Cay Reef Association v R* [2009] UKPC 44, [2010] 2 LRC 530, at [47]; *R (Perry) v Hackney LBC* [2014] EWHC 1721 (Admin), [2014] JPL 1329, at [23].

73 SI 2004/3391.

- where permission to proceed is granted, the defendant authority will owe a duty to the court to co-operate and give candid disclosure of the relevant facts and (so far as they are not apparent from contemporaneous documents which have been disclosed) the reasoning behind the decision challenged in the judicial review proceedings (the 'duty of candour').[74]

5.33 Nonetheless, circumstances may arise where a claimant requires disclosure of documents held by the defendant. Under CPR 31.12 the court may make an order for specific disclosure or specific inspection. It will not do so, however, unless disclosure appears to be necessary in order to resolve the matter fairly and justly.[75] In considering whether or not to require disclosure, the court will need to balance those factors weighing in favour of and against disclosure.[76] The court may be readier to order disclosure where the proportionality of an interference with a Convention right is in issue, but even then disclosure is not automatic,[77] and if ordered should be carefully limited to the issues which require it in the interests of justice.[78] The court will not allow 'fishing expeditions' – where a claimant seeks disclosure merely in the hope that something will emerge to support his claim.[79]

5.34 Where disclosure is objected to on the ground that the documents sought are confidential, the court may receive the documents first to determine whether, and to what extent, they should be disclosed, including whether any part of the documents should be redacted.[80]

5.35 The court may order disclosure before the commencement of proceedings,[81] but this would constitute a significant departure from the normal

74 *Belize Alliance of Conservation Non-Governmental Organisations v Department of the Environment of Belize* [2004] UKPC 6, [2004] Env LR 38, at [86]; *Tweed v Parades Commission* [2006] UKHL 53, [2007] 1 AC 650, at [31], [54]. The duty of candour applies where it is not possible for the court to assess the merits of an issue that has been raised unless the public authority against whom the claim is brought furnishes the court with information which it alone is in a position to provide. It should not be relied upon to transfer to the defendant the onus of proving matters which a claimant is under a duty and in a position to prove: *Marshall v Deputy Governor of Bermuda* [2010] UKPC 9, at [27–29]. See *R. (Hoareau) v Secretary of State for Foreign State for Foreign and Commonwealth Affairs* [2018] EWHC 1508 (Admin) for principles governing disclosure and the relationship between disclosure and the duty of candour. See Chapter 4 for further discussion on the duty of candour.

75 *Tweed v Parades Commission for Northern Ireland*, at [3], [32], [33], [41], [52].

76 See, eg, *Sky Blue Sports & Leisure Ltd v Coventry City Council* [2013] EWHC 3366 (Admin), [2014] BLGR 34 (disclosure sought prior to the grant of permission); *R (Leyton Orient FC) v London Legacy Development Corporation* [2013] EWHC 3653 (Admin); *R (Perry) v Hackney LBC* [2014] EWHC 1721 (Admin), [2014] JPL 1329.

77 *Tweed v Parades Commission for Northern Ireland*, at [3], [32], [38], [51], [56], [57].

78 Ibid, [32].

79 Ibid, [31], [56].

80 Ibid, [5], [41], [58].

81 Senior Courts Act 1981, s 33(2); CPR 31.16; *British Union for the Abolition of Vivisection (BUAV) v Secretary of State for the Home Department* [2014] EWHC 43 (Admin), [2014] ACD 69, at [32–33].

procedures for judicial review and is unlikely to be appropriate except in a most exceptional case.[82]

D CASE MANAGEMENT OF STATUTORY CHALLENGES

Applications to the High Court

5.36 An application under an enactment giving the High Court jurisdiction to quash or prohibit any order, scheme, certificate or plan, any amendment or approval of a plan, any decision of a Minister or government department or any action on the part of a Minister or government department must be made in accordance with Part 8 of the CPR.[83] This is a broad class, which for the purposes of the Planning Court includes applications under:

- ss 287 and 288 of the Town and Country Planning Act 1990 (TCPA 1990);
- s 63 of the Planning (Listed Buildings and Conservation Areas) Act 1990 (P(LBCA)A 1990);
- s 22 of the Planning (Hazardous Substances) Act 1990;
- s 113 of the Planning and Compulsory Purchase Act 2004;
- s 22 of the Transport and Works Act 1992;
- s 105D of, and Sch 2, para 2 to, the Highways Act 1980;
- para 35, Sch 9 to the Road Traffic Regulation Act 1984;
- para 7, Sch 11 and Sch 15, para 12 to the Wildlife and Countryside Act 1981;
- s 23 of the Acquisition of Land Act 1981 (ALA 1981).

5.37 The main procedural steps in an application to the Planning Court under Part 8 of the CPR comprise:

- the filing and service of a claim form;[84]
- the filing and service of an acknowledgment of service in the relevant practice form not more than 21 days after service of the claim form;[85]

82 *British Union for the Abolition of Vivisection (BUAV) v Secretary of State for the Home Department*, at [54–57].

83 CPR r 8.1(6) and PD 8C paras 2.1-2.4 and 4.1.

84 See CPR 8.2 and CPR PD 8C paras 2.1-2.4 and 4.1. Whether or not a document constitutes a valid application to the High Court is a matter of fact and degree. If the claim documents do not identify any grounds within the relevant enactment on which the application is made, it may be struck out: *R (A) v Secretary of State for Communities and Local Government* [2011] EWCA Civ 1253, [2012] JPL 579, at [63–66].

85 See CPR PD 8C paras 5.3-5.5; *Bovale Ltd v Secretary of State for Communities and Local Government* [2009] EWCA Civ 171, [2009] 1 WLR 2274, at [52–55]; for consequences of failing to file an acknowledgement of service see CPR PD 8C paras 6.1-6.2.

- where the leave of the court is required, the grant or refusal of permission to proceed which may be determined on the papers or at an oral hearing[86];
- the determination of any application for interim relief;
- a substantive hearing.

5.38 Part 8 of the CPR does not require the respondent to a statutory challenge to file a document setting out his grounds for contesting the claim, but a Planning Court judge may nonetheless direct one to be provided.[87]

Disclosure

5.39 For essentially the same reasons as apply in judicial review proceedings, disclosure is not usually ordered in statutory applications to the High Court,[88] but an order for standard or specific disclosure, including disclosure before the commencement of proceedings, may be made where it is necessary for the fair and just disposal of the case.[89]

Appeals to the High Court

5.40 Certain statutory appeals also constitute Planning Court claims, principally appeals under s 289 of the TCPA 1990 and s 65 of the P(LBCA) A 1990. For these appeals the procedure in CPR Part 52 as modified by PD 52D para 26.1 is to be followed. In summary this comprises:

- the service and filing of an application for permission to appeal, together with a draft appellant's notice and supporting witness evidence, within

86 See CPR PD 8C paras 7.1-9.2.

87 See CPR PD 54E para 3.5.

88 See CPR PD 8C para 14.3; see **5.32** above. In *Dinedor Hill Action Association v County of Herefordshire DC* [2008] EWHC 1741 (Admin), [2009] 1 P&CR 4, it was held, at para 31, that the principle that a public authority defendant in judicial review proceedings should put before the court all relevant material applies equally to proceedings under ss 287 and 288 of the Town and Country Planning Act 1990.

89 See CPR 31.1(2), 31.5, 31.12, 31.16; *R (Archway Sheet Metal Works) Ltd v Secretary of State for Communities and Local Government* [2014] EWHC 4450 (Admin), at [16]. It is only in rare cases that it would be appropriate to order disclosure of a planning inspector's notes: *Miller v Minister of Housing and Local Government* (1968) 19 P&CR 263, 274–275; *Brien v Secretary of State for the Environment and Bromley London Borough Council* [1995] JPL 523; *Belmont Riding Centre v Secretary of State for the Environment, Transport and the Regions* [2001] PLCR 12, at [59–61].

28 days after notice of the decision appealed against is given to the applicant;[90]

- the filing and service by any respondent to the application of any witness statement or affidavit to be relied on at the permission hearing at least two days before the hearing;[91]
- a permission hearing;[92]
- if permission is granted, the service of the appellant's notice;[93]
- where necessary or so directed, the filing and service of a respondent's notice;[94]
- a substantive hearing.[95]

5.41 In a statutory appeal, any person may apply for permission to file evidence, or to make representations at the appeal hearing.[96]

5.42 The court may remit the matter to the Secretary of State or, in Wales, the Welsh Ministers to the extent necessary to enable the Secretary of State or the Welsh Ministers to provide the court with such further information in connection with the matter as the court may direct.[97]

Standing

5.43 The right to challenge various decisions, plans, schemes and orders in the High Court is in a number of Acts expressed to be exercisable by a 'person

90 See CPR PD 52D para 26.1(1)–(4), (12). The 28-day period is fixed by the CPR and may be extended by the court under CPR 3.1(2)(a), although as in judicial review proceedings the claimant would need to show good reason for an extension of time: see para **5.28** above, and see *R (Hysaj) v Secretary of State for the Home Department (Practice Note)* [2014] EWCA Civ 1633, [2015] 1 WLR 2472. A failure to serve and file the documents specified by rules of court may invalidate the appeal: see *Wenman v Secretary of State for the Environment* [1995] JPL 1040, but now see CPR 3.10 and the approach adopted in *R (Wandsworth LBC) v Secretary of State for Transport, Local Government and the Regions* [2003] EWHC 622 Admin, [2004] 1 P&CR 32; *Corus UK Ltd v Erewash BC* [2006] EWCA Civ 1175, [2007] 1 P&CR 22; *R (Westminster City Council) v Secretary of State for Communities and Local Government* [2014] EWHC 1248 (Admin); *Harrogate Borough Council v Secretary of State for Communities and Local Government* [2014] EWHC 1506 (Admin).

91 See CPR PD 52D para 26.1(8).

92 Ibid, para 26.1(5)–(11).

93 Ibid, para 26.1(11)(c), (12)

94 See CPR 52.13; CPR PD 54E para 3.5. For the principles applicable to an application for an extension of time to file a respondent's notice, see *Salford Estates (No 2) Ltd v Altomart Ltd (Practice Note)* [2014] EWCA Civ 1408, [2015] 1 WLR 1825. For consequences of not filing where required to do so under r 52.13(2)(b) see *Sahota v Singh* [2018] EWHC 1685 (Ch), ChD

95 See CPR PD 52D para 26.1(13)–(16).

96 See CPR 52.25; CPR PD 52D paras 3.6–3.8.

97 CPR PD 52D para 26.1(14).

aggrieved'.[98] Whether or not a claimant is a 'person aggrieved' will depend on the particular legislation involved and the nature of the grounds on which the claimant claims to be aggrieved. Persons will ordinarily be regarded as aggrieved if they made objections or representations as part of the procedure which preceded the decision challenged, and their complaint is that the decision was not properly made. There may be circumstances, however, in which a person who has not participated in the process may none the less be 'aggrieved', such as where an inadequate description of the development was given to the public, misleading the claimant so that he did not object or take part in the procedure leading to the impugned decision. Where a person has demonstrated a genuine concern about the legality of a development which is bound to have a significant impact on the environment, he may be a person aggrieved even if his proprietary interests are unaffected.[99]

Permission

5.44 Some statutory challenges in the Planning Court require the court's permission to proceed.[100] In considering the merits of an application for permission, the test applied by the court is the same as that in judicial review proceedings: is the claim arguable.[101]

E INTERIM RELIEF

Judicial review proceedings

5.45 CPR 25.1 contains a non-exhaustive list of interim remedies a court may grant, including an interim injunction, an interim declaration and an order for disclosure before a claim is brought. In addition, the court has power in judicial review proceedings to grant a stay suspending the effect of the decision under

98 See, eg, ss 287 and 288 of the Town and Country Planning Act 1990; s 63 of the Planning (Listed Buildings and Conservation Areas) Act 1990; s 22 of the Planning (Hazardous Substances) Act 1990; s 113 of the Planning and Compulsory Purchase Act 2004; s 22 of the Transport and Works Act 1992; s 105D of, and Sch 2, para 2 to, the Highways Act 1980, Sch 11, para 7 and Sch 15, para 12 to the Wildlife and Countryside Act 1981; and s 23 of the Acquisition of Land Act 1981.

99 *Walton v Scottish Ministers* [2012] UKSC 44, [2013] Env LR 16, at [83–88], [102–103], [151–154]; compare *JB Trustees Ltd v Secretary of State for Communities and Local Government* [2013] EWHC 3555 (Admin), [2014] JPL 656, at [32–47].

100 Challenges brought under s 289 of the Town and Country Planning Act 1990 (TCPA 1990) and s 65 of the Planning (Listed Buildings and Conservation Areas) Act 1990 (P(LBCA)A 1990). Further to section 91 of and Schedule 16 to the Criminal Justice and Courts Act 2015, leave is also required in challenges brought under ss 287 and 288 of the TCPA 1990, s 63 of the P(LBCA)A 1990, s 22 of the Planning (Hazardous Substances) Act 1990 and s 113 of the Planning and Compulsory Purchase Act 2004.

101 *Wendy Fair Markets Ltd v Secretary of State for the Environment* [1996] JPL 649, 653, 654; *Walsall MBC v Secretary of State for Communities and Local Government* [2013] EWCA Civ 370, [2013] JPL 1183, at [24], [27].

challenge. Interim injunctions, stays and interim declarations are considered below. Orders for pre-claim disclosure are dealt with at para **5.35** above.

Interim injunctions

5.46 An interim injunction may be sought at any stage of the proceedings, including before a claim is issued.[102] In judicial review proceedings an application for an interim injunction will be determined having regard to the guidelines in *American Cyanamid Co v Ethicon Ltd*[103] but with modifications appropriate to the public law element of the case.[104] First, the applicant must demonstrate that there is a serious question to be tried. In the context of public law proceedings, this involves considering whether there is a real (ie more than fanciful) prospect of the claim succeeding at the substantive hearing.[105] Second, the court must consider whether the balance of convenience lies in favour of granting or refusing the interim relief that is sought.

5.47 Applications for interim relief in public law proceedings differ from interim applications in private law proceedings because, in general, no damages are payable as a result of an unlawful administrative act and nor will the public authority suffer financial loss from being prevented from implementing its policy.[106] This means that, in general, there is a strong public interest in permitting a public authority's decision to continue and therefore an applicant for interim relief must make out a strong case.

5.48 In assessing the balance of convenience, the public interest must be taken into account.[107] In many cases before the Planning Court the decision under challenge will have been taken within a statutory framework intended to protect and promote the public interest. There is, for instance, a well-recognised public interest in protecting the environment and regulating the use of land, to which the town and country planning regime gives effect.[108] There may, of course, be competing public interests: in ensuring that a lawful process is followed and in giving effect to a decision that benefits the public.

102 Senior Courts Act 1981, ss 31(2), 37(1); CPR 25.2. The procedure is governed by CPR 25.2, 25.3, PD 25A and Part 23 (which contains general rules about applications). See also The Administrative Court: Judicial Review Guide (July 2020), para 15.6.

103 [1975] AC 396, 407G–408H.

104 *R (Lochailort Investments Ltd) v Mendip District Council* [2019] EWHC 2633 (QB); [2020] JPL 439, at [13].

105 *R (Medical Justice) v Secretary of State for the Home Department* [2010] EWHC 1425 (Admin), [6]; The Administrative Court: Judicial Review Guide, para 15.10

106 *R (Medical Justice) v Secretary of State for the Home Department* [2010] EWHC 1425 (Admin), [12]; The Administrative Court: Judicial Review Guide, para 15.10.

107 *R v Secretary of State for Transport, Ex p Factortame Ltd (No 2)* at [673B–C].

108 *South Bucks v Porter* [2003] UKHL 26, [2003] 2 AC 558, at [10]; *Lawrence v Fen Tigers* [2014] UKSC 13, [2014] AC 822, at [89], [91], [95], [156], [193].

5.49 Special factors may require the court to go beyond the balance of convenience and explore the merits in more detail, such as where the grant or refusal of an interim injunction will in effect be decisive of the whole case.[109]

5.50 One option available to the Planning Court, where the merits of the underlying claim are unclear, and there appears to be no particular urgency in granting interim relief, is to either order that the permission application be expedited or that it be 'rolled up' with the substantive hearing.[110] This allows the Planning Court to hear full argument for both sides before making a decision on relief.

5.51 The grant of a mandatory interim injunction is more likely to result in irremediable prejudice to the party affected, and a court may therefore require a high degree of assurance that at the substantive hearing it will appear that the injunction was rightly granted.[111]

5.52 Although in civil litigation the party seeking an interim injunction is usually required to give an undertaking in damages, this is not invariably the case.[112] In Aarhus Convention claims the court must consider whether the effect of requiring an undertaking in damages would render the proceedings prohibitively expensive for the party seeking the injunction.[113] If an applicant is unable to offer a sufficient undertaking, that is not fatal to the application but it is an important factor which weighs against the grant of interim relief.[114]

5.53 Ultimately, the court has a wide discretion to take the course which seems most likely to minimise the risk of an unjust result.[115]

Stays

5.54 Where in a claim for judicial review permission to proceed is given, the court may direct that there be a stay of the proceedings to which the claim

109 *NWL Ltd v Woods (The Nawala) (No 2)* [1979] 1 WLR 1294, at [1306B–1307B]; *Belize Alliance of Conservation Non-Governmental Organisations v Department of the Environment of Belize*, at [35]; and see, eg, *R (GSTS Pathology LLP) v Revenue and Customs Commissioners* [2013] EWHC 1801 (Admin), [2013] STC 2017, at [63–66].

110 Administrative Court: Judicial Review Guide (July 2020), para 15.10

111 *National Commercial Bank Jamaica Ltd v Olint Corporation Ltd* [2009] UKPC 16, [2009] 1 WLR 1405, at [19].

112 CPR PD 25A paras 5.1(1), 5.1A; *Kirklees MBC v Wickes Building Supplies Ltd* [1993] AC 227 (undertaking not required of local authority seeking to enforce the law); *R v Darlington BC, Ex p Darlington Taxi Owners* [1994] COD 424; *R v Servite Houses, Ex p Goldsmith (interim relief)* (2000) 3 CCL Rep 354; *Belize Alliance of Conservation Non-Governmental Organisations v Department of the Environment of Belize*, at [37–39].

113 See CPR PD 25A paras 5.1A, 5.1B; *European Commission v UK* Case C-530/11, [2014] QB 988, at [64–68].

114 R (Coleman) v Barnet London Borough Council [2012] EWHC 3100 (Admin), at [14].

115 *R v Secretary of State for Transport, Ex p Factortame Ltd (No 2)*, 659E–F; *Belize Alliance of Conservation Non-Governmental Organisations v Department of the Environment of Belize*, at [39]; *National Commercial Bank Jamaica Ltd v Olint Corporation Ltd*, at [17].

relates.[116] This power extends to administrative decisions and the processes by which they are reached.[117] The effect of a stay of proceedings is to suspend them until the determination of the challenge. 'What this means in practice will depend on the context and the stage that has been reached in the proceedings. If the inferior court or administrative body has not yet made a final decision, then the effect of the stay will be to prevent the taking of the steps that are required for the decision to be made. If a final decision has been made, but it has not been implemented, then the effect of the stay will be to prevent its implementation. In each of these situations, so long as the stay remains in force, no further steps can be taken in the proceedings, and any decision taken will cease to have effect: it is suspended for the time being.'[118] A stay may be granted even when the decision under challenge has been fully implemented.[119]

5.55 The court will not normally grant a stay for the purpose of enabling the defendant to reconsider the decision under challenge in the claim.[120] If the defendant agrees to reconsider the decision, the appropriate course of action is to withdraw the claim for judicial review. A fresh claim can be brought in respect of the subsequent decision.

5.56 If a third party who is not a party to the judicial review proceedings would be detrimentally affected by the grant of a stay, the court should apply the principles applicable to the grant of an interim injunction.[121] In the absence of special circumstances, an undertaking in damages should also be given by the party seeking the stay.[122]

Interim declarations

5.57 In determining an application for an interim declaration, the court will usually apply the *American Cyanamid* guidelines, as modified in public law cases.[123] Where the effect of an interim declaration would be to render

116 CPR 54.10(2)(a).

117 *R v Secretary of State for Education and Science, Ex p Avon County Council (No 2)* [1991] 1 QB 558; *R v Secretary of State for the Home Department, Ex p Muboyayi* [1992] QB 244; *R (H) v Ashworth Special Hospital Authority* [2002] EWCA Civ 923, [2003] 1 WLR 923; *Cala Homes (South) Ltd v Secretary of State for Communities and Local Government* [2010] EWHC 3278 (Admin), [2011] JPL 553.

118 Per Dyson LJ in *R (H) v Ashworth Special Hospital Authority*, at [45].

119 *R (H) v Ashworth Special Hospital Authority*, at [46], [48], [94],

120 Administrative Court: Judicial Review Guide (July 2020), para 12.8.3

121 *R v Inspectorate of Pollution, Ex p Greenpeace Ltd* [1994] 1 WLR 570, 573D–G, 576F–H.

122 *R v Inspectorate of Pollution, Ex p Greenpeace Ltd*, 577B–C; *R v Darlington BC, Ex p Darlington Taxi Owners*; *Belize Alliance of Conservation Non-Governmental Organisations v Department of the Environment of Belize*, at [38].

123 *R v Secretary of State for the Environment, Ex p The Royal Society for the Protection of Birds* [1997] Env LR 431, 439–441; *R v Secretary of State for Trade and Industry, Ex p Trades Union Congress* [2001] 1 CMLR 8, at [17–19], [26], [61]; *Transport for London v Griffin* [2012] EWHC 1105 (QB), at [26].

inoperative a provision of national legislation, the applicant will in all save the most exceptional cases be required to show a strong prima facie case.[124]

Duty of full and fair disclosure

5.58 A party who applies for interim relief without notice to the opposing party must make full and fair disclosure of all the facts material for the court to know in determining the application.[125] Not only must all material facts be disclosed, the applicant must also draw the court's attention to the significant factual, legal and procedural aspects of the case.[126] A failure to observe this duty may lead to the order for interim relief being set aside and the parties or their representatives may be required to explain why information or evidence was not disclosed to the court.[127]

Statutory challenges

5.59 The remedies of interim injunction and interim declaration are available in all claims, including statutory challenges brought under Part 8 of the CPR. In most such challenges, however, they are unlikely to be needed because where an Act confers a right to challenge the validity of an order or other instrument by application to the High Court, the court is usually given the power to suspend the order or instrument until the final determination of the proceedings. For example, powers of interim suspension are given in the case of challenges to: the grant of planning permission by the Secretary of State;[128] a local development plan;[129] a Transport and Works Act order;[130] a traffic regulation order;[131] and a compulsory purchase order.[132]

Giving interim effect to enforcement notices and listed building enforcement notices

5.60 In an appeal brought under s 289 of the TCPA 1990 in respect of an enforcement notice or under s 65 of the P(LBCA)A 1990 in respect of a listed building enforcement notice, the court may, on such terms if any as it thinks fit (which may include terms requiring the local planning authority to give an undertaking as to damages or any other matter), order that the notice shall have

124 *R v Secretary of State for Trade and Industry, Ex p Trades Union Congress*, at [18], [21], [24], [26], [33].
125 See, for example, *Brink's MAT Ltd v Elcombe* [1988] 1 WLR 1350, 1356F–1357B, 1358B–C, 1359B.
126 *Memory Corporation Plc v Sidhu (No 2)* [2000] 1 WLR 1443, 1454D–H, 1459H–1460B.
127 *Brink's MAT Ltd v Elcombe; Memory Corporation Plc v Sidhu (No 2)*; The Administrative Court: Judicial Review Guide (July 2020), para 14.1.3
128 Town and Country Planning Act 1990, s 288(5)(a).
129 Planning and Compulsory Purchase Act 2004, s 113(5).
130 Transport and Works Act 1992, s 22(2)(a).
131 Road Traffic Regulation Act 1984, Sch 9, para 36(1)(a).
132 Acquisition of Land Act 1981, s 24(1).

effect, or have effect to such extent as may be specified in the order, pending the final determination of the appeal and any re-hearing and determination by the Secretary of State.[133] If no such order is made, the notice will be of no effect until the final determination of the underlying appeal.[134]

F FINAL RELIEF

Judicial review claims

5.61 On an application for judicial review the court may grant:

- a mandatory order;
- a prohibitory order;
- a quashing order;
- a declaration;
- an injunction.[135]

5.62 The court may also award damages, restitution or the recovery of a sum due, provided: (a) the application includes a claim for such an award arising from any matter to which the application relates; and (b) the court is satisfied that such an award would have been made if the claim had been made in an action begun by the applicant at the time of making the application.[136]

5.63 If, on an application for judicial review, the court quashes the decision to which the application relates, it may in addition:

(a) remit the matter to the court, tribunal or authority which made the decision, with a direction to reconsider the matter and reach a decision in accordance with the findings of the Planning Court, or

(b) substitute its own decision for the decision in question (but only if (i) the decision in question was made by a court or tribunal, (ii) the decision is quashed on the ground that there has been an error of law, and (iii) without the error there would have been only one decision which the court or tribunal could have reached).[137]

133 Town and Country Planning Act 1990, s 289(4A); Planning (Listed Buildings and Conservation Areas) Act 1990, s 65(3A).
134 Town and Country Planning Act 1990, s 175(4); Planning (Listed Buildings and Conservation Areas) Act 1990, s 39(3).
135 Senior Courts Act 1981, ss 29, 31(2), 37(1).
136 Ibid, s 31(4).
137 Ibid, s 31(5), (5A); CPR 54.19.

Discretionary nature of relief

5.64 The grant of relief is in the discretion of the court.[138] Although the starting point is that an unlawful decision will ordinarily be quashed,[139] relief may be refused (or attenuated relief granted) where, inter alia, there has been undue delay[140] (see further below) or a lack of prejudice to the claimant,[141] where the error complained of made no difference to the decision under challenge[142] (see further below), where the grant of relief would be pointless[143] or where there would be substantial prejudice to the public interest or a third party.[144]

Delay

5.65 Where the court considers that there has been undue delay in making an application for judicial review, the court may refuse to grant any relief sought on the application if it considers that the granting of the relief sought would be likely to cause substantial hardship to, or substantially prejudice the rights of, any person or would be detrimental to good administration.[145] Eight 'broad principles' on delay were set out by the Court of Appeal in *R (Thornton Hall Hotel Ltd) v Wirral Metropolitan Borough Council* when allowing a late challenge to proceed some five years after the decision but in a highly unusual factual context. The Court emphasised that the case was an exceptional one.[146]

138 *R (Edwards) v Environment Agency* [2008] UKHL 22, [2008] Env LR 34, at [63].

139 *Berkeley v Secretary of State for the Environment* [2001] 2 AC 603, 616F; *R (Edwards) v Environment Agency*, at [63]; *R (Gardner) v Harrogate Borough Council* [2008] EWHC 2942 (Admin), [2009] JPL 872, at [40]; *Tata Steel UK Ltd v Newport City Council* [2010] EWCA Civ 1626, at [7], [8], [15].

140 Senior Courts Act 1981, s 31(6).

141 See *Walton v Scottish Ministers* [2012] UKSC 44, [2013] Env LR 16, at [111], [112], [138], [139]; and see, eg, *R (Midcounties Co-operative Ltd) v Wyre Forest DC* [2009] EWHC 964 (Admin); *R (CBRE Lionbrook (General Partners) Limited) v Rugby Borough Council* [2014] EWHC 646 (Admin); *R (Perry) v London Borough of Hackney* [2014] EWHC 3499 (Admin).

142 Senior Courts Act 1981, s 31(2A); *Simplex v Secretary of State for the Environment* (1989) 57 P&CR 306, 326–327, 329; *R (Smith) v North East Derbyshire Primary Care Trust* [2006] EWCA Civ 1291, [2006] 1 WLR 3315, at [10].

143 See, eg, *R (Edwards) v Environment Agency*. The court may defer consideration of the issue of relief so that the significance of an established error may be investigated: see, eg, *R (Lady Hart of Chilton) v Babergh DC* [2014] EWHC 3261 (Admin), at [104–105].

144 See *Walton v Scottish Ministers*, at [103], [105], [114], [128], [131], [155], [156]; and see, eg, *R (Gavin) v Haringey LBC* [2003] EWHC 2591 (Admin), [2004] 2 P&CR 13; *R (Guiney) v Greenwich LBC* [2008] EWHC 2012 (Admin), [2009] JPL 211; *Kendall v Rochford DC* [2014] EWHC 3866 (Admin), at [122–126].

145 Senior Courts Act 1981, s 31(6); *Caswell v Dairy Produce Quota Tribunal for England and Wales* [1990] 2 AC 738; *R (Gavin) v Haringey LBC*, at [82–84], [90–92].

146 *R (Thornton Hall Hotel Ltd) v Wirral Metropolitan Borough Council* [2019] EWCA Civ 737, [2019] PTSR 1794, at [21].

No significant effect on outcome

5.66 At common law, where a court is satisfied that an established error made no difference to the decision under challenge, in other words that the decision (absent the error) would inevitably have been the same, the court *may* decline to quash the decision.[147] This discretionary ground has been modified by the statutory test enacted by the Criminal Courts and Justice Act 2015 which amended section 31(2A)–(2C) of the SCA 1981:

> '(2A) The court
>
> (a) must refuse to grant relief on an application for judicial review, and
>
> (b) may not make an award under subsection (4)[148] on such an application,
>
> if it appears to the court to be highly likely that the outcome for the applicant would not have been substantially different if the conduct complained of had not occurred.
>
> (2B) The court may disregard the requirements in subsection (2A)(a) and (b) if it considers that it is appropriate to do so for reasons of exceptional public interest.
>
> (2C) If the court grants relief or makes an award in reliance on subsection (2B), the court must certify that the condition in subsection (2B) is satisfied.'

5.67 The statutory test modifies the *Simplex* test in three ways.[149] First, the court is now under a duty (rather than having a discretion) to refuse relief if the test is satisfied. Second, the threshold for satisfying the test is lowered: the outcome does not inevitably have to be the same; it will suffice if it is merely 'highly likely'. Third, it is not necessary to show that the outcome would have been exactly the same; it is enough that the outcome would not have been 'substantially different' for the claimant. Nonetheless, the threshold continues to be a high one and the Planning Court will need to be careful to avoid straying into an assessment of the merits (rather than the legality) of the policy or decision under challenge. It will often be difficult or impossible for a court to conclude that this test is satisfied[150] – although there are plenty of reported cases in which the Planning Court has been able to do just that.[151]

147 *Simplex (GE (Holdings) Ltd v Secretary of State for the Environment* [1988] 3 PLR 25, at [42].

148 Senior Courts Act 1981, s 31(4) empowers the court to award damages, restitution or the recovery of a sum due.

149 *R (Plan B Earth) v Secretary of State for Transport* [2020] EWCA Civ 214, at [272].

150 Ibid, [273].

151 .See, eg, *R (Advearse) v Dorset Council* [2020] EWHC 807, *R (Heathrow Hub Ltd) v Secretary of State for Transport* [2020] EWCA Civ 213, *R (Wingfield) v Canterbury City Council* [2019] EWHC 1974 (Admin).

Statutory challenges

5.68 For statutory challenges, where the court is usually empowered to quash the order, document, plan or other instrument in question, the decision of the Supreme Court in *Walton v Scottish Ministers*[152] provides helpful guidance on the approach to be taken to the grant of relief. As in judicial review proceedings, the grant of relief is discretionary.

5.69 Where a substantive error of law is made out and there is no good ground to refuse relief, the court's powers will be circumscribed by the statutory remedies provided.[153]

5.70 A successful challenge to a decision of the Secretary of State in an enforcement notice, listed building enforcement notice or tree replanting notice appeal will result in the matter being remitted to the Secretary of State for re-hearing and determination in accordance with the opinion of the court.[154]

Costs

5.71 The court's costs jurisdiction is considered in Chapter 6.

G OTHER POWERS

Declarations of incompatibility

5.72 Where the court is satisfied that a provision of primary or subordinate legislation is incompatible with a Convention right (and in the latter case considers that primary legislation prevents removal of the incompatibility) it may make a declaration of incompatibility.[155] The court may not make a declaration of incompatibility unless 21 days' notice, or such other period of notice as the court directs, has been given to the Crown.[156]

References to Europe

5.73 Where a question as to the interpretation or validity of EU law is raised in proceedings and the court considers that a decision on the question is

152 [2012] UKSC 44, [2013] Env LR 16, at [103–114], [124–131], [133], [139], [155], [156].

153 See, eg, *Jones v Welsh Assembly Government* [2008] EWHC 3515 (Admin); *Whitworth v Secretary of State for Environment, Food and Rural Affairs* [2010] EWCA Civ 1468, at [48–52]; *Walton v Scottish Ministers*, at [141–145].

154 CPR PD 52D para 26.1(15). As to the effect of remittal see *R (Perrett) v Secretary of State for Communities and Local Government* [2009] EWCA Civ 1365 [2010] JPL 999.

155 Human Rights Act 1998, s 4. A declaration of incompatibility is a discretionary remedy: see *R (Nasseri) v Secretary of State for the Home Department* [2009] UKHL 23; [2010] 1 AC 1, at [18], [19].

156 CPR 19.4A.

necessary to enable it to give judgment, it may request the Court of Justice to give a ruling thereon.[157] However, from 1 January 2021, the Court of Justice will only have jurisdiction over cases which were pending on 30 December 2020.[158] Thereafter domestic courts will no longer be able to make requests for rulings.[159] The Court of Justice's rulings on pending cases are binding on domestic courts.[160]

Contempt

5.74 Where a party disobeys a court order, breaches an undertaking, makes a false statement of truth or engages in conduct that disrupts proceedings or is calculated to obstruct or prejudice the administration of justice, the court has power to punish that party for contempt of court.[161] The court may impose a sentence of up to two years' imprisonment,[162] order sequestration of the contemnor's assets and/or impose a fine. Part 81 of the Civil Procedure Rules and Practice Direction 81 set out a detailed code of rules to be followed in contempt proceedings. The Court's powers to punish for a contempt of court extend to non-parties, as the BBC found to its cost when it recorded and then broadcast as a news item footage from a remote hearing of the Planning Court in the case of *R (Finch) v Surrey County Council* [2020] EWHC 3566 (Admin). In subsequent contempt proceedings the BBC was fined £28,000 by the Divisional Court [2021] EWHC 170 (QB).

157 Treaty on the Functioning of the European Union, Art 267; CPR Part 68, PD 68.

158 Article 86(2), Agreement on the withdrawal of the United Kingdom of Great Britain and Northern Ireland from the European Union and the European Atomic Energy Community

159 European Union (Withdrawal) Act 2018, s 6(1)(b)

160 Article 87(1), Agreement on the withdrawal of the United Kingdom of Great Britain and Northern Ireland from the European Union and the European Atomic Energy Community

161 See CPR Part 81, PD 81. The onus of proof is on the party alleging contempt, which must be proved beyond reasonable doubt. In order to establish that someone is in contempt it is necessary to show (i) that he knew of the terms of the order; (ii) that he acted (or failed to act) in a manner which involved a breach of the order; and (iii) that he knew of the facts which made his conduct a breach: *Masri v Consolidated Contractors International Company SAL* [2011] EWHC 1024 (Comm), at [150].

162 Contempt of Court Act 1981, s 14(1).

CHAPTER 6

Costs

James Findlay QC, and Alex Williams

A	Introduction	6.1
B	General principles relating to costs	6.4
	– Court's discretion and the general rule	6.4
	– Method of assessing the amount of costs	6.7
	– Basis of assessment	6.9
	– Relevance of conduct	6.10
	– Costs against non–parties	6.13
	– Partial success	6.16
	– Special methods of funding	6.17
C	Judicial reviews in the Planning Court – costs at the permission stage	6.18
	– Where permission is granted	6.19
	– Where permission is refused	
D	Statutory challenges in the Planning Court – costs at the permission stage	6.28
E	Costs following discontinuance/consent to relief	6.31
	– Discontinuance	6.32
	– Settled or withdrawn claims	6.33
F	Costs upon final determination	6.39
	– Exercise of discretion in judicial review/planning appeals	6.39
	– Multiple defendants and interested parties	6.42
	– Part 36 offers in judicial reviews	6.45
	– Interveners	6.46
G	Protective costs orders and cost capping	6.49
	– Summary	6.49
	– Background and *Corner House*	6.50
	– Aarhus Convention: overview of relevant provisions	6.53
	– Aarhus Convention: application	6.59

	– The meaning of 'not prohibitively expensive'	6.62
	– Problems with using PCOs to achieve compliance with the Aarhus Convention: *Commission v UK*	6.65
	– Fixed costs regime under CPR Part 45	6.70
	– Problems with the fixed costs regime	6.82
	– Criminal Justice and Courts Act 2015: non environmental cases	6.85
	– Criminal Justice and Courts Act 2015: environmental cases	6.100
H	Conclusion	6.102

A INTRODUCTION

6.1 Litigation is expensive. Aside from the merits of the case, the question of costs is usually the decisive factor in deciding whether or not to bring or defend proceedings. Planning Court litigation is no different. A proper understanding of the applicable costs regime is vital to the decision making process and to assessment of risk.

6.2 It is not our purpose to set out the law on costs in full. However, there are certain principles and practices which are specific to public law litigation in the Planning Court which need to be understood by those involved in litigation in that court. In particular, the costs landscape in environmental litigation has been significantly affected by the growth in orders which grant parties protection from the risk of costs. Such orders are now common in the Planning Court and awareness of the provisions is vital.

6.3 In this chapter we will first summarise the general principles which apply to the determination of costs, which are common to most civil litigation, and then address specific areas of interest to those involved in Planning Court litigation.

B GENERAL PRINCIPLES RELATING TO COSTS

Court's discretion and the general rule

6.4 The general principles guiding the High Court's apportionment and assessment of the costs of litigation are contained within Part 44 of the Civil Procedure Rules and related Practice Directions. These are common to most areas of civil litigation, and apply equally in the Planning Court unless alternative specific provision is made. A detailed discussion of rules relating to costs is beyond the scope of this book, and specialist texts are available.[1] What follows is a broad overview of the costs landscape.

6.5 The fundamental principle behind the rules relating to costs is that they are always at the discretion of the court.[2] The court has a discretion as to whether costs are payable at all, the amount which is payable, and the time within which payment is to be made.[3] Examples of the kinds of costs orders that the court may make are contained in CPR 44.2(6). The court's discretion is to be exercised judicially and having regard to all of the circumstances, including the conduct of the parties, whether a party has been partially successful, and any admissible offers to settle the proceedings.[4] The court can take into account a wide range of factors when making orders for costs; and because the discretion is broad, it is difficult successfully to appeal against such orders.

6.6 The general rule, all other things being equal, is that the successful party will recover its costs from the losing party.[5] Such outcome is not inevitable, nor will it necessarily be a full award. The court may make different orders, for example that only a proportion (or a stated amount) of the winning party's costs are to be paid, following an assessment of all of the circumstances of the case.[6]

Method of assessing the amount of costs

6.7 Where the court decides to exercise its discretion to order a party to pay costs, there will need to be an assessment of the amount of costs which are to be paid, unless they are agreed. A party will rarely if ever recover all the costs it has actually expended on a case. As a broad rule of thumb, a full costs award will mean recovery of about two thirds of actual costs incurred if costs are awarded on a standard basis.[7] The assessment of the amount to be recovered may be by way of a summary assessment by the judge at the end of a hearing, or by the process of detailed assessment which is contained in CPR Part 47. We say nothing further about detailed assessment, save that there are generally advantages to both parties in avoiding it and agreeing the level costs if possible, as the additional cost expended in assessment may not be justified by the outcome. As to summary assessment, it is important that practitioners bear the prospect of it in mind. The general rule is that it will be carried out at the conclusion of any hearing which has lasted not more than one day.[8] In order to carry out such an assessment, the court will need to be provided with a schedule setting out the costs which are claimed. Signed statements of costs must be filed and served on the other

1 See Middleton and Rowley *Cook on Costs 2020* (LexisNexis, 2019) and Friston *Civil Costs: Law and Practice* (3rd edn, Jordan Publishing Ltd, 2016).
2 Senior Courts Act 1981, s 51(1).
3 CPR 44.2(1).
4 Ibid, 44.2(4).
5 Ibid, 44.2(2)(a).
6 Ibid, 44.2(6)(a) and (b).
7 On the meaning of the standard basis, see **7.9** below.
8 CPR PD 44, para 9.2.

parties not less than 24 hours before the hearing, and must contain specified information.[9] Form N260 is routinely used. The court will take into account any failure to file and serve a statement in deciding what order to make about costs, including the costs of any further hearing or detailed assessment hearing that may be necessary as a result of that failure.[10]

6.8 In Planning Court cases, a summary assessment is likely to be carried out in cases where an *ex tempore* judgment is delivered at the end of the hearing (eg in oral permission hearings) or in very short appeals or challenges. Where judgment is reserved, the usual practice of the court is not to hear submissions on costs until judgment is delivered, and it is likely to order that the amount of costs is to be determined by detailed assessment if the parties are not able to agree a figure. In practice, when judgment is reserved a draft judgment is delivered in advance of the formal judgment being handed down. This gives parties a chance to agree an appropriate order or make submissions, usually in writing, as to what the orders as to costs should be.

Basis of assessment

6.9 The amount of costs which are payable may be assessed by the court on either the standard basis or the indemnity basis. An award of indemnity costs is usually made in order to mark the court's disapproval of the paying party's conduct before or during the litigation. There is a substantial body of case law addressing the circumstances in which indemnity costs should be ordered. Again, that is beyond the scope of this book, but a helpful summary is provided in *Civil Procedure* (*'The White Book'*) (Sweet and Maxwell). Where costs are assessed on the standard basis, the court will determine whether the costs were proportionately and reasonably incurred or proportionate and reasonable in amount.[11] Where the assessment is carried out on the indemnity basis the question of proportionality does not arise. The court will determine whether the costs were unreasonably incurred or unreasonable in amount.[12] An assessment on the indemnity basis will invariably mean that the paying party is ordered to pay a greater amount of costs than would be the case on the standard basis.

Relevance of conduct

6.10 In deciding what order to make about costs, one of the matters to which the court will have regard is the conduct of the parties, including conduct before as well as during the proceedings.[13] In particular, the extent to which the parties have followed relevant pre-action protocols will be taken into account. For judicial

9 CPR PD 44, para 9.5 makes provision for timing and contains a list of the information which must be included in a costs schedule.
10 CPR PD 44, para 9.6.
11 CPR 44.4(1)(a).
12 Ibid, 44.4(1)(b).
13 Ibid, 44.2(4)(a) and (5)(a).

review claims, the Pre-Action Protocol for Judicial Review should be followed.[14] In other cases, the Practice Direction on Pre-Action Conduct will be relevant. For example and depending on the facts of the case, it may be possible to argue that had the pre-action protocol procedure been followed the defendant would have taken some action which would have avoided the need to incur the costs of commencing proceedings. The claimant's recovery may therefore be limited even if the claimant is successful. The pre-action protocol has more limited utility in certain planning cases (for example challenges to the grant of planning permission) where the decision maker does not have jurisdiction to withdraw the decision which is complained of,[15] and in those types of case the extent to which it was complied with may carry limited weight in the court's decision on costs. However, in our experience use of the pre-action protocol is helpful even in such situations, as by assisting in defining the issues it may reduce costs and/or may persuade one side or the other that its case is weak and so to take the appropriate action.

6.11 A further conduct-related issue that may arise in judicial review claims in the Planning Court is the failure of the defendant to file a timely acknowledgment of service in accordance with CPR r 54.8. Although a defendant may still participate in the hearing of the substantive claim (if permission is granted),[16] the court may take into account the failure to file an acknowledgment of service when determining the issue of costs.[17] The obvious rationale for this rule is that costs will be incurred in the substantive hearing which might have been avoided, in whole or in part, had the defendant put forward its arguments at the permission stage.

6.12 Parties are expected to consider alternative dispute resolution in all proceedings, although the opportunities for that may also be limited in planning challenges where the decision maker has no power to withdraw its decision. However, it should not be ignored in an appropriate case. More helpful guidance is provided in section 10.2 of Fordham *Judicial Review Handbook*.[18]

Costs against non-parties

6.13 The court has power to award costs against non-parties under s 51 of the Senior Courts Act 1981; however, it has been said that such an order 'will

14 See further discussion on this in Chapter 3 – Preparing and Pursuing Claims.

15 *R (Gleeson) v Secretary of State for Communities and Local Government* [2014] PTSR 1226, [2014] EWCA Civ 1118, at [23–25]; applied in *R (Thornton Hall Hotel Ltd) v Wirral Metropolitan Borough Council* [2018] EWHC 560 (Admin) at [30] (although not on appeal, at [2019] EWCA Civ 737, which upheld the judgment of Kerr J below). See further on this issue the discussion in Chapter 3.

16 But not the permission hearing: CPR 54.9(1)(a).

17 CPR 54.9(2).

18 (6th edn, Hart Publishing, 2012). At the time of writing the 7th edition is due for publication in March 2021.

always be exceptional',[19] and an application for an order against a non-party should be treated with 'considerable caution'.[20] The critical factor in each case 'is the nature and degree of [the non-party's] connection with the proceedings.'[21] A distinction has generally been drawn between those with no personal interest in the litigation, who do not stand to benefit from it and do not seek to control its course (where an order would not normally be made), and non-parties who not only fund the proceedings but also control or will benefit from them (where an order is more likely to be made). In the latter case the non-party is 'not so much facilitating access to justice by the party funded as himself gaining access to justice for his own purposes. He himself is 'the real party' to the litigation'.[22] If that is the case, it will 'normally provide strong grounds for making an order that the [non-party] bear some or all of the other side's costs if the litigation is unsuccessful'.[23]

6.14 The Criminal Justice and Courts Act 2015 contains provisions specifically for judicial review cases which allow for the amendment of the Civil Procedure Rules which, if and when brought into force,[24] may facilitate an increase in the extent to which the court is prepared to make orders against non-parties. Claimants will be required to provide information about the financing of the claim as one of the conditions for the court granting permission to apply for judicial review.[25] The claimant may be required to give information about the source, nature and extent of financial resources which are available or likely to be available to meet liabilities arising in connection with the application. If the claimant is a body corporate that is unable to demonstrate that it is likely to be able to meet such liabilities, it may be required to provide information

19 Although this has been said to mean simply that there should be something taking the case 'outside the ordinary run of cases where parties pursue or defend claims for their own benefit and at their own expense': *Dymocks Franchise Systems (NSW) Pty Ltd v Todd* [2004] UKPC 39 [2004] 1 WLR 2807 at [2815]; applied in *Various Claimants v Giambrone & Law (a firm) and others* [2019] 4 WLR 7, at[11] (appeal outstanding at time of writing). Lord Reed in *XYZ v Travellers Insurance Company Ltd* [2019] UKSC 48 in obiter comments has called into question the whole basis of any test of significance in powerful obiter remarks, see in particular at [112], albeit in a case which concerned insurers.

20 *Symphony Group plc v Hodgson* [1993] 3 WLR 830 at [841].

21 *Deutsche Bank AG v Sebastian Holdings Inc and another* [2016] EWCA Civ 23, at [21].

22 *Dymocks Franchise Systems (NSW) Pty Ltd v Todd* [2004] UKPC 39 [2004] 1 WLR 2807 at [2815].

23 *Deutsche Bank AG v Sebastian Holdings Inc and another* [2016] EWCA Civ 23, at [25].

24 Although, after 5 years, they still have not been. The government stated on 13 March 2020 that there were 'no plans to bring into force ss.85 and 86', noting also that the Aarhus Committee 'finds we meet the [Aarhus Convention's] requirements… as regards costs orders against funders of litigation': paragraph 10, *UK Government Oral Statement in Relation to the Compliance Committee's Review of the UK's 2nd Annual Progress Report on Decision VI/8k*. This was a bolder statement than in September 2019, when the government said there were no plans to bring the provisions into force 'in the foreseeable future', as recorded at paragraph 82 in Aarhus Convention Compliance Committee, *Second Progress Review of the Implementation of Decision VI/8k on Compliance by the United Kingdom of Great Britain and Northern Ireland with its Obligations under the Convention* (6 March 2020). Both sources are available at www.unece.org/environmental-policy/conventions/public-participation/aarhus-convention/tfwg/envppcc/implementation-of-decisions-of-the-meeting-of-the-parties-on-compliance-by-individual-parties/sixth-meeting-of-the-parties-2017/decision-vi8k-concerning-united-kingdom.html.

25 CJCA 2015, s 85(1), amending s 31(3) of the Senior Courts Act 1981.

about its members and their ability to provide financial support.[26] The rules may provide that only a person whose financial support exceeds or is likely to exceed a level set out in the rules need be identified under these provisions.[27] However, at present there seems to be no plan for the government to bring the relevant sections into force.[28]

6.15 The financial information provided pursuant to these provisions must be taken into account by the court when it determines the issue of costs,[29] and the court *must* consider whether to order costs to be paid by a person, other than a party, who is identified as providing (or likely or able to provide) financial support for the purposes of the proceedings.[30]

Partial success

6.16 CPR 44.2 specifically contemplates a situation where a party has succeeded on only part of its case, and provides that this is one of the factors that the court may take into account when deciding what order to make on costs.[31] This situation may arise quite frequently in public law challenges, where claims are brought on a variety of different grounds, only one of which needs to succeed in order to invalidate the decision which is challenged. A partial award of costs in these circumstances reflects the fact that costs have been incurred as a result of the claimant pursuing grounds which ultimately did not succeed.[32]

Special methods of funding

6.17 Finally, we draw attention to the existence of CFAs and Legal Aid in terms of funding proceedings. Guidance in respect of CFAs can be found in *Cook on Costs*,[33] and readers are advised to consult the Legal Aid Agency or a solicitor for the up to date position on public funding.

26 CJCA 2015, s 85(2), inserting new s 31(3A) into the Senior Courts Act 1981. The purpose of this latter requirement is undoubtedly to seek to deter the increasing use of limited companies to act as claimants, shielding the individuals concerned from the cost risks that they would otherwise face if bringing the claim in an individual capacity.

27 CJCA 2015, s 85(2), inserting new s 31(3B) into the Senior Courts Act 1981.

28 See paragraph 10, *UK Government Oral Statement in Relation to the Compliance Committee's Review of the UK's 2nd Annual Progress Report on Decision VI/8k* (n 24 above).

29 CJCA 2015, s 86(1)–(2).

30 Ibid, s 86(3).

31 CPR 44.2(4)(b).

32 The amount of time and costs which have been expended in dealing with the unsuccessful grounds will often be the determinative factor. Two cases at opposite ends of the spectrum are *R (Essex County Council) v Secretary of State for Education* [2012] ELR 383, [2012] EWHC 1460 (Admin), where the Secretary of State was ordered to pay only 50% of the claimant's costs (the majority of time and costs having been incurred on the two unsuccessful grounds) and *R (Luton Borough Council) v Secretary of State for Education* [2011] ELR 222, [2011] EWHC 556 (Admin) where the claimants recovered all of their costs despite failing on a number of grounds, because the additional grounds had not significantly increased the expenditure of costs or time.

33 Middleton and Rowley *Cook on Costs 2020* (LexisNexis, 2019).

C JUDICIAL REVIEWS IN THE PLANNING COURT – COSTS AT THE PERMISSION STAGE

6.18 Claims issued in or transferred to the Planning Court typically require the permission of the court to proceed. Permission will only be granted if the court is satisfied that the claimant's grounds of challenge are arguable. The requirement for permission is common to all judicial review claims, and also applies to certain statutory challenges including under ss 288 and 289 Town and Country Planning Act 1990 and s 113 of the Planning and Compulsory Purchase Act 2004. Particular rules apply to the determination of costs at the permission stage.

Where permission is granted

6.19 Where the court grants permission for a judicial review claim to proceed to a substantive hearing or grants permission to appeal (whether on the papers or at an oral hearing), the general rule is that the costs incurred at the permission stage will be the claimant's costs in the case. This is the order which is deemed to have been made in the absence of any express mention of costs in the order granting permission, unless the court makes a different order on the issue.[34] The Planning Court retains the discretion, as always, to make a different order for the costs of the permission application if that is appropriate in the circumstances of the case; although this is rare.[35] The effect of the order which is deemed to have been made is that the claimant/appellant will be awarded his costs for the permission stage if he ultimately succeeds in the claim/appeal, but the defendant will not recover the costs it has incurred on the permission application if the claim fails. Defendants may consider it worth seeking a different costs order, such as costs reserved[36] or costs in the case[37] so that if they succeed in resisting the claim they can recover their costs of this stage. But they would need to justify that possibility, for example by arguing that they were required to attend the hearing for some reason.

Where permission is refused

Permission refused on the papers – costs of acknowledgment of service

6.20 Where a judicial review claim is refused on the papers, the claimant will usually be ordered to pay the costs which were incurred by the defendant

34 CPR 44.10(2)(a) and (b).

35 Situations where it may be appropriate to make a different order include where permission has been granted on a significantly narrower basis than was sought; or where the defendant/respondent's conduct at the permission stage has warranted particular criticism.

36 The determination of reserved costs will take place at an unspecified later date; it will usually fall to one of the parties to raise the issue at the appropriate stage.

37 The party which is successful at the conclusion of the proceedings will be awarded the costs which were 'in the case', ie they follow the outcome of the case.

in filing its acknowledgment of service and summary grounds of defence.[38] The procedure under CPR Part 54 obliges the defendant to file an acknowledgment of service and summary grounds for defending the claim if he wishes to take part at the permission stage; it is therefore considered to be fair to award the defendant the costs of so doing if the claim is successfully resisted at the permission stage.[39] However, it should also be noted that the courts do not expect 'substantial expense' to be incurred at this stage and the level of award should reflect that.[40] In our experience there is significant variation between judges as to whether they will award costs on paper refusals and, if so, how they approach quantification. It is common to make provision for the claimant to make written submissions as to quantum before a final order is made.

6.21 The Court of Appeal has suggested that the general rule – that the defendant recovers its costs of acknowledging service from claimant – may not apply where the defendant is in breach of the pre-action protocol.[41] This is presumably because proper compliance with the pre-action protocol might have dissuaded the applicant from proceeding with the claim, which would in turn avoid costs being incurred at the permission stage. Pre-action conduct is of course a matter to which the court is explicitly required to have regard under CPR 44.4(3)(a)(i): see above.

6.22 The Court of Appeal has also held that there is no general limit on the number of parties who may be entitled to the costs of filing an acknowledgement of service and filing summary grounds; the claimant may therefore be liable to multiple parties.[42] This is subject to the general rule that costs must be reasonable and proportionate; it may not be proportionate, for instance, for an interested party simply to duplicate the defendant's submissions.

Permission refused following oral reconsideration

6.23 The usual rule is that neither defendants nor interested parties will recover their costs of attending an oral permission hearing. It is embodied in paragraphs 8.5 and 8.6 of Practice Direction 54A, which provide that defendants and interested parties need not attend oral permission hearings unless the court directs otherwise, but that if they do attend the court will not generally make an order for costs against the claimant.[43]

38 *Re Leach* [2001] EWHC 445 (Admin), affirmed as applicable under the CPR by *R (Mount Cook Land Ltd) v Westminster City Council* [2004] 2 P & CR 22 and, more recently, in *Campaign to Protect Rural England (Kent Branch) v Secretary of State for Communities and Local Government* [2019] EWCA Civ 1230.

39 *R (Mount Cook Land Ltd) v Westminster City Council* [2004] 2 P & CR 22, at [54].

40 *R (Davey) v Aylesbury Vale District Council* [2007] EWCA Civ 1166 at [32]–[33].

41 *R (Mount Cook Land Ltd) v Westminster City Council* [2004] 2 P & CR 22, at [76(1)].

42 *Campaign to Protect Rural England (Kent Branch) v Secretary of State for Communities and Local Government* [2019] EWCA Civ 1230, at [20]–[25].

43 At [8.5] and [8.6].

6.24 The leading case on this issue is *R (Mount Cook Land Ltd) v Westminster City Council.*[44] The Court of Appeal confirmed (at paragraph 76(2)) that the general rule is as now stated in paragraphs 8.5 and 8.6 of PD54A. There is an obligation on defendants to take the initial procedural step of filing an acknowledgment of service under CPR 54.8. Thus, as noted above, they should recover their costs for so doing; but different considerations apply to the costs of defendants who choose voluntarily to attend oral permission hearings and argue their cases.[45]

6.25 Although the Court of Appeal reiterated the general rule, it also made clear that judges could exercise their broad costs discretion to depart from the general rule where there were exceptional circumstances which justified doing so. Examples of features that might amount to exceptional circumstances were said to include: (i) the hopelessness of the claim; (ii) the persistence of the claimant after being alerted to the facts/law demonstrating the hopelessness of the claim; (iii) the extent to which the claimant has sought to abuse the judicial review procedure for collateral ends;[46] (iv) whether, as a result of the deployment of full argument and documentary evidence by both sides, the unsuccessful claimant has effectively had an early substantive hearing of the claim.[47] The use by the claimant of substantial resources to pursue an unfounded claim, and which are available to meet a costs order, was also said to be a relevant factor in the exercise of the court's discretion.[48]

6.26 Other instances where costs for attendance are regularly awarded include where the claimant is seeking any form of interim relief – in effect the defendant has been brought to court.

6.27 In many cases defendants attend permission hearings in the knowledge they are unlikely to recover costs on the basis that if they can assist in securing dismissal of the claim at that stage the relatively minor cost of such attendance is worthwhile expending.

D STATUTORY CHALLENGES IN THE PLANNING COURT – COSTS AT THE PERMISSION STAGE

6.28 The Criminal Justice and Courts Act 2015 introduced a new permission stage for statutory appeals brought under s 288 of the Town and Country Planning Act 1990 and s 113 of the Planning and Compulsory Purchase Act 2004. CPR Practice Direction 8C governs the procedure for both types of appeal.

44 [2004] 2 P & CR 22.
45 See *Mount Cook* at [74].
46 For example in *Mount Cook* itself the claimant was clearly deploying its considerable resources to use the public law route (as well as other legal proceedings) to bring pressure on a third party to surrender its lease or submit to the claimant's development proposals.
47 At [76(5]).
48 At [76(6)].

As in judicial review, respondents wishing to take part in the proceedings must file an acknowledgment of service but need not attend an oral permission hearing unless the court orders otherwise.[49] In practice, the courts therefore apply the *Mount Cook* principles applicable in judicial review.[50] If the claimant is refused permission on the papers, there is no general limit on the number of defendants and interested parties who may claim their reasonable and proportionate costs of acknowledging service and filing summary grounds from the claimant.[51]

6.29 Section 289 appeals involve different considerations. In *R v Secretary of State for Wales ex p Rozhon*,[52] the Court of Appeal held that the costs of the oral hearing to determine whether to grant leave to appeal on a point of law under s 289 would normally follow the event. Therefore, where leave was refused, the unsuccessful applicant would be ordered to pay the costs of the respondent's attendance at the hearing.[53] This general rule can be contrasted with the rule in judicial review proceedings, where the respondent's costs of attending an oral permission hearing are not generally recoverable. It is apparent from the judgment in *Rozhon* that this difference in practice is attributable to the fact that: (i) s 289 appeals are not initially considered on the papers and an oral hearing is obligatory, and parties served with the s 289 appeal are entitled to attend;[54] whereas there is an initial paper consideration of applications for leave to apply for judicial review, and at the time *Rozhon* was decided this paper stage usually took place without notice to defendants.

6.30 It will be apparent that the judicial review procedure has changed significantly since *Rozhon* was decided; in particular, the pre-action protocol is designed to ensure the early involvement of the defendant, and the defendant is required to file an acknowledgment of service and summary grounds in order to oppose the claim. It is therefore apparent that part of the rationale underlying the decision in that case is no longer applicable. Nevertheless, currently *Rozhon* remains good law and was referred to by the Court of Appeal in the *Mount Cook* case, where Auld LJ contrasted the new regime for costs in judicial review claims under the CPR with the position in s 289 appeals as explained in *Rozhon*.[55]

49 PD 8C, paras 5.2; 8.1–8.2.

50 As acknowledged by Laing J in *Elghanian v Secretary of State for Communities and Local Government* (unreported, 18 April 2018) at [16].

51 *Campaign to Protect Rural England (Kent Branch) v Secretary of State for Communities and Local Government* [2019] EWCA Civ 1230, at [26-36].

52 (1993) 91 LGR 667.

53 *Rozhon* was applied more recently by Hickinbottom J in the later case of *Williams v Secretary of State for Communities and Local Government* [2009] EWHC 475 (Admin) at [93–100], where it was held that 'the event' for these purposes was the outcome of the appeal itself, in a case where leave had been granted but the substantive appeal had failed. The judge therefore held that the respondent was entitled to the costs it had incurred at the permission stage. Care should be taken with this authority, because the judge's conclusions on this issue were expressly made without hearing full argument on the issue; it was clear to him that it was 'not the case for authoritatively deciding this issue as one of principle' ([98]).

54 This remains the position; the rules are contained in CPR PD 52D, para 26.1.

55 At [70]. See also *Williams*, (n 3); and *Elghanian v Secretary of State for Communities and Local Government* (unreported, 18 April 2018) at [12].

That position may change, but, if so, it is perhaps more likely to come about by amendment to the CPR.

E COSTS FOLLOWING DISCONTINUANCE/CONSENT TO RELIEF

6.31 As with all civil litigation, claims in the Planning Court do not always proceed to a final hearing, even where permission has been granted (in cases where that is a requirement). There are a wide variety of reasons why that might be the case.

Discontinuance

6.32 First, the claimant may have a change of heart and unilaterally discontinue the claim in accordance with the procedure set out in CPR Part 38. In such cases the claimant will be liable for the defendant's costs unless the court orders otherwise: see CPR 38.6. In many cases the claimant may be able to secure a more favourable costs outcome by negotiation, but they cannot count on it. If there is a costs dispute, the court will normally seek to have it resolved by written submissions, which is indeed the general practice when cases do not proceed to a full hearing.

Settled or withdrawn claims

6.33 Although the Civil Procedure Rules make no express provision for the 'withdrawal' of a claim (as opposed to its discontinuance under Part 38), there is a recognised practice of withdrawing proceedings within the Administrative Court, and therefore within the Planning Court, which has been recognised judicially.[56] Alternatively, the parties may agree to either the dismissal of the claim, or the quashing of the decision, by consent, thereby avoiding a substantive hearing.

Where agreement reached on all issues, including costs

6.34 Where the parties reach agreement that the case should not proceed, it is likely that agreement will also have been reached as to the appropriate order for costs. In those circumstances, the consent order which will be filed with the court and which disposes of the proceedings will also include the agreed order for costs. The parties are required to file two copies of the signed draft order together with a short statement which explains why the order is justified and referring to any authorities and statutory provisions relied upon.[57] If the court is satisfied that the order should be made, it will be made without the need for attendance by the

56 Practice Statement (Administrative Court: Uncontested Proceedings) [2008] 1 WLR 1377 at [1377G–H].

57 Ibid at [1377C–D]. This is usually contained in the recitals to the draft order.

parties. If the court is not satisfied on the basis of the information provided by the parties that the order can properly be made, the proceedings will be listed for a hearing.[58] If the proceedings are being settled on terms which grant a remedy to the claimant but before the question of permission has been determined, the draft order will need to make provision for permission to be granted in order to give the court jurisdiction to grant a remedy.

Where no agreement reached on costs

6.35 These issues were considered in detail by the Court of Appeal in *R (M) v Croydon LBC*,[59] where changes in the law by virtue of a Supreme Court judgment and the approach of the courts to expert evidence of the type considered in the case were instrumental in leading the defendant to concede the claim. The court reviewed earlier cases on costs on settlement of judicial review claims,[60] and identified three general principles, being that any decision relating to costs is primarily a matter for the discretion of the trial judge, that the general rule is that a successful party can look to the unsuccessful one for his costs and that how a party is funded will rarely if ever make a difference to that party's right to recover costs. It gave guidance as to the approach the courts would take in three distinct types of case:

(1) In cases where the terms of the settlement are such that the claimant has been wholly successful, the claimant should normally recover all of his costs, unless there is some good reason for ordering otherwise. The fact that the defendant has acted realistically by settling rather than proceeding to a full hearing was not a basis for refusing to award costs to the claimant; the point of the pre-action protocols is to encourage early resolution of claims and defendants should concede before the claim is issued if they wish to avoid costs.

(2) Where the claimant has only been partially successful under the terms of the settlement, the court may or may not be in a position to form a view as to the appropriate costs order, depending on the circumstances of the case. The factors that the court would consider when determining the appropriate costs order in this type of case would include the reasonableness of the claimant pursuing the unsuccessful elements of the claim; how important the unsuccessful elements were in comparison with the successful elements; and the impact of the unsuccessful elements on the overall costs of the proceedings. No order for costs may be the fairest outcome. In some cases it might be helpful to consider who would have won if the matter had proceeded to trial, if tolerably clear.[61]

58 Ibid at [1377D–E].

59 [2012] 1 WLR 2607.

60 *R (Boxall) v Waltham Forest LBC* (2000) 4 CCLR 258; *R (Scott) v Hackney LBC* [2009] EWCA Civ 217 and *R (Bahta) v Secretary of State for the Home Department* [2011] 5 Costs LR 857.

61 As had happened in *Boxall*.

(3) Where the terms of the settlement did not actually reflect the claimant's claim, it would often be very difficult for the court to determine whether there was a 'successful' party and, if so, who it was. There would be an even stronger argument for making no order for costs as the default position; although in some cases it might be sensible to look at the underlying claims and to consider whether it was tolerably clear who would have won if the matter had not been settled.

6.36 The court also emphasised that it was in the interests of both parties to settle the issue of costs. The court has jurisdiction but no obligation to resolve freestanding disputes about costs, and it is necessary to have regard to the proportionality of the work and cost involved in making submissions, and the material the judge is asked to consider, to the amounts at stake. There is a risk that the court may conclude that no order can be made in favour of either party without disproportionate expenditure of judicial time, and no order for costs would be appropriate in such cases.[62] In this regard, the courts strongly discourage satellite litigation where the costs issue requires determination of the underlying merits of the substantive claim.[63] There is also limited if any scope to resolve conflicting evidence and the production of witness evidence going to costs issues would be inappropriate.[64]

6.37 Sometimes a defendant takes action which avoids the need for the claim to proceed to a hearing. For example, it may re-determine a decision in such a way that the claimant no longer wishes to pursue its claim. A similar approach is taken to that where the defendant consents to relief (ie the court may need to examine the extent to which the claimant has been successful in obtaining the relief sought), but regard has to be had to the circumstances. It may be that the defendant's re-determination of its decision was without prejudice to the defendant's initial stance and so the proper order is no order as to costs. Causation is a relevant and potentially decisive factor in the exercise of the court's discretion here: the fact that the claimant has obtained the relief sought does not necessarily mean that the existence of the proceedings has caused or contributed to that result, which may have happened anyway.[65] On the other hand, success may mean obtaining a result earlier than it would otherwise have been obtained.[66] However, the reality is that if a defendant takes action which avoids the challenge, it will probably be for the defendant to justify why it should not pay the costs. If, however, proceedings are avoided as a result of actions taken by a third party, then it is more likely that costs will lie where they fall.

6.38 As noted above, in almost every case, the court is likely to determine any disputes on the papers and it will favour short, succinct submissions: see the

62 At [47] and [77].

63 *Khan v Secretary of State for the Home Department* [2018] EWCA Civ 1684, at [50] and [69], which also confirmed that *R(M)* remains the leading authority on the issue –at [45].

64 *R (Parveen) v Redbridge LBC* [2020] EWCA Civ 194, at [40].

65 *R (Parveen) v Redbridge LBC* [2020] EWCA Civ 194, at [31].

66 Ibid, at [37].

guidance at paras 7-8 of Annex 5 to the Administrative Court Judicial Review Guide (July 2020).

F COSTS UPON FINAL DETERMINATION

Exercise of discretion in judicial review/planning appeals

6.39 As noted above, costs usually follow the event. If the claimant wins, then the order is usually straightforward and will cover all the costs the claimant has incurred in bringing the proceedings, subject to the issue of assessment referred to above. However, if the defendant wins then consideration has to be given to a number of factors.

6.40 In *Davey v Aylesbury Vale*[67] the Court of Appeal gave useful guidance as to the approach to be taken in such circumstances, see Sedley LJ, at paragraph 21, as read with the Master of the Rolls' comments at paragraphs 29–31. The guidance can be summarised as follows:

(1) Whilst costs ordinarily follow the event and the onus is on a claimant who has lost to show that some different approach should be adopted, on the conclusion of full judicial review proceedings in a defendant's favour, the nature and purpose of the particular claim is relevant to the exercise of the judge's discretion as to costs. In contrast to a judicial review claim brought wholly or mainly for commercial or proprietary reasons, a claim brought partly or wholly in the public interest, albeit unsuccessful, may properly result in a restricted or no order for costs.

(2) If awarding costs against the claimant, the judge should consider whether they are to include preparation costs in addition to acknowledgment costs. It will be for the defendant to justify these in the sense that it was reasonable and proportionate to incur such costs. There may be no sufficient reason why such costs, if incurred, should be recoverable, but the onus would be on the claimant to show why certain costs should not be recovered.

(3) It is highly desirable that these questions should be dealt with by the trial judge and left to the costs judge only in relation to the reasonableness of individual items.

(4) If at the conclusion of such proceedings the judge makes an undifferentiated order for costs in a defendant's favour: (i) the order has to be regarded as including any reasonably incurred preparation costs; but (ii) as noted above, costs of attending a permission hearing will not be recovered.

6.41 Whilst such guidance dates from 2007, in our view it is still considered applicable,[68] although it is important to note that it pre-dates changes to the CPR

67 [2007] EWCA Civ 1166, [2008] 1 WLR 878.

68 See, eg, *R (Wilson and Others) v Prime Minister* [2019] EWCA Civ 304 at [68] and [72] and, in the planning field, *Dignity Funerals Limited v Breckland District Council and Another* [2017] EWHC 1492 (Admin) at [124].

in 2013 to emphasise the importance of proportionality in the assessment of costs as well as the changes giving effect to the Aarhus cap.[69]

Multiple defendants and interested parties

6.42 In many planning cases there will be more than one defendant, or there will be one or more interested parties. However, the starting point is that only one set of costs will be allowed. The Court of Appeal set out the position in *Bolton Metropolitan District Council v Secretary of State for Environment (Practice Note)*[70] (and note that there is no difference in practice whether the first defendant is the Secretary of State or a planning authority):

(1) The Secretary of State, when successful in defending his decision, will normally be entitled to the whole of his costs. He should not be required to share his award of costs by apportionment, whether by agreement with other parties, or by further order of the court.

(2) The developer will not normally be entitled to his costs unless he can show that there was likely to be a separate issue on which he was entitled to be heard, that is to say an issue not covered by counsel for the Secretary of State; or unless he has an interest which requires separate representation. The mere fact that he is the developer will not of itself justify a second set of costs in every case.

(3) A second set of costs is more likely to be awarded at first instance than in the Court of Appeal or Supreme Court, by which time the issues should have crystallised, and the extent to which there are indeed separate interests should have been clarified.

(4) An award of a third set of costs will rarely be justified, even if there are in theory three or more separate interests.

6.43 The court will have regard to all factors including the importance of the case, whether a party has a separate interest and the extent to which different arguments are advanced and/or the party can assist the court. The matter is very much for the court's discretion and, even if exercised, may only result in a partial award of costs in respect of particular costs, eg a witness statement, or up to a certain stage in the proceedings, ie when it became clear that the defendant would defend.

6.44 Third parties can have costs awarded against them, but that is very rare. Examples might include if they had behaved in such a way as to cause further costs to be unreasonably incurred or had singlehandedly and unsuccessfully pursued a particular line of argument.

69 As noted by Coulson LJ in *Campaign to Protect Rural England v Secretary of State for Communities and Local Government* [2019] EWCA Civ 1230, at [45].

70 [1995] 1 WLR 1176 at [1178F–1179A].

Part 36 offers in judicial reviews

6.45 Although it may rarely arise in Planning Court cases, CPR Part 36 does apply in judicial review cases, as the licensing case of *R (Hemming) v Westminster City Council* demonstrates.[71] Many planning cases will not fit within the confines of Part 36, but in such cases 'without prejudice offers save as to costs' may well be effective. In either case, both the claimant and defendant should give consideration to such measures in order to seek to limit their liability to adverse costs orders, or to maximise any award of costs in their favour.

Interveners

6.46 In some cases, parties not directly involved in a case may wish to make submissions on matters, usually of principle. For example NGOs, such as Friends of the Earth, may wish to input into certain environmental cases. It is unlikely that interveners will feature in Planning Court cases. Intervention is more common in appeals.

6.47 Where interveners do appear, the general rule prior to the commencement of s 87 of the Criminal Justice and Courts Act 2015 was that they would bear the costs of the intervention and would not be ordered to pay the costs of any other party. This reflected the fact that the role of the intervener is to assist the court on broader issues of policy and public interest, rather than advocating in favour of either party's arguments in the particular case in which they intervene.

6.48 The position has changed under s 87 of the Criminal Justice and Courts Act 2015. Sections 87(3) and (4) prevent the court from ordering another party to pay the intervener's costs unless there are exceptional circumstances that make it appropriate to do so. Sections 87(5)–(8) allow for the court to order an intervener to pay costs which another party has incurred as a result of the intervener's involvement in that stage of the proceedings. The power can only be exercised if another party makes an application. The court must be satisfied that: (a) the intervener has acted, in substance, as the sole or principal applicant, defendant, appellant or respondent; (b) the intervener's evidence and representations, taken as a whole, have not been of significant assistance to the court; (c) a significant part of the intervener's evidence and representations relates to matters that it is not necessary for the court to consider in order to resolve the issues that are the subject of the stage in the proceedings; or (d) the intervener has behaved unreasonably. If one of those conditions is met, the court must make a costs order unless there are exceptional circumstances that make it inappropriate to do so (having regard to any criteria which are specified in rules of court).[72]

71 [2013] EWCA Civ 591, at [139]–[144]. The case was subsequently appealed to the Supreme Court, but not on this point.

72 No criteria have yet been specified by CPR 46.15.

G PROTECTIVE COSTS ORDERS AND COST CAPPING

Summary

6.49 A protective costs order ('PCO') or cost capping order is an order which limits or removes a party's potential liability to pay costs associated with the claim. There are three situations in which orders of this nature may arise in the Planning Court. First, in 'Aarhus Convention claims', the CPR makes provision for fixed costs for both claimants and defendants. Secondly, the Criminal Justice and Courts Act 2015 makes provision for cost capping in judicial review claims. Lastly, common law '*Corner House*' principles currently still apply to appeals and statutory applications in the Planning Court, and may apply to other cases which do not fall within either CPR 45 or the 2015 Act. Each of these situations is addressed in this section, beginning with the *Corner House* principles as they were first in time.

Background and Corner House

6.50 The concept of an order limiting or removing a claimant's potential liability to pay the costs of other parties within public law litigation was first recognised in the non-planning case of *R v Lord Chancellor ex p Child Poverty Action Group.*[73] Such orders are based on the fact that public law litigation is often pursued in the public interest rather than for private or commercial reasons. Claimants face the risk of significant costs orders being made against them if their public law claims do not succeed, and the courts developed the protective costs order ('PCO)' in order to mitigate this risk.

6.51 In *R (Corner House Research) v Secretary of State for Trade and Industry*[74] the Court of Appeal confirmed that a PCO could be made at any stage in proceedings, and on such conditions as the court thinks fit. The court laid down criteria which would be applied when determining an application for a PCO. The criteria are as follows:

(i) the issues raised are of general public importance;[75]

(ii) the public interest requires that those issues should be resolved;[76]

73 [1999] 1 WLR 347.

74 [2005] 1 WLR 2600, [2005] EWCA Civ 192.

75 Cases which clarify the true construction of a statutory provision which applies to and potentially affects the whole population are of general public importance. An issue which is of public importance but which affects only a section of the population may still be of 'general' public importance, although it will not be in the first rank of general public importance. It may be relevant to consider the number of people potentially affected (directly or indirectly) by the outcome: *R (Compton) v Wiltshire Primary Care Trust (Practice Note)* [2009] 1 WLR 1436, [2008] EWCA Civ 749.

76 The court must ask whether the issues require resolution not generally but *in the instant* proceedings: *Maugham v Uber London Ltd* [2019] EWHC 391 (Ch) at [58]. There is an overlap between this requirement and the first requirement that the claim raises an issue of general public importance. Relevant factors may include the apparent level of public support or interest in the claim (*Compton*, at [21–22]) and the extent to which the issues have already been considered judicially (*Goodson v HM Coroner for Bedfordshire and Luton* [2006] CP Rep 6, [2005] EWCA Civ 1172).

(iii) the applicant has no private interest in the outcome of the case;[77]

(iv) having regard to the financial resources of the applicant and the respondent(s)[78] and to the amount of costs that are likely to be involved, it is fair and just to make the order; and

(v) if the order is not made the applicant will probably discontinue the proceedings and will be acting reasonably in doing so.[79]

It is for the court, in its discretion, to decide whether it is fair and just to make the order in the light of the considerations set out above. The Court of Appeal further held that it will be likely to enhance the merits of the application if those acting for the applicant do so on a pro bono basis.

6.52 Applications for *Corner House*-type PCOs should be made on the face of the claim form and supported by evidence, and any grounds for resisting such an order should be set out in the acknowledgement of service.[80] The issue will be considered on the papers; if the application is refused then the claimant may seek an oral reconsideration; but if a PCO is granted it should not be set aside in the absence of a compelling reason for doing so.[81] The Court of Appeal considered

77 In *Eweida v British Airways plc* [2010] 1 Costs LR 43 the Court of Appeal reviewed the authorities and held that the requirement that there should be no private interest remained good law. A line of cases which had been taken as stating otherwise (*Morgan v Hinton Organics (Wessex) Ltd* [2009] 2 P & CR 30, *R (Buglife: The Invertebrate Conservation Trust) v Thurrock Thames Gateway Development Corpn* [2009] Env LR 315 and *R (Bullmore) v West Hertfordshire Hospitals NHS Trust* [2007] EWHC 1350 (Admin) did not modify the principle on a proper analysis. The correct position appears to be that the fact that a claimant has a private interest would not necessarily and in all circumstances be fatal to a PCO application, but it is a factor to be taken into account when balancing the other *Corner House* criteria: *R (Litvinenko) v Secretary of State for the Home Department* [2013] EWHC 3135 (Admin), *R (Young) v Oxford City Council* [2012] EWCA Civ 46, *Austin v Miller Argent (South Wales) Ltd* [2015] 1 WLR 62, at [37]. A private interest is something more than feeling some degree of commitment to or intensity about the intended result of the proceedings, since people do not bring legal proceedings about matters to which they are indifferent: *Dulgheriu v Ealing LBC* [2018] EWHC 1302 (Admin) at [44].

78 The claimant must show that it would not be reasonable for him to run the risk of a costs order being made against him without the protection of a PCO. In *R (British Union for the Abolition of Vivisection) v Secretary of State for the Home Department* [2006] EWHC 250 (Admin) a PCO was granted in favour of a claimant with an annual income exceeding £1 million, where the court concluded that the claimant would be likely to discontinue to proceedings, and would be acting reasonably in so doing. When considering financial resources, the court can consider whether the applicant's solicitors have agreed to support their client by indemnifying him against any liability for the costs and disbursements of his opponent: *R (Roszowski) v Secretary of State for the Home Department* [2017] EWCA Civ 412, at [23]. It can also consider whether a claim brought by an applicant of limited means is in fact financed by an organisation with considerable financial resources: *Dulgheriu v Ealing LBC* [2018] EWHC 1302 (Admin) at [63].

79 In *R (Roszowski) v Secretary of State for the Home Department* [2017] EWCA Civ 412, at [16]–[22] this was read more exactingly, as a requirement that the applicant *would* (not would probably) discontinue.

80 *Corner House,* at [78].

81 Ibid, at [79].

that indemnity costs should be ordered in response to an unmeritorious application to set aside a PCO granted on the papers.[82]

Aarhus Convention: overview of relevant provisions

6.53 The Convention on Access to Information, Public Participation in Decision Making and Access to Justice in Environmental Matters ('the Aarhus Convention') was signed in 1998. It has paved the way for a dramatic increase in the use of PCOs to limit the potential costs liability of claimants in cases involving environmental matters.

6.54 Article 9 of the Convention deals with access to justice in environmental matters. Articles 9(1) and (2) require that the public has access to legal proceedings to determine issues relating to the provision of environmental information, and to challenge decisions, acts or omissions on proposed activities which are subject to public participation provisions. They ensure that the public are able to enforce the substantive obligations contained in Articles 4 and 6 respectively.

6.55 Article 9(3) is of broader application and provides that, in addition to the procedures referred to in Articles 9(1) and (2),

> 'each party shall ensure that, where they meet the criteria, if any, laid down in its national law, members of the public have access to administrative or judicial procedures to challenge acts and omissions by private persons and public authorities which contravene provisions of its national law relating to the environment.'

6.56 Although 'environment' is not defined in the Aarhus Convention, the definition of 'environmental information' provides an indication of the breadth of the concept. According to this definition, administrative measures likely to affect the state of the land are classed as 'environmental'. This appears to include most, if not all, planning matters.[83]

6.57 The concept of 'national law relating to the environment' is also a broad one, and in the UK it includes the town and country planning system, through which Parliament has chosen to implement much of the UK's environmental protection. This is the case notwithstanding that much of the detail of the system is contained in policies rather than in statutory regulation.[84]

82 Ibid.

83 This was conceded by the Secretary of State in *Venn v Secretary of State for Communities and Local Government* [2014] EWCA Civ 1539, at [11] and endorsed by the court at [18].

84 *Venn* at [15]–[17]. Art 9(3) has been held to include a challenge to the Secretary of State's decision to authorise a private company to enter onto land for the purposes of site investigation prior to the construction of a new nuclear power station: *R (Dowley) v Secretary of State for Communities and Local Government* [2016] EWHC 2618 (Admin) at [98]–[102].

6.58 Article 9(4) requires that the legal proceedings referred to in Articles 9(1)–(3) must provide adequate and effective remedies, be fair, equitable timely and not prohibitively expensive. The requirement that environmental challenges must not be 'prohibitively expensive' has underpinned the expansion in cost protection in this area.

Aarhus Convention: application

6.59 The principles of Articles 9(1), (2) and (4), but not Article 9(3), of the Aarhus Convention have been implemented in certain EU directives and then transposed into UK law. Where the claim concerns decisions covered by those Directives, the court's general discretion in relation to costs has been held to be insufficient to provide adequate certainty that proceedings are not prohibitively expensive.[85] Such certainty is required at the outset of cases, and must not be dependent on discretion post-determination. In *Garner v Elmbridge BC*[86] the Court of Appeal held that in such Directive cases the *Corner House* requirements for the claim to raise an issue of general public importance, which the public interest required to be resolved, cannot apply to justify the refusal of a PCO.[87]

6.60 In addition to the implementation of Aarhus principles in EU and thus UK law, Articles 9(3) and 9(4) have been incorporated (at least in part) by reference in CPR Part 45, which makes provision for a fixed costs regime for 'Aarhus Convention claims'. The relevant provisions of CPR Part 45 are discussed in greater detail below. Where CPR Part 45 applies, costs are determined in accordance with its rules rather than by reference to *Corner House* criteria.

6.61 In cases falling within the scope of Article 9(3), but where the claimant is not relying on any provision of EU or UK law which implements the Aarhus Convention (and where the fixed costs regime in CPR Part 45 does not apply), the court is not obliged to grant a PCO in order to give effect to the Convention.[88] To do so would be to usurp the legislative function.[89] In such cases, the Convention is no more than a matter to which the court should have regard when deciding whether to grant a PCO under normal *Corner House* principles.[90] The Court of Appeal restated the basic position in *Venn v Secretary of State for Communities and Local Government*.[91]

85 *Morgan v Hinton Organics (Wessex) Ltd* [2009] Env LR 30, at [47(ii]). See also the earlier decision in Case C-427/07 *Commission* v *Ireland* [2009] ECR I-6277, at [93] and [94].
86 [2010] EWCA Civ 1006.
87 *Garner v Elmbridge BC* [2012] PTSR 250.
88 Although the UK and the EU are signatories to the Aarhus Convention, it is not directly applicable in UK law. Article 9(3) does not have direct effect and so cannot be directly relied upon to form the basis of a PCO application in the absence of the EU rights already referred to: *Lesoochranárske zoskupenie VLK v Ministerstvo žvotného prostredia Slovenskej Republicky* (Case C-240/09).
89 *Austin v Miller Argent (South Wales) Ltd* [2015] 1 WLR 62, at [37].
90 *Morgan v Hinton Organics* [2009] Env LR 30; *Austin v Miller Argent (South Wales) Ltd* [2015] 1 WLR 62.
91 [2014] EWCA Civ 1539, at [32]–[35].

The meaning of 'not prohibitively expensive'

6.62 The correct approach to this question was clarified, at least in part, by the Supreme Court in *R (Edwards) v Environment Agency*,[92] following a reference to the Court of Justice of the European Union.[93] The CJEU had affirmed that the Aarhus Convention does not affect the powers of national courts to award 'reasonable costs', and that the costs in question are 'all the costs arising from participation in the judicial proceedings'.[94]

6.63 Lord Carnwath JSC said that the following significant points could be extracted from the CJEU's judgment:[95]

(i) First, the test is not purely subjective. The cost of proceedings must not exceed the financial resources of the person concerned nor appear to be objectively unreasonable.

(ii) The court did not give definitive guidance as to how to assess what is 'objectively unreasonable'. In particular it did not in terms adopt Sullivan LJ's suggested alternative of an 'objective' assessment based on the ability of an 'ordinary' member of the public to meet the potential liability for costs. While the court did not apparently reject that as a possible factor in the overall assessment, 'exclusive' reliance on the resources of an 'average applicant' was not appropriate, because it might have little connection with the situation of the person concerned.

(iii) The court could also take into account what might be called the 'merits' of the case.[96]

92 [2014] 1 WLR 55, [2013] UKSC 78.

93 *R (Edwards) v Environment Agency (No 2)* (Case C-260/11) [2013] 1 WLR 2914, CJEU.

94 Ibid, at [25]–[27].

95 Ibid, at [23].

96 The Supreme Court observed that it was not clear how the CJEU saw this factor being brought into account. The following analysis was suggested at para 28 (by reference to factors referred to by the CJEU):

'(i) A reasonable prospect of success. Lack of a reasonable prospect of success in the claim may, it seems, be a reason for allowing the defendants to recover a higher proportion of their costs. The fact that 'frivolity' is mentioned separately (see below), suggests that something more demanding is envisaged than, for example, the threshold test of reasonable arguability.

(ii) The importance of what is at stake for the claimant … this is likely to be a factor increasing the proportion of costs fairly recoverable … a person with 'extensive individual economic interests' at stake in the proceedings may reasonably be expected to bear higher risks in terms of costs.

(iii) The importance of what is at stake for the protection of the environment. Conversely … this is likely to be a factor reducing the proportion of costs recoverable, or eliminating recovery altogether …

(iv) The complexity of the relevant law and procedure … a complex case is likely to require higher expenditure by the defendants, and thus, objectively, to justify a higher award of costs. Although mention is only made of complexity of law or procedure, the same presumably should apply to technical or factual complexity.

(v) The potentially frivolous nature of the claim at its various stages. The defendants should not have to bear the costs of meeting a frivolous claim. In domestic judicial review procedures, whether at first instance or on appeal, this issue is likely to be resolved in favour of the claimant by the grant of permission.'

(iv) That the claimant has not in fact been deterred for carrying on the proceedings is not 'in itself' determinative.

(v) The same criteria are to be applied on appeal as at first instance.[97]

6.64 In 'Aarhus Convention claims' under CPR Part 45, fixed costs are prescribed and accordingly there is no scope for the kind of analysis set out in the *Edwards* judgment.

Problems with using PCOs to achieve compliance with the Aarhus Convention: Commission v UK[98]

6.65 In 2014 the CJEU delivered a judgment in infraction proceedings against the UK. The European Commission argued that the UK had not properly transposed Directive 2003/35/EC,[99] because the availability of PCOs (on *Corner House* criteria) was based on case-law which remained contradictory and the process was subject to legal uncertainty (among other complaints). It is important to note at the outset that the CJEU was not considering the Aarhus provisions of CPR 45, which were not in force at the relevant date.

6.66 The CJEU upheld those arguments. It said that correct transposition would only be achieved if national courts were obliged by a rule of law to ensure that the proceedings are not prohibitively expensive for the claimant, which was not the case.[100] Unequivocal rules were required in order for specific rights conferred by EU to be effective, and transposition via the mechanism of the PCO was not sufficiently clear and precise.[101]

6.67 The CJEU could not take into account the modification of the *Corner House* criteria brought about in *Garner* (although the Commission had acknowledged that this had been a favourable development) because the judgment post-dated the Commission's reasoned opinion,[102] but given the rest of the CJEU's reasoning it seems unlikely that consideration of *Garner* would have led to any different outcome.

6.68 The Commission had also criticised the practice of capping the defendant's potential liability to the claimant when making a PCO (known as a 'reciprocal cost cap'), but the CJEU concluded that the Commission had not provided sufficient information to enable it to examine the issue. This issue remains a feature of PCOs in the Planning Court whether under CPR 45 or *Corner House*.

97 Here the CJEU had meant that 'the same principles should be applied to the assessment at each stage, taking account of costs previously incurred': *Edwards* at [24].

98 Case C-530/11.

99 Implementing Aarhus principles in EU law by amending the environmental impact assessment and integrated pollution prevention and control directives.

100 At [55].

101 At [56].

102 At [57].

6.69 The impact of the CJEU's judgment is more limited than might otherwise be the case because of the entry into force of new fixed costs provisions in CPR Part 45 and the changes which have been brought about by the Criminal Justice and Courts Act 2015. These are considered in the following sections.

Fixed costs regime under CPR Part 45[103]

6.70 Part 45 now contains a fixed costs regime for Aarhus Convention claims, such a claim being defined as a claim brought by one or more members of the public by judicial review or review under statute[104] which challenges the legality of any decision, act or omission of a body exercising public functions and which is within the scope of Articles 9(1) to (3) of the Aarhus Convention.[105]

6.71 Where the fixed costs regime applies, a claimant or defendant may not be ordered to pay costs exceeding the amounts specified.[106] This includes payments by claimants to interested parties, whose recoverable costs may therefore be limited too.[107] Where the claimant is ordered to pay costs, the specified amount is £5,000 if the claimant is claiming only as an individual and not as, or on behalf of, a business or other legal person (in all other cases it is £10,000).[108] Where the defendant is ordered to pay costs, the specified amount is £35,000.[109] The principle of reciprocal cost caps is therefore carried forward and given general application under this regime. After some inconsistent approaches in first instant decisions, the Court of Appeal has confirmed that the various caps are inclusive of any VAT that is payable on the underlying fees.[110]

6.72 The courts must approach Aarhus caps in two distinct stages: first, apply the usual costs principles under CPR Part 44 to determine the amount payable; second, apply the costs cap only if the amount at stage one exceeds £35,000. In cases where the defendant alleges that the claimant deserves only a proportion of their costs, it is not appropriate to conflate these two stages by assessing the claimant's costs as some proportion or part of the capped figure.[111]

6.73 Similarly, the Aarhus caps apply regardless of when the costs assessment takes place; beyond the requirements of reasonableness and proportionality there is nothing in principle to prevent a party recovering up to the value

103 The relevant provisions of CPR Part 45 have been amended since they first came into force in 2013. At the time of writing the most recent iteration came into force on 1 October 2019.

104 As of 1 October 2019, Part 45 therefore covers s 288 reviews wherever they fall within the scope of Arts 9(1)-(3); previously s 288 reviews falling within the scope of Art 9(3) were excluded.

105 CPR 45.41(2)(a). For 'member of the public', see Art 2(4) of the Aarhus Convention.

106 Ibid 45.43(1).

107 *Campaign to Protect Rural England (Kent Branch) v Secretary of State for Communities and Local Government* [2019] EWCA Civ 1230, at [47].

108 CPR 45.43(2).

109 Ibid 45.43(3).

110 *R (Friends of the Earth Ltd) v Secretary of State for Transport* [2021] EWCA Civ 13, at [32].

111 *R (Shave) v Maidstone Borough Council* [2020] EWHC 1895 (Admin) at [68].

of the cap even at the permission stage, if that is when the claim happens to be determined.[112]

6.74 In the case of multiple claimants or defendants, the specified amounts apply in relation to each such claimant or defendant individually and may not be exceeded, irrespective of the number of receiving parties.[113]

6.75 On an application, these specified limits may be varied or even removed altogether in relation to any party.[114] The court must be satisfied that removing/ varying the limit would not render the costs of the proceedings prohibitively expensive for the claimant.[115] In the case of a variation reducing the claimant's or increasing the defendant's maximum costs liability, the court must also be satisfied that the proceedings would be prohibitively expensive for the claimant without the variation.[116] Proceedings are prohibitively expensive if their likely costs either exceed the claimant's financial resources or are objectively unreasonable having regard to the factors mentioned in CPR 45.44(3)(b), which include the situation of the parties, the claimant's prospects of success, and the complexity of the law and procedure. The likely costs of the proceedings include the claimant's own costs.[117]

6.76 Applications to vary must be made and determined according to CPR 45.44(5) to (7). Claimants must therefore make the application in the claim form, defendants in the acknowledgment of service; and applications must be supported with reasons.[118] Later applications are only possible if a significant change in circumstances has meant that the proceedings would now be either prohibitively expensive (if the variation were not made) or no longer prohibitively expensive (if the variation were made) for the claimant.[119] Late applications must be accompanied by the information contained in CPR 45.44(7). On a hearing to determine the variation application, the circumstances may require the court to hold the hearing in private on account of the confidentiality of the information: see CPR 39.2(3)(c).

6.77 Interested parties can also apply to vary costs caps, even though CPR Part 45 only mentions applications by claimants and defendants. Once it is appreciated that interested parties may be subject to a costs cap limiting their recoverable costs, it would be unjust not to allow them to ask the court to

112 *Campaign to Protect Rural England (Kent Branch) v Secretary of State for Communities and Local Government* [2019] EWCA Civ 1230, at [50].

113 CPR 45.43(4).

114 Ibid 45.44(1).

115 Ibid 45.44(2)(a).

116 Ibid 45.44(2)(b).

117 *R (Royal Society for the Protection of Birds) v Secretary of State for Justice* [2017] EWHC 2309 (Admin) at [58].

118 CPR 45.45(5).

119 Ibid 45.45(6). As an example of a late application for a variation in practice, see the discussion in *CPRE Surrey & Another v Waverley BC and others* [2018] EWHC 2969 (Admin).

vary that cap.[120] Despite the lack of any procedural rules expressly governing applications by interested parties, we would suggest that the courts will at the very least insist that applications be made promptly once the grounds for doing so appear, and consonantly with the overriding objective.

6.78 In order to benefit from the fixed costs regime, the claimant must state that the claim is an Aarhus Convention claim in his claim form; as well as filing and serving, with the claim form, a schedule of the claimant's financial resources.[121] If the defendant disagrees that the claim is an Aarhus claim, it must set out that denial in its acknowledgment of service and set out its grounds.[122] The court will then determine the issue at the earliest opportunity.[123]

6.79 If the court concludes that (contrary to the claimant's assertion) the claim is not an Aarhus Convention claim, it will normally make no order for the costs of the proceedings to determine the issue.[124] If the court concludes that (contrary to the defendant's denial) the claim is an Aarhus Convention claim, it will normally order that the defendant pay the claimants' costs of those proceedings on the standard basis, and that the order may be enforced notwithstanding that this would increase the defendant's total liability for costs beyond the specified £35,000 limit.[125]

6.80 Clearly, therefore, the rules are designed to ensure that proceedings cannot be rendered prohibitively expensive for claimants simply by virtue of the defendant challenging the applicability of the fixed costs regime.

6.81 In practice, in many cases there is now no issue that there should be a PCO and the rules are such that if there is no denial of entitlement the court does not even have to make an actual order.

Problems with the fixed costs regime

6.82 Although CPR Part 45 has been broadened such that it now applies to all statutory appeals there are still many areas in respect of which there appears to be tension with the Convention. These still include the types of claim covered, rules as to eligibility for costs protection, the level of costs caps and their variation, procedures with multiple claimants, costs protection in appeal, pre-action costs, costs protection for interveners and funders of litigation. See, in greater detail in the UN's Aarhus Compliance Committee's most recent progress review, the

120 *R (Bertoncini) v Hammersmith and Fulham LBC* (unreported, QBD (Planning Court), 2 June 2020) at [10]. The judge concluded his judgment with this comment (at [26]): 'The voice of the interested party is in my view an important one.'
121 CPR 45.42(1).
122 Ibid 45.45(1).
123 Ibid 45.45(2).
124 Ibid 45.45(3)(a).
125 Ibid 45.45(3)(b).

suggestion that CPR Part 45 still had some way to go in terms of guaranteeing the Convention's requirements in several respects.[126] Generally, it is important to remember that the fixed costs regime is not itself fixed. There will likely be further amendments to the fixed costs regime in future, notwithstanding Brexit, as the UK will remain a signatory to the Treaty. We advise readers to be particularly careful to ensure that they work from the most recent iteration of the relevant procedural rules at all times, and not to assume that previous cases were decided on the same iteration.

6.83 One continuing issue is that on its current formulation CPR Part 45 only applies to claims brought by one or more 'members of the public', a term that falls to be construed according to the Aarhus Convention itself.[127] Article 2(4) of the Convention defines the public as 'one or more natural or legal persons, and, in accordance with national legislation or practice, their associations, organizations and groups'. Article 2(2), also relevant, defines a public authority to include government 'at national, regional and other level'. The UN's Aarhus Compliance Committee has found that a London borough council cannot constitute a member of the public for the purpose of the Convention, since otherwise the state would be proceeding against itself in 'an internal dispute' on the international plane.[128] At almost the same time the Court of Appeal concluded otherwise.[129]

6.84 With respect to the current version of the CPR, the 'members of the public' restriction under CPR 45.41(2)(a) appears to exclude local authority claimants. This is not without its difficulties, including whether it includes or excludes parish councils. It does seem that unincorporated associations will be covered.[130]

126 Aarhus Convention Compliance Committee, *Second Progress Review of the Implementation of Decision VI/8k on Compliance by the United Kingdom of Great Britain and Northern Ireland with its Obligations under the Convention* (6 March 2020), available at www.unece.org/environmental-policy/conventions/public-participation/aarhus-convention/tfwg/envppcc/implementation-of-decisions-of-the-meeting-of-the-parties-on-compliance-by-individual-parties/sixth-meeting-of-the-parties-2017/decision-vi8k-concerning-united-kingdom.html.

127 CPR 45.41(2).

128 ACCC/C/2014/100 (7 August 2015): available at www.unece.org/fileadmin/DAM/env/pp/compliance/C2014-100/Correspondence_with_Party_concerned/ToPartiesC100_07.08.2015.pdf.

129 See *R (HS2 Action Alliance Ltd) v Secretary of State for Transport* [2015] EWCA Civ 203, at [15], in which case a planning authority sought to challenge a major scheme and did obtain costs protection, but, note, that this was determined by reference to an earlier and broader definition and it would now be excluded. In an unreported permission hearing in *Crondall Parish Council v SSHCLG* (CO/3900/2018, 28 November 2018) Mr John Howell QC sitting as a Deputy High Court Judge held that a parish council was a member of 'the public' for the purpose of the Aarhus Convention, notwithstanding that it was also a 'public authority', and so entitled to costs protection.

130 *Aireborough Neighbourhood Development Forum v Leeds City Council and others* [2020] EWHC 45 (Admin) at [28] and [31]. Lieven J was dealing with the issue of standing but her obiter comment as to Aarhus' application is indicative of support for such proposition.

Criminal Justice and Courts Act 2015: non-environmental cases

6.85 The Criminal Justice and Courts Act 2015 makes provision for 'cost capping orders' in ss 88–90.[131] The overall effect is to put cost protection on a statutory rather than common law footing. The *Corner House* criteria are largely replicated within the statutory criteria.

6.86 It is important to note that these provisions only apply to judicial review proceedings as defined in s 88(12).[132]

6.87 For claims which do fall within the definition of judicial review proceedings, the court can only make a cost capping order in accordance with ss 88–90, and cannot grant such orders on common law principles. For the avoidance of doubt, ss 88–90 do not apply to proceedings that fall within the CPR Part 45 fixed costs regime for Aarhus Convention claims.[133]

6.88 Significantly, the court can only make a cost capping order if leave to apply for judicial review has been granted.[134] Substantial costs can be incurred by parties prior to the determination of permission, particularly in high profile or complex cases; and there is also the possibility that permission is refused on the papers but later granted following an application for oral reconsideration. The non-availability of costs protection for this stage of proceedings has therefore been controversial.

6.89 The court can only grant a cost capping order if the following criteria are satisfied:[135]

(1) The proceedings are public interest proceedings;

(2) In the absence of a cost capping order, the application would withdraw the application for judicial review or cease to participate in the proceedings; and

(3) It would be reasonable for the applicant to do so.

6.90 Proceedings are 'public interest proceedings' only if they raise an issue which is of general public importance; the public interest requires the issue to be resolved; and the proceedings are likely to provide an appropriate means of resolving it.[136] The first two of these criteria are the same as the first two

131 Defined as orders 'limiting or removing the liability of a party to judicial review proceedings to pay another party's costs in connection with any stage of the proceedings': s 88(2).

132 The definition includes applications for leave to apply for judicial review, substantive applications for judicial review and appeals (and applications for leave to appeal) from those proceedings.

133 Criminal Justice and Courts Act 2015 (Disapplication of Sections 88 and 89) Regulations 2017/100, reg 2.

134 CJCA 2015, s 88(3).

135 Ibid, s 88(6).

136 Ibid, s 88(7). On how to determine the 'issue', see *R (Beety) v Nursing and Midwifery Council* [2017] EWHC 3579 (Admin) at [9]: it 'has to be gleaned from a consideration of the claim as put forward and what may be put forward by way of defence'.

Corner House criteria, but the requirement for the court to consider whether the particular proceedings are an appropriate means of resolving the issue is new. Appropriateness is a question of degree for the judge; in this regard it may be relevant, for instance, that a public consultation will enable a number of the main public interest issues to be aired and examined out of court.[137]

6.91 It is also notable that the criteria for defining public interest proceedings (as well as the overall criteria for granting a cost capping order in s 88(6)) are both mandatory and cumulative: the criteria must all be satisfied. This is a further contrast between the new provisions and the previous law under *Corner House,* where the courts consistently emphasised that the criteria were not to be applied as if they were statutory provisions or in an overly prescriptive manner. Under s 88, it was plainly Parliament's intention to restrict costs capping orders to cases with a high degree of public interest.[138]

6.92 When determining whether proceedings are public interest proceedings, the court must also have regard to the number of people likely to be directly affected if relief is granted to the applicant, the significance of the effect on these people, and whether the proceedings involve a point of law of general public importance.[139] Although these factors were not spelled out as separate criteria by the Court of Appeal in *Corner House*, they are factors which have been considered by courts in subsequent cases.[140] The Lord Chancellor is empowered to amend the matters to which the court must have regard when determining whether proceedings are public interest proceedings by secondary legislation.[141]

6.93 The notion of a 'point of law' being of general public importance under s 88(8) is different to the separate criterion of an 'issue' of general public importance under s 88(7)(a). The issue may be important without the law, as one judge has put it, being 'an obvious Supreme Court point'.[142]

6.94 In deciding whether to make a costs capping order, and its terms, the court must consider the financial resources of the parties (including anyone who does or may provide the parties with financial support), the extent to which the applicant for the order (or anyone who has provided the applicant with financial support) is likely to benefit if relief is granted to the applicant for judicial review, whether legal representatives for the applicant for the order are acting pro bono, and whether the applicant for the order is an appropriate person to represent the

137 *R (Hawking) v Secretary of State for Health and Social Care* [2018] EWHC 989 (Admin) at [14].

138 Ibid, at [17].

139 CJCA 2015, s 88(8).

140 The issue of how many people would be affected by the outcome, and the significance of the effect, were explored in some detail in *R (Compton) v Wiltshire Primary Care Trust* [2009] 1 WLR 1436, [2008] EWCA Civ 749, at [21–23], [62–63] and [77–78]. With reference to s 88 specifically, see *R (Beety) v Nursing and Midwifery Council* [2017] EWHC 3579 (Admin) at [18]; *R (We Love Hackney Ltd) v Hackney LBC* [2019] EWHC 1007 (Admin) at [44]–[48].

141 CJCA 2015, s 88(9).

142 *R (Beety) v Nursing and Midwifery Council* [2017] EWHC 3579 (Admin) at [20].

interests of other persons or the public interest generally.[143] The pro bono factor, while relevant, should not be read more bluntly as preventing a costs capping order being made unless the lawyers act for nothing.[144]

6.95 Section 89(2) introduces reciprocal capping. If the costs capping order removes or limits the liability of the applicant for judicial review to pay the costs of another party if relief is not granted, it must also limit or remove the liability of the other party to pay the applicant's costs if it is. However, there is nothing in s 89(2) to suggest that the reciprocal cap must mirror the cap in favour of the applicant for the costs capping order.[145]

6.96 Once the court has imposed a costs cap, there is nothing in principle to prevent it from reducing recoverable costs further still, in the exercise of its general costs discretion under CPR Part 44.2. Parties are otherwise potentially encouraged into lax practice and unreasonable litigation conduct if they can count on receiving the full amount of the capped costs.[146]

6.97 An application for a costs capping order must be made on notice and supported by evidence setting out why it should be made, a summary of the applicant's financial resources,[147] and the costs and disbursements the applicant considers the parties are likely to incur in the future conduct of the proceedings.[148] The applicant must serve a copy of the application notice and supporting documents on every other party, save that the applicant can apply to dispense with the need to serve financial resources evidence on one or more parties.[149]

6.98 If the applicant is a body corporate, its application must also provide evidence setting out whether it can demonstrate that it is likely to have financial resources available to meet liabilities arising in connection with the proceedings.[150] If the body corporate is unable to demonstrate that it is likely to have such financial resources, the court must consider making directions for the provision of information about the body's members and their ability to provide financial support for the purposes of the proceedings.[151]

6.99 As with the Aarhus fixed costs regime under CPR Part 45, a party can apply to vary a costs capping order. Any such application must be made on notice, with copies of the application notice and any supporting documents being

143 CCJA 2015, s 89.

144 *R (Beety) v Nursing and Midwifery Council* [2017] EWHC 3579 (Admin) at [37]–[38].

145 Ibid, at [40].

146 *R (Elan-Cane) v Secretary of State for the Home Department* [2020] EWCA Civ 363, at [148]–[150].

147 On which see also Practice Direction 46, para 10.1. Financial resources are not simply assets and income; they may include other monies, such as an inheritance, which a party might be able to obtain or has an expectation of coming into possession of within a reasonable period: *R (Harvey) v Leighton Linslade Town Council* [2019] EWHC 760 (Admin) at [115].

148 CPR 46.17(1).

149 Ibid 46.17(2)-(3).

150 Ibid 46.17(1)(iv).

151 Ibid 46.18.

served on the other parties.[152] As with the application for the costs capping order itself, the applicant to vary can apply to dispense with the need to serve financial resources evidence on one or more parties.[153]

Criminal Justice and Courts Act 2015: environmental cases

6.100 Section 90 of the Act allows for the possibility of a new cost capping regime being introduced for environmental cases. It provides that the Lord Chancellor may make regulations disapplying ss 88 and 89 in relation to 'judicial review proceedings which … have as their subject an issue relating entirely or partly to the environment'. No draft regulations bringing about a new environmental costs capping regime have been published at the time of writing. Consequently the fixed costs regime in CPR Part 45 remains in place for such claims.[154]

6.101 As already noted, the cost capping provisions of the Criminal Justice and Courts Act 2015 only apply to judicial review claims, not statutory appeals and applications, and this will be equally true for any regulations made under s 90.

H CONCLUSION

6.102 As stated at the outset of this chapter, the intention has not been to provide a comprehensive analysis of the costs rules which apply in the Planning Court. However, it is hoped that readers will have gained a basic overview and will understand where to look to obtain more detailed information.

152 Ibid 46.19(1).
153 Ibid 46.19(3).
154 As made clear by reg 2 of the Criminal Justice and Courts Act 2015 (Disapplication of Sections 88 and 89) Regulations 2017/100.

CHAPTER 7

Key legal principles in Planning Court claims

Clare Parry, Josef Cannon, Dr Ashley Bowes and Dr Sam Fowles

A	Introduction	7.1
B	Grounds of challenge	7.3
	– Misinterpretation of policy	7.4
	– NPPF	7.11
	– Material and immaterial considerations and s 70 Town and Country Planning Act 1990	7.43
	– Reasons	7.48
	– Procedural regularity	7.58
	– Consistency of decisions	7.60
	– Errors of law	7.66
	– Errors of fact	7.68
	– Rationality	7.71
	– Legitimate expectation	7.75
	– Procedural fairness	7.79
	– Bias	7.85
	– Duty to make enquiries	7.89
	– Fettering discretion	7.97
C	Approach taken by Court to challenges	7.100
	– Challenges no reflecting way case put to Inspector/ Council	7.100
	– Council decision making	7.102
	– Approach to Inspectors' decision letters	7.116
	– Secretary of State's approach to Inspector's recommendations	7.124
	– Improper purposes	7.126
D	Relief/discretion to quash	7.127
	– Examples of refusal to quash	7.128

	– Examples of refusing to exercise the discretion not to quash	7.129
	– In European cases	7.130
E	Substantive Issues	7.132
	– Conditions	7.133
	– Interpretation	7.134
	– Condition/limitation distinction	7.136
	– *Grampian* conditions	7.137
	– *Whitley* conditions	7.139
	– Section 106 agreements	7.149
	– Community Infrastructure Levy	7.143
	– Planning permissions	7.144
	– Fallback	7.148
	– General Permitted Development Order ('GPDO')	7.150
	– Meeting full objectively assessed need	7.152
	– Enforcement	7.153
	– Heritage	7.158
	– NPPF	7.161
	– Alternative sites/schemes	7.164
	– Consultee requests	7.166
	– Reservoirs	7.168
	– Village greens	7.169
	– Commons	7.171
	– Relationship with other regulatory regimes	7.172
	– Local plans/neighbourhood plans	7.174
F	Human Rights/Equality	7.178
	– Human Rights Act 1998	7.178
	– Best interests of children	7.185
	– Equality Act 2010	7.187
G	European Legislation	7.189
	– EIA	7.189
	– Habitats Regulations	7.193
	– Strategic Environmental Assessment/Sustainability Appraisal	7.201
H	Litigation procedure	7.209
	– Statements of common ground/agreed issues in the judicial review	7.210
	– Whether to apply *Mitchell*	7.212

	– Time limits	7.214
	– Pre-action letters	7.221
	– Striking out	7.222
	– Failure properly to complete claim form	7.223
	– What can be challenged under s 288 or 289	7.225
	– Judicially reviewing development plans in progress	7.226
	– Cross examination	7.227
	– Disclosure and the duty of candour	7.229
	– Issue estoppel	7.233
	– Totally without merit claims	7.235
	– Alternative remedy	7.237
	– Procedural exclusivity	7.240
I	Information	7.243
	– Availability of relevant documents	7.244
	– Viability assessments/confidential information	7.245
	– Right to see draft s 106 agreements	7.247

A INTRODUCTION

7.1 The jurisprudence applied by the Planning Court has not departed radically from the approach formerly taken by the Administrative Court prior to its creation. As discussed in Chapter 1, whilst in procedural terms the Planning Court is a specialist court within the Administrative Court, the law that it applies sits within the overall jurisprudence of administrative or public law, and attempts to suggest that planning law should development its own principles outside of those wider principles have been rebuffed by the courts. However, the categorisation of certain claims as 'significant' allied to the creation of a specialist list of judges to hear those cases has undoubtedly enabled the speedier delivery of high-quality judgments in the broad planning context.

7.2 This chapter seeks, by reference to particular cases, to identify the main issues with which the Planning Court has grappled on a frequent basis. It identifies groups of cases in which those issues have been considered and seeks to identify briefly the approach the Court has taken to those issues. Under each heading or subheading cases which have considered the particular issue are identified and the conclusions of the case briefly stated along with the paragraph(s) in the judgments where those conclusions can most easily be identified. In the fast-moving world of increasing cases and of online judgments, this chapter does not pretend to have covered every issue or to be fully comprehensive. Nor can it be entirely up to date. However, it is intended to provide a useful point of reference as a starting point for the reader interested in the scope and nature of the work commonly dealt with in the Planning Court.

B GROUNDS OF CHALLENGE

7.3 The grounds of challenge in a challenge under s 288 of the Town and Country Planning act 1991 were helpfully summarised by Lindblom J (as he then was) in *Bloor Homes East Midlands Ltd v SSCLG)*[1] [17], approved in *Barwood Strategic II LLP v East Staffordshire Borough Council*[2] [8]–[9]. The Planning Court has repeatedly cited this summary with approval.

Misinterpretation of policy

7.4 The approach in *Tesco v Dundee*[3] that interpretation of policy is a matter of law for the courts to determine is a settled principle that has been followed by the Planning Court. As such it does not depend on the evidence which happens to be presented in one particular forum *(R (on the application of Clientearth) v Secretary of State for Business, Energy and Industrial Strategy)*[4] [136]. The Appellate Courts have, however, emphasised the limitations of this process (*Suffolk Coastal DC v Hopkins Homes Ltd*[5] [23–34], *R (on the application of Samuel Smith Old Brewery (Tadcaster) and others) v North Yorkshire County Council*[6] [21]). The Planning Court has also highlighted the important distinction between the interpretation of policy and its application in the context of a particular planning decision. [7]

7.5 As the interpretation of policy is a matter of law the Court is unlikely to be assisted by other Inspectors' decisions on the issue (*Wiltshire Council v SSHCLG*[8] [20]). Nor can previous indications that a policy does not apply change the objective meaning of that policy (*Mills v SSHCLG*[9] [23]).

7.6 Policy statements are not analogous to a statute or contract, they are full of broad statements which may be mutually irreconcilable. Their application requires planning judgement which can only be challenged on the grounds of irrationality or perversity (*Suffolk Coastal DC v Hopkins Homes Ltd*[10] [22–23], [25] [74]). The Court does not approach the interpretation of policy with the same linguistic rigour it applies to the construction of a statute or a contract (*Gladman Developments Ltd v Canterbury City Council*[11] [22]).

1 [2014] EWHC 754 (Admin).
2 [2017] EWCA Civ 893.
3 [2012] UKSC 13.
4 [2020] EWHC 1303 (Admin).
5 [2017] UKSC 37.
6 [2020] UKSC 3.
7 *Trustees of Barker Mill Estates v SSCLG & Test Valley Borough Council* [2016] EWHC 3028 (Admin) at [22], [27].
8 [2020] EWHC 954.
9 [2019] EWHC 3476 (Admin).
10 [2017] UKSC 37.
11 [2019] EWCA Civ 669.

7.7 *R (on the application of Clientearth) v Secretary of State for Business, Energy and Industrial Strategy)*[12] [104] (planning policies should be interpreted bearing in mind they are intended to guide practical decision making. Decision makers can expect policy to be expressed as clearly and simply as possible and the courts to provide a straightforward interpretation of such policy (*Mills v SSHCLG*[13] [10]). The supporting text is not a part of the policy and cannot trump the policy. This approach was upheld by the Court of Appeal when dismissing ClientEarth's appeal in [2021] EWCA Civ 43, [56].

7.8 It is fundamental to interpret statements of policy in their proper context and to read the document as a whole not selectively *(R (on the application of Clientearth)*[14] [67], [129]. The context in which words appear in policy is very important and care needs to be taken when relying on authorities for the meaning of words drawn from other contexts (*Wiltshire Council v SSCLG*[15] [23]). Regard should be had to the overall policy objective or mischief the policy seeks to address (*Wiltshire Council*[16] [27], [29]).

7.9 The policy writer's stated intention as to what a policy means carries little if any weight in its interpretation unless supported by documents contemporaneous to when the policy was created, such as a change from a draft to a final version of the policy (*Wiltshire Council*[17] [28]). It would not be right to use documents relating to the examination history of a policy to put a gloss on the policy (*Mills v SSHCLG* [22].

7.10 Planning policy should not be subject to excessive legalism in challenges before the planning court *Gladman Developments Limited v SSHCL*[18] [115]). The Court of Appeal took the same approach when dismissing Gladman's appeal in [2021] EWCA Civ 104. General principles on the interpretation of planning policy also apply to the interpretation of government policy more generally including the National Planning Policy Framework ('NPPF') (*Suffolk Coastal DC v Hopkins Homes Ltd*[19] [22]–[26]) and to the national policy statements (*R (on the application of Arthur Scarisbrick) v SSCLG v Whitemoss Landfill Ltd*[20] [19]).

NPPF

7.11 Since the introduction of the NPPF the courts have had to grapple with the correct approach to individual policies in the document. All references are to the version of the NPPF published in February 2019 unless otherwise stated.

12 [2020] EWHC 1303 (Admin).
13 [2019] EWHC 3476 (Admin).
14 [2020] EWHC 1303 (Admin).
15 [2020] EWHC 954.
16 Ibid.
17 Ibid.
18 [2020] EWHC 518 (Admin).
19 [2017] UKSC 37.
20 [2017] EWCA Civ 787.

7.12 The Planning Court has said that it should not normally be necessary to carry out a textual comparison with the 2012 version of the NPPF in order to understand the NPPF 2019 (*Paul Newman Homes v SSHCLG*[21] [20], [27], [38]). This decision was upheld by the Court of Appeal in [2021] EWCA Civ 15.

7.13 The NPPF is a material consideration to be taken into account in planning decision making but it is policy not statute and does not displace the statutory presumption in favour of the development plan (*Suffolk Coastal DC*[22] [21]).

7.14 When interpreting the NPPF it is not the business of the interpreter to go searching for possible ambiguities or conflicts in order to detract from the obvious meaning of the words to be interpreted (*City and Country Bramshill Ltd v SSHCLG*[23] [26]).

7.15 The presumption in favour of sustainable development is set out in paragraph 11 of the NPPF. The broad structure of paragraph 11 and its application in the context of s 38(6) of the Planning and Compulsory Purchase Act 2004 were discussed in *Monkhill Ltd v SSHCLG*[24] at [39]–[45]. The Court of Appeal endorsed the approach taken by the Planning Court in [2021] EWCA Civ 74.

7.16 *Paul Newman Homes v SSHCLG*[25] [32] shows that where one or more relevant development plan policies exist it cannot be said that there are 'no relevant development plan policies' so that the trigger for the tilted balance does not apply. There is no requirement that such a relevant policy be up to date. Relevance connotes no more than some real role in the determination of the application. What is relevant can include general development control policies and mundane policies even if they are not remotely controversial in their application.

7.17 For the purposes of the part of paragraph 11 which states 'where the policies which are most important for determining the application are out of date', a policy is not considered to be out of date simply because it is found in a plan whose plan period has expired, although that may be relevant to the decision (*Peel Investments (North) v SSCLG*[26] [58]). *Paul Newman Homes*[27] [35] The first task is to identify the basket of policies from the development plan which constitutes the most important for determining the application, the second task is to decide whether that basket viewed overall is out of date. The fact that one or more of the policies in the basket might be out of date would be relevant but not determinative of this exercise. [36] A single up to date policy could prevent it being said that 'the policies which are the most important for determining the application are out of date'.

21 [2019] EWHC 2367 (Admin).
22 [2017] UKSC 37.
23 [2019] EWHC 3819 (Admin).
24 [2019] EWHC 1993 (Admin).
25 [2019] EWHC 2367 (Admin).
26 [2019] EWHC 2143 (Admin).
27 [2019] EWHC 2367 (Admin).

7.18 The approach to older development plan policies was discussed in *Gladman Developments Limited v Daventry District Council and SSCLG*[28] at [40]–[44]. The fact that the Council has granted permission on sites in breach of a policy would not in and of itself justify a conclusion that the policy was out of date *Gladman Developments Limited v SSHCLG and Central Bedfordshire Council*[29] [37]. It is a relevant consideration that current housing needs could not be met within the existing settlement boundaries – the weight to be placed on this consideration is a matter for an Inspector not the courts (*Telford and Wrekin BC v SSCLG*[30] [25]).

7.19 Paragraph 11(d)(ii) of the NPPF does not require any relevant development plan policies to be excluded from the tilted balance (*Gladman Developments Limited v SSHCLG*[31] [90]–[92]). This was confirmed by the Court of Appeal when dismissing Gladman's appeal in [2021] EWCA Civ 104.

7.20 *Keep Bourne End Green v Buckinghamshire Council*[32] concerns the plan-making process and notes that the guidance in the NPPF is the department's view on what makes a strategy sound as required by statute, it is not prescriptive, provided Inspectors and authorities have reached a conclusion which is not irrational their decision cannot be questioned in the courts – the mere fact that they have not followed the policy guidance in every respect does not make the conclusion unlawful. Soundness is a matter to be judged by the Inspector and the Council and raises no issue of law unless their decision is irrational, or they have ignored material considerations [58]).

7.21 The supply and delivery of housing is frequently controversial in planning decisions. The requirement to maintain a five-year supply of housing is a purely quantitative one (*Peel Investments (North) v SSCLG*[33] [81]).

7.22 *City and Country Bramshill Ltd v SSHCLG*[34] confirmed that an isolated home in the countryside connotes a dwelling that is physically separate from or remote from a settlement and it is a matter of fact and planning judgment for the decision maker in the circumstances of the case. A settlement for these purposes could include a hamlet or cluster of dwellings [22]. A decision maker must identify the relevant settlement for the purpose of the operation of paragraph 79 and then decide whether the development of houses is remote from it, both are questions of planning judgment [23]. The remote from settlement test applies even if the proposed houses lie within the curtilage of previously developed land and the size of the proposed settlement does not determine whether the houses are to be treated as isolated or not [24].

28 [2016] EWCA Civ 1146.
29 [2019] EWHC 127 (Admin).
30 [2016] EWHC 3073 (Admin).
31 [2020] EWHC 518 (Admin).
32 [2020] EWHC 1984 (Admin).
33 [2019] EWHC 2143 (Admin).
34 [2019] EWHC 3819 (Admin).

7.23 For retail policy, the application of the sequential test under paragraph 86 and 87[35] of the NPPF does not depend on the identity of the applicant or proposed operator (*Aldergate Properties Ltd v Mansfield DC*[36]).

7.24 *Asda Stores v Leeds City Council*[37] (paragraph 90 of the NPPF does not create a tilted balance in favour of refusal where a proposal fails the sequential test or has a significant adverse impact, despite saying that in such circumstances permission 'should' be refused [43]–[46]).

7.25 Green belt policy has been an important strand of national policy for nearly 70 years. The NPPF was designed to consolidate and simplify previously expressed policy rather than effect major policy change (*R (on the application of Samuel Smith Old Brewery (Tadcaster) and others) v North Yorkshire County Council*) [3][38]). The matters relevant to openness in the green belt are a matter of planning judgement and not law [39].

7.26 'Dwelling' for the purpose of the exception 'subdivision of a residential building' in NPPF paragraph 79(d) means one physical residential building and the exception does not apply to other outbuildings (*Wiltshire Council v SSHCLG*[39] [4] [26]–[34].

7.27 In relation to the requirement to demonstrate exceptional circumstances to move a green belt boundary, what is meant by exceptional circumstances is deliberately not defined showing there is a planning judgment to be made. It is deliberately broad and not subject to dictionary definition (*Compton Parish Council (2173), Julian Cranwell (2174), Ockham Parish Council (2175) v Guildford Borough Council*[40] [68]). Whether circumstances are capable of amounting to exceptional circumstances is a question of law, but caution and restraint would be applied in reaching a decision that a factor relied on in a planning decision was not capable in law of amounting to exceptional circumstances [69]. Exceptional circumstances is a less demanding test than the very special circumstances test for allowing development in the green belt, and there is no requirement that release from the green belt is a last resort [70]. The exceptional circumstances can be found in the accumulation or combination of circumstances of varying natures [71]. Housing needs can be part of the judgment of exceptional circumstances [72]. Exceptional does not mean that the circumstances would be unlikely to recur in a similar fashion elsewhere [74].

7.28 With regard to open space and recreation, the effect of paragraph 97 of the NPPF is that where open space is lost there is no requirement to provide a

35 The case considered the equivalent paragraphs in the NPPF 2012 but nothing turns on this.
36 [2016] EWHC 1670 (Admin).
37 [2019] EWHC 3578 (Admin).
38 [2020] UKSC 3.
39 [2020] EWHC 954.
40 [2019] EWHC 3242 (Admin).

precisely similar quantity in replacement but it does require an equivalent quality and quantity (*Peter Day v Shropshire Council*[41] [44]).

7.29 Particular spaces can be protected by Local Green Space policies. It is not appropriate to add a judicial gloss to the policy criteria for designating Local Green Space, such as saying that there is a high bar to their designation (*Lochailort Investments Limited v Mendip District Council*[42] [34]), the requirements are less onerous than the requirements for designating green belt land [35]. However, once designated, a local policy for control of development within a local green space cannot be stricter than the policies applicable to development in the green belt (*Lochailort Investments Ltd* in the Court of Appeal [33][43]).

7.30 Paragraph 80 of the NPPF in relation to economic development does not exclude enabling development from its scope but it does not expressly relate to, let alone favour it (*Thorpe Hall Leisure Ltd v SSHCLG*[44] [110]).

7.31 In relation to sustainable transport, paragraph 111 of the Framework requires a developer to produce a transport assessment which is sufficiently satisfactory for a conclusion about the severity of the traffic impact to be reached (*Satnam Millenium Ltd v SSHCLG*[45] [58]). Paragraph 109 of the Framework is not to be understood in isolation from paragraph 111 [60].

7.32 For policies protecting the natural environment, the words 'valued landscape' are not susceptible to precise definition, legal or otherwise and it is common to refer to the Guidelines for Landscape and Visual Impact guidance (*Campaign to Protect Rural England v Herefordshire Council*[46] [64]). It is not enough to show that individuals subjectively value the landscape [65]. The means by which the planning system should achieve the objective of protecting and enhancing valued landscapes are not stated but two ways it may obviously do so are plan making and the determination of appeals in accordance with the relevant provisions of the development plan (unless material considerations indicate otherwise) [66]. The officer did not fall into error in their report by not referring expressly to paragraph 170(a) of the NPPF or reaching a conclusion on what extent the landscape should be regarded as 'valued'.

7.33 In paragraph 172, what is a major development in an Area of Outstanding Natural Beauty (AONB) is not to be determined solely by its impact on the qualities of the AONB (*Compton Parish Council (2173), Julian Cranwell (2174), Ockham Parish Council (2175) v Guildford Borough Council*[47] [210]). Whether a proposal is a major development in accordance with the definition set out in footnote 55 of the NPPF is essentially a matter of planning judgment for the

41 [2019] EWHC 3539 (Admin).
42 [2020] EWHC 1146 (Admin).
43 [2020] EWCA Civ 1259.
44 [2020] EWHC 44 (Admin).
45 [2019] EWHC 2631 (Admin).
46 [2019] EWHC 3458 (Admin).
47 [2019] EWHC 3242 (Admin).

decision maker (*Monkhill Ltd v SSHCLG*[48] [9]). The first part of paragraph 172 in *Monkhill* is capable of sustaining a clear reason for refusal, including in the context of paragraph 11(d)(i) of the NPPF [53].

7.34 The Air Quality Directive is not a parallel consenting regime to which paragraph 183 of the NPPF is directed (*Gladman Developments v SSCHLG*[49] [44]–[48]).

7.35 Viability is a frequent issue that is disputed, especially because of the implications for the delivery of affordable housing. As to the obligation to provide background material see *The Queen on the application of Holborn Studios Limited v London Borough of Hackney v GHL (Eagle Wharf Road) Limited*[50] [71].

7.36 The re-use of previously developed land (PDL) is encouraged and the partial use of a building for agriculture or forestry does not turn it into an agricultural or forestry building so as to exclude it from the definition of PDL (*Bates v Maldon District Council*[51] [27]).

7.37 The NPPF is supplemented by a web-based series of further guidance, in the form of the Planning Practice Guidance (PPG). The PPG has to be treated with considerable caution when the court is asked to find that there has been a misinterpretation of the planning policy it contains. It is not consulted on or subject to external scrutiny. It is not drafted for or by lawyers and there is no public system for checking for inconsistencies or tensions between paragraphs. It will rarely be amenable to the type of legal analysis by the courts applied in *Tesco v Dundee*. *(Solo Retail Limited v Torridge DC*[52] [33]).

7.38 Authorities are not free to adopt any interpretation they choose of other guidance (such as the BRE guide on daylight and sunlight) within the bounds of rationality. Documents that fall to be construed objectively by a court include documents promulgated by an authority or other institution (*Rainbird v Tower Hamlets LBC*[53] [81]). In interpreting such documents it is necessary to have in mind that it is not an enactment but advice aimed primarily at designers [82]. In so far as it contains technical or scientific terms the court may be assisted by expert evidence [82].

Decision taking

7.39 Compliance with the duty in s 38(6) of the Planning and Compulsory Purchase Act 2004 does not require a view to be expressed about whether a

48 [2019] EWHC 1993 (Admin).
49 [2019] EWCA Civ 1543.
50 [2017] EWHC 2823 (Admin).
51 [2018] EWHC 3421 (Admin); see also Court of Appeal at [2019] EWCA Civ 1272.
52 [2019] EWHC 489 (Admin).
53 [2019] EWHC 3458 (Admin).

development does or does not comply with every relevant policy in the development plan (*Safe Rottingdean Ltd v Brighton and Hove City Council*[54] [103]). There is no hard and fast rule about how s 38(6) is to be complied with [104]. Section 38(6) requires a conclusion on whether the proposal accords with the development plan or not, but this can be lawfully achieved without specifically referring to the statutory duty [109].

7.40 For an example of where the Planning Court considered that it was not sufficiently clear whether s 38(6) had been complied with see *Gare v Babergh District Council*[55] [52]. This can be contrasted with *Corbett v Cornwall* Council[56] where the Court found that in undertaking their role of assisting planning committees it can fairly be said that the professional officers of a planning authority and members who sit regularly on a planning committee will not often be shown to have misinterpreted the policies of its development plan [66].

7.41 It is sufficient for the purposes of s 38(6) for a proposal to accord with the development plan taken as a whole, it does not need to comply with every policy in the development plan considered individually (*Martin v Folkestone and Hythe District Council*[57] [25]).

7.42 Useful principles on the approach to lawful decision taking can be found in *BDW Trading Ltd (t/a David Wilson Homes (Central Mercia and West Midlands)) v Secretary of State for Communities and Local Government*[58] (summary of the legal principles [20]). *R (Corbett) v Cornwall Council*[59] (a breach of a single policy may trigger a breach of the plan as a whole but it is not necessarily the case that a breach of a single policy must render a proposal in breach of the plan [31]; where policies pull in different directions, it is for the decision maker to resolve whether the proposal is in accordance with the plan as a whole [27]–[28]). *Canterbury City Council v Secretary of State for Communities & Local Government*[60](decision maker must understand the meaning of individual policies and their true effect in combination [21] and [31]). *Hopkins Homes Ltd v SSCLG*[61]. NPPF is a material consideration in every planning case but when considering whether it has been correctly interpreted the expertise of the decision maker should be respected.

54 [2019] EWHC 2632 (Admin).
55 [2019] EWHC 2041 (Admin).
56 [2020] EWCA Civ 508.
57 [2020] EWHC 1614 (Admin).
58 [2016] EWCA Civ 493.
59 [2020] EWCA Civ 508.
60 [2019] EWCA Civ 669.
61 [2017] UKSC 37.

Material and immaterial considerations and s 70 Town and Country Planning Act 1990

7.43 A frequent ground of challenge in the Planning Court is an allegation that the decision-maker has taken into account an immaterial consideration or has failed to take into account a material consideration.

7.44 *R (Wright) v Resilient Energy Severndale Ltd*[62] summarises earlier case law and establishes that to be a material consideration it must be one which relates to the character of the use of the land and which fairly and reasonably relates to the permitted development. *R (Samuel Smith Old Brewery (Tadcaster))) and others) v North Yorkshire County Council*[63] shows that absent a statutory obligation to take a material consideration into account, it is a matter of judgment for the decision taker whether to take a factor into account[29]–[32]. Consequently, to show a decision maker has failed to have regard to a material consideration it is not sufficient to show it is a potentially relevant matter [31]–[32]. This approach was followed in *R (Client Earth) v Secretary of State for Business, Energy & Industrial Strategy*[64] where the Planning Court held that a decision maker does not err in law if he has no regard to a matter, it has to be shown that some legal principle compelled (not merely empowered) him to do so or that the matter was 'so obviously material' [99]) as to require consideration).

7.45 The impact of having a gliding club nearby in terms of noise and risk to occupants of a house, were relevant considerations in deciding whether to grant prior approval for the conversion of a barn to residential use (*Coventry Gliding Club Ltd v Harborough District* Council [65] [14]).

7.46 Whether the proposed development is deliverable is not, in the absence of particular circumstances, a material consideration (*Satnam Millenium Ltd v SSHCLG*[66] [92]). At least reasons must be given as to why non-deliverability is a relevant factor in a particular case [93].

7.47 The Secretary of State when forming national planning policy must take into account 'obviously material considerations' (on concession by Counsel) (*Stephenson v SSHCLG*[67] [33]). Part of the NPPF relating to fracking was successfully challenged due to failure to take into account scientific evidence produced by the claimant as an obviously material consideration [68].

62 [2019] UKSC 53.
63 [2020] UKSC 3.
64 [2020] EWHC 1303 (Admin)
65 [2019] EWHC 3059 (Admin).
66 [2019] EWHC 2631 (Admin).
67 [2019] EWHC 519.

Reasons

7.48 Although the statutory duty to give reasons has been removed a common law duty to give reasons may be implied in order to meet the requirements of fairness. This is likely to occur where permission has been granted in the face of an officer's advice or substantial public opposition, or involve major departures from the development plans or other policies of recognised importance (*R (CPRE Kent) v Dover District Council*[68] [51]–[58]). This part of the judgement of Lord Carnworth is, however, strictly obiter as noted in *Save Britain's Heritage v SSCLG*[69] [27] when discussing whether there could be an obligation at common law to give reasons for a procedural decision not to 'call in' an application.

7.49 While the common law may in certain circumstances impose a duty to give reasons to fill the gaps this cannot extend to imposing a duty on the executive to give reasons in all circumstances, even where Parliament did not intend that reasons should be provided, which was the case for procedural decisions as to who should be the decision maker (*Save Britain's Heritage*[70] [29]).

7.50 The standard of reasoning set out in *South Bucks v Porter (No 2)*[71] is applicable in all planning decision making (*R (CPRE Kent) v Dover District Council*[72] [59]). A common law duty to give reasons did not apply where the committee acted in accordance with recommendations in the Officer's report, even though there was public disquiet at the application (*Peter Day v Shropshire Council*[73] [126]).

7.51 By way of contrast, there was a common law duty to give reasons where Members were disagreeing with Officer's advice, in circumstances where it was the second time the site had come before Members (the first determination having been quashed), and the public would be left in real doubt as to the approach that would be taken to a key policy in future cases (*Gare v Babergh District Council*[74] [35]).

7.52 There must be genuine as opposed to forensic doubt as to what the decision maker decided and why (*Starbones Limited v SSHCLG*[75] [75], [76]).

7.53 *R (on the application of Clientearth) v Secretary of State for Business, Energy and Industrial Strategy*[76] [146] shows that the fact that the Secretary of State is disagreeing with the Panel's conclusion does not give rise to a heightened obligation to give reasons for their decision, the courts have discouraged parties

68 [2017] UKSC 79.
69 [2018] EWCA Civ 2137.
70 Ibid.
71 [2004] 1 WLR 1953.
72 [2017] UKSC 79.
73 [2019] EWHC 3539 (Admin).
74 [2019] EWHC 2041 (Admin).
75 [2020] EWHC 526 (Admin).
76 [2020] EWHC 1303 (Admin).

from seeking to judge the adequacy of reasons in one case by comparison with decision letters criticised in other cases. [149] In a reasons case it must be shown both that the claimant has suffered substantial prejudice and that the impugned reasons may well conceal a public law error or that they raise a substantial doubt as to whether the decision contains an error which would provide a ground for quashing it.

7.54 Reasons do not have to be discursive (*London Borough of Tower Hamlets v SSHCLG*[77] [40], [74]). The standard of reasons expected on issues such as visual impact and design is generally lower (*Starbones Limited v SSHCLG*[78] [38]), including where the Secretary of State is disagreeing with an Inspector's conclusions on these matters [38] and [39]. Where a Secretary of State disagrees with his Inspector's report there is no heightened standard of reasons but he must explain the reasons for his disagreement [40]. The Secretary of State is not required to address every point raised in the Inspector's report to him [69].

7.55 There is a duty on an Inspector conducting a local plan examination to give reasons and the standard of reasons is that set out in *South Bucks District Council v Porter*: *CPRE v Waverley DC*[79] [72]). An Inspector's reasons may well satisfy the requisite standard if they are more succinctly expressed than reasons in a s 78 appeal [75], there is a distinction between the duties of an Inspector examining the soundness of a plan and conducting a se 78 appeal [71]–[72]. Although that will not excuse the failure to properly deal with a point that was 'absolutely central to the process' (*Aireborough Neighbourhood Development Forum v Leeds City Council*[80] [107]). The inquisitorial nature of the public examination of a plan has implications for the reasons an Inspector has to give (*Cooper Estates Strategic Land Ltd v Royal Tonbridge Wells BC*[81] [26–29]). A local plan Inspector deciding whether to allocate a site which is subject to a previous appeal decision is not required to identify on an issue by issue basis where they agreed with the appeal inspector (*Compton Parish Council (2173), Julian Cranwell (2174), Ockham Parish Council (2175) v Guildford Borough Council*[82] [167]).

7.56 An examiner examining a neighbourhood plan must give reasons which meet the test set out in *South Buckinghamshire v Porter*. However, the statutory process for examining a neighbourhood plan will affect what may be considered the 'principal controversial issues'. The main focus is on whether or not the plan meets the basic conditions (*Lochailort Investments Limited v Mendip District Council*[83] [167]–[170]). A local authority is obliged to give reasons for its decision whether a neighbourhood plan should be put to a referendum or not but

77 [2019] EWHC 2219 (Admin).
78 [2020] EWHC 526 (Admin).
79 [2019] EWCA Civ 1826.
80 [2020] EWHC 1461 (Admin).
81 [2017] EWHC 224 (Admin).
82 [2019] EWHC 3242 (Admin).
83 [2020] EWHC 1146 (Admin).

they are entitled to rely on the reasons given by the examiner where appropriate [167].

7.57 Where a planning decision is taken in line with an officer's report then there is an assumption that the reasons for that decision are set out in that report (*Bates v Maldon District Council*[84] [19vi]). Where reliance is placed on an officer's report and minutes as providing, by inference, reasons for a decision then those documents should provide reasons to the standard set out in *South Bucks v Porter*: *Gare v Babergh District Council*[85] [41]. In *Gare* the judge rejected the contrary view taken by Andrews J in *Pagham Parish Council v Arun District Council*[86] *[35].* Relying on a paper chase of documents to satisfy the duty to give reasons will make it harder for the decision maker to satisfy that duty: *Gare v Babergh District Council*[87] [43]. The Court has deplored the pleading of an unparticularised reasons challenge (*Keep Bourne End Green v Buckinghamshire Council*[88] [28]–[30]).

Procedural regularity

7.58 Late publication of reports which breached no formal time limits caused no prejudice to interested parties and there was time for any interested party to respond if they wished to do so bearing in mind the limited nature of any new information disclosed for the first time in the reports (*Campaign to Protect Rural England v Herefordshire Council*[89] [89]). In relation to the withholding of documents from the public on the basis of s 100D(5) of the Local Government Act 1972, the statutory intention behind s 100D(5) is to ensure that documents on which the Officer's report is based are open to be viewed by members of the public [92]. In this case the economic needs assessment disclosed exempt information and if open to inspection by the public would disclose the applicant's confidential information in breach of the obligation of confidence. On this basis it was not required to be included in the list of background documents or made available for inspection by members of the public [96].

7.59 A consultation on the main modifications proposed to a local plan was inadequate because it was not apparent from the terms of the consultation that under the modifications a designation of playing fields as local green space would no longer apply (*Jopling v Richmond-Upon-Thames London Borough Council*[90] [56]–[59]).

84 [2019] EWCA Civ 1272.
85 [2019] EWHC 2041 (Admin).
86 [2019] EWHC 1721 (Admin).
87 [2019] EWHC 2041 (Admin).
88 [2020] EWHC 1984 (Admin).
89 [2019] EWHC 3458 (Admin).
90 [2019] EWHC 190 (Admin).

Consistency of decisions

7.60 The circumstances in which a decision can be impugned for failing to take into account a previous decision were reviewed by the Court of Appeal in *Baroness Cumberlege v SSCLG*[91] [78]–[106]. Previous decisions on applications for planning permission are capable of being a material consideration in a subsequent application [81], and consistency in the application of development control decisions in a given area is desirable [82]. This may mean that a previous decision is one that it would be unreasonable for a decision maker to fail to take into account [100] – whether that is the case will depend on the circumstances. However, there is no requirement to refer to all previous decisions which may have been material [85]. It is not the case that the possible obligation to consider a previous decision only applies to decisions drawn to the decision maker's attention, if the decision maker has grounds for thinking there is a decision which has not been drawn to his attention he may be required to take reasonable steps to discover whether or not there is such a decision [94]. Whether a decision maker is required to take steps to find out if another decision exists depends on matters including whether the decision maker was or ought to be aware that such a decision may exist, the significance any such decision may have in relation to the decision to be made and what steps may have been required to find whether the decision did exist and to obtain it [100]. The Secretary of State can usually rely on advocates to draw matter to his attention during the inquiry but after the inquiry he may have to take further steps to find relevant decisions depending on the circumstances [101]. The Secretary of State and his inspectors are not to be treated as being cognisant of all appeal decisions taken [103]. A Secretary of State is not required to be aware of the contents of each and every decision he or his predecessors have taken, but ought reasonably to avoid apparently inconsistent decisions and the obligation to explain inconsistencies may be more stringent in practice [105].

7.61 *R (Cooper) v Ashford Borough Council*[92] [45] (a decision maker is not obliged to provide reasons for distinguishing an earlier decision where the developments differ in a number of material respects or where the reasons for distinguishing are evident from the later assessment. Further, [53] the consistency principle cannot be relied on when the earlier decision was evidently a mistake).

7.62 The fact that previous Inspectors have interpreted a policy in a particular way cannot change the objective meaning of the policy (*Mills v SSHCLG* [24]). For a case where the earlier advice was considered 'confused' see *Risby v East Hertfordshire DC*.[93]

7.63 *Banks v SSCLG*[94] (the case of *North Wiltshire* does not create some special rule requiring reasons when a purportedly or actually indistinguishable

91 [2018] EWCA Civ 1305 (Admin).
92 [2016] EWHC 1525 (Admin).
93 [2019] EWHC 3474 (Admin).
94 [2018] EWHC 3141.

previous decision was raised [112]. There is no different rule for reasons in respect of previous decisions than for any other material consideration, it depends on the importance of the issue, and whether it was a principal area of controversy. Materiality is not of itself a sufficient basis for a duty to give reasons explaining how a consideration was dealt with [112]).

7.64 *R (oao Bates) v Maldon District Council*[95] (a previous planning decision in relation to the same land is capable of being a material consideration both because it may provide a fall-back position and because in any event there is a public interest in the consistency of decision making [19i]. The public interest in the consistency of decision making is not a principle of law but a principle of good practice traditionally supported by the courts [19ii]. A decision maker must consider whether there has been a material change of circumstances since an earlier decision and must always exercise his own judgment, he is not bound by the earlier decision or to give the earlier decision any particular weight [19iii]. Where a planning decision differs from an earlier decision maker on a crucial planning issue he is required to grasp the intellectual nettle of the disagreement and explain his reasons for disagreeing [19viii]).

7.65 The approach to be applied when applying the principle of consistency to a quashed decision was reviewed in *R (Davison) v Elmbridge Borough Council*[96] [56]: (i) the principle of consistency is not limited to the formal decision but extends to the reasoning underling the decision; (ii) the quashed decision is not capable of having legal effect and the decision maker is not bound by it but starts afresh; (iii) the previous decision is capable of being a material consideration and a failure to take it into account will be unlawful if no reasonable decision maker could have failed to take it into account; (iv) the decision maker may need to analyse the reasons the decision was quashed and take into account the parts unaffected by the quashing; and (v) the greater the inconsistency the more explanation is needed.

Error of law

7.66 If a decision maker wrongly directs themselves in their decision making this will frequently lead to a decision being quashed. The Planning Court has repeatedly referred to *Michael Mansell v Tonbridge and Malling BC and Others*[97] [42] for the proper approach to an Officer's Report to Committee.

7.67 Recent examples of decisions where a judge has found an error of law include *Shave v Maidstone Borough Council*[98] where it was an error of law to conclude that there was no justification to seek more details about the location of lodges because planning permission was only required for a change of use [44]–

95 [2019] EWCA Civ 1272.
96 [2019] EWHC 1409 (Admin) .
97 [2017] EWCA Civ 1314.
98 [2020] EWHC 1895 (Admin).

[48]. In *Hall v City of Bradford Metropolitan District Council*[99] there was an error of law in that officers did not provide the committee with any information about the potential impact of the proposal on a conservation area [47]. In *London Borough of Islington v SSHCLG*[100] an Inspector wrongly allowed an appeal against an enforcement notice on ground (d) by not asking the legally correct question of whether the building had been used as a single dwelling throughout the whole of the four years proceeding the enforcement notice so that the authority could have taken enforcement action at any time during that time period [25]. In *USB Waste Essex Ltd v Essex County Council*[101] the County Council wrongly issued a certificate of lawfulness in circumstances where they had misdirected themselves as to the meaning of the underlying planning permission [58]. In *Mawbey v Lewisham LBC*[102] the Council made an error of law in taking an incorrect (too narrow) interpretation of a 'mast' [42]. In *Brent LBC v SSHCLG*[103] an Inspector made an error of law in failing to address a submission that there had been a material change of use by way of intensification [55]. In *Canterbury City Council v SSHCLG*[104] it was an error of law to fail to undertake an Appropriate Assessment where the need to do so had been screened out by taking account of mitigation measures [48].

Error of fact

7.68 In limited circumstances an error of fact can give rise to a challenge in the Planning Court. The guidance of error of fact in public law cases is derived from *E v Home Secretary.*[105]. The application of the guidance in *E v Home Secretary* to planning cases was discussed in *Watt v Hackney*[106] [48]–[53]. There was an error of fact in the daylight/sunlight assessment which led to the permission being quashed.

7.69 Examples of cases where the Planning Court has considered an allegation of mistake of fact include the following. *Flynn v Southwark LBC:*[107] when read as a whole the report did not suggest that grant funding had been confirmed therefore the error of fact contended for did not arise [54]. *Ikram v SSHCLG:*[108] no error of fact because the error contended for was not 'established' [92]. *Johnson v Windsor & Maidenhead:*[109] no error of fact because error contended for was not 'established', it was not appropriate for the Court to seek to resolve competing recollections of events in order to decide what occurred

99 [2019] EWHC 2899 (Admin).
100 [2019] EWHC 2691 (Admin).
101 [2019] EWHC 1924 (Admin).
102 [2019] EWCA Civ 1016.
103 [2019] EWHC 1399 (Admin).
104 [2019] EWHC 1211 (Admin).
105 [2004] EWCA Civ 49; [2004] QB 1044.
106 [2016] EWHC 1978 (Admin).
107 [2019] EWHC 3575 (Admin).
108 [2019] EWHC 1869 (Admin).
109 [2019] EWHC 160 (Admin).

[79]. *DLA Delivery v Baroness Cumberlege*:[110] the Inspector made a mistake of fact as to the relationship between the proposed development and a 7km zone of influence for Ashdown Forest SAC which would alone have justified an order quashing the Secretary of State's decision [70]. *Richborough Estates v SSHCLG:*[111] an incomplete summary of the evidence did not amount to an error of fact, and an error of fact should not be sought by the sort of forensic dissection of documents undertaken by the Claimant [54]. *Wokingham BC v SSCLG*[112] [89]–[91]: the Inspector made an error of fact in relation to the response to developer's inquiries which supported the conclusion that his decision was flawed.

7.70 *Ecotricity Next Generation Ltd v SSCLG*[113] (the inspector mistakenly considered the turbine would be seen in views of the church, which was unfair to the applicant, and an error of law arising from an error of fact [40]–[42]).

Rationality

7.71 The intensity of review on reasonableness or rationality grounds was discussed in *Spurrier v Secretary of State for Transport*[114] [141]–[172]. The factors on which the degree of scrutiny of review particularly depend include: (i) the nature of any right or interest it seeks to protect; (ii) the process by which the decision under challenge was reached; and (iii) the nature of the ground of challenge [151]. Generally, in matters involving planning judgment, the approach to irrationality challenges is that there is a heavy onus on the claimant and/or the claimant faces a particularly daunting task to show that a judgment was irrational, but that does not confine judicial review to issues of bad faith or manifest absurdity [169]–[171]. This reflects the inability of the court to determine issues of planning judgment for itself, especially in judicial review proceedings where there is a factual conflict or a conflict of expert opinion [171]. The various challenges to the National Policy Statement before the courts should be approached with this intensity of review bearing in mind the matters challenged involved planning judgment [172]. The court should accord an enhanced margin of appreciation to decisions involving or based upon 'scientific, technical and predictive assessments' by those with appropriate expertise [179].

7.72 *R (on the application of Clientearth) v Secretary of State for Business, Energy and Industrial Strategy*[115] (where a decision maker decides to have regard to a matter is generally for his judgment as to how far to go into it, something which can only be challenged on irrationality grounds [256]).

7.73 Many cases in the Planning Court show the formidable obstacles faced by a claimant seeking to argue that a decision is irrational. Examples include *Renew*

110 [2018] EWCA Civ 1305.
111 [2018] EWHC 33 (Admin).
112 [2017] EWHC 1863 (Admin).
113 [2015] EWHC 189 (Admin).
114 [2019] EWHC 1070 (Admin).
115 [2020] EWHC 1303 (Admin).

Land Developments Ltd v Welsh Ministers:[116] the Court of Appeal overturning the decision of the High Court and concluding that it had not been irrational for an Inspector to conclude there was a loss of open space in circumstances where the space in question was privately owned and could be fenced off in any event [36]. *WSPA v Welsh Ministers:*[117] the irrationality threshold is a 'formidable mountain'; it was not irrational to find that economic benefits outweighed harm to historic sites and settings even if that conclusion was 'unpopular and even deeply surprising' [42], [47]).

7.74 Rare examples of successful rationality challenges include the following. *Satnam Millenium Ltd v SSHCLG:*[118] it was irrational to take into account the harms of the proposed scheme without considering the benefits, if the scheme was not deliverable the benefits could not occur [63]. *McLennan v Medway Council:*[119] it was irrational to reject as irrelevant the effect the development would have on a renewable energy system [37]. *Veolia ES (UK) Ltd v SSCLG:*[120] the Secretary of State following Inspector's view that granting planning permission would prejudice the local waste plan process was 'quite bizarre' and irrational, but not quashed as it would have made no difference to the outcome [54]–[58]). *Lee Valley Regional Park Authority, R (on the application of) v Broxbourne Borough Council & Anor:*[121] it was irrational on the facts to find that the spread of urban housing over the presently open site would not result in significant loss of openness [60]–[61]).

Legitimate expectation

7.75 A legitimate expectation in the planning context can arise in two different ways: by an express promise or by a practice even where there has been no express promise (*Save Britain's Heritage v SSCLG*[122] [35]). It is important to keep the difference between these two types of cases in mind [36]. If a legitimate expectation was created by a practice the expectation may well disappear when the practice changes, but this is not the position in cases where the expectation arose out of an express promise [43]. Where a promise was made to give reasons for call in decisions a change to that policy had to be announced publicly [48]. Where a public body indicates a clear and unambiguous policy that will operate in a particular type of case, an individual is entitled to expect that policy to be operated until a reasonable decision is taken that the policy be modified or withdrawn, or implementation interferes with the body's other statutory duties [39]. In promise cases there is no requirement for the applicant to show detrimental reliance [50].

116 [2020] EWCA Civ 143.
117 [2014] EWHC 1896 (Admin).
118 [2019] EWHC 2631 (Admin).
119 [2019] EWHC 1738 (Admin).
120 [2015] EWHC 91 (Admin).
121 [2015] EWHC 185 (Admin).
122 [2018] EWCA Civ 2137.

7.76 Where it is said that a legitimate expectation arises from a practice what is required is that there must be a practice which is impliedly tantamount to an express promise (*Heathrow Hub Limited, Runway Innovations Limited v The Secretary of State for Transport*[123] [69]). There must be a consistent practice which is sufficient to generate an implied representation to the same effect [75].

7.77 A legitimate expectation can only be based on a promise which is 'clear, unambiguous and devoid of relevant qualification' – whether this is the case depends on how, on a fair reading, it would have been reasonably understood. It is not essential that the person relied on it to their detriment (*Douglas Bond v Vale of White Horse District* Council[124] [60]). When considering whether the public body was entitled to frustrate the substantive legitimate expectation the question is whether it was so unfair that to take a different course will amount to an abuse of power, the critical question being whether there is sufficient public interest to override the legitimate expectation. It is for the public body to place material before the court justifying its change of approach [61]–[62]. The principles of good administration in having accurate documents setting out important planning policy justified the Council in resiling from its representation in relation to not altering an error in a development plan [67].

7.78 Whether a legitimate expectation arises may depend on the nature or circumstances in which an assurance is give. Formal declarations of policy or procedure issued after appropriate public consultation or pursuant to particular statutory provisions may readily be seen as giving rise to a legitimate expectation – less formal documents that merely purport to give guidance or advice may less readily be interpreted as giving rise to one (*Campaign to Protect Rural England v Herefordshire Council*[125] [23]). Paragraphs in the Council's polytunnel guidance did not give rise to an enforceable legitimate expectation [35]–[48].

Procedural fairness

7.79 Many challenges in the Planning Court have involved an allegation that there is some unfairness in the procedure adopted by the decision maker. The principal authority on procedural fairness is *Hopkins Developments Ltd v SSCLG*[126] where the Court explained that: (i) any party to a planning inquiry is entitled to know the case which he has to meet and to have a reasonable opportunity to adduce evidence and make submissions in relation to the opposing case; and (ii) if there is procedural unfairness which materially prejudices a party to a planning inquiry that may be good grounds for quashing the Inspector's decision [62].

123 [2020] EWCA Civ 213.
124 [2019] EWHC 3080 (Admin).
125 [2019] EWHC 3458 (Admin).
126 [2014] EWCA Civ 470.

7.80 *The Mayor of London v SSCLG:*[127] the procedural unfairness alleged must have materially prejudiced the claimant [76], [91], there was no unfairness in an Inspector not accepting something agreed in the statement of common ground (SOCG) where the other side had evidently resiled from the SOCG [86] and the point was not relied on as a substantial matter in the appeal [83]–[86]. There was no material prejudice as the claimant had not set out even the gist of the evidence he would have called [91]).

7.81 Where there is an allegation of breach of natural justice the question for the court is whether the claimant knew the case it had to meet and had a reasonable opportunity to adduce evidence and/or make submissions to meet it (*Spitfire Bespoke Homes Ltd v SSHCLG*[128] [49]). The principles of natural justice apply as much to written appeal procedures as they do to oral hearings [49]. Where a point had been put in issue by the Council in their written statement and responded to by the appellant in their response, it was difficult to discern the basis on which it could be said there had been procedural unfairness, let alone unfairness leading to substantial prejudice [63].

7.82 There was no procedural unfairness where an Inspector failed to identify that he was concerned about the reasonableness of a suggested condition (*Hook v SSHCLG*[129] [56]). It is for the developer to be alert to the fact that he might lose his primary case and thus to the potential need to put forward any fall-back case (*Kerry v SSHCLG*[130] [46]–[52]). Where an Inspector identified one of the main issues as the effectiveness of any measures put forward to deal with air pollution, it was not unfair for the Inspector to conclude against the appellant on this point notwithstanding that the appellant was following a recognised arithmetical model of mitigation (*Gladman Developments v SSCLG*[131] [49]–[61]).

7.83 *Barlow (on behalf of Harthill Against Fracking) v SSHCLG:*[132] no procedural unfairness where a Planning Inspector failed to adjourn for four weeks to enable an interested party to respond to a traffic management report provided on behalf of the appellant [5].

7.84 *Sykes v Cheshire West and Chester BC*: what fairness requires of a local authority in deciding whether to accept an amendment to a planning permission is a question which is ultimately for the Court to decide. The Court's role is not simply to review the reasonableness of the decision maker's judgment [29]. A change from a facility only accessible to members to a facility available to the general public was a volte-face and it was unfair that objectors did not have an opportunity to respond [34]. In saying that this would have made no difference to objectors the test sets a low threshold [37]. Evidence provided speculating as to what had occurred if the procedure had been different was unhelpful and

127 [2020] EWHC 1176 (Admin).
128 [2020] EWHC 958 (Admin).
129 [2020] EWCA Civ 486.
130 [2020] EWHC 908 (Admin).
131 [2019] EWCA Civ 1543.
132 [2019] EWHC 146 QB.

counterintuitive, the whole concept of natural justice and the ability to have a full and fair hearing is predicated on decision-makers having heard further representations and deciding according [37].

Bias

7.85 Like the Administrative Court, the Planning Court has been slow to accept the argument that the decision of a committee or official was vitiated by bias or predetermination. The test for bias is now found in *Porter v McGill*[133] [102]–[103].

7.86 The test for apparent bias was considered in the planning context by Sales LJ in *Turner v SSCLG.*[134] The test applicable is whether having had regard to all the circumstances, a fair-minded observer would conclude there was a real possibility that the Inspector was biased [8]. The test is less rigorous than there being a probability of bias but higher than there being any possibility of bias [10]. An assertion by the Inspector that they are not biased in not likely to be helpful [8]. The Court is to look at all of the material before it not just that available to the hypothetical fair-minded observer at the time of the decision [10]. The hypothetical observer is a legal construct and the Court will be cautious about treating the evidence from any particular person who attends the inquiry as the personification of that observer [16]. The hypothetical observer will appreciate: (i) the Inspector's inquisitorial role which makes it appropriate for him to focus debate at the inquiry; (ii) that the Inspector has to efficiently run the inquiry which may require robust case management; (iii) an Inspector is entitled to encourage focussed questioning and short and focussed answers in the cross examination of witnesses; (iv) an Inspector is to be expected to have done a good deal of preparation before an Inquiry and to focus debate on the issues which are of assistance for him in writing a report; and (v) the Inspector is entitled to give indications in the course of the inquiry about points which seem to be unrealistic or bad [18].The Inspector's code of conduct is designed to promote best practice and does not create a standard by which an appearance of bias is to be judged [19]. The Court considered a wide range of criticisms of the Inspector's behaviour but concluded they were all well within the spectrum of robust case management [44].

7.87 In *Satnam Millenium Ltd v Secretary of State for Housing Communities and Local Government*[135] the judge reviewed a number of authorities on apparent bias in the planning context, but doubted the value of the continued citation of cases which preceded or did not expressly apply the test in *Porter v Magill*[136] [202]. It was too general an approach to say that if an Inspector has a conversation about the case with one party in the absence of the other there is

133 [2002] 2 AC 357.
134 [2015] EWCA Civ 582.
135 [2019] EWHC 2631 (Admin).
136 [2002] AC 357.

a real risk that justice will not be seen to be done [202]. Giving local residents significant time to make representations and ask questions and scheduling those representations amid other evidence could not warrant any fair-minded observer alleging, let alone concluding, that there was a real possibility of bias [231]. An Inspector having chats (not about the merits of the case) with individuals where the room layout gave rise to this did not show a real risk of bias [235-6], nor did discussions with the Council about the logistics of the inquiry room [239] or a conversation with Highways England in a public place that was subsequently referred to in inquiry session [240]. It would be appropriate for parties concerned about unreported conversations taking place with the Inspector to raise it with him [242], otherwise they may be taken to have waived their right to complain about them [243].

7.88 In *Kuznetsov v SSCLG*[137] the Court rejected that an Inspector was biased despite the Inspector having written an email to their case officer saying of the claimant 'If it hadn't been so time-wasting it would have been laughable' and 'very unfortunately he came back 10 minutes later'. The emails had to be read in context of an Inspector trying to help the claimant but becoming frustrated by them taking bad points [68]–[71].

Duty to make inquiries

7.89 The Planning Court has explored in a number of cases the extent of the duty on a decision maker to investigate matters. A decision maker must ask himself the right question and take reasonable steps to acquaint himself with the correct information to enable him to answer it correctly, this includes the need to allow the time reasonably necessary to obtain the relevant information and understand it and take it into account (*R (CPRE Kent) v Dover District Council*[138] [62]).

7.90 A planning officer failed to take reasonable steps to ascertain the extent of a recreation ground created by a Borough Council (*Peter Day v Shropshire Council*[139] [54]).

7.91 *CPRE Surrey v Waverley Borough Council*[140] [65]–[66]: within the context of the statutory scheme for examining a local plan, an Inspector examining such a plan was not obliged to seek more information than had been provided to him at the examination [65] even though there were uncertainties in the evidence [66].

7.92 Any administrative decision maker is under a duty to acquaint himself with information relevant to the decision in order to be able to make a properly informed decision, but the scope and content of that duty is context specific. It is

137 [2017] EWHC 2713 (Admin).
138 [2017] UKSC 79.
139 [2019] EWHC 3539 (Admin).
140 [2019] EWCA Civ 1826.

for the decision maker and not the Court to decide on the manner and intensity of inquiry to be undertaken into any relevant factor. A decision by a local planning authority as to the extent to which it considers it necessary to investigate relevant matters is challengeable only on conventional public law grounds (*Jayes v Flintshire County Council*[141] [14]). Where an Officer had limited information about the impact of the refusal of planning permission on children on a Site, it was open to her to make more inquiries [56]–[59] but this did not amount to an error of law.

7.93 A wide margin of discretion should be applied to councils advised by specialist planning officers in considering the extent to which it is necessary to investigate certain issues in greater or lesser detail(*Plant v Lambeth London Borough Council*[142] [70]).

7.94 In light of the duty to take reasonable steps to acquaint himself with the relevant information identified in *Secretary of State for Education and Science v Tameside Metropolitan Borough Council,*[143] there is no absolute rule that the Secretary of State is not obliged to have regard to a decision not placed before him (*DLA Delivery Ltd v Baroness Cumberlege of Newick*[144] [32]). In the High Court in the same case, the Court said that while there was a duty to take reasonable steps to acquaint himself with the relevant information in order to answer the question before him correctly, the court should only strike down a decision if no reasonable authority possessed of that material could have supposed that the inquiries they made were sufficient. Whether further inquiries were required would depend not only on the significance of the information that might be obtained if they are made but on the likelihood such information exists and the difficulties in finding out whether it does and obtaining it [75].

7.95 It is for the decision maker to decide on the manner and intensity of any inquiry subject to *Wednesbury* review (*Winters v SSCLG*[145] [35]). In that case the Inspector did not fail in his investigative duty where he had observed work on site and sought representations from the relevant parties [39].

7.96 An Inspector is not expected to make inquiries of her own motion and go behind the statement of comment ground where it was 'far from an obvious point' (*Renew Land Developments Limited v Welsh Ministers*[146] [40]).

Fettering discretion

7.97 A decision maker must keep an open mind and must not take any steps that would prevent them approaching their decision with an open mind.

141 [2018] EWCA Civ 1089.
142 [2016] EWHC 3324 (Admin).
143 [1977] AC 1014.
144 [2018] EWCA Civ 1305.
145 [2017] EWHC 357 (Admin).
146 [2020] EWCA Civ 143.

7.98 This history of and principles of the rule against fettering discretion were discussed at [19] in *SSCLG v West Berkshire District Council.*[147] A policy must not be inflexible, it ought not to fetter the exercise of a statutory discretion and it must envisage that the decision maker has power to depart from its terms if the individual circumstances of the case require (*Moore v SSCLG*[148] [38]). However, a policy maker is entitled to express policy in unqualified terms (*SSCLG l*[149] [21]).

7.99 The Secretary of State and an Inspector had not unlawfully fettered their discretion and applied a test of considering whether there were very good planning reasons for departing from a previous decision (*St Albans City and District Council v SSCLG*[150] [47]–[59]).

C. APPROACH TAKEN BY COURT IN CHALLENGES

Challenges not reflecting way case put to Inspector/Council

7.100 The Planning Court has been astute to prevent parties developing a challenge before the Planning Court that does not reflect the way they put their case to the decision maker: see Client Earth *(R. (on the application of Clientearth) v Secretary of State for Business, Energy and Industrial Strategy)*[151] *at 192]*

7.101 *R (on the application of Wynn-Williams) v SSCLG* [152] (the court should only very rarely allow new points to be taken at the s 288 stage; in any event the new point had no merit in the circumstances [26], [27], [28], [31], [32], [33]). *A4 Metal Recycling v SSCLG & Anor*[153] (the place and time for raising all matters of assessment or planning judgment is the process leading to the inspector's decision; it is not appropriate to raise such matters for the first time on appeal under s 288 [11]). *Luton Borough Council, R (on the application of) v Central Bedfordshire Council & Ors*[154] (late (ie after the grant of planning permission) raising of issues deprecated where the subsequent judicial review was based (in part) on failure to deal with that issue [107]).

Council decision making

Approach to officer's reports

7.102 The Planning Court has followed the Administrative Court in refusing to take a legalistic or pedantic approach to officers' reports to committees and on delegated decisions.

147 [2016] EWCA Civ 441.
148 [2016] EWHC 2736 (Admin).
149 [2016] EWCA Civ 441.
150 [2015] EWHC 655 (Admin).
151 [2020] EWHC 1303 (Admin)
152 [2014] EWHC 3374 (Admin).
153 [2014] EWHC 2524 (Admin).
154 [2014] EWHC 4325 (Admin).

7.103 The Court of Appeal set out the key principles in *Mansell v Tonbridge & Malling Borough Council*[155] [142]. Earlier cases should be read in the light of these remarks but remain instructive. *Earl Shilton Action Group v Hinckley & Bosworth Borough Council & Ors*[156] (officers' reports are not to be construed as if they are statutes but read overall and fairly; do they show that author identified the issues and material matters to be weighed? Reports are addressed to a 'knowledgeable readership' which can be presumed to have some knowledge of the planning regime and their area; there is no application to officers' reports of the rule of statutory construction that all words are intended to mean something; the challenge was dismissed as unarguable [11], [30]). *Hayes, R (on the application of) v Wychavon District Council & Anor*[157] (officer's report should not be subject to the same level of scrutiny as a decision letter; the relevant legal principles were summarised; the 'regrettable' drafting/cut-and-paste errors in the report were not sufficient to vitiate decision; unlikely to have misled anyone [23], [26], [66], [67]). *Warners Retail (Moreton) Ltd v Cotswold District Council*[158] (the legal principles were summarised; the overall effect of reports did not mislead [17], [50]). *Corrie, R (on the application of) v Suffolk County Council & Ors*[159] (officer's report did not need to refer to every point raised in the consultation [73]). *R (on the application of East Meon Forge and Cricket Ground Protection Association) v East Hampshire District Council* (the principles were re-iterated; the advice in the officer's report was 'controversial' but not 'wholly illogical' and as such not sufficient to vitiate the decision; failure to report information about financial circumstances of the claimant (relevant to viability of alternative restoration scheme) having said that it would be reported upon was 'poor professional practice' but was not sufficient to vitiate the decision as it would not have influenced the decision [32]–[34], [61], [62], [74], [75], [94]). *Khan, R (on the application of) v London Borough of Sutton*[160] (the report must be considered as a whole and in context that it was addressed to an informed local readership; there was no unlawful flaw on the facts [42]–[44], [59]). *Carnegie (on behalf of the Oaks Action Group), R (on the application of) v London Borough of Ealing*[161] (the Principles were set out; there was no requirement to set out within a report views of other officers that differ from the author's own; the overall planning judgment contained in Report did not mislead [21]–[23], [50], [51], [55]). *Ash Parish Council, R (on the application of) v Guildford Borough Council & Anor*[162] (Despite 'undoubtedly infelicitous' wording and errors, overall the report did not significantly mislead [15], [42], [46]–[52]). *Law v Essex County Council*[163] (officer's report did not mislead, the audience were an informed readership with local knowledge [52]).

155 [2017] EWCA Civ 1314.
156 [2014] EWHC 1764 (Admin).
157 [2014] EWHC 1987 (Admin).
158 [2014] EWHC 2504 (Admin).
159 [2014] EWHC 2490 (Admin).
160 [2014] EWHC 3663 (Admin).
161 [2014] EWHC 3807 (Admin).
162 [2014] EWHC 3864 (Admin).
163 [2015] EWHC 329 (Admin).

Comments by individual committee members in course of debate

7.104 Now that Council decision-making is often broadcast by webcam or otherwise recorded, challenges sometimes arise based on comments made by members of the committee during the debate on a planning application.

7.105 *Tesco Stores Ltd, R (on the application of) v Forest of Dean District Council & Ors*[164] (the general tenor of discussions at planning committee is what is important, rather than individual comments by members in the course of the discussion; what a member says in discussion may not be why he votes a particular way; caution must be applied when seeking to understand the reasoning by reference to transcripts of discussions [23], [63], [72], [73]).

Background knowledge of area expected from members

7.106 Members of a committee can be expected to have a reasonable knowledge of the local area.

7.107 *R. (on the application of Lady Hart of Chilton) v Babergh District Council*[165] (members' local knowledge is likely to include significant local employment trends [92], [93]).

Relying on officers to evaluate documents

7.108 Where commercially sensitive documents are provided with a planning application the committee sometimes have to rely on officers to summarise and evaluate those documents for them.

7.109 *Perry, R (on the application of) v Newmark Properties Ltd & Ors*[166] (officer's function includes sifting technical detail and distilling material information into reports and to do so is lawful [68]–[70]).

Justiciability of composition of committees

7.110 The Planning Court is unlikely to become involved in essentially political decisions about who sits on a planning committee, even when the question of who sits on a committee can be determinative of the outcome of applications.

164 [2014] EWHC 3348 (Admin).
165 [2014] EWHC 3261 (Admin).
166 [2014] EWHC 3499 (Admin).

7.111 *Carnegie (On Behalf of the Oaks Action Group), R (on the application of) v London Borough of Ealing*[167] (decisions about substitutions to committees are not matters for courts: they are part of the political process [33], [37]).

Decisions being sent back to committee following change in circumstances

7.112 As there is frequently a gap between the decision of the committee and the issuing of a grant of planning permission, it is frequently said that there has been a change in circumstances between the decision and the grant, relying on the well-known case of *R (Kides) v South Cambridgeshire District Council.*[168] Instances of such arguments succeeding are, however, few and far between.

7.113 *Police and Crime Commissioner for Leicestershire, R (on the application of) v Hallam Land Management Ltd & Ors*[169] (challenge upon basis that decision to grant subject to s.106 agreement being finalised was vitiated where actual s.106 did not (it was said) secure the contributions anticipated, was rejected [66], [67]). *R (on the application of Couves) v Gravesham Borough Council*[170] (there were changes of circumstances between the resolution and the grant; although the officer had not said in terms that they could not reasonably have altered the committee's view that was the only conclusion that can be drawn from what he says about those changes [93]; the statement in *Kides* about when an officer could 'safely' grant without referring back to committee was a safety factor and not a legal requirement [91], [93]).

Delegation schemes

7.114 Where officers make decisions themselves this is done in accordance with a delegation scheme. The Planning Court regularly has to investigate the contents of delegation schemes to ensure that the power to make the decision falls within it.

7.115 *R (on the application of Pemberton International Ltd) v London Borough of Lambeth*[171] (the scheme must be read as a whole; although the scheme was criticised as unclear and in need of amendment it was not unlawful [52]–[54], [61]). *R (on the application of Longacre Properties Ltd) v Winchester City Council*[172] (the scheme should be approached with a degree of common sense and officers should not have to cast around within scheme for inconsistencies [48], [50], [56], [57]). *R (on the application of Couves) v Gravesham Borough Council*[173] (there were elements of uncertainty about the delegation scheme and

167 [2014] EWHC 3807 (Admin).
168 [2002] EWCA Civ 1370.
169 [2014] EWHC 1719 (Admin).
170 [2015] EWHC 504 (Admin).
171 [2014] EWHC 1998 (Admin).
172 [2014] EWHC 3373 (Admin).
173 [2015] EWHC 504 (Admin).

the resolution under it but it was significant that no members or officers had raised any concerns about what was being done [40], [49]).

Approach to Inspectors' decision letters

7.116 The Planning Court has also adopted a permissive approach to the interpretation of Planning Inspectors' decision letters, which should be read as a whole, without excessive legalism and with a dollop of common sense.

7.117 *FCC Environment v (1) SSCLG (2) East Riding of Yorkshire Council*[174] (decision letters must be read in a common sense way and not with the scrutiny one might associate with reading a contract or a statute [30], [31]). *Taylor Wimpey West London v SSCLG & Ors*[175] (common sense reading of a decision letter meant that, even though the inspector had not expressed himself as clearly as he might, there was no error disclosed [50], [55]). *A4 Metal Recycling v SSCLG & Anor*[176] (writing a decision letter is not akin to answering an examination paper; the inspector is an expert and the decision letter can be treated as his considered judgment as such; the inspector is entitled to form judgments based on his impressions on a site visit [5]). *Copas v SSCLG*[177] (decision letters must be read fairly, and as a whole; on the facts the inspector had not left out of account any material considerations [22], [53]). *Howell & Ors v SSCLG* [2014] EWHC 3627 (decision letters must be read in good faith, fairly and as a whole, in a straightforward way and without excessive legalism [73]). *Britaniacrest Recycling Ltd v SSCLG*[178] (the decision maker has a wide judgment as to how issues are approached and decisions are not to be subjected to 'the analytical attention of a medieval schoolman' [27]).

Reading as a whole

7.118 *Lord Mayor And Citizens of the City of Westminster v The SSCLG & Anor*[179] (although reading passages in isolation might just permit the reading contended for by claimant, that is not the right way to read it – it should be read as a whole [29]). *Fuller v SSCLG*[180] (inspector's decision must be read as a whole: when that was done, the Claimant's challenge fell away [22]).

Reading fairly

7.119 *Lark Energy Ltd v SSCLG & Anor*[181] (The decision letter must be read fairly, and without excessive legalism; words should be read in their full context:

174 [2014] EWHC 2035 (Admin).
175 [2014] EWHC 2082 (Admin).
176 [2014] EWHC 2524 (Admin).
177 [2014] EWHC 2634 (Admin).
178 [2015] EWHC 1019 (Admin).
179 [2014] EWHC 1234 (Admin).
180 [2015] EWHC 142 (Admin).
181 [2014] EWHC 2035 (Admin).

on the issue of whether an inspector compared the scheme before him with the 'fallback' only, or instead carried out a proper balance of the planning merits of the scheme, including that fallback, there was no error [31], [32], [37]–[40]). *Arsenal Football Club Plc v SSCLG & Anor*[182] (decisions must not be read as if they are statutes; a fair reading includes the requirement to read a decision in the context of the way the respective cases were put to the decision-maker, as that may explain the structure of the decision [31]–[33], [38]).

Benefit of the doubt

7.120 *Lark Energy Ltd*[183] (the Court was prepared to give the Secretary of State the benefit of the doubt in his overall conclusions section of report and as such no error was disclosed [41]).

Deference

7.121 *Guinness & Anor v The SSCLG*[184] (the inspector was entitled to come to her own view about whether harm was done to a by reason of the installation of double glazing, even where the existing windows were of equally poor design [24]–[28]). *Pugh v SSCLG & Ors*[185] (it was for the inspector to form his own view as to the effect of the development on heritage assets, and he was entitled to adopt a particular assessment if it accorded with his own [43]). *Fuller v SSCLG*[186] (considerable deference was given to an inspector, who decided that no decision was needed on the main issue in the case by imposing a condition rather than stopping the development going ahead [22]–[23]). *Trail Riders Fellowship v Secretary of State for the Environment, Food and Rural Affairs*[187] (inspector's decision as to status of a route was not overturned: he was entitled to reach a conclusion either way and the court should not substitute its own view).

Non-material errors

7.122 *Shortt v SSCLG*[188] (where inspector had misapplied a legal test, but done so in respect of a point that was ultimately not determinative, the decision was not quashed [17]). *North Cote Farms Ltd v SSCLG & Anor*[189] (no express discussion of s 38(6) or any finding of whether the proposal was or was not in accordance with the development plan, but there did not need to be, as both parties agreed that only minimal weight should be given to the old development

182 [2014] EWHC 2620 (Admin).
183 [2014] EWHC 2035 (Admin).
184 [2014] EWHC 4114 (Admin).
185 [2015] EWHC 3 (Admin).
186 [2015] EWHC 142 (Admin).
187 [2015] EWHC 85 (Admin).
188 [2014] EWHC 2480 (Admin).
189 [2015] EWHC 292 (Admin).

plan, which was not in accordance with NPPF; the omission made no difference to the outcome [64]).

Contradictory passages

7.123 *Moore & Ors v SSCLG*[190] (where there were contradictory passages in a decision letter, but that contradiction was apparent rather than substantive, and the second such passage was clearly an error, the challenge was dismissed on this ground (but upheld on other grounds) [56]–[63]).

Secretary of State's approach to Inspector's recommendations

7.124 In a number of areas (green belt, renewable energy) the Secretary of State has adopted a policy of 'calling in' substantial numbers of planning applications (for example, under s 77 of the TCPA 1990 or s 12 of the P(LBCA) 1990). This has led to challenges which have forced the Planning Court to consider the scope of his power to disagree with the recommendations of his inspector.

7.125 *Ecotricity (Next Generation) Ltd R (on the application of) v SSCLG*[191] (the Secretary of State gave sufficient reasons for disagreeing with his inspector on whether the proposal would have significant adverse impact on landscape character or visual amenity; there was no obligation for the Secretary of State to conduct his own site view before disagreeing with his inspector on visual impact – he had sufficient detail before him to reach the conclusion he did [11], [15], [17]–[22]).[192] *Wind Prospect Developments Ltd v SSCLG*[193] (there was no requirement for the Secretary of State to conduct a site visit where he had maps, illustrations and predicted views of the proposed turbines; he was entitled to differ from his inspector in the judgment reached on visual impact [15]–[27]). *O'Connor v SSCLG*[194] (the Secretary of State had failed to take any account of the inspector's conclusions about flood risk zones and his conclusion was not reasonably open to him given the inspector's conclusions [45]).

Improper purposes

7.126 *GRA Acquisition Ltd, R (on the application of) v Oxford City Council*[195] (there was no evidence of an improper purpose or agenda for designation of a stadium as a conservation area: there was no allegation of bad faith and no evidence to support a contention that the reasons were other than those stated [60]).

190 [2014] EWHC 3592 (Admin).
191 [2014] EWHC 2699 (Admin).
192 Appeal against decision of Planning Court subsequently dismissed by the Court of Appeal on 28 April 2015, at the time of writing unreported.
193 [2014] EWHC 4041 (Admin).
194 [2014] EWHC 3821 (Admin).
195 [2015] EWHC 76 (Admin).

D RELIEF/DISCRETION TO QUASH

7.127 Frequently a decision maker argues that even if they have made an error the Court should exercise their discretion to refuse to quash.

Examples of refusal to quash

7.128 *R (on the application of Longacre Properties Ltd) v Winchester City Council*[196] (although it had not been made out on the facts, if there had been a breach of the requirement to consult a particular member, it would have made no difference because the member had given unchallenged evidence as to what his response would have been; as such the discretion not to quash would have been exercised [73]–[76], [79]). *R (on the application of Lady Hart of Chilton) v Babergh District Council*[197] (where the only successful ground of challenge was that the Council had failed to notify the Secretary of State of the planning application in order that he could consider calling it in, the relief granted was to allow the Secretary of State an opportunity to call it in; if he took that opportunity, the decision would be quashed, if he did not, it would not [104]–[105]). *Ash Parish Council, R (on the application of) v Guildford Borough Council & Anor*[198] (although the claim failed, had it succeeded relief would have been withheld because it was a case where the outcome would have been the same notwithstanding the alleged error [54]). *Dear v SSCLG & Anor*[199] (where the effect of the errors identified was academic, no order to quash on those grounds [35]–[36]). *Veolia ES (UK) Ltd v SSCLG*[200] (the Secretary of State's decision would inevitably have been the same had he not made the errors identified, and so there would be no quashing on those grounds of the decision that followed; but the decision was quashed on another ground where the errors on that ground could not be said to have made no difference [54]–[58]; [108]). *Law v Essex County Council*[201] (although the claim failed, the court would have taken into account the prejudice to good administration caused by quashing the decision when considering the discretion to quash, together with the hardship caused to the defendant; and taken together the discretion to withhold relief would have been exercised in this case [55]–[56]). *Venn v SSCLG*[202] (the inspector had acted unfairly in relation to a report on light [42] however the decision would not be quashed given the peripheral importance of that report [48]). *R (on the application of Smech Properties Ltd) v Runnymede Borough Council*[203] (where Council had granted permission on the incorrect basis that they had a five year land supply the decision would not be quashed as the situation would have been even more dire had it been properly understood [121]).

196 [2014] EWHC 3373 (Admin).
197 [2014] EWHC 3261 (Admin).
198 [2014] EWHC 3844 (Admin).
199 [2015] EWHC 29 (Admin).
200 [2015] EWHC 91 (Admin).
201 [2015] EWHC 329 (Admin).
202 [2015] EWHC 1186 (Admin).
203 [2015] EWHC 823 (Admin).

Examples of refusing to exercise the discretion not to quash

7.129 *R (on the application of McClellan) v Lambeth London Borough Council*[204] (where the cabinet failed to take into account a material consideration, and the judgment was a fine balance, there was no exercise of discretion not to quash [23]–[26]). *R (on the application of Pemberton International Ltd) v Lambeth London Borough Council*[205] (where the decision maker had failed to have regard to complaints about breaches of condition, it was not possible to say that the same decision would inevitably have been reached had the error not been made; the discretion to refuse to quash was not exercised [71], [73]). *R (on the application of Midcounties Co-operative Ltd) v Forest of Dean District Council*[206] (it was impossible to say that the decision would have been the same in a complex case involving interrelating planning issues; failure to take into account all material considerations vitiated the decision and despite further delay being occasioned by quashing, there was no basis not to quash [80-[82]). *Joicey, R (on the application of) v Northumberland County Council*[207] (there was a serious breach of the Council's statutory obligations in respect of disclosure, and there was no reason to deny the Claimant his remedy [46]–[59]). *Robert Hitchins Ltd, R (on the application of) v Worcestershire County Council & Ors*[208] (where a successful claimant continued to retain a sufficient interest in the case (as a party liable to make transport contributions under a s106 agreement), there was no good reason to deny the declaration sought [70]–[74]). *South Gloucestershire Council v SSCLG*[209] (where serious errors of law were made with potentially profound consequences for the future, the decision should be quashed notwithstanding sympathy for the consequent effect of quashing on the applicant. The matter was remitted to an inspector [69]–[73]). *Gottlieb, R (on the application of) v Winchester City Council*[210] (where there had been a serious breach of the procurement regime which was both procedural and substantive, for the second time in respect of that particular scheme of works, it would have to be an exceptional course to allow the unlawful decision to stand; in the circumstances the decision would be quashed. The successful claimant (a local Councillor) had sufficient standing and a legitimate interest in seeing the procurement regime adhered to generally [154]). *Silus Investments SA, R (on the application of) v London Borough of Hounslow*[211] (where the Claimant had been denied his right to participate in the planning process leading to the designation of a conservation area, it could not be said that his participation would inevitably have made no difference; such an approach would suggest that the Council had a 'closed mind' [67]). *R (on the application of Cheshire East Council) v SSCLG*[212] (it is an exceptional course to uphold an inspector's decision when there has been

204 [2014] EWHC 1964 (Admin).
205 [2014] EWHC 1998 (Admin).
206 [2014] EWHC 3059 (Admin).
207 [2014] EWHC 3657 (Admin).
208 [2014] EWHC 3809 (Admin).
209 [2014] EWHC 4555 (Admin).
210 [2015] EWHC 220 (Admin).
211 [2015] EWHC 358 (Admin).
212 [2015] EWHC 410 (Admin).

an error of law in the decision making process and there is a danger that the court may be tempted to make its own judgment of the planning merits in deciding whether or not to do so [66]). *Ecotricity v SSCLG*[213] (unhesitatingly rejected the submission that discretionary relief should be refused if there was procedural unfairness because of an alternative remedy of a new planning application supported by appropriate evidence [70]).

In European cases

7.130 The Supreme Court in *Walton* recognised that the discretion not to quash could apply even where there was a breach of European derived legislation. The Planning Court has had to grapple with the consequences of this.

7.131 *Hughes, R (the application of) v South Lakeland District Council*[214] (where a Screening Opinion was found to be flawed, and there was evidence from the author that if she was to undertake the process again she would come to the same view, the discretion not to quash would be exercised. It was inevitable that the Screening Opinion would have produced the same outcome regardless of the errors. Although a European matter, it was putting it too high to say that the discretion not to quash was severely circumscribed [41]–[46]). *Kendall v Rochford District Council*[215] (it was correct to withhold even limited relief in the circumstances: although the consultation on the draft plan had been lawful, there had been a breach of the Directive and Regulations; there was no real (or substantial) prejudice to the claimant and the outcome would have been exactly the same had the breach not occurred [126]). *Davies, R (On the Application of) v Carmarthenshire County Council & Anor*[216] (the court had decided that the Screening Opinion was flawed, and would not have exercised its discretion to withhold relief in the circumstances [42], [46]). *R (on the application of Westerleigh Group Ltd) v Aylesbury Vale District Council*[217] (it was not appropriate to refuse to quash a planning authority's decision in an Habitats Regulation case on the basis of Natural England's role in policing those regulations [96]–[98]; it could not be said the committee would inevitably have made the same decision if the error had been corrected [98]).

E SUBSTANTIVE ISSUES

7.132 Over its first five years the Planning Court has had to deal with a large number of discrete issues of substance. The selection of cases discussed below is by no means comprehensive but follows the structure of the topics discussed in the First Edition of this work, with updating as appropriate.

213 [2015] EWHC 801 (Admin).
214 [2014] EWHC 3979 (Admin).
215 [2014] EWHC 3866 (Admin).
216 [2015] EWHC 230 (Admin).
217 [2015] EWHC 885 (Admin).

Conditions

7.133 The court has in a number of cases emphasised the high threshold for the court quashing a condition on the ground that it is irrational. *Joicey, R (on the Application of) v Northumberland County Council*[218] (the court confirmed that there was a judicial reluctance to become involved in the evaluation of a condition so long as it is fairly and reasonably related to the development in question; complexity in a condition does not make it unlawful [70]). *Howell & Ors v SSCLG*[219] (the court although troubled by the condition emphasised that to quash it, the condition would have to 'fail the high threshold of rationality'; the inspector did not have to develop a condition himself to deal with an issue when no such condition had been suggested to him at the Inquiry [68]–[70]). *R (on the application of Isherwood Carter) v Swansea City and County Council*[220] (it would be irrational for a Council to impose a condition it knew could not be fulfilled, but there was no need to have positive evidence that a condition could be met before imposing such a condition [40]).

Interpretation

7.134 The correct approach to the interpretation of planning conditions has been a regular issue for the Administrative Court over the years and the Planning Court has also had to grapple with it.

7.135 *IXPL Ltd, R (on the application of) v Harlow Council*[221] (it was not appropriate to apply the *ejusdem generis* rule of construction to planning conditions as conditions are to be read by a reasonable reader not versed in the niceties of commercial construction [33]). By contrast, *Greaves and another v Boston Borough Council*[222] (a noise condition is to be read by experts so the fact that it contained terms not understood by the general public did not make it unlawful or unenforceable [35]–[39]). *Menston Action Group, R (on the application of) v Bradford Metropolitan District Council & Anor*[223] (the Court set out the existing law on the interpretation of conditions at [9]; a condition should if at all possible be construed in accordance with the law [12]; as the interpretation the Claimant were seeking to put on the condition would have made it contrary to law that interpretation could not be accepted [18]–[19]). This latter point was recently re-affirmed by the Court of Appeal in *DB Symmetry Ltd v Swindon Borough Council* [224] (The courts have also leant in favour of an interpretation of a condition that would render it lawful rather than interpreting it in a way which would mean that it could not have been lawfully imposed [68], [88]).

218 [2014] EWHC 3657 (Admin).
219 [2014] EWHC 3627 (Admin).
220 [2015] EWHC 75 (Admin).
221 [2014] EWHC 3860 (Admin).
222 [2014] EWHC 3590 (Admin).
223 [2015] EWHC 184 (Admin).
224 [2020] EWCA Civ 1331.

Condition/limitation distinction

7.136 Since *I'm Your Man v Secretary of State* (1999) 77 P&CR 251; [1999] PLCR 109 the courts have wrestled with the relationship between conditions and limitations. *Cotswold Grange Country Park LLP v SSCLG*[225] (the number of caravans in the description of a permission was a limitation not a condition, and therefore unenforceable [30]).

Grampian conditions

7.137 A *Grampian* condition prevents any development until certain steps are undertaken, and are frequently used where there is a contingent step that may or may not occur. However, the Planning Court has had to deal with the approach a decision maker should take to the imposition of such conditions.

7.138 *FCC Environment v (1) SSCLG (2) East Riding of Yorkshire Council*[226] (if there are no prospects at all of satisfactory mitigation becoming available during the lifetime of a permission then a Grampian condition should be refused; there is nothing which provides that simply because there is some prospect of a Grampian condition being complied with permission must be granted [12], [13], [16], [17]).

Whitley conditions

7.139 Since *Hart Aggregates* not all failures to comply with commencement conditions will lead to the decision being quashed, only failures to comply with those conditions going to the heart of the permission.

7.140 *Silver v SSCLG*[227] (a planning inspector was best placed to judge whether a condition went to the heart of a condition in the exercise of his planning judgment; provided that approach was not irrational the court would be unwilling to interfere [53]).

Section 106 agreements

7.141 The circumstances in which a s 106 agreement has been imposed and the interpretation of that agreement are also a common source of litigation.

7.142 *R (on the application of Midcounties Co-operative Ltd) v Forest of Dean District Council*[228] (permission quashed because a committee were required

225 [2014] EWHC 1138 (Admin).
226 [2014] EWHC 2035 (Admin).
227 [2014] EWHC 2729 (Admin).
228 [2014] EWHC 3059 (Admin).

to consider properly how the s 106 contributions proposed would mitigate the harm it was intended to address and had acted without any evidence on this issue [53]–[58]). By contrast *Tesco Stores Ltd, R (on the application of) v Forest of Dean District Council & Ors*[229] (despite officers' concerns, members were entitled to conclude that they had sufficient information to enable them to be satisfied that the s 106 agreement before them met the statutory tests and would ameliorate the harm to the town centre [127]). *R (on the application of Lady Hart of Chilton) v Babergh District Council*[230] (the court rejected a claim that that the s 106 agreement failed to deliver the required benefits; the court accepted that there had been a long negotiation and the Council could rationally conclude that the agreement put forward represented the best terms available so as to have prospects of securing the substantial socio-economic benefits for which the Council had granted planning permission [12], [55]–[58]). *Oxfordshire County Council v SSCLG*[231] (an Inspector was entitled to conclude that a Council's administrative monitoring fees for the s 106 agreement were unlawful as a standardised fee rather than an individualised assessment of costs to be incurred for that development; the fees were not necessary to make the development acceptable in planning terms [54]–[55]).

Community Infrastructure Levy

7.143 *R (on the application of Hourhope Ltd) v Shropshire Council*[232] (for the purposes of the Community Infrastructure Levy Regulations 2010,[233] reg 40(7), the requirement that a building be 'in use' required more than that a building had a use to which it might theoretically be put [18], whether a property is 'in use' will requires an assessment of all the circumstances and evidence as to which activities take place [25]).

Planning permissions

Implementation

7.144 It is frequently important for the parties to know (often years later) whether a particular permission has been implemented.

7.145 *Silver v SSCLG*[234] (in assessing whether a series of works had implemented a planning permission it was right to look at the whole of what had been done; there were sufficient differences between the works and the permission for the inspector rationally to conclude that the works had not implemented the

229 [2014] EWHC 3348 (Admin).
230 [2014] EWHC 3261 (Admin).
231 [2015] EWHC 186 (Admin).
232 [2015] EWHC 518 (Admin).
233 SI 2010/948.
234 [2014] EWHC 2729 (Admin).

permission [34]–[43]). *Hillside Parks Ltd v Snowdonia National Park Authority*[235] (the right to continue with a part-implemented planning permission could be lost if subsequent development under later permissions made it impossible to complete the original development in all respects as originally authorised [67], [72]).

Interpretation

7.146 In two cases the Planning Court considered looking at extrinsic material to interpret a planning permission.

7.147 *Howell & Ors v SSCLG*[236] (there was an ambiguity in the grant of permission for a wind turbine and as such it was permissible to look at other documentation including the Environmental Statement in deciding whether the permission was for a specific model of turbine [83]–[84]). *Djurberg v SSCLG*[237] (the court considered detailed evidence of the state of the land at the time of a grant of permission to conclude whether a previous grant of permission covered an existing situation [29], [38], [39]).

Fallback

7.148 It is frequently relevant to consider what could be done without planning permission and the relative harm this would cause in comparison with what is now proposed.

7.149 *Lark Energy Ltd v SSCLG & Anor*[238] (an inspector was entitled to compare the merits of what was proposed with what had been granted but on a fair reading of the decision letter he had – as he must – reached a view as to the acceptability of what was proposed, not just carried out a comparison [29], [30], [34], [35]). *R (on the application of Wynn-Williams) v SSCLG* (the case of *Gambone* which adopted a two stage approach ((i) was the fallback likely to come forwards; (ii) was the fallback more harmful) was helpful but did not need to be mechanistically applied; here it had been properly applied [9], [43]–[46], [51], [52]). *A4 Metal Recycling v SSCLG & Anor*[239] (determination of the appropriate fallback was a matter for the inspector's assessment and judgment; he was entitled to reject the claimant's arguments that various uses were lawful and conclude they did not constitute a fallback, particularly in light of a refusal of a certificate of lawfulness for those uses [7], [25], [26], [27]).

235 [2020] EWCA Civ 1440.
236 [2014] EWHC 3627 (Admin).
237 [2014] EWHC 4137 (Admin).
238 [2014] EWHC 2006 (Admin).
239 [2014] EWHC 2524 (Admin).

General Permitted Development Order ('GPDO')

7.150 The courts have upheld the need to interpret the GPDO in a broad and common sense matter, but have frequently had to resolve highly technical debates.

7.151 *Evans v SSCLG*[240] (rear first floor extension is not permitted on Article 1(5) land [24], [25]; if any part of a building is unlawful, permitted development rights for the building as a whole are excluded [37]). *Valentino Plus Ltd v SSCLG*[241] (mixed use in Class F meant a number of uses in the same building; a restrictive interpretation to the effect that those uses had to have a functional link was not required [14]–[18]).

Meeting full objectively assessed need

7.152 Housing provision meeting full objectively assessed need is an important concept in the NPPF. *Satnam Millennium Ltd v Warrington Borough Council*[242] (the court explains the relationship between objectively assessed need for an area and for local market housing area [25]; it is not unlawful for a local authority to set an annual housing figure below the objectively assessed need for its area in light of wider housing market factors [25], [31], nor to assume that neighbouring authorities would 'pick up' excess need [36]; but it was unlawful to leave out of account any assessment of affordable housing need [43]).

Enforcement

7.153 *Silver v SSCLG*[243] (an inspector was entitled to conclude that a notice was not a nullity as looking at it within its four corners it was not defective or hopelessly ambiguous and uncertain [57]). *Jackson v SSCLG*[244] (the deceit principles in *Welwyn v SSHD* remain good law and have not been wholly replaced by the planning enforcement order scheme [61]–[68]).

Green belt

7.154 Pressure on the green belt has led to litigation in the Planning Court clarifying the correct approach to various aspects of green belt policy. See also the discussion above in relation to the interpretation of the NPPF.

240 [2014] EWHC 4111 (Admin).
241 [2015] EWHC 19 (Admin).
242 [2015] EWHC 370 (Admin).
243 [2014] EWHC 2729 (Admin).
244 [2015] EWHC 20 (Admin).

Very special circumstances

7.155 *Redhill Aerodrome Ltd v SSCLG & Ors*[245] (paragraph 88 of the NPPF says 'very special circumstances will not exist unless the potential harm to the Green Belt by reason of inappropriateness, and any other harm, is clearly outweighed by other considerations; any other harm in this context refers to any harm that is relevant for planning purposes and is not limited to harm to the green belt). *Luton Borough Council, R (on the application of) v Central Bedfordshire Council & Ors*[246] (the 'very special circumstances' test does not require a decision maker to chop a mixed use proposal up into separate components and to apply the test separately in relation to each [167]).

Green belt release

7.156 *Gallagher Homes Ltd v Solihull Metropolitan Borough Council*[247] (what might constitute exceptional circumstances justifying green belt release was considered; the test has not changed since the introduction of the NPPF; a proposal to extend the green belt must be subject to the same stringent regime as a proposal to diminish it [124]). *R (on the application of IM Properties Development Ltd) v Lichfield District Council*[248] (there is no doctrine that green belt land is to be released as a last resort or only when it can be shown that the original basis for inclusion was false; it is an exercise of planning judgment as to whether exceptional circumstances necessitating revision have been demonstrated [87]–[91], [95]–[96]).

Openness

7.157 *Connors v SSCLG*[249] (the correct starting point for a temporary permission in the green belt is that even on a temporary basis the development would be inappropriate, would cause harm, and can only be approved in very special circumstances [162]). *R (Samuel Smith Old Brewery (Tadcaster) and others v North Yorkshire County Council* [250] (assessing openness in the green belt is a matter for planning judgment and not law and need not necessarily include visual impacts [39]).

245 [2014] EWCA Civ 1386 (Admin).
246 [2014] EWHC 4325 (Admin).
247 [2014] EWHC 1283 (Admin).
248 [2014] EWHC 2440 (Admin).
249 [2014] EWHC 2358 (Admin).
250 [2020] UKSC 3.

Heritage

Settings of listed buildings and conservation areas

7.158 Since the Court of Appeal in *Barnwell* emphasised the importance of statutory duties concerning listed buildings and conservation areas, the Planning Court has had to grapple with a number of challenges where it is said that the decision maker has paid insufficient heed to those matters.

7.159 *R (Loader) v Rother DC*[251] (decision makers must give the views of Historic England great weight and only depart from them with cogent reasons [40). *R (Liverpool Open and Green Spaces Community Interest Company) v Liverpool City Council*[252] (a failure to tell members of the committee about 'strong conservation objections' from internal conservation consultee was an error of law). *Catesby Estates Ltd v SSCLG*[253] (setting of a heritage asset is not limited to direct visual relationship, other considerations may be relevant).*The Forge Field Society & Ors v Sevenoaks District Council*[254] (nothing in *Barnwell* changes the position that a planning authority's assessment of the likely harm on the setting of a listed building or a conservation area is a matter for the authority's own judgment; but the finding of harm to the setting of a listed building or conservation area gives rise to a strong presumption against planning permission being granted; although the committee report properly referred to the statutory test this was insufficient when the relevant paragraphs dealing with harm to heritage assets treated less than substantial harm as a less than substantial objection [48]–[59]). *WSPA v Welsh Ministers*[255] (the minister clearly had special regard to the impact on the setting of the listed buildings; there was no difference between the statutory phrase 'special regard' and the phrase used which was 'particular regard' [20], [21], [40]). *R (on the application of Lady Hart of Chilton) v Babergh District Council*[256] (a committee was entitled to disagree with a heritage officer's assessment and find that substantial harm to heritage assets was justified; the relevant part of the NPPF and the relevant statutory provisions had been drawn fully to their attention [80] to [89]). *Carnegie (On Behalf of the Oaks Action Group), R (on the application of) v London Borough of Ealing*[257] (where after diligent inquiry no harm had been found to the setting of the heritage asset there was no need to go further than that in the officer's report [25], [26], [27], [58]). *R (Pagham Parish Council) v Arun District Council*[258] (an 'impact' is not necessarily to be equated to a harmful impact [38]) but note *R(Hall) v Bradford MBC*[259] (even negligible harm is sufficient to engage the statutory duty [33]–[34]). *Catesby Estates Ltd v Steer*[260] (the concept of 'significance' whilst

251 [2016] EWCA Civ 795.
252 [2020] EWCA Civ 861.
253 [2018] EWCA Civ 1697.
254 [2014] EWHC 1895 (Admin).
255 [2014] EWHC 1896 (Admin).
256 [2014] EWHC 3261 (Admin).
257 [2014] EWHC 3807 (Admin).
258 [2019] EWHC 1721 (Admin)
259 [2019] EWHC 2899 (Admin)
260 [2018] EWCA Civ 1697.

not mentioned in the statutory tests, is a relevant determining factor in assessing whether the statutory test is met [30]). *Dill v SSHCLG*[261] (status of a listed building can be considered on appeal against a listed building enforcement notice [25]; the court upheld the *Skerritts* test for what is a building [52]).

7.160 *Hughes, R (on the application of) v South Lakeland District Council*[262] (the officer's report fell into the error identified in *Barnwell*; the report struck a straightforward balance without reference to the necessary presumption; as such the permission must fall [54]–[60]). *Mordue v SSCLG*[263] (the reasons given by a decision maker do not need to recite that 'considerable importance and weight' has been applied to the statutory duty in order to discharge the duty [27]–[28]). *Gerber v Wiltshire Council*[264] (where on a proper analysis the authority did consider that a development would have an effect on a listed building they were required to consult English Heritage; furthermore the Council was unable to demonstrate that it had complied with the obligation under section 66(1) [56]).

NPPF

7.161 The meaning of the heritage provisions of the NPPF continues to be fodder for challenge.

7.162 *R(Williams) v Powys CC*[265] (where s 66 Planning (Listed Buildings and Conservation Areas) Act 1990 is engaged but is not drawn to members' attention, that is likely to amount to an error of law [66]) *Mordue v SSCLG*[266] (where decision maker works through the NPPF paragraphs, s/he will have discharged the statutory duty, and thus where an expert planning decision maker refers to a paragraph within the NPPF heritage provisions the appropriate inference is that s/he has taken them all into account, absent positive indications to the contrary [28]). *Bramshill v SSHCLG*[267] (where there is a finding of harm, that should be weighed against the public benefits of the scheme in accordance with the NPPF, a decision maker should not perform a 'mini-balance' of that harm against heritage benefits so as to avoid a finding of harm overall [111]) but note *Palmer v Herefordshire Council*[268] (if mitigation measures are put in place which would avoid the harm, then a decision maker is in those circumstances entitled to find the statutory duty is met [29]; however see *Safe Rottingdean Ltd v Brighton & Hove City Council*[269] which appears to take matters a step further.

261 [2020] UKSC 20.
262 [2014] EWHC 3979 (Admin).
263 [2015] EWCA Civ 1243.
264 [2015] EWHC 524 (Admin).
265 [2017] EWCA Civ 427.
266 [2015] EWCA Civ 1243.
267 [2019] EWHC 3437 (Admin).
268 [2016] EWCA Civ 1061.
269 [2019] EWHC 2632 (Admin).

Conservation areas

7.163 *R (on the application of McClellan) v Lambeth London Borough Council*[270] (s 72 of the Planning (Listed Buildings and Conservations Area) Act 1990 did not apply to the decision whether to remove the Council's tree from a conservation area [18]). *GRA Acquisition Ltd, R (on the application of) v Oxford City Council*[271] (the question of what constituted an 'area' for the designation of a conservation area had to be established; the Council could rationally conclude that the Oxford racetrack was such an area [36]–[38]). *Silus Investments SA, R (on the application of) v London Borough of Hounslow*[272] (the Council had been properly advised that it was not lawful to designate a conservation area just to save a single building and had not improperly designated the area [48]–[49]). *Organisation for Promotion of Environmental Needs Ltd, R (on the application of) v London Borough of Hackney*[273] (the authority was entitled to conclude on what was before it that a development could not go ahead retaining a façade [55], [58]).

Alternative sites/schemes

7.164 It is frequently argued by opponents of schemes that the decision maker should have regard to some alternative site or alternative scheme.

7.165 *The Forge Field Society & Ors, R (on the application of) v Sevenoaks District Council*[274] (alternative sites had to be considered given the planning benefits of the scheme but also the clear objections to it; it was not for the court to consider whether other development sites were feasible and carried less harm; the Council had to consider those matters and failed to do so [84]–[94]). *R (on the application of East Meon Forge and Cricket Ground Protection Association) v East Hampshire District Council*[275] (exceptionally an alternative scheme to that proposed did have to be considered because it was central to the reasoning of the conservation officer [76]–[80]). *Horsham District Council v SSCLG*[276] (the Inspector's exercise of his judgement was lawful in circumstances where there was no tangible alternative scheme put before him; the suggestion that the inspector could not approve the scheme if he thought a better one might have been proposed was misconceived [54]–[60]). *Luton Borough Council, R (on the application of) v Central Bedfordshire Council & Ors*[277] (alternative sites were not obviously material and the defendant did not act irrationally in failing to consider alternative sites; there was no error in failing to consider expressly whether to consider alternative sites [149]–[153]). *R (on the application of*

270 [2014] EWHC 1964 (Admin).
271 [2015] EWHC 76 (Admin).
272 [2015] EWHC 358 (Admin).
273 [2014] EWHC 4272 (Admin).
274 [2014] EWHC 1895 (Admin).
275 [2014] EWHC 3543 (Admin).
276 [2015] EWHC 109 (Admin).
277 [2014] EWHC 4325 (Admin).

Westerleigh Group Ltd) v Aylesbury Vale District Council[278] (in order to show that a decision maker erred in failing to have regard to alternative sites it was necessary to find some legal principle that compelled (not merely empowered) him to do so; there was none here [73]).

Consultee requests

7.166 The court has reiterated the importance of paying careful regard to the responses of a statutory consultee.

7.167 *R (on the application of East Meon Forge and Cricket Ground Protection Association) v East Hampshire District Council*[279] (planning permission was unlawful because the Council failed to have regard to Sport England's sound representations; Sport England was a statutory consultee [123]).

Reservoirs

7.168 *R (on the application of Heath & Hampstead Society) v City of London*[280] (the purpose of the Reservoirs Act 1975 was to prevent the escape of water not to mitigate the effects of an escape; therefore the Defendant was entitled in light of the advice from various engineers to conclude preventative action should be taken [52], [101]).

Village greens

7.169 Challenges to village green decisions fall within the jurisdiction of the Planning Court. However, possibly because of the effect of reforms which prevent the making of a village green application where a planning application has been made, the court has only had to deal with limited challenges to the decision of a Registration Authority.

7.170 *Naylor v Essex County Council*[281] (use could be 'as of right' where local authority do not own the land but operate it under a statutory regime [39], [59]; a registration authority was entitled to assume that they were provided with all relevant information, and to allege an additional investigative duty it would be necessary to show no reasonable authority would fail to obtain the information [60]–[64]; physical exclusion of users and carrying out of an incompatible use are two different ways of showing interruption of user [69]–[72]; matters of judgment by the registration authority were not to be impugned [74]). *R (Lancashire County Council) v SSEFRA; R (NHS Property Services Ltd) v Surrey County Council*[282]

278 [2015] EWHC 885 (Admin).
279 [2014] EWHC 3543 (Admin).
280 [2014] EWHC 3868 (Admin).
281 [2014] EWHC 2560 (Admin).
282 [2019] UKSC 58.

(land held by local authorities for statutory purposes which were incompatible with the enjoyment of public rights over a village green could not be subject to a successful registration because of the doctrine of statutory incompatibility. This long-running litigation was commenced in the Planning Court).

Commons

7.171 *R (on the application of Littlejohns) v Devon County Council*[283] (the intent of the Commons Registration Act 1965 was that all common land and rights of common should be registered and registration should be conclusive [36] Parliament did not expect or intend new rights to be registered over existing common land [37] if new rights arose by prescription over existing commons they would be extinguished as soon as they arose by virtue of non-registration [41] the 2006 Act did not revive any such rights [49]).

Relationship with other regulatory regimes

7.172 Often decision makers in planning are forced to consider the relationship between their decision and other regulatory regimes such as Environmental Permit schemes.

7.173 *R (on the application of Frack Free Balcombe Residents Association) v West Sussex County Council*[284] (the local authority was entitled to assume that environmental controls in other regimes would be properly applied [100]–[104]).

Local plans/neighbourhood plans

7.174 The complex series of steps necessary to put together a local or neighbourhood plan continue to be a source of litigation in the Planning Court, which has tended to uphold the decision making of local and neighbourhood plan inspectors.

Challenges/inspector's role

7.175 *Grand Union Investments Ltd v Dacorum Borough Council*[285] (testing the soundness of a plan is not a task for the courts, it is a matter of planning judgment; the court's jurisdiction is limited to review on traditional public law grounds; guidance to soundness in the NPPF is policy not law and should not be treated as law; the assessment of soundness was an essentially practical exercise [56]–[59], [67]). *BDW Trading Ltd (t/a Barratt Homes) & Anor v Cheshire West*

283 [2015] EWHC 730 (Admin).
284 [2014] EWHC 4108 (Admin).
285 [2014] EWHC 1894 (Admin).

& Chester Borough Council & Ors[286] (whether a plan adequately addressed reasonable alternatives was a matter of planning judgment [74]). *Gladman Development Ltd v Wokingham Borough Council*[287] (an Inspector considering a development plan document dealing with allocation of housing was not required to consider objective assessment of needs [60]).

Duty to co-operate under s 33A Planning and Compulsory Purchase Act 2004

7.176 *Samuel Smith Old Brewery (Tadcaster) v Selby District Council*[288] (where the duty to co-operate came into force during a period of suspension of the plan the authority was not subject to it [9], [26]–[37]). *R (Central Bedfordshire Council) v SSCLG*[289] (the duty is active and ongoing [50]). *Sevenoaks District Council v SSHCLG*[290] (the courts will not interfere with a judgment by a Planning Inspector, based on her assessment of the available evidence, that the duty had not been met [51], [55]).

Neighbourhood plans

7.177 *Larkfleet Homes Ltd, R (on the application of) v Rutland County Council & Anor*[291] ('clearly wrong' to suggest that housing policies are strategic in nature and thus cannot be dealt with in neighbourhood development plans; neighbourhood plans can deal with site allocation [19]). *R (on the application of Gladman Developments Ltd) v Aylesbury Vale DC*[292] (a neighbourhood development plan can include policies for housing including locational policies even where there is no development plan document setting out strategic policies for housing; the examiner was entitled to conclude the neighbourhood plan was in conformity with strategic policies notwithstanding that such strategic policies had not yet been adopted; the examiner was entitled to conclude that the plan represented sustainable development notwithstanding that others wanted more housing, and future development plan documents might require more; the examiner was entitled to conclude it was appropriate to make the neighbourhood plan even though there might in future be a need for further growth [58]–[79]). *Crane v SSCLG*[293] (neighbourhood plans are an important part of the localism agenda [1]).

286 [2014] EWHC 1470 (Admin).
287 [2014] EWHC 2320 (Admin).
288 [2014] EWHC 3441 (Admin).
289 [2015] EWHC 2167 (Admin).
290 [2020] EWHC 3054 (Admin).
291 [2014] EWHC 4095 (Admin).
292 [2014] EWHC 4323 (Admin).
293 [2015] EWHC 425 (Admin).

F HUMAN RIGHTS/EQUALITY

Human Rights Act 1998

7.178 The role of the Human Rights Act 1998 in planning is relatively well established and the Planning Court has dealt with relatively few cases in which this was a central issue.

Article 8

7.179 Article 8 is a qualified right providing freedom from interference with an individual's home, family and private life.

7.180 *Connors v SSCLG*[294] (rights derived from Article 8 are a material consideration; the decision not to grant planning permission in the green belt for a gypsy and traveller site pursued a legitimate and highly important aim and was proportionate [157], [158], [172]); *R (on the application of Mahoney) v SSCLG*[295] (s 33(2) of the Land Compensation Act 1973, which precludes the making of a home loss payment to a caravan dweller unless no suitable alternative is available to him on reasonable terms, is not incompatible with Article 14 of the ECHR when read with Article 8 and Article 1 of the First Protocol; the case does not fall within Article 8 [40]).

Article 6

7.181 Article 6 enshrines the right to a fair trial.

7.182 *Moore v SSCLG*[296] (a policy to call in all gypsy and traveller applications in the green belt was in breach of Article 6 because it meant that applications were not determined within a reasonable time [150]). *R (on the application of Binning Property Ltd v Secretary of State for Housing, Communities, and Local Government*[297] (the filter requirement in the procedure for an appeal under s 289 of the Town and Country Planning Act 1990 complies with Article 6. The High Court's jurisdiction to finally refuse permission to appeal is compatible with Article 6 because it enables the Court to ensure that Court resources are used in an effective way and not wasted on unarguable challenges. This conclusion is not disturbed by subsequent legislative and procedural changes bearing on s 289. *R (Cash) v SSCLG* (Inspectors have a wide margin of discretion. Where an inspector clearly engages with the Article 8 rights in play and considers them with care it is unlikely that the court will interfere with the inspector's conclusions on proportionality.)

294 [2014] EWHC 2358 (Admin).
295 [2015] EWHC 589 (Admin).
296 [2015] EWHC 44 (Admin).
297 [2019] EWCA Civ 250.

Article 14

7.183 Article 14 prevents discrimination in the exercise of other rights.

7.184 *Connors v SSCLG*[298] (the court has jurisdiction to decide whether decisions dismissing appeals involve any element of discrimination under Article 14; equality of treatment is a fundamental value and allegations of discriminatory treatment need careful scrutiny; it is not possible to find any evidence in the statistics supporting a differential treatment of gypsy and traveller sites in the green belt as against other sites in the green belt [144], [145], [148]). *R (Wilson) v Wychavon District Council*[299] (The use of stop notices against residential caravans might discriminate against Gypsies and Travellers but stop notices are necessary because caravans can be moved onto land, and have an immediate impact on the environment, very quickly, which makes other enforcement powers ineffective in practice.) *Wells v UK*[300] (refusing planning permission in order to protect the environment, while being more likely to impact on Gypsies and Travellers, is not disproportionate and therefore acceptable under Article 14.)

Best interests of children

7.185 Where children are affected by certain decisions, the decision maker is bound to give primary consideration to their best interests.

7.186 *Connors*[301] (although a primary consideration the best interests of the child are not determinative; whether the decision maker has performed the exercise of taking into account the best interests of the child; where harm to the green belt was given significant weight in accordance with policy this did not show that the best interests of the child were being treated as having less weight than any other consideration [167], [170]). *Dear v SSCLG & Anor*[302] (whether the decision maker has given proper weight to the best interests of the child as a primary consideration is a matter of substance not form; provided the decision maker ascribes the correct weight to the best interests of the child at the outset he can then adjust the weight to be given to it in the decision making process [47]–[50]). *R (Cash) v SSCLG*[303] (while the best interests of the child must be the primary consideration for the decision-maker and no other consideration should be given greater weight, it is not necessarily determinative of the matter. Where an inspector conducted a proportionality assessment in relation to each household which might be forced to move as a result of enforcement action, she was entitled to find that other considerations outweighed the best interests of

298 [2014] EWHC 2358 (Admin).
299 [2007] EWCA Civ 52.
300 [2007] ECHR App No 00037794/05.
301 [2014] EWHC 2358 (Admin).
302 [2015] EWHC 29 (Admin).
303 [2015] EWHC 2357 (Admin).

the children involved. *Flintshire County Council v Jayes*[304] (where the adverse impact on the children involved outweighs the planning harm then the interests of the children become, in effect, determinative [42-63]).

Equality Act 2010

7.187 The Equality Act 2010 brings together various pieces of anti-discrimination legislation, preventing direct and indirect discrimination on various protected grounds and introducing a duty to consider how a decision will impact on the aims of achieving equality (the public sector equality duty).

7.188 *Moore v SSCLG*[305] (the practice of calling in all gypsy and traveller cases was discriminatory within the meaning of s 19(1); it has not been shown this was a proportionate way of achieving a legitimate objective; there was a failure to comply with the public sector equality duty in introducing it [125]–[126], [135]–[137]). *R (West Berkshire DC) v SSCLG*[306] (compliance with the public sector equality duty may be achieved in substance if an equality assessment is undertaken after a decision is made and satisfies the statutory requirements [66-68], [73], [77], [83], 85-88]). *R (Williams) v Caerphilly CBC*[307] (compliance with the public sector equality duty is a matter of substance not form. A Decision-maker who does not undertake a formal assessment but nevertheless considers the substantive issues, will have complied with the duty. [31-33], [36-38].) *R (Stroud) v North West Leicestershire DC*[308] (the duty to have 'due regard' for matters does not necessarily require the decision-maker to look for all possible implications but, rather, to consider them properly when raised on the facts. The court should not interpret the public sector equality duty in an unnecessarily cumbersome or formal manner [22-38]).

G EUROPEAN LEGISLATION

EIA

7.189 Although challenges to screening opinions or an Environmental Statement adopted in accordance with the EIA Directive are rarely successful, they continue to feature in a large number of cases before the Planning Court.

Screening opinions

7.190 *Kenyon v SSHCLG*[309] (screener not obliged to set out in detail all the information which might be relevant in the screening opinion. The conclusions

304 [2018] EWCA Civ 1089.
305 [2015] EWHC 44 (Admin).
306 [2016] EWCA Civ 441.
307 [2019] EWHC 1618 (Admin).
308 [2018] EWHC 2886.
309 [2020] EWCA Civ 202.

need not be justified by reference to lengthy written reasons [54]). *R (Champion) v North Norfolk District Council*[310] (there must be a real rather than a hypothetical risk of significant effects [15]; not all uncertainties must be ruled out in order to adopt a negative screening opinion [52]). *R (Plan B Earth) v Secretary of State for Transport*[311] (the review by the Court is the *Wednesbury* standard [75] & [136]). *R (Cairns) v Hertfordshire Council*[312] (by contrast to the *Habitats* regime, a screener may take into account mitigation measures when undertaking the screening assessment [28]). *R (Corrie) v Suffolk County Council* [313] (where there has been a change in circumstances following a screening opinion, a claimant arguing that the screening opinion should be revisited has to show that it was irrational for the Council not to consider this and that it gave rise to a realistic prospect of the Secretary of State coming to a different conclusion; the claimant should have challenged the Secretary of State's screening opinion, rather than waiting for the grant of permission [66]–[69], [70]). *Howard v Wigan Metropolitan Borough Council*[314] (screening opinions should be read as a whole and not subjected to a semantic analysis; when this was done it was clear that the decision maker had regard to all issues and the screening opinion was not arguably perverse [12], [15]). *R (Swire) v SSHCLG*[315](a rare example of a screening opinion being quashed because the measures to remediate the potential harm to human health posed by BSE-related contamination had yet to be identified when the decision not to require an EIA was taken [106]).

Adequacy of the Environmental Statement

7.191 *R(Larkfleet) v South Kestevan DC*[316] (the scope of the ES is a question of judgment for the decision maker, the Court will only intervene to prevent the mischief of 'project splitting' to make a larger project artificially smaller for the purposes of assessment [37]). *R (Squire) v Shropshire Council*[317] (a rare example of a planning permission being quashed because the ES failed to consider odour and dust from the storage and spreading of manure on nearby land). *R (Khan) v London Borough of Sutton*[318] (it is for a local authority to decide whether an Environmental Statement meets the requirements of the regulations; the Environmental Statement only requires such information as is reasonably required to assess the environmental effects of the development and which the applicant can reasonably be required to compile having regard to current knowledge; until an end user was known it was virtually impossible to describe the likely significant effects of off-site pipe work and not to do so did not vitiate the environmental statement [119]–[122], [128]).

310 [2015] UKSC 52.
311 [2020] EWCA Civ 214.
312 [2018] EWHC 2050 (Admin).
313 [2014] EWHC 2490 (Admin).
314 [2014] EWHC 4296 (Admin).
315 [2020] EWHC 1298 (Admin)
316 [2015] EWCA Civ 887.
317 [2019] EWCA Civ 888.
318 [2014] EWHC 3663 (Admin).

Development consents

7.192 *R (on the application of Cherkley Campaign Ltd) v Mole Valley District Council*[319] (the provision of the landscape ecological management plan pursuant to condition did not engage the EIA process [17]). *R (XSWFX) v Ealing LBC*[320] (screening does not just cover 'development consent' but also 'subsequent applications'). *R (Champion) v North Norfolk District Council*[321] (screening decisions must be kept under review [15]).

Habitats Regulations

7.193 The Planning Court has adopted a similarly robust approach to claimants who seek to challenge an appropriate assessment carried out pursuant to the Habitats Directive or a decision not to carry out an appropriate assessment.

Appropriate assessment

7.194 *Wealden District Council v SSCLG*[322](summary of the applicable legal principles [44]). *Gladman Developments Ltd v SSCLG*[323] (European law has established that when deciding whether an appropriate assessment is required, it is not permissible to take account of mitigation measures [63]). *R (Langton) v Secretary of State for Environment, Food and Rural Affairs*[324] (license conditions were not mitigation measures, rather were 'integral features of the project', such that it was permissible to take them into account in the screening exercise [157]).

In-combination effects

7.195 *Forest of Dean Friends of the Earth v Forest of Dean District Council*[325] (it is necessary to be flexible when assessing in-combination effects in plans that have not yet fully been worked up [38]).

Court's role on challenge

7.196 *Smyth v SSCLG*[326](the assessment whether a project is likely to have significant effects is primarily one for the relevant competent authority to undertake, subject to review by the court on *Wednesbury* grounds only [80]).

319 [2014] EWHC 3291 (Admin).
320 [2020] EWHC 1485 (Admin).
321 [2015] UKSC 52.
322 [2017] EWHC 351 (Admin).
323 [2019] EWHC 2001 (Admin).
324 [2018] EWHC 2190 (Admin).
325 [2014] EWHC 1353 (Admin).
326 [2015] EWCA Civ 174.

R (Hudson) v Legoland Windsor Ltd[327](in-spite of a failure to conduct an appropriate assessment, Lang J declined to quash the permission as there had been consultation with Natural England and the matters considered in the officer's report [91]).

In enforcement notices

7.197 *Cash v Wokingham Borough Council*[328] (a claim that an enforcement notice was invalid because compliance with it would put the applicant in breach of the Habitats Regulations was rejected; the Habitats Regulations should be interpreted purposively as a shield to protect delicate habitats not a sword [16], [18], [20], [35]).

Natural England Objection

7.198 In all areas of the Habitats Directive, it is clear that the view of Natural England (or NRW in Wales) will be a very important factor in the Planning Court's decision making.

7.199 *Ashdown Forest Economic Development LLP v SSCLG*[329] (a decision maker performing duties under the Habitats Regulations should give the views of Natural England considerable weight [110]). *Wealden District Council v SSCLG*[330] (the views of Natural England are not binding and may be departed from with cogent reasons [91] & [95]).

Local authority/inspector role in relation to protected species licences

7.200 *Cheshire East Council v SSCLG*[331] (a planning inspector is ordinarily entitled to grant permission unless he concludes that the proposals are likely to require a licence and are unlikely to be licensed; where no-one was contending the grant of a licence was unlikely, the inspector was entitled to conclude it would not be unlikely; the inspector is not required to make a detailed assessment of matters that are primarily the responsibility of Natural England [48], [50], [51]–[55], [61]–[64]). *R (on the application of Westerleigh Group Ltd) v Aylesbury Vale District Council*[332] (on the facts of this particular case the Council were obliged to at least bring a site to the attention of the committee as a potential satisfactory alternative [94]).

327 [2019] EWHC 3505 (Admin).
328 [2014] EWHC 3748 (Admin).
329 [2014] EWHC 406 (Admin).
330 [2016] EWHC 247 (Admin).
331 [2014] EWHC 3536 (Admin).
332 [2015] EWHC 885 (Admin).

Strategic Environmental Assessment/Sustainability Appraisal

Reasonable alternatives

7.201 Since *Heard v Broadland District Council*, the question of whether a decision maker has properly considered reasonable alternatives as part of their strategic environmental impact assessment has been a feature of many challenges to those assessments.

7.202 *Ashdown Forest Economic Development LLP v Wealden District Council*[333] (the identification of reasonable alternatives is a matter of evaluative judgment for the decision maker [42]). *Grand Union Investments Ltd v Dacorum Borough Council*[334] (the requirement to consider reasonable alternatives is to consider reasonable alternatives to the implementation of a plan not to every modification of the plan; it assumes there are alternatives that can be assessed to the same extent [91]–[95]). *R (Friends of the Earth England, Wales and Northern Ireland) v Welsh Ministers*[335] (the authorities on reasonable alternative are summarised at [88]). *No Adastral New Town Ltd v Suffolk Coastal DC*[336] (prior deficiencies in the sustainability appraisal could be cured by subsequent public examination and consultation [59]).

Court's approach to likely significant effects

7.203 A decision maker is only obliged to carry out an SEA where there is a likely significant effect from the plan or programme.

7.204 *Grand Union Investments Ltd v Dacorum Borough Council*[337] (Council's assessment of likely significant effects can only be impugned on *Wednesbury* grounds [90], [91]).

Change in circumstances

7.205 *Samuel Smith Old Brewery (Tadcaster) v Selby District Council*[338] (decision that there was no significant change requiring further SA work was a planning judgment and lawful [84], [85]).

Framework for future consent

7.206 Important factors to consider when resolving whether an SEA is required is whether the plan or programme sets the framework for future

333 [2015] EWCA Civ 681.
334 [2014] EWHC 1894 (Admin).
335 [2015] EWHC 776 (Admin).
336 [2015] EWCA Civ 88.
337 [2014] EWHC 1894 (Admin).
338 [2014] EWHC 3441 (Admin).

consents and whether it is regulated by any legislative, regulatory or administrative provision.

7.207 *R (on the application of HS2 Action Alliance Ltd) v Secretary of State for Transport*[339] (the HS2 command paper does not set the framework for future development and so did not require an SEA [38]). *Friends of the Earth Ltd v SSHCLG*[340] (the NPPF is not regulated by any qualifying procedure and so did not require an SEA [47]).

Consultation

7.208 *Kendall v Rochford District Council*[341] (consulting by e-mail only is not sufficient under the SEA Regulations).

H LITIGATION PROCEDURE

7.209 The Planning Court has, in a number of cases, had to rule on disputes about what is the correct approach to litigation in the Planning Court.

Statements of common ground

7.210 Parties have been encouraged to provide agreed statements of facts and issues to help narrow the areas of dispute.

7.211 *Tesco Stores Ltd, R (on the Application of) v Forest of Dean District Council & Ors*[342] (Court commented on the helpfulness of the agreed statement of facts and issues that had been completed as part of the judicial review [13]).

Mitchell principles

7.212 The question of whether the full force of the *Mitchell* judgment should apply in public law cases has arisen before the Planning Court.

7.213 *Harrogate Borough Council v SSCLG & Anor*[343] (*Mitchell* was applied [56], [57], [64]). *R (on the application of Cherkley Campaign Ltd) v Mole Valley District Council*[344] (*Mitchell/Denton* applied to an application to extend time, modified to recognise this is a public law context [17], [35]–[41]).

339 [2014] UKSC 3.
340 [2019] EWHC 518 (Admin).
341 [2014] EWHC 3866 (Admin).
342 [2014] EWHC 3348 (Admin).
343 [2014] EWHC 1506 (Admin).
344 [2014] EWHC 3291 (Admin).

Time limits

7.214 *R (on the application of Cherkley Campaign Ltd) v Mole Valley District Council*[345] ('I accept the point made by Mr Katkowski that since the advent of the new planning court in April 2014 a stricter approach to time limits is now the order of the day' [35]–[41]).

7.215 *Croke v SSCLG*[346] (the six-week time limit for issuing a s 288 challenge is strict and cannot be extended by the exercise of judicial discretion save in exceptional circumstances [33]–[39]; obiter if the court office wrongly refuses to accept a claim on the basis that it is (erroneously) said to be on the wrong form, that might justify an extension of time as 'exceptional circumstances' [58]; upholding the Planning Court decision of HHJ Alice Robinson, siting as a deputy High Court Judge).

7.216 *R (Thornton Hall Hotel Ltd) v Wirral Metropolitan Borough Council and another*[347] (the Court of Appeal upheld the Planning Court's decision to permit an extension of time for issuing judicial review proceedings in a case where the delay was in excess of five years where the 'extremely unusual' circumstances compelled it).

7.217 *Nottingham City Council v Calverton Parish Council*[348] (where there is a six-week time limit for challenging a development plan document and it ends on a day when the court office is closed, the last day for making the challenge is the next day the court is open).

7.218 *Harrogate Borough Council v SSCLG & Anor*[349] (although there was a small amount of prejudice to the interested party the Court was prepared to extend time for service of the claim, where it had been issued in time [32]). Where the claim form was erroneously served on the old address for the Government Legal Department such that it arrived at the proper address late, and there was no prejudice, time for service was extended (*South Derbyshire District Council v Secretary of State for Housing Communities and Local Government*[350]).

7.219 *SSCLG v San Vicente*[351] (CPR 17.4 (only allowing new grounds where they arise out of substantially the same facts) does not apply to new grounds being added after expiry of the six-week time limit for bringing a s 288 challenge [36-53]. Rule 17.1(2) applies instead [58]); *Cheshire East Council v SSCLG*[352] (the Court has discretion to grant permission to add a new ground after the six-week time limit had expired; there was no prejudice to any party in allowing

345 [2014] EWHC 3291 (Admin).
346 [2019] EWCA Civ 54.
347 [2019] EWCA Civ 737.
348 [2015] EWHC 503 (Admin).
349 [2014] EWHC 1506 (Admin).
350 [2020] EWHC 872 (Admin).
351 [2013] EWCA Civ 817.
352 [2014] EWHC 3536 (Admin).

the amendments; given the issues were arguable and there was no prejudice the public interest was in favour of the amendment; that the claimant may have contributed to the error complained of did not detract from that [42]–[44]).

7.220 A 'successful objector' in respect of a compulsory acquisition request within proceedings for a DCO must apply within 28 days of notification that the examination has completed; where, before the examination has completed, land with which an objector's objection is concerned is removed from the proposed DCO, time starts to run from that point, not from the point of final completion of the examination (*R (Trago Mills Ltd) v SSCLG*[353] [84]–[85]).

Pre-action letters

7.221 *Harrogate Borough Council v SSCLG & Anor*[354] (there was no need to use a pre-action protocol letter in s 288 decisions; there is no legal power to settle the matter without court proceedings [45]).

Striking out

7.222 *R (on the application of Cheshire East Council) v SSCLG*[355] (the Court would have struck out a ground that was academic [48]). *Coates v SSCLG*[356] (the Court of Appeal upheld a decision to strike out a s 288 claim against the decision of planning inspector, and a refusal to adjourn to allow the claimant to plead amended grounds, under CPR 3.4.). In *R (Hillingdon LBC) v Secretary of State for Transport*[357] an attempted judicial review challenge to the proposed contents of a draft national policy statement was struck out: s 13(1) of the Planning Act 2008 only permitted such challenges within the six-week period beginning with designation of the national policy statement (or its publication, whichever was the latest).

Failure properly to complete claim form

7.223 Given the tight time limit of six weeks to bring a claim, parties sometimes resort to issuing an incomplete claim form in order to ensure that they comply with the time limit. This approach has not found favour with the Planning Court.

7.224 *Carnegie (On Behalf of the Oaks Action Group), R (on the application of) v Ealing*[358] (a claim form which failed to identify a basis of claim and simply referred back to the letter before action was clearly defective; however it was

353 [2016] EWHC 1792 (Admin).
354 [2014] EWHC 1506 (Admin).
355 [2014] EWHC 2824 (Admin).
356 [2017] EWCA Civ 940.
357 [2017] EWHC 121 (Admin).
358 [2014] EWHC 3807 (Admin).

not a nullity; an extension of time was required; although the approach of the claimant was to be deprecated an extension of time was granted given that the pre-action protocol letter was attached and the grounds of claim very closely followed the pre-action protocol letter [60]–[67]).

What can be challenged under s 288 or 289

7.225 What can be challenged under s 288 or 289 is carefully circumscribed by legislation and the Planning Court has been astute to protect the proper boundaries of such a challenge.

Judicially reviewing development plans in progress

7.226 *R (on the application of IM Properties Development Ltd) v Lichfield District Council*[359] (judicial review cannot be brought to a decision to adopt a main modification during the plan examination process; the correct procedure is to wait and challenge the plan in accordance with the statutory scheme [65]–[72]). However, a challenge to the steps taken in preparation of a submission draft of a local plan (before it submission for examination) was not ousted by s 113 of the Planning and Compulsory Purchase Act 2004 (*R (CK Properties (Theydon Bois) Ltd v Epping Forest District Council*[360] [51-53]).

Cross examination

7.227 Normally public law applications in the Planning Court are decided without resorting to cross examination of witnesses and instances where cross examination is permitted are usually exceptional.

7.228 *Jedwell v Denbighshire County Council*[361] (Court of Appeal overturned decision to refuse to permit cross-examination, holding that cross-examination can be permitted in judicial review proceedings 'in an appropriate case', matter remitted to Planning Court [50-59] where cross-examination was permitted[362]); *R (on the application of Longacre Properties Ltd) v Winchester City Council*[363] (exceptionally in judicial review permission given to cross examine a number of witnesses [4], [12]). *R (Save Britain's Heritage) v Liverpool City Council* [364] (permission given to cross-examine in 'one of those rare cases where it is in the interests of justice' [34]); *Greaves and another v Boston Borough Council*[365] (cross examination of experts on noise permitted but it is not appropriate in

359 [2014] EWHC 2440 (Admin).
360 [2018] EWHC 1649 (Admin).
361 [2015] EWCA Civ 1232.
362 [2016] EWHC 458 (Admin).
363 [2014] EWHC 3373 (Admin).
364 [2016] EWHC 48 (Admin).
365 [2014] EWHC 3590 (Admin).

judicial review proceedings and the Court derived almost no benefit from it; it would seldom if ever be appropriate to permit cross examination in such circumstances [22], [23]); *Juliet Benson v SSCLG*[366] (cross-examination of an Inspector permitted in a s 289 challenge, but scope of questions restricted)

Disclosure and the duty of candour

7.229 *Westminster City Council v Secretary of State for Housing Communities and Local Government*[367] (the duty of candour extends to early and regular review of the merits of a case before the Planning Court, and in particular to seek to avoid late or last-minute settlement where the case should have been compromised much earlier [46]; and to early disclosure of a Report to the Chief Executive which explained the basis of the decision impugned (*R (Pearl) v Maldon District Council and Brown*[368] [46]).

7.230 *R (Legard) v Royal Borough of Kensington and Chelsea and others* [369] (there was no breach of the duty where, although e-mails later accepted to be disclosable had not been disclosed until late in the proceedings: although the duty is a continuous one, the 'ease and convenience of modern communication (in particular email) creates considerable difficulties for disclosure', and the claimant's case had evolved as the proceedings went on [174]).

7.231 *R (Midcounties C-Operative Ltd v Forest of Dean District Council and another* [370] (where a local authority decides not to defend its own decision in judicial review proceedings, but does not concede the claim, the Planning Court has set out that it should nonetheless consider whether it has complied with its duty of candour, by disclosing all relevant documents, and whether that duty requires it to file a witness statement to assist the court in understanding the details of the case – or indeed an acknowledgment of service, even in only outline form[149]–[151]).

7.232 *R (Larkfleet Ltd) v South Kesteven District Council and another*[371] (disclosure not normally ordered in judicial review proceedings but was on one narrow point in this case relating to whether two projects were in fact linked).

Issue estoppel

7.233 *R (on the application of Cherkley Campaign Ltd) v Mole Valley District Council*[372] (an issue estoppel arose where a ground had been pleaded and refused

366 [2018] EWHC 2354 (Admin).
367 [2020] EWHC 1472 (Admin).
368 [2018] EWHC 212 (Admin).
369 [2018] EWHC 32 (Admin.)
370 [2015] EWHC 1251 (Admin).
371 [2014] EWHC 3887 (Admin).
372 [2014] EWHC 3291 (Admin).

permission in a first judicial review where there had been no application to renew on that ground [29]).

7.234 The Planning Court has repeatedly reminded those consenting to judgment on a legal challenge of the importance of clearly setting out the ambit of the error which is accepted, in order *inter alia* that the law on issue estoppel can properly be applied: *R (Kemball) v SSCLG*[373] [39], *Trustees of the Barker Mill Estates v Test Valley Borough Council*[374] [111]–[112] and *Westminster City Council v Secretary of State for Housing Communities and Local Government*[375] [51].

Totally without merit claims

7.235 The Court can prevent a right to make an oral application for permission in judicial review cases that have been refused on the papers by marking the cases 'totally without merit'.

7.236 *Commercial Estates Group Ltd v SSCLG & Ors*[376] (it is not appropriate for a judge hearing an oral renewal retrospectively to vary the order refusing permission to certify it as totally without merit; there is no purpose to making such an order on an oral renewal hearing [45]–[47]).

Alternative remedy

7.237 One ground for refusing permission to proceed before the Planning Court is that the applicant has an alternative remedy. See also the discussion on alternative remedies and academic claims in Chapter 5.

7.238 *Perry, R (on the application of) v Newmark Properties Ltd & Ors*[377] (a complaint to the information commissioner constituted an alternative remedy on a case involving an allegation of breach of the Environmental Information Regulations [106]).

7.239 *R (Piffs ELM Ltd) v Tewkesbury Borough Council and others*[378] (claimant in judicial review claim against refusal of its application for planning permission should pursue its statutory appeal to an inspector instead; judicial review in such circumstances would be appropriate only in exceptional cases involving abuse of power [56]–[59].

373 [2015] EWHC 3338 (Admin).
374 [2016] EWHC 3028 (Admin).
375 [2020] EWHC 1472 (Admin).
376 [2014] EWHC 3089 (Admin).
377 [2014] EWHC 3499 (Admin).
378 [2016] EWHC 3248 (Admin).

Procedural exclusivity

7.240 The Planning Court has been careful to ensure that the use of methods such as an application for a declaration cannot be used to avoid the strict procedural requirements of a public law challenge.

7.241 *Cash v Wokingham Borough Council*[379] (challenges to an enforcement notice not brought by appeal must be brought by judicial review; failure to do so circumvents the protections for public authorities and will ordinarily be an abuse of process [3], [26]).

7.242 *Connors v SSCLG*[380] (an application under s 288 cannot be used to challenge decisions under s 79 or a decision to call in appeals; there is jurisdiction under s 288 to consider a challenge to a direction under an appeal [135], [138], [139]).

I INFORMATION

7.243 A matter that frequently forms part of challenges to the Planning Court has been a suggestion that there was a failure to put documents in the public domain during the planning process. While the Court has taken a strong line on decision makers who fail to follow statutory processes, in *Joicey* they have also been clear that there is no right for the public (either in the decision-making process or court proceedings) to see confidential information, especially viability assessments.

Availability of relevant documents

7.244 *R (on the application of Lady Hart of Chilton) v Babergh District Council*[381] (provision of an addendum report shortly before the committee meeting was not a breach of s 100B of the Local Government Act 1972 [95]–[98]). *Joicey, R (on the application of) v Northumberland County Council*[382] (failure to provide an important noise assessment until shortly before the committee meeting was a breach of the Local Government Act 1972; failure to put it on the website was a breach of the Council's statement of community involvement [34]–[36], [43]–[45]).

379 [2014] EWHC 3748 (Admin).
380 [2014] EWHC 2358 (Admin).
381 [2014] EWHC 3261 (Admin).
382 [2014] EWHC 3657 (Admin).

Viability assessments/confidential information

7.245 Viability arguments arise frequently in planning cases and developers seek to support their arguments with reference to viability assessments that are usually provided on a confidential basis. See also the discussion above in the context of interpretation of the NPPF.

7.246 *Perry, R (on the application of) v Newmark Properties Ltd & Ors*[383] (the viability assessment contained confidential information as it contained assumptions about build costs sales and residual values which are of the utmost commercial sensitivity [48]–[61]; the councillors were not entitled to see the information [90]; there was no right to the public to access the information under the Local Government Act [78], [87]–[94], [96]). *Equiom (Isle of Man) Ltd & Ors v London Borough of Croydon*[384] (there was no error in failing to disclose a viability report to councillors and objectors; reliance on Aarhus does not advance the claim [14]–[21]). *Luton Borough Council, R (on the application of) v Central Bedfordshire Council & Ors*[385] (there was no unfairness causing material prejudice where the claimants had failed to raise the issue of non-disclosure of viability information at the appropriate time [195]). *Turner v SSCLG*[386] (the Planning Court refused to quash the decision of an inspector on a called-in inquiry where the original viability assessment had not been disclosed, and the council's report on the assessment was disclosed two days prior to the inquiry starting). *R (Plant) v Lambeth LBC*[387] (a consultation document should have explained that the local authority's inability to service its debt was a real constraint on the availability of funds for refurbishment of a housing estate. The consultation should have included this information but the failure did not justify the quashing of the decision because there was no substantial prejudice, unfairness, or failure to ensure participation in decision making flowing from it [104]–[106], [109], [114]–[115]).

Right to see draft s 106 agreements

7.247 *Police and Crime Commissioner for Leicestershire, R (on the application of) v Hallam Land Management Ltd & Ors*[388] (there is no right to see every iteration of a draft s 106 agreement or to have every iteration put on the planning register; in any event no prejudice could be shown because there was no evidence they had ever looked at the planning register [80]).

383 [2014] EWHC 3499 (Admin).
384 [2014] EWHC 3660 (Admin).
385 [2014] EWHC 4325 (Admin).
386 [2015] EWHC 375 (Admin).
387 [2016] EWHC 3324 (Admin).
388 [2014] EWHC 1719 (Admin).

APPENDIX A

CPR Provisions

CIVIL PROCEDURE RULES 1998

SI 1998/3132

Part 3
The court's case [and costs][1] management powers

[Section I
Case Management][1]

3.1 The court's general powers of management

(1) The list of powers in this rule is in addition to any powers given to the court by any other rule or practice direction or by any other enactment or any powers it may otherwise have.

(2) Except where these Rules provide otherwise, the court may–

(a) extend or shorten the time for compliance with any rule, practice direction or court order (even if an application for extension is made after the time for compliance has expired);

(b) adjourn or bring forward a hearing;

[(bb) require that any proceedings in the High Court be heard by a Divisional Court of the High Court;][2]

(c) require a party or a party's legal representative to attend the court;

(d) hold a hearing and receive evidence by telephone or by using any other method of direct oral communication;

(e) direct that part of any proceedings (such as a counterclaim) be dealt with as separate proceedings;

(f) stay(GL) the whole or part of any proceedings or judgment either generally or until a specified date or event;

(g) consolidate proceedings;

(h) try two or more claims on the same occasion;

(i) direct a separate trial of any issue;

(j) decide the order in which issues are to be tried;

(k) exclude an issue from consideration;

(l) dismiss or give judgment on a claim after a decision on a preliminary issue;

[(ll) order any party to file and [exchange a costs budget][3];][4]

(m) take any other step or make any other order for the purpose of managing the case and furthering the overriding objective[, including hearing an Early Neutral Evaluation with the aim of helping the parties settle the case][5].

(3) When the court makes an order, it may–

(a) make it subject to conditions, including a condition to pay a sum of money into court; and

(b) specify the consequence of failure to comply with the order or a condition.

[(3A) Where the court has made a direction in accordance with paragraph (2)(bb) the proceedings shall be heard by a Divisional Court of the High Court and not by a single judge.][2]

(4) Where the court gives directions it [will][6] take into account whether or not a party has complied with [the Practice Direction (Pre-Action Conduct) and][7] any relevant pre-action protocol[(GL)].

(5) The court may order a party to pay a sum of money into court if that party has, without good reason, failed to comply with a rule, practice direction or a relevant pre-action protocol.

(6) When exercising its power under paragraph (5) the court must have regard to–

(a) the amount in dispute; and

(b) the costs which the parties have incurred or which they may incur.

[(6A) Where a party pays money into court following an order under paragraph (3) or (5), the money shall be security for any sum payable by that party to any other party in the proceedings …[8].

…[8]][9]

(7) A power of the court under these Rules to make an order includes a power to vary or revoke the order.

[(8) The court may contact the parties from time to time in order to monitor compliance with directions. The parties must respond promptly to any such enquiries from the court.][1]

Amendments

1 Inserted by the Civil Procedure (Amendment) Rules 2013, SI 2013/262, r 5(a), (c), (d) (1 April 2013).

2 Inserted by the Civil Procedure (Amendment No. 2) Rules 2017, SI 2017/889, rr 2, 3 (1 October 2017).

3 Substituted by the Civil Procedure (Amendment No.7) Rules 2013, SI 2013/1974, r 4(a) (1 October 2013: substitution has effect subject to saving specified in the Civil Procedure (Amendment No.7) Rules 2013, r 30).

4 Inserted by the Civil Procedure (Amendment No.3) Rules 2005, SI 2005/2292, r 3 (1 October 2005).

5 Inserted by the Civil Procedure (Amendment No. 4) Rules 2015, SI 2015/1569, rr 2, 4 (1 October 2015).

6 Substituted by the Civil Procedure (Amendment No.3) Rules 2008, SI 2008/3327, r 3(a) (6 April 2009).

7 Inserted by the Civil Procedure (Amendment No.3) Rules 2008, SI 2008/3327, r 3(b) (6 April 2009).

8 Repealed by the Civil Procedure (Amendment No.3) Rules 2006, SI 2006/3435, r 3 (6 April 2007).

9 Inserted by the Civil Procedure (Amendment) Rules 1999, SI 1999/1008, r 4 (26 April 1999).

[3.1A Case management – unrepresentated parties

(1) This rule applies in any proceedings where at least one party is unrepresented.

(2) When the court is exercising any powers of case management, it must have regard to the fact that at least one party is unrepresented.

(3) Both the parties and the court must, when drafting case management directions in the multi-track and fast track, take as their starting point any relevant standard directions which can be found online at www.justice.gov.uk/courts/procedure-rules/civil and adapt them as appropriate to the circumstances of the case.

(4) The court must adopt such procedure at any hearing as it considers appropriate to further the overriding objective.

(5) At any hearing where the court is taking evidence this may include—

(a) ascertaining from an unrepresented party the matters about which the witness may be able to give evidence or on which the witness ought to be cross-examined; and

(b) putting, or causing to be put, to the witness such questions as may appear to the court to be proper.][1]

Amendment

1 Inserted by the Civil Procedure (Amendment No. 4) Rules 2015, SI 2015/1569, rr 2, 5 (1 October 2015).

3.2 Court officer's power to refer to a judge

Where a step is to be taken by a court officer–

(a) the court officer may consult a judge before taking that step;

(b) the step may be taken by a judge instead of the court officer.

3.3 Court's power to make order of its own initiative

(1) Except where a rule or some other enactment provides otherwise, the court may exercise its powers on an application or of its own initiative.

(Part 23 sets out the procedure for making an application)

(2) Where the court proposes to make an order of its own initiative–

(a) it may give any person likely to be affected by the order an opportunity to make representations; and

(b) where it does so it must specify the time by and the manner in which the representations must be made.

(3) Where the court proposes–

(a) to make an order of its own initiative; and

(b) to hold a hearing to decide whether to make the order,

it must give each party likely to be affected by the order at least 3 days' notice of the hearing.

(4) The court may make an order of its own initiative without hearing the parties or giving them an opportunity to make representations.

(5) Where the court has made an order under paragraph (4)–

(a) a party affected by the order may apply to have it set aside[(GL)], varied or stayed[(GL)]; and

(b) the order must contain a statement of the right to make such an application.

(6) An application under paragraph (5)(a) must be made–

(a) within such period as may be specified by the court; or

(b) if the court does not specify a period, not more than 7 days after the date on which the order was served on the party making the application.

[(7) If the court of its own initiative strikes out a statement of case or dismisses an application [(including an application for permission to appeal or for permission to apply for judicial review)][1], and it considers that the claim or application is totally without merit–

(a) the court's order must record that fact; and

(b) the court must at the same time consider whether it is appropriate to make a civil restraint order.][2]

Amendments

1 Inserted by the Civil Procedure (Amendment No.3) Rules 2005, SI 2005/2292, r 4 (1 October 2005).

2 Inserted by the Civil Procedure (Amendment No.2) Rules 2004, SI 2004/2072, r 4 (1 October 2004).

3.4 Power to strike out a statement of case

(1) In this rule and rule 3.5, reference to a statement of case includes reference to part of a statement of case.

(2) The court may strike out(GL) a statement of case if it appears to the court–

(a) that the statement of case discloses no reasonable grounds for bringing or defending the claim;

(b) that the statement of case is an abuse of the court's process or is otherwise likely to obstruct the just disposal of the proceedings; or

(c) that there has been a failure to comply with a rule, practice direction or court order.

(3) When the court strikes out a statement of case it may make any consequential order it considers appropriate.

(4) Where–

(a) the court has struck out a claimant's statement of case;

(b) the claimant has been ordered to pay costs to the defendant; and

(c) before the claimant pays those costs, [the claimant][1] starts another claim against the same defendant, arising out of facts which are the same or substantially the same as those relating to the claim in which the statement of case was struck out,

the court may, on the application of the defendant, stay(GL) that other claim until the costs of the first claim have been paid.

(5) Paragraph (2) does not limit any other power of the court to strike out(GL) a statement of case.

[(6) If the court strikes out a claimant's statement of case and it considers that the claim is totally without merit–

(a) the court's order must record that fact; and

(b) the court must at the same time consider whether it is appropriate to make a civil restraint order.][2]

Amendments

1 Substituted by the Civil Procedure (Amendment) Rules 2014, SI 2014/407, r 6(a) (22 April 2014 being the date on which the Crime and Courts Act 2013, s 17(1), (2) come into force for all purposes).

2 Inserted by the Civil Procedure (Amendment No.2) Rules 2004, SI 2004/2072, r 5 (1 October 2004).

3.5 Judgment without trial after striking out

(1) This rule applies where–

(a) the court makes an order which includes a term that the statement of case of a party shall be struck out if the party does not comply with the order; and

(b) the party against whom the order was made does not comply with it.

(2) A party may obtain judgment with costs by filing a request for judgment if–

(a) the order referred to in paragraph (1)(a) relates to the whole of a statement of case; and

(b) where the party wishing to obtain judgment is the claimant, the claim is for–

(i) a specified amount of money;

(ii) an amount of money to be decided by the court;

(iii) delivery of goods where the claim form gives the defendant the alternative of paying their value; or

(iv) any combination of these remedies.

[(3) Where judgment is obtained under this rule in a case to which paragraph (2)(b)(iii) applies, it will be judgment requiring the defendant to deliver the goods, or (if [the defendant][1] does not do so) pay the value of the goods as decided by the court (less any payments made).][2]

[(4)][3] The request must state that the right to enter judgment has arisen because the court's order has not been complied with.

[(5)][3] A party must make an application in accordance with Part 23 if [they wish][1] to obtain judgment under this rule in a case to which paragraph (2) does not apply.

Amendments

1 Substituted by the Civil Procedure (Amendment) Rules 2014, SI 2014/407, r 6(c) (22 April 2014 being the date on which the Crime and Courts Act 2013, s 17(1), (2) come into force for all purposes).

2 Inserted by the Civil Procedure (Amendment) Rules 2000, SI 2000/221, r 3(c) (2 May 2000).

3 Substituted by the Civil Procedure (Amendment) Rules 2000, SI 2000/221, r 3(a), (b) (2 May 2000).

[[3.5A Judgment without trial after striking out a claim in the County Court Money Claims Centre

(1) If a claimant files a request for judgment in the County Court Money Claims Centre in accordance with rule 3.5, in a claim which includes an amount of money to be decided by the court, the claim will be sent to the preferred hearing centre.

(2) If a claim is sent to a preferred hearing centre pursuant to paragraph (1), any further correspondence should be sent to, and any further requests should be made at, the hearing centre to which the claim was sent.][1]][2]

Amendments

1 Substituted by the Civil Procedure (Amendment) Rules 2014, SI 2014/407, r 6(d) (22 April 2014 being the date on which the Crime and Courts Act 2013, s 17(1), (2) come into force for all purposes).

2 Inserted by the Civil Procedure (Amendment No.4) Rules 2011, SI 2011/3103, r 4(b) (19 March 2012).

3.6 Setting aside judgment entered after striking out

(1) A party against whom the court has entered judgment under rule 3.5 may apply to the court to set the judgment aside.

(2) An application under paragraph (1) must be made not more than 14 days after the judgment has been served on the party making the application.

(3) If the right to enter judgment had not arisen at the time when judgment was entered, the court must set aside[(GL)] the judgment.

(4) If the application to set aside[(GL)] is made for any other reason, rule 3.9 (relief from sanctions) shall apply.

[3.6A

If—

(a) a party against whom judgment has been entered under rule 3.5 applies to set the judgment aside;

(b) the claim is for a specified sum;

(c) the claim was started in the County Court Money Claims Centre; and

(d) the claim has not been sent to a County Court hearing centre,

the claim will be sent to—

(i) if the defendant is an individual, the defendant's home court; and

(ii) if the defendant is not an individual, the preferred hearing centre.][1]

Amendment

1 Inserted by the Civil Procedure (Amendment) Rules 2014, SI 2014/407, r 6(e) (22 April 2014 being the date on which the Crime and Courts Act 2013, s 17(1), (2) come into force for all purposes).

3.7 Sanctions for non-payment of certain fees [by the claimant][1]

[(1) [Except where rule 3.7A1 applies, this rule applies to fees payable tby the claimant where][2]—

(a) …[3]

(b) …[3]

(c) …[3]; …[4]

(d) the court has made an order giving permission to proceed with a claim for judicial review[: or][5]

[(e) the fee payable for a hearing specified by the [Civil Proceedings Fees Order 2008 (Fees Order 2008)][2] is not paid.][6]

…[3]

(Rule 54.12 provides for the service of the order giving permission to proceed with a claim for judicial review)

(2) The court will serve a notice on the claimant requiring payment of the fee specified in the relevant Fees Order if, at the time the fee is due, the claimant has not paid it or made an application for [full or part][5] remission.][7]

(3) The notice will specify the date by which the claimant must pay the fee.

(4) If the claimant does not—

(a) pay the fee; or

(b) make an application for [full or part][5] remission of the fee,

by the date specified in the notice—

- (i) [the claim will automatically be struck out without further order of the court][8]; and
- (ii) the claimant [will][9] be liable for the costs which the defendant has incurred unless the court orders otherwise.

(Rule [44.9][10] provides for the basis of assessment where a right to costs arises under this rule [and contains provisions about when a costs order is deemed to have been made and applying for an order under section 194(3) of the Legal Services Act 2007][11])

[(5) Where an application for—

(a) full or part remission of a fee is refused, the court will serve notice on the claimant requiring payment of the full fee by the date specified in the notice; or

(b) part remission of a fee is granted, the court will serve notice on the claimant requiring payment of the balance of the fee by the date specified in the notice.][5]

(6) If the claimant does not pay the fee by the date specified in the notice—

(a) [the claim will automatically be struck out without further order of the court][8]; and

(b) the claimant [will][9] be liable for the costs which the defendant has incurred unless the court orders otherwise.

[(7) If–

(a) a claimant applies to have the claim reinstated; and

(b) the court grants relief,

the relief [will][9] be conditional on the claimant either paying the fee or filing evidence of [full or part][5] or remission of the fee within the period specified in paragraph (8).

(8) The period referred to in paragraph (7) is–

(a) if the order granting relief is made at a hearing at which a claimant is present or represented, 2 days from the date of the order;

(b) in any other case, 7 days from the date of service of the order on the claimant.][12]

Amendments

1 Inserted by the Civil Procedure (Amendment) Rules 2017, SI 2017/95, rr 4, 5(2) (6 March 2017).

2 Substituted by the Civil Procedure (Amendment) Rules 2017, SI 2017/95, rr 4, 5(3)(a), (c), (4) (6 March 2017).

3 Repealed by the Civil Procedure (Amendment) Rules 2017, SI 2017/95, rr 4, 5(3)(b), (d) (6 March 2017).

4 Repealed by the Civil Procedure (Amendment No.2) Rules 2007, SI 2007/3543, r 3(a) (6 April 2008).

5 Substituted by the Civil Procedure (Amendment No.2) Rules 2007, SI 2007/3543, r 3(b), (d), (e), (f), (g) (6 April 2008).

6 Inserted by the Civil Procedure (Amendment No.2) Rules 2007, SI 2007/3543, r 3(c) (6 April 2008).

7 Substituted by the Civil Procedure (Amendment No. 4) Rules 2000, SI 2000/2092, r 4 (2 October 2000).

8 Substituted by the Civil Procedure (Amendment No.3) Rules 2005, SI 2005/2292, r 5 (1 October 2005).

9 Substituted by the Civil Procedure (Amendment) Rules 2008, SI 2008/2178, r 4(a), (c), (d) (1 October 2008).

10 Substituted by the Civil Procedure (Amendment No.7) Rules 2013, SI 2013/1974, r 4(b) (1 October 2013: substitution has effect subject to saving specified in the Civil Procedure (Amendment No.7) Rules 2013, r 30).

11 Inserted by the Civil Procedure (Amendment) Rules 2008, SI 2008/2178, r 4(b) (1 October 2008).

12 Substituted by the Civil Procedure (Amendment No. 2) Rules 2003, SI 2003/1242, r 4 (2 June 2003).

[3.7A1 Sanctions for non-payment of the trial fee by the claimant

(1) In this rule and in rule 3.7AA—

(a) 'Fees Order 2008' means the Civil Proceedings Fees Order 2008;

(b) 'fee notice' means a notice of—

  (i) the amount of a trial fee;

  (ii) the trial fee payment date; and

  (iii) the consequences of non-payment of the trial fee;

(c) 'trial date' means the date of the trial in relation to which the trial fee is payable, and if the trial in relation to which the trial fee is payable is scheduled to commence during the course of a specified period, 'trial date' means the date of the Monday of the first week of that specified period;

(d) 'trial fee' means fee 2.1 set out in the Table in Schedule 1 to the Fees Order 2008 and payable for the trial of a case on the multi-track, fast track or small claims track;

(e) 'trial fee payment date' means the date by which the trial fee must be paid, calculated in accordance with the Fees Order 2008;

(f) 'revised trial fee payment date' means, if an application for fee remission is denied in whole or part, the revised date by which the fee or part of it is to be paid, calculated in accordance with the Fees Order 2008.

(2) This rule applies in relation to trial fees where that fee is to be paid by the claimant and the court notifies the parties in writing of the trial date.

(3) When the court notifies the parties in writing of the trial date, the court must also send a fee notice to the claimant.

(4) The fee notice may be contained in the same document as the notice of trial date, or may be a separate document.

(5) Where an application for full or part remission of a trial fee is refused, when the court sends written notice to the claimant of the refusal, the court must also notify the claimant in writing—

(a) that the claimant is required to pay the full trial fee by the revised trial fee payment date; and

(b) of the consequences of non-payment of the trial fee.

(6) Where part remission of a fee is granted, when the court sends written notice to the claimant of the part remission, the court must also notify the claimant in writing—

(a) that the claimant is required to pay the balance of the trial fee by the revised trial fee payment date; and

(b) of the consequences of non-payment of the balance of the trial fee.

(7) If—

(a) the claimant has had notice in accordance with this rule to pay the trial fee;

(b) the claimant has not applied to have the trial fee remitted in whole or part; and

(c) the trial fee has not been paid on or before the trial fee payment date,

the claim will automatically be struck out without further order of the court, and unless the court orders otherwise, the claimant will be liable for the costs which the defendant has incurred.

(8) If—

(a) the claimant has had notice in accordance with this rule to pay the trial fee;

(b) the claimant has applied to have the trial fee remitted in whole or part;

(c) remission is refused or only part remission of the trial fee is granted;

(d) following the decision on remission, the claimant has had notice in accordance with this rule to pay the full trial fee or balance of it; and

(e) the full trial fee or balance of it (as appropriate) has not been paid on or before the revised trial fee payment date,

the claim will automatically be struck out without further order of the court, and, unless the court orders otherwise, the claimant will be liable for the costs which the defendant has incurred.

(Rule 44.9 provides for the basis of assessment where a right to costs arises under this rule and contains provisions about when a costs order is deemed to have been made and applying for an order under section 194(3) of the Legal Services Act 2007(**3**).)

(9) If—

(a) a claimant applies to have the claim reinstated; and

(b) the court grants relief,

the relief must be conditional on the claimant either paying the trial fee or filing evidence of full or part remission of that fee within the period specified in paragraph (10).

(10) The period referred to in paragraph (9) is—

(a) if the order granting relief is made at a hearing at which the claimant is present or represented, 2 days from the date of the order;

(b) in any other case, 7 days from the date of service of the order on the claimant.

(11) If a fee is not paid for a claim where there is also a counterclaim, the counterclaim will still stand.][1]

Amendment

1 Inserted by the Civil Procedure (Amendment) Rules 2017, SI 2017/95, rr 4, 5(5) (6 March 2017).

[3.7A [Sanctions for non-payment of certain fees by the defendant][1]

[(1) [Except where rule 3.7AA applies, this rule applies to fees payable by the defendant where—][2]

(a) a defendant files a counterclaim without—

(i) payment of the fee specified by the [Civil Proceedings Fees Order 2008 (Fees Order 2008)][2]; or

(ii) making an application for full or part remission of the fee; or

(b) the proceedings continue on the counterclaim alone and—

(i) …[3]

(ii) …[3]

(iii) …[3]

(iv) the fee payable for a hearing specified by the [Fees Order 2008][2] is not paid.][4]

(2) The court will serve a notice on the defendant requiring payment of the fee specified in the [Fees Order 2008][2] if, at the time the fee is due, the defendant has not paid it or made an application for [full or part][4] remission.

(3) The notice will specify the date by which the defendant must pay the fee.

(4) If the defendant does not—

(a) pay the fee; or

(b) make an application for [full or part][4] remission of the fee,

by the date specified in the notice, the counterclaim will automatically be struck out without further order of the court.

[(5) Where an application for—

(a) full or part remission of a fee is refused, the court will serve notice on the defendant requiring payment of the full fee by the date specified in the notice; or

(b) part remission of a fee is granted, the court will serve notice on the defendant requiring payment of the balance of the fee by the date specified in the notice.][4]

(6) If the defendant does not pay the fee by the date specified in the notice, the counterclaim will automatically be struck out without further order of the court.

(7) If—

(a) the defendant applies to have the counterclaim reinstated; and

(b) the court grants relief,

the relief will be conditional on the defendant either paying the fee or filing evidence of [full or part][4] remission of the fee within the period specified in paragraph (8).

(8) The period referred to in paragraph (7) is—

(a) if the order granting relief is made at a hearing at which the defendant is present or represented, 2 days from the date of the order;

(b) in any other case, 7 days from the date of service of the order on the defendant.][5]

Amendments

1 Inserted by the Civil Procedure (Amendment) Rules 2017, SI 2017/95, rr 4, 5(6) (6 March 2017).

2 Substituted by the Civil Procedure (Amendment) Rules 2017, SI 2017/95, rr 4, 5(7)(a), (b), (c)(ii), (8) (6 March 2017).

3 Repealed by the Civil Procedure (Amendment) Rules 2017, SI 2017/95, rr 4, 5(7)(c)(i) (6 March 2017).

4 Substituted by the Civil Procedure (Amendment No.2) Rules 2007, SI 2007/3543, r 4 (6 April 2008).

5 Inserted by the Civil Procedure (Amendment No.3) Rules 2005, SI 2005/2292, r 6 (1 October 2005).

[3.7AA Sanctions for non-payment of the trial fee by the defendant, where proceedings continue on the counterclaim alone

(1) This rule applies in relation to trial fees where that fee is to be paid by the defendant and the court notifies the defendant in writing of the trial date.

(Definitions contained in rule 3.7A1(1) apply to this rule also.)

(2) When the court notifies the parties in writing of the trial date, the court must also send a fee notice to the defendant.

(3) The fee notice may be contained in the same document as the notice of trial date, or may be a separate document.

(4) Where an application for full or part remission of a trial fee is refused, when the court sends written notice to the defendant of the refusal, the court must also notify the defendant in writing—

(a) that the defendant is required to pay the full trial fee by the revised trial fee payment date; and

(b) of the consequences of non-payment of the trial fee.

(5) Where part remission of a fee is granted, when the court sends written notice to the defendant of the part remission, the court must also notify the defendant in writing—

(a) that the defendant is required to pay the balance of the trial fee by the revised trial fee payment date; and

(b) of the consequences of non-payment of the balance.

(6) If—

(a) the defendant has had notice in accordance with this rule to pay the trial fee;

(b) the defendant has not applied to have the trial fee remitted in whole or part; and

(c) the trial fee has not been paid on or before the trial fee payment date,

the counterclaim will automatically be struck out without further order of the court.

(7) If—

(a) the defendant has had notice in accordance with this rule to pay the trial fee;

(b) the defendant has applied to have the trial fee remitted in whole or part;

(c) remission is refused or only part remission of the trial fee is granted;

(d) following the decision on remission, the defendant has had notice in accordance with this rule to pay the full trial fee or balance of it; and

(e) the full trial fee or balance of it (as appropriate) has not been paid on or before the revised trial fee payment date,

the counterclaim will automatically be struck out without further order of the court.

(8) If—

(a) a defendant applies to have the counterclaim reinstated; and

(b) the court grants relief,

the relief will be conditional on the defendant either paying the trial fee or filing evidence of full or part remission of the fee within the period specified in paragraph (9).

(9) The period referred to in paragraph (8) is—

(a) if the order granting relief is made at a hearing at which the defendant is present or represented, 2 days from the date of the order;

(b) in any other case, 7 days from the date of service of the order on the defendant.][1]

Amendment

1 Inserted by the Civil Procedure (Amendment) Rules 2017, SI 2017/95, rr 4, 5(9) (6 March 2017).

[3.7B Sanctions for dishonouring cheque

(1) This rule applies where any fee is paid by cheque and that cheque is subsequently dishonoured.

(2) The court will serve a notice on the paying party requiring payment of the fee which will specify the date by which the fee must be paid.

(3) If the fee is not paid by the date specified in the notice—

(a) where the fee is payable by the claimant, the claim will automatically be struck out without further order of the court;

(b) where the fee is payable by the defendant, the defence will automatically be struck out without further order of the court,

and the paying party shall be liable for the costs which any other party has incurred unless the court orders otherwise.

([Rule 44.9][1] provides for the basis of assessment where a right to costs arises under this rule)

(4) If—

(a) the paying party applies to have the claim or defence reinstated; and

(b) the court grants relief,

the relief shall be conditional on that party paying the fee within the period specified in paragraph (5).

(5) The period referred to in paragraph (4) is—

(a) if the order granting relief is made at a hearing at which the paying party is present or represented, 2 days from the date of the order;

(b) in any other case, 7 days from the date of service of the order on the paying party.

(6) For the purposes of this rule, 'claimant' includes a Part 20 claimant and 'claim form' includes a Part 20 claim.][2]

Amendments

1 Substituted by the Civil Procedure (Amendment No.7) Rules 2013, SI 2013/1974, r 4(c) (1 October 2013: substitution has effect subject to saving specified in the Civil Procedure (Amendment No.7) Rules 2013, r 30).

2 Inserted by the Civil Procedure (Amendment No.3) Rules 2005, SI 2005/2292, r 7 (1 October 2005).

3.8 Sanctions have effect unless defaulting party obtains relief

(1) Where a party has failed to comply with a rule, practice direction or court order, any sanction for failure to comply imposed by the rule, practice direction or court order has effect unless the party in default applies for and obtains relief from the sanction.

(Rule 3.9 sets out the circumstances which the court [will][1] consider on an application to grant relief from a sanction)

(2) Where the sanction is the payment of costs, the party in default may only obtain relief by appealing against the order for costs.

(3) Where a rule, practice direction or court order–

(a) requires a party to do something within a specified time, and

(b) specifies the consequence of failure to comply,

the time for doing the act in question may not be extended by agreement between the parties [except as provided in paragraph (4)][2].

[(4) In the circumstances referred to in paragraph (3) and unless the court orders otherwise, the time for doing the act in question may be extended by prior written agreement of the parties for up to a maximum of 28 days, provided always that any such extension does not put at risk any hearing date.][2]

Amendments

1 Substituted by the Civil Procedure (Amendment) Rules 2013, SI 2013/262, r 5(f) (1 April 2013: substitution has effect subject to transitional provisions specified in the Civil Procedure (Amendment) Rules 2013, r 22(2)).

2 Inserted by the Civil Procedure (Amendment No. 5) Rules 2014, SI 2014/1233, r 3 (5 June 2014).

3.9 Relief from sanctions

[(1) On an application for relief from any sanction imposed for a failure to comply with any rule, practice direction or court order, the court will consider all the circumstances of the case, so as to enable it to deal justly with the application, including the need—

(a) for litigation to be conducted efficiently and at proportionate cost; and

(b) to enforce compliance with rules, practice directions and orders.][1]

(2) An application for relief must be supported by evidence.

Amendment

1 Substituted by the Civil Procedure (Amendment) Rules 2013, SI 2013/262, r 5(g) (1 April 2013: substitution has effect subject to transitional provisions specified in the Civil Procedure (Amendment) Rules 2013, r 22(2)).

3.10 General power of the court to rectify matters where there has been an error of procedure

Where there has been an error of procedure such as a failure to comply with a rule or practice direction–

(a) the error does not invalidate any step taken in the proceedings unless the court so orders; and

(b) the court may make an order to remedy the error.

[3.11 Power of the court to make civil restraint orders

A practice direction may set out–

(a) the circumstances in which the court has the power to make a civil restraint order against a party to proceedings;

(b) the procedure where a party applies for a civil restraint order against another party; and

(c) the consequences of the court making a civil restraint order.][1]

Amendment

1 Inserted by the Civil Procedure (Amendment No.2) Rules 2004, SI 2004/2072, r 6 (1 October 2004).

[Section II
Costs Management

3.12 Application of this Section and the purpose of costs management

[(1) This Section and Practice Direction 3E apply to all Part 7 multi-track cases, except—

(a) where the claim is commenced on or after 22nd April 2014 and the amount of money claimed as stated on the claim form is £10 million or more; or

(b) where the claim is commenced on or after 22nd April 2014 and is for a monetary claim which is not quantified or not fully quantified or is for a non-monetary claim and in any such case the claim form contains a statement that the claim is valued at £10 million or more; or

[(c) where in proceedings commenced on or after 6th April 2016 a claim is made by or on behalf of a person under the age of 18 (a child) (and on a child reaching majority this exception will continue to apply unless the court otherwise orders); or

(d) where the proceeding are the subject of fixed costs or scale costs; or

(e) the court otherwise orders.][1]

(1A) This Section and Practice Direction 3E will apply to any other proceedings (including applications) where the court so orders.][2]

(2) The purpose of costs management is that the court should manage both the steps to be taken and the costs to be incurred by the parties to any proceedings [(or variation costs as provided in rule 3.15A)][3] so as to further the overriding objective.][4]

Amendments

1 Substituted by the Civil Procedure (Amendment) Rules 2016, SI 2016/234, r 5 (6 April 2016).

2 Substituted by the Civil Procedure (Amendment No. 4) Rules 2014, SI 2014/867, r 4(a) (22 April 2014: substitution has effect subject to transitional provisions specified in the Civil Procedure (Amendment No. 4) Rules 2014, r 25).

3 Inserted by the Civil Procedure (Amendment No. 3) Rules 2020, SI 2020/747, rr 3, 4(1) (1 October 2020).

4 Inserted by the Civil Procedure (Amendment) Rules 2013, SI 2013/262, r 5(h) (1 April 2013).

[3.13 Filing and exchanging budgets [and budget discussion reports][1]

[(1) Unless the court otherwise orders, all parties except litigants in person must file and exchange budgets—

(a) where the stated value of the claim on the claim form is less than £50,000, with their directions questionnaires; or

(b) in any other case, not later than 21 days before the first case management conference.

(2) In the event that a party files and exchanges a budget under paragraph (1), all other parties, not being litigants in person, must file an agreed budget discussion report no later than 7 days before the first case management conference.][2]

[(3) The court—

(a) may, on its own initiative or on application, order the parties to file and exchange costs budgets in a case where the parties are not otherwise required by this Section to do so;

(b) shall (other than in an exceptional case) make an order to file and exchange costs budgets if all parties consent to an application for such an order.

(4) The court may, in a substantial case, direct that budgets are to be limited in the first instance to part only of the proceedings and extended later to cover the whole proceedings.

(5) Every budget must be dated and verified by a statement of truth signed by a senior legal representative of the party.

(6) Even though a litigant in person is not required to prepare a budget, each other party (other than a litigant in person) must provide the litigant in person with a copy of that party's budget.][3]][4]

Amendments

1 Inserted by the Civil Procedure (Amendment) Rules 2016, SI 2016/234, r 6(a) (6 April 2016).

2 Substituted by the Civil Procedure (Amendment) Rules 2016, SI 2016/234, r 6(b) (6 April 2016).

3 Inserted by the Civil Procedure (Amendment No. 3) Rules 2020, SI 2020/747, rr 3, 4(2) (1 October 2020).

4 Inserted by the Civil Procedure (Amendment) Rules 2013, SI 2013/262, r 5(h) (1 April 2013).

[3.14 Failure to file a budget

Unless the court otherwise orders, any party which fails to file a budget despite being required to do so will be treated as having filed a budget comprising only the applicable court fees.][1]

Amendment

1 Inserted by the Civil Procedure (Amendment) Rules 2013, SI 2013/262, r 5(h) (1 April 2013).

[3.15 Costs management orders

(1) In addition to exercising its other powers, the court may manage the costs to be incurred [(the budgeted costs)][1] by any party in any proceedings.

(2) The court may at any time make a 'costs management order'. [Where costs budgets have been filed and exchanged the court will make a costs management order unless it is satisfied that the litigation can be conducted justly and at proportionate cost in accordance with the overriding objective without such an order being made. By a costs management order the court will—][2]

(a) record the extent to which the [budgeted costs][3] are agreed between the parties;

(b) in respect of [the budgeted costs][3] which are not agreed, record the court's approval after making appropriate revisions[;

(c) record the extent (if any) to which incurred costs are agreed.][1]

(3) If a costs management order has been made, the court will thereafter control the parties' budgets in respect of recoverable costs.

[(4) Whether or not the court makes a costs management order, it may record on the face of any case management order any comments it has about the incurred costs which are to be taken into account in any subsequent assessment proceedings.][1]

[(5) Save in exceptional circumstances—

(a) the recoverable costs of initially completing Precedent H (the form to be used for a costs budget) shall not exceed the higher of—

(i) £1,000; or

(ii) 1% of the total of the incurred costs (as agreed or allowed on assessment) and the budgeted costs (agreed or approved); and

(b) all other recoverable costs of the budgeting and costs management process shall not exceed 2% of the total of the incurred costs (as agreed or allowed on assessment) and the budgeted (agreed or approved) costs.

(Precedent H is annexed to Practice Direction 3E.)

(6) The court may set a timetable or give other directions for future reviews of budgets.

(7) After a party's budgeted costs have been approved or agreed, the party must re-file and re-serve the budget—

(a) in the form approved or agreed with re-cast figures; and

(b) annexed to the order approving the budgeted costs or recording the parties' agreement.

(8) A costs management order concerns the totals allowed for each phase of the budget, and while the underlying detail in the budget for each phase used by the party to calculate the totals claimed is provided for reference purposes to assist the court in fixing a budget, it is not the role of the court in the costs management hearing to fix or approve the hourly rates claimed in the budget.][4]][5]

Amendments

1 Inserted by the Civil Procedure (Amendment) Rules 2017, SI 2017/95, rr 4, 5(10)(a), (b)(iii), (c) (6 March 2017).

2 Substituted by the Civil Procedure (Amendment No. 4) Rules 2014, SI 2014/867, r 5 (22 April 2014).

3 Substituted by the Civil Procedure (Amendment) Rules 2017, SI 2017/95, rr 4, 5(10)(b)(i), (ii) (6 March 2017).

4 Inserted by the Civil Procedure (Amendment No. 3) Rules 2020, SI 2020/747, rr 3, 4(3) (1 October 2020).

5 Inserted by the Civil Procedure (Amendment) Rules 2013, SI 2013/262, r 5(h) (1 April 2013).

[3.15A Revision and variation of costs budgets on account of significant developments ('variation costs')

(1) A party ('the revising party') must revise its budgeted costs upwards or downwards if significant developments in the litigation warrant such revisions.

(2) Any budgets revised in accordance with paragraph (1) must be submitted promptly by the revising party to the other parties for agreement, and subsequently to the court, in accordance with paragraphs (3) to (5).

(3) The revising party must—

(a) serve particulars of the variation proposed on every other party, using the form prescribed by Practice Direction 3E;

(b) confine the particulars to the additional costs occasioned by the significant development; and

(c) certify, in the form prescribed by Practice Direction 3E, that the additional costs are not included in any previous budgeted costs or variation.

(4) The revising party must submit the particulars of variation promptly to the court, together with the last approved or agreed budget, and with an explanation of the points of difference if they have not been agreed.

(5) The court may approve, vary or disallow the proposed variations, having regard to any significant developments which have occurred since the date when the previous budget was approved or agreed, or may list a further costs management hearing.

(6) Where the court makes an order for variation, it may vary the budget for costs related to that variation which have been incurred prior to the order for variation but after the costs management order.][1]

Amendment

1 Inserted by the Civil Procedure (Amendment No. 3) Rules 2020, SI 2020/747, rr 3, 4(4) (1 October 2020).

[3.16 Costs management conferences

(1) Any hearing which is convened solely for the purpose of costs management (for example, to approve a revised budget) is referred to as a 'costs management conference'.

(2) Where practicable, costs management conferences should be conducted by telephone or in writing.][1]

Amendment

1 Inserted by the Civil Procedure (Amendment) Rules 2013, SI 2013/262, r 5(h) (1 April 2013).

[3.17 Court to have regard to budgets and to take account of costs

(1) When making any case management decision, the court will have regard to any available budgets of the parties and will take into account the costs involved in each procedural step.

(2) Paragraph (1) applies whether or not the court has made a costs management order.

[(3) Subject to rule 3.15A, the court—

(a) may not approve costs incurred before the date of any costs management hearing; but

(b) may record its comments on those costs and take those costs into account when considering the reasonableness and proportionality of all budgeted costs.

(4) If an interim application is made but is not included in a budget, the court may, if it considers it reasonable not to have included the application in the budget, treat the costs of such interim application as additional to the approved budgets.][1]][2]

Amendments

1 Inserted by the Civil Procedure (Amendment No. 3) Rules 2020, SI 2020/747, rr 3, 4(5) (1 October 2020).

2 Inserted by the Civil Procedure (Amendment) Rules 2013, SI 2013/262, r 5(h) (1 April 2013).

[3.18 Assessing costs on the standard basis where a costs management order has been made

In any case where a costs management order has been made, when assessing costs on the standard basis, the court will—

(a) have regard to the receiving party's last approved or agreed [budgeted costs][1] for each phase of the proceedings; …[2]

(b) not depart from such approved or agreed [budgeted costs][2] unless satisfied that there is good reason to do so[; and

(c) take into account any comments made pursuant to rule 3.15(4) or [3.17(3)][3] and recorded on the face of the order][4].

(Attention is drawn to [rules 44.3(2)(a) and 44.3(5)][5], which concern proportionality of costs.)][6]

Amendments

1 Substituted by the Civil Procedure (Amendment) Rules 2017, SI 2017/95, rr 4, 5(11)(a)(i), (b) (6 March 2017).

2 Repealed by the Civil Procedure (Amendment) Rules 2017, SI 2017/95, rr 4, 5(11)(a)(ii) (6 March 2017).

3 Substituted by the Civil Procedure (Amendment No. 3) Rules 2020, SI 2020/747, rr 3, 4(6) (1 October 2020).

4 Inserted by the Civil Procedure (Amendment) Rules 2017, SI 2017/95, rr 4, 5(10)(c) (6 March 2017).

5 Substituted by the Civil Procedure (Amendment) Rules 2016, SI 2016/234, r 6(b) (6 April 2016).

6 Inserted by the Civil Procedure (Amendment) Rules 2013, SI 2013/262, r 5(h) (1 April 2013).

[Section III
Costs Capping

3.19 Costs capping orders – General

[(1) For the purposes of this Section—

(a) 'costs capping order' means an order limiting the amount of future costs (including disbursements) which a party may recover pursuant to an order for costs subsequently made; and

(b) 'future costs' means costs incurred in respect of work done after the date of the costs capping order but excluding the amount of any additional liability.

(2) This Section does not apply to judicial review costs capping orders under Part 4 of the Criminal Justice and Courts Act 2015 or to protective costs orders.

(Rules 46.16 to 46.19 make provision for judicial review costs capping orders under Part 4 of the Criminal Justice and Courts Act 2015.)][1]

(3) ...[2]

(4) A costs capping order may be in respect of–

(a) the whole litigation; or

(b) any issues which are ordered to be tried separately.

(5) The court may at any stage of proceedings make a costs capping order against all or any of the parties, if—

(a) it is in the interests of justice to do so;

(b) there is a substantial risk that without such an order costs will be disproportionately incurred; and

(c) it is not satisfied that the risk in subparagraph (b) can be adequately controlled by–

(i) case management directions or orders made under this Part; and

(ii) detailed assessment of costs.

(6) In considering whether to exercise its discretion under this rule, the court will consider all the circumstances of the case, including—

(a) whether there is a substantial imbalance between the financial position of the parties;

(b) whether the costs of determining the amount of the cap are likely to be proportionate to the overall costs of the litigation;

(c) the stage which the proceedings have reached; and

(d) the costs which have been incurred to date and the future costs.

(7) A costs capping order, once made, will limit the costs recoverable by the party subject to the order unless a party successfully applies to vary the order. No such variation will be made unless—

(a) there has been a material and substantial change of circumstances since the date when the order was made; or

(b) there is some other compelling reason why a variation should be made.][3]

Amendments

1 Substituted by the Civil Procedure (Amendment No. 2) Rules 2016, SI 2016/707, r 4(a) (9 August 2016).

2 Repealed by the Civil Procedure (Amendment No. 2) Rules 2016, SI 2016/707, r 4(b) (9 August 2016).

3 Inserted by the Civil Procedure (Amendment) Rules 2013, SI 2013/262, r 5(h) (1 April 2013).

[3.20 Application for a costs capping order

(1) An application for a costs capping order must be made on notice in accordance with Part 23.

(2) The application notice must–

(a) set out–

(i) whether the costs capping order is in respect of the whole of the litigation or a particular issue which is ordered to be tried separately; and

(ii) why a costs capping order should be made; and

(b) be accompanied by a budget setting out–

(i) the costs (and disbursements) incurred by the applicant to date; and

(ii) the costs (and disbursements) which the applicant is likely to incur in the future conduct of the proceedings.

(3) The court may give directions for the determination of the application and such directions may–

(a) direct any party to the proceedings–

(i) to file a schedule of costs in the form set out in paragraph 3 of Practice Direction 3F – Costs capping;

(ii) to file written submissions on all or any part of the issues arising;

(b) fix the date and time estimate of the hearing of the application;

(c) indicate whether the judge hearing the application will sit with an assessor at the hearing of the application; and

(d) include any further directions as the court sees fit.][1]

Amendment

1 Inserted by the Civil Procedure (Amendment) Rules 2013, SI 2013/262, r 5(h) (1 April 2013).

[3.21 Application to vary a costs capping order

An application to vary a costs capping order must be made by application notice pursuant to Part 23.][1]

Amendment

1 Inserted by the Civil Procedure (Amendment) Rules 2013, SI 2013/262, r 5(h) (1 April 2013).

Part 8
Alternative procedure for claims

8.1 Types of claim in which Part 8 procedure may be followed

(1) The Part 8 procedure is the procedure set out in this Part.

(2) A claimant may use the Part 8 procedure where–

(a) he seeks the court's decision on a question which is unlikely to involve a substantial dispute of fact; or

(b) paragraph (6) applies.

[(2A) In the County Court, a claim under the Part 8 procedure may be made at any County Court hearing centre unless an enactment, rule or practice direction provides otherwise.

(Practice Direction 8A includes further direction in respect of claims which are not made at the appropriate County Court hearing centre in the first instance.)][1]

(3) The court may at any stage order the claim to continue as if the claimant had not used the Part 8 procedure and, if it does so, the court may give any directions it considers appropriate.

(4) Paragraph (2) does not apply if a practice direction provides that the Part 8 procedure may not be used in relation to the type of claim in question.

(5) Where the claimant uses the Part 8 procedure he may not obtain default judgment under Part 12.

(6) A rule or practice direction may, in relation to a specified type of proceedings–

(a) require or permit the use of the Part 8 procedure; and

(b) disapply or modify any of the rules set out in this Part as they apply to those proceedings.

(Rule 8.9 provides for other modifications to the general rules where the Part 8 procedure is being used)

[...[2]][3]

Amendments

1 Inserted by the Civil Procedure (Amendment) Rules 2014, SI 2014/407, r 7 (22 April 2014 being the date on which the Crime and Courts Act 2013, s 17(1), (2) come into force for all purposes).

2 Repealed by the Civil Procedure Rules 1998 (Amendment) (EU Exit) Regulations 2019, SI 2019/521, regs 2, 5 (31 January 2020).

3 Inserted by the Civil Procedure (Amendment) Rules 2008, SI 2008/2178, r 7 (12 December 2008 for purposes specified in the Civil Procedure (Amendment) Rules 2008, r 1(3)(a); 1 January 2009 otherwise).

8.2 Contents of the claim form

Where the claimant uses the Part 8 procedure the claim form must state–

(a) that this Part applies;

(b)

(i) the question which the claimant wants the court to decide; or

(ii) the remedy which the claimant is seeking and the legal basis for the claim to that remedy;

(c) if the claim is being made under an enactment, what that enactment is;

(d) if the claimant is claiming in a representative capacity, what that capacity is; and

(e) if the defendant is sued in a representative capacity, what that capacity is.

(Part 22 provides for the claim form to be verified by a statement of truth)

(Rule 7.5 provides for service of the claim form)

...[1]

Amendment

1 Repealed by the Civil Procedure (Amendment No.7) Rules 2013, SI 2013/1974, r 6(a) (1 October 2013: repeal has effect subject to saving specified in the Civil Procedure (Amendment No.7) Rules 2013, r 30).

[8.2A Issue of claim form without naming defendants

[(1) A practice direction may set out the circumstances in which a claim form may be issued under this Part without naming a defendant.

(2) The practice direction may set out those cases in which an application for permission must be made by application notice before the claim form is issued.][1]

(3) The application notice for permission–

(a) need not be served on any other person; and

(b) must be accompanied by a copy of the claim form that the applicant proposes to issue.

(4) Where the court gives permission it will give directions about the future management of the claim.][2]

Amendments

1 Substituted by the Civil Procedure (Amendment) Rules 2001, SI 2001/256, r 5 (26 March 2001).

2 Inserted by the Civil Procedure (Amendment) Rules 2000, SI 2000/221, r 5 (2 May 2000).

8.3 Acknowledgment of service

(1) The defendant must–

(a) file an acknowledgment of service in the relevant practice form not more than 14 days after service of the claim form; and

(b) serve the acknowledgment of service on the claimant and any other party.

(2) The acknowledgment of service must state–

(a) whether the defendant contests the claim; and

(b) if the defendant seeks a different remedy from that set out in the claim form, what that remedy is.

(3) The following rules of Part 10 (acknowledgment of service) apply–

(a) rule 10.3(2) (exceptions to the period for filing an acknowledgment of service); and

(b) rule 10.5 (contents of acknowledgment of service).

...[1]

...[2]

Amendments

1 Repealed by the Civil Procedure (Amendment No.7) Rules 2013, SI 2013/1974, r 6(b) (1 October 2013: repeal has effect subject to saving specified in the Civil Procedure (Amendment No.7) Rules 2013, r 30).

2 Repealed by the Civil Procedure (Amendment No. 5) Rules 2001, SI 2001/4015, r 11 (25 March 2002).

8.4 Consequence of not filing an acknowledgment of service

(1) This rule applies where–

(a) the defendant has failed to file an acknowledgment of service; and

(b) the time period for doing so has expired.

(2) The defendant may attend the hearing of the claim but may not take part in the hearing unless the court gives permission.

8.5 Filing and serving written evidence

(1) The claimant must file any written evidence on which he intends to rely when he files his claim form.

(2) The claimant's evidence must be served on the defendant with the claim form.

(3) A defendant who wishes to rely on written evidence must file it when he files his acknowledgment of service.

(4) If he does so, he must also, at the same time, serve a copy of his evidence on the other parties.

(5) The claimant may, within 14 days of service of the defendant's evidence on him, file further written evidence in reply.

(6) If he does so, he must also, within the same time limit, serve a copy of his evidence on the other parties.

(7) The claimant may rely on the matters set out in his claim form as evidence under this rule if the claim form is verified by a statement of truth.

8.6 Evidence—general

(1) No written evidence may be relied on at the hearing of the claim unless–

(a) it has been served in accordance with rule 8.5; or

(b) the court gives permission.

(2) The court may require or permit a party to give oral evidence at the hearing.

(3) The court may give directions requiring the attendance for cross-examination[(GL)] of a witness who has given written evidence.

(Rule 32.1 contains a general power for the court to control evidence)

8.7 Part 20 claims

Where the Part 8 procedure is used, Part 20 (counterclaims and other additional claims) applies except that a party may not make a Part 20 claim (as defined by rule 20.2) without the court's permission.

8.8 Procedure where defendant objects to use of the Part 8 procedure

(1) Where the defendant contends that the Part 8 procedure should not be used because–

(a) there is a substantial dispute of fact; and

(b) the use of the Part 8 procedure is not required or permitted by a rule or practice direction, he must state his reasons when he files his acknowledgment of service.

(Rule 8.5 requires a defendant who wishes to rely on written evidence to file it when he files his acknowledgment of service)

(2) When the court receives the acknowledgment of service and any written evidence it will give directions as to the future management of the case.

(Rule 8.1(3) allows the court to make an order that the claim continue as if the claimant had not used thePart 8 procedure)

8.9 Modifications to the general rules

Where the Part 8 procedure is followed–

(a) provision is made in this Part for the matters which must be stated in the claim form and the defendant is not required to file a defence and therefore–

(i) Part 16 (statements of case) does not apply;

(ii) Part 15 (defence and reply) does not apply;

(iii) any time limit in these Rules which prevents the parties from taking a step before a defence is filed does not apply; and

(iv) the requirement under rule 7.8 to serve on the defendant a form for defending the claim does not apply;

(b) the claimant may not obtain judgment by request on an admission and therefore–

(i) rules 14.4 to 14.7 do not apply; and

(ii) the requirement under rule 7.8 to serve on the defendant a form for admitting the claim does not apply; and

(c) the claim shall be treated as allocated to the multi-track and therefore Part 26 does not apply.

[Part 44
General rules about costs

Section I
General

44.1 Interpretation and application

(1) In Parts 44 to 47, unless the context otherwise requires—

'authorised court officer' means any officer of—

(i) [the County Court][1];

(ii) a district registry;

(iii) [the Family Court;][2]

[(iiia) the High Court; or][3]

(iv) the Costs Office,

whom the Lord Chancellor has authorised to assess costs;

'conditional fee agreement' means an agreement enforceable under section 58 of the Courts and Legal Services Act 1990;

'costs' includes fees, charges, disbursements, expenses, remuneration, reimbursement allowed to a litigant in person under rule 46.5 and any fee or reward charged by a lay representative for acting on behalf of a party in proceedings allocated to the small claims track;

'costs judge' means a taxing master of the Senior Courts;

'Costs Office' means the Senior Courts Costs Office;

'costs officer' means—

(i) a costs judge;

(ii) a [District Judge][4]; or

(iii) an authorised court officer;

'detailed assessment' means the procedure by which the amount of costs is decided by a costs officer in accordance with Part 47;

'the Director (legal aid)' means the person designated as the Director of Legal Aid Casework pursuant to section 4 of the Legal Aid, Sentencing and Punishment of Offenders Act 2012, or a person entitled to exercise the functions of the Director;

'fixed costs' means costs the amounts of which are fixed by these rules whether or not the court has a discretion to allow some other or no amount, and include—

(i) the amounts which are to be allowed in respect of legal representatives' charges in the circumstances set out in Section I of Part 45;

(ii) fixed recoverable costs calculated in accordance with rule 45.11;

(iii) the additional costs allowed by rule 45.18;

(iv) fixed costs determined under rule 45.21;

(v) costs fixed by rules 45.37 and 45.38;

'free of charge' has the same meaning as in section 194(10) of the 2007 Act;

'fund' includes any estate or property held for the benefit of any person or class of person and any fund to which a trustee or personal representative is entitled in that capacity;

'HMRC' means HM Revenue and Customs;

'legal aid' means civil legal services made available under arrangements made for the purposes of Part 1of the Legal Aid, Sentencing and Punishment of Offenders Act 2012;

'paying party' means a party liable to pay costs;

'the prescribed charity' has the same meaning as in section 194(8) of the 2007 Act;

'pro bono representation' means legal representation provided free of charge;

'receiving party' means a party entitled to be paid costs;

'summary assessment' means the procedure whereby costs are assessed by the judge who has heard the case or application;

'VAT' means Value Added Tax;

'the 2007 Act' means the Legal Services Act 2007.

('Legal representative' has the meaning given in rule 2.3).

(2) The costs to which Parts 44 to 47 apply include—

(a) the following costs where those costs may be assessed by the court—

(i) costs of proceedings before an arbitrator or umpire;

(ii) costs of proceedings before a tribunal or other statutory body; and

(iii) costs payable by a client to their legal representative; and

(b) costs which are payable by one party to another party under the terms of a contract, where the court makes an order for an assessment of those costs.

(3) Where advocacy or litigation services are provided to a client under a conditional fee agreement, costs are recoverable under Parts 44 to 47 notwithstanding that the client is liable to pay the legal representative's fees and expenses only to the extent that sums are recovered in respect of the proceedings, whether by way of costs or otherwise.][5]

Amendments

1 Substituted by the Civil Procedure (Amendment) Rules 2014, SI 2014/407, r 4(a)(i) (22 April 2014 being the date on which the Crime and Courts Act 2013, s 17(1), (2) come into force for all purposes).

2 Substituted by the Civil Procedure (Amendment) Rules 2014, SI 2014/407, r 18(a) (22 April 2014 being the date on which the Crime and Courts Act 2013, s 17(1), (2) come into force for all purposes).

3 Inserted by the Civil Procedure (Amendment) Rules 2014, SI 2014/407, r 18(b) (22 April 2014 being the date on which the Crime and Courts Act 2013, s 17(1), (2) come into force for all purposes).

4 Substituted by the Civil Procedure (Amendment) Rules 2014, SI 2014/407, r 4(a)(iv) (22 April 2014 being the date on which the Crime and Courts Act 2013, s 17(1), (2) come into force for all purposes).

5 Substituted by the Civil Procedure (Amendment) Rules 2013, SI 2013/262, r 16, Schedule (1 April 2013).

[44.2 Court's discretion as to costs

(1) The court has discretion as to—

(a) whether costs are payable by one party to another;

(b) the amount of those costs; and

(c) when they are to be paid.

(2) If the court decides to make an order about costs—

(a) the general rule is that the unsuccessful party will be ordered to pay the costs of the successful party; but

(b) the court may make a different order.

(3) The general rule does not apply to the following proceedings—

(a) proceedings in the Court of Appeal on an application or appeal made in connection with proceedings in the Family Division; or

(b) proceedings in the Court of Appeal from a judgment, direction, decision or order given or made in probate proceedings or family proceedings.

(4) In deciding what order (if any) to make about costs, the court will have regard to all the circumstances, including—

(a) the conduct of all the parties;

(b) whether a party has succeeded on part of its case, even if that party has not been wholly successful; and

(c) any admissible offer to settle made by a party which is drawn to the court's attention, and which is not an offer to which costs consequences under Part 36 apply.

(5) The conduct of the parties includes—

(a) conduct before, as well as during, the proceedings and in particular the extent to which the parties followed the Practice Direction – Pre-Action Conduct or any relevant pre-action protocol;

(b) whether it was reasonable for a party to raise, pursue or contest a particular allegation or issue;

(c) the manner in which a party has pursued or defended its case or a particular allegation or issue; and

(d) whether a claimant who has succeeded in the claim, in whole or in part, exaggerated its claim.

(6) The orders which the court may make under this rule include an order that a party must pay—

(a) a proportion of another party's costs;

(b) a stated amount in respect of another party's costs;

(c) costs from or until a certain date only;

(d) costs incurred before proceedings have begun;

(e) costs relating to particular steps taken in the proceedings;

(f) costs relating only to a distinct part of the proceedings; and

(g) interest on costs from or until a certain date, including a date before judgment.

(7) Before the court considers making an order under paragraph (6)(f), it will consider whether it is practicable to make an order under paragraph (6)(a) or (c) instead.

(8) Where the court orders a party to pay costs subject to detailed assessment, it will order that party to pay a reasonable sum on account of costs, unless there is good reason not to do so.][1]

Amendment

1 Substituted by the Civil Procedure (Amendment) Rules 2013, SI 2013/262, r 16, Schedule (1 April 2013).

[44.3 Basis of assessment

(1) Where the court is to assess the amount of costs (whether by summary or detailed assessment) it will assess those costs—

(a) on the standard basis; or

(b) on the indemnity basis,

but the court will not in either case allow costs which have been unreasonably incurred or are unreasonable in amount.

(Rule 44.5 sets out how the court decides the amount of costs payable under a contract.)

(2) Where the amount of costs is to be assessed on the standard basis, the court will—

(a) only allow costs which are proportionate to the matters in issue. Costs which are disproportionate in amount may be disallowed or reduced even if they were reasonably or necessarily incurred; and

(b) resolve any doubt which it may have as to whether costs were reasonably and proportionately incurred or were reasonable and proportionate in amount in favour of the paying party.

(Factors which the court may take into account are set out in rule 44.4.)

(3) Where the amount of costs is to be assessed on the indemnity basis, the court will resolve any doubt which it may have as to whether costs were reasonably incurred or were reasonable in amount in favour of the receiving party.

(4) Where—

(a) the court makes an order about costs without indicating the basis on which the costs are to be assessed; or

(b) the court makes an order for costs to be assessed on a basis other than the standard basis or the indemnity basis,

the costs will be assessed on the standard basis.

(5) Costs incurred are proportionate if they bear a reasonable relationship to—

(a) the sums in issue in the proceedings;

(b) the value of any non-monetary relief in issue in the proceedings;

(c) the complexity of the litigation;

(d) any additional work generated by the conduct of the paying party; and

(e) any wider factors involved in the proceedings, such as reputation or public importance.

(6) Where the amount of a solicitor's remuneration in respect of non-contentious business is regulated by any general orders made under the Solicitors Act 1974, the amount of the costs to be allowed in respect of any such business which falls to be assessed by the court will be decided in accordance with those general orders rather than this rule and rule 44.4.

[(7) Paragraphs (2)(a) and (5) do not apply in relation to—

(a) cases commenced before 1st April 2013; or

(b) costs incurred in respect of work done before 1st April 2013,

and in relation to such cases or costs, rule 44.4.(2)(a) as it was in force immediately before 1st April 2013 will apply instead.][1]][2]

Amendments

1 Substituted by the Civil Procedure (Amendment No.2) Rules 2013, SI 2013/515, r 5 (1 April 2013).

2 Substituted by the Civil Procedure (Amendment) Rules 2013, SI 2013/262, r 16, Schedule (1 April 2013).

[44.4 Factors to be taken into account in deciding the amount of costs

(1) The court will have regard to all the circumstances in deciding whether costs were—

(a) if it is assessing costs on the standard basis—

 (i) proportionately and reasonably incurred; or

 (ii) proportionate and reasonable in amount, or

(b) if it is assessing costs on the indemnity basis—

 (i) unreasonably incurred; or

 (ii) unreasonable in amount.

(2) In particular, the court will give effect to any orders which have already been made.

(3) The court will also have regard to—

(a) the conduct of all the parties, including in particular—

 (i) conduct before, as well as during, the proceedings; and

 (ii) the efforts made, if any, before and during the proceedings in order to try to resolve the dispute;

(b) the amount or value of any money or property involved;

(c) the importance of the matter to all the parties;

(d) the particular complexity of the matter or the difficulty or novelty of the questions raised;

(e) the skill, effort, specialised knowledge and responsibility involved;

(f) the time spent on the case;

(g) the place where and the circumstances in which work or any part of it was done; and

(h) the receiving party's last approved or agreed budget.

(Rule 35.4(4) gives the court power to limit the amount that a party may recover with regard to the fees and expenses of an expert.)][1]

Amendment

1 Substituted by the Civil Procedure (Amendment) Rules 2013, SI 2013/262, r 16, Schedule (1 April 2013).

[44.5 Amount of costs where costs are payable under a contract

(1) [Subject to paragraphs (2) and (3)][1], where the court assesses (whether by summary or detailed assessment) costs which are payable by the paying party to the receiving party under the terms of a contract, the costs payable under those terms are, unless the contract expressly provides otherwise, to be presumed to be costs which—

(a) have been reasonably incurred; and

(b) are reasonable in amount,

and the court will assess them accordingly.

(2) The presumptions in paragraph (1) are rebuttable. Practice Direction 44 – General rules about costs sets out circumstances where the court may order otherwise.

(3) Paragraph (1) does not apply where the contract is between a solicitor and client.][2]

Amendments

1 Substituted by the Civil Procedure (Amendment) Rules 2016, SI 2016/234, r 8 (6 April 2016).

2 Substituted by the Civil Procedure (Amendment) Rules 2013, SI 2013/262, r 16, Schedule (1 April 2013).

[44.6 Procedure for assessing costs

(1) Where the court orders a party to pay costs to another party (other than fixed costs) it may either—

(a) make a summary assessment of the costs; or

(b) order detailed assessment of the costs by a costs officer,

unless any rule, practice direction or other enactment provides otherwise.

(Practice Direction 44 – General rules about costs sets out the factors which will affect the court's decision under paragraph (1).)

(2) A party may recover the fixed costs specified in Part 45 in accordance with that Part.][1]

Amendment

1 Substituted by the Civil Procedure (Amendment) Rules 2013, SI 2013/262, r 16, Schedule (1 April 2013).

[44.7 Time for complying with an order for costs

(1) A party must comply with an order for the payment of costs within 14 days of—

(a) the date of the judgment or order if it states the amount of those costs;

(b) if the amount of those costs (or part of them) is decided later in accordance with Part 47, the date of the certificate which states the amount; or

(c) in either case, such other date as the court may specify.

(Part 47 sets out the procedure for detailed assessment of costs.)][1]

Amendment

1 Substituted by the Civil Procedure (Amendment) Rules 2013, SI 2013/262, r 16, Schedule (1 April 2013).

[44.8 Legal representative's duty to notify the party

Where—

(a) the court makes a costs order against a legally represented party; and

(b) the party is not present when the order is made,

the party's legal representative must notify that party in writing of the costs order no later than 7 days after the legal representative receives notice of the order.

(Paragraph 10.1 of Practice Direction 44 defines 'party' for the purposes of this rule.)][1]

Amendment

1 Substituted by the Civil Procedure (Amendment) Rules 2013, SI 2013/262, r 16, Schedule (1 April 2013).

[44.9 Cases where costs orders deemed to have been made

(1) Subject to paragraph (2), where a right to costs arises under—

(a) rule 3.7 [or 3.7A1][1] (defendant's right to costs where claim is struck out for non-payment of fees);

[(a1) rule 3.7B (sanctions for dishonouring cheque);][2]

(b) [rule 36.13][3](1) or (2) (claimant's entitlement to costs where a Part 36 offer is accepted); or

(c) rule 38.6 (defendant's right to costs where claimant discontinues),

a costs order will be deemed to have been made on the standard basis.

(2) Paragraph 1(b) does not apply where a Part 36 offer is accepted before the commencement of proceedings.

(3) Where such an order is deemed to be made in favour of a party with pro bono representation, that party may apply for an order under section 194(3) of the 2007 Act.

(4) Interest payable under section 17 of the Judgments Act 1838 or section 74 of the County Courts Act 1984 on the costs deemed to have been ordered under paragraph (1) will begin to run from the date on which the event which gave rise to the entitlement to costs occurred.][4]

Amendments

1 Inserted by the Civil Procedure (Amendment) Rules 2017, SI 2017/95, rr 4, 7 (6 March 2017).

2 Inserted by the Civil Procedure (Amendment No.7) Rules 2013, SI 2013/1974, r 19 (1 October 2013: insertion has effect subject to saving specified in the Civil Procedure (Amendment No.7) Rules 2013, r 30).

3 Substituted by the Civil Procedure (Amendment No. 8) Rules 2014, SI 2014/3299, r 9 (6 April 2015: substitution has effect subject to transitional provisions specified in the Civil Procedure (Amendment No. 8) Rules 2014, r 18).

4 Substituted by the Civil Procedure (Amendment) Rules 2013, SI 2013/262, r 16, Schedule (1 April 2013).

[44.10 Where the court makes no order for costs

(1) Where the court makes an order which does not mention costs—

(a) subject to paragraphs (2) and (3), the general rule is that no party is entitled—

(i) to costs; or

(ii) to seek an order under section 194(3) of the 2007 Act,

in relation to that order; but

(b) this does not affect any entitlement of a party to recover costs out of a fund held by that party as trustee or personal representative, or under any lease, mortgage or other security.

(2) Where the court makes—

(a) an order granting permission to appeal;

(b) an order granting permission to apply for judicial review; or

(c) any other order or direction sought by a party on an application without notice,

and its order does not mention costs, it will be deemed to include an order for applicant's costs in the case.

(3) Any party affected by a deemed order for costs under paragraph (2) may apply at any time to vary the order.

(4) The court hearing an appeal may, unless it dismisses the appeal, make orders about the costs of the proceedings giving rise to the appeal as well as the costs of the appeal.

(5) Subject to any order made by the transferring court, where proceedings are transferred from one court to another, the court to which they are transferred may deal with all the costs, including the costs before the transfer.][1]

Amendment

1 Substituted by the Civil Procedure (Amendment) Rules 2013, SI 2013/262, r 16, Schedule (1 April 2013).

[44.11 Court's powers in relation to misconduct

(1) The court may make an order under this rule where—

(a) a party or that party's legal representative, in connection with a summary or detailed assessment, fails to comply with a rule, practice direction or court order; or

(b) it appears to the court that the conduct of a party or that party's legal representative, before or during the proceedings or in the assessment proceedings, was unreasonable or improper.

(2) Where paragraph (1) applies, the court may—

(a) disallow all or part of the costs which are being assessed; or

(b) order the party at fault or that party's legal representative to pay costs which that party or legal representative has caused any other party to incur.

(3) Where—

(a) the court makes an order under paragraph (2) against a legally represented party; and

(b) the party is not present when the order is made,

the party's legal representative must notify that party in writing of the order no later than 7 days after the legal representative receives notice of the order.][1]

Amendment

1 Substituted by the Civil Procedure (Amendment) Rules 2013, SI 2013/262, r 16, Schedule (1 April 2013).

[44.12 Set Off

(1) Where a party entitled to costs is also liable to pay costs, the court may assess the costs which that party is liable to pay and either—

(a) set off the amount assessed against the amount the party is entitled to be paid and direct that party to pay any balance; or

(b) delay the issue of a certificate for the costs to which the party is entitled until the party has paid the amount which that party is liable to pay.][1]

Amendment

1 Substituted by the Civil Procedure (Amendment) Rules 2013, SI 2013/262, r 16, Schedule (1 April 2013).

[Section II
Qualified One-Way Costs Shifting

44.13 Qualified one-way costs shifting: scope and interpretation

(1) This Section applies to proceedings which include a claim for damages—

(a) for personal injuries;

(b) under the Fatal Accidents Act 1976; or

(c) which arises out of death or personal injury and survives for the benefit of an estate by virtue of section 1(1) of the Law Reform (Miscellaneous Provisions) Act 1934,

but does not apply to applications pursuant to section 33 of the Senior Courts Act 1981 or section 52 of the County Courts Act 1984 (applications for pre-action disclosure), or where rule 44.17 applies.

(2) In this Section, 'claimant' means a person bringing a claim to which this Section applies or an estate on behalf of which such a claim is brought, and includes a person making a counterclaim or an additional claim.][1]

Amendment

1 Substituted by the Civil Procedure (Amendment) Rules 2013, SI 2013/262, r 16, Schedule (1 April 2013).

[44.14 Effect of qualified one-way costs shifting

(1) Subject to rules 44.15 and 44.16, orders for costs made against a claimant may be enforced without the permission of the court but only to the extent that the

aggregate amount in money terms of such orders does not exceed the aggregate amount in money terms of any orders for damages and interest made in favour of the claimant.

(2) Orders for costs made against a claimant may only be enforced after the proceedings have been concluded and the costs have been assessed or agreed.

(3) An order for costs which is enforced only to the extent permitted by paragraph (1) shall not be treated as an unsatisfied or outstanding judgment for the purposes of any court record.][1]

Amendment

1 Substituted by the Civil Procedure (Amendment) Rules 2013, SI 2013/262, r 16, Schedule (1 April 2013).

[44.15 Exceptions to qualified one-way costs shifting where permission not required

Orders for costs made against the claimant may be enforced to the full extent of such orders without the permission of the court where the proceedings have been struck out on the grounds that—

(a) the claimant has disclosed no reasonable grounds for bringing the proceedings;

(b) the proceedings are an abuse of the court's process; or

(c) the conduct of—

(i) the claimant; or

(ii) a person acting on the claimant's behalf and with the claimant's knowledge of such conduct,

is likely to obstruct the just disposal of the proceedings.][1]

Amendment

1 Substituted by the Civil Procedure (Amendment) Rules 2013, SI 2013/262, r 16, Schedule (1 April 2013).

[44.16 Exceptions to qualified one-way costs shifting where permission required

(1) Orders for costs made against the claimant may be enforced to the full extent of such orders with the permission of the court where the claim is found on the balance of probabilities to be fundamentally dishonest.

(2) Orders for costs made against the claimant may be enforced up to the full extent of such orders with the permission of the court, and to the extent that it considers just, where—

(a) the proceedings include a claim which is made for the financial benefit of a person other than the claimant or a dependant within the meaning of section 1(3) of the Fatal Accidents Act 1976 (other than a claim in respect of the gratuitous provision of care, earnings paid by an employer or medical expenses); or

(b) a claim is made for the benefit of the claimant other than a claim to which this Section applies.

(3) Where paragraph (2)(a) applies, the court may, subject to rule 46.2, make an order for costs against a person, other than the claimant, for whose financial benefit the whole or part of the claim was made.][1]

Amendment

1 Substituted by the Civil Procedure (Amendment) Rules 2013, SI 2013/262, r 16, Schedule (1 April 2013).

[44.17 Transitional provision

This Section does not apply to proceedings where the claimant has entered into a pre-commencement funding arrangement (as defined in rule 48.2).][1]

Amendment

1 Substituted by the Civil Procedure (Amendment) Rules 2013, SI 2013/262, r 16, Schedule (1 April 2013).

Part III
Damages-Based Agreements

[44.18 Award of costs where there is a damages-based agreement

(1) The fact that a party has entered into a damages-based agreement will not affect the making of any order for costs which otherwise would be made in favour of that party.

(2) Where costs are to be assessed in favour of a party who has entered into a damages-based agreement—

(a) the party's recoverable costs will be assessed in accordance with rule 44.3; and

(b) the party may not recover by way of costs more than the total amount payable by that party under the damages-based agreement for legal services provided under that agreement.][1]

Amendment

1 Substituted by the Civil Procedure (Amendment) Rules 2013, SI 2013/262, r 16, Schedule (1 April 2013).

[Part 45
Fixed costs

Part I
Fixed costs

45.1 Scope of this Section

(1) This Section sets out the amounts which, unless the court orders otherwise, are to be allowed in respect of legal representatives' charges.

(2) This Section applies where—

(a) the only claim is a claim for a specified sum of money where the value of the claim exceeds £25 and—

(i) judgment in default is obtained under rule 12.4(1);

(ii) judgment on admission is obtained under rule 14.4(3);

(iii) judgment on admission on part of the claim is obtained under rule 14.5(6);

(iv) summary judgment is given under Part 24;

(v) the court has made an order to strike out a defence under rule 3.4(2)(a) as disclosing no reasonable grounds for defending the claim; or

(vi) rule 45.4 applies;

(b) the only claim is a claim where the court gave a fixed date for the hearing when it issued the claim and judgment is given for the delivery of goods, and the value of the claim exceeds £25;

(c) the claim is for the recovery of land, including a possession claim under Part 55, whether or not the claim includes a claim for a sum of money and the defendant gives up possession, pays the amount claimed, if any, and the fixed commencement costs stated in the claim form;

(d) the claim is for the recovery of land, including a possession claim under Part 55, where one of the grounds for possession is arrears of rent, for which the court gave a fixed date for the hearing when it issued the claim and judgment is given for the possession of land (whether or not the order for possession is suspended on terms) and the defendant—

(i) has neither delivered a defence, or counterclaim, nor otherwise denied liability; or

(ii) has delivered a defence which is limited to specifying his proposals for the payment of arrears of rent;

(e) the claim is a possession claim under Section II of Part 55 (accelerated possession claims of land let on an assured shorthold tenancy) and a possession order is made where the defendant has neither delivered a defence, or counterclaim, nor otherwise denied liability;

(f) the claim is a demotion claim under Section III of Part 65 or a demotion claim is made in the same claim form in which a claim for possession is made under Part 55 and that demotion claim is successful; or

(g) a judgment creditor has taken steps under Parts 70 to 73 to enforce a judgment or order.

(Practice Direction 7B sets out the types of case where a court will give a fixed date for a hearing when it issues a claim.)

(3) No sum in respect of legal representatives' charges will be allowed where the only claim is for a sum of money or goods not exceeding £25.

(4) Any appropriate court fee will be allowed in addition to the costs set out in this Section.

(5) The claim form may include a claim for fixed commencement costs.][1]

Amendment

1 Substituted by the Civil Procedure (Amendment) Rules 2013, SI 2013/262, r 16, Schedule (1 April 2013).

[45.2 Amount of fixed commencement costs in a claim for the recovery of money or goods

(1) The amount of fixed commencement costs in a claim to which rule 45.1(2)(a) or (b) applies—

(a) will be calculated by reference to Table 1; and

(b) the amount claimed, or the value of the goods claimed if specified, in the claim form is to be used for determining the band in Table 1 that applies to the claim.

(2) The amounts shown in Table 4 are to be allowed in addition, if applicable.

Table 1

Fixed costs on commencement of a claim for the recovery of money or goods			
Relevant band	Where the claim form is served by the court or by any method other than personal service by the claimant	Where– the claim form is served personally by the claimant; and there is only one defendant	Where there is more than one defendant, for each additional defendant personally served at separate addresses by the claimant

Where— the value of the claim exceeds £25 but does not exceed £500	£50	£60	£15
Where— the value of the claim exceeds £500 but does not exceed £1,000	£70	£80	£15
Where— the value of the claim exceeds £1,000 but does not exceed £5,000; or the only claim is for delivery of goods and no value is specified or stated on the claim form	£80	£90	£15
Where— the value of the claim exceeds £5,000	£100	£110	£15

][1]

Amendment

1 Substituted by the Civil Procedure (Amendment) Rules 2013, SI 2013/262, r 16, Schedule (1 April 2013).

[45.3 When defendant only liable for fixed commencement costs

Where—

(a) the only claim is for a specified sum of money; and

(b) the defendant pays the money claimed within 14 days after being served with the particulars of claim, together with the fixed commencement costs stated in the claim form,

the defendant is not liable for any further costs unless the court orders otherwise.][1]

Amendment

1 Substituted by the Civil Procedure (Amendment) Rules 2013, SI 2013/262, r 16, Schedule (1 April 2013).

[45.4 Costs on entry of judgment in a claim for the recovery of money or goods

Where—

(a) the claimant has claimed fixed commencement costs under rule 45.2; and

(b) judgment is entered in a claim to which rule 45.1(2)(a) or (b) applies in the circumstances specified in Table 2, the amount to be included in the judgment for the claimant's legal representative's charges is the total of—

(i) the fixed commencement costs; and

(ii) the relevant amount shown in Table 2.

Table 2

Fixed Costs on Entry of Judgment in a claim for the recovery of money or goods		
	Where the amount of the judgment exceeds £25 but does not exceed £5,000	Where the amount of the judgment exceeds £5,000
Where judgment in default of an acknowledgment of service is entered under rule 12.4(1) (entry of judgment by request on claim for money only)	£22	£30
Where judgment in default of a defence is entered under rule 12.4(1) (entry of judgment by request on claim for money only)	£25	£35
Where judgment is entered under rule 14.4 (judgment on admission), or rule 14.5 (judgment on admission of part of claim) and claimant accepts the defendant's proposal as to the manner of payment	£40	£55
Where judgment is entered under rule 14.4 (judgment on admission), or rule 14.5 (judgment on admission of part of claim) and court decides the date or time of payment	£55	£70
Where summary judgment is given under Part 24 or the court strikes out a defence under rule 3.4(2)(a), in either case, on application by a party	£175	£210
Where judgment is given on a claim for delivery of goods under a regulated agreement within the meaning of the Consumer Credit Act 1974 and no other entry in this table applies	£60	£85

][1]

Amendment

1 Substituted by the Civil Procedure (Amendment) Rules 2013, SI 2013/262, r 16, Schedule (1 April 2013).

[45.5 Amount of fixed commencement costs in a claim for the recovery of land or a demotion claim

(1) The amount of fixed commencement costs in a claim to which rule 45.1(2)(c), (d) or (f) applies will be calculated by reference to Table 3.

(2) The amounts shown in Table 4 are to be allowed in addition, if applicable.

Table 3

Fixed costs on commencement of a claim for the recovery of land or a demotion claim		
Where the claim form is served by the court or by any method other than personal service by the claimant	Where— the claim form is served personally by the claimant; and there is only one defendant	Where there is more than one defendant, for each additional defendant personally served at separate addresses by the claimant
£69.50	£77.00	£15.00

][1]

Amendment

1 Substituted by the Civil Procedure (Amendment) Rules 2013, SI 2013/262, r 16, Schedule (1 April 2013).

[45.6 Costs on entry of judgment in a claim for the recovery of land or a demotion claim

(1) Where—

(a) the claimant has claimed fixed commencement costs under rule 45.5; and

(b) judgment is entered in a claim to which rule 45.1(2)(d) or (f) applies, the amount to be included in the judgment for the claimant's legal representative's charges is the total of—

(i) the fixed commencement costs; and

(ii) the sum of £57.25.

(2) Where an order for possession is made in a claim to which rule 45.1(2)(e) applies, the amount allowed for the claimant's legal representative's charges for preparing and filing—

(a) the claim form;

(b) the documents that accompany the claim form; and

(c) the request for possession,

is £79.50.][1]

Amendment

1 Substituted by the Civil Procedure (Amendment) Rules 2013, SI 2013/262, r 16, Schedule (1 April 2013).

[45.7 Miscellaneous fixed costs

Table 4 shows the amount to be allowed in respect of legal representative's charges in the circumstances mentioned.

Table 4

Miscellaneous Fixed Costs	
For service by a party of any document other than the claim form required to be served personally including preparing and copying a certificate of service for each individual served	£15.00
Where service by an alternative method or at an alternative place is permitted by an order under rule 6.15 for each individual served	£53.25
Where a document is served out of the jurisdiction –	
(a) in Scotland, Northern Ireland, the Isle of Man or the Channel Islands;	£68.25
(b) in any other place	£77.00

][1]

Amendment

1 Substituted by the Civil Procedure (Amendment) Rules 2013, SI 2013/262, r 16, Schedule (1 April 2013).

[45.8 Fixed enforcement costs

Table 5 shows the amount to be allowed in respect of legal representatives' costs in the circumstances mentioned. The amounts shown in Table 4 are to be allowed in addition, if applicable.

Table 5

Fixed Enforcement Costs	
For an application under rule 70.5(4) that an award may be enforced as if payable under a court order, where the amount outstanding under the award:	
exceeds £25 but does not exceed £250	£30.75
exceeds £250 but does not exceed £600	£41.00
exceeds £600 but does not exceed £2,000	£69.50
exceeds £2,000	£75.50
On attendance to question a judgment debtor (or officer of a company or other corporation) who has been ordered to attend court under rule 71.2 where the questioning takes place before a court officer, including attendance by a responsible representative of the legal representative	for each half hour or part, £15.00
On the making of a final third party debt order under rule 72.8(6)(a) or an order for the payment to the judgment creditor of money in court under rule 72.10(1)(b):	
if the amount recovered is less than £150	one-half of the amount recovered
Otherwise	£98.50
[On the making of a final charging order under rule 73.10(6A)(a), 73.10(7)(a) or 73.10A(3)(a)][1]:	£110.00
	The court may also allow reasonable disbursements in respect of search fees and the registration of the order.
Where a certificate is issued and registered under Schedule 6 to the Civil Jurisdiction and Judgments Act 1982, the costs of registration	£39.00
Where permission is given under [rule 83.13][2] to enforce a judgment or order giving possession of land and costs are allowed on the judgment or order, the amount to be added to the judgment or order for costs –	
(a) basic costs	£42.50
(b) where notice of the proceedings is to be to more than one person, for each additional person	£2.75
[Where a writ of control as defined in rule 83.1(2)(k) is issued against any party	£51.75][3]
Where a writ of execution as defined in [rule 83.1(2)(l)][2], is issued against any party	£51.75
Where a request is filed for the issue of a warrant of [control under rule 83.15][2], for a sum exceeding £25	£2.25

[Where a request is filed for the issue of a warrant of delivery under rule 83.15 for a sum exceeding £25	£2.25][3]
Where an application for an attachment of earnings order is made and costs are allowed under [rule 89.10][4] or CCR Order 28, rule 10, for each attendance on the hearing of the application	£8.50

][5]

Amendments

1 Substituted by the Civil Procedure (Amendment) Rules 2020, SI 2020/82, rr 2, 4 (6 April 2020).

2 Substituted by the Civil Procedure (Amendment No. 4) Rules 2014, SI 2014/867, r 8(a), (c), (d) (22 April 2014).

3 Inserted by the Civil Procedure (Amendment No. 4) Rules 2014, SI 2014/867, r 8(b), (e) (22 April 2014).

4 Substituted by the Civil Procedure (Amendment) Rules 2016, SI 2016/234, r 9 (6 April 2016).

5 Substituted by the Civil Procedure (Amendment) Rules 2013, SI 2013/262, r 16, Schedule (1 April 2013).

[Section VI
Fast Track Trial Costs

45.37 Scope of this Section

(1) This Section deals with the amount of costs which the court may award as the costs of an advocate for preparing for and appearing at the trial of a claim in the fast track (referred to in this rule as 'fast track trial costs').

(2) For the purposes of this Section—

'advocate' means a person exercising a right of audience as a representative of, or on behalf of, a party;

'fast track trial costs' means the costs of a party's advocate for preparing for and appearing at the trial, but does not include—

(i) any other disbursements; or

(ii) any value added tax payable on the fees of a party's advocate; and

'trial' includes a hearing where the court decides an amount of money or the value of goods following a judgment under Part 12 (default judgment) or Part 14 (admissions) but does not include–

(i) the hearing of an application for summary judgment under Part 24; or

(ii) the court's approval of a settlement or other compromise under rule 21.10.][1]

Amendment

1 Substituted by the Civil Procedure (Amendment) Rules 2013, SI 2013/262, r 16, Schedule (1 April 2013).

[45.38 Amount of fast track trial costs

(1) Table 9 shows the amount of fast track trial costs which the court may award (whether by summary or detailed assessment).

Table 9

Value of the claim	Amount of fast track trial costs which the court may award
No more than £3,000	£485
More than £3,000 but not more than £10,000	£690
More than £10,000 but not more than £15,000	£1,035
For proceedings issued on or after 6th April 2009, more than £15,000	£1,650

(2) The court may not award more or less than the amount shown in the table except where—

(a) it decides not to award any fast track trial costs; or

(b) rule 45.39 applies,

but the court may apportion the amount awarded between the parties to reflect their respective degrees of success on the issues at trial.

(3) Where the only claim is for the payment of money—

(a) for the purpose of quantifying fast track trial costs awarded to a claimant, the value of the claim is the total amount of the judgment excluding—

(i) interest and costs; and

(ii) any reduction made for contributory negligence[; and][1]

(b) for the purpose of quantifying fast track trial costs awarded to a defendant, the value of the claim is—

(i) the amount specified in the claim form (excluding interest and costs);

(ii) if no amount is specified, the maximum amount which the claimant reasonably expected to recover according to the statement of value included in the claim form under rule 16.3; or

(iii) more than £15,000, if the claim form states that the claimant cannot reasonably say how much is likely to be recovered.

(4) Where the claim is only for a remedy other than the payment of money, the value of the claim is deemed to be more than £3,000 but not more than £10,000, unless the court orders otherwise.

(5) Where the claim includes both a claim for the payment of money and for a remedy other than the payment of money, the value of the claim is deemed to be the higher of—

(a) the value of the money claim decided in accordance with paragraph (3); or

(b) the deemed value of the other remedy decided in accordance with paragraph (4),

unless the court orders otherwise.

(6) Where—

(a) a defendant has made a counterclaim against the claimant;

(b) the counterclaim has a higher value than the claim; and

(c) the claimant succeeds at trial both on the claim and the counterclaim,

for the purpose of quantifying fast track trial costs awarded to the claimant, the value of the claim is the value of the defendant's counterclaim calculated in accordance with this rule.][2]

Amendments

1 Substituted by the Civil Procedure (Amendment No.7) Rules 2013, SI 2013/1974, r 20(h) (1 October 2013: substitution has effect subject to saving specified in the Civil Procedure (Amendment No.7) Rules 2013, r 30).

2 Substituted by the Civil Procedure (Amendment) Rules 2013, SI 2013/262, r 16, Schedule (1 April 2013).

[45.39 Power to award more or less than the amount of fast track trial costs

(1) This rule sets out when a court may award—

(a) an additional amount to the amount of fast track trial costs shown in Table 9 in rule 45.38(1); or

(b) less than those amounts.

(2) If—

(a) in addition to the advocate, a party's legal representative attends the trial;

(b) the court considers that it was necessary for a legal representative to attend to assist the advocate; and

(c) the court awards fast track trial costs to that party,

the court may award an additional £345 in respect of the legal representative's attendance at the trial.

(3) If the court considers that it is necessary to direct a separate trial of an issue then the court may award an additional amount in respect of the separate trial but that amount is limited in accordance with paragraph (4) of this rule.

(4) The additional amount the court may award under paragraph (3) will not exceed two-thirds of the amount payable for that claim, subject to a minimum award of £485.

(5) Where the party to whom fast track trial costs are to be awarded is a litigant in person, the court will award—

(a) if the litigant in person can prove financial loss, two-thirds of the amount that would otherwise be awarded; or

(b) if the litigant in person fails to prove financial loss, an amount in respect of the time spent reasonably doing the work at the rate specified in Practice Direction 46.

(6) Where a defendant has made a counterclaim against the claimant, and—

(a) the claimant has succeeded on his claim; and

(b) the defendant has succeeded on his counterclaim,

the court will quantify the amount of the award of fast track trial costs to which—

(i) but for the counterclaim, the claimant would be entitled for succeeding on his claim; and

(ii) but for the claim, the defendant would be entitled for succeeding on his counterclaim,

and make one award of the difference, if any, to the party entitled to the higher award of costs.

(7) Where the court considers that the party to whom fast track trial costs are to be awarded has behaved unreasonably or improperly during the trial, it may award that party an amount less than would otherwise be payable for that claim, as it considers appropriate.

(8) Where the court considers that the party who is to pay the fast track trial costs has behaved improperly during the trial the court may award such additional amount to the other party as it considers appropriate.][1]

Amendment

1 Substituted by the Civil Procedure (Amendment) Rules 2013, SI 2013/262, r 16, Schedule (1 April 2013).

[45.40 Fast track trial costs where there is more than one claimant or defendant

(1) Where the same advocate is acting for more than one party—

(a) the court may make only one award in respect of fast track trial costs payable to that advocate; and

(b) the parties for whom the advocate is acting are jointly entitled to any fast track trial costs awarded by the court.

(2) Where—

(a) the same advocate is acting for more than one claimant; and

(b) each claimant has a separate claim against the defendant,

the value of the claim, for the purpose of quantifying the award in respect of fast track trial costs is to be ascertained in accordance with paragraph (3).

(3) The value of the claim in the circumstances mentioned in paragraph (2) or (5) is—

(a) where the only claim of each claimant is for the payment of money—

(i) if the award of fast track trial costs is in favour of the claimants, the total amount of the judgment made in favour of all the claimants jointly represented; or

(ii) if the award is in favour of the defendant, the total amount claimed by the claimants,

and in either case, quantified in accordance with rule 45.38(3);

(b) where the only claim of each claimant is for a remedy other than the payment of money, deemed to be more than £3,000 but not more than £10,000; and

(c) where claims of the claimants include both a claim for the payment of money and for a remedy other than the payment of money, deemed to be—

(i) more than £3,000 but not more than £10,000; or

(ii) if greater, the value of the money claims calculated in accordance with subparagraph (a) above.

(4) Where—

(a) there is more than one defendant; and

(b) any or all of the defendants are separately represented,

the court may award fast track trial costs to each party who is separately represented.

(5) Where—

(a) there is more than one claimant; and

(b) a single defendant,

the court may make only one award to the defendant of fast track trial costs, for which the claimants are jointly and severally liable.

(6) For the purpose of quantifying the fast track trial costs awarded to the single defendant under paragraph (5), the value of the claim is to be calculated in accordance with paragraph (3) of this rule.][1]

Amendment

1 Substituted by the Civil Procedure (Amendment) Rules 2013, SI 2013/262, r 16, Schedule (1 April 2013).

[Part 52
Appeals

Section I
Scope and interpretatioin

52.1 Scope and interpretation

(1) The rules in this Part apply to appeals to—

(a) the civil division of the Court of Appeal;

(b) the High Court; and

(c) the County Court.

(2) This Part does not apply to an appeal in detailed assessment proceedings against a decision of an authorised court officer.

(3) In this Part—

(a) 'appeal' includes an appeal by way of case stated;

(b) 'appeal court' means the court to which an appeal is made;

(c) 'lower court' means the court, tribunal or other person or body from whose decision an appeal is brought;

(d) 'appellant' means a person who brings or seeks to bring an appeal;

(e) 'respondent' means—

(i) a person other than the appellant who was a party to the proceedings in the lower court and who is affected by the appeal; and

(ii) a person who is permitted by the appeal court to be a party to the appeal; and

(f) 'appeal notice' means an appellant's or respondent's notice.

(4) This Part is subject to any rule, enactment or practice direction which sets out special provisions with regard to any particular category of appeal.][1]

Amendment

1 Substituted by the Civil Procedure (Amendment No. 3) Rules 2016, SI 2016/788, rr 4, 10, Schedule (3 October 2016).

[52.2 Parties to comply with Practice Directions 52A to 52E

All parties to an appeal must comply with Practice Directions 52A to 52E.][1]

Amendment

1 Substituted by the Civil Procedure (Amendment No. 3) Rules 2016, SI 2016/788, rr 4, 10, Schedule (3 October 2016).

[Section II Permission to appeal – General

52.3 Permission to appeal

(1) An appellant or respondent requires permission to appeal—

(a) where the appeal is from a decision of a judge in the County Court or the High Court, or to the Court of Appeal from a decision of a judge in the family court, except where the appeal is against—

(i) a committal order;

(ii) a refusal to grant habeas corpus; or

(iii) a secure accommodation order made under section 25 of the Children Act 1989 [or section 119 of the Social Services and Well-being (Wales) Act 2014][1]; or

(b) as provided by Practice Directions 52A to 52E.

(Other enactments may provide that permission is required for particular appeals.)

(2) An application for permission to appeal may be made—

(a) to the lower court at the hearing at which the decision to be appealed was made; or

(b) to the appeal court in an appeal notice.

(Rule 52.12 sets out the time limits for filing an appellant's notice at the appeal court. Rule 52.13 sets out the time limits for filing a respondent's notice at the appeal court. Any application for permission to appeal to the appeal court must be made in the appeal notice (see rules 52.12(1) and 52.13(3)).)

(3) Where the lower court refuses an application for permission to appeal—

(a) a further application for permission may be made to the appeal court; and

(b) the order refusing permission must specify—

(i) the court to which any further application for permission should be made; and

(ii) the level of judge who should hear the application.][2]

Amendments

1 Inserted by the Civil Procedure (Amendment No. 2) Rules 2017, SI 2017/889, rr 2, 6(a) (1 October 2017).

2 Substituted by the Civil Procedure (Amendment No. 3) Rules 2016, SI 2016/788, rr 4, 10, Schedule (3 October 2016).

[52.4 Determination of applications for permission to appeal to the County Court and High Court

(1) Where an application for permission to appeal is made to an appeal court other than the Court of Appeal, the appeal court will determine the application on paper without an oral hearing, [unless the court otherwise directs, or][1] as provided for under paragraph (2).

(2) Subject to paragraph (3) and except where a rule or practice direction provides otherwise, where the appeal court, without a hearing, refuses permission to appeal, the person seeking permission may request the decision to be reconsidered at an oral hearing.

(3) Where in the appeal court a judge of the High Court, a Designated Civil Judge or a Specialist Circuit Judge refuses permission to appeal without an oral hearing and considers that the application is totally without merit, the judge may make an order that the person seeking permission may not request the decision to be reconsidered at an oral hearing.

(4) For the purposes of paragraph (3), 'Specialist Circuit Judge' means any Circuit Judge in the County Court nominated to hear cases in the [Circuit Commercial][1], Chancery or Technology and Construction Court lists.

(5) Rule 3.3(5) (party able to apply to set aside, etc., a decision made of court's own initiative) does not apply to an order made under paragraph (3) that the person seeking permission may not request the decision to be reconsidered at an oral hearing.

(6) A request under paragraph (2) must be filed within 7 days after service of the notice that permission has been refused.][2]

Amendments

1 Substituted by the Civil Procedure (Amendment No. 2) Rules 2017, SI 2017/889, rr 2, 6(b) (1 October 2017).

2 Substituted by the Civil Procedure (Amendment No. 3) Rules 2016, SI 2016/788, rr 4, 10, Schedule (3 October 2016).

[52.5 Determination of applications for permission to appeal to the Court of Appeal

(1) Where an application for permission to appeal is made to the Court of Appeal, the Court of Appeal will determine the application on paper without an oral hearing, except as provided for under paragraph (2).

(2) The judge considering the application on paper may direct that the application be determined at an oral hearing, and must so direct if the judge is of the opinion that the application cannot be fairly determined on paper without an oral hearing.

(3) An oral hearing directed under paragraph (2) must be listed—

(a) no later than 14 days from the date of the direction under that paragraph; and

(b) before the judge who made that direction,

unless the court directs otherwise.

(4) The Court of Appeal may, in any direction under paragraph (2)—

(a) identify any issue or issues on which the party seeking permission should specifically focus its submissions at the oral hearing in order to assist the court to determine the application; and

(b) direct the respondent to serve and file written submissions and to attend the oral hearing.][1]

Amendment

1 Substituted by the Civil Procedure (Amendment No. 3) Rules 2016, SI 2016/788, rr 4, 10, Schedule (3 October 2016).

[52.6 Permission to appeal test – first appeals

(1) Except where rule 52.7 applies, permission to appeal may be given only where—

(a) the court considers that the appeal would have a real prospect of success; or

(b) there is some other compelling reason for the appeal to be heard.

(2) An order giving permission under this rule or under rule 52.7 may—

(a) limit the issues to be heard; and

(b) be made subject to conditions.

(Rule 3.1(3) also provides that the court may make an order subject to conditions.)

(Rule 25.15 provides for the court to order security for costs of an appeal.)][1]

Amendment

1 Substituted by the Civil Procedure (Amendment No. 3) Rules 2016, SI 2016/788, rr 4, 10, Schedule (3 October 2016).

[52.7 Permission to appeal test – second appeals

(1) Permission is required from the Court of Appeal for any appeal to that court from a decision of the County Court, the family court or the High Court which was itself made on appeal, or a decision of the Upper Tribunal which was made on appeal from a decision of the First-tier Tribunal on a point of law where the Upper Tribunal has refused permission to appeal to the Court of Appeal.

(2) The Court of Appeal will not give permission unless it considers that—

(a) the appeal would—

(i) have a real prospect of success; and

(ii) raise an important point of principle or practice; or

(b) there is some other compelling reason for the Court of Appeal to hear it.][1]

Amendment

1 Substituted by the Civil Procedure (Amendment No. 3) Rules 2016, SI 2016/788, rr 4, 10, Schedule (3 October 2016).

[Section III Permission to appeal – judicial review appeals, planning statutory review appeals and appeals from the Employment Appeal Tribunal

52.8 Judicial review appeals from the High Court

(1) Where permission to apply for judicial review has been refused at a hearing in the High Court, an application for permission to appeal may be made to the Court of Appeal.

(2) Where permission to apply for judicial review of a decision of the Upper Tribunal has been refused by the High Court on the papers or where permission to apply for judicial review has been refused on the papers and recorded as being totally without merit in accordance with rule 23.12, an application for permission to appeal may be made to the Court of Appeal.

(3) An application under paragraph (1) must be made within 7 days of the decision of the High Court to refuse to give permission to apply for judicial review.

(4) An application under paragraph (2) must be made within 7 days of service of the order of the High Court refusing permission to apply for judicial review.

(5) On an application under paragraph (1) or (2), the Court of Appeal may, instead of giving permission to appeal, give permission to apply for judicial review.

(6) Where the Court of Appeal gives permission to apply for judicial review in accordance with paragraph (5), the case will proceed in the High Court unless the Court of Appeal orders otherwise.][1]

Amendment

1 Substituted by the Civil Procedure (Amendment No. 3) Rules 2016, SI 2016/788, rr 4, 10, Schedule (3 October 2016).

[52.9 Judicial review appeals from the Upper Tribunal

(1) Where permission to bring judicial review proceedings has been refused by the Upper Tribunal at a hearing and permission to appeal has been refused by

the Upper Tribunal, an application for permission to appeal may be made to the Court of Appeal.

(2) Where an application for permission to bring judicial review proceedings has been determined by the Upper Tribunal on the papers and recorded as being totally without merit and permission to appeal has been refused by the Upper Tribunal, an application for permission to appeal may be made to the Court of Appeal.

(3) An application under this rule to the Court of Appeal must be made within 7 days of—

(a) the decision of the Upper Tribunal refusing permission to appeal to the Court of Appeal, where that decision was made at a hearing; or

(b) service of the order of the Upper Tribunal refusing permission to appeal to the Court of Appeal, where the decision to refuse permission was made on the papers.][1]

Amendment

1 Substituted by the Civil Procedure (Amendment No. 3) Rules 2016, SI 2016/788, rr 4, 10, Schedule (3 October 2016).

[52.10 Planning statutory review appeals

(1) Where permission to apply for a planning statutory review has been refused at a hearing in the High Court, an application for permission to appeal may be made to the Court of Appeal.

(See Part 8 and Practice Direction 8C.)

(2) Where permission to apply for a planning statutory review has been refused by the High Court on the papers and recorded as totally without merit in accordance with rule 23.12, an application for permission to appeal may be made to the Court of Appeal.

(3) An application under paragraph (1) must be made within 7 days of the decision of the High Court to refuse to give permission to apply for a planning statutory review.

(4) An application under paragraph (2) must be made within 7 days of service of the order of the High Court refusing permission to apply for a planning statutory review.

(5) On an application under paragraph (1) or (2) the Court of Appeal may, instead of giving permission to appeal, give permission to apply for a planning statutory review.

(6) Where the Court of Appeal gives permission to apply for a planning statutory review in accordance with paragraph (5), the case will proceed in the High Court unless the Court of Appeal orders otherwise.][1]

Amendment

1 Substituted by the Civil Procedure (Amendment No. 3) Rules 2016, SI 2016/788, rr 4, 10, Schedule (3 October 2016).

[52.11 Appeals from the Employment Appeal Tribunal

(1) Where on an appeal to the Employment Appeal Tribunal either—

(a) the appellant or special advocate has been given notice under rule 3(7) of the Employment Appeal Tribunal Rules 1993 ('the 1993 Rules') and an order has been made under rule 3(7ZA) of those Rules; or

(b) a direction has been made under rule 3(10) of the 1993 Rules that no further action shall be taken on the notice of appeal,

the appellant may apply to the Court of Appeal for permission to appeal.

(2) An application under paragraph (1) must be made within 7 days of the date of—

(a) service of the notice under rule 3(7) of the 1993 Rules; or

(b) the direction made under rule 3(10) of those Rules,

as the case may be.

(3) The Court of Appeal may, instead of giving permission to appeal, direct that the notice under rule 3(7) of the 1993 Rules or (as the case may be) the direction under rule 3(10) of those Rules shall be of no effect so that the appeal shall proceed in the Employment Appeal Tribunal as if the notice or direction had not been given or made, but such a direction shall not be given unless the test for the grant of permission to appeal under rule 52.6(2) is met.][1]

Amendment

1 Substituted by the Civil Procedure (Amendment No. 3) Rules 2016, SI 2016/788, rr 4, 10, Schedule (3 October 2016).

[Section IV
Additional rules

52.12 Appellant's notice

(1) Where the appellant seeks permission from the appeal court, it must be requested in the appellant's notice.

(2) The appellant must file the appellant's notice at the appeal court within—

(a) such period as may be directed by the lower court (which may be longer or shorter than the period referred to in sub-paragraph (b)); or

(b) where the court makes no such direction, and subject to the specific provision about time limits in rules 52.8 to 52.11 and Practice Direction 52D, 21 days after the date of the decision of the lower court which the appellant wishes to appeal.

(3) Subject to paragraph (4) and unless the appeal court orders otherwise, an appellant's notice must be served on each respondent—

(a) as soon as practicable; and

(b) in any event not later than 7 days,

after it is filed.

(4) Where an appellant seeks permission to appeal against a decision to refuse to grant an interim injunction under section 41 of the Policing and Crime Act 2009, the appellant is not required to serve the appellant's notice on the respondent.][1]

Amendment

1 Substituted by the Civil Procedure (Amendment No. 3) Rules 2016, SI 2016/788, rr 4, 10, Schedule (3 October 2016).

[52.13 Respondent's notice

(1) A respondent may file and serve a respondent's notice.

(2) A respondent who—

(a) is seeking permission to appeal from the appeal court; or

(b) wishes to ask the appeal court to uphold the decision of the lower court for reasons different from or additional to those given by the lower court,

must file a respondent's notice.

(3) Where the respondent seeks permission from the appeal court it must be requested in the respondent's notice.

(4) A respondent's notice must be filed within—

(a) such period as may be directed by the lower court; or

(b) where the court makes no such direction, 14 days after the date in paragraph (5).

(5) The date referred to in paragraph (4) is—

(a) the date the respondent is served with the appellant's notice where—

(i) permission to appeal was given by the lower court; or

(ii) permission to appeal is not required;

(b) the date the respondent is served with notification that the appeal court has given the appellant permission to appeal; or

(c) the date the respondent is served with notification that the application for permission to appeal and the appeal itself are to be heard together.

(6) Unless the appeal court orders otherwise, a respondent's notice must be served on the appellant and any other respondent—

(a) as soon as practicable; and

(b) in any event not later than 7 days,

after it is filed.

(7) This rule does not apply where rule 52.12(4) applies.][1]

Amendment

1 Substituted by the Civil Procedure (Amendment No. 3) Rules 2016, SI 2016/788, rr 4, 10, Schedule (3 October 2016).

[52.14 Transcripts at public expense

(1) Subject to paragraph (2), the lower court or the appeal court may direct, on the application of a party to the proceedings, that an official transcript of the judgment of the lower court, or of any part of the evidence or the proceedings in the lower court, be obtained at public expense for the purposes of an appeal.

(2) Before making a direction under paragraph (1), the court must be satisfied that—

(a) the applicant qualifies for fee remission or is otherwise in such poor financial circumstances that the cost of obtaining a transcript would be an excessive burden; and

(b) it is necessary in the interests of justice for such a transcript to be obtained.][1]

Amendment

1 Substituted by the Civil Procedure (Amendment No. 3) Rules 2016, SI 2016/788, rr 4, 10, Schedule (3 October 2016).

[52.15 Variation of time

(1) An application to vary the time limit for filing an appeal notice must be made to the appeal court.

(2) The parties may not agree to extend any date or time set by—

(a) these Rules;

(b) Practice Directions 52A to 52E; or

(c) an order of the appeal court or the lower court.

(Rule 3.1(2)(a) provides that the court may extend or shorten the time for compliance with any rule, practice direction or court order (even if an application for extension is made after the time for compliance has expired).)

(Rule 3.1(2)(b) provides that the court may adjourn or bring forward a hearing.)][1]

Amendment

1 Substituted by the Civil Procedure (Amendment No. 3) Rules 2016, SI 2016/788, rr 4, 10, Schedule (3 October 2016).

[52.16 Stay[(GL)]

Unless—

(a) the appeal court or the lower court orders otherwise; or

(b) the appeal is from the Immigration and Asylum Chamber of the Upper Tribunal,

an appeal shall not operate as a stay of any order or decision of the lower court.][1]

Amendment

1 Substituted by the Civil Procedure (Amendment No. 3) Rules 2016, SI 2016/788, rr 4, 10, Schedule (3 October 2016).

[52.17 Amendment of appeal notice

An appeal notice may not be amended without the permission of the appeal court.][1]

Amendment

1 Substituted by the Civil Procedure (Amendment No. 3) Rules 2016, SI 2016/788, rr 4, 10, Schedule (3 October 2016).

[52.18 Striking out[(GL)] appeal notices and setting aside[(GL)] or imposing conditions on permission to appeal

(1) The appeal court may—

(a) strike out the whole or part of an appeal notice;

(b) set aside permission to appeal in whole or in part;

(c) impose or vary conditions upon which an appeal may be brought.

(2) The court will only exercise its powers under paragraph (1) where there is a compelling reason for doing so.

(3) Where a party was present at the hearing at which permission was given, that party may not subsequently apply for an order that the court exercise its powers under sub-paragraphs (1)(b) or (1)(c).][1]

Amendment

1 Substituted by the Civil Procedure (Amendment No. 3) Rules 2016, SI 2016/788, rr 4, 10, Schedule (3 October 2016).

[52.19 Orders to limit the recoverable costs of an appeal [– general][1]

(1) [Subject to rule 52.19A, in][2] any proceedings in which costs recovery is normally limited or excluded at first instance, an appeal court may make an order that the recoverable costs of an appeal will be limited to the extent which the court specifies.

(2) In making such an order the court will have regard to—

(a) the means of both parties;

(b) all the circumstances of the case; and

(c) the need to facilitate access to justice.

(3) If the appeal raises an issue of principle or practice upon which substantial sums may turn, it may not be appropriate to make an order under paragraph (1).

(4) An application for such an order must be made as soon as practicable and will be determined without a hearing unless the court orders otherwise.][3]

Amendments

1 Inserted by the Civil Procedure (Amendment) Rules 2017, SI 2017/95, rr 4, 9(1)(a) (28 February 2017).

2 Substituted by the Civil Procedure (Amendment) Rules 2017, SI 2017/95, rr 4, 9(1)(b) (6 March 2017).

3 Substituted by the Civil Procedure (Amendment No. 3) Rules 2016, SI 2016/788, rr 4, 10, Schedule (3 October 2016).

[52.19A Orders to limit the recoverable costs of an appeal – appeals in Aarhus Convention claims

(1) In this rule, 'Aarhus Convention claim' and 'prohibitively expensive' have the same meanings as in Section VII of Part 45, and 'claimant' means a claimant to whom rules 45.43 to 45.45 apply.

(2) In an appeal against a decision made in an Aarhus Convention claim to which rules 45.43 to 45.45 apply, the court must—

(a) consider whether the costs of the proceedings will be prohibitively expensive for a party who was a claimant; and

(b) if they will be, make an order limiting the recoverable costs to the extent necessary to prevent this.

(3) When the court considers the financial resources of a party for the purposes of this rule, it must have regard to any financial support which any person has provided or is likely to provide to that party.][1]

Amendment

1 Inserted by the Civil Procedure (Amendment) Rules 2017, SI 2017/95, rr 4, 9(2) (28 February 2017).

[52.20 Appeal court's powers

(1) In relation to an appeal the appeal court has all the powers of the lower court.

(Rule 52.1(4) provides that this Part is subject to any enactment that sets out special provisions with regard to any particular category of appeal. Where such an enactment gives a statutory power to a tribunal, person or other body, it may be the case that the appeal court may not exercise that power on an appeal.)

(2) The appeal court has power to—

(a) affirm, set aside or vary any order or judgment made or given by the lower court;

(b) refer any claim or issue for determination by the lower court;

(c) order a new trial or hearing;

(d) make orders for the payment of interest;

(e) make a costs order.

(3) In an appeal from a claim tried with a jury the Court of Appeal may, instead of ordering a new trial—

(a) make an order for damages; or

(b) vary an award of damages made by the jury.

(4) The appeal court may exercise its powers in relation to the whole or part of an order of the lower court.

(Part 3 contains general rules about the court's case management powers.)

(5) If the appeal court—

(a) refuses an application for permission to appeal;

(b) strikes out an appellant's notice; or

(c) dismisses an appeal,

and it considers that the application, the appellant's notice or the appeal is totally without merit, the provisions of paragraph (6) must be complied with.

(6) Where paragraph (5) applies—

(a) the court's order must record the fact that it considers the application, the appellant's notice or the appeal to be totally without merit; and

(b) the court must at the same time consider whether it is appropriate to make a civil restraint order.][1]

Amendment

1 Substituted by the Civil Procedure (Amendment No. 3) Rules 2016, SI 2016/788, rr 4, 10, Schedule (3 October 2016).

[52.21 Hearing of appeals

(1) Every appeal will be limited to a review of the decision of the lower court unless—

(a) a practice direction makes different provision for a particular category of appeal; or

(b) the court considers that in the circumstances of an individual appeal it would be in the interests of justice to hold a re-hearing.

(2) Unless it orders otherwise, the appeal court will not receive—

(a) oral evidence; or

(b) evidence which was not before the lower court.

(3) The appeal court will allow an appeal where the decision of the lower court was—

(a) wrong; or

(b) unjust because of a serious procedural or other irregularity in the proceedings in the lower court.

(4) The appeal court may draw any inference of fact which it considers justified on the evidence.

(5) At the hearing of the appeal, a party may not rely on a matter not contained in that party's appeal notice unless the court gives permission.][1]

Amendment

1 Substituted by the Civil Procedure (Amendment No. 3) Rules 2016, SI 2016/788, rr 4, 10, Schedule (3 October 2016).

[52.22 Non-disclosure of Part 36 offers and payments

(1) [Unless the appeal court otherwise orders, the][1] fact that a Part 36 offer or payment into court has been made must not be disclosed to any judge of the appeal court who is to hear or determine—

(a) an application for permission to appeal; or

(b) an appeal,

until all questions (other than costs) have been determined.

(2) Paragraph (1) does not apply if the Part 36 offer or payment into court is relevant to the substance of the appeal.

(3) Paragraph (1) does not prevent disclosure in any application in the appeal proceedings if disclosure of the fact that a Part 36 offer or payment into court has been made is properly relevant to the matter to be decided.

(Rule 36.4 has the effect that a Part 36 offer made in proceedings at first instance will not have consequences in any appeal proceedings. Therefore, a fresh Part 36 offer needs to be made in appeal proceedings. However, this rule applies to a Part 36 offer whether made in the original proceedings or in the appeal.)][2]

Amendments

1 Substituted by the Civil Procedure (Amendment) Rules 2020, SI 2020/82, rr 2, 5(1) (6 April 2020).

2 Substituted by the Civil Procedure (Amendment No. 3) Rules 2016, SI 2016/788, rr 4, 10, Schedule (3 October 2016).

[Section V
Special provisions relating to the Court of Appeal

52.23 Assignment of appeals to the Court of Appeal

(1) Where the court from or to which an appeal is made or from which permission to appeal is sought ('the relevant court') considers that—

(a) an appeal which is to be heard by the County Court or the High Court would raise an important point of principle or practice; or

(b) there is some other compelling reason for the Court of Appeal to hear it,

the relevant court may order the appeal to be transferred to the Court of Appeal.

(The Master of the Rolls has the separate statutory power to direct that an appeal which would be heard by the County Court or the High Court should be heard instead by the Court of Appeal – see section 57 of the Access to Justice Act 1999.)

(2) The Master of the Rolls or the Court of Appeal may remit an appeal to the court in which the original appeal was or would have been brought.][1]

Amendment

1 Substituted by the Civil Procedure (Amendment No. 3) Rules 2016, SI 2016/788, rr 4, 10, Schedule (3 October 2016).

[52.24 Who may exercise the powers of the Court of Appeal

(1) A court officer assigned to the Civil Appeals Office who is—

(a) a barrister; …[1]

(b) a solicitor[; or][2]

[(c) a Fellow of the Chartered Institute of Legal Executives,][2]

may exercise the jurisdiction of the Court of Appeal with regard to the matters set out in paragraph (2) with the consent of the Master of the Rolls.

(2) The matters referred to in paragraph (1) are—

(a) any matter incidental to proceedings in the Court of Appeal;

(b) any other matter where there is no substantial dispute between the parties; and

(c) the dismissal of an appeal or application where a party has failed to comply with any order, rule or practice direction.

(3) A court officer may not decide an application for—

(a) permission to appeal;

(b) bail pending an appeal;

(c) an injunction(GL);

(d) a stay(GL) of execution of any order or decision of the lower court other than a temporary stay over a period when the Court of Appeal is not sitting or cannot conveniently be convened;

(e) a stay of proceedings in the lower court.

(4) Decisions of a court officer will be made without an oral hearing, unless a court officer directs otherwise.

(5) A party may request any decision of a court officer to be reviewed by a single judge, and—

(a) the review will be determined on paper without an oral hearing; except that

(b) the judge determining the review on paper may direct that the review be determined at an oral hearing, and must so direct if the judge is of the opinion that the review cannot be fairly determined on paper without an oral hearing.

(6) A party may request a decision of a single judge made without a hearing (other than a decision made on a review under paragraph (5) and a decision determining an application for permission to appeal) to be reconsidered, and—

(a) the reconsideration will be determined by the same or another judge on paper without an oral hearing; except that

(b) the judge determining the reconsideration on paper may direct that the reconsideration be determined at an oral hearing, and must so direct if the judge is of the opinion that the reconsideration cannot be fairly determined on paper without an oral hearing.

(7) A request under paragraph (5) or (6) must be filed within 7 days after the party is served with notice of the decision.

(8) A single judge may refer any matter for a decision by a court consisting of two or more judges.

(Section 54(4) of the Access to Justice Act 1999 provides that there is no appeal from the decision of a single judge on an application for permission to appeal.)

(Section 58(2) of the Senior Courts Act 1981 provides that there is no appeal to the Supreme Court from decisions of the Court of Appeal that—

(a) are taken by a single judge or any officer or member of staff of that court in proceedings incidental to any cause or matter pending before the civil division of that court; and

(b) do not involve the determination of an appeal or of an application for permission to appeal,

and which may be called into question by rules of court. Paragraphs (5) and (6) of this rule provide the procedure for the calling into question of such decisions.)][3]

Amendments

1 Repealed by the Civil Procedure (Amendment) Rules 2020, SI 2020/82, rr 2, 5(2)(a) (6 April 2020).

2 Inserted by the Civil Procedure (Amendment) Rules 2020, SI 2020/82, rr 2, 5(2)(b), (c) (6 April 2020).

3 Substituted by the Civil Procedure (Amendment No. 3) Rules 2016, SI 2016/788, rr 4, 10, Schedule (3 October 2016).

[Section VI
Special provisions relating to statutory appeals

52.25 Statutory appeals – court's power to hear any person

(1) In a statutory appeal any person may apply for permission—

(a) to file evidence; or

(b) to make representations at the appeal hearing.

(2) An application under paragraph (1) must be made promptly.][1]

Amendment

1 Substituted by the Civil Procedure (Amendment No. 3) Rules 2016, SI 2016/788, rr 4, 10, Schedule (3 October 2016).

[52.26 Appeals under the Law of Property Act 1922

An appeal lies to the High Court against a decision of the Secretary of State under paragraph 16 of Schedule 15 to the Law of Property Act 1922.][1]

Amendment

1 Substituted by the Civil Procedure (Amendment No. 3) Rules 2016, SI 2016/788, rr 4, 10, Schedule (3 October 2016).

[52.27 Appeals from certain tribunals

(1) A person who was a party to proceedings before a tribunal referred to in section 11(1) of the Tribunals and Inquiries Act 1992 and is dissatisfied in point of law with the decision of the tribunal may appeal to the High Court.

(2) The tribunal may, on its own initiative or at the request of a party to the proceedings before it, state, in the form of a special case for the decision of the High Court, a question of law arising in the course of the proceedings.][1]

Amendment

1 Substituted by the Civil Procedure (Amendment No. 3) Rules 2016, SI 2016/788, rr 4, 10, Schedule (3 October 2016).

[52.28 Appeals under certain planning legislation

(1) Where the Secretary of State has given a decision in proceedings on an appeal under Part VII of the Town and Country Planning Act 1990 against an enforcement notice—

(a) the appellant;

(b) the local planning authority; or

(c) another person having an interest in the land to which the notice relates,

may appeal to the High Court against the decision on a point of law.

(2) Where the Secretary of State has given a decision in proceedings on an appeal under Part VIII of that Act against a notice under section 207 of that Act—

(a) the appellant;

(b) the local planning authority; or

(c) another person (other than the appellant) on whom the notice was served,

may appeal to the High Court against the decision on a point of law.

(3) Where the Secretary of State has given a decision in proceedings on an appeal under section 39 of the Planning (Listed Buildings and Conservation Areas) Act 1990 against a listed building enforcement notice—

(a) the appellant;

(b) the local planning authority; or

(c) any other person having an interest in the land to which the notice relates,

may appeal to the High Court against the decision on a point of law.][1]

Amendment

1 Substituted by the Civil Procedure (Amendment No. 3) Rules 2016, SI 2016/788, rr 4, 10, Schedule (3 October 2016).

[52.29 Appeals under certain legislation relating to pensions

Where an appeal lies to the High Court—

(a) under section 151(4) of the Pension Schemes Act 1993 from a determination or direction of the Pensions Ombudsman; or

(b) under section 217(1) of the Pensions Act 2004 from a determination or direction of the Pension Protection Fund Ombudsman,

the permission of the High Court is required for such an appeal to be brought.][1]

Amendment

1 Substituted by the Civil Procedure (Amendment No. 3) Rules 2016, SI 2016/788, rr 4, 10, Schedule (3 October 2016).

[Section VII
Reopening final appeals

52.30 Reopening of final appeals

(1) The Court of Appeal or the High Court will not reopen a final determination of any appeal unless—

(a) it is necessary to do so in order to avoid real injustice;

(b) the circumstances are exceptional and make it appropriate to reopen the appeal; and

(c) there is no alternative effective remedy.

(2) In paragraphs (1), (3), (4) and (6), 'appeal' includes an application for permission to appeal.

(3) This rule does not apply to appeals to the County Court.

(4) Permission is needed to make an application under this rule to reopen a final determination of an appeal even in cases where under rule 52.3(1) permission was not needed for the original appeal.

(5) There is no right to an oral hearing of an application for permission unless, exceptionally, the judge so directs.

(6) The judge must not grant permission without directing the application to be served on the other party to the original appeal and giving that party an opportunity to make representations.

(7) There is no right of appeal or review from the decision of the judge on the application for permission, which is final.

(8) The procedure for making an application for permission is set out in Practice Direction 52A.][1]

Amendment

1 Substituted by the Civil Procedure (Amendment No. 3) Rules 2016, SI 2016/788, rr 4, 10, Schedule (3 October 2016).

[Part 54
Judicial review and statutory review

[Section I
Judicial review] 1

54.1 Scope and interpretation

(1) [This Section of this Part][2] contains rules about judicial review.

(2) [In this Section][2]—

(a) a 'claim for judicial review' means a claim to review the lawfulness of—

  (i) an enactment; or

  (ii) a decision, action or failure to act in relation to the exercise of a public function.

(b) …[3]

(c) …[3]

(d) …[3]

(e) 'the judicial review procedure' means the Part 8 procedure as modified by [this Section][2];

(f) 'interested party' means any person (other than the claimant and defendant) who is directly affected by the claim; and

(g) 'court' means the High Court, unless otherwise stated.

(Rule 8.1(6)(b) provides that a rule or practice direction may, in relation to a specified type of proceedings, disapply or modify any of the rules set out in Part 8 as they apply to those proceedings)][4]

Amendments

1 Inserted by the Civil Procedure (Amendment) Rules 2003, SI 2003/364, r 4, Sch 1, Pt 1 (1 April 2003 being the commencement date for the Nationality, Immigration and Asylum Act 2002, Pt 5).

2 Substituted by the Civil Procedure (Amendment) Rules 2003, SI 2003/364 rule 5(a), (b) (1 April 2003 being the commencement date for the Nationality, Immigration and Asylum Act 2002, Pt 5).

3 Repealed by the Civil Procedure (Amendment No. 5) Rules 2003, SI 2003/3361, r 12 (1 May 2004).

4 Inserted by the Civil Procedure (Amendment No. 4) Rules 2000, SI 2000/2092, r 22, Schedule (2 October 2000).

[54.1A Who may exercise the powers of the High Court

(1) A court officer assigned to the Administrative Court office who is—

(a) a barrister; …[1]

(b) a solicitor[; or][2]

[(c) a Fellow of the Chartered Institute of Legal Executives,][3]

may exercise the jurisdiction of the High Court with regard to the matters set out in paragraph (2) with the consent of the President of the Queen's Bench Division.

(2) The matters referred to in paragraph (1) are—

(a) any matter incidental to any proceedings in the High Court;

(b) any other matter where there is no substantial dispute between the parties; and

(c) the dismissal of an appeal or application where a party has failed to comply with any order, rule or practice direction.

(3) A court officer may not decide an application for—

(a) permission to bring judicial review proceedings;

(b) an injunction;

(c) a stay of any proceedings, other than a temporary stay of any order or decision of the lower court over a period when the High Court is not sitting or cannot conveniently be convened, unless the parties seek a stay by consent.

(4) Decisions of a court officer may be made without a hearing.

(5) A party may request any decision of a court officer to be reviewed by a judge of the High Court.

(6) At the request of a party, a hearing will be held to reconsider a decision of a court officer, made without a hearing.

(7) A request under paragraph (5) or (6) must be filed within 7 days after the party is served with notice of the decision.][4]

Amendments

1 Repealed by the Civil Procedure (Amendment) Rules 2020, SI 2020/82, rr 2, 7(a) (6 April 2020).

2 Substituted by the Civil Procedure (Amendment) Rules 2020, SI 2020/82, rr 2, 7(b) (6 April 2020).

3 Inserted by the Civil Procedure (Amendment) Rules 2020, SI 2020/82, rr 2, 7(c) (6 April 2020).

4 Inserted by the Civil Procedure (Amendment No.2) Rules 2012, SI 2012/2208, r 9(b) (1 October 2012).

[54.2 When this [Section][1] must be used

The judicial review procedure must be used in a claim for judicial review where the claimant is seeking—

(a) a mandatory order;

(b) a prohibiting order;

(c) a quashing order; or

(d) an injunction under section 30 of the [Senior Courts Act 1981][2] (restraining a person from acting in any office in which he is not entitled to act).][3]

Amendments

1 Substituted by the Civil Procedure (Amendment) Rules 2003, SI 2003/364 rule 5(c) (1 April 2003 being the commencement date for the Nationality, Immigration and Asylum Act 2002, Pt 5).

2 Substituted by the Constitutional Reform Act 2005, s 59, Sch 11, para 1(2) (1 October 2009).

3 Inserted by the Civil Procedure (Amendment No. 4) Rules 2000, SI 2000/2092, r 22, Schedule (2 October 2000).

[54.3 When this [Section][1] may be used

(1) The judicial review procedure may be used in a claim for judicial review where the claimant is seeking—

(a) a declaration; or

(b) an injunction[(GL)].

(Section 31(2) of the [Senior Courts Act 1981][2] sets out the circumstances in which the court may grant a declaration or injunction in a claim for judicial review)

(Where the claimant is seeking a declaration or injunction in addition to one of the remedies listed in rule 54.2, the judicial review procedure must be used)

(2) A claim for judicial review may include a claim for damages[, restitution or the recovery of a sum due][3] but may not seek [such a remedy][4] alone.

(Section 31(4) of the [Senior Courts Act 1981][2] sets out the circumstances in which the court may award damages[, restitution or the recovery of a sum due][3] on a claim for judicial review)][5]

Amendments

1 Substituted by the Civil Procedure (Amendment) Rules 2003, SI 2003/364 rule 5(c) (1 April 2003 being the commencement date for the Nationality, Immigration and Asylum Act 2002, Pt 5).

2 Substituted by the Constitutional Reform Act 2005, s 59, Sch 11, para 1(2) (1 October 2009).

3 Inserted by the Civil Procedure (Amendment No. 5) Rules 2003, SI 2003/3361, r 13(a)(i), (b) (1 May 2004).

4 Substituted by the Civil Procedure (Amendment No. 5) Rules 2003, SI 2003/3361, r 13(a)(ii) (1 May 2004).

5 Inserted by the Civil Procedure (Amendment No. 4) Rules 2000, SI 2000/2092, r 22, Schedule (2 October 2000).

[54.4 Permission required

The court's permission to proceed is required in a claim for judicial review whether started under this [Section][1] or transferred to the Administrative Court.][2]

Amendments

1 Substituted by the Civil Procedure (Amendment) Rules 2003, SI 2003/364 rule 5(d) (1 April 2003 being the commencement date for the Nationality, Immigration and Asylum Act 2002, Pt 5).

2 Inserted by the Civil Procedure (Amendment No. 4) Rules 2000, SI 2000/2092, r 22, Schedule (2 October 2000).

[54.5 Time limit for filing claim form

[(A1) In this rule—

'the planning acts' has the same meaning as in section 336 of the Town and Country Planning Act 1990;

['decision governed by the Public Contracts Regulations 2015' means any decision the legality of which is or may be affected by a duty owed to an economic operator by virtue of regulations 89 or 90 of those Regulations (and for this purpose it does not matter that the claimant is not an economic operator); and][1]

'economic operator' has the same meaning as in [regulation 2(1) of the Public Contracts Regulations 2015][1].][2]

(1) The claim form must be filed—

(a) promptly; and

(b) in any event not later than 3 months after the grounds to make the claim first arose.

(2) The time [limits][3] in this rule may not be extended by agreement between the parties.

(3) This rule does not apply when any other enactment specifies a shorter time limit for making the claim for judicial review.

[(4) Paragraph (1) does not apply in the cases specified in paragraphs (5) and (6).

(5) Where the application for judicial review relates to a decision made by the Secretary of State or local planning authority under the planning acts, the claim form must be filed not later than six weeks after the grounds to make the claim first arose.

(6) Where the application for judicial review relates to a decision governed by [the Public Contracts Regulations 2015][1], the claim form must be filed within the time within which an economic operator would have been required by [[regulation 92(2)][4]][1] of those Regulations (and disregarding the rest of that regulation) to start any proceedings under those Regulations in respect of that decision.][2]][5]

Amendments

1 Substituted by the Public Contracts Regulations 2015, SI 2015/102, reg 116(b), Sch 6, para 11 (26 February 2015: substitution has effect subject to savings and transitional provisions specified in the Public Contracts Regulations 2015, Pt 5).

2 Inserted by the Civil Procedure (Amendment No. 4) Rules 2013, SI 2013/1412, r 4(a)(i), (iii) (1 July 2013: insertion has effect subject to transitional provision specified in the Civil Procedure (Amendment No. 4) Rules 2013, r 5(2)).

3 Substituted by the Civil Procedure (Amendment No. 4) Rules 2013, SI 2013/1412, r 4(a)(ii) (1 July 2013: substitution has effect subject to transitional provision specified in the Civil Procedure (Amendment No. 4) Rules 2013, r 5(2)).

4 Substituted by the Civil Procedure (Amendment No. 3) Rules 2016, SI 2016/788, rr 4, 11 (3 October 2016).

5 Inserted by the Civil Procedure (Amendment No. 4) Rules 2000, SI 2000/2092, r 22, Schedule (2 October 2000).

[54.6 Claim form

(1) In addition to the matters set out in rule 8.2 (contents of the claim form) the claimant must also state—

(a) the name and address of any person he considers to be an interested party;

(b) that he is requesting permission to proceed with a claim for judicial review; ...[1]

(c) any remedy (including any interim remedy) he is claiming[; and][2]

[(d) where appropriate, the grounds on which it is contended that the claim is an Aarhus Convention claim.

(Rules 45.41 to 45.44 make provision about costs in Aarhus Convention claims.)][3]

(Part 25 sets out how to apply for an interim remedy)

(2) The claim form must be accompanied by the documents required by [Practice Direction 54A][4].][5]

Amendments

1 Repealed by the Civil Procedure (Amendment) Rules 2013, SI 2013/262, r 18(a) (1 April 2013: revocation has effect subject to transitional provisions specified in the Civil Procedure (Amendment) Rules 2013, r 22(8)).

2 Substituted by the Civil Procedure (Amendment) Rules 2013, SI 2013/262, r 18(b) (1 April 2013: substitution has effect subject to transitional provisions specified in the Civil Procedure (Amendment) Rules 2013, r 22(8)).

3 Inserted by the Civil Procedure (Amendment) Rules 2013, SI 2013/262, r 18(c) (1 April 2013: insertion has effect subject to transitional provisions specified in the Civil Procedure (Amendment) Rules 2013, r 22(8)).

4 Substituted by the Civil Procedure (Amendment No.2) Rules 2009, SI 2009/3390, r 29(b) (6 April 2010).

5 Inserted by the Civil Procedure (Amendment No. 4) Rules 2000, SI 2000/2092, r 22, Schedule (2 October 2000).

[54.7 Service of claim form

The claim form must be served on—

(a) the defendant; and

(b) unless the court otherwise directs, any person the claimant considers to be an interested party,

within 7 days after the date of issue.][1]

Amendment

1 Inserted by the Civil Procedure (Amendment No. 4) Rules 2000, SI 2000/2092, r 22, Schedule (2 October 2000).

[54.7A Judicial review of decisions of the Upper Tribunal

(1) This rule applies where an application is made, following refusal by the Upper Tribunal of permission to appeal against a decision of the First Tier Tribunal, for judicial review—

(a) of the decision of the Upper Tribunal refusing permission to appeal; or

(b) which relates to the decision of the First Tier Tribunal which was the subject of the application for permission to appeal.

(2) Where this rule applies—

(a) the application may not include any other claim, whether against the Upper Tribunal or not; and

(b) any such other claim must be the subject of a separate application.

(3) The claim form and the supporting documents required by paragraph (4) must be filed no later than 16 days after the date on which notice of the Upper Tribunal's decision was sent to the applicant.

(4) The supporting documents are—

(a) the decision of the Upper Tribunal to which the application relates, and any document giving reasons for the decision;

(b) the grounds of appeal to the Upper Tribunal and any documents which were sent with them;

(c) the decision of the First Tier Tribunal, the application to that Tribunal for permission to appeal and its reasons for refusing permission; and

(d) any other documents essential to the claim.

(5) The claim form and supporting documents must be served on the Upper Tribunal and any other interested party no later than 7 days after the date of issue.

(6) The Upper Tribunal and any person served with the claim form who wishes to take part in the proceedings for judicial review must, no later than 21 days after service of the claim form, file and serve on the applicant and any other party an acknowledgment of service in the relevant practice form.

(7) The court will give permission to proceed only if it considers—

(a) that there is an arguable case, which has a reasonable prospect of success, that both the decision of the Upper Tribunal refusing permission to appeal and the decision of the First Tier Tribunal against which permission to appeal was sought are wrong in law; and

(b) that either—

(i) the claim raises an important point of principle or practice; or

(ii) there is some other compelling reason to hear it.

(8) If the application for permission is refused on paper without an oral hearing, rule 54.12(3) (request for reconsideration at a hearing) does not apply.

(9) If permission to apply for judicial review is granted—

(a) if the Upper Tribunal or any interested party wishes there to be a hearing of the substantive application, it must make its request for such a hearing no later than 14 days after service of the order granting permission; and

(b) if no request for a hearing is made within that period, the court will make a final order quashing the refusal of permission without a further hearing.

(10) The power to make a final order under paragraph (9)(b) may be exercised by the Master of the Crown Office or a Master of the Administrative Court.][1]

Amendments

1 Inserted by the Civil Procedure (Amendment No.2) Rules 2012, SI 2012/2208, r 9(c) (1 October 2012).

[54.8 Acknowledgment of service

(1) Any person served with the claim form who wishes to take part in the judicial review must file an acknowledgment of service in the relevant practice form in accordance with the following provisions of this rule.

(2) Any acknowledgment of service must be—

(a) filed not more than 21 days after service of the claim form; and

(b) served on—

(i) the claimant; and

(ii) subject to any direction under rule 54.7(b), any other person named in the claim form,

as soon as practicable and, in any event, not later than 7 days after it is filed.

(3) The time limits under this rule may not be extended by agreement between the parties.

(4) The acknowledgment of service—

(a) must—

(i) where the person filing it intends to contest the claim, set out a summary of his grounds for doing so; and

[(ia) where the person filing it intends to contest the application for permission on the basis that it is highly likely that the outcome for the claimant would not have been substantially different if the conduct complained of had not occurred, set out a summary of the grounds for doing so; and][1]

(ii) state the name and address of any person the person filing it considers to be an interested party; and

(b) may include or be accompanied by an application for directions.

(5) Rule 10.3(2) does not apply.

[(Section 31(3C) of the Senior Courts Act 1981 requires the court, where it is asked to do so by the defendant, to consider whether the outcome for the claimant would have been substantially different if the conduct complained of had not occurred.)][1]][2]

Amendments

1 Inserted by the Civil Procedure (Amendment No. 2) Rules 2015, SI 2015/670, rr 7, 8 (13 April 2015: insertion has effect subject to saving provision specified in the Civil Procedure (Amendment No. 2) Rules 2015, r 12(2)).

2 Inserted by the Civil Procedure (Amendment No. 4) Rules 2000, SI 2000/2092, r 22, Schedule (2 October 2000).

[54.9 Failure to file acknowledgment of service

(1) Where a person served with the claim form has failed to file an acknowledgment of service in accordance with rule 54.8, he—

(a) may not take part in a hearing to decide whether permission should be given unless the court allows him to do so; but

(b) provided he complies with rule 54.14 or any other direction of the court regarding the filing and service of—

(i) detailed grounds for contesting the claim or supporting it on additional grounds; and

(ii) any written evidence,

may take part in the hearing of the judicial review.

(2) Where that person takes part in the hearing of the judicial review, the court may take his failure to file an acknowledgment of service into account when deciding what order to make about costs.

(3) Rule 8.4 does not apply.][1]

Amendment

1 Inserted by the Civil Procedure (Amendment No. 4) Rules 2000, SI 2000/2092, r 22, Schedule (2 October 2000).

[54.10 Permission given

(1) Where permission to proceed is given the court may also give directions.

[(2) Directions under paragraph (1) may include—

(a) a stay(GL) of proceedings to which the claim relates;

(b) directions requiring the proceedings to be heard by a Divisional Court.][1]

(Rule 3.7 provides a sanction for the non-payment of the fee payable when permission to proceed has been given)][2]

Amendments

1 Substituted by the Civil Procedure (Amendment No.3) Rules 2010, SI 2010/2577, r 3 (20 October 2010).

2 Inserted by the Civil Procedure (Amendment No. 4) Rules 2000, SI 2000/2092, r 22, Schedule (2 October 2000).

[54.11 Service of order giving or refusing permission

The court will serve—

(a) the order giving or refusing permission; and

[(ai) any certificate (if not included in the order) that permission has been granted for reasons of exceptional public interest in accordance with section 31(3F) of the Senior Courts Act 1981; and][1]

(b) any directions,

on—

(i) the claimant;

(ii) the defendant; and

(iii) any other person who filed an acknowledgment of service.][2]

Amendments

1 Inserted by the Civil Procedure (Amendment No. 2) Rules 2015, SI 2015/670, r 9 (13 April 2015: insertion has effect subject to saving provision specified in the Civil Procedure (Amendment No. 2) Rules 2015, r 12(2)).

2 Inserted by the Civil Procedure (Amendment No. 4) Rules 2000, SI 2000/2092, r 22, Schedule (2 October 2000).

[54.11A Permission decision where court requires a hearing

(1) This rule applies where the court wishes to hear submissions on—

(a) whether it is highly likely that the outcome for the claimant would not have been substantially different if the conduct complained of had not occurred; and if so

(b) whether there are reasons of exceptional public interest which make it nevertheless appropriate to give permission.

(2) The court may direct a hearing to determine whether to give permission.

(3) The claimant, defendant and any other person who has filed an acknowledgment of service must be given at least 2 days' notice of the hearing date.

(4) The court may give directions requiring the proceedings to be heard by a Divisional Court.

(5) The court must give its reasons for giving or refusing permission.][1]

Amendment

1 Inserted by the Civil Procedure (Amendment No. 2) Rules 2015, SI 2015/670, r 10 (13 April 2015: insertion has effect subject to saving provision specified in the Civil Procedure (Amendment No. 2) Rules 2015, r 12(2)).

[54.12 Permission decision without a hearing

(1) This rule applies where the court, without a hearing—

(a) refuses permission to proceed; or

(b) gives permission to proceed—

(i) subject to conditions; or

(ii) on certain grounds only.

(2) The court will serve its reasons for making the decision when it serves the order giving or refusing permission in accordance with rule 54.11.

(3) [Subject to paragraph (7), the][1] claimant may not appeal but may request the decision to be reconsidered at a hearing.

(4) A request under paragraph (3) must be filed within 7 days after service of the reasons under paragraph (2).

(5) The claimant, defendant and any other person who has filed an acknowledgment of service will be given at least 2 days' notice of the hearing date.

[(6) The court may give directions requiring the proceedings to be heard by a Divisional Court.][2]

[(7) Where the court refuses permission to proceed and records the fact that the application is totally without merit in accordance with rule 23.12, the claimant may not request that decision to be reconsidered at a hearing.][3]][4]

Amendments

1 Substituted by the Civil Procedure (Amendment No. 4) Rules 2013, SI 2013/1412, r 4(b)(i) (1 July 2013: substitution has effect subject to transitional provision specified in SI 2013/1412 rule 5(1))

2 Inserted by the Civil Procedure (Amendment No.3) Rules 2010, SI 2010/2577, r 4 (20 October 2010).

3 Inserted by the Civil Procedure (Amendment No. 4) Rules 2013, SI 2013/1412, r 4(b)(ii) (1 July 2013: insertion has effect subject to transitional provision specified in SI 2013/1412 rule 5(1))

4 Inserted by the Civil Procedure (Amendment No. 4) Rules 2000, SI 2000/2092, r 22, Schedule (2 October 2000).

[54.13 Defendant etc. may not apply to set aside[(GL)]

Neither the defendant nor any other person served with the claim form may apply to set aside[(GL)] an order giving permission to proceed.][1]

Amendment

1 Inserted by the Civil Procedure (Amendment No. 4) Rules 2000, SI 2000/2092, r 22, Schedule (2 October 2000).

[54.14 Response

(1) A defendant and any other person served with the claim form who wishes to contest the claim or support it on additional grounds must file and serve—

(a) detailed grounds for contesting the claim or supporting it on additional grounds; and

(b) any written evidence,

within 35 days after service of the order giving permission.

(2) The following rules do not apply—

(a) rule 8.5(3) and 8.5(4) (defendant to file and serve written evidence at the same time as acknowledgment of service); and

(b) rule 8.5(5) and 8.5(6) (claimant to file and serve any reply within 14 days).][1]

Amendment

1 Inserted by the Civil Procedure (Amendment No. 4) Rules 2000, SI 2000/2092, r 22, Schedule (2 October 2000).

[54.15 Where claimant seeks to rely on additional grounds

The court's permission is required if a claimant seeks to rely on grounds other than those for which he has been given permission to proceed.][1]

Amendment

1 Inserted by the Civil Procedure (Amendment No. 4) Rules 2000, SI 2000/2092, r 22, Schedule (2 October 2000).

[54.16 Evidence

(1) Rule 8.6[(1)][1] does not apply.

(2) No written evidence may be relied on unless—

(a) it has been served in accordance with any—

(i) rule under this [Section][2]; or

(ii) direction of the court; or

(b) the court gives permission.][3]

Amendments

1 Inserted by the Civil Procedure (Amendment) Rules 2002, SI 2002/2058, r 21 (2 December 2002).

2 Substituted by the Civil Procedure (Amendment) Rules 2003, SI 2003/364 rule 5(d) (1 April 2003 being the commencement date for the Nationality, Immigration and Asylum Act 2002, Pt 5).

3 Inserted by the Civil Procedure (Amendment No. 4) Rules 2000, SI 2000/2092, r 22, Schedule (2 October 2000).

[54.17 Court's powers to hear any person

(1) Any person may apply for permission—

(a) to file evidence; or

(b) make representations at the hearing of the judicial review.

(2) An application under paragraph (1) should be made promptly.][1]

Amendment

1 Inserted by the Civil Procedure (Amendment No. 4) Rules 2000, SI 2000/2092, r 22, Schedule (2 October 2000).

[54.18 Judicial review may be decided without a hearing

The court may decide the claim for judicial review without a hearing where all the parties agree.][1]

Amendment

1 Inserted by the Civil Procedure (Amendment No. 4) Rules 2000, SI 2000/2092, r 22, Schedule (2 October 2000).

[54.19 Court's powers in respect of quashing orders

(1) This rule applies where the court makes a quashing order in respect of the decision to which the claim relates.

[(2) The court may—

(a)

(i) remit the matter to the decision-maker; and

(ii) direct it to reconsider the matter and reach a decision in accordance with the judgment of the court; or

(b) in so far as any enactment permits, substitute its own decision for the decision to which the claim relates.

(Section 31 of the Supreme Court Act 1981 enables the High Court, subject to certain conditions, to substitute its own decision for the decision in question.)][1]

(3) …[2]][3]

Amendments

1 Substituted by the Civil Procedure (Amendment No.2) Rules 2007, SI 2007/3543, r 7(b) (6 April 2008).

2 Repealed by the Civil Procedure (Amendment No.2) Rules 2007, SI 2007/3543, r 7(c) (6 April 2008).

3 Inserted by the Civil Procedure (Amendment No. 4) Rules 2000, SI 2000/2092, r 22, Schedule (2 October 2000).

[54.20 Transfer

The court may—

(a) order a claim to continue as if it had not been started under this [Section][1]; and

(b) where it does so, give directions about the future management of the claim.

(Part 30 (transfer) applies to transfers to and from the Administrative Court)][2]

Amendments

1 Substituted by the Civil Procedure (Amendment) Rules 2003, SI 2003/364 rule 5(e) (1 April 2003 being the commencement date for the Nationality, Immigration and Asylum Act 2002, Pt 5).

2 Inserted by the Civil Procedure (Amendment No. 4) Rules 2000, SI 2000/2092, r 22, Schedule (2 October 2000).

[Section II
Planning Court

54.21 General

(1) This Section applies to Planning Court claims.

(2) In this Section, 'Planning Court claim' means a judicial review or statutory challenge which —

(a) involves any of the following matters —

(i) planning permission, other development consents, the enforcement of planning control and the enforcement of other statutory schemes;

(ii) applications under the Transport and Works Act 1992;

(iii) wayleaves;

(iv) highways and other rights of way;

(v) compulsory purchase orders;

(vi) village greens;

(vii) European Union environmental legislation and domestic transpositions, including assessments for development consents, habitats, waste and pollution control;

(viii) national, regional or other planning policy documents, statutory or otherwise; or

(ix) any other matter the judge appointed under rule 54.22(2) [considers appropriate][1]; and

(b) has been issued or transferred to the Planning Court.

(Part 30 (Transfer) applies to transfers to and from the Planning Court.)][2]

Amendments

1 Inserted by the Civil Procedure (Amendment No. 6) Rules 2014, SI 2014/2044, r 9 (1 October 2014).

2 Inserted by the Civil Procedure (Amendment No. 3) Rules 2014, SI 2014/610, r 3 (6 April 2014).

[54.22 Specialist list

(1) The Planning Court claims form a specialist list.

(2) A judge nominated by the President of the Queen's Bench Division will be in charge of the Planning Court specialist list and will be known as the Planning Liaison Judge.

[(3) The President of the Queen's Bench Division will be responsible for the nomination of specialist planning judges to deal with Planning Court claims which are significant within the meaning of Practice Direction 54E, and of other judges to deal with other Planning Court claims.][1]][2]

Amendments

1 Inserted by the Civil Procedure (Amendment No. 5) Rules 2014, SI 2014/1233, r 4 (5 June 2014).

2 Inserted by the Civil Procedure (Amendment No. 3) Rules 2014, SI 2014/610, r 3 (6 April 2014).

[54.23 Application of the Civil Procedure Rules

These Rules and their practice directions will apply to Planning Court claims unless this section or a practice direction provides otherwise.][1]

Amendment

1 Inserted by the Civil Procedure (Amendment No. 3) Rules 2014, SI 2014/610, r 3 (6 April 2014).

[54.24 Further provision about Planning Court claims

Practice Direction 54E makes further provision about Planning Court claims, in particular about the timescales for determining such claims.][1]

Amendment

1 Inserted by the Civil Procedure (Amendment No. 3) Rules 2014, SI 2014/610, r 3 (6 April 2014).

APPENDIX B

Practice Directions and Protocols

PRACTICE DIRECTION – PRE-ACTION CONDUCT

Introduction

1 Pre-action protocols explain the conduct and set out the steps the court would normally expect parties to take before commencing proceedings for particular types of civil claims. They are approved by the Master of the Rolls and are annexed to the Civil Procedure Rules (CPR). (The current pre-action protocols are listed in paragraph 18.)

2 This Practice Direction applies to disputes where no pre-action protocol approved by the Master of the Rolls applies. A person who knowingly makes a false statement in a pre-action protocol letter or other document prepared in 14 anticipation of legal proceedings may be subject to proceedings for contempt of court.

Objectives of pre-action conduct and protocols

3 Before commencing proceedings, the court will expect the parties to have exchanged sufficient information to—

(a) understand each other's position;

(b) make decisions about how to proceed;

(c) try to settle the issues without proceedings;

(d) consider a form of Alternative Dispute Resolution (ADR) to assist with settlement;

(e) support the efficient management of those proceedings; and

(f) reduce the costs of resolving the dispute.

Proportionality

4 A pre-action protocol or this Practice Direction must not be used by a party as a tactical device to secure an unfair advantage over another party. Only reasonable and proportionate steps should be taken by the parties to identify, narrow and resolve the legal, factual or expert issues.

5 The costs incurred in complying with a pre-action protocol or this Practice Direction should be proportionate (CPR 44.3(5)). Where parties incur disproportionate costs in complying with any pre-action protocol or this Practice Direction, those costs will not be recoverable as part of the costs of the proceedings.

Steps before issuing a claim at court

6 Where there is a relevant pre-action protocol, the parties should comply with that protocol before commencing proceedings. Where there is no relevant pre-action protocol, the parties should exchange correspondence and information to comply with the objectives in paragraph 3, bearing in mind that compliance should be proportionate. The steps will usually include—

(a) the claimant writing to the defendant with concise details of the claim. The letter should include the basis on which the claim is made, a summary of the facts, what the claimant wants from the defendant, and if money, how the amount is calculated;

(b) the defendant responding within a reasonable time – 14 days in a straight forward case and no more than 3 months in a very complex one. The reply should include confirmation as to whether the claim is accepted and, if it is not accepted, the reasons why, together with an explanation as to which facts and parts of the claim are disputed and whether the defendant is making a counterclaim as well as providing details of any counterclaim; and

(c) the parties disclosing key documents relevant to the issues in dispute.

Experts

7 Parties should be aware that the court must give permission before expert evidence can be relied upon (see CPR 35.4(1)) and that the court may limit the fees recoverable. Many disputes can be resolved without expert advice or evidence. If it is necessary to obtain expert evidence, particularly in low value claims, the parties should consider using a single expert, jointly instructed by the parties, with the costs shared equally.

Settlement and ADR

8 Litigation should be a last resort. As part of a relevant pre-action protocol or this Practice Direction, the parties should consider whether negotiation or some other form of ADR might enable them to settle their dispute without commencing proceedings.

9 Parties should continue to consider the possibility of reaching a settlement at all times, including after proceedings have been started. Part 36 offers may be made before proceedings are issued.

10 Parties may negotiate to settle a dispute or may use a form of ADR including—

(a) mediation, a third party facilitating a resolution;

(b) arbitration, a third party deciding the dispute;

(c) early neutral evaluation, a third party giving an informed opinion on the dispute; and

(d) Ombudsmen schemes.

(Information on mediation and other forms of ADR is available in the Jackson ADR Handbook (available from Oxford University Press) or at—

http://www.civilmediation.justice.gov.uk/

11 If proceedings are issued, the parties may be required by the court to provide evidence that ADR has been considered. A party's silence in response to an invitation to participate or a refusal to participate in ADR might be considered unreasonable by the court and could lead to the court ordering that party to pay additional court costs.

Stocktake and list of issues

12 Where a dispute has not been resolved after the parties have followed a pre-action protocol or this Practice Direction, they should review their respective positions. They should consider the papers and the evidence to see if proceedings can be avoided and at least seek to narrow the issues in dispute before the claimant issues proceedings.

Compliance with this Practice Direction and the Protocols

13 If a dispute proceeds to litigation, the court will expect the parties to have complied with a relevant pre-action protocol or this Practice Direction. The court will take into account non-compliance when giving directions for the management of proceedings (see CPR 3.1(4) to (6)) and when making orders for costs (see CPR 44.3(5)(a)). The court will consider whether all parties have complied in substance with the terms of the relevant pre-action protocol or this Practice Direction and is not likely to be concerned with minor or technical infringements, especially when the matter is urgent (for example an application for an injunction).

14 The court may decide that there has been a failure of compliance when a party has—

(a) not provided sufficient information to enable the objectives in paragraph 3 to be met;

(b) not acted within a time limit set out in a relevant protocol, or within a reasonable period; or

(c) unreasonably refused to use a form of ADR, or failed to respond at all to an invitation to do so.

15 Where there has been non-compliance with a pre-action protocol or this Practice Direction, the court may order that

(a) the parties are relieved of the obligation to comply or further comply with the pre-action protocol or this Practice Direction;

(b) the proceedings are stayed while particular steps are taken to comply with the pre-action protocol or this Practice Direction;

(c) sanctions are to be applied.

16 The court will consider the effect of any non-compliance when deciding whether to impose any sanctions which may include—

(a) an order that the party at fault pays the costs of the proceedings, or part of the costs of the other party or parties;

(b) an order that the party at fault pay those costs on an indemnity basis;

(c) if the party at fault is a claimant who has been awarded a sum of money, an order depriving that party of interest on that sum for a specified period, and/or awarding interest at a lower rate than would otherwise have been awarded;

(d) if the party at fault is a defendant, and the claimant has been awarded a sum of money, an order awarding interest on that sum for a specified period at a higher rate, (not exceeding 10% above base rate), than the rate which would otherwise have been awarded.

Limitation

17 This Practice Direction and the pre-action protocols do not alter the statutory time limits for starting court proceedings. If a claim is issued after the relevant limitation period has expired, the defendant will be entitled to use that as a defence to the claim. If proceedings are started to comply with the statutory time limit before the parties have followed the procedures in this Practice Direction or the relevant pre-action protocol, the parties should apply to the court for a stay of the proceedings while they so comply.

Protocols in force

18 The table sets out the protocols currently in force and from which date.

Protocol	Came into force
Personal Injury	6 April 2015
Resolution of Clinical Disputes	6 April 2015
Construction and Engineering	9 November 2016 2nd edition
Defamation	02 October 2000
Professional Negligence	16 July 2000
Judicial Review	6 April 2015
Disease and Illness	8 December 2003
Housing Disrepair	6 April 2015
Possession Claims by Social Landlords	6 April 2015
Possession Claims for Mortgage Arrears	6 April 2015
Dilapidation of Commercial Property	1 January 2012
Low Value Personal Injury Road Traffic Accident Claims	30 April 2010 extended from 31 July 2013
Low Value Personal Injury Employers' and Public Liability Claims	31 July 2013

PRACTICE DIRECTION 8A – ALTERNATIVE PROCEDURE FOR CLAIMS

This Practice Direction supplements CPR Part 8 and Schedule 1 & Schedule 2 to the CPR

Contents of this Practice Direction

Terminology

1.1 In this Practice Direction, 'Schedule rules' means provisions contained in the Schedules to the CPR, which were previously contained in the Rules of the Supreme Court (1965) or the County Court Rules (1981).

Application of this Practice Direction

2.1 Section A contains general provisions about claims and applications to which Part 8 applies. Section B comprises a table listing claims, petitions and applications under various enactments which must be made under Part 8. Section C contains certain additions and modifications to the Part 8 procedure that apply to the particular claims and applications identified.

2.2 Some of the claims and applications listed in the table in Section B are dealt with in the Schedule Rules in the CPR. The table in Section B contains cross-reference to the relevant Schedule Rules.

Section A
General provisions applicable to Part 8 claims

Types of claim in which the Part 8 procedure may be used

3.1 The types of claim for which the Part 8 procedure may be used include–

(1) a claim by or against a child or protected party, as defined in rule 21.1(2), which has been settled before the commencement of proceedings and the sole purpose of the claim is to obtain the approval of the court to the settlement; or

(2) a claim for provisional damages which has been settled before the commencement of proceedings and the sole purpose of the claim is to obtain a consent judgment.

3.2

(1) The Part 8 procedure must be used for those claims, petitions and applications listed in the table in Section B.

(2) Where a claim is listed in the table in Section B and is identified as a claim to which particular provisions of Section C apply, the Part 8 procedure shall apply subject to the additions and modifications set out in the relevant paragraphs in Section C.

3.3 The Part 8 procedure must also be used for any claim or application in relation to which an Act, rule or practice direction provides that the claim or application is brought by originating summons, originating motion or originating application.

3.4 Where it appears to a court officer that a claimant is using the Part 8 procedure inappropriately, he may refer the claim to a judge for the judge to consider the point.

3.5 The court may at any stage order the claim to continue as if the claimant had not used the Part 8 procedure and, if it does so, the court will allocate the claim to a track and give such directions as it considers appropriate.

Issuing the claim

4.1

(1) Part 7 and Practice Direction 7A contain a number of rules and directions applicable to all claims, including those to which Part 8 applies. Those rules and directions should be applied where appropriate.

(2) Subject to the provisions in rule 8.1(2A), in the County Court a claim under the Part 8 procedure may be made in any County Court hearing centre. However, when a claim is given a hearing date the court may direct that proceedings should be transferred to another hearing centre if appropriate to do so. A claimant should consider the potential delay which may result if a claim is not made at the appropriate hearing centre in the first instance.

4.2 Where a claimant uses the Part 8 procedure, the claim form (practice form N208) should be used and must state the matters set out in rule 8.2 and, if rule 8.1(6) applies, must comply with the requirements of the rule or practice direction in question. In particular, the claim form must state that Part 8 applies; a Part 8 claim form means a claim form which so states.

Responding to the claim

5.1 The provisions of Part 15 (defence and reply) do not apply where the claim form is a Part 8 claim form.

5.2 Where a defendant who wishes to respond to a Part 8 claim form is required to file an acknowledgment of service, that acknowledgment of service should be in practice form N210.

5.3 Where a defendant objects to the use of the Part 8 procedure, and his statement of reasons includes matters of evidence, the acknowledgment of service must be verified by a statement of truth.

Managing the claim

6.1 The court may give directions immediately a Part 8 claim form is issued either on the application of a party or on its own initiative. The directions may include fixing a hearing date where–

(1) there is no dispute, such as in child and protected party settlements; or

(2) where there may be a dispute, but a hearing date could conveniently be given.

6.2 Where the court does not fix a hearing date when the claim form is issued, it will give directions for the disposal of the claim as soon as practicable after the defendant has acknowledged service of the claim form or, as the case may be, after the period for acknowledging service has expired.

6.3 Certain applications may not require a hearing.

6.4 The court may convene a directions hearing before giving directions.

Evidence

7.1 A claimant must file the written evidence on which he relies when his Part 8 claim form is issued (unless the evidence is contained in the claim form itself).

7.2 Evidence will normally be in the form of a witness statement or an affidavit but a claimant may rely on the matters set out in his claim form provided that it has been verified by a statement of truth.

(For information about (1) statements of truth see Part 22 and Practice Direction 22, and (2) written evidence see Part 32 and Practice Direction 32.)

7.3 A defendant wishing to rely on written evidence, must file it with his acknowledgment of service.

7.4 A party may apply to the court for an extension of time to serve and file evidence under rule 8.5 or for permission to serve and file additional evidence under rule 8.6(1).

(For information about applications see Part 23 and Practice Direction 23A.)

7.5

(1) The parties may, subject to the following provisions, agree in writing on an extension of time for serving and filing evidence under rule 8.5(3) or rule 8.5(5).

(2) An agreement extending time for a defendant to file evidence under rule 8.5(3)–

(a) must be filed by the defendant at the same time as he files his acknowledgement of service; and

(b) must not extend time by more than 14 days after the defendant files his acknowledgement of service.

(3) An agreement extending time for a claimant to file evidence in reply under rule 8.5(5) must not extend time to more than 28 days after service of the defendant's evidence on the claimant.

Hearing

8.1 The court may on the hearing date–

(1) proceed to hear the case and dispose of the claim;

(2) give case management directions.

8.2 Case management directions may include the specific allocation of a case to a track.

8.3 CPR rules 26.5(3) and (4) and rules 26.6 to 26.10 apply to the allocation of a claim under paragraph 8.2.

Section B
Claims and applications that must be made under Part 8

9.1 The claimant must use the Part 8 procedure if the claim is listed in the table below.

9.2 Section C of this Practice Direction contains special provisions modifying the Part 8 procedure, and where it does so, those provisions should be followed. The table below refers to the relevant paragraph of Section C where it applies.

9.3 Some of the claims and applications listed in the table below are dealt with in the Schedule Rules, and those rules modify the Part 8 procedure. A cross-reference to the relevant Schedule Rule is contained in the table below.

9.4 For applications that may or must be brought in the High Court, where no other rule or practice direction assigns the application to a Division of the court, the table specifies the Division to which the application is assigned.

Type of Claim or Application	Paragraph of Section C	Division	Schedule Rule
Application under section 14 of the Bills of Sale Act 1878 (Rectification of register)	Paragraph 10A	Queen's Bench Central Office	
Application under section 15 of the Bills of Sale Act 1878 (Entry of satisfaction)	Paragraph 11	Queen's Bench Central Office	
Application under section 16 of the Bills of Sale Act 1878 (Search of the bills of sale register)	Paragraph 11A	Queen's Bench Central Office	
Application under the proviso to section 7 of the Bills of Sale Act (1878) Amendment Act 1882 (Restraining removal or sale of goods seized)		Queen's Bench Central Office	
Application under the Public Trustee Act 1906 (free-standing proceedings)	Paragraph 12	Chancery	
Application under section 7 of the Deeds of Arrangement Act 1914 (Rectification of register)	Paragraph 12A	Queen's Bench Central Office	
Proceedings under the Trustee Act 1925		Chancery	
Applications under section 2(3) of the Public Order Act 1936	Paragraph 13	Chancery	
Proceedings under jurisdiction conferred by section 1 of the Railway and Canal Commission (Abolition) Act 1949	Paragraph 14	Chancery	
Administration of Justice Act 1960 (Applications under the Act)		Divisional Court	RSC O.109, r.1(3)
Administration of Justice Act 1960 (Appeals under section 13 of the Act)		Divisional Court	RSC O.109, r.2(4)
Proceedings under section 14 of the Commons Registration Act 1965		Chancery	
Application under the Mines (Working Facilities and Support) Act 1966	Paragraph 15	Chancery	
Proceedings under section 21 or 25 of the Law of Property Act 1969		Chancery	

Type of Claim or Application	Paragraph of Section C	Division	Schedule Rule
Local Government Act 1972 (claims under section 92 – proceedings for disqualification)		Queen's Bench Central Office	
Application under article 10 of the Mortgaging of Aircraft Order 1972 (Rectification of register)	Paragraph 15A	Chancery	
Application to register an assignment of book debts (section 344 of the Insolvency Act 1986)	Paragraph 15B	Queen's Bench Central Office	
Proceedings under the Control of Misleading Advertisements Regulations 1988		Chancery<	
Application under section 42 of the Senior Courts Act 1981	Paragraph 16	Administrative Court	
Proceedings in the High Court under the Representation of the People Acts	Paragraph 17A	Queen's Bench Central Office	
Applications under Part II of the Mental Health Act 1983	Paragraph 18	Administrative Court	
Applications under section 13 of the Coroners Act 1988	Paragraph 19	Administrative Court	
Application for an injunction to prevent environmental harm under section 187B or 214A of the Town and Country Planning Act 1990; section 44A of the Planning (Listed Buildings and Conservation Areas) Act 1990; or section 26AA of the Planning (Hazardous Substances) Act 1990	Paragraph 20	Queen's Bench	
Confiscation and forfeiture in connection with criminal proceedings (I. Drug Trafficking Act 1994 and Criminal Justice (International Co-operation) Act 1990 – Application for a confiscation order)		Queen's Bench	RSC O.115, r.2B(1)
Confiscation and forfeiture in connection with criminal proceedings (I. Drug Trafficking Act 1994 and Criminal Justice (International Co-operation) Act 1990 – Application for a restraint order or charging order)		Queen's Bench	RSC O.115, r.3(1)

Type of Claim or Application	Paragraph of Section C	Division	Schedule Rule
Confiscation and forfeiture in connection with criminal proceedings (I. Drug Trafficking Act 1994 and Criminal Justice (International Co-operation) Act 1990 – Realisation of property)		Queen's Bench	RSC O.115, r.7(1)
Criminal Procedure and Investigations Act 1996 (Application under section 54(3))		Administrative Court	
Confiscation and forfeiture in connection with criminal proceedings (III. Terrorism Act 2000 – Application for a restraint order)		Queen's Bench	RSC O.115, r.26(1)
Proceedings under the Financial Services and Markets Act 2000	Paragraph 21	Chancery	
Application for an injunction under section 12 or 26 of the Energy Act 2008	Paragraph 20	Queen's Bench	
Stakeholder applications – mode of application, unless there are existing proceedings (Rule 86.2(3))		Chancery or Queen's Bench	RSC O.17, r.3(1)
Criminal proceedings (estreat of recognizances)		Queen's Bench	RSC O.79, r.8(2
Criminal proceedings (bail)		Queen's Bench	RSC O.79, r.9(2)
Application under an enactment giving the High Court jurisdiction to quash or prohibit any order, scheme, certificate or plan, any amendment or approval of a plan, any decision of a Minister or government department or any action on the part of a Minister or government department	Paragraph 22	Administrative Court	
Application under section 66 of the Anti-Social Behaviour, Crime and Policing Act 2014 to question the validity of a public spaces protection order or variation of such an order	Paragraph 22	Administrative Court	
Proceedings under the Telecommunications Restriction Orders (Custodial Institutions) (England and Wales) Regulations 2015	Paragraph 23	N/A (County Court)	N/A

Type of Claim or Application	Paragraph of Section C	Division	Schedule Rule
Proceedings under the Drug Dealing Telecommunications Restriction Orders Regulations 2017	Paragraph 24	N/A (County Court)	N/A
Proceedings transferred to the High Court from the Magistrates' Court under section 303R of the Proceeds of Crime Act 2002 or under paragraph 10J of Part 4A of Schedule 1 to the Anti-terrorism, Crime and Security Act 2001	Paragraph 25	Queen's Bench	N/A

Section C
Special provisions

10.1 The following special provisions apply to the applications indicated.

Applications under section 14 of the Bills of Sale Act 1878

10A.1 This paragraph applies to an application under section 14 of the Bills of Sale Act 1878 for an order to rectify an omission or mis-statement in relation to the registration, or renewal of the registration, of a bill of sale–

(1) by inserting in the register the true name, residence or occupation of a person; or

(2) by extending the time for registration of the bill of sale or an affidavit of its renewal.

10A.2 The application must be made–

(1) by claim form under Part 8; or

(2) by witness statement.

10A.3 Where the application is made by witness statement–

(1) Part 23 applies to the application;

(2) the witness statement constitutes the application notice under that Part;

(3) the witness statement does not need to be served on any other person; and

(4) the application will normally be dealt with without a hearing.

10A.4 The application must set out–

(1) the particulars of the bill of sale and of the omission or mis-statement; and

(2) the grounds on which the application is made.

10A.5 The application must be made to a Master of the Queen's Bench Division and accompanied by payment of the prescribed fee.

Applications under Section 15 of the Bills of Sale Act 1878

11.1 This paragraph applies where an application is made under section 15 of the Bills of Sale Act 1878 for an order that a memorandum of satisfaction be written on a registered copy of a bill of sale.

11.2 If the person entitled to the benefit of the bill of sale has not consented to the satisfaction, the claim form–

(1) must be served on that person; and

(2) must be supported by evidence that the debt (if any) for which the bill of sale was made has been satisfied or discharged.

11.3 If the person entitled to the benefit of the bill of sale has consented to the satisfaction, the application may be made by–

(1) claim form under Part 8; or

(2) witness statement.

11.4 Where paragraph 11.3 applies and the application is made by Part 8 claim form, the claim form–

(1) must contain details of the consent;

(2) must be supported by a witness statement by a person who witnessed the consent verifying the signature on it; and

(3) must not be served on any person other than the person entitled to the benefit of the bill of sale.

11.5 Where paragraph 11.3 applies and the application is made by witness statement–

(1) Part 23 will apply to the application;

(2) the witness statement will constitute the application notice under that Part;

(3) the witness statement does not need to be served on any other person; and

(4) the application will normally be dealt with without a hearing.

Applications under section 16 of the Bills of Sale Act 1878

11A.1 This paragraph applies to an application under section 16 of the Bills of Sale Act 1878 for a search of the bills of sale register and for a certificate of the results of the search.

11A.2 The application must be made–

(1) by claim form under Part 8; or

(2) by written request.

11A.3 The application must give sufficient information to enable the relevant bill of sale to be identified.

11A.4 The application must be made to a Master of the Queen's Bench Division and accompanied by payment of the prescribed fee.

Application under the Public Trustee Act 1906

12.1 An application under the Public Trustee Act 1906 must be made–

(1) where no proceedings have been issued, by a Part 8 claim;

(2) in existing proceedings, by a Part 23 application.

12.2 Without prejudice to sections 10(2) and 13(7) of the Public Trustee Act 1906, the jurisdiction of the High Court under the Act is exercised by a single judge of the Chancery Division sitting in private.

Applications under section 7 of the Deeds of Arrangement Act 1914

12A.1 This paragraph applies to an application under section 7 of the Deeds of Arrangement Act 1914 for an order to rectify an omission or mis-statement in relation to the registration of a deed of arrangement–

(1) by inserting in the register the true name, residence or description of a person; or

(2) by extending the time for registration.

12A.2 The application must be made–

(1) by claim form under Part 8; or

(2) by witness statement.

12A.3 Where the application is made by witness statement–

(1) Part 23 applies to the application;

(2) the witness statement constitutes the application notice under that Part;

(3) the witness statement does not need to be served on any other person; and

(4) the application will normally be dealt with without a hearing.

12A.4 The application must set out–

(1) the particulars of the deed of arrangement and of the omission or mis-statement; and

(2) the grounds on which the application is made.

12A.5 The application must be made to a Master of the Queen's Bench Division and accompanied by payment of the prescribed fee.

Application under section 2(3) of the Public Order Act 1936

13.1 The Attorney General may determine the persons who should be made defendants to an application under section 2(3) of the Public Order Act 1936.

13.2 If the court directs an inquiry under section 2(3), it may appoint the Official Solicitor to represent any interests it considers are not sufficiently represented and ought to be represented.

Proceedings under section 1 of the Railway and Canal Commission (Abolition) Act 1949

14.1 Paragraphs 15.3 to 15.14 apply, with appropriate modifications, to proceedings in which jurisdiction has been conferred on the High Court by section 1 of the Railway and Canal Commission (Abolition) Act 1949, except to the extent that–

(1) an Act;

(2) a rule;

(3) a practice direction,

provides otherwise.

Application under the Mines (Working Facilities and Support) Act 1966

15.1 In this paragraph–

(1) 'the Act' means the Mines (Working Facilities and Support) Act 1966;

(2) 'the applicant' means the person who has applied for the grant of a right under the Act.

15.2 This paragraph applies where the Secretary of State refers an application to the High Court under any provision of the Act.

15.3 The Secretary of State must–

(1) file a reference signed by him or a person authorised to sign on his behalf in the Chancery Division of the High Court;

(2) file, along with the reference, any documents and plans deposited with him by the applicant in support of his application; and

(3) within 3 days of filing the reference, give notice to the applicant that the reference has been filed.

15.4 Within 10 days of receiving the notice referred to in paragraph 15.3(3), the applicant must issue a claim form.

15.5 The claim form–

(1) must identify the application under the Act and the remedy sought; and

(2) need not be served on any other party.

15.6 Within 7 days of the claim form being issued, the applicant must–

(1) apply for the claim to be listed for a hearing before a Master; and

(2) give notice of the hearing date to the Secretary of State.

15.7 The applicant must, not less than 2 days before the date fixed for a hearing, file at court–

(1) a witness statement in support of the claim, giving details of all persons known to the applicant to be interested in, or affected by, the application; and

(2) a draft of any proposed advertisement or notice of the application.

15.8 At the hearing, the Master will–

(1) fix a date by which any notice of objection under paragraph 15.9 must be filed;

(2) fix a date for a further hearing of the claim; and

(3) give directions about–

(a) any advertisement that is to be inserted or notice of the application and hearing date that is to be given; and

(b) what persons are to be served with a copy of the application or any other document in the proceedings.

15.9 Any person who wishes to oppose the application must, within the time fixed by the court under paragraph 15.8, serve notice of objection on the applicant, stating–

(a) his name and address;

(b) the name and address of his solicitor, if any;

(c) the grounds of his objection;

(d) any alternative method for effecting the objects of the application that he alleges may be used; and

(e) the facts on which he relies.

15.10 Any document that is required to be served on the person who has given notice of objection ('the objector') may be served by posting it to the following address–

(1) where the notice of objection gives the name and address of a solicitor, to the solicitor;

(2) in any other case, to the objector at the address stated in the notice of objection.

15.11 The objector may appear, or be represented at any further hearing, and may take such part in the proceedings as the court allows.

15.12 The applicant must, not less than two days before the date set for the further hearing, file at court–

(1) any notices of objection served on him;

(2) a list of objectors, together with–

(a) their names and addresses;

(b) the names and addresses of their solicitors, if any; and

(c) a summary of their respective grounds of objection.

15.13 If the objector does not appear, or is not represented, at the further hearing–

(1) his notice of objection will have no effect; and

(2) he will not be entitled to take any further part in the proceedings unless the court orders otherwise.

15.14 At the further hearing, the court will–

(1) give directions about the future conduct of the claim, including–

(a) any further information the applicant is required to give in relation to any of the grounds or facts relied on in support of the application;

(b) any further information the objector is required to give in relation to any of the grounds or facts relied on in opposition to the application;

(c) whether the applicant may serve a reply to any notice of objection;

(d) whether any particular fact should be proved by a witness statement;

(e) whether any statements of case or points of claim or defence are to be served; and

(2) adjourn the claim for hearing before a judge.

Applications under article 10 of the Mortgaging of Aircraft Order 1972

15A.1 This paragraph applies to an application under article 10 of the Mortgaging of Aircraft Order 1972 for an order to amend the Register of Aircraft Mortgages.

15A.2 The application must be made by claim form under Part 8.

15A.3 Every person (other than the claimant) who appears in the register as mortgagor or mortgagee of the aircraft concerned must be made a defendant to the claim.

15A.4 A copy of the claim form must be sent to the Civil Aviation Authority.

15A.5 The application will be assigned to the Chancery Division.

15A.6 The Civil Aviation Authority is entitled to be heard in the proceedings.

Applications under section 344 of the Insolvency Act 1986 for registration of assignments of book debts

15B.1 This paragraph applies to an application under section 344 of the Insolvency Act 1986 to register an assignment of book debts.

15B.2 The application must be made–

(1) by claim form under Part 8; or

(2) by witness statement.

15B.3 The application must be made to a Master of the Queen's Bench Division and accompanied by payment of the prescribed fee.

15B.4 Where the application is made by witness statement–

(1) Part 23 applies to the application;

(2) the witness statement constitutes the application notice under that Part;

(3) the witness statement does not need to be served on any other person; and

(4) the application will normally be dealt with without a hearing.

15B.5 The application–

(1) must have exhibited to it a true copy of the assignment and of every schedule to it;

(2) must set out the particulars of the assignment and the parties to it; and

(3) must verify the date and time of the execution of the assignment, and its execution in the presence of a witness.

15B.6 Upon the court being satisfied, the documents so exhibited will be filed and the particulars of the assignment and of the parties to it entered in the register.

Application under section 42 of the Senior Courts Act 1981

16.1 An application under section 42 of the Senior Courts Act 1981 is heard and determined by a Divisional Court.

16.2 The claim form must be filed at the Administrative Court and–

(1) be accompanied by a witness statement in support; and

(2) be served on the person against whom the order is sought.

Application for detailed assessment of a returning officer's account

17.1

(1) An application by–

- (a) the Secretary of State under section 30 of the Representation of the People Act 1983 or paragraph 4 of Schedule 1 to the Recall of MPs Act 2015;
- (b) the Welsh Ministers under article 24 of the National Assembly for Wales (Representation of the People) Order 2007; or

(c) the Electoral Commission under paragraph 17 of Schedule 3 to the European Union Referendum Act 2015,

for the detailed assessment of a returning officer's account must be made by claim form.

(2) In this paragraph and paragraphs 17.3 to 17.5 and 17.8, references to the returning officer are to be read–

(a) for applications under the Recall of MPs Act 2015, as references to the petition officer;

(b) for applications under the National Assembly for Wales (Representation of the People) Order 2007, as references to–

(i) the constituency returning officer, in relation to a constituency election; and

(ii) the constituency and regional returning officer, in relation to a regional election; and

(c) for applications under the European Union Referendum Act 2015, as references to the counting officer or Regional Counting Officer.

17.2 When it issues the claim form, the court will fix a date for the hearing of the detailed assessment to be dealt with if the application is granted.

17.3 The returning officer may, on the application, apply to the court to examine any claim made against him in respect of matters charged in the account.

17.4 To make an application under paragraph 17.3, the returning officer must file an application within 7 days of being served with a copy of the application for detailed assessment.

17.5 When an application is filed under paragraph 17.3, the court will–

(a) fix a date for the hearing;

(b) give notice of the hearing date to the returning officer; and

(c) serve a copy of the application and notice of hearing on the claimant.

17.6 The examination and detailed assessment may take place on the same day, provided that the examination is determined before the detailed assessment is concluded.

17.7 The district judge may hear and determine–

(a) an application for detailed assessment;

(b) any application under paragraph 17.3.

17.8 The court will serve a copy of the order made in the application on–

(a) the Secretary of State;

(b) the returning officer; and

(c) in an application under paragraph 17.3, the claimant.

Other proceedings under the Representation of the People Acts

17A.1

(1) This paragraph applies to proceedings under the Representation of the People Acts (other than proceedings under section 30 of the Representation of the People Act 1983) amd the European Union Referendum (Conduct) Regulations 2016 ('the 2016 Regulations').

(2) The jurisdiction of the High Court under those Acts in matters relating to Parliamentary and local government elections, or under the 2016 Regulations, will be exercised by a Divisional Court except that–

  (a) any jurisdiction, under a provision of any of those Acts, or under the 2016 Regulations, exercisable by a single judge will be exercised by a single judge;

  (b) any jurisdiction, under any such provision, exercisable by a Master will be exercised by a Master; and

  (c) where the court's jurisdiction in matters relating to Parliamentary elections is exercisable by a single judge, that jurisdiction in matters relating to local government elections is also exercisable by a single judge.

Application under Mental Health Act 1983

18.1 In this paragraph–

(1) a section referred to by a number refers to the section so numbered in the Mental Health Act 1983 and 'Part II' means Part II of that Act;

(2) 'hospital manager' means the manager of a hospital as defined in section 145(1) of the Act; and

(3) 'place of residence' means, in relation to a patient who is receiving treatment as an in-patient in a hospital or other institution, that hospital or institution.

18.2 The claim form must be filed–

(1) in the County Court hearing centre serving the patient's place of residence is situated; or

(2) in the case of an application under section 30, in the court or County Court hearing centre that made the order under section 29 which the application seeks to discharge or vary.

18.3 Where an application is made under section 29 for an order that the functions of the nearest relative of the patient are to be exercisable by some other person–

(1) the nearest relative must be made a respondent, unless–

  (a) the application is made on the grounds that the patient has no nearest relative or that it is not reasonably practicable to ascertain whether he has a nearest relative; or

(b) the court orders otherwise; and

(2) the court may order that any other person shall be made a respondent.

18.4 Subject to paragraph 18.5, the court may accept as evidence of the facts relied upon in support of the application, any report made–

(1) by a medical practitioner; or

(2) by any of the following acting in the course of their official duties–

(a) a probation officer;

(b) an officer of a local authority;

(c) an officer of a voluntary body exercising statutory functions on behalf of a local authority; or

(d) an officer of a hospital manager.

18.5 The respondent must be informed of the substance of any part of the report dealing with his fitness or conduct that the court considers to be material to the determination of the claim.

18.6 An application under Part II shall be heard in private unless the court orders otherwise.

18.7 The judge may, for the purpose of determining the application, interview the patient. The interview may take place in the presence of, or separately from, the parties. The interview may be conducted elsewhere than at the court. Alternatively, the judge may direct the district judge to interview the patient and report to the judge in writing.

Applications under section 13 of the Coroners Act 1988

19.1 An application under section 13 of the Coroners Act 1988 is heard and determined by a Divisional Court.

19.2 The application must, unless made by the Attorney General, be accompanied by the Attorney General's fiat.

19.3 The claim form must–

(1) state the grounds for the application;

(2) be filed at the Administrative Court; and

(3) be served upon all persons directly affected by the application within six weeks of the grant of the Attorney General's fiat.

Application for injunction to prevent environmental harm or unlicensed activities

20.1 This paragraph relates to applications under–

(1) section 187B or 214A of the Town and Country Planning Act 1990;

(2) section 44A of the Planning (Listed Buildings and Conservation Areas) Act 1990;

(3) section 26AA of the Planning (Hazardous Substances) Act 1990; or

(4) section 12 or 26 of the Energy Act 2008.

20.2 An injunction may be granted under those sections against a person whose identity is unknown to the applicant.

20.3 In this paragraph, an injunction refers to an injunction under one of those sections and 'the defendant' is the person against whom the injunction is sought.

20.4 In the claim form, the applicant must describe the defendant by reference to–

(1) a photograph;

(2) a thing belonging to or in the possession of the defendant; or

(3) any other evidence.

20.5 The description of the defendant under paragraph 20.4 must be sufficiently clear to enable the defendant to be served with the proceedings.

(The court has power under Part 6 to dispense with service or make an order permitting service by an alternative method or at an alternative place).

20.6 The application must be accompanied by a witness statement. The witness statement must state–

(1) that the applicant was unable to ascertain the defendant's identity within the time reasonably available to him;

(2) the steps taken by him to ascertain the defendant's identity;

(3) the means by which the defendant has been described in the claim form; and

(4) that the description is the best the applicant is able to provide.

20.7 When the court issues the claim form it will–

(1) fix a date for the hearing; and

(2) prepare a notice of the hearing date for each party.

20.8 The claim form must be served not less than 21 days before the hearing date.

20.9 Where the claimant serves the claim form, he must serve notice of the hearing date at the same time, unless the hearing date is specified in the claim form.

(CPR rules 3.1(2) (a) and (b) provide for the court to extend or shorten the time for compliance with any rule or practice direction, and to adjourn or bring forward a hearing)

20.10 The court may on the hearing date–

(1) proceed to hear the case and dispose of the claim; or

(2) give case management directions.

Proceedings under the Financial Services and Markets Act 2000

21.1 This paragraph applies to proceedings in the High Court under the Financial Services and Markets Act 2000.

21.2 Proceedings in the High Court under the Act (other than applications for a mandatory order) and actions for damages for breach of a statutory duty imposed by the Act shall be assigned to the Chancery Division.

21.3 Such proceedings and actions must be begun by claim form (except for applications by petition by the Financial Conduct Authority or the Prudential Regulation Authority under section 367 of the Act).

21.4 The Financial Conduct Authority or the Prudential Regulation Authority may make representations to the court where there is a question about the meaning of any rule or other instrument made by, or with the approval or consent of, the Financial Conduct Authority or the Prudential Regulation Authority.

21.5 When the court makes a voting rights suspension order under section 89NA of the Act, the Financial Conduct Authority must within 7 days, or such period as the Court may direct, serve a copy of the order on the company which issued the shares to which it relates.

Application to quash certain orders, schemes, etc

22.1 This paragraph applies where the High Court has jurisdiction under any enactment, on the application of any person to quash or prohibit any–

(1) order, scheme, certificate or plan of;

(2) amendment or approval of a plan of;

(3) decision of;

(4) action on the part of,

a Minister or government department.

22.2 The jurisdiction shall be exercisable by a single judge of the Queen's Bench Division.

22.3 The claim form must be filed at the Administrative Court and served within the time limited by the relevant enactment for making the application. Practice Direction 54D applies to applications under this paragraph.

22.4 Subject to paragraph 22.6, the claim form must be served on the appropriate Minister or government department and on the person indicated in the following table.

If the application relates to– 1 a compulsory purchase order made by an authority other than the appropriate Minister or government department; or 2 a clearance order under the Housing Act 1985.	The authority that made the order.
If the application relates to a scheme or order– 1 to which Section 2 of the Highways Act 1980 applies; and 2 which was made by an authority other than the Secretary of State	The authority that made the scheme or order.
If the application relates to a structure plan, local plan or other development plan within the meaning of the Town and Country Planning Act 1990	The local planning authority who prepared the plan.
If the application relates to any decision or order, or any action on the part of a Minister of the Crown to which section 21 of the Land Compensation Act 1961 applies.	a The authority directly concerned with such decision, order or action; or b if that authority is the applicant, on every person who would, if he were aggrieved by the decision, order or action, be entitled to apply to the High Court under section 21 of the Land Compensation Act.
If the application relates to a scheme to which Schedule 32 of the Local Government, Planning and Land Act 1980 applies	The body which adopted the scheme.

22.5 In paragraph 22.4, 'the appropriate Minister or government department' means the Minister of the Crown or government department–

(1) by whom the order, scheme, certificate, plan, amendment, approval or decision in question was or may be made, authorised, confirmed, approved or given;

(2) on whose part the action in question was or may be taken.

22.6 Where the application relates to an order made under the Road Traffic Regulation Act 1984, the claim form must be served–

(1) if the order was made by a Minister of the Crown, on that Minister;

(2) if the order was made by a local authority with the consent, or following a direction, of a Minister of the Crown, on that authority and also on that Minister;

(3) in any other case, on the local authority by whom the order was made.

22.7 Evidence at the hearing of an application under this paragraph is by witness statement.

22.8 The applicant must–

(1) file a witness statement in support of the application in the Administrative Court within 14 days after service of the claim form; and

(2) serve a copy of the witness statement and of any exhibit on the respondent at the time of filing.

22.9 The respondent must–

(1) file any witness statement in opposition to the application in the Administrative Court within 21 days after service on him of the applicant's witness statement; and

(2) serve a copy of his witness statement and of any exhibit on the applicant at the time of filing.

22.10 Omitted

22.11 Unless the court otherwise orders, the application will not be heard earlier than 14 days after the time for filing a witness statement by the respondent has expired.

22.12 Where an application is made under section 66 of the Anti-Social Behaviour, Crime and Policing Act 2014 to question the validity of a public spaces protection order or of a variation of such an order —

(a) the claim form must be served on the local authority by which the order or variation was made or varied; and

(b) paragraphs 22.2, 22.3 and 22.7 to 22.11 apply.

Proceedings under the Telecommunications Restriction Orders (Custodial Institutions) (England and Wales) Regulations 2015

23.1 This paragraph applies to proceedings under the Telecommunications Restriction Orders (Custodial Institutions) (England and Wales) Regulations 2015 ('the TRO Regulations').

23.2 An application under regulation 3(1) for a Telecommunications Restriction Order ('TRO') must be made at the Clerkenwell and Shoreditch County Court hearing centre.

23.2A If the claimant indicates in the claim form that the claimant is also applying for a non-disclosure order under regulation 8 of the TRO Regulations, the claimant's evidence in respect of the TRO application must not be served until the court has determined the non-disclosure application. If the non-disclosure application is not granted, the court must give the claimant an opportunity to withdraw the TRO application. If the non-disclosure application is not granted and the claimant withdraws the claim, then the court must return the TRO claim form, and any documents submitted in connection with the TRO application, to the claimant.

23.3 The court must when it issues the claim form fix a date for hearing of the application for a TRO, which must unless the court orders otherwise be no later than 21 days after the date of issue.

23.4 In accordance with regulation 10 of the TRO Regulations, if a hearing is held, it must be held in private unless the court orders otherwise.

23.5 Rule 44.2(2)(a) (the general rule on costs) does not apply to proceedings to which this paragraph applies.

(Regulation 6 of the TRO Regulations makes specific provision for costs in relation to an application for a TRO.)

23.6 Rule 5.4B (supply of court documents to a party) applies subject to any order made by the court under regulation 5(2) of the TRO Regulations.

23.7 Unless the court orders otherwise, rule 5.4C (supply of court documents to a non-party) does not apply to any proceedings to which this paragraph applies.

Proceedings under the Drug Dealing Telecommunication Restriction Orders Regulations 2017

24.1 This paragraph applies to proceedings under The Drug Dealing Telecommunication Restriction Orders Regulations 2017 ('the DDTRO Regulations'); and references in this paragraph to a regulation by number alone are to a regulation in the DDTRO Regulations.

24.2 An application under regulation 3(1) for a Drug Dealing Telecommunication Restriction Order ('DDTRO') must be made at one of the following County Court hearing centres:

- Clerkenwell and Shoreditch
- Manchester
- Liverpool
- Birmingham
- Newcastle
- Bristol.

24.3 The court must when it issues the claim form fix a date for hearing of the application for a DDTRO, which must unless the court orders otherwise be no later than 21 days after the date of issue.

24.4 In accordance with regulation 4(2), an application for a DDTRO must be made and heard without notice of the application or hearing having been given to an affected person or their legal representative and be heard and determined in the absence of an affected person or their legal representative.

24.5 Rule 5.4B (supply of court documents to a party) applies subject to any order made by the court under regulation 9(1) of the DDTRO Regulations.

24.6 Unless the court orders otherwise, rule 5.4C (supply of court documents to a non-party) does not apply to any proceedings to which this paragraph applies.

24.7 In accordance with regulation 9(4), an application for a non-disclosure order may be determined in advance of, or at the same time as, a DDTRO application or appeal.

24.8 In accordance with regulation 9(7), if the claimant indicates in the claim form that the claimant is also applying for a non-disclosure order under regulation 9 of the DDTRO Regulations, the claimant's evidence in respect of the DDTRO application must not be served until the court has determined the non-disclosure application. If the non-disclosure application is not granted, the court must give the claimant an opportunity to withdraw the DDTRO application. If the nondisclosure application is not granted and the claimant withdraws the claim, then the court must return the DDTRO claim form, and any documents submitted in connection with the DDTRO application, to the claimant.'.

Proceedings under Chapter 3A of Part 5 of the Proceeds of Crime Act 2002 and Part 4A of Schedule 1 to the Anti-terrorism, Crime and Security Act 2001

25.1 This paragraph applies to applications which are transferred from a magistrates' court to the High Court under Section 303R of the Proceeds of Crime Act 2002 or paragraph 10J of Schedule 1 to the Anti-terrorism Crime and Security Act 2001 ('transferred forfeiture applications').

25.2 The Part 8 procedure applies to transferred forfeiture applications with the following modifications.

25.3 Rules 8.2 and 8.2A(2)-(4), and paragraphs 4.1, 4.2, and paragraphs 7.1 to 7.5 of this practice direction, do not apply, and—

(1) the application made to the magistrates' court ('the MC document') shall be treated as equivalent to a Part 8 claim form (whether or not any defendant is named in it);

(2) no separate claim form is to be issued;

(3) the applicant to the magistrates' court shall be 'the claimant';

(4) the address of the claimant given in the MC document shall be the claimant's address for service;

(5) any person named in the MC document as being a person the application was being brought against or who has sought to oppose or who has failed or refused to agree to the application whilst it was in the magistrates' court shall be a defendant; and

(6) any evidence filed by the claimant with the magistrates' court prior to the transfer of the application to the High Court shall be treated as evidence filed by the claimant in support of the Part 8 Claim; and any evidence so filed by

any defendant or other person shall be treated as evidence filed in relation to the Part 8 Claim.

25.4 On receipt of a transferred forfeiture application—

(1) the court shall give the proceedings a number;

(2) the proceedings are to be heard in the Queen's Bench Division unless the court shall otherwise order;

(3) if the court considers it is necessary, the court shall order that the claimant must provide the court with any of the information listed in rule 8.2(b) to (e), and with the names (or other means of identification) of the defendant(s), where that information is not otherwise provided in the MC document; and

(4) the court shall order a directions hearing to be listed on the first available date after twenty-eight days after the end of the service period (see paragraph 25.5), at which the court will—

 (i) fix a date for the hearing of the application or for a further directions hearing;

 (ii) give directions as to the exchange of evidence between the parties;

 (iii) give directions as to any other matters which are required in advance of that hearing, for example regarding the joinder of or service upon any further persons.

25.5 Rule 7.5 shall not apply and, subject to any direction made by the Court in accordance with paragraph 25.6 (or order made under rules 6.15, 6.16, 6.27 or 6.28), the claimant shall serve (in like manner as provided by Part 6 of the Rules in relation to service of claim forms or as provided by any enactment) upon the defendant the following documents within two months of the date of the order made under paragraph 25.4 ('the service period')—

(1) the transferred application, and any evidence described in paragraph 25.3(6);

(2) a statement of who are the defendants (unless such is apparent from the MC document) which must also be filed at court;

(3) the order transferring the application to the High Court under Section 303R of the Proceeds of Crime Act 2002 or paragraph 10J of Schedule 1 to the Anti-terrorism Crime and Security Act 2001 (as appropriate);

(4) the order made under paragraph 25.4; and (5) an acknowledgment of service form.

25.6 The court may extend the service period by making a direction of its own initiative or on application of any party, whether before or after the expiry of the period described in paragraph 25.5. An application for a direction to extend the service period is to be supported by evidence, with the court having a general discretion (and, for the avoidance of doubt, no sanction is imposed by paragraph 25.5), and rule 3.1(2)(a) shall apply and rules 7.6 and 7.7 shall not apply.

25.7 Rule 8.3 applies with the modification that the acknowledgment of service must be filed not more than 14 days after service of the documents listed in paragraph 25.5.

25.8 Rule 8.5 does not apply, and, except as provided by paragraphs 25.3(6) above, the parties—

(1) may (but without any obligation to do so) file and serve evidence not less than 7 days before the first directions hearing; and

(2) must file and serve evidence in accordance with the directions given by the court,

and any such evidence must (unless the court otherwise directs) be in the form of a witness statement or an affidavit.

25.9 Rule 8.6 applies with the modification that no written evidence may be relied on at the hearing of the claim unless—

(1) it is as described in paragraphs 25.3(6) or 25.8(1) or it has been filed and served in accordance with the court's directions; or

(2) the court gives permission (for which any party may apply).

PRACTICE DIRECTION 8C – ALTERNATIVE PROCEDURE FOR STATUTORY REVIEW OF CERTAIN PLANNING MATTES

This Practice Direction supplements CPR Part 8

General provisions applicable to planning statutory review

1.1 This Practice Direction, which is made pursuant to rule 8.1(6), relates to claims for statutory review under—

(a) section 287 of the Town and Country Planning Act 1990;

(b) section 288 of the Town and Country Planning Act 1990;

(c) section 63 of the Planning (Listed Buildings and Conservation Areas) Act 1990;

(d) section 22 of the Planning (Hazardous Substances) Act 1990; and

(e) section 113 of the Planning and Compulsory Purchase Act 2004.

1.2 In this Practice Direction "claim for planning statutory review" means a claim under any of the statutory provisions set out in paragraph 1.1.

1.3 The Part 8 procedure must be used in a claim for planning statutory review.

1.4 Part 8 applies to a claim for planning statutory review with the modifications set out in this Practice Direction.

1.5 Practice Direction 8A does not apply to a claim for planning statutory review.

1.6 Practice Direction 54D applies to applications under this Practice Direction.

1.7 Practice Direction 54E applies to applications under this Practice Direction.

(Rule 8.1(6)(b) provides that a rule or practice direction may, in relation to a specified type of proceedings, dis-apply or modify any of the rules set out in Part 8 as they apply to those proceedings.)

Claim form

2.1 A Part 8 claim form (in practice form N208) must be used and must be filed at the Administrative Court within the time limited by the statutory provisions set out in paragraph 1.1.

2.2 In addition to the matters set out in rule 8.2 (contents of the claim form) the claimant must also state –

(a) the name and address of any person that the claimant considers must be served in accordance with paragraph 4.1;

(b) that the claimant is requesting permission to proceed with a claim for planning statutory review;

(Permission is required to apply for planning statutory review under the provisions listed in paragraph 1.1 (a) to (e) of this Practice Direction.)

(c) a detailed statement of the claimant's grounds for bringing the claim for planning statutory review;

(d) a statement of the facts relied on;

(e) any application for directions; and

(f) the remedy being claimed (including any interim remedy).

(Part 25 sets out how to apply for an interim remedy.)

2.3 The claim form must be accompanied by the following documents–

(a) any written evidence in support of the claim;

(b) a copy of any decision, order, relevant document or action that the claimant seeks to have quashed;

(c) copies of any documents on which the claimant proposes to rely;

(d) copies of any relevant statutory material; and

(e) a list of essential documents for advance reading by the court (with page references to the passages relied on).

2.4 Where it is not possible to file all the above documents, the claimant must indicate which documents have not been filed and the reasons why they are not currently available.

Bundle of documents at permission stage

3.1 The claimant must file two copies of a paginated and indexed bundle containing all the documents referred to in paragraphs 2.1 to 2.3.

3.2 Attention is drawn to rules 8.5(1) and 8.5(7).

Service of the claim form

4.1 The claim form must be served on the appropriate Minister or government department and, where different, on the person indicated in the following table:

If the application is brought under – 1. section 287 of the Town and Country Planning Act 1990; or 2. section 113 of the Planning and Compulsory Purchase Act 2004.	The authority who prepared the relevant document.
If the application relates to any decision or order, or any action on the part of a Minister of the Crown to which – 1. section 288 of the Town and Country Planning Act 1990 applies; or 2. section 63 of the Planning (Listed Buildings and Conservation Areas) Act 1990 applies.	a. The authority directly concerned with the decision, order or action; or b. if that authority is the claimant, on every person who would, if he were aggrieved by the decision, order, relevant document or action, be entitled to apply to the High Court under section 288 of the Town and Country Planning Act 1990 or section 63 of the Planning (Listed Buildings and Conservation Areas) Act 1990 as the case may be.
If the application relates to any decision on the part of a Minister of the Crown to which section 22 of the Planning (Hazardous Substances) Act 1990 applies.	a. The hazardous substance authority who made the decision on the application to which the proceedings relate; or b. if that authority is the claimant, on every person who would, if he were aggrieved by the decision, be entitled to apply to the High Court under section 22 of the Planning (Hazardous Substances) Act 1990.
If the application is brought under – 1. section 287 of the Town and Country Planning Act 1990; or 2. section 113 of the Planning and Compulsory Purchase Act 2004.	The authority who prepared the relevant document.

If the application relates to any decision or order, or any action on the part of a Minister of the Crown to which – 1. section 288 of the Town and Country Planning Act 1990 applies; or 2. section 63 of the Planning (Listed Buildings and Conservation Areas) Act 1990 applies.	a. The authority directly concerned with the decision, order or action; or b. if that authority is the claimant, on every person who would, if he were aggrieved by the decision, order, relevant document or action, be entitled to apply to the High Court under section 288 of the Town and Country Planning Act 1990 or section 63 of the Planning (Listed Buildings and Conservation Areas) Act 1990 as the case may be.
If the application relates to any decision on the part of a Minister of the Crown to which section 22 of the Planning (Hazardous Substances) Act 1990 applies.	a. The hazardous substance authority who made the decision on the application to which the proceedings relate; or b. if that authority is the claimant, on every person who would, if he were aggrieved by the decision, be entitled to apply to the High Court under section 22 of the Planning (Hazardous Substances) Act 1990.

4.2 In paragraph 4.1 "the appropriate Minister or government department" means the Minister of the Crown of the government department –

(a) by whom the decision or order was or may be made;

(b) on whose part the action in question was or may be taken.

4.3 Except as required by paragraphs 7.3 or 10.1, the Administrative Court will not serve documents and service must be effected by the parties.

4.4 The claim form must be served within the time limited by the relevant enactment for making a claim for planning statutory review set out in paragraph 1.1.

Acknowledgment of service

5.1 Rules 8.3(1) and 8.3(2) do not apply to a claim for planning statutory review.

5.2 Any person served with the claim form who wishes to take part in the planning statutory review must file an acknowledgment of service in the relevant practice form in accordance with paragraphs 5.3 to 5.6.

5.3 Any acknowledgment of service must be –

(a) filed not more than 21 days after service of the claim form; and

(b) served on –

   (i) the claimant; and

   (ii) any other person named in the claim form, as soon as practicable and, in any event, not later than 7 days after it is filed.

5.4 The time limits under paragraph 5.3 may not be extended by agreement between the parties.

5.5 The acknowledgment of service –

(a) must –

  (i) where the person filing it intends to contest the claim, set out a summary of his grounds for doing so;

  (ii) state the name and address of any person the person filing it considers should be served in accordance with paragraph 4.1; and

  (iii) comply with rule 10.5; and

(b) may include or be accompanied by an application for directions.

5.6 Rule 10.3(2) does not apply.

5.7 The provisions of Part 15 (defence and reply) to do not apply.

Failure to file acknowledgment of service

6.1 Where a person served with the claim form has failed to file an acknowledgment of service in accordance with paragraphs 5.1 to 5.7, rule 8.4 does not apply and that person–

(a) may not take part in a hearing to decide whether permission should be given unless the court allows him to do so; but

(b) provided that person complies with paragraphs 12.1 to 12.3 or any other direction of the court regarding the filing and service of –

  (i) detailed grounds for contesting the claim or supporting it on additional grounds; and

  (ii) any written evidence,

may take part in the hearing of the planning statutory review.

6.2 Where that person takes part in the hearing of the planning statutory review, the court may take the failure to file an acknowledgment of service into account when deciding what order to make about costs.

Permission decision without a hearing

7.1 The court will generally consider the question of permission without a hearing.

7.2 Paragraphs 7.3 to 7.8 apply where the court, without a hearing –

(a) refuses permission to proceed; or

(b) gives permission to proceed –

  (i) subject to conditions; or

  (ii) on certain grounds only.

7.3 The court will serve its reasons for making the decision when it serves the order giving or refusing permission in accordance with paragraph 10.1.

7.4 Subject to paragraph 7.8, the claimant may not appeal but may request the decision to be reconsidered at a hearing.

7.5 A request under paragraph 7.4 must be filed within 7 days after service of the reasons under paragraph 7.3.

7.6 The claimant, defendant and any other person who has filed an acknowledgment of service will be given at least 2 days' notice of the hearing date.

7.7 The court may give directions requiring the proceedings to be heard by a Divisional Court.

7.8 Where the court refuses permission to proceed and records the fact that the application is totally without merit in accordance with rule 23.12, the claimant may not request that decision to be reconsidered at a hearing.

Permission hearing

8.1 Neither the defendant nor any other person need attend a hearing on the question of permission unless the court directs otherwise.

8.2 Where the defendant or any party does attend a hearing, the court will not generally make an order for costs against the claimant.

Permission given

9.1 Where permission to proceed is given the court may also give directions.

9.2 Directions under paragraph 9.1 may include –

(a) a stay of proceedings to which the claim relates;

(b) directions requiring the proceedings to be heard by a Divisional Court; or

(c) directions about serving the claim form and any evidence on other persons.

Service of order giving or refusing permission

10.1 The court will serve –

(a) the order giving or refusing permission; and

(b) any directions,

on –

- (i) the claimant;
- (ii) the defendant; and
- (iii) any other person who filed an acknowledgment of service.

Defendant etc. may not apply to set aside

11.1 Neither the defendant nor any other person served with the claim form may apply to set aside an order giving permission to proceed.

Response

12.1 A defendant and any other person served with the claim form who wishes to contest the claim or support it on additional grounds must file and serve –

(a) detailed grounds for contesting the claim or supporting it on additional grounds; and

(b) any written evidence,

within 35 days after service of the order giving permission.

12.2 Where the party filing the detailed grounds intends to rely on documents not already filed, that party must file a paginated bundle of those documents when filing the detailed grounds.

12.3 The following rules do not apply –

(a) rule 8.5 (3) and 8.5 (4) (defendant to file and serve written evidence at the same time as acknowledgment of service); and

(b) rule 8.5 (5) and 8.5 (6) (claimant to file and serve any reply within 14 days).

Where claimant seeks to rely on additional grounds

13.1 Where the claimant intends to apply to rely on additional grounds at the hearing of the planning statutory review, the claimant must give notice to the court and to any other person served with the claim form no later than 7 clear days before the hearing.

13.2 The court's permission is required if a claimant seeks to rely on grounds other than those for which the claimant has been given permission to proceed.

Evidence

14.1 Rule 8.6 (1) does not apply.

14.2 No written evidence may be relied on unless–

(a) it has been served in accordance with–

  (i) this Practice Direction; or

  (ii) direction of the court; or

(b) the court gives permission.

14.3 Disclosure is not required unless the court orders otherwise.

Skeleton arguments

15.1 The claimant must file and serve a skeleton argument not less than 21 working days before the date of the hearing of the statutory review.

15.2 The defendant and any other party wishing to make representations at the hearing of the planning statutory review must file and serve a skeleton argument not less than 14 working days before the date of the hearing.

15.3 Skeleton arguments must contain–

(a) a time estimate for the complete hearing, including delivery of judgment;

(b) a list of issues;

(c) a list of the legal points to be taken (together with any relevant authorities with page references to the passages relied on);

(d) a chronology of events (with page references to the bundle of documents (see paragraph 16);

(e) a list of essential documents for the advance reading of the court (with page references to the passages relied on) (if different from that filed with the claim form) and a time estimate for that reading; and

(f) a list of persons referred to.

Bundle of documents at hearing stage

16.1 The claimant must file a paginated and indexed bundle of all relevant documents required for the hearing of the planning statutory review when filing the claimant's skeleton argument.

16.2 The bundle must also include those documents required by the defendant and any other party who is to make representations at the hearing.

Planning statutory review may be decided without a hearing

17.1 The court may decide the claim for planning statutory review without a hearing where all the parties agree.

Agreed final order

18.1 If the parties agree about the final order to be made in a claim for planning statutory review, the claimant must file at the court a document (with 2 copies) signed by all the parties setting out the terms of the proposed agreed order together with a short statement of the matters relied on as justifying the proposed agreed order and copies of any authorities or statutory provisions relied on.

18.2 The court will consider the documents referred to in paragraph 18.1 and will make the order if satisfied that the order should be made.

18.3 If the court is not satisfied that the order should be made, a hearing date will be set.

18.4 Where the agreement relates to an order for costs only, the parties need only file a document signed by all the parties setting out the terms of the proposed order.".

PRACTICE DIRECTION 45 – FIXED COSTS

This Practice Direction supplements Part 45

Section I
Fixed costs

Fixed costs in small claims

1.1 Under Rule 27.14 the costs which can be awarded to a claimant in a small claim include the fixed costs payable under Part 45 attributable to issuing the claim.

1.2 Those fixed costs are the sum of–

(a) the fixed commencement costs calculated in accordance with Table 1 of Rule 45.2;

(b) the appropriate court fee or fees paid by the claimant.

Claims to which Part 45 does not apply

1.3 In a claim to which Part 45 does not apply, no amount shall be entered on the claim form for the charges of the claimant's legal representative, but the words 'to be assessed' shall be inserted.

Section II
Road traffic accidents: fixed recoverable costs in costs-only proceedings

Scope

2.1 Section II of Part 45 ('the Section') provides for certain fixed costs to be recoverable between parties in respect of costs incurred in disputes which are settled prior to proceedings being issued. The Section applies to road traffic accident disputes as defined in rule 45.9(4)(a), where the accident which gave rise to the dispute occurred on or after 6th October 2003.

2.2 The Section does not apply to disputes where the total agreed value of the damages is within the small claims limit or exceeds £10,000. Rule 26.8(2) sets out how the financial value of a claim is assessed for the purposes of allocation to track.

2.3 Fixed recoverable costs are to be calculated by reference to the amount of agreed damages which are payable to the receiving party. In calculating the amount of these damages–

(a) account must be taken of both general and special damages and interest;

(a) any interim payments made must be included;

(c) where the parties have agreed an element of contributory negligence, the amount of damages attributed to that negligence must be deducted;

(d) any amount required by statute to be paid by the compensating party directly to a third party (such as sums paid by way of compensation recovery payments and National Health Service expenses) must not be included.

2.4 The Section applies to cases which fall within the scope of the Uninsured Drivers Agreement dated 13 August 1999. The section does not apply to cases which fall within the scope of the Untraced Drivers Agreement dated 14 February 2003.

Fixed recoverable costs formula

2.5 The amount of fixed costs recoverable is the sum of–

(a) £800;

(b) 20% of the agreed damages up to £5,000; and

(c) 15% of the agreed damages between £5,000 and £10,000.

For example, agreed damages of £7,523 would result in recoverable costs of £2,178.45 i.e.

£800 + (20% of £5,000) + (15% of £2,523).

Additional costs for work in specified areas

2.6 The area referred to in rules 45.11(2), 45.18(5), 45.29C(2), 45.29E(2), 45.25F(5), 45.29G(2) and 45.29H consists of (within London) the area served by the County Court hearing centres at Barnet, Brentford, Central London, Clerkenwell and Shoreditch, Edmonton, Ilford, Mayors and City of London, Romford, Wandsworth and Willesden and (outside London) the County Court hearing centres at Bromley, Croydon, Dartford, Gravesend and Uxbridge.

Multiple claimants

2.7 Where two or more potential claimants instruct the same legal representative, the provisions of the section apply in respect of each claimant.

Information to be included in the claim form

2.8 Costs only proceedings are commenced using the procedure set out in rule 46.14. A claim form should be issued in accordance with Part 8. Where the claimant is claiming an amount of costs which exceed the amount of the fixed recoverable costs the claim form must give details of the exceptional circumstances to justify the additional costs.

2.9 The claimant must also include on the claim form details of any disbursements. The disbursements that may be claimed are set out in rule 45.12(1). If the disbursement falls within 45.12(2)(c) (disbursements that have arisen due to a particular feature of the dispute) the claimant must give details of the particular feature of the dispute that made the disbursement necessary.

Disbursements

2.10 If the parties agree the amount of the fixed recoverable costs and the only dispute is as to the payment of, or amount of, a disbursement, then proceedings should be issued under rule 46.14.

Section IIIA
Claims which no longer continue under the RTA or EL/PL protocols – disbursements

Claims for loss of earnings: Rule 45.29I(2)(g)

2A.1 Where, under rule 45.29I(2)(g) (loss of earnings), the court allows a claim for any loss of earnings or leave by a party or witness due to attending a hearing or staying away from home for the purpose of attending a hearing, the specified sums, per day, for each person are—

(a) £90, where the value of the claim for damages is not more than £10,000; and

(b) £135, where the value of the claim for damages is more than £10,000.

Section IV
Scale costs for proceddings in the Intellectual Property Enterprise Court

Tables A and B

3.1 Tables A and B set out the maximum amount of scale costs which the court will award for each stage of a claim in the Intellectual Property Enterprise Court.

3.2 Table A sets out the scale costs for each stage of a claim up to determination of liability.

3.3 Table B sets out the scale costs for each stage of an inquiry as to damages or account of profits.

Table A

Stage of a claim	Maximum amount of costs
Particulars of claim	£7,000
Defence and counterclaim	£7,000
Reply and defence to counterclaim	£7,000
Reply to defence to counterclaim	£3,500
Attendance at a case management conference	£3,000
Making or responding to an application	£3,000
Providing or inspecting disclosure or product/process description	£6,000
Performing or inspecting experiments	£3,000
Preparing witness statements	£6,000
Preparing experts' report	£8,000
Preparing for and attending trial and judgment	£16,000
Preparing for determination on the papers	£5,500

Table B

Stage of a claim	Maximum amount of costs
Points of claim	£3,000
Points of defence	£3,000
Attendance at a case management conference	£3,000
Making or responding to an application	£3,000
Providing or inspecting disclosure	£3,000
Preparing witness statements	£6,000
Preparing experts' report	£6,000
Preparing for and attending trial and judgment	£8,000
Preparing for determination on the papers	£3,000

Section VI
Fast track trial costs

Scope

4.1 Section VI of Part 45 applies to the costs of an advocate for preparing for and appearing at the trial of a claim in the fast track.

4.2 It applies only where, at the date of the trial, the claim is allocated to the fast track. It does not apply in any other case, irrespective of the final value of the claim.

4.3 In particular it does not apply to a disposal hearing at which the amount to be paid under a judgment or order is decided by the court (see paragraph 12.4 of Practice Direction 26)).

Section VII
Costs limits in Aarhus Convention claims

Limit on costs recoverable from a party in an Aarhus Convention claim: Rule 45.43

5.1 Omitted

5.2 Omitted

Section VIII
Claims which no longer continue under the RTA or EL/PL protocols – disbursements

Claims for loss of earnings: Rule 45.29I(2)(g)

6.1 Where, under rule 45.29I(2)(g) (loss of earnings), the court allows a claim for any loss of earnings or leave by a party or witness due to attending a hearing or staying away from home for the purpose of attending a hearing, the specified sums, per day, for each person are–

(a) £90, where the value of the claim for damages is not more that £10,000; and

(b) £135, where the value of the claim for damages is more that £10,000.

PRACTICE DIRECTION 52D – STATUTORY APPEALS AND APPEALS SUBJECT TO SPECIAL PROVISION

This Practice Direction supplements CPR Part 52

Section I
Introduction

1.1 This Practice Direction applies to all statutory appeals, and to other appeals which are subject to special provision, but not to appeals by way of case stated (to which Practice Direction 52E applies).

Section II
Routes of appeal

2.1 In this Practice Direction, the court to which an appeal lies is prescribed by statute.

Section III
General provisions about statutory appeals

3.1 This Section contains general provisions about statutory appeals (paragraphs 3.2 – 3.8). For where this Practice Direction or a statute makes additional special provision see also Section 4.

3.2 Where any of the provisions in this Section provide for documents to be filed at the appeal court, those documents are in addition to any documents required under Part 52 or Practice Direction 52B or 52C.

3.3 Subject to rule 52.9—

(1) where the appellant wishes to appeal against a decision of the Upper Tribunal, the appellant's notice must be filed within 28 days of the date on which notice of the Upper Tribunal's decision on permission to appeal to the Court of Appeal is sent to the appellant.

3.3A Where a statement of reasons for a decision is given later than the notice of that decision, the period for filing the appellant's notice is calculated from the date on which the statement is sent to the appellant.

Service of appellant's notice: rule 52.12(3)

3.4

(1) The appellant must serve the appellant's notice on the respondent and on the chairman of the tribunal, Minister of State, government department or other person from whose decision the appeal is brought.

(2) In the case of an appeal from the decision of a tribunal that has no chairman or member who acts as a chairman, the appellant's notice must be served on the member (or members if more than one) of the tribunal.

Variation of time: rule 52.15

3.5 Where any statute prescribes a period within which an appeal must be filed then, unless the statute otherwise provides, the appeal court may not extend that period.

Applications by third parties (rule 52.25)

3.6 Where all the parties consent, the court may deal with an application under rule 52.25 without a hearing.

3.7 An application for permission must be made by letter to the relevant court office, identifying the appeal, explaining who the applicant is and indicating why and in what form the applicant wants to participate in the hearing.

3.8 If the applicant is seeking a prospective order as to costs, the letter must say what kind of order and on what grounds.

Section IV
Specific appeals

Provisions about specific appeals

4.1 This Section sets out special provisions about the appeals listed in the Table below. This Section is not exhaustive and does not create, amend or remove any right of appeal.

4.2 Part 52 applies to all appeals to which this Section applies subject to any special provisions set out in this Section.

4.3 Where any of the provisions in this Section provide for documents to be filed at the appeal court, these documents are in addition to any documents required under Part 52 or Practice Direction 52B or 52C.

Certain appeals to the High Court to be heard in Chancery Division

5.1 Any appeal to the High Court, and any case stated or question referred for the opinion of that court under any of the following enactments shall be heard in the Chancery Division–

(1) section 38(3) of the Clergy Pensions Measure 1961;

(2) Omitted

(3) the Industrial and Provident Societies Act 1965;

(4) section 222(3) of the Inheritance Tax Act 1984;

(5) the Land Registration Act 2002;

(6) paragraph 16 of Schedule 15 to the Law of Property Act 1922;

(7) section 215 or 217 of the Pensions Act 2004;

(8) section 151 of the Pension Schemes Act 1993;

(9) section 13 and 13B of the Stamp Act 1891;

(10) regulation 8(3) of the Stamp Duty Reserve Tax Regulations 1986.

Table

Statute (or description of appeal)	Appropriate Court	Relevant paragraph in this Practice Direction
Agricultural Land Tribunal	High Court	18.1
Architects Act 1997, s. 22	High Court	19.1
Chiropractors Act 1994, s. 31	High Court	19.1
Civil Partnership – conditional order for dissolution or nullity	CA	6.1
Clergy Pensions Measure 1961, s. 38(3)	High Court	5.1
Competition: Chapters I and II of Part I of the Competition Act 1998	CA	7.1
Competition Appeal Tribunal	CA	8.1
Contempt of Court	CA	9.1
Court of Protection	CA	10.1
Decree nisi of divorce or nullity of marriage	CA	6.1
Dentists Act 1984, ss. 29 and 44	High Court	19.1
Employment Appeal Tribunal	CA	11.1
Extradition Act 2003	High Court	21.1
Friendly Societies Act 1974	High Court	5.1 and 22.1
Friendly Societies Act 1992	High Court	5.1 and 22.1
Health Professions Order 2001, art. 38	High Court	19.1
Housing Act 1996, ss.204 and 204A	County Court	28.1
Immigration and Asylum Act 1999, Part II	County Court	29.1
Immigration and Asylum Appeals	CA	12.1
Inheritance Tax Act 1984, s. 222	High Court	5.1 and 23.1
Land Registration Act 2002	High Court	5.1 and 24.1
Law of Property Act 1922, para. 16 of Sch. 15	High Court	5.1
Local Government (Miscellaneous Provisions) Act 1976	County Court	30.1
Medical Act 1983, s. 40	High Court	19.1
Medicines Act 1968, ss. 82(3) and 83	High Court	19.1
Merchant Shipping Act 1995	High Court	25.1
Nurses, Midwives and Health Visitors Act 1997, s.12	High Court	19.1
Nursing and Midwifery Order 2001 art. 38	High Court	19.1
Opticians Act 1989, s. 23	High Court	19.1
Osteopaths Act 1993, s. 31	High Court	19.1
Patents Court: on appeal from Comptroller	CA	13.1
Patents: Revocation of patent	CA	14.1
Pensions Act 2004, ss. 215 and 217	High Court	5.1

Statute (or description of appeal)	Appropriate Court	Relevant paragraph in this Practice Direction
Pension Schemes Act 1993, s. 151	High Court	5.1
Pharmacy Act 1954	High Court	19.1
Pharmacy Order 2010, art. 58	High Court	19.1
Planning (Listed Buildings and Conservation Areas) Act 1990, s. 65	High Court	26.1
Proscribed Organisations Appeal Commission	CA	15.1
Representation of the People Act 1983, s. 56	County Court	31.1–31.3
Serious Crime Prevention Orders	CA	16.1
Solicitors Disciplinary Tribunal	High Court	27.1
Special Immigration Appeals Commission	CA	17.1
tamp Duty Reserve Tax Regulations 1986, reg. 8	High Court	5.1 and 23.1
Town and Country Planning Act 1990, s. 289	High Court	26.1
UK Borders Act 2007, s. 11	County Court	32.1
Welsh statutory appeals	High Court	27A.1–27A.7

Appeals to the Court of Appeal

Appeal against decree nisi of divorce or nullity of marriage or conditional dissolution or nullity order in relation to civil partnership

6.1

(1) The appellant must file the appellant's notice at the Court of Appeal within 28 days after the date on which the decree was pronounced or conditional order made.

(2) The appellant must file the following documents with the appellant's notice–

(a) the decree or conditional order; and

(b) a certificate of service of the appellant's notice.

(3) The appellant's notice must be served on the appropriate District Judge (see sub-paragraph (6)) in addition to the persons to be served under rule 52.12(3) and in accordance with that rule.

(4) The lower court may not alter the time limits for filing of the appeal notices.

(5) Where an appellant intends to apply to the Court of Appeal for an extension of time for serving or filing the appellant's notice the appellant must give notice of that intention to the appropriate District Judge (see sub-paragraph 6) before the application is made.

(6) In this paragraph 'the appropriate District Judge' means, where the lower court is–

(a) the County Court, the District Judge of the County Court hearing centre in question;

(b) a district registry, the District Judge of that registry;

(c) the Principal Registry of the Family Division, the senior District Judge of that division.

Appeals relating to the application of Chapters I and II of Part I of the Competition Act 1998

7.1

(1) This paragraph applies to any appeal to the Court of Appeal relating to the application Chapter I or Chapter II of Part I of the Competition Act 1998.

(2) In this paragraph–

(a) 'the Act' means the Competition Act 1998;

(b) Omitted

(c) Omitted

(d) 'competition authority' means–

(i) the Competition and Markets Authority; or

(ii) a regulator as defined in section 54 of the Act;

(e) Omitted

(3) Any party whose appeal notice raises an issue relating to the application of Chapter I or II of Part I of the Act, must–

(a) state that fact in the appeal notice; and

(b) serve a copy of the appeal notice on the Competition and Markets Authority at the same time as it is served on the other party to the appeal (addressed to the General Counsel, the Competition and Markets Authority, The Cabot, 25 Cabot Square, London E14 4QZ).

(4) Omitted

(5) A competition authority may make written observations to the Court of Appeal, or apply for permission to make oral observations, on issues relating to the application of Chapter I or II.

(6) If a competition authority intends to make written observations to the Court of Appeal, it must give notice of its intention to do so by letter to the Civil Appeals Office at the earliest opportunity.

(7) An application by a competition authority for permission to make oral representations at the hearing of an appeal must be made by letter to the

Civil Appeals Office at the earliest opportunity, identifying the appeal and indicating why the applicant wishes to make oral representations.

(8) If a competition authority files a notice under sub-paragraph (6) or an application under sub-paragraph (7), it must at the same time serve a copy of the notice or application on every party to the appeal.

(9) Any request by a competition authority for the court to send it any documents relating to an appeal should be made at the same time as filing a notice under sub-paragraph (6) or an application under sub-paragraph (7).

(10) When the Court of Appeal receives a notice under sub-paragraph (6) it may give case management directions to the competition authority, including directions about the date by which any written observations are to be filed.

(11) The Court of Appeal will serve on every party to the appeal a copy of any directions given or order made–

(a) on an application under sub-paragraph (7); or

(b) under sub-paragraph (10).

(12) Omitted

(13) Omitted

(14) Omitted

Appeal from Competition Appeal Tribunal

8.1

(1) Where the appellant applies for permission to appeal at the hearing at which the decision is delivered by the tribunal and–

(a) permission is given; or

(b) permission is refused and the appellant wishes to make an application to the Court of Appeal for permission to appeal,

the appellant's notice must be filed at the Court of Appeal within 14 days after the date of that hearing.

(2) Where the appellant applies in writing to the Registrar of the tribunal for permission to appeal and–

(a) permission is given; or

(b) permission is refused and the appellant wishes to make an application to the Court of Appeal for permission to appeal,

the appellant's notice must be filed at the Court of Appeal within 14 days after the date of receipt of the tribunal's decision on permission.

(3) Where the appellant does not make an application to the tribunal for permission to appeal, but wishes to make an application to the Court of

Appeal for permission, the appellant's notice must be filed at the Court of Appeal within 14 days after the end of the period within which the appellant may make a written application to the Registrar of the tribunal.

Appeals in cases of contempt of court (section 13 Administration of Justice Act 1960)

9.1 In an appeal under section 13 of the Administration of Justice Act 1960 (appeals in cases of contempt of court), the appellant must serve the appellant's notice on the court or the Upper Tribunal from whose order or decision the appeal is brought in addition to the persons to be served under rule 52.12(3) and in accordance with that rule.

Appeal from the Court of Protection

10.1

(1) In this paragraph–

(a) 'P' means a person who lacks, or who is alleged to lack, capacity within the meaning of the Mental Capacity Act 2005 to make a decision or decisions in relation to any matter that is subject to an order of the Court of Protection;

(b) 'the person effecting notification' means–

(i) the appellant;

(ii) an agent duly appointed by the appellant; or

(iii) such other person as the Court of Protection may direct, who is required to notify P in accordance with this paragraph; and

(c) 'final order' means a decision of the Court of Appeal that finally determines the appeal proceedings before it.

(2) Where P is not a party to the proceedings, unless the Court of Appeal directs otherwise, the person effecting notification must notify P–

(a) that an appellant's notice has been filed with the Court of Appeal and–

(i) who the appellant is;

(ii) what final order the appellant is seeking;

(iii) what will happen if the Court of Appeal makes the final order sought by the appellant; and

(iv) that P may apply under rule 52.25 (Statutory appeals: court's power to hear any person) by letter for permission to file evidence or make representations at the appeal hearing;

(b) of the final order, the effect of the final order and what steps P can take in relation to it; and

(c) of such other events and documents as the Court of Appeal may direct.

(Paragraphs 3.6 to 3.8 of this Practice Direction 52D contain provisions on how a third party can apply for permission to file evidence or make representations at an appeal hearing.)

(3) The person effecting notification must provide P with the information specified in sub-paragraph (2)–

(a) within 14 days of the date on which the appellant's notice was filed with the Court of Appeal;

(b) within 14 days of the date on which the final order was made; or

(c) within such time as the Court of Appeal may direct,

as the case may be.

(4) The person effecting notification must provide P in person with the information specified in sub-paragraph (2) in a way that is appropriate to P's circumstances (for example, using simple language, visual aids or any other appropriate means).

(5) Where P is to be notified as to–

(a) the existence or effect of a document other than the appellant's notice or final order; or

(b) the taking place of an event,

the person effecting notification must explain to P–

(i) in the case of a document, what the document is and what effect, if any, it has; or

(ii) in the case of an event, what the event is and its relevance to P.

(6) The person effecting notification must, within 7 days of notifying P, file a certificate of notification (form N165) which certifies–

(a) the date on which P was notified; and

(b) that P was notified in accordance with this paragraph.

(7) Where the person effecting notification has not notified P in accordance with this paragraph, a certificate of non-notification (form N165) must be filed with the Court of Appeal stating the reason why notification has not been effected.

(8) Where the person effecting notification must file a certificate of non-notification with the Court of Appeal, the certificate must be filed within the following time limits–

(a) where P is to be notified in accordance with sub-paragraph (2)(a) (appellant's notice), within 21 days of the appellant's notice being filed with the Court of Appeal;

(b) where P is to be notified in accordance with sub-paragraph (2)(b) (final order), within 21 days of the final order being made by the Court of Appeal; or

(c) where P is to be notified of such other events and documents as may be directed by the Court of Appeal, within such time as the Court of Appeal directs.

(9) The appellant or such other person as the Court of Appeal may direct may apply to the Court of Appeal seeking an order–

(a) dispensing with the requirement to comply with the provisions of this paragraph; or

(b) requiring some other person to comply with the provisions of this paragraph.

(10) An application made under sub-paragraph (9) may be made in the appellant's notice or by Part 23 application notice.

(Paragraphs 6.1 to 6.3 of Practice Direction 52A contain provisions about the dismissal of applications or appeals by consent. Paragraph 6.5 of Practice Direction 52A contains provisions about allowing unopposed appeals or applications involving a child or protected party.)

Appeal from Employment Appeal Tribunal

11.1

(1) This paragraph applies to an appeal to the Court of Appeal from the Employment Appeal Tribunal (EAT) under section 37 of the Employment Tribunals Act 1996.

(2) If an application for permission to appeal to the Court of Appeal is refused by the EAT or is not made, then such an application must be made to the Court of Appeal within 21 days of the date of the sealed order of the EAT.

(3) An application for extension of time for filing an appellant's notice may be entertained by the EAT but such applications should normally be made to the Court of Appeal.

Immigration and Asylum Appeals

12.1 The provisions of paragraph 28 of Practice Direction 52C (bundle of documents in immigration appeals and asylum appeals) apply to appeals from the Upper Tribunal Immigration and Asylum Chamber.

Appeal from Patents Court on appeal from Comptroller

13.1 Where the appeal is from a decision of the Patents Court which was itself made on an appeal from a decision of the Comptroller-General of Patents,

Designs and Trade Marks, the appellant must serve the appellant's notice on the Comptroller in addition to the persons to be served under rule 52.12(3) and in accordance with that rule.

Appeal against order for revocation of patent

14.1

(1) This paragraph applies where an appeal lies to the Court of Appeal from an order for the revocation of a patent.

(2) The appellant must serve the appellant's notice on the Comptroller-General of Patents, Designs and Trade Marks (the 'Comptroller') in addition to the persons to be served under rule 52.12(3) and in accordance with that rule.

(3) Where, before the appeal hearing, the respondent decides not to oppose the appeal or not to attend the appeal hearing, the respondent must immediately serve notice of that decision on–

(a) the Comptroller; and

(b) the appellant.

(4) Where the respondent serves a notice in accordance with sub-paragraph (3), copies of the following documents must also be served on the Comptroller with that notice–

(a) the petition;

(b) any statements of claim;

(c) any written evidence filed in the claim.

(5) Within 14 days after receiving the notice in accordance with sub-paragraph (3), the Comptroller must serve on the appellant a notice stating an intention to attend the appeal hearing or otherwise.

(6) The Comptroller may attend the appeal hearing and oppose the appeal–

(a) in any case where notice has been given under paragraph (5) of the intention to attend; and

(b) in any other case (including, in particular, a case where the respondent withdraws his opposition to the appeal during the hearing) if the Court of Appeal so directs or permits.

Appeal from Proscribed Organisations Appeal Commission

15.1 The appellant's notice must be filed at the Court of Appeal within 14 days after the date when the Proscribed Organisations Appeal Commission–

(a) granted; or

(b) where section 6(2)(b) of the Terrorism Act 2000 applies, refused permission to appeal.

Appeals in relation to serious crime prevention orders

16.1

(1) This paragraph applies to an appeal under section 23(1) of the Serious Crime Act 2007 or section 16 of the Senior Courts Act 1981 in relation to a serious crime prevention order and is made.

(2) The appellant must serve the appellant's notice on any person who made representations in the proceedings by virtue of section 9(1), (2) or (3) of the Serious Crime Act 2007 in addition to the persons to be served under rule 52.12(3) and in accordance with that rule.

Appeal from Special Immigration Appeals Commission

17.1

(1) An application for permission to appeal to the Court of Appeal must first be made to the Special Immigration Appeals Commission pursuant section 7(2) of the Special Immigration Appeals Commission Act 1997 and paragraph 27 of the SIAC (Procedure) Rules 2003 (as amended).

(2) The appellant's notice must be filed at the Court of Appeal within 21 days of the date on which the Special Immigration Appeals Commission's decision granting or refusing permission to appeal to the Court of Appeal is given.

Appeals to the High Court

Reference of question of law by Agricultural Land Tribunal

18.1

(1) A question of law referred to the High Court by an Agricultural Land Tribunal under section 6 of the Agriculture (Miscellaneous Provisions) Act 1954 shall be referred by way of case stated by the Tribunal.

(2) Where the proceedings before the tribunal arose on an application under section 11 of the Agricultural Holdings Act 1986, an–

   (a) application notice for an order under section 6 that the tribunal refers a question of law to the court; and

   (b) appellant's notice by which an appellant seeks the court's determination on a question of law,

   must be served on the authority having power to enforce the statutory requirement specified in the notice in addition to every other party to those proceedings and on the secretary of the tribunal.

(3) Where, in accordance with sub-paragraph (2), a notice is served on the authority mentioned in that paragraph, that authority may attend the appeal hearing and make representations to the court.

Appeals against decisions affecting the registration of architects and health care professionals

19.1

(1) This paragraph applies to an appeal to the High Court under–

   (a) section 22 of the Architects Act 1997;

   (b) section 31 of the Chiropractors Act 1994;

   (c) section 29 or section 44 of the Dentists Act 1984;

   (d) article 38 of the Health Professions Order 2001;

   (e) section 40 of the Medical Act 1983;

   (f) section 82(3) and 83(2) of the Medicines Act 1968;

   (g) section 12 of the Nurses, Midwives and Health Visitors Act 1997;

   (h) article 38 of the Nursing and Midwifery Order 2001;

   (i) section 23 of the Opticians Act 1989;

   (j) section 31 of the Osteopaths Act 1993;

   (k) section 10 of the Pharmacy Act 1954;

   (l) article 58 of the Pharmacy Order 2010.

(2) Every appeal to which this paragraph applies must be supported by written evidence and, if the court so orders, oral evidence and will be by way of re-hearing.

(3) The appellant must file the appellant's notice within 28 days after the decision that the appellant wishes to appeal.

(4) In the case of an appeal under an enactment specified in column 1 of the following table, the persons to be made respondents are the persons specified in relation to that enactment in column 2 of the table and the person to be served with the appellant's notice is the Registrar of the relevant Council.

1	2
Enactment	Respondent
Architects Act 1997, s. 22	Architects Act 1997, s. 22 The Architects' Registration Council of the United Kingdom
Chiropractors Act 1994, s. 31	The General Chiropractic Council
Dentists Act 1984, ss. 29 and 44	The General Dental Council
Health Professions Order 2001, art. 38	The Health Professions Council
Medical Act 1983, s. 40	The General Medical Council
Medicines Act 1968, ss. 82(3) and 83(2)	The Pharmaceutical Society of Great Britain

1	2
Enactment	Respondent
Nurses, Midwives and Health Visitors Act 1997, s.12; Nursing and Midwifery Order 2001, art. 38	The Nursing and Midwifery Council
Opticians Act 1989, s.23	The General Optical Council
Osteopaths Act 1993, s. 31	The General Osteopathic Council
Pharmacy Act 1954, s.10	The Royal Pharmaceutical Society of Great Britain
Pharmacy Order 2010, art. 58	The General Pharmaceutical Council

Appeals under regulation 74 of the European Public Limited-Liability Company Regulations 2004

20.1 Omitted

21.1 Omitted.

Appeals affecting industrial and provident societies etc.

22.1

(1) This paragraph applies to all appeals under–

(a) the Friendly Societies Act 1974;

(b) the Friendly Societies Act 1992 and;

(c) the Industrial and Provident Societies Act 1965.

(2) At any stage on an appeal, the court may–

(a) direct that the appellant's notice be served on any person;

(b) direct that notice be given by advertisement or otherwise of–

(i) the bringing of the appeal;

(ii) the nature of the appeal; and

(iii) the time when the appeal will or is likely to be heard; or

(c) give such other directions as it thinks proper to enable any person interested in–

(i) the society, trade union, alleged trade union or industrial assurance company; or

(ii) the subject matter of the appeal,

to appear and be heard at the appeal hearing.

Appeals under section 222 of the Inheritance Tax Act 1984 and regulation 8(3) of the Stamp Duty Reserve Tax Regulations 1986

23.1

(1) This paragraph applies to appeals to the High Court under section 222(3) of the Inheritance Tax Act 1984 (the '1984 Act') and regulation 8(3) of the Stamp Duty Reserve Tax Regulations 1986 (the '1986 Regulations').

(2) The appellant's notice must–

(a) state the date on which the Commissioners for Her Majesty's Revenue and Customs (the 'Board') gave notice to the appellant under section 221 of the 1984 Act or regulation 6 of the 1986 Regulations of the determination that is the subject of the appeal;

(b) state the date on which the appellant gave to the Board notice of appeal under section 222(1) of the 1984 Act or regulation 8(1) of the 1986 Regulations and, if notice was not given within the time permitted, whether Her Majesty's Revenue and Customs (HMRC) have given their consent or the tribunal has given permission for notice to be given after the time permitted, and where applicable, the date of such consent or permission; and

(c) either state that the appellant and the Board have agreed that the appeal may be to the High Court or contain an application for permission to appeal to the High Court.

(3) The appellant must file the following documents with the appellant's notice–

(a) 2 copies of the notice referred to in sub-paragraph 2(a);

(b) 2 copies of the notice of appeal (under section 222(1) of the 1984 Act or regulation 8(1) of the 1986 Regulations) referred to in paragraph 2(b); and

(c) where the appellant's notice contains an application for permission to appeal, written evidence setting out the grounds on which it is alleged that the matters to be decided on the appeal are likely to be substantially confined to questions of law.

(4) The appellant must–

(a) file the appellant's notice at the court; and

(b) serve the appellant's notice on the Board,

within 30 days of the date on which the appellant gave to the Board notice of appeal under section 222(1) of the 1984 Act or regulation 8(1) of the 1986 Regulations or, if HMRC have given consent or the tribunal has given permission for notice to be given after the time permitted, within 30 days of the date on which such consent or permission was given.

(5) The court will set a date for the hearing of not less than 40 days from the date that the appellant's notice was filed.

(6) Where the appellant's notice contains an application for permission to appeal–

(a) a copy of the written evidence filed in accordance with sub-paragraph (3)(c) must be served on the Board with the appellant's notice; and

(b) the Board–

(i) may file written evidence; and

(ii) if it does so, must serve a copy of that evidence on the appellant, within 30 days after service of the written evidence under sub-paragraph (6)(a).

(7) The appellant may not rely on any grounds of appeal not specified in the notice referred to in sub-paragraph (2)(b) on the hearing of the appeal without the permission of the court.

Appeal against a decision of the adjudicator under section 111 of the Land Registration Act 2002

24.1

(1) A person who is aggrieved by a decision of the adjudicator and who wishes to appeal that decision must obtain permission to appeal.

(2) The appellant must serve on the adjudicator a copy of the appeal court's decision on a request for permission to appeal as soon as reasonably practicable and in any event within 14 days of receipt by the appellant of the decision on permission.

(3) The appellant must serve on the adjudicator and the Chief Land Registrar a copy of any order by the appeal court to stay a decision of the adjudicator pending the outcome of the appeal as soon as reasonably practicable and in any event within 14 days of receipt by the appellant of the appeal court's order to stay.

(4) The appellant must serve on the adjudicator and the Chief Land Registrar a copy of the appeal court's decision on the appeal as soon as reasonably practicable and in any event within 14 days of receipt by the appellant of the appeal court's decision.

Appeals under the Merchant Shipping Act 1995

25.1

(1) his paragraph applies to appeals under the Merchant Shipping Act 1995 and for this purpose a re-hearing and an application under section 61 of the Merchant Shipping Act 1995 are treated as appeals.

(2) The appellant must file any report to the Secretary of State containing the decision from which the appeal is brought with the appellant's notice.

(3) Where a re-hearing by the High Court is ordered under sections 64 or 269 of the Merchant Shipping Act 1995, the Secretary of State must give reasonable notice to the parties whom he considers to be affected by the re-hearing.

Appeals under s 289(6) of the Town and Country Planning Act 1990 and s 65(5) of the Planning (Listed Buildings and Conservation Areas) Act 1990 26.1

26.1

(1) An application for permission to appeal to the High Court under section 289 of the Town and Country Planning Act 1990 ('the TCP Act') or section 65 of the Planning (Listed Buildings and Conservation Areas) Act 1990 ('the PLBCA Act') must be made within 28 days after notice of the decision is given to the applicant.

(2) The application–

(a) must be in writing and must set out the reasons why permission should be granted; and

(b) if the time for applying has expired, must include an application to extend the time for applying, and must set out the reasons why the application was not made within that time.

(3) The applicant must, before filing the application, serve a copy of it on the persons referred to in sub-paragraph (12) with the draft appellant's notice and a copy of the witness statement or affidavit to be filed with the application.

(4) The applicant must file the application in the Administrative Court Office with–

(a) a copy of the decision being appealed;

(b) a draft appellant's notice;

(c) a witness statement or affidavit verifying any facts relied on; and

(d) a witness statement or affidavit giving the name and address of, and the place and date of service on, each person who has been served with the application. If any person who ought to be served has not been served, the witness statement or affidavit must state that fact and the reason why the person was not served.

(5) An application will be heard–

(a) by a single judge; and

(b) unless the court otherwise orders, not less than 21 days after it was filed at the Administrative Court Office.

(6) Practice direction 54D applies to applications and appeals under this paragraph.

(7) Any person served with the application is entitled to appear and be heard.

(8) Any respondent who intends to use a witness statement or affidavit at the hearing–

(a) must file it in the Administrative Court Office; and

(b) must serve a copy on the applicant as soon as is practicable and in any event, unless the court otherwise allows, at least 2 days before the hearing.

(9) The court may allow the applicant to use a further witness statement or affidavit.

(10) Where on the hearing of an application the court is of the opinion that a person who ought to have been served has not been served, the court may adjourn the hearing, on such terms as it directs, in order that the application may be served on that person.

(11) Where the court grants permission–

(a) it may impose terms as to costs and as to giving security;

(b) it may give directions; and

(c) the relevant appellant's notice must be served and filed within 7 days of the grant.

(12) The persons to be served with the appellant's notice are–

(a) the Secretary of State;

(b) the local planning authority who served the notice or gave the decision, as the case may be, or, where the appeal is brought by that authority, the appellant or applicant in the proceedings in which the decision appealed against was given;

(c) in the case of an appeal brought by virtue of section 289(1) of the TCP Act or section 65(1) of the PLBCA Act, any other person having an interest in the land to which the notice relates; and

(d) in the case of an appeal brought by virtue of section 289(2) of the TCP Act, any other person on whom the notice to which those proceedings related was served.

(13) The appeal will be heard and determined by a single judge unless the court directs that the matter be heard and determined by a Divisional Court.

(14) The court may remit the matter to the Secretary of State to the extent necessary to enable the Secretary of State to provide the court with such further information in connection with the matter as the court may direct.

(15) Where the court is of the opinion that the decision appealed against was erroneous in point of law, it will not set aside or vary that decision but will remit the matter to the Secretary of State for re-hearing and determination in accordance with the opinion of the court.

(16) The court may give directions as to the exercise, until an appeal brought by virtue of section 289(1) of the TCP Act is finally concluded and any re-hearing and determination by the Secretary of State has taken place, of the power to serve, and institute proceedings (including criminal proceedings) concerning–

(a) a stop notice under section 183 of that Act; and

(b) a breach of condition notice under section 187A of that Act.

(17) An appeal brought by virtue of sections 289(1) or (2) of the TCP Act or section 65(1) of the PLBCA Act will be treated as if it is a review under statute for the purposes of rules 45.41 to 45.44 and may therefore be an Aarhus Convention claim for the purposes of those rules.

Appeals from decisions of the Law Society or the Solicitors Disciplinary Tribunal to the High Court

27.1

(1) This paragraph applies to appeals from the Law Society or the Solicitors Disciplinary Tribunal ('the Tribunal') to the High Court under the Solicitors Act 1974, Administration of Justice Act 1985, the Courts and Legal Services Act 1990, the European Communities (Lawyer's Practice) Regulations 2000 or the European Communities (Recognition of Professional Qualifications) Regulations 2015.

(2) The appellant must file the appellant's notice in the Administrative Court.

(3) Unless the court otherwise orders the appellant must serve the appellant's notice on–

(a) every party to the proceedings before the Tribunal; and

(b) the Law Society.

Appeals from decisions of the Bar Standards Board or Disciplinary Tribunals to the High Court

27.1A

(1) This paragraph applies to appeals to the High Court under section 24 of the Crime and Courts Act 2013—

(a) from decisions of the Bar Standards Board on review under the Bar Qualification Rules; or

(b) from decisions of Disciplinary Tribunals of the Council of the Inns of Court.

(2) The appellant must file the appellant's notice in the Administrative Court.

(3) Unless the court otherwise orders, the appellant must serve the appellant's notice on—

 (a) every party to the proceedings before the Bar Standards Board or the Disciplinary Tribunal as appropriate; and

 (b) the Council of the Inns of Court in the case of appeals from decisions of the Disciplinary Tribunal.

Appeals to the High Court – Wales only

Welsh statutory appeals

Introduction

27A.1

(1) This paragraph and paragraphs 27A.2 to 27A.7 apply to certain appeals to the High Court under enactments relating to Wales only ('Welsh statutory appeals').

(2) For these purposes, Welsh statutory appeals are appeals under the following enactments–

 (a) section 79 of the Local Government Act 2000;

 (b) section 32(1) of the Education (Wales) Act 2014; and

 (c) section 59 of the Welsh Language (Wales) Measure 2011.

Service of documents in a Welsh statutory appeal to be by parties

27A.2 The Administrative Court will not serve documents in a Welsh statutory appeal, and service must be effected by the parties as provided in the following paragraphs.

Appellant's notice in a Welsh statutory appeal

27A.3

(1) The appellant must file the appellant's notice in the Administrative Court Office of the High Court at the District Registry in Cardiff.

(2) If the appellant's notice is filed at an Administrative Court Office other than in Cardiff the proceedings will be transferred to Cardiff.

(3) The appellant must file the appellant's notice–

 (a) within the time specified in the relevant statutory provision listed in paragraph 27A.1; or

 (b) if the relevant statutory provision specifies no time, within 28 days of the date of the decision the appellant wishes to appeal.

(4) The appellant must file with the appellant's notice–

(a) a statement of facts relied on and grounds for bringing the appeal;

(b) a copy of the decision the appellant wishes to appeal;

(c) any written evidence in support of the appeal.

(5) The appellant must–

(a) within 7 days of the date on which the appeal was filed, serve a sealed copy of the appellant's notice and the documents in sub-paragraph (4) on–

(i) the authority or tribunal which made the decision the appellant wishes to appeal; and

(ii) the respondent to the appeal, and

(b) file a certificate of service confirming the date of service under subparagraph (a).

Respondent's notice in a Welsh statutory appeal

27A.4 If the respondent intends to contest the appeal the respondent must, within 21 days of service under paragraph 27A.3(5)(a), file–

(a) a respondent's notice;

(b) any written evidence in contesting the appeal.

Time of permission hearing in a Welsh statutory appeal

27A.5 Where the relevant statutory provision requires the appellant to obtain the permission of the Court to appeal, a permission hearing will be listed no earlier than 7 days after the expiry of the time limit in paragraph 27A.4.

Listing of a Welsh statutory appeal

27A.6 Unless the Court orders otherwise, the appeal will not be heard earlier than 28 days after the later of–

(a) the expiry of the time limit in paragraph 27A.4; or

(b) if applicable, the date on which permission to appeal is granted.

Further documentation for hearing of a Welsh statutory appeal

27A.7

(1) Sub-paragraphs (2) to (4) apply only where permission to appeal has been granted or where permission is not required.

(2) The appellant must, not less than 21 days before the date of the hearing of the appeal, file–

(a) a paginated and indexed bundle of the appellant's and respondent's notices and the documents filed with them; and

(b) a skeleton argument.

(3) The respondent and any other party wishing to make representations at the hearing of the appeal must file a skeleton argument not less than 14 days before the date of the hearing of the appeal.

(4) The appellant must file a paginated and indexed bundle of all statutory materials and case law relied upon by the appellant and the respondent not less than 7 days before the hearing of the appeal.

Appeals to the County Court

Appeals under sections 204 and 204A of the Housing Act 1996

28.1

(1) An appellant should include appeals under section 204 and section 204A of the Housing Act 1996 in one appellant's notice.

(2) If it is not possible to do so (for example because an urgent application under section 204A is required) the appeals may be included in separate appellant's notices.

(3) An appeal under section 204A may include an application for an order under section 204A(4)(a) requiring the authority to secure that accommodation is available for the applicant's occupation.

(4) If, exceptionally, the court makes an order under section 204A(4)(a) without notice, the appellant's notice must be served on the authority together with the order. Such an order will normally require the authority to secure that accommodation is available until a hearing date when the authority can make representations as to whether the order under section 204A(4)(a) should be continued.

(5) Unless the court orders otherwise–

(a) the appellant shall file and serve its proposed case management directions for the appeal together with the appellant's notice;

(b) the respondent shall within 14 days thereafter either agree those directions or file and serve alternative proposed directions;

(c) within 14 days after service of the appellant's notice the respondent must disclose any documents relevant to the decision under appeal, in so far as not previously disclosed;

(d) within 14 days after receipt of any documents disclosed under sub-paragraph (c) the appellant may make any amendments to its grounds of appeal which arise out of those documents.

Appeal under Part II of the Immigration and Asylum Act 1999 (carriers' liability)

29.1

(1) A person appealing to the County Court under section 35A or section 40B of the Immigration and Asylum Act 1999 ('the Act') against a decision by the Secretary of State to impose a penalty under section 32 or a charge under section 40 of the Act must, subject to sub-paragraph (2), file the appellant's notice within 28 days after receiving the penalty notice or charge notice.

(2) Where the appellant has given notice of objection to the Secretary of State under section 35(4) or section 40A(3) of the Act within the time prescribed for doing so, the appellant must file the appellant's notice within 28 days after receiving notice of the Secretary of State's decision in response to the notice of objection.

(3) Sections 35A and 40B of the Act provide that any appeal under those sections shall be a re-hearing of the Secretary of State's decision to impose a penalty or charge, and therefore rule 52.21(1) does not apply.

Local Government (Miscellaneous Provisions) Act 1976

30.1 Where one of the grounds upon which an appeal against a notice under sections 21, 23 or 35 of the Local Government (Miscellaneous Provisions) Act 1976 is brought is that–

(a) it would have been fairer to serve the notice on another person; or

(b) that it would be reasonable for the whole or part of the expenses to which the appeal relates to be paid by some other person,

that person must be made a respondent to the appeal, unless the court, on application of the appellant made without notice, otherwise directs.

Representation of the People Act 1983, National Assembly for Wales (Representation of the People) Order 2007 and Recall of MPs Act 2015 – appeals against decisions of registration officers

31.1

(1) This paragraph applies in relation to an appeal against a decision of a registration officer, being a decision referred to in–

(a) section 56(1) of the Representation of the People Act 1983 ('the Act');

(b) article 5(1) of the National Assembly for Wales (Representation of the People) Order 2007 ('the 2007 Order'); or

(c) regulation 74(1) of the Recall of MPs Act 2015 (Recall Petition) Regulations 2016 ('the 2016 Regulations').

(2) Where a person ('the appellant') has given notice of such an appeal in accordance with the relevant requirements of–

(a) section 56, and the regulations made under section 53 ('the 2001 Regulations') of the Act;

(b) article 5 of, and paragraph 9 of Schedule 1 to, the 2007 Order; or

(c) regulations 74 and 77 of the 2016 Regulations,

the registration officer must, within 7 days after receiving the notice, forward by post to the County Court–

(i) the notice; and

(ii) the statement required by the 2001 Regulations, by paragraph 9 of Schedule 1 to the 2007 Order or by regulation 77 of the 2016 Regulations as the case may be.

(3) The respondents to the appeal will be–

(a) the registration officer; and

(b) if the decision of the registration officer was given in favour of any other person than the appellant, that other person.

(4) On the hearing of the appeal–

(a) the statement forwarded to the court by the registration officer, and any document containing information submitted to the court by the registration officer pursuant to the 2001 Regulations, 2007 Order and 2016 Regulations, are admissible as evidence of the facts stated in them; and

(b) the court–

(i) may draw any inference of fact that the registration officer might have drawn; and

(ii) may give any decision and make any order that the registration officer ought to have given or made.

(5) A respondent to an appeal (other than the registration officer) is not liable for nor entitled to costs, unless he appears before the court in support of the registration officer's decision.

(6) Rule 52.12 (appellant's notice) does not apply to an appeal to which this paragraph applies.

Representation of the People Act 1983 – special provision in relation to anonymous entries in the register

31.2

(1) In this paragraph–

(a) 'anonymous entry' has the meaning given by section 9B(4) of the Representation of the People Act 1983;

(b) 'appeal notice' means the notice required by regulation 32 of the Representation of the People (England and Wales) Regulations 2001.

(2) This paragraph applies to an appeal to the County Court to which paragraph 31.1 (Representation of the People Act 1983 – appeals against decisions of registration officers) applies if a party to the appeal is a person–

(a) whose entry in the register is an anonymous entry; or

(b) who has applied for such an entry.

(3) This paragraph also applies to an appeal to the Court of Appeal from a decision of the County Court in an appeal to which paragraph 31.1 applies.

(4) The appellant may indicate in the appeal notice that an application for an anonymous entry has been applied for, or that the entry in the register is an anonymous entry.

(5) The respondent or any other person who applies to become a party to the proceedings may indicate in a respondent's notice or an application to join the proceedings that the entry in the register is an anonymous entry, or that an application has been made for an anonymous entry.

(6) Where the appellant gives such an indication in the appeal notice, the court will refer the matter to a District Judge for directions about the further conduct of the proceedings, and, in particular, directions about how the matter should be listed in the court list.

(7) Where the court otherwise becomes aware that a party to the appeal is a person referred to in sub-paragraph (2), the court will give notice to the parties that no further step is to be taken until the court has given any necessary directions for the further conduct of the matter.

Representation of the People Act 1983, National Assembly for Wales (Representation of the People) Order 2007 and Recall of MPs Act 2015 – appeals selected as test cases

31.3

(1) Where two or more appeals under–

(a) section 56, and the 2001 Regulations;

(b) article 5 of, and paragraph 9 of Schedule 1 to, the 2007 Order; or

(c) regulations 74 and 77 of the 2016 Regulations,

involve the same point of law, the court may direct that one appeal ('the testcase appeal') is to be heard first as a test case.

(2) The court will send a notice of the direction to each party to all of those appeals.

(3) Where a notice under sub-paragraph (2) is served on any party to an appeal (other than the test-case appeal), that party may (within 7 days after the notice is served on that party) give notice to the court requesting the appeal to be heard and–

(a) the court will hear that appeal after the test-case appeal is disposed of;

(b) the court will give the parties to that appeal notice of the day on which it will be heard; and

(c) the party who gave the notice is not entitled to receive any costs of the separate hearing of that appeal unless the judge otherwise orders.

(4) Where no notice is given under sub-paragraph (3) within the period limited by that paragraph–

(a) the decision on the test-case appeal binds the parties to each of the other appeals;

(b) without further hearing, the court will make, in each other appeal, an order similar to the order in the test-case appeal; and

(c) the party to each other appeal who is in the same interest as the unsuccessful party to the selected appeal is liable for the costs of the test-case appeal in the same manner and to the same extent as the unsuccessful party to that appeal and an order directing the party to pay such costs may be made and enforced accordingly.

(5) Sub-paragraph (4)(a) does not affect the right to appeal to the Court of Appeal of any party to an appeal other than the test-case appeal.

Appeals under section 11 of the UK Borders Act 2007

32.1

(1) A person appealing to the County Court under section 11 of the UK Borders Act 2007 ('the Act') against a decision by the Secretary of State to impose a penalty under section 9(1) of the Act, must, subject to sub-paragraph (2), file the appellant's notice within 28 days after receiving the penalty notice.

(2) Where the appellant has given notice of objection to the Secretary of State under section 10 of the Act within the time prescribed for doing so, the appellant's notice must be filed within 28 days after receiving notice of the Secretary of State's decision in response to the notice of objection.

PRACTICE DIRECTION 54A – JUDICIAL REVIEW

This Practice Direction supplements Part 54

Section I
General provisions relating to judicial review

1.1 In addition to Part 54 and this practice direction attention is drawn to:

- section 31 of the Senior Courts Act 1981; and
- the Human Rights Act 1998

The Court

2.1 Part 54 claims for judicial review are dealt with in the Administrative Court.

(Practice Direction 54D) contains provisions about where a claim for judicial review may be started, administered and heard.)

2.2 Omitted

2.3 Omitted

2.4 Omitted

3.1 Omitted

3.2 Omitted

Rule 54.5 – Time limit for filing claim form

4.1 Where the claim is for a quashing order in respect of a judgment, order or conviction, the date when the grounds to make the claim first arose, for the purposes of rule 54.5(1)(b), is the date of that judgment, order or conviction.

Rule 54.6 – Claim form

Interested parties

5.1 Where the claim for judicial review relates to proceedings in a court or tribunal, any other parties to those proceedings must be named in the claim form as interested parties under rule 54.6(1)(a) (and therefore served with the claim form under rule 54.7(b)).

5.2 For example, in a claim by a defendant in a criminal case in the Magistrates or Crown Court for judicial review of a decision in that case, the prosecution must always be named as an interested party.

Human rights

5.3 Where the claimant is seeking to raise any issue under the Human Rights Act 1998, or seeks a remedy available under that Act, the claim form must include the information required by paragraph 15 of Practice Direction 16.

Devolution issues

5.4 Where the claimant intends to raise a devolution issue, the claim form must:

(1) specify that the applicant wishes to raise a devolution issue and identify the relevant provisions of the Government of Wales Act 2006, the Northern Ireland Act 1998 or the Scotland Act 1998; and

(2) contain a summary of the facts, circumstances and points of law on the basis of which it is alleged that a devolution issue arises.

5.5 In this practice direction 'devolution issue' has the same meaning as in paragraph 1, Schedule 9 to the Government of Wales Act 2006, paragraph 1, Schedule 10 to the Northern Ireland Act 1998; and paragraph 1, Schedule 6 to the Scotland Act 1998.

Claim form

5.6 The claim form must include or be accompanied by–

(1) a detailed statement of the claimant's grounds for bringing the claim for judicial review;

(2) a statement of the facts relied on;

(3) any application to extend the time limit for filing the claim form;

(4) any application for directions.

5.7 In addition, the claim form must be accompanied by

(1) any written evidence in support of the claim or application to extend time;

(2) a copy of any order that the claimant seeks to have quashed;

(3) where the claim for judicial review relates to a decision of a court or tribunal, an approved copy of the reasons for reaching that decision;

(4) copies of any documents on which the claimant proposes to rely;

(5) copies of any relevant statutory material; and

(6) a list of essential documents for advance reading by the court (with page references to the passages relied on).

5.8 Where it is not possible to file all the above documents, the claimant must indicate which documents have not been filed and the reasons why they are not currently available.

Bundle of documents

5.9 The claimant must file one copy of a paginated and indexed bundle containing all the documents referred to in paragraphs 5.6 and 5.7 unless the case is to be heard before a Divisional Court. For Divisional Court cases the number of bundles required will be one set for each judge hearing the case.

5.10 Attention is drawn to rules 8.5(1) and 8.5(7).

Rule 54.7 – Service of claim form

6.1 Except as required by rules 54.11 or 54.12(2), the Administrative Court will not serve documents and service must be effected by the parties.

6.2 Where the defendant or interested party to the claim for judicial review is–

(a) the Immigration and Asylum Chamber of the First-tier Tribunal, the address for service of the claim form is Home Office, Status Park 2, 4 Nobel Drive, Harlington, Hayes, Middlesex UB3 5EY;

(b) the Crown, service of the claim form must be effected on the solicitor acting for the relevant government department as if the proceedings were civil proceedings as defined in the Crown Proceedings Act 1947.

(Practice Direction 66 gives the list published under section 17 of the Crown Proceedings Act 1947 of the solicitors acting in civil proceedings (as defined in that Act) for the different government departments on whom service is to be effected, and of their addresses.)

(Part 6 contains provisions about the service of claim forms.)

Rule 54.8 – Acknowledgment of service

7.1 Attention is drawn to rule 8.3(2) and the relevant practice direction and to rule 10.5.

Rule 54.10 – Permission given

Directions

8.1 Case management directions under rule 54.10(1) may include directions about serving the claim form and any evidence on other persons.

8.2 Where a claim is made under the Human Rights Act 1998, a direction may be made for giving notice to the Crown or joining the Crown as a party. Attention is drawn to rule 19.4A and paragraph 6 of Practice Direction 19A.

8.3 Omitted

Permission without a hearing

8.4 The court will generally, in the first instance, consider the question of permission without a hearing.

Permission hearing

8.5 Neither the defendant nor any other interested party need attend a hearing on the question of permission unless the court directs otherwise.

8.6 Where the defendant or any party does attend a hearing, the court will not generally make an order for costs against the claimant.

Rule 54.11 – Service of order giving or refusing permission

9.1 An order refusing permission or giving it subject to conditions or on certain grounds only must set out or be accompanied by the court's reasons for coming to that decision.

Rule 54.14 – Response

10.1 Where the party filing the detailed grounds intends to rely on documents not already filed, he must file a paginated bundle of those documents when he files the detailed grounds.

Rule 54.15 – Where claimant seeks to rely on additional grounds

11.1 Where the claimant intends to apply to rely on additional grounds at the hearing of the claim for judicial review, he must give notice to the court and to any other person served with the claim form no later than 7 clear days before the hearing (or the warned date where appropriate).

Rule 54.16 – Evidence

12.1 Disclosure is not required unless the court orders otherwise.

Rule 54.17 – Court's powers to hear any person

13.1 Where all the parties consent, the court may deal with an application under rule 54.17 without a hearing.

13.2 Where the court gives permission for a person to file evidence or make representations at the hearing of the claim for judicial review, it may do so on conditions and may give case management directions.

13.3 An application for permission should be made by letter to the Administrative Court office, identifying the claim, explaining who the applicant is and indicating why and in what form the applicant wants to participate in the hearing.

13.4 If the applicant is seeking a prospective order as to costs, the letter should say what kind of order and on what grounds.

13.5 Applications to intervene must be made at the earliest reasonable opportunity, since it will usually be essential not to delay the hearing.

Rule 54.20 – Transfer

14.1 Attention is drawn to rule 30.5.

14.2 In deciding whether a claim is suitable for transfer to the Administrative Court, the court will consider whether it raises issues of public law to which Part 54 should apply.

Skeleton arguments

15.1 The claimant must file and serve a skeleton argument not less than 21 working days before the date of the hearing of the judicial review (or the warned date).

15.2 The defendant and any other party wishing to make representations at the hearing of the judicial review must file and serve a skeleton argument not less than 14 working days before the date of the hearing of the judicial review (or the warned date).

15.3 Skeleton arguments must contain:

(1) a time estimate for the complete hearing, including delivery of judgment;

(2) a list of issues;

(3) a list of the legal points to be taken (together with any relevant authorities with page references to the passages relied on);

(4) a chronology of events (with page references to the bundle of documents (see paragraph 16.1);

(5) a list of essential documents for the advance reading of the court (with page references to the passages relied on) (if different from that filed with the claim form) and a time estimate for that reading; and

(6) a list of persons referred to.

Bundle of documents to be filed

16.1 The claimant must file a paginated and indexed bundle of all relevant documents required for the hearing of the judicial review when he files his skeleton argument.

16.2 The bundle must also include those documents required by the defendant and any other party who is to make representations at the hearing.

Agreed final order

17.1 If the parties agree about the final order to be made in a claim for judicial review, the claimant must file at the court a document (with 2 copies) signed by all the parties setting out the terms of the proposed agreed order together with a short statement of the matters relied on as justifying the proposed agreed order and copies of any authorities or statutory provisions relied on.

17.2 The court will consider the documents referred to in paragraph 17.1 and will make the order if satisfied that the order should be made.

17.3 If the court is not satisfied that the order should be made, a hearing date will be set.

17.4 Where the agreement relates to an order for costs only, the parties need only file a document signed by all the parties setting out the terms of the proposed order.

Section II
Applications for permission to apply for judicial review in immigration and asylum cases – challenging removal

18.1

(1) This Section applies where–

(a) a person has been served with a copy of directions for his removal from the United Kingdom by the UK Border Agency of the Home Office and notified that this Section applies; and

(b) that person makes an application for permission to apply for judicial review before his removal takes effect.

(2) This Section does not prevent a person from applying for judicial review after he has been removed.

(3) The requirements contained in this Section of this Practice Direction are additional to those contained elsewhere in the Practice Direction.

18.2

(1) A person who makes an application for permission to apply for judicial review must file a claim form and a copy at court, and the claim form must–

(a) indicate on its face that this Section of the Practice Direction applies; and

(b) be accompanied by–

(i) a copy of the removal directions and the decision to which the application relates; and

(ii) any document served with the removal directions including any document which contains the UK Border Agency's factual summary of the case; and

(c) contain or be accompanied by the detailed statement of the claimant's grounds for bringing the claim for judicial review; or

(d) if the claimant is unable to comply with paragraph (b) or (c), contain or be accompanied by a statement of the reasons why.

(2) The claimant must, immediately upon issue of the claim, send copies of the issued claim form and accompanying documents to the address specified by the UK Border Agency.

(Rule 54.7 also requires the defendant to be served with the claim form within 7 days of the date of issue. Rule 6.10 provides that service on a Government Department must be effected on the solicitor acting for that Department, which in the case of the UK Border Agency is the Treasury Solicitor. The address for the Treasury Solicitor may be found in the Annex to Part 66 of these Rules.)

18.3 Where the claimant has not complied with paragraph 18.2(1)(b) or (c) and has provided reasons why he is unable to comply, and the court has issued the claim form, the Administrative Court–

(a) will refer the matter to a Judge for consideration as soon as practicable; and

(b) will notify the parties that it has done so.

18.4 If, upon a refusal to grant permission to apply for judicial review, the Court indicates that the application is clearly without merit, that indication will be included in the order refusing permission.

Section III
Applications for permission to apply for judicial review of decisions of the Upper Tribunal

19.1 A person who makes an application for permission to apply for judicial review of the decision of the Upper Tribunal refusing permission to appeal must file a claim form which must–

(a) state on its face that the application is made under Rule 54. 7A;

(b) set out succinctly the grounds on which it is argued that the criteria in Rule 54.7A(7) are met; and

(c) be accompanied by the supporting documents required under Rule 54.7A(4).

19.2 If the Upper Tribunal or any interested party wishes there to be a hearing of the substantive application under Rule 54.7A(9), it must make its request in writing (by letter copied to the claimant) for such a hearing no later than 14 days after service of the order granting permission.

PRACTICE DIRECTION 54D – ADMINISTRATIVE COURT (VENUE)

This Practice Direction supplements Part 54

Scope and purpose

1.1 This Practice Direction concerns the place in which a claim before the Administrative Court should be started and administered and the venue at which it will be determined.

1.2 This Practice Direction is intended to facilitate access to justice by enabling cases to be administered and determined in the most appropriate location. To achieve this purpose it provides flexibility in relation to where claims are to be administered and enables claims to be transferred to different venues.

1.3 This Practice Direction is subject to the requirement in rule 7.1A that any claim against Welsh public bodies which challenge the lawfulness of their decisions must be issued and heard in Wales."

Venue – general provisions

2.1 The claim form in proceedings in the Administrative Court may be issued at the Administrative Court Office of the High Court at–

(1) the Royal Courts of Justice in London; or

(2) at the District Registry of the High Court at Birmingham, Cardiff, Leeds, or Manchester unless the claim is one of the excepted classes of claim set out in paragraph 3 of this Practice Direction which may only be started and determined at the Royal Courts of Justice in London.

2.2 Any claim started in Birmingham will normally be determined at a court in the Midland region (geographically covering the area of the Midland Circuit); in Cardiff in Wales; in Leeds in the North-Eastern Region (geographically covering the area of the North Eastern Circuit); in London at the Royal Courts of Justice; and in Manchester, in the North-Western Region (geographically covering the Northern Circuit).

Excepted classes of claim

3.1 The excepted classes of claim referred to in paragraph 2.1(2) are–

(1) proceedings to which Part 76 or Part 79 applies, and for the avoidance of doubt–

  (a) proceedings relating to control orders (within the meaning of Part 76);

  (b) financial restrictions proceedings (within the meaning of Part 79);

  (c) proceedings relating to terrorism or alleged terrorists (where that is a relevant feature of the claim); and

  (d) proceedings in which a special advocate is or is to be instructed;

(2) proceedings to which RSC Order 115 applies;

(3) proceedings under the Proceeds of Crime Act 2002;

(4) appeals to the Administrative Court under the Extradition Act 2003;

(5) proceedings which must be heard by a Divisional Court; and

(6) proceedings relating to the discipline of solicitors.

3.2 If a claim form is issued at an Administrative Court office other than in London and includes one of the excepted classes of claim, the proceedings will be transferred to London.

Urgent applications

4.1 During the hours when the court is open, where an urgent application needs to be made to the Administrative Court outside London, the application must be made to the judge designated to deal with such applications in the relevant District Registry.

4.2 Any urgent application to the Administrative Court during the hours when the court is closed, must be made to the duty out of hours High Court judge by telephoning 020 7947 6000.

Assignment to another venue

5.1 The proceedings may be transferred from the office at which the claim form was issued to another office. Such transfer is a judicial act.

5.2 The general expectation is that proceedings will be administered and determined in the region with which the claimant has the closest connection, subject to the following considerations as applicable–

(1) any reason expressed by any party for preferring a particular venue;

(2) the region in which the defendant, or any relevant office or department of the defendant, is based;

(3) the region in which the claimant's legal representatives are based;

(4) the ease and cost of travel to a hearing;

(5) the availability and suitability of alternative means of attending a hearing (for example, by videolink);

(6) the extent and nature of media interest in the proceedings in any particular locality;

(7) the time within which it is appropriate for the proceedings to be determined;

(8) whether it is desirable to administer or determine the claim in another region in the light of the volume of claims issued at, and the capacity, resources and workload of, the court at which it is issued;

(9) whether the claim raises issues sufficiently similar to those in another outstanding claim to make it desirable that it should be determined together with, or immediately following, that other claim; and

(10) whether the claim raises devolution issues and for that reason whether it should more appropriately be determined in London or Cardiff.

5.3

(1) When an urgent application is made under paragraph 4.1 or 4.2, this will not by itself decide the venue for the further administration or determination of the claim.

(2) The court dealing with the urgent application may direct that the case be assigned to a particular venue.

(3) When an urgent application is made under paragraph 4.2, and the court does not make a direction under sub-paragraph (2), the claim will be assigned in the first place to London but may be reassigned to another venue at a later date.

5.4 The court may on an application by a party or of its own initiative direct that the claim be determined in a region other than that of the venue in which the claim is currently assigned. The considerations in paragraph 5.2 apply.

5.5 Once assigned to a venue, the proceedings will be both administered from that venue and determined by a judge of the Administrative Court at a suitable court within that region, or, if the venue is in London, at the Royal Courts of Justice. The choice of which court (of those within the region which are identified by the Presiding Judge of the circuit suitable for such hearing) will be decided, subject to availability, by the considerations in paragraph 5.2.

5.6 When giving directions under rule 54.10, the court may direct that proceedings be reassigned to another region for hearing (applying the considerations in paragraph 5.2). If no such direction is given, the claim will be heard in the same region as that in which the permission application was determined (whether on paper or at a hearing).

PRACTICE DIRECTION 54E – PLANNING COURT CLAIMS

This Practice Direction supplements Part 54

General

1.1 This Practice Direction applies to Planning Court claims.

1.2 In this Practice Direction 'planning statutory review' means a review under the provisions listed in paragraph 1.1(a) to (e) of PD8C.

How to start a Planning Court claim

2.1 Planning Court claims must be issued or lodged in the Administrative Court Office of the High Court in accordance with Practice Direction 54D.

2.2 The form must be marked the 'Planning Court'.

Categorisation of Planning Court claims

3.1 Planning Court claims may be categorised as 'significant' by the Planning Liaison Judge.

3.2 Significant Planning Court claims include claims which—

(a) relate to commercial, residential, or other developments which have significant economic impact either at a local level or beyond their immediate locality;

(b) raise important points of law;

(c) generate significant public interest; or

(d) by virtue of the volume or nature of technical material, are best dealt with by judges with significant experience of handling such matters.

3.3 A party wishing to make representations in respect of the categorisation of a Planning Court claim must do so in writing, on issuing the claim or lodging an acknowledgment of service as appropriate.

3.4 The target timescales for the hearing of significant (as defined by paragraph 3.2) Planning Court claims, which the parties should prepare to meet, are as follows, subject to the overriding objective of the interests of justice—

(a) applications for permission to apply for judicial review or planning statutory review are to be determined within three weeks of the expiry of the time limit for filing of the acknowledgment of service;

(b) oral renewals of applications for permission to apply for judicial review or planning statutory review are to be heard within one month of receipt of request for renewal;

(c) applications for permission under section 289 of the Town and Country Planning Act 1990 are to be determined within one month of issue;

(d) planning statutory reviews are to be heard within six months of issue; and

(e) judicial reviews are to be heard within ten weeks of the expiry of the period for the submission of detailed grounds by the defendant or any other party as provided in Rule 54.14.

3.5 The Planning Court may make case management directions, including a direction to any party intending to contest the claim to file and serve a summary of his grounds for doing so.

3.6 Notwithstanding the categorisation under paragraph 3.1 of a Planning Court claim as significant or otherwise, the Planning Liaison Judge may direct the expedition of any Planning Court claim if he considers it to necessary to deal with the case justly.

PRE-ACTION PROTOCOL FOR JUDICIAL REVIEW

Introduction

1. This Protocol applies to proceedings **within England and Wales only**. It does not affect the time limit specified by Rule 54.5(1) of the Civil Procedure

Rules (CPR), which requires that any claim form in an application for judicial review must be filed promptly and in any event not later than 3 months after the grounds to make the claim first arose. Nor does it affect the shorter time limits specified by Rules 54.5(5) and (6), which set out that a claim form for certain planning judicial reviews must be filed within 6 weeks and the claim form for certain procurement judicial reviews must be filed within 30 days.[1]

2. This Protocol sets out a code of good practice and contains the steps which parties should generally follow before making a claim for judicial review.

3. The aims of the protocol are to enable parties to prospective claims to—

(a) understand and properly identify the issues in dispute in the proposed claim and share information and relevant documents;

(b) make informed decisions as to whether and how to proceed;

(c) try to settle the dispute without proceedings or reduce the issues in dispute;

(d) avoid unnecessary expense and keep down the costs of resolving the dispute; and

(e) support the efficient management of proceedings where litigation cannot be avoided.

4. Judicial review allows people with a sufficient interest in a decision or action by a public body to ask a judge to review the lawfulness of—

- an enactment; or
- a decision, action or failure to act in relation to the exercise of a public function.[2]

5. Judicial review should only be used where no adequate alternative remedy, such as a right of appeal, is available. Even then, judicial review may not be appropriate in every instance. Claimants are strongly advised to seek appropriate legal advice as soon as possible when considering proceedings. Although the Legal Aid Agency will not normally grant full representation before a letter before claim has been sent and the proposed defendant given a reasonable time to respond, initial funding may be available, for eligible claimants, to cover the work necessary to write this. (See Annex C for more information.)

6. This protocol will not be appropriate in very urgent cases. In this sort of case, a claim should be made immediately. Examples are where directions have been set for the claimant's removal from the UK or where there is an urgent need for an interim order to compel a public body to act where it has unlawfully refused to do so, such as where a local housing authority fails to secure interim accommodation for a homeless claimant. A letter before claim, and a claim itself, will not stop the implementation of a disputed decision, though a proposed defendant may agree to take no action until its response letter has been provided. In other cases, the claimant may need to apply to the court for an urgent interim order. Even in very urgent cases, it is good practice to alert the defendant by telephone and to send by email (or fax) to the defendant the draft Claim Form which the claimant

intends to issue. A claimant is also normally required to notify a defendant when an interim order is being sought.

7. All claimants will need to satisfy themselves whether they should follow the protocol, depending upon the circumstances of the case. Where the use of the protocol is appropriate, the court will normally expect all parties to have complied with it in good time before proceedings are issued and will take into account compliance or non-compliance when giving directions for case management of proceedings or when making orders for costs.[3]

8. The Upper Tribunal Immigration and Asylum Chamber (UTIAC) has jurisdiction in respect of judicial review proceedings in relation to most immigration decisions.[4] The President of UTIAC has issued a Practice Statement to the effect that, in judicial review proceedings in UTIAC, the parties will be expected to follow this protocol, where appropriate, as they would for proceedings in the High Court.

Alternative Dispute Resolution

9. The courts take the view that litigation should be a last resort. The parties should consider whether some form of alternative dispute resolution ('ADR') or complaints procedure would be more suitable than litigation, and if so, endeavour to agree which to adopt. Both the claimant and defendant may be required by the court to provide evidence that alternative means of resolving their dispute were considered. Parties are warned that if the protocol is not followed (including this paragraph) then the court must have regard to such conduct when determining costs. However, parties should also note that a claim for judicial review should comply with the time limits set out in the Introduction above. Exploring ADR may not excuse failure to comply with the time limits. If it is appropriate to issue a claim to ensure compliance with a time limit, but the parties agree there should be a stay of proceedings to explore settlement or narrowing the issues in dispute, a joint application for appropriate directions can be made to the court.

10. It is not practicable in this protocol to address in detail how the parties might decide which method to adopt to resolve their particular dispute. However, summarised below are some of the options for resolving disputes without litigation which may be appropriate, depending on the circumstances—

- Discussion and negotiation.
- Using relevant public authority complaints or review procedures.
- Ombudsmen – the Parliamentary and Health Service and the Local Government Ombudsmen have discretion to deal with complaints relating to maladministration. The British and Irish Ombudsman Association provide information about Ombudsman schemes and other complaint handling bodies and this is available from their website atwww.bioa.org.uk. Parties may wish to note that the Ombudsmen are not able to look into a complaint once court action has been commenced.

- Mediation – a form of facilitated negotiation assisted by an independent neutral party.

11. The Civil Justice Council and Judicial College have endorsed The Jackson ADR Handbook by Susan Blake, Julie Browne and Stuart Sime (2013, Oxford University Press). The Citizens Advice Bureaux website also provides information about ADR: http://www.ad viceguide.org.uk/england/law_e/law_legal_system_e/law_taking_legal_action_e/alternatives_to_court.htm. Information is also available at: http://www.civilmediation.justice.gov.uk/

12. If proceedings are issued, the parties may be required by the court to provide evidence that ADR has been considered. A party's silence in response to an invitation to participate in ADR or refusal to participate in ADR might be considered unreasonable by the court and could lead to the court ordering that party to pay additional court costs.

Requests for information and documents at the pre-action stage

13. Requests for information and documents made at the pre-action stage should be proportionate and should be limited to what is properly necessary for the claimant to understand why the challenged decision has been taken and/or to present the claim in a manner that will properly identify the issues. The defendant should comply with any request which meets these requirements unless there is good reason for it not to do so. Where the court considers that a public body should have provided relevant documents and/or information, particularly where this failure is a breach of a statutory or common law requirement, it may impose costs sanctions.

The letter before claim

14. In good time before making a claim, the claimant should send a letter to the defendant. The purpose of this letter is to identify the issues in dispute and establish whether they can be narrowed or litigation can be avoided.

15. Claimants should normally use the suggested standard format for the letter outlined at Annex A. For Immigration, Nationality and Asylum cases, the Home Office has a standardised form which can be used. It can be found online at:https://www.gov.uk/government/publications/chapter-27-judicial-review-guidance-part-1

16. The letter should contain the date and details of the decision, act or omission being challenged, a clear summary of the facts and the legal basis for the claim. It should also contain the details of any information that the claimant is seeking and an explanation of why this is considered relevant. If the claim is considered to be an Aarhus Convention claim (see Rules 45.41 to 45.44 and Practice Direction 45), the letter should state this clearly and explain the reasons, since specific rules as to costs apply to such claims. If the claim is considered appropriate for

allocation to the Planning Court and/or for classification as "significant" within that court, the letter should state this clearly and explain the reasons.

17. The letter should normally contain the details of any person known to the claimant who is an Interested Party. An Interested Party is any person directly affected by the claim.[5] They should be sent a copy of the letter before claim for information. Claimants are strongly advised to seek appropriate legal advice when considering proceedings which involve an Interested Party and, in particular, before sending the letter before claim to an Interested Party or making a claim.

18. A claim should not normally be made until the proposed reply date given in the letter before the claim has passed, unless the circumstances of the case require more immediate action to be taken. The claimant should send the letter before claim in good time so as to enable a response which can then be taken into account before the time limit for issuing the claim expires, unless there are good reasons why this is not possible.

19. Any claimant intending to ask for a protective costs order (an order that the claimant will not be liable for the costs of the defendant or any other party or to limit such liability) should explain the reasons for making the request, including an explanation of the limit of the financial resources available to the claimant in making the claim.

The letter of response

20. Defendants should normally respond within 14 days using the standard format at Annex B. Failure to do so will be taken into account by the court and sanctions may be imposed unless there are good reasons.[6] Where the claimant is a litigant in person, the defendant should enclose a copy of this Protocol with its letter.

21. Where it is not possible to reply within the proposed time limit, the defendant should send an interim reply and propose a reasonable extension, giving a date by which the defendant expects to respond substantively. Where an extension is sought, reasons should be given and, where required, additional information requested. This will not affect the time limit for making a claim for judicial review[7] nor will it bind the claimant where he or she considers this to be unreasonable. However, where the court considers that a subsequent claim is made prematurely it may impose sanctions.

22. If the claim is being conceded in full, the reply should say so in clear and unambiguous terms.

23. If the claim is being conceded in part or not being conceded at all, the reply should say so in clear and unambiguous terms, and—

(a) where appropriate, contain a new decision, clearly identifying what aspects of the claim are being conceded and what are not, or, give a clear timescale within which the new decision will be issued;

(b) provide a fuller explanation for the decision, if considered appropriate to do so;

(c) address any points of dispute, or explain why they cannot be addressed;

(d) enclose any relevant documentation requested by the claimant, or explain why the documents are not being enclosed;

(e) where documents cannot be provided within the time scales required, then give a clear timescale for provision. The claimant should avoid making any formal application for the provision of documentation/information during this period unless there are good grounds to show that the timescale proposed is unreasonable;

(f) where appropriate, confirm whether or not they will oppose any application for an interim remedy; and

(g) if the claimant has stated an intention to ask for a protective costs order, the defendant's response to this should be explained.

If the letter before claim has stated that the claim is an Aarhus Convention claim but the defendant does not accept this, the reply should state this clearly and explain the reasons. If the letter before claim has stated that the claim is suitable for the Planning Court and/or categorisation as "significant" within that court but the defendant does not accept this, the reply should state this clearly and explain the reasons.

24. The response should be sent to all Interested Parties[8] identified by the claimant and contain details of any other persons who the defendant considers are Interested Parties.

Annex A
Letter before claim

Section I
Information required in a letter before claim

1 Proposed claim for judicial review

To (Insert the name and address of the proposed defendant – see details in section 2.)

2 The claimant

(Insert the title, first and last name and the address of the claimant.)

3 The defendant's reference details

(When dealing with large organisations it is important to understand that the information relating to any particular individual's previous dealings with it may not be immediately available, therefore it is important to set out the relevant reference numbers for the matter in dispute and/or the identity of those within the public body who have been handling the particular matter in dispute – see details in section 3.)

4 The details of the claimants' legal advisers, if any, dealing with this claim

(Set out the name, address and reference details of any legal advisers dealing with the claim.)

5 The details of the matter being challenged

(Set out clearly the matter being challenged, particularly if there has been more than one decision.)

6 The details of any Interested Parties

(Set out the details of any Interested Parties and confirm that they have been sent a copy of this letter.)

7 The issue

(Set out a brief summary of the facts and relevant legal principles, the date and details of the decision, or act or omission being challenged, and why it is contended to be wrong.)

8 The details of the action that the defendant is expected to take

(Set out the details of the remedy sought, including whether a review or any interim remedy are being requested.)

9 ADR proposals

(Set out any proposals the claimant is making to resolve or narrow the dispute by ADR.)

10 The details of any information sought

(Set out the details of any information that is sought which is related to identifiable issues in dispute so as to enable the parties to resolve or reduce those issues. This may include a request for a fuller explanation of the reasons for the decision that is being challenged.)

11 The details of any documents that are considered relevant and necessary

(Set out the details of any documentation or policy in respect of which the disclosure is sought and explain why these are relevant.)

12 The address for reply and service of court documents

(Insert the address for the reply.)

13 Proposed reply date

(The precise time will depend upon the circumstances of the individual case. However, although a shorter or longer time may be appropriate in a particular case, 14 days is a reasonable time to allow in most circumstances.)

Section 2
Address for sending the letter before claim

Public bodies have requested that, for certain types of cases, in order to ensure a prompt response, letters before claim should be sent to specific addresses.

- Where the claim concerns a decision in an Immigration, Asylum or Nationality case (including in relation to an immigration decision taken abroad by an Entry Clearance Officer)— The claim should be sent electronically to the following Home Office email address: UKVIPAP@homeoffice.gsi.gov.uk

Alternatively the claim may be sent by post to the following Home Office postal address:

Litigation Operations Allocation Hub Status Park 2 4 Nobel Drive Harlington Hayes Middlesex UB3 5EY

The Home Office has a standardised form which claimants may find helpful to use for communications with the Home Office in Immigration, Asylum or Nationality cases pursuant to this Protocol, to assist claimants to include all relevant information and to promote speedier review and response by the Home Office. The Home Office form may be filled out in electronic or hard copy format. It can be found online at:https://www.gov.uk/government/publications/chapter-27-judicial-review-guidance-part-1

- Where the claim concerns a decision by the Legal Aid Agency— The address on the decision letter/notification; Legal Director Corporate Legal Team Legal Aid Agency 102 Petty France London SW1H 9AJ
- Where the claim concerns a decision by a local authority— The address on the decision letter/notification; and their legal department[9]
- Where the claim concerns a decision by a department or body for whom the Treasury Solicitor acts and the Treasury Solicitor has already been involved in the case, a copy should also be sent, quoting the Treasury Solicitor's reference, to— The Treasury Solicitor, 102 Petty France, Westminster, London SW1W 9GL
- Where the claim concerns a decision by Her Majesty's Revenue and Customs— the address on the letter notifying the decision; and The General Counsel and Solicitor to HM Revenue and Customs, HM Revenue and Customs, South West Wing, Bush House, Strand, London WC2B 4RD
- In all other circumstances, the letter should be sent to the address on the letter notifying the decision. 9 The relevant address should be available from a range of sources such as the Phone Book; Business and Services Directory, Thomson's Local Directory, CAB, etc.

Section 3.
Specific reference details required

Public bodies have requested that the following information should be provided, if at all possible, in order to ensure prompt response. Where the claim concerns an Immigration, Asylum or Nationality case, dependent upon the nature of the case—

- The Home Office reference number;
- The Port reference number;
- The Asylum and Immigration Tribunal reference number;
- The National Asylum Support Service reference number; or, if these are unavailable:
- The full name, nationality and date of birth of the claimant.

Where the claim concerns a decision by the Legal Aid Agency—

- The certificate reference number.

Annex B
Response to a letter before claim

Information required in a response to a letter before claim

1 The claimant

(Insert the title, first and last names and the address to which any reply should be sent.)

2 From

(Insert the name and address of the defendant.)

3 Reference details

(Set out the relevant reference numbers for the matter in dispute and the identity of those within the public body who have been handling the issue.)

4 The details of the matter being challenged

(Set out details of the matter being challenged, providing a fuller explanation of the decision, where this is considered appropriate.)

5 Response to the proposed claim

(Set out whether the issue in question is conceded in part, or in full, or will be contested. Where an interim reply is being sent and there is a realistic prospect of settlement, details should be included. If the claimant is a litigant in person, a copy of the Pre-Action Protocol should be enclosed with the letter.)

6 Details of any other Interested Parties

(Identify any other parties who you consider have an interest who have not already been sent a letter by the claimant.)

7 ADR proposals

(Set out the defendant's position on any ADR proposals made in the letter before claim and any ADR proposals by the defendant.)

8 Response to requests for information and documents

(Set out the defendant's answer to the requests made in the letter before claim including reasons why any requested information or documents are not being disclosed.)

9 Address for further correspondence and service of court documents

(Set out the address for any future correspondence on this matter)

Annex C
Notes on public funding for legal costs in judicial review

Public funding for legal costs in judicial review is available from legal professionals and advice agencies which have contracts with the Legal Aid Agency. Funding may be provided for—

- Legal Help to provide initial advice and assistance with any legal problem; or
- Legal Representation to allow you to be represented in court if you are taking or defending court proceedings. This is available in two forms—

Investigative Help is limited to funding to investigate the strength of the proposed claim. It includes the issue and conduct of proceedings only so far as is necessary to obtain disclosure of relevant information or to protect the client's position in relation to any urgent hearing or time limit for the issue of proceedings. This includes the work necessary to write a letter before claim to the body potentially under challenge, setting out the grounds of challenge, and giving that body a reasonable opportunity, typically 14 days, in which to respond.

Full Representation is provided to represent you in legal proceedings and includes litigation services, advocacy services, and all such help as is usually given by a person providing representation in proceedings, including steps preliminary or incidental to proceedings, and/or arriving at or giving effect to a compromise to avoid or bring to an end any proceedings. Except in emergency cases, a proper letter before claim must be sent and the other side must be given an opportunity to respond before Full Representation is granted.

Further information on the type(s) of help available and the criteria for receiving that help may be found in the Legal Aid Agency's pages on the Ministry of Justice website at:https://www.justice.gov.uk/legal-aid

A list of contracted firms and Advice Agencies may be found at: http://find-legal-advice.justice.gov.uk"

Footnotes

1 The court has a discretion to extend time. It cannot be taken that compliance with the protocol will of itself be sufficient to excuse delay or justify an extension of time, but it may be a relevant factor. Under rule 54.5(2), judicial review time limits cannot be extended by agreement between the parties. However, a court will take account of a party's agreement 'not to take a time point' so far as concerns delay while they were responding to a letter before claim.

2 Civil Procedure Rules, Rule 54.1(2).

3 Civil Procedure Rules, Practice Directions 44-48.

4 See the Direction made by the Lord Chief Justice dated 21 August 2013 (as amended on 17 October 2014), available in the UTIAC section of the www. justice.gov.uk website. Also, the High Court can order the transfer of judicial review proceedings to the UTIAC.

5 See Civil Procedure Rules, Rule 54.1(2).

6 See Civil Procedure Rules, Practice Direction – Pre-Action Conduct and Protocols, paragraphs 2-3.

7 See Civil Procedure Rules, Rule 54.5(1).

8 See Civil Procedure Rules, Rule 54.1(2)(f).

9 The relevant address should be available from a range of sources such as the Phone Book; Business and Services Directory, Thomson's Local Directory, CAB, etc.

APPENDIX C

Forms

N215PC CERTIFICATE OF SERVICE (PLANNING COURT)

Certificate of service

Name of court	Claim No.
Name of Claimant	
Name of Defendant	

On what day did you serve? ☐☐/☐☐/☐☐☐☐

The date of service is ☐☐/☐☐/☐☐☐☐

What documents did you serve?
Please attach copies of the documents you have not already filed with the court.

On whom did you serve?
(If appropriate include their position e.g. partner, director).

How did you serve the documents?
(please tick the appropriate box)

☐ by first class post or other service which provides for delivery on the next business day

☐ by delivering to or leaving at a permitted place

☐ by personally handing it to or leaving it with (................time left, where document is other than a claim form) *(please specify)*

☐ by other means permitted by the court *(please specify)*

☐ by Document Exchange

☐ by fax machine (................time sent, where document is other than a claim form) *(you may want to enclose a copy of the transmission sheet)*

☐ by other electronic means (................time sent, where document is other than a claim form) *(please specify)*

Give the address where service effected, include fax or DX number, e-mail address or other electronic identification

Being the ☐ claimant's ☐ defendant's ☐ solicitor's ☐ litigation friend

☐ usual residence

☐ last known residence

☐ place of business

☐ principal place of business

☐ last known place of business

☐ last known principal place of business

☐ principal office of the partnership

☐ principal office of the corporation

☐ principal office of the company

☐ place of business of the partnership/company/corporation within the jurisdiction with a connection to claim

☐ other *(please specify)*

I believe that the facts stated in this certificate are true.

Full name

Signed

(Claimant) (Defendant) ('s solicitor) ('s litigation friend)

Position or office held

(If signing on behalf of firm or company)

Date ☐☐/☐☐/☐☐☐☐

N215 Certificate of service (09.11)

Rules relating to the service of documents are contained in Part 6 of the Civil Procedure Rules (www.justice.gov.uk) and you should refer to the rules for information.

Calculation of deemed day of service of a claim
A claim form served within the UK in accordance with Part 6 of the Civil Procedure rules is deemed to be served on the second business day after the claimant has completed the steps required by CPR 7.5(1).

Calculation of the deemed day of service of documents other than the claim form (CPR 6.26)

Method of service	**Deemed day of service**
First class post or other service which provides for delivery on the next business day	The second day after it was posted, left with, delivered to or collected by the relevant service provider provided that day is a business day; or if not, the next business day after that day
Document exchange	The second day after it was left with, delivered to or collected by the relevant service provider provided that day is a business day; or if not, the next business day after that day
Delivering the document to or leaving it at a permitted address	If it is delivered to or left at the permitted address on a business day before 4.30pm, on that day; or in any other case, on the next business day after that day
Fax	If the transmission of the fax is completed on a business day before 4.30pm, on that day; or in any other case, on the next business day after the day on which it was transmitted
Other electronic method	If the email or other electronic transmission is sent on a business day before 4.30pm, on that day; or in any other case, on the next business day after the day on which it was sent
Personal service	If the document is served personally before 4.30pm on a business day, it is served on that day; or in any other case, on the next business day after that day

In this context 'business day' means any day except Saturday, Sunday or a bank holiday; (under the Banking and Financial Dealings Act 1971 in the part of the UK where service is to take place) includes Good Friday and Christmas Day.

N461PC JUDICIAL REVIEW CLAIM FORM

Judicial Review
Claim Form

In the High Court of Justice Administrative Court	
Help with Fees - Ref no. (if applicable)	H W F - ☐☐☐ - ☐☐☐

Notes for guidance are available which explain how to complete the judicial review claim form. Please read them carefully before you complete the form.

For Court use only	
Administrative Court Reference No.	
Date filed	

Seal

Is your claim in respect of refusal of an application for fee remission? ☐Yes ☐No

SECTION 1 Details of the claimant(s) and defendant(s)

Claimant(s) name and address(es)

name

address

Telephone no. **Fax no.**

E-mail address

Claimant's or claimant's legal representatives' address to which documents should be sent.

name

address

Telephone no. **Fax no.**

E-mail address

Claimant's Counsel's details

name

address

Telephone no. **Fax no.**

E-mail address

1st Defendant

name

Defendant's or (where known) Defendant's legal representatives' address to which documents should be sent.

name

address

Telephone no. **Fax no.**

E-mail address

2nd Defendant

name

Defendant's or (where known) Defendant's legal representatives' address to which documents should be sent.

name

address

Telephone no. **Fax no.**

E-mail address

SECTION 2 Details of other interested parties

Include name and address and, if appropriate, details of DX, telephone or fax numbers and e-mail

name

address

Telephone no.

Fax no.

E-mail address

name

address

Telephone no.

Fax no.

E-mail address

SECTION 3 Details of the decision to be judicially reviewed

Decision:

Date of decision:

Name and address of the court, tribunal, person or body who made the decision to be reviewed.

name

address

SECTION 4 Permission to proceed with a claim for judicial review

I am seeking permission to proceed with my claim for Judicial Review.

Is this application being made under the terms of Section 18 Practice Direction 54 (Challenging removal)? ☐ Yes ☐ No

Are you making any other applications? If Yes, complete Section 8. ☐ Yes ☐ No

Is the claimant in receipt of a Civil Legal Aid Certificate? ☐ Yes ☐ No

Are you claiming exceptional urgency, or do you need this application determined within a certain time scale? If Yes, complete Form N463 and file this with your application. ☐ Yes ☐ No

Have you complied with the pre-action protocol? If No, give reasons for non-compliance in the box below. ☐ Yes ☐ No

Have you issued this claim in the region with which you have the closest connection? (Give any additional reasons for wanting it to be dealt with in this region in the box below). If No, give reasons in the box below. ☐ Yes ☐ No

Does the claim include any issues arising from the Human Rights Act 1998?
If Yes, state the articles which you contend have been breached in the box below. ☐ Yes ☐ No

SECTION 5 Detailed statement of grounds

☐ set out below ☐ attached

SECTION 6 Aarhus Convention claim

I contend that this claim is an Aarhus Convention claim ☐ Yes ☐ No

If Yes, indicate in the following box if you do not wish the costs limits under CPR 45.43 to apply.

If you have indicated that the claim is an Aarhus claim set out the grounds below, including (if relevant) reasons why you want to vary the limit on costs recoverable from a party.

SECTION 7 Details of remedy (including any interim remedy) being sought

SECTION 8 Other applications

I wish to make an application for:-

3 of 6

SECTION 9 Statement of facts relied on

Statement of Truth

I believe (The claimant believes) that the facts stated in this claim form are true.

Full name ____________________

Name of claimant's solicitor's firm ____________________

Signed ____________________ Position or office held ____________________

Claimant ('s solicitor) (if signing on behalf of firm or company)

SECTION 10 Supporting documents

If you do not have a document that you intend to use to support your claim, identify it, give the date when you expect it to be available and give reasons why it is not currently available in the box below.

Please tick the papers you are filing with this claim form and any you will be filing later.

☐ Statement of grounds	☐ included	☐ attached
☐ Statement of the facts relied on	☐ included	☐ attached
☐ Application to extend the time limit for filing the claim form	☐ included	☐ attached
☐ Application for directions	☐ included	☐ attached
☐ Any written evidence in support of the claim or application to extend time		
☐ Where the claim for judicial review relates to a decision of a court or tribunal, an approved copy of the reasons for reaching that decision		
☐ Copies of any documents on which the claimant proposes to rely		
☐ A copy of the legal aid or Civil Legal Aid Certificate *(if legally represented)*		
☐ Copies of any relevant statutory material		
☐ A list of essential documents for advance reading by the court *(with page references to the passages relied upon)*		
☐ Where a claim relates to an Aarhus Convention claim, a schedule of the claimant's significant assets, liabilities, income and expenditure.	☐ included	☐ attached

If Section 18 Practice Direction 54 applies, please tick the relevant box(es) below to indicate which papers you are filing with this claim form:

☐ a copy of the removal directions and the decision to which the application relates	☐ included	☐ attached
☐ a copy of the documents served with the removal directions including any documents which contains the Immigration and Nationality Directorate's factual summary of the case	☐ included	☐ attached
☐ a detailed statement of the grounds	☐ included	☐ attached

Reasons why you have not supplied a document and date when you expect it to be available:-

Signed ______________________________________ Claimant ('s Solicitor)______________________________

N462PC JUDICIAL REVIEW ACKNOWLEDGMENT OF SERVICE

N462PC

Judicial Review

Acknowledgment of Service

In the High Court of Justice Planning Court in the Administrative Court	
Claim No.	
Claimant(s) *(including ref.)*	
Defendant(s)	
Interested Parties	

Name and address of person to be served

name

address

SECTION A

Tick the appropriate box

1. I intend to contest all of the claim	☐	complete sections B, C, D and F
2. I intend to contest part of the claim	☐	
3. I do not intend to contest the claim	☐	complete section F
4. The defendant (interested party) is a court or tribunal and **intends** to make a submission.	☐	complete sections B, C and F
5. The defendant (interested party) is a court or tribunal and **does not intend** to make a submission.	☐	complete sections B and F
6. The applicant has indicated that this is a claim to which the Aarhus Convention applies.	☐	complete sections E and F
7. The **Defendant** asks the Court to consider whether the outcome for the claimant would have been **substantially different** if the conduct complained of had not occurred [see s.31(3C) of the Senior Courts Act 1981]	☐	A summary of the grounds for that request must be set out in/accompany this Acknowledgment of Service

Note: If the application seeks to judicially review the decision of a court or tribunal, the court or tribunal need only provide the Administrative Court with as much evidence as it can about the decision to help the Administrative Court perform its judicial function.

SECTION B

Insert the name and address of any person you consider should be added as an interested party.

name	name
address	address
Telephone no. / Fax no.	Telephone no. / Fax no.
E-mail address	E-mail address

SECTION C

Summary of grounds for contesting the claim. If you are contesting only part of the claim, set out which part before you give your grounds for contesting it. If you are a court or tribunal filing a submission, please indicate that this is the case.

SECTION D

Give details of any directions you will be asking the court to make, or tick the box to indicate that a separate application notice is attached.

If you are seeking a direction that this matter be heard at an Administrative Court venue other than that at which this claim was issued, you should complete, lodge and serve on all other parties Form N464PC with this acknowledgment of service.

SECTION E

Response to the claimant's contention that the claim is an Aarhus claim

Do you deny that the claim is an Aarhus Convention claim? ☐ Yes ☐ No

If Yes, please set out your grounds for denial in the box below.

Do you wish to vary the costs limits under CPR 45.43(2)? ☐ Yes ☐ No

If Yes, state the reason why you want to vary the limits on costs recoverable from a party.

3 of 4

SECTION F

*delete as appropriate

*(I believe)(The defendant believes) that the facts stated in this form are true.

*I am duly authorised by the defendant to sign this statement.

(if signing on behalf of firm or company, court or tribunal)

Position or office held

(To be signed by you or by your solicitor or litigation friend)

Signed

Date

Give an address to which notices about this case can be sent to you

name

address

Telephone no.

Fax no.

E-mail address

If you have instructed counsel, please give their name address and contact details below.

name

address

Telephone no.

Fax no.

E-mail address

Completed forms, together with a copy, should be lodged with the Administrative Court Office (court address, over the page), at which this claim was issued within 21 days of service of the claim upon you, and further copies should be served on the Claimant(s), any other Defendant(s) and any interested parties within 7 days of lodgement with the Court.

Administrative Court addresses

- Administrative Court in **London**

  Administrative Court Office, Room C315, Royal Courts of Justice, Strand, London, WC2A 2LL.

- Administrative Court in **Birmingham**

  Administrative Court Office, Birmingham Civil Justice Centre, Priory Courts, 33 Bull Street, Birmingham B4 6DS.

- Administrative Court in **Wales**

  Administrative Court Office, Cardiff Civil Justice Centre, 2 Park Street, Cardiff, CF10 1ET.

- Administrative Court in **Leeds**

  Administrative Court Office, Leeds Combined Court Centre, 1 Oxford Row, Leeds, LS1 3BG.

- Administrative Court in **Manchester**

  Administrative Court Office, Manchester Civil Justice Centre, 1 Bridge Street West, Manchester, M3 3FX.

4 of 4

N463PC JUDICIAL REVIEW APPLICATION FOR URGENT CONSIDERATION

Judicial Review
Application for urgent consideration

In the High Court of Justice Planning Court in the Administrative Court	
Claim No.	
Claimant(s) *(including ref.)*	
Defendant(s)	
Interested Party(ies)	

This form must be completed by the Claimant or the Claimant's advocate if exceptional urgency is being claimed and the application needs to be determined within a certain time scale.

The claimant, or the claimant's solicitors must serve this form on the defendant(s) and any interested parties with the N461PC Judicial review claim form.

To the Defendant(s) and Interested Party(ies)
Representations as to the urgency of the claim may be made by defendants or interested parties to the relevant Administrative Court Office by fax or email:-

For cases proceeding in

London
Fax: 020 7947 6802 **email:** administrativecourtoffice.generaloffice@hmcts.x.gsi.gov.uk

Birmingham
Fax: 0121 250 6730 **email:** administrativecourtoffice.birmingham@hmcts.x.gsi.gov.uk

Cardiff
Fax: 02920 376461 **email:** administrativecourtoffice.cardiff@hmcts.x.gsi.gov.uk

Leeds
Fax: 0113 306 2581 **email:** administrativecourtoffice.leeds@hmcts.x.gsi.gov.uk

Manchester
Fax: 0161 240 5315 **email:** administrativecourtoffice.manchester@hmcts.x.gsi.gov.uk

SECTION 1 Reasons for urgency

SECTION 2 Proposed timetable *(tick the boxes and complete the following statements that apply)*

☐ a) The N461PC application for permission should be considered within ________ hours/days

If consideration is sought within 48 hours, you must complete Section 3 below

☐ b) Abridgement of time is sought for the lodging of acknowledgments of service

☐ c) If permission for judicial review is granted, a substantive hearing is sought by ______________ (date)

N463PC Judicial review Application for urgent consideration (04.14) *1 of 2*

SECTION 3 Justification for request for immediate consideration

If it is decided that your application will be dealt with as an immediate application, we will notify you of the outcome by email as soon as the judge has reached a determination. You will subsequently be sent a hard copy of the judges order in the post. Please provide an email address to which you would like notification sent.

Email address:

Please note: if you do not provide a valid email address, you will only be notified of the outcome by post, which will take at least 2 – 3 days to be processed and delivered.

Date and time when it was first appreciated that an immediate application might be necessary.

Date

Time

Please provide reasons for any delay in making the application.

What efforts have been made to put the defendant and any interested party on notice of the application?

SECTION 4 Interim relief *(state what interim relief is sought and why in the box below)*

A draft order must be attached.

SECTION 5 Service

A copy of this form of application was served on the defendant(s) and interested parties as follows:

Defendant

☐ by fax machine to — time sent

Fax no. — time

☐ by handing it to or leaving it with

name

☐ by e-mail to

e-mail address

Date served

Date

Interested party

☐ by fax machine to — time sent

Fax no. — time

☐ by handing it to or leaving it with

name

☐ by e-mail to

e-mail address

Date served

Date

I confirm that all relevant facts have been disclosed in this application

Name of claimant's advocate

name

Claimant (claimant's advocate)

Signed

N464PC APPLICATION FOR DIRECTIONS AS TO VENUE FOR ADMINISTRATION AND DETERMINATION

Application for directions as to venue for administration and determination

In the High Court of Justice Planning Court in the Administrative Court	
Claim No.	
Claimant(s)/ Appellant(s)	
Defendant(s)/ Respondent(s)	
Interested Party(ies)	

Name and address of party making application

name

address

I/We apply to the court for a direction that this matter be administered and determined at the:

- ☐ Royal Courts of Justice in **London**
- ☐ District Registry of the High Court at **Birmingham**
- ☐ District Registry of the High Court at **Cardiff**
- ☐ District Registry of the High Court at **Leeds**
- ☐ District Registry of the High Court at **Manchester**

for the following reason(s): *(please refer to paragraph 5.2 of PD54D set out overleaf)*

(To be signed by you or by your solicitor or litigation friend) **Signed**

Date

Name

(if signing on behalf of firm or company, court) **Position or office held**

Please send your completed form to the Administrative Court Office which is currently administering this matter, within 21 days of service of the proceedings upon you. You must also serve copies of your completed application on all other parties.

N464PC Application for directions as to venue for administration and determination (04.14)

Practice Direction 54D 5.2

5.2 The general expectation is that proceedings will be administered and determined in the region with which the claimant/appellant has the closest connection, subject to the following considerations as applicable -

1) any reason expressed by any party for preferring a particular venue;
2) the region in which the defendant/respondent or any relevant office or department of the defendant/respondent is based;
3) the region in which the claimant's/appellant's legal representatives are based;
4) the ease and cost of travel to a hearing;
5) the availability and suitability of alternative means of attending a hearing (for example, by videolink);
6) the extent and nature of media interest in the proceedings in any particular locality;
7) the time within which it is appropriate for the proceedings to be determined;
8) whether it is desirable to administer or determine the claim in another region in the light of the volume of claims issued at, and the capacity, resources and workload of, the court at which it is issued;
9) whether the claim raises issues sufficiently similar to those in another outstanding claim to make it desirable that it should be determined together with, or immediately following, that other claim; and
10) whether the claim raises devolution issues and for that reason whether it should more appropriately be determined in London or Cardiff.

N465PC RESPONSE TO APPLICATION AS TO VENUE FOR ADMINISTRATION AND DETERMINATION

Response to application for directions as to venue for administration and determination

You must serve this form **within 7 days** of receiving form *N464PC Application for directions as to venue for administration and determination.*

Name and address of party responding to application

name

address

In the High Court of Justice Planning Court in the Administrative Court	
Claim No.	
Claimant(s)/ Appellant(s)	
Defendant(s)/ Respondent(s)	
Interested Party(ies)	

I/We oppose the application for directions as to the venue for administration and determination, for the following reason(s):-

(To be signed by you or by your solicitor or litigation friend) **Signed**

Date

Name

(if signing on behalf of firm or company, court) **Position or office held**

Please send your completed form to the Administrative Court Office which is currently administering this matter, **within 7 days** of receiving form N464PC Application for directions as to venue from administration and determination. You must also serve copies of your completed form on all other parties.

N465PC Response to application as to venue for administration and determination (04.14)

PC001 REQUEST FOR AN ADJOURNMENT (BIRMINGHAM)

Request for an adjournment

Planning Court at Birmingham
Birmingham Civil Justice Centre
Priory Courts
5th Floor
33 Bull Street
Birmingham B4 6DS
DX 701987 Birmingham 7

All requests must be made no later than 2 working days before the hearing.
A request for an adjournment can be considered only when the views of all parties have been received.
It is the responsibility of the party seeking the adjournment to ensure the views of all parties are included in this form before it is lodged with the court. All parties must sign this form before the court can deal with your request for an adjournment. Where there are more than 3 parties, please use additional forms. Please note that there is a fee payable for any application to adjourn made within 14 days of the hearing date, unless you are entitled to fee remission, in which case you must lodge an Application for a Remission of Fee (Form Ex160) with your application.

Case Title			
Case Ref No:		Date of hearing:	/ /

For completion by the party seeking the adjournment

Are you the ☐ Claimant ☐ Defendant ☐ Interested Party

Reasons for requesting adjourment:

Has a request for adjournment been made previously? ☐ Yes ☐ No

If Yes, please supply details:

Signed:		Print name:		Date:	/ /

For completion by other parties

Are you the ☐ Claimant ☐ Defendant ☐ Interested Party

Do you oppose the adjournment? ☐ Yes ☐ No

If Yes, please give reasons:

Signed:		Print name:		Date:	/ /

For completion by other parties

Are you the ☐ Claimant ☐ Defendant ☐ Interested Party

Do you oppose the adjournment? ☐ Yes ☐ No

If Yes, please give reasons:

Signed:		Print name:		Date:	/ /

Send your completed form and the appropriate fee or form Ex160 to the address above.

PC001 (09.08)

PC001 REQUEST FOR AN ADJOURNMENT (CARDIFF)

Request for an adjournment

Planning Court for Wales
Cardiff Civil Justice Centre
2 Park Street
Cardiff
CF10 1ET

All requests must be made no later than 2 working days before the hearing.
A request for an adjournment can be considered only when the views of all parties have been received.
It is the responsibility of the party seeking the adjournment to ensure the views of all parties are included in this form before it is lodged with the court. All parties must sign this form before the court can deal with your request for an adjournment. Where there are more than 3 parties, please use additional forms. Please note that there is a fee payable for any application to adjourn made within 14 days of the hearing date, unless you are entitled to fee remission, in which case you must lodge an Application for a Remission of Fee (Form Ex160) with your application.

Case Title			
Case Ref No:		Date of hearing:	/ /

For completion by the party seeking the adjournment

Are you the ☐ Claimant ☐ Defendant ☐ Interested Party

Reasons for requesting adjourment:

Has a request for adjournment been made previously? ☐ Yes ☐ No

If Yes, please supply details:

Signed:		Print name:		Date:	/ /

For completion by other parties

Are you the ☐ Claimant ☐ Defendant ☐ Interested Party

Do you oppose the adjournment? ☐ Yes ☐ No

If Yes, please give reasons:

Signed:		Print name:		Date:	/ /

For completion by other parties

Are you the ☐ Claimant ☐ Defendant ☐ Interested Party

Do you oppose the adjournment? ☐ Yes ☐ No

If Yes, please give reasons:

Signed:		Print name:		Date:	/ /

Send your completed form and the appropriate fee or form Ex160 to the address above.

PC001 (09.08)

PC001 REQUEST FOR AN ADJOURNMENT (LEEDS)

Request for an adjournment

Planning Court in Leeds
Leeds Combined Court
1 Oxford Row
Leeds
West Yorkshire
LS1 3BG

All requests must be made no later than 2 working days before the hearing.
A request for an adjournment can be considered only when the views of all parties have been received.
It is the responsibility of the party seeking the adjournment to ensure the views of all parties are included in this form before it is lodged with the court. All parties must sign this form before the court can deal with your request for an adjournment. Where there are more than 3 parties, please use additional forms. Please note that there is a fee payable for any application to adjourn made within 14 days of the hearing date, unless you are entitled to fee remission, in which case you must lodge an Application for a Remission of Fee (Form Ex160) with your application.

Case Title

Case Ref No: Date of hearing: / /

For completion by the party seeking the adjournment
Are you the ☐ Claimant ☐ Defendant ☐ Interested Party
Reasons for requesting adjourment:

Has a request for adjournment been made previously? ☐ Yes ☐ No
If Yes, please supply details:

Signed: Print name: Date: / /

For completion by other parties
Are you the ☐ Claimant ☐ Defendant ☐ Interested Party
Do you oppose the adjournment? ☐ Yes ☐ No
If Yes, please give reasons:

Signed: Print name: Date: / /

For completion by other parties
Are you the ☐ Claimant ☐ Defendant ☐ Interested Party
Do you oppose the adjournment? ☐ Yes ☐ No
If Yes, please give reasons:

Signed: Print name: Date: / /

Send your completed form and the appropriate fee or form Ex160 to the address above.

PC001 (09.08)

PC001 REQUEST FOR AN ADJOURNMENT (LONDON)

Request for an adjournment

Planning Court
Room C324
Royal Courts of Justice
Strand
London WC2A 2LL

All requests must be made no later than 2 working days before the
A request for an adjournment can be considered only when the views of all parties have been received.
It is the responsibility of the party seeking the adjournment to ensure the views of all parties are included in this form before it is lodged with the court. All parties must sign this form before the court can deal with your request for an adjournment. Where there are more than 3 parties, please use additional forms. Please note that there is a fee payable for any application to adjourn made within 14 days of the hearing date, unless you are entitled to fee remission, in which case you must lodge an Application for a Remission of Fee (Form Ex160) with your application.

Case Title

Case Ref No: Date of hearing: / /

For completion by the party seeking the adjournment
Are you the ☐ Claimant ☐ Defendant ☐ Interested Party
Reasons for requesting adjourment:

Has a request for adjournment been made previously? ☐ Yes ☐ No
If Yes, please supply details:

Signed: Print name: Date: / /

For completion by other parties
Are you the ☐ Claimant ☐ Defendant ☐ Interested Party

Do you oppose the adjournment? ☐ Yes ☐ No
If Yes, please give reasons:

Signed: Print name: Date: / /

For completion by other parties
Are you the ☐ Claimant ☐ Defendant ☐ Interested Party

Do you oppose the adjournment? ☐ Yes ☐ No
If Yes, please give reasons:

Signed: Print name: Date: / /

PC001 (09.08)

Send your completed form and the appropriate fee or form Ex160 to the address above.

PC001 REQUEST FOR AN ADJOURNMENT (MANCHESTER)

Request for an adjournment

Planning Court in Manchester
12th Floor
Manchester Civil Justice Centre
1 Bridge Street West
Manchester
M60 9DJ

All requests must be made no later than 2 working days before the hearing.
A request for an adjournment can be considered only when the views of all parties have been received.
It is the responsibility of the party seeking the adjournment to ensure the views of all parties are included in this form before it is lodged with the court. All parties must sign this form before the court can deal with your request for an adjournment. Where there are more than 3 parties, please use additional forms. Please note that there is a fee payable for any application to adjourn made within 14 days of the hearing date, unless you are entitled to fee remission, in which case you must lodge an Application for a Remission of Fee (Form Ex160) with your application.

Case Title			
Case Ref No:		Date of hearing:	/ /

For completion by the party seeking the adjournment

Are you the ☐ Claimant ☐ Defendant ☐ Interested Party

Reasons for requesting adjourment:

Has a request for adjournment been made previously? ☐ Yes ☐ No

If Yes, please supply details:

Signed:		Print name:		Date:	/ /

For completion by other parties

Are you the ☐ Claimant ☐ Defendant ☐ Interested Party

Do you oppose the adjournment? ☐ Yes ☐ No

If Yes, please give reasons:

Signed:		Print name:		Date:	/ /

For completion by other parties

Are you the ☐ Claimant ☐ Defendant ☐ Interested Party

Do you oppose the adjournment? ☐ Yes ☐ No

If Yes, please give reasons:

Signed:		Print name:		Date:	/ /

Send your completed form and the appropriate fee or form Ex160 to the address above.

PC001 (09.08)

PCPF244 APPLICATION NOTICE (PART 23)

Application Notice (Part 23)
IN THE HIGH COURT OF JUSTICE
QUEENS BENCH DIVISION
THE PLANNING COURT

Claim No:

Claimant:

Defendant:

APPLICATION NOTICE

Part A - I/We (1) the [Solicitor on behalf of the](2)
Apply for an order, a draft of which is attached, for(3)
I/We wish to have the application dealt with [at a hearing/without a hearing*] before a [Judge/Master] with a time estimate of hour(s) minutes agreed/not agreed.
*delete where applicable

This application will be heard before the Hon. Mr Justice / Master

on day the of at am/pm in Court/Room**
(**enter venue for hearing)

Part B - I/We wish to rely on [*] the attached Witness Statement/Affidavit
[*] my statement of case
[*] the evidence in Part C on the reverse of this application.
*tick as appropriate

Dated ------------------------

Signed ------------------------------ (name)--

position or office held --
*(Claimant)(Litigation friend)(Claimant's Solicitor)(Signing on behalf of firm or company)
*delete as appropriate

---

(1) State full name of Claimant or his/her Solicitor
(2) State title of party e.g. Claimant, Defendant etc.
(3) State briefly the nature of the order sought and the reason it is sought including the material facts relied on and identifying any rule or statutory provision.

Part C - Evidence

Statement of Truth (to be signed when part C is completed)
*(I believe)(The Claimant believes) that the facts stated in this application notice are true.
*I am duly authorised by the Claimant to sign this statement

Full name--

Name of Claimant's Solicitor's firm --

Signed ------------------------------position or office held --------------------------------
*(Claimant)(Litigation friend)(Claimant's Solicitor)(Signing on behalf of firm or company)
*delete as appropriate

To: Respondent/Respondent's Solicitor's address, DX or e-mail	To: Claimant/Claimant's Solicitor's address, DX or e-mail
Ref No. Tel No. Fax No.	Ref No. Tel No. Fax No.

N208 CLAIM FORM (CPR PART 8)

Claim Form
(CPR Part 8)

In the	
Claim no.	
Fee Account no.	
Help with Fees - Ref no. (if applicable)	**H W F -** **-**

Claimant

SEAL

Defendant(s)

Does your claim include any issues under the Human Rights Act 1998? ☐ Yes ☐ No

Details of claim *(see also overleaf)*

Defendant's name and address

	£
Court fee	
Legal representative's costs	
Issue date	

For further details of the courts **www.gov.uk/find-court-tribunal**.
When corresponding with the Court, please address forms or letters to the Manager and always quote the claim number.

N208 Claim form (CPR Part 8) (08.18)

Claim no.	

Details of claim *(continued)*

Statement of Truth
*(I believe)(The Claimant believes) that the facts stated in these particulars of claim are true.
* I am duly authorised by the claimant to sign this statement.

Full name ______________________________

Name of claimant's legal representative's firm ______________________________

signed ______________________________ position or office held ______________________________

*(Claimant)(Litigation friend)
(Legal representative)

(if signing on behalf of firm or company)

**delete as appropriate*

Claimant's or claimant's legal representative's address to which documents should be sent if different from overleaf. If you are prepared to accept service by DX, fax or e-mail, please add details.

Find out how HM Courts and Tribunals Service uses personal information you give them when you fill in a form: https://www.gov.uk/government/organisations/hm-courts-and-tribunals-service/about/personal-information-charter

N260 STATEMENT OF COSTS (SUMMARY ASSESSMENT)

N260

Statement of Costs (summary assessment)

(CPR PD44 9.5)

In the	
Court	
Case Reference	

Case Title

Statement of Costs for the hearing on **(interim application/fast track trial)**

Description of fee earners*

(a) *(name) (grade) (hourly rate claimed)*	
(b) *(name) (grade) (hourly rate claimed)*	
(c) *(name) (grade) (hourly rate claimed)*	
(d) *(name) (grade) (hourly rate claimed)*	

Attendances on

Personal attendances

(a) *(number)*		hours at £		£
(b) *(number)*		hours at £		£
(c) *(number)*		hours at £		£
(d) *(number)*		hours at £		£

Letters out/emails

(a) *(number)*		hours at £		£
(b) *(number)*		hours at £		£
(c) *(number)*		hours at £		£
(d) *(number)*		hours at £		£

Telephone

(a) *(number)*		hours at £		£
(b) *(number)*		hours at £		£
(c) *(number)*		hours at £		£
(d) *(number)*		hours at £		£

N260 Statement of Costs (summary assessment) (06.15)

Attendances on opponents (including negotiations):

Personal attendances

(a) *(number)*		hours at £		£	
(b) *(number)*		hours at £		£	
(c) *(number)*		hours at £		£	
(d) *(number)*		hours at £		£	

Letters out/emails

(a) *(number)*		hours at £		£	
(b) *(number)*		hours at £		£	
(c) *(number)*		hours at £		£	
(d) *(number)*		hours at £		£	

Telephone

(a) *(number)*		hours at £		£	
(b) *(number)*		hours at £		£	
(c) *(number)*		hours at £		£	
(d) *(number)*		hours at £		£	

Attendance on others:

Personal attendances

(a) *(number)*		hours at £		£	
(b) *(number)*		hours at £		£	
(c) *(number)*		hours at £		£	
(d) *(number)*		hours at £		£	

Letters out/emails

(a) *(number)*		hours at £		£	
(b) *(number)*		hours at £		£	
(c) *(number)*		hours at £		£	
(d) *(number)*		hours at £		£	

Telephone

(a) *(number)*		hours at £		£	
(b) *(number)*		hours at £		£	
(c) *(number)*		hours at £		£	
(d) *(number)*		hours at £		£	

Site inspections etc.

(a) *(number)*		hours at £		£
(b) *(number)*		hours at £		£
(c) *(number)*		hours at £		£
(d) *(number)*		hours at £		£

Work done on documents, as set out in schedule:

Attendance at hearing:

(a) *(number)*		hours at £		£
(b) *(number)*		hours at £		£
(c) *(number)*		hours at £		£
(d) *(number)*		hours at £		£
(e) Fixed costs				£

(a) *(number)*		hours travel and waiting time £		£
(b) *(number)*		hours travel and waiting time £		£
(c) *(number)*		hours travel and waiting time £		£
(d) *(number)*		hours travel and waiting time £		£

Sub Total £

(A) Solicitors and Chartered Legal Executives with over eight years post qualification experience including at least eight years litigation experience.

(B) Solicitors and Chartered Legal Executives with over four years post qualification experience including at least four years litigation experience.

(C) Other solicitors and Chartered Legal Executives and fee earners of equivalent experience.

(D) Trainee solicitors, paralegals and other fee earners.

"Chartered Legal Executive" means a Fellow of the Chartered Institute of Legal Executives (CILEx). Those who are not Fellows of CILEx are not entitled to call themselves Chartered Legal Executives and in principle are therefore not entitled to the same hourly rate as a Chartered Legal Executive.

Brought forward £

Counsel's fees *(name) (year of call)*

Fee for [advice/conference/documents]	£
Fee for hearing	£

Other expenses

Court fees	£
Others *(give brief description)*	£
Total	£
Amount of VAT claimed	
on solicitors and counsel's fees	£
on other expenses	£
Grand Total £	

The costs stated above do not exceed the costs which the is liable to pay in respect of the work which this statement covers. Counsel's fees and other expenses have been incurred in the amounts stated above and will be paid to the persons stated.

Signed

Dated

Name of Partner signing

Name of firm of solicitors

Schedule of work done on documents

Item	Description of work *(one line only)*	(A) hours	(B) hours	(C) hours	(D) hours	Total £
1						
2						
3						
4						
5						
6						
7						
8						
9						
10						
11						
12						
13						
14						
15						
16						
17						
18						
19						
20						
21						
22						
23						
24						
25						
26						
27						
28						
29						
30						
Total						

Index

[all references are to paragraph number]

A

Aarhus Convention claims
generally, 3.68–3.73
Acknowledgment of service
generally, 3.110
judicial review claims, 4.16–4.24
response, 3.110–3.116
statutory reviews, 4.49
Adjournment of hearings
case management, 5.4
Amendment of claims
case management, 5.12
Appeals to High Court
statutory challenges, 5.40–5.42
Applications to High Court
statutory challenges, 5.36–5.44
Attendance at court
case management, 5.4
Administrative Court
generally, 1.2
Alternative remedy
litigation procedure, 7.237–7.239
Alternative sites and schemes
jurisprudence, 7.164–7.165
Appeals
Court of Appeal, to, 3.172
permission to appeal, 3.170–3.171
Supreme Court, to, 3.173
Applications to the High Court
generally, 5.36–5.39

B

Background knowledge
Council decision making, 7.106–7.107
Benefit of doubt
decision letters of Inspectors, 7.120
Best interests of children
human rights, 7.185–7.186
Bias
grounds of challenge, 7.85–7.88

C

Case management
amendment of claims, 5.12
available powers, 5.4
clerical errors, 5.11
conditions of payment, 5.8
Case management – *contd*
control of evidence, 5.18–5.20
general powers, 5.3–5.44
generally, 2.31–2.34
inherent jurisdiction, 5.21
interim, 3.147–3.151
introduction, 5.3–5.5
judicial review claims, of
delay, 5.26–5.29
disclosure, 5.32–5.35
introduction, 5.22
permission to proceed, 5.23–5.25
rolled up hearings, 5.31
urgent claims, 5.30
orders, as to, 5.8–5.9
overriding objective, 5.6–5.7
protective costs orders, 5.14–5.16
relief from sanctions, 5.10
remedying errors, 5.11
revocation of orders, 5.9
statutory challenges, of
appeals to High Court, 5.40–5.42
applications to High Court, 5.36–5.44
disclosure, 5.39
permission to proceed, 5.44
relevant applications, 5.36
standing, 5.43
striking out, 5.13
substitution of parties, 5.12
transfer of proceedings, 5.17
variation of orders, 5.9
written evidence, 5.20
Case preparation
generally, 3.155–3.163
Change of use
planning regulation, 1.26–1.31
Clerical errors
case management, 5.11
Commencement
case management, 2.31–2.34
rules, 2.18
significant claims, 2.19–2.23
timetabling, 2.24–2.30
venues, 2.35–2.38
Comments by individual committee members
Council decision making, 7.104–7.105
Commons
legal principles, 7.171

Community Infrastructure Levy
s 106 TCPA agreements, 7.143
Composition of committees
Council decision making, 7.110–7.111
Compromise
responses to Planning Court claims, 4.107
Compulsory purchase orders
Planning Court claims, 2.3
Conditional fee agreements (CFAs)
generally, 6.17
Conditions
distinction from limitation, 7.136
Grampian conditions, 7.137–7.138
interpretation, 7.134–7.135
introduction, 7.133
Whitley conditions, 7.139–7.140
Conditions of payment
case management, 5.8
Conduct of planning claims
acknowledgment of service
generally, 3.110
response, 3.110–3.116
appeals, 3.172–3.173
calculation of time for purposes of issue, 3.77–3.83
case management, 3.147–3.151
case preparation, 3.155–3.163
conduct of hearings, 3.164–3.165
costs, 3.169
extension of time limits, 3.84–3.88
hearings
case preparation, 3.155–3.163
conduct, 3.164–3.165
costs, 3.169
permission to appeal, 3.170–3.171
relief, 3.166–3.168
interim relief
introduction, 3.130–3.131
judicial review claims, 3.132–3.138
statutory challenges, 3.139–3.146
introduction, 3.1–3.5
issue
categories of claims, 3.107–3.109
generally, 3.89–3.93
introduction, 3.24–3.26
judicial review claims, 3.94–3.96
'significant' claims, 3.107–3.109
statutory challenges, 3.97–3.106
permission to appeal, 3.170–3.171
permission to proceed
appealing refusal, 3.128–3.129
hearing, 3.125–3.127
judicial review claims, 3.117–3.122
statutory challenges, 3.123–3.124
pre-action conduct, 3.6–3.14
pre-action disclosure, 3.22–3.23
pre-action protocol, 3.15–3.21
Conduct of planning claims – *contd*
preparation
generally, 3.24–3.26
standing in judicial review planning challenges, 3.27–3.37
standing in statutory challenges, 3.54–3.64
provision of information
Aarhus Convention, 3.68–3.73
financial resources, 3.65–3.67
relief, 3.166–3.168
response to acknowledgment of service, 3.110–3.116
service
judicial review claims, 3.94
statutory challenges, 3.101
settlement, 3.152–3.154
'significant' claims, 3.107–3.109
standing in judicial review planning challenges
generally, 3.27–3.28
individuals, 3.38–3.53
local action groups, 3.29–3.37
'sufficient interest', 3.27
standing in statutory challenges, 3.54–3.64
time limits
calculation of time for purposes of issue, 3.77–3.83
extension, 3.84–3.88
generally, 3.74–3.76
Confidential information
jurisprudence, 7.246
Consent to judgment
responses to Planning Court claims, 4.108
Conservation areas
generally, 7.163
planning regulation, 1.42
setting, 7.158–7.160
Consistency of decisions
grounds of challenge, 7.60–7.66
Consolidation of proceedings
case management, 5.4
Consultee requests
legal principles, 7.166–7.167
Contempt
case management, 5.74
Contradictory passages
decision letters of Inspectors, 7.123
Control of evidence
case management, 5.18–5.20
Cost capping orders
Aarhus Convention
application, 6.59–6.61
relevant provisions, 6.53–6.58
application, 6.59–6.61
background, 6.50–6.52

Cost capping orders – *contd*
case management, 5.14–5.16
Criminal Justice and Courts Act 2015
environmental cases, 6.100–6.101
non environmental cases, 6.85–6.99
environmental cases, 6.100–6.101
fixed costs
generally, 6.70–6.81
problems with, 6.82–6.84
non environmental cases, 6.85–6.99
'not prohibitively expensive', 6.62–6.64
problems with use, 6.65–6.69
relevant provisions, 6.53–6.58
summary, 6.49
Costs
amount, 6.7–6.8
assessment
basis, 6.9
method, 6.7–6.8
conclusion, 6.102
conditional fee agreements, 6.17
conduct, 6.10–6.12
CPR and practice directions, 6.4
discontinuance, on, 6.31–6.32
discretion of court
final determination, on, 6.39–6.41
general principles, 6.4–6.6
final determination, on
discretion, 6.39–6.41
interested parties, 6.42–6.44
interveners, 6.46–6.48
multiple defendants, 6.42–6.44
Part 36 offers, 6.45
fixed costs
generally, 6.70–6.81
problems with, 6.82–6.84
funding methods, 6.17
general principles
assessment of amount, 6.7–6.9
conduct, 6.10–6.12
discretion of court, 6.4–6.6
funding methods, 6.17
non-parties, 6.13–6.15
partial success, 6.16
general rule, 6.4–6.6
interveners, 6.46–6.48
introduction, 6.1–6.3
judicial review claims
Part 36 offers, 6.45
permission stage, at, 6.18–6.27
judicial review claims at permission stage
acknowledgment of service, 6.20–6.23
introduction. 6.18
oral reconsideration, 6.24–6.27
permission granted, where, 6.19
permission refused, where, 6.20–6.27
non-parties, 6.13–6.15
Costs – *contd*
overview, 3.169
partial success, 6.16
permission stage, at
judicial review claims, 6.18–6.27
s 288 TCPA appeals, 6.28
s 289 TCPA appeals, 6.29–6.30
permission stage in judicial review claims, at
acknowledgment of service, 6.20–6.23
introduction. 6.18
oral reconsideration, 6.24–6.27
permission granted, where, 6.19
permission refused, where, 6.20–6.27
protective costs orders
Aarhus Convention, 6.53–6.61
application, 6.59–6.61
background, 6.50–6.52
Criminal Justice and Courts Act 2015, 6.85–6.101
environmental cases, 6.100–6.101
fixed costs, 6.70–6.84
non environmental cases, 6.85–6.99
'not prohibitively expensive', 6.62–6.64
problems with use, 6.65–6.69
relevant provisions, 6.53–6.58
summary, 6.49
s 288 TCPA appeals, 6.28
s 289 TCPA appeals, 6.29–6.30
settlement of claims
agreement reached on all issues, 6.34
generally, 6.33
no agreement reached, 6.35–6.38
statutory challenges, 5.71, 7.28
withdrawal of claims, 6.33
Costs budgets
case management, 5.4
Council decision making
background knowledge of areas expected, 7.106–7.107
comments by individual committee members during debate, 7.104–7.105
composition of committees, 7.110–7.111
delegation schemes, 7.114–7.115
evaluation of documents by officers, 7.108–7.109
justiciability of committee, 7.110–7.111
officer's reports, 7.102–7.103
return of decisions to committee after change in circumstances, 7.112–7.113
Court of Appeal
resisting Planning Court claims, 4.110–4.111
Cross examination
litigation procedure, 7.227–7.228

D

Damages
judicial review claims, 5.62
Decision-making
enforcement notice appeals
case management, 5.40–5.44
compromise, 4.107
consent to judgment, 4.108
costs, 6.29–6.30
evidence, 4.102–4.104
interim orders, 4.99–4.101
introduction, 4.85–4.87
overlap between ss 288 and 289 TCPA, 4.94–4.96
permission to proceed, 4.97–4.98
powers of court, 4.105–4.106
practice directions, 4.88–4.93
pre-action responses, 4.2–4.12
redetermination, 4.109
standing, 5.43
Inspectors' letters
benefit of doubt, 7.120
contradictory passages, 7.123
deference, 7.121
fair reading, 7.119
introduction, 7.116–7.117
non-material errors, 7.122
reading documents as a whole, 7.118
reading fairly, 7.119
planning regulation
change of use, 1.26–1.31
deemed planning permission, 1.25
'development', 1.24
development management, 1.23
generally, 1.23
operational development, 1.25
Declarations
judicial review claims, 5.61
Declarations of incompatibility
powers of Planning Court, 5.72
Deemed planning permission
planning regulation, 1.25
Deference
decision letters of Inspectors, 7.121
Delay
judicial review claims
case management, 5.26–5.29
final relief, 5.65
Delegation schemes
Council decision making, 7.114–7.115
'Development'
planning regulation, 1.24
Development consents
environmental impact assessment, 7.192
Planning Court claims, 2.3
Development control
planning regulation, 1.23
Development management
planning regulation, 1.23
Development plans
judicial review, 7.226
neighbourhood plans, 7.177
planning regulation, 1.15–1.16
reasons for making decision, 7.48
reading documents as a whole, 7.41–7.42
Disclosure
case management
judicial review claims, 5.32–5.35
statutory challenges, 5.39
duty of candour, 4.32–4.34
generally, 5.32–5.35
interim orders
judicial review, 4.32–4.36
statutory challenges, 4.62
interim relief
judicial review, 5.58
statutory challenges, 5.58
judicial review claims
case management, 5.32–5.35
duty of candour, 4.32–4.34
interim orders, 4.32–4.36
interim relief, 5.58
statutory challenges
case management, 5.39
interim orders, 4.62
interim relief, 5.58
Discretion
costs
final determination, on, 6.39–6.41
general principles, 6.4–6.6
final relief for judicial review claims, 5.64
grounds of challenge, 7.97–7.99
quashing decisions
European cases, 7.130–7.131
exercise, 7.127–7.131
introduction, 7.127
refusal to exercise discretion not to quash, 7.129
refusal to quash, 7.128–7.131
Discrimination
Article 14 ECHR, 7.183–7.184
Equality Act 2010, 7.187–7.188
Duty to co-operate
local planning, 7.176
Duty to make inquiries
grounds of challenge, 7.89–7.96

E

Enforcement
legal principles, 7.153
Planning Court claims, 2.3
planning regulation, 1.33

Enforcement notices
Habitats Regulations, 7.197
statutory challenges, 5.60
Environmental impact assessment (EIA)
adequacy, 7.191
development consents, 7.192
introduction, 7.189
planning regulation, 1.35
screening opinions, 7.190
Environmental regulation
EIA Directive, 1.35
general, 1.34–1.43
Habitats Directive, 1.36–1.39
impact assessment, 1.35
SEA Directive, 1.35
Equality
human rights, 7.187–7.188
Error of fact
grounds of challenge, 7.68–7.70
Error of law
grounds of challenge, 7.66–7.67
European legislation
environmental impact assessment
adequacy, 7.191
development consents, 7.192
introduction, 7.189
screening opinions, 7.190
Habitats Regulations
appropriate assessment, 7.194
court's role, 7.196
introduction, 7.193
in combination effects, 7.195
in enforcement notices, 7.197
objection by Natural England, 7.198–7.199
protected species licences, 7.200
legal principles
environmental impact assessment, 7.189–7.192
Habitats Regulations, 7.193–7.200
strategic environmental assessment, 7.201–7.208
strategic environmental assessment (SEA)
change in circumstances, 7.205
consultation, 7.208
future consent framework, 7.206–7.207
likely significant effects, 7.203–7.204
reasonable alternatives, 7.201–7.202
EU legislation
Planning Court claims, 2.3
Evaluation of documents by officers
Council decision making, 7.108–7.109
Evidence
case management, 5.18–5.20
judicial review claims, 4.40–4.43
statutory challenges, 4.102–4.104
Extension of time
case management, 5.4
generally, 3.84–3.88

F

Failure to properly complete claim form
litigation procedure, 7.223–7.224
Fair reading
decision letters of Inspectors, 7.119
Fair trial
jurisprudence, 7.181–7.182
Fairness
grounds of challenge, 7.79–7.84
Fallback
legal principles, 7.148–7.149
Fettering discretion
grounds of challenge, 7.97–7.99
Final relief
judicial review claims, of
damages, 5.62
declarations, 5.61
delay, 5.65
discretionary nature, 5.64
generally, 5.61–5.63
injunctions, 5.61
mandatory orders, 5.61
no significant effect on outcome, 5.66–5.67
prohibitory orders, 5.61
quashing orders, 5.61
restitution, 5.62
statutory challenges, of
costs, 5.71
generally, 5.68–5.70
Financial resources
generally, 3.65–3.67
Full objectively assessed needs
legal principles, 7.152

G

General permitted development
planning regulation, 1.25
GPDO
legal principles, 7.150–7.151
Grampian conditions
jurisprudence, 7.137–7.138
Green belt
introduction, 7.154
openness, 7.157
release, 7.156
very special circumstances, 7.155
Grounds of defence
judicial review
detailed grounds, 4.37–4.39
summary grounds, 4.16–4.27
statutory reviews, 4.54–4.57

H

Habitats
appropriate assessment, 7.194
court's role, 7.196
introduction, 7.193
in combination effects, 7.195
in enforcement notices, 7.197
objection by Natural England, 7.198–7.199
Planning Court claims, 2.3
planning regulation, 1.36–1.39
protected species licences, 7.200
Heritage
conservation areas, 7.163
NPPF, 7.161–7.162
setting of listed buildings and conservation areas, 7.158–7.160
Highways
Planning Court claims, 2.3
Human rights
anti-discrimination
Article 14 ECHR, 7.183–7.184
Equality Act 2010, 7.187–7.188
Article 6 ECHR, 7.181–7.182
Article 8 ECHR, 7.179–7.180
Article 14 ECHR, 7.183–7.184
best interests of children, 7.185–7.186
equality, 7.187–7.188
freedom from discrimination
Article 14 ECHR, 7.183–7.184
Equality Act 2010, 7.187–7.188
introduction, 7.178
planning regulation, 1.40
right to fair trial, 7.181–7.182
right to respect for private and family life, 7.179–7.180

I

Immaterial considerations
grounds of challenge, 7.43–7.47
Implementation of planning permissions
jurisprudence, 7.145–7.145
Improper purposes
approach of court to challenges, 7.126
Information rights
availability of relevant documents, 7.244
confidential information, 7.246
introduction, 7.243
s 106 agreements, 7.247
viability assessments, 7.245–7.246
Inherent jurisdiction
case management, 5.21
Injunctions
interim relief
introduction, 4.28–4.29
judicial review claims, 5.46–5.53
judicial review claims, 5.61
Inspectors' decision letters
benefit of doubt, 7.120
contradictory passages, 7.123
deference, 7.121
fair reading, 7.119
introduction, 7.116–7.117
non-material errors, 7.122
reading documents as a whole, 7.118
reading fairly, 7.119
Interim declarations
judicial review claims, 5.57
Interim injunctions
applications, 3.130
judicial review claims
applications, 3.132
generally, 5.46–5.53
introduction, 4.28–4.29
statutory reviews, 4.60
Interim orders
judicial review, 4.28–4.36
statutory appeals, 4.99–4.101
statutory reviews, 4.58–4.62
Interim relief
applications
introduction, 3.130–3.131
judicial review, 3.132–3.138
statutory challenges, 3.139–3.146
case management, 5.22
judicial review claims, of
applications, 3.132–3.138
declarations, 5.57
disclosure, 5.58
generally, 4.28–4.29
injunctions, 5.46–5.53
powers of the court, 5.45–5.58
pre-action disclosure, 5.45
stay of proceedings, 5.54–5.56
statutory challenges, of
applications, 3.139–3.146
generally, 4.58–4.60
giving interim effect to enforcement notices, 5.60
powers of the court, 5.59–5.60
Interpretation
conditions, 7.134–7.135
planning permissions, 7.146–7.147
Issue
categories of claims, 3.107–3.109
generally, 3.89–3.93
introduction, 3.24–3.26
judicial review claims, 3.94–3.96
'significant' claims, 3.107–3.109
statutory challenges, 3.97–3.106
Issue estoppel
litigation procedure, 7.233–7.234

J

Judges
generally, 2.12–2.17
Judicial review
acknowledgment of service, 4.16–4.24
case management
delay, 5.26–5.29
disclosure, 5.32–5.35
introduction, 5.22
permission to proceed, 5.23–5.25
rolled up hearings, 5.31
urgent claims, 5.30
costs
Part 36 offers, 6.45
permission stage, at, 6.18–6.27
costs at permission stage
acknowledgment of service, 6.20–6.23
introduction. 6.18
oral reconsideration, 6.24–6.27
permission granted, where, 6.19
permission refused, where, 6.20–6.27
damages, 5.62
declarations, 5.61
defence
detailed grounds, 4.37–4.39
evidence, 4.40–4.43
summary grounds, 4.16–4.27
delay
case management, 5.26–5.29
final relief, 5.65
detailed grounds of defence, 4.37–4.39
development plans, 7.226
disclosure
duty of candour, 4.32–4.34
generally, 5.32–5.35
interim relief, 5.58
introduction, 4.32–4.36
evidence of defence, 4.40–4.43
final relief
damages, 5.62
declarations, 5.61
delay, 5.65
discretionary nature, 5.64
generally, 5.61–5.63
injunctions, 5.61
mandatory orders, 5.61
no significant effect on outcome, 5.66–5.67
prohibitory orders, 5.61
quashing orders, 5.61
restitution, 5.62
grounds of defence
detailed, 4.37–4.39
summary, 4.16–4.27
hearings, 4.44–4.45

Judicial review – *contd*
injunctions
generally, 5.61
interim, 5.46–5.53
introduction, 4.28–4.29
interim declarations, 5.57
interim injunctions
applications, 3.132
generally, 5.46–5.53
introduction, 4.28–4.29
interim orders, 4.28–4.36
interim relief
applications, 3.132–3.138
declarations, 5.57
disclosure, 5.58
generally, 4.28–4.29
injunctions, 5.46–5.53
powers of the court, 5.45–5.58
pre-action disclosure, 5.45
stay of proceedings, 5.54–5.56
issue, 3.94–3.96
jurisdiction of Planning Court, 2.6–2.8
legal principles in Planning Court claims
see also **Legal principles**
anti-discrimination, 7.187–7.188
approach of court to challenges, 7.100–7.126
discretion to quash, 7.127–7.131
equality, 7.187–7.188
European legislation, 7.189–7.208
grounds of challenge, 7.42–7.99
human rights, 7.178–7.186
information, 7.243–7.247
introduction, 7.1–7.2
litigation procedure, 7.209–7.242
substantive issues, 7.132–7.177
letters before claim, 4.3–4.7
mandatory orders, 5.61
permission to proceed
appealing refusal, 3.128–3.129
generally, 5.23–5.25
hearing, 3.125–3.127
introduction, 3.117–3.122
Practice Directions, 4.13–4.15
pre-action disclosure, 5.45
pre-action protocol, 4.2–4.12
prohibitory orders, 5.61
protective costs orders, 4.28
quashing orders, 5.61
restitution, 5.62
rolled up hearings
generally, 5.31
summary grounds of defence, 4.26–4.27
service, 3.94
standing
generally, 3.27–3.28

Judicial review – *contd*
standing – *contd*
individuals, 3.38–3.53
local action groups, 3.29–3.37
'sufficient interest', 3.27
stay of proceedings, 5.54–5.56
striking out, 4.30
substantive hearings, 4.44–4.45
summary grounds of defence, 4.16–4.27
totally without merit orders, 4.31
urgent claims, 5.30
Jurisdiction
generally, 2.3–2.11
introduction, 2.2
'Planning Court claim', 2.3
powers of Planning Court, and, 5.1–5.2
Justiciability of committee
Council decision making, 7.110–7.111

L

Land use
planning regulation, 1.17
Legal principles
alternative remedy, 7.237–7.239
alternative sites and schemes, 7.164–7.165
anti-discrimination
Article 14 ECHR, 7.183–7.184
Equality Act 2010, 7.187–7.188
application of *Mitchell*, 7.212–7.213
approach of court to challenges
background knowledge of areas expected, 7.106–7.107
benefit of doubt, 7.120
comments by individual committee members during debate, 7.104–7.105
composition of committees, 7.110–7.111
contradictory passages, 7.123
Council decision making, 7.102–7.115
decision letters of Inspectors, 7.116–7.123
deference, 7.121
delegation schemes, 7.114–7.115
evaluation of documents by officers, 7.108–7.109
fair reading, 7.119
improper purposes, 7.126
justiciability of committee, 7.110–7.111
non-material errors, 7.122
officer's reports, 7.102–7.103
reading documents as a whole, 7.118
reading fairly, 7.119
reflection of way case put to Inspector, 7.100–7.101

Legal principles – *contd*
approach of court to challenges – *contd*
return of decisions to committee after change in circumstances, 7.112–7.113
Secretary of State's response to Inspector's recommendations, 7.124–7.125
background knowledge of areas expected, 7.106–7.107
benefit of doubt, 7.120
best interests of children, 7.185–7.186
bias, 7.85–7.88
comments by individual committee members during debate, 7.104–7.105
commons, 7.171
Community Infrastructure Levy, 7.143
composition of committees, 7.110–7.111
conditions
distinction from limitation, 7.136
Grampian conditions, 7.137–7.138
interpretation, 7.134–7.135
introduction, 7.133
Whitley conditions, 7.139–7.140
confidential information, 7.246
conservation areas
generally, 7.163
setting, 7.158–7.160
consistency of decisions, 7.60–7.66
consultee requests, 7.166–7.167
contradictory passages, 7.123
Council decision making
background knowledge of areas expected, 7.106–7.107
comments by individual committee members during debate, 7.104–7.105
composition of committees, 7.110–7.111
delegation schemes, 7.114–7.115
evaluation of documents by officers, 7.108–7.109
justiciability of committee, 7.110–7.111
officer's reports, 7.102–7.103
return of decisions to committee after change in circumstances, 7.112–7.113
cross examination, 7.227–7.228
decision letters of Inspectors
benefit of doubt, 7.120
contradictory passages, 7.123
deference, 7.121
fair reading, 7.119
introduction, 7.116–7.117
non-material errors, 7.122
reading documents as a whole, 7.118
reading fairly, 7.119
decision taking, 7.39–7.42

Legal principles – *contd*
deference, 7.121
delegation schemes, 7.114–7.115
development consents
environmental impact assessment, 7.192
development plans
judicial review, 7.226
neighbourhood plans, 7.177
reasons for making decision, 7.48
reading documents as a whole, 7.41–7.42
disclosure
duty of candour, 7.229–7.232
discretion to quash
European cases, 7.130–7.131
exercise, 7.127–7.131
introduction, 7.127
refusal to exercise discretion not to quash, 7.129
refusal to quash, 7.128–7.131
discrimination
Article 14 ECHR, 7.183–7.184
Equality Act 2010, 7.187–7.188
duty of candour, 7.229–7.232
duty to co-operate, 7.176
duty to make inquiries, 7.89–7.96
enforcement, 7.153
enforcement notices
Habitats Regulations, 7.197
environmental impact assessment (EIA)
adequacy, 7.191
development consents, 7.192
introduction, 7.189
screening opinions, 7.190
equality
Article 14 ECHR, 7.183–7.184
Equality Act 2010, 7.187–7.188
error of fact, 7.68–7.70
error of law, 7.66–7.67
European legislation
environmental impact assessment, 7.189–7.192
Habitats Regulations, 7.193–7.200
strategic environmental assessment, 7.201–7.208
evaluation of documents by officers, 7.108–7.109
failure to properly complete claim form, 7.223–7.224
fair reading, 7.119
fair trial, 7.181–7.182
fairness, 7.79–7.84
fallback, 7.148–7.149
fettering discretion, 7.97–7.99
full objectively assessed needs, 7.152
GPDO, 7.150–7.151

Legal principles – *contd*
Grampian conditions, 7.137–7.138
green belt
introduction, 7.154
openness, 7.157
release, 7.156
very special circumstances, 7.155
grounds of challenge
bias, 7.85–7.88
consistency of decisions, 7.60–7.66
decision taking, 7.39–7.42
duty to make inquiries, 7.89–7.96
error of fact, 7.68–7.70
error of law, 7.66–7.67
fairness, 7.79–7.84
fettering discretion, 7.97–7.99
immaterial considerations, 7.43–7.47
introduction, 7.42
legitimate expectation, 7.75–7.78
making inquiries, 7.89–7.96
material considerations, 7.43–7.47
misinterpretation of policy, 7.4–7.38
NPPF, 7.11–7.38
procedural fairness, 7.79–7.84
procedural regularity, 7.58–7.59
rationality, 7.71–7.74
reading documents as a whole, 7.41–7.42
reasons to be given, 7.48–7.57
s 38(6) PCPA 2004, 7.39–7.41
supply of housing, 7.21
Habitats Regulations
appropriate assessment, 7.194
court's role, 7.196
introduction, 7.193
in combination effects, 7.195
in enforcement notices, 7.197
objection by Natural England, 7.198–7.199
protected species licences, 7.200
heritage
conservation areas, 7.163
NPPF, 7.161–7.162
setting of listed buildings and conservation areas, 7.158–7.160
human rights
anti-discrimination, 7.187–7.188
Article 6 ECHR, 7.181–7.182
Article 8 ECHR, 7.179–7.180
Article 14 ECHR, 7.183–7.184
best interests of children, 7.185–7.186
equality, 7.187–7.188
freedom from discrimination, 7.183–7.184
introduction, 7.178
right to fair trial, 7.181–7.182

Legal principles – *contd*
human rights – *contd*
right to respect for private and family life, 7.179–7.180
immaterial considerations, 7.43–7.47
implementation of planning permissions, 7.145–7.145
improper purposes, 7.126
information
availability of relevant documents, 7.244
confidential information, 7.246
introduction, 7.243
s 106 agreements, 7.247
viability assessments, 7.245–7.246
interpretation
conditions, 7.134–7.135
planning permissions, 7.146–7.147
introduction, 7.1–7.2
issue estoppel, 7.233–7.234
judicial review of development plans, 7.226
justiciability of committee, 7.110–7.111
legitimate expectation, 7.75–7.78
listed buildings
setting, 7.158–7.160
litigation procedure
agreed issues, 7.210–7.211
alternative remedy, 7.237–7.239
application of *Mitchell*, 7.212–7.213
cross examination, 7.227–7.228
development plans, 7.226
duty of candour in disclosure, 7.229–7.232
failure to properly complete claim form, 7.223–7.224
introduction, 7.209
issue estoppel, 7.233–7.234
judicial review of development plans, 7.226
pre-action protocol letter, 7.221
procedural exclusivity, 7.240–7.242
s 288 TCPA challenges, 7.225
s 289 TCPA challenges, 7.225
statements of common ground, 7.210–7.211
striking out, 7.222
time limits, 7.214–7.220
totally without merit, 7.235–7.236
local plans
duty to co-operate, 7.176
Inspector's role, 7.175
introduction, 7.174
neighbourhood plans, 7.177
making inquiries, 7.89–7.96
material considerations, 7.43–7.47

Legal principles – *contd*
meeting full objectively assessed needs, 7.152
misinterpretation of policy
decision taking, 7.39–7.42
generally, 7.4–7.10
NPPF, 7.11–7.38
Natural England's objections
Habitats Regulations, 7.198–7.199
neighbourhood plans, 7.177
non-material errors, 7.122
NPPF
generally, 7.11–7.38
heritage, 7.161–7.162
officer's reports, 7.102–7.103
openness, 7.157
planning permissions
implementation, 7.144–7.145
interpretation, 7.146–7.147
pre-action protocol letter, 7.221
private and family life, 7.179–7.180
procedural exclusivity, 7.240–7.242
procedural fairness, 7.79–7.84
procedural regularity, 7.58–7.59
protected species licences, 7.200
quashing decisions
European cases, 7.130–7.131
exercise, 7.127–7.131
introduction, 7.127
refusal to exercise discretion not to quash, 7.129
refusal to quash, 7.128–7.131
rationality, 7.71–7.74
reading documents as a whole
approach of court, 7.118
decision letters, 7.116–7.118
decision taking, 7.41–7.42
delegation schemes, 7.115
error of fact, 7.69
misinterpretation of policy, 7.8
officer's reports, 7.103
screening opinions, 7.190
reading fairly, 7.119
reasons to be given, 7.48–7.57
reflection of way case put to Inspector, 7.100–7.101
refusal to quash
European cases, 7.130–7.131
exercise of discretion, 7.128
introduction, 7.127
refusal to exercise discretion, 7.129
relationship with other regulatory regimes, 7.172–7.173
reservoirs, 7.168
return of decisions to committee after change in circumstances, 7.112–7.113
right to fair trial, 7.181–7.182

Legal principles – *contd*
right to respect for private and family life, 7.179–7.180
s 38(6) PCPA 2004
decision taking, 7.39–7.41
misinterpretation of policy, 7.15
non-material errors, 7.122
s 106 TCPA agreements
Community Infrastructure Levy, 7.143
generally, 7.141–7.143
information rights, 7.247
s 288 TCPA challenges, 7.225
s 289 TCPA challenges, 7.225
screening opinions, 7.190
Secretary of State's response to Inspector's recommendations, 7.124–7.125
setting of listed buildings and conservation areas, 7.158–7.160
strategic environmental assessment (SEA)
change in circumstances, 7.205
consultation, 7.208
future consent framework, 7.206–7.207
likely significant effects, 7.203–7.204
reasonable alternatives, 7.201–7.202
statements of common ground, 7.210–7.211
striking out, 7.222
substantive issues
alternative sites and schemes, 7.164–7.165
commons, 7.171
Community Infrastructure Levy, 7.143
conditions, 7.133–7.140
conservation areas, 7.158–7.160, 7.163
consultee requests, 7.166–7.167
duty to co-operate, 7.176
enforcement, 7.153
fallback, 7.148–7.149
full objectively assessed needs, 7.152
GPDO, 7.150–7.151
Grampian conditions, 7.137–7.138
green belt, 7.154–7.157
green belt release, 7.156
heritage, 7.158–7.163
implementation of planning permissions, 7.145–7.145
Inspector's role, 7.175
interpretation of conditions, 7.134–7.135
interpretation of planning permissions, 7.146–7.147
introduction, 7.132
limitation/condition distinction, 7.136
listed buildings, 7.158–7.160
local plans, 7.174–7.177

Legal principles – *contd*
substantive issues – *contd*
meeting full objectively assessed needs, 7.152
neighbourhood plans, 7.177
NPPF, 7.161–7.162
openness, 7.157
planning permissions, 7.144–7.147
relationship with other regulatory regimes, 7.172–7.173
reservoirs, 7.168
s 106 agreements, 7.141–7.143
setting of listed buildings and conservation areas, 7.158–7.160
very special circumstances, 7.155
village greens, 7.169–7.170
Whitley conditions, 7.139–7.140
supply of housing, 7.21
time limits, 7.214–7.220
totally without merit, 7.235–7.236
very special circumstances, 7.155
viability assessments, 7.245–7.246
village greens, 7.169–7.170
Whitley conditions, 7.139–7.140

Legitimate expectation
grounds of challenge, 7.75–7.78

Letters of claim
generally, 4.3–4.7

Liaison Judge
generally, 2.4

Listed buildings
planning regulation, 1.41
setting, 7.158–7.160

Litigation procedure
see also **Patents Court claims**
agreed issues, 7.210–7.211
alternative remedy, 7.237–7.239
application of *Mitchell*, 7.212–7.213
cross examination, 7.227–7.228
development plans, 7.226
disclosure
duty of candour, 7.229–7.232
failure to properly complete claim form, 7.223–7.224
introduction, 7.209
issue estoppel, 7.233–7.234
judicial review of development plans, 7.226
pre-action protocol letter, 7.221
procedural exclusivity, 7.240–7.242
s 288 TCPA challenges, 7.225
s 289 TCPA challenges, 7.225
statements of common ground, 7.210–7.211
striking out, 7.222
time limits, 7.214–7.220
totally without merit, 7.235–7.236

Local planning authorities
decision-making, 1.23
development and use of land, 1.21
enforcement, 1.33
human rights, 1.40
land survey, 1.10
NPPF, 1.18
planning 'exceptionalism', 1.50
role of court, 1.53
Local plans
duty to co-operate, 7.176
Inspector's role, 7.175
introduction, 7.174
neighbourhood plans, 7.177
planning regulation, 1.21

M

Mandatory orders
judicial review claims, 5.61
Material change of use
generally, 1.26–1.31
Material considerations
grounds of challenge, 7.43–7.47
Meeting full objectively assessed needs
legal principles, 7.152
Misinterpretation of policy
decision taking, 7.39–7.42
generally, 7.4–7.38
Mitchell decisions
litigation procedure, 7.212–7.213

N

National Planning Policy Framework (NPPF)
generally, 7.11–7.38
heritage, 7.161–7.162
planning regulation, 1.17
National Planning Policy Guidance
planning regulation, 1.17
Natural England's objections
Habitats Regulations, 7.198–7.199
Neighbourhood plans
generally, 7.177
planning regulation, 1.21
Non-material errors
decision letters of Inspectors, 7.122
Non-party costs
generally, 6.13–6.15
NPPF
generally, 7.11–7.38
heritage, 7.161–7.162

O

Officer's reports
Council decision making, 7.102–7.103
Openness
jurisprudence, 7.157
Operational development
planning regulation, 1.25
Oral renewal hearings
summary grounds of defence, 4.24–4.25
totally without merit applications, 4.31
Orders
case management, 5.8–5.9
Overriding objective
case management, 5.6–5.7

P

Part 8 challenges
See also **Statutory reviews**
case management, 5.36–5.38
compromise, 4.107
consent to judgment, 4.108
development plans, as to, 4.68–4.75
disclosure
case management, 5.39
interim orders, 4.62
grant of planning permission or listed building consent, as to, 4.76–4.84
interim orders and relief, 4.58–4.62
interim injunctions, 4.60
interim orders, 4.58–4.62
interim relief
applications, 3.139–3.146
generally, 4.58–4.60
giving interim effect to enforcement notices, 5.60
powers of the court, 5.59–5.60
introduction, 4.46–4.47
overlap between ss 288 and 289 TCPA, 4.94–4.96
practice directions, 4.48–4.53
pre-action responses, 4.2–4.12
redetermination, 4.109
refusal of planning permission or listed building consent, as to, 4.76–4.84
standing, 5.43
summary grounds of defence, 4.54–4.57
time limit, 4.63–4.67
Part 52 challenges
See also **Statutory appeals**
case management, 5.40–5.44
compromise, 4.107
consent to judgment, 4.108
costs, 6.29–6.30
evidence, 4.102–4.104
interim orders, 4.99–4.101
interim relief
applications, 3.139–3.146
generally, 4.58–4.60

Part 52 challenges – *contd*
interim relief – *contd*
giving interim effect to enforcement notices, 5.60
powers of the court, 5.59–5.60
introduction, 4.85–4.87
overlap between ss 288 and 289 TCPA, 4.94–4.96
permission to proceed
generally, 4.97–4.98
introduction, 5.44
powers of court, 4.105–4.106
practice directions, 4.88–4.93
pre-action responses, 4.2–4.12
redetermination, 4.109
standing, 5.43
Permission to appeal
generally, 3.170–3.171
Permission to proceed
appealing refusal, 3.128–3.129
hearing, 3.125–3.127
judicial review claims
generally, 5.23–5.25
introduction, 3.117–3.122
statutory challenges
generally, 5.44
introduction, 3.123–3.124
Planning conditions
distinction from limitation, 7.136
Grampian conditions, 7.137–7.138
interpretation, 7.134–7.135
introduction, 7.133
Whitley conditions, 7.139–7.140
Planning Court
background, 1.1–1.4
claims
see also **Proceedings in Planning Court**
conduct, 3.1–3.173
introduction, 2.1–2.2
jurisdiction, 2.3–2.17
legal principles, 7.1–7.247
meaning, 2.3
preparation and pursuit, 3.1–3.173
procedures, 2.18–2.34
resisting, 4.1–4.113
venues, 2.35–2.38
creation, 1.1–1.4
establishment, 2.4
introduction, 2.1–2.2
judges, 2.12–2.17
judicial review, 2.6–2.8
jurisdiction
generally, 2.3–2.11
introduction, 2.2
'Planning Court claim', 2.3
powers, 5.1–5.2
Planning Court – *contd*
legal principles
see also **Legal principles**
anti-discrimination, 7.187–7.188
approach of court to challenges, 7.100–7.126
discretion to quash, 7.127–7.131
equality, 7.187–7.188
European legislation, 7.189–7.208
grounds of challenge, 7.42–7.99
human rights, 7.178–7.186
information, 7.243–7.247
introduction, 7.1–7.2
litigation procedure, 7.209–7.242
substantive issues, 7.132–7.177
Liaison Judge, 2.4
overview, 1.1–1.4
powers
see also **Powers of Planning Court**
case management, 5.3–5.44
contempt, 5.74
declarations of incompatibility, 5.72
final relief, 5.61–5.71
interim relief, 5.45–5.60
introduction, 5.1–5.2
reference to European Court, 5.73
procedural rules, 2.18
procedures
case management, 2.31–2.34
conduct of claims, 3.1–3.173
preparation and pursuit of claims, 3.1–3.173
resisting claims, 4.1–4.113
rules, 2.18
significant claims, 2.19–2.23
timetabling, 2.24–2.30
venues, 2.35–2.38
purpose, 1.2
relevant CPR and practice directions, 2.2
significant Planning Court claims, 2.19–2.23
specialist judges, 2.12–2.17
'statutory challenge', 2.7–2.20
Planning enforcement
Planning Court claims, 2.3
Planning permission
change of use, 1.26–1.31
conditions
distinction from limitation, 7.136
Grampian, 7.137–7.138
interpretation, 7.134–7.135
introduction, 7.133
Whitley, 7.139–7.140
'development', 1.24
development management, 1.23
implementation, 7.144–7.145
interpretation, 7.146–7.147

Planning permission – *contd*
operational development, 1.25
Planning Court claims, 2.3
planning regulation, 1.23–1.31
Planning policy documents
Planning Court claims, 2.3
Planning Policy Guidance Notes
planning regulation, 1.17
Planning Policy Statements
planning regulation, 1.17
Planning regulation
central government's role, 1.17
change of use, 1.26–1.31
conservation area consent, 1.42
court's role, 1.52–1.59
current regime, 1.12–1.14
decision making
change of use, 1.26–1.31
deemed planning permission, 1.25
'development', 1.24
development management, 1.23
generally, 1.23
operational development, 1.25
deemed planning permission, 1.25
demise of 'exceptionalism', 1.44–1.51
'development', 1.24
development control, 1.23
development management, 1.23
development plans, 1.15–1.16
enforcement, 1.33
environmental regulation
EIA Directive, 1.35
general, 1.34–1.43
Habitats Directive, 1.36–1.39
impact assessment, 1.35
SEA Directive, 1.35
'exceptionalism', 1.44–1.51
forward planning, 1.15–1.22
general permitted development, 1.25
historical overview, 1.08–1.11
human rights, 1.40
land use, 1.17
listed building consent, 1.41
local planning authorities
decision-making, 1.23
development and use of land, 1.21
enforcement, 1.33
human rights, 1.40
land survey, 1.10
NPPF, 1.18
planning 'exceptionalism', 1.50
role of court, 1.53
local plans, 1.21
material change of use, 1.26–1.31
National Planning Policy
Framework, 1.17–1.18
National Planning Policy Guidance, 1.17
Planning regulation – *contd*
neighbourhood plans, 1.21
operational development, 1.25
planning permission
change of use, 1.26–1.31
deemed planning permission, 1.25
'development', 1.24
development management, 1.23
generally, 1.23
operational development, 1.25
Planning Policy Guidance Notes, 1.17
Planning Policy Statements, 1.17
regional development agencies, 1.20
regional planning, 1.20
role of the court, 1.52–1.59
statement of community
involvement, 1.22
structure plans, 1.20
tree preservation, 1.43
use, 1.26–1.31
Planning statutory appeals
See also **Statutory challenges**
case management, 5.40–5.44
compromise, 4.107
consent to judgment, 4.108
costs, 6.29–6.30
evidence, 4.102–4.104
interim orders, 4.99–4.101
interim relief
applications, 3.139–3.146
generally, 4.58–4.60
giving interim effect to enforcement
notices, 5.60
powers of the court, 5.59–5.60
introduction, 4.85–4.87
overlap between ss 288 and
289 TCPA, 4.94–4.96
permission to proceed
generally, 4.97–4.98
introduction, 5.44
powers of court, 4.105–4.106
practice directions, 4.88–4.93
pre-action responses, 4.2–4.12
redetermination, 4.109
standing, 5.43
Planning statutory reviews
See also **Statutory challenges**
case management, 5.36–5.38
compromise, 4.107
consent to judgment, 4.108
development plans, as to, 4.68–4.75
disclosure
case management, 5.39
interim orders, 4.62
grant of planning permission or listed
building consent, as to, 4.76–4.84
interim orders and relief, 4.58–4.62

Planning statutory reviews – *contd*
interim injunctions, 4.60
interim orders, 4.58–4.62
interim relief
applications, 3.139–3.146
generally, 4.58–4.60
giving interim effect to enforcement notices, 5.60
powers of the court, 5.59–5.60
introduction, 4.46–4.47
overlap between ss 288 and 289 TCPA, 4.94–4.96
practice directions, 4.48–4.53
pre-action responses, 4.2–4.12
redetermination, 4.109
refusal of planning permission or listed building consent, as to, 4.76–4.84
standing, 5.43
summary grounds of defence, 4.54–4.57
time limit, 4.63–4.67
Pollution control
Planning Court claims, 2.3
Powers of Planning Court
adjournment of hearings, 5.4
attendance at court, 5.4
case management
amendment of claims, 5.12
available powers, 5.4
clerical errors, 5.11
conditions of payment, 5.8
control of evidence, 5.18–5.20
general powers, 5.3–5.44
inherent jurisdiction, 5.21
introduction, 5.3–5.5
judicial review claims, of, 5.22–5.35
orders, as to, 5.8–5.9
overriding objective, 5.6–5.7
protective costs orders, 5.14–5.16
relief from sanctions, 5.10
remedying errors, 5.11
revocation of orders, 5.9
statutory challenges, of, 5.36–5.44
striking out, 5.13
substitution of parties, 5.12
transfer of proceedings, 5.17
variation of orders, 5.9
written evidence, 5.20
case management (judicial review claims)
delay, 5.26–5.29
disclosure, 5.32–5.35
introduction, 5.22
permission to proceed, 5.23–5.25
rolled up hearings, 5.31
urgent claims, 5.30

Powers of Planning Court – *contd*
case management (statutory challenges)
appeals to High Court, 5.40–5.42
applications to High Court, 5.36–5.44
disclosure, 5.39
permission to proceed, 5.44
relevant applications, 5.36
standing, 5.43
consolidation of proceedings, 5.4
contempt, 5.74
costs
see also **Costs**
conclusion, 6.102
discontinuance, on, 6.31–6.32
final determination, on, 6.39–6.48
general principles, 6.4–6.17
introduction, 6.1–6.3
permission stage, at, 6.18–6.30
protective costs orders, 6.49–6.101
settlement, on, 6.33–6.38
costs budgets, 5.4
declarations of incompatibility, 5.72
extension of time limits, 5.4
final relief
judicial review claims, of, 5.61–5.67
statutory challenges, of, 5.68–5.71
final relief (judicial review claims)
damages, 5.62
declarations, 5.61
delay, 5.65
discretionary nature, 5.64
generally, 5.61–5.63
injunctions, 5.61
mandatory orders, 5.61
no significant effect on outcome, 5.66–5.67
prohibitory orders, 5.61
quashing orders, 5.61
restitution, 5.62
final relief (statutory challenges)
costs, 5.71
generally, 5.68–5.70
interim relief
judicial review claims, of, 5.45–5.58
statutory challenges, of, 5.59–5.60
interim relief (judicial review claims)
disclosure, 5.58
interim declarations, 5.57
interim injunctions, 5.46–5.53
introduction, 5.45
pre-action disclosure, 5.45
stay of proceedings, 5.54–5.56
interim relief (statutory challenges)
generally, 5.59
giving interim effect to enforcement notices, 5.60
introduction, 5.1–5.2

Powers of Planning Court – *contd*
jurisdiction, 5.1–5.2
preliminary issues, 5.4
reference to European Court, 5.73
separate trials, 5.4
shortening time limits, 5.4
stay of proceedings, 5.4
telephone hearings, 5.4
time limits, 5.4
Practice directions
judicial review, 4.13–4.15
planning statutory appeals, 4.88–4.93
planning statutory reviews, 4.48–4.53
Pre-action conduct
generally, 3.6–3.14
Pre-action disclosure
generally, 3.22–3.23
judicial review claims, 5.45
Pre-action protocol
generally, 4.2–4.12
introduction, 3.15–3.21
jurisprudence, 7.221
letters before claim, 4.3–4.7
Preliminary issues
case management, 5.4
Private and family life
human rights, 7.179–7.180
Procedural exclusivity
litigation procedure, 7.240–7.242
Procedural fairness
grounds of challenge, 7.79–7.84
Procedural regularity
grounds of challenge, 7.58–7.59
Proceedings in Planning Court
Aarhus Convention claims, 3.68–3.73
acknowledgment of service
generally, 3.110
response, 3.110–3.116
appeals
Court of Appeal, to, 3.172
Supreme Court, to, 3.173
case management
generally, 2.31–2.34
interim, 3.147–3.151
case preparation, 3.155–3.163
commencement
case management, 2.31–2.34
rules, 2.18
significant claims, 2.19–2.23
timetabling, 2.24–2.30
venues, 2.35–2.38
compromise, 4.107
conduct
acknowledgment of service, 3.110
appeals, 3.172–3.173
case management, 3.147–3.151
case preparation, 3.155–3.163

Proceedings in Planning Court – *contd*
conduct – *contd*
costs, 3.169
hearings, 3.155–3.171
interim relief, 3.130–3.146
introduction, 3.1–3.5
issue, 3.89–3.109
permission to appeal, 3.170–3.171
permission to proceed, 3.117–3.129
pre-action conduct, 3.6–3.14
pre-action disclosure, 3.22–3.23
pre-action protocol, 3.15–3.21
preparation, 3.24–3.26
provision of information, 3.65–3.73
relief, 3.166–3.168
response to acknowledgment of service, 3.110–3.116
settlement, 3.152–3.154
standing, 3.27–3.64
time limits, 3.74–3.88
consent to judgment, 4.108
costs, 3.169
Court of Appeal, and, 4.110–4.111
decisions on enforcement notice appeals, to
case management, 5.40–5.44
compromise, 4.107
consent to judgment, 4.108
costs, 6.29–6.30
evidence, 4.102–4.104
interim orders, 4.99–4.101
introduction, 4.85–4.87
overlap between ss 288 and 289 TCPA, 4.94–4.96
permission to proceed, 4.97–4.98
powers of court, 4.105–4.106
practice directions, 4.88–4.93
pre-action responses, 4.2–4.12
redetermination, 4.109
standing, 5.43
disclosure
duty of candour, 4.32–4.34
interim relief, 5.58
judicial review claims, 4.32–4.36, 5.32–5.35
statutory reviews, 5.39
evidence
case management, 5.18–5.20
judicial review claims, 4.40–4.43
statutory challenges, 4.102–4.104
extension of time, 3.84–3.88
financial resources, 3.65–3.67
hearings
case preparation, 3.155–3.163
conduct, 3.164–3.165
costs, 3.169
permission to appeal, 3.170–3.171
relief, 3.166–3.168

Proceedings in Planning Court – *contd*
injunctions
judicial review claims, 5.61
interim injunctions
applications, 3.130–3.132
judicial review claims, 4.28–4.29, 5.46–5.53
statutory reviews, 4.60
interim orders
judicial review, 4.28–4.36
statutory appeals, 4.99–4.101
statutory reviews, 4.58–4.62
interim relief
applications, 3.130–3.146
case management, 5.22
judicial review, 4.28–4.29
powers of the court, 5.45–5.60
statutory challenges, 4.58–4.60
interim relief applications
introduction, 3.130–3.131
judicial review claims, 3.132–3.138
statutory challenges, 3.139–3.146
interim relief for judicial review
applications, 3.132–3.138
declarations, 5.57
disclosure, 5.58
generally, 4.28–4.29
injunctions, 5.46–5.53
powers of the court, 5.45–5.58
pre-action disclosure, 5.45
stay of proceedings, 5.54–5.56
interim relief for statutory challenges
applications, 3.139–3.146
generally, 4.58–4.60
giving interim effect to enforcement notices, 5.60
powers of the court, 5.59–5.60
issue
categories of claims, 3.107–3.109
generally, 3.89–3.93
introduction, 3.24–3.26
judicial review claims, 3.94–3.96
'significant' claims, 3.107–3.109
statutory challenges, 3.97–3.106
judicial review claims
see also **Judicial review**
acknowledgment of service, 4.16
case management, 5.22–5.35
costs, 6.18–6.27
detailed grounds of defence, 4.37–4.39
evidence of defence, 4.40–4.43
final relief, 5.61–5.66
hearings, 4.44–4.45
interim orders, 4.28–4.36
interim relief, 3.132–3.138, 5.45–5.56
issue, 3.94–3.96
jurisdiction, 2.6–2.8

Proceedings in Planning Court – *contd*
judicial review claims – *contd*
permission to proceed, 3.117–3.122
practice directions, 4.13–4.15
pre-action protocol, 4.2–4.12
rolled up hearings, 5.31
standing, 3.27–3.53
summary grounds of defence, 4.16–4.27
legal principles
see also **Legal principles**
anti-discrimination, 7.187–7.188
approach of court to challenges, 7.100–7.126
discretion to quash, 7.127–7.131
equality, 7.187–7.188
European legislation, 7.189–7.208
grounds of challenge, 7.42–7.99
human rights, 7.178–7.186
information, 7.243–7.247
introduction, 7.1–7.2
litigation procedure, 7.209–7.242
substantive issues, 7.132–7.177
letters of claim, 4.3–4.7
meaning of 'Planning Court claim', 2.3
oral renewal hearings
summary grounds of defence, 4.24–4.25
totally without merit applications, 4.31
permission to appeal, 3.170–3.171
permission to proceed
appealing refusal, 3.128–3.129
hearing, 3.125–3.127
judicial review claims, 3.117–3.122
statutory challenges, 3.123–3.124
pre-action conduct, 3.6–3.14
pre-action disclosure, 3.22–3.23
pre-action protocol
generally, 3.15–3.21
letters of claim, 4.3–4.7
preparation
generally, 3.24–3.26
standing in judicial review planning challenges, 3.27–3.37
standing in statutory challenges, 3.54–3.64
procedure
agreed issues, 7.210–7.211
alternative remedy, 7.237–7.239
application of *Mitchell*, 7.212–7.213
cross examination, 7.227–7.228
development plans, 7.226
duty of candour in disclosure, 7.229–7.232
failure to properly complete claim form, 7.223–7.224

Proceedings in Planning Court – *contd*
procedure – *contd*
introduction, 7.209
issue estoppel, 7.233–7.234
judicial review of development plans, 7.226
pre-action protocol letter, 7.221
procedural exclusivity, 7.240–7.242
s 288 TCPA challenges, 7.225
s 289 TCPA challenges, 7.225
statements of common ground, 7.210–7.211
striking out, 7.222
time limits, 7.214–7.220
totally without merit, 7.235–7.236
protective costs orders
case management, 5.14–5.16
judicial review claims, 4.28
provision of information
Aarhus Convention, 3.68–3.73
financial resources, 3.65–3.67
redetermination, 4.109
refusal of permission to proceed, 3.128–3.129
relief, 3.166–3.168
resisting claims
see also **Resisting Planning Court claims**
compromise, 4.107
consent to judgment, 4.108
introduction, 4.1
judicial review, 4.13–4.45
pre-action protocol letters of claim, 4.2–4.12
redetermination, 4.109
statutory appeals, 4.85–4.106
statutory reviews, 4.46–4.84
resisting in Court of Appeal, 4.110–4.111
resisting in Supreme Court, 4.112
response to acknowledgment of service, 3.110–3.116
rolled up hearings
generally, 5.31
summary grounds of defence, 4.26–4.27
rules, 2.18
settlement, 3.152–3.154
significant claims
generally, 2.19–2.23
issue, 3.107–3.109
standing in judicial review planning challenges
generally, 3.27–3.28
individuals, 3.38–3.53
local action groups, 3.29–3.37
'sufficient interest', 3.27

Proceedings in Planning Court – *contd*
standing in statutory challenges
appeals, 5.43
generally, 3.54–3.64
statutory appeals
case management, 5.40–5.44
compromise, 4.107
consent to judgment, 4.108
costs, 6.29–6.30
evidence, 4.102–4.104
interim orders, 4.99–4.101
introduction, 4.85–4.87
overlap between ss 288 and 289 TCPA, 4.94–4.96
permission to proceed, 4.97–4.98
powers of court, 4.105–4.106
practice directions, 4.88–4.93
pre-action responses, 4.2–4.12
redetermination, 4.109
standing, 5.43
statutory challenges
appeals, 4.85–4.103
compromise, 4.107
consent to judgment, 4.108
Court of Appeal, in, 4.110–4.111
interim relief, 3.139–3.146
issue, 3.97–3.106
overlap between ss 288 and 289 TCPA, 4.94–4.96
permission to proceed, 3.123–3.124
redetermination, 4.109
reviews, 4.46–4.84
Supreme Court, in, 4.112
statutory reviews
case management, 5.36–5.38
compromise, 4.107
consent to judgment, 4.108
development plans, as to, 4.68–4.75
disclosure, 5.39
grant of planning permission or listed building consent, as to, 4.76–4.84
interim orders and relief, 4.58–4.62
introduction, 4.46–4.47
overlap between ss 288 and 289 TCPA, 4.94–4.96
practice directions, 4.48–4.53
pre-action responses, 4.2–4.12
redetermination, 4.109
refusal of planning permission or listed building consent, as to, 4.76–4.84
standing, 5.43
summary grounds of defence, 4.54–4.57
time limit, 4.63–4.67
striking out
case management, 5.13
judicial review, 4.30

Proceedings in Planning Court – *contd*
striking out – *contd*
litigation procedure, 7.222
summary grounds of defence
judicial review, 4.16–4.27
statutory reviews, 4.54–4.57
Supreme Court, and, 4.112
time limits
calculation of time for purposes of issue, 3.77–3.83
extension, 3.84–3.88
generally, 3.74–3.76
statutory reviews, 4.63–4.67
timetabling, 2.24–2.30
venues, 2.35–2.38
Prohibitory orders
judicial review claims, 5.61
Protected species licences
Habitats Regulations, 7.200
Protective costs orders
Aarhus Convention
application, 6.59–6.61
problems with compliance, 6.65–6.69
relevant provisions, 6.53–6.58
application, 6.59–6.61
background, 6.50–6.52
case management, 5.14–5.16
Criminal Justice and Courts Act 2015
environmental cases, 6.100–6.101
non environmental cases, 6.85–6.99
environmental cases, 6.100–6.101
fixed costs
generally, 6.70–6.81
problems with, 6.82–6.84
judicial review claims, 4.28
non environmental cases, 6.85–6.99
'not prohibitively expensive', 6.62–6.64
problems with use, 6.65–6.69
relevant provisions, 6.53–6.58
summary, 6.49
Provision of information
Aarhus Convention, 3.68–3.73
financial resources, 3.65–3.67

Q

Quashing decisions
European cases, 7.130–7.131
exercise, 7.127–7.131
introduction, 7.127
refusal to exercise discretion not to quash, 7.129
refusal to quash, 7.128–7.131
Quashing orders
judicial review claims, 5.61

R

Rationality
grounds of challenge, 7.71–7.74
Reading documents as a whole
approach of court, 7.118
decision letters, 7.116–7.118
decision taking, 7.41–7.42
delegation schemes, 7.115
error of fact, 7.69
misinterpretation of policy, 7.8
officer's reports, 7.103
screening opinions, 7.190
Reading fairly
decision letters of Inspectors, 7.119
Reasons to be given
grounds of challenge, 7.48–7.57
Redetermination
responses to Planning Court claims, 4.109
Reference to European Court
powers of Planning Court, 5.73
Refusal of permission to proceed
generally, 3.128–3.129
Refusal to quash
European cases, 7.130–7.131
exercise of discretion, 7.128
introduction, 7.127
refusal to exercise discretion, 7.129
Regional development agencies
planning regulation, 1.20
Regional planning
planning regulation, 1.20
Relationship with other regulatory regimes
legal principles, 7.172–7.173
Relief
hearings, 3.166–3.168
Relief from sanctions
case management, 5.10
Remedying errors
case management, 5.11
Reservoirs
jurisprudence, 7.168
Resisting Planning Court claims
compromise, 4.107
consent to judgment, 4.108
Court of Appeal, in, 4.110–4.111
introduction, 4.1
judicial review claims
detailed grounds of defence, 4.37–4.39
evidence, 4.40–4.43
hearings, 4.,44–4.45
interim orders and relief, 4.28–4.36
practice directions, 4.13–4.15
summary grounds of defence, 4.16–4.27
letters before claim, 4.3–4.7
pre-action protocol, 4.2–4.12

Resisting Planning Court claims – *contd*
redetermination, 4.109
statutory appeals
case management, 5.40–5.44
compromise, 4.107
consent to judgment, 4.108
costs, 6.29–6.30
evidence, 4.102–4.104
interim orders, 4.99–4.101
introduction, 4.85–4.87
overlap between ss 288 and 289 TCPA, 4.94–4.96
permission to proceed, 4.97–4.98
powers of court, 4.105–4.106
practice directions, 4.88–4.93
pre-action responses, 4.2–4.12
redetermination, 4.109
standing, 5.43
statutory reviews
case management, 5.36–5.38
compromise, 4.107
consent to judgment, 4.108
development plans, as to, 4.68–4.75
disclosure, 5.39
grant of planning permission or listed building consent, as to, 4.76–4.84
interim orders and relief, 4.58–4.62
introduction, 4.46–4.47
overlap between ss 288 and 289 TCPA, 4.94–4.96
practice directions, 4.48–4.53
pre-action responses, 4.2–4.12
redetermination, 4.109
refusal of planning permission or listed building consent, as to, 4.76–4.84
standing, 5.43
summary grounds of defence, 4.54–4.57
time limit, 4.63–4.67
Supreme Court, in, 4.112
Restitution
judicial review claims, 5.62
Return of decisions to committee after change in circumstances
Council decision making, 7.112–7.113
Revocation of orders
case management, 5.9
Right to fair trial
jurisprudence, 7.181–7.182
Right to respect for private and family life
human rights, 7.179–7.180
Rights of way
Planning Court claims, 2.3
Rolled up hearings
generally, 5.31
summary grounds of defence, 4.26–4.27

S

Sanctions, relief from
case management, 5.10
Screening opinions
jurisprudence, 7.190
SEA Directive
planning regulation, 1.35
Secretary of State
response to Inspector's recommendations, 7.124–7.125
Section 38(6) PCPA 2004 challenges
case management, 5.36–5.39
generally, 4.76–4.84
legal principles
decision taking, 7.39–7.41
misinterpretation of policy, 7.15
non-material errors, 7.122
practice directions, 4.48
Section 61N TCPA challenges
calculation of time, 3.82
generally 4.47
Section 63 P(LBCA)A 1990 challenges
case management, 5.36–5.39
generally, 4.76–4.84
interim relief, 3.145
issuing claims, 3.97
practice directions, 4.48
Section 65 P(LBCA)A 1990 challenges
calculation of time, 3.81
issuing claims, 3.105
permission hearing, 3.126
permission to proceed, 3.124
refusal of permission, 3.129
response to acknowledgement of service, 3.116
Section 106 TCPA agreements
Community Infrastructure Levy, 7.143
generally, 7.141–7.143
information rights, 7.247
Section 113 PCPA 2004 challenges
case management, 5.36–5.39
generally, 4.68–4.75
interim relief, 3.142–3.143
introduction, 3.3
issuing claims, 3.97
practice directions, 4.48
standing, 3.61
Section 287 TCPA challenges
interim relief, 3.140
issuing claims, 3.97
practice directions, 4.48
Section 288 TCPA challenges
See also **Statutory reviews**
case management, 5.36–5.38
compromise, 4.107
consent to judgment, 4.108
development plans, as to, 4.68–4.75

Section 288 TCPA challenges – *contd*
disclosure
case management, 5.39
interim orders, 4.62
grant of planning permission or listed building consent, as to, 4.76–4.84
interim orders and relief, 4.58–4.62
interim injunctions, 4.60
interim orders, 4.58–4.62
interim relief
applications, 3.139–3.146
generally, 4.58–4.60
giving interim effect to enforcement notices, 5.60
powers of the court, 5.59–5.60
introduction, 4.46–4.47
issuing claims, 3.97
overlap between ss 288 and 289 TCPA, 4.94–4.96
practice directions, 4.48–4.53
pre-action responses, 4.2–4.12
redetermination, 4.109
refusal of planning permission or listed building consent, as to, 4.76–4.84
standing, 5.43
summary grounds of defence, 4.54–4.57
time limit, 4.63–4.67
Section 289 TCPA challenges
See also **Statutory appeals**
case management, 5.40–5.44
compromise, 4.107
consent to judgment, 4.108
costs, 6.29–6.30
evidence, 4.102–4.104
interim orders, 4.99–4.101
interim relief
applications, 3.139–3.146
generally, 4.58–4.60
giving interim effect to enforcement notices, 5.60
powers of the court, 5.59–5.60
introduction, 4.85–4.87
issuing claims, 3.105
overlap between ss 288 and 289 TCPA, 4.94–4.96
permission to proceed
generally, 4.97–4.98
introduction, 5.44
powers of court, 4.105–4.106
practice directions, 4.88–4.93
pre-action responses, 4.2–4.12
redetermination, 4.109
standing, 5.43
Separate trials
case management, 5.4
Service
judicial review claims, 3.94
statutory challenges, 3.101
Setting of listed buildings and conservation areas
legal principles, 7.158–7.160
Settlement
costs
agreement reached on all issues, 6.34
generally, 6.33
no agreement reached, 6.35–6.38
generally, 3.152–3.154
Shortening time limits
case management, 5.4
Significant claims
generally, 2.19–2.23
issue, 3.107–3.109
Standing
judicial review planning challenges
generally, 3.27–3.28
individuals, 3.38–3.53
local action groups, 3.29–3.37
'sufficient interest', 3.27
statutory challenges
case management, 5.43
generally, 3.54–3.64
Statutory appeals
See also **Statutory challenges**
case management, 5.40–5.44
compromise, 4.107
consent to judgment, 4.108
costs, 6.29–6.30
evidence, 4.102–4.104
interim orders, 4.99–4.101
interim relief
applications, 3.139–3.146
generally, 4.58–4.60
giving interim effect to enforcement notices, 5.60
powers of the court, 5.59–5.60
introduction, 4.85–4.87
overlap between ss 288 and 289 TCPA, 4.94–4.96
permission to proceed
generally, 4.97–4.98
introduction, 5.44
powers of court, 4.105–4.106
practice directions, 4.88–4.93
pre-action responses, 4.2–4.12
redetermination, 4.109
standing, 5.43
Statutory challenges
appeals to High Court
case management, 5.40–5.44
compromise, 4.107
consent to judgment, 4.108
costs, 6.29–6.30

Statutory challenges – *contd*
appeals to High Court – *contd*
evidence, 4.102–4.104
interim orders, 4.99–4.101
introduction, 4.85–4.87
overlap between ss 288 and 289 TCPA, 4.94–4.96
permission to proceed, 4.97–4.98
powers of court, 4.105–4.106
practice directions, 4.88–4.93
pre-action responses, 4.2–4.12
redetermination, 4.109
standing, 5.43
applications to High Court, 5.36–5.44
approval of listed building consent, as to,
case management, 5.36–5.39
generally, 4.76–4.84
practice directions, 4.48
case management
appeals to High Court, 5.40–5.42
applications to High Court, 5.36–5.44
disclosure, 5.39
permission to proceed, 5.44
relevant applications, 5.36
standing, 5.43
compromise, 4.107
consent to judgment, 4.108
costs, 5.71
decisions on enforcement notice appeals, to
case management, 5.40–5.44
compromise, 4.107
consent to judgment, 4.108
costs, 6.29–6.30
evidence, 4.102–4.104
interim orders, 4.99–4.101
introduction, 4.85–4.87
overlap between ss 288 and 289 TCPA, 4.94–4.96
permission to proceed, 4.97–4.98
powers of court, 4.105–4.106
practice directions, 4.88–4.93
pre-action responses, 4.2–4.12
redetermination, 4.109
standing, 5.43
development plans, as to
case management, 5.36–5.39
generally, 4.68–4.75
practice directions, 4.48
disclosure
duty of candour, 4.32–4.34
interim orders, 4.32–4.36, 4.62
interim relief, 5.58
judicial review, 5.32–5.35
statutory challenges, 5.39
enforcement notice appeals, to
case management, 5.40–5.44

Statutory challenges – *contd*
enforcement notice appeals, to – *contd*
compromise, 4.107
consent to judgment, 4.108
costs, 6.29–6.30
evidence, 4.102–4.104
interim orders, 4.99–4.101
introduction, 4.85–4.87
overlap between ss 288 and 289 TCPA, 4.94–4.96
permission to proceed, 4.97–4.98
powers of court, 4.105–4.106
practice directions, 4.88–4.93
pre-action responses, 4.2–4.12
redetermination, 4.109
standing, 5.43
enforcement notices, 5.60
final relief
costs, 5.71
generally, 5.68–5.70
grant of listed building consent, as to
case management, 5.36–5.39
generally, 4.76–4.84
practice directions, 4.48
grant of planning permission, as to
case management, 5.36–5.39
costs, 6.28
generally, 4.76–4.84
practice directions, 4.48
grounds
see also **Grounds of challenge**
consistency of decisions, 7.60–7.66
decision taking, 7.39–7.42
duty to make inquiries, 7.89–7.96
error of fact, 7.68–7.70
error of law, 7.66–7.67
fairness, 7.79–7.84
fettering discretion, 7.97–7.99
immaterial considerations, 7.43–7.47
introduction, 7.42
legitimate expectation, 7.75–7.78
making inquiries, 7.89–7.96
material considerations, 7.43–7.47
misinterpretation of policy, 7.4–7.38
NPPF, 7.11–7.38
procedural fairness, 7.79–7.84
rationality, 7.71–7.74
reasons to be given, 7.48–7.57
interim injunctions
applications, 3.130
judicial review, 4.28–4.29
powers of the court, 5.46–5.53
statutory reviews, 4.60
interim orders, 4.28–4.36
interim relief
applications, 3.132–3.138
declarations, 5.57

Statutory challenges – *contd*
interim relief – *contd*
disclosure, 5.58
generally, 4.28–4.29
injunctions, 5.46–5.53
powers of the court, 5.45–5.58
pre-action disclosure, 5.45
stay of proceedings, 5.54–5.56
introduction, 2.7–2.10
issue, 3.97–3.106
legal principles
see also **Legal principles**
anti-discrimination, 7.187–7.188
approach of court to challenges, 7.100–7.126
discretion to quash, 7.127–7.131
equality, 7.187–7.188
European legislation, 7.189–7.208
grounds of challenge, 7.42–7.99
human rights, 7.178–7.186
information, 7.243–7.247
introduction, 7.1–7.2
litigation procedure, 7.209–7.242
substantive issues, 7.132–7.177
letters before claim, 4.3–4.7
neighbourhood development orders, and, 4.47
Part 8 claims, in
case management, 5.36–5.38
compromise, 4.107
consent to judgment, 4.108
development plans, as to, 4.68–4.75
disclosure, 5.39
grant of planning permission or listed building consent, as to, 4.76–4.84
interim orders and relief, 4.58–4.62
introduction, 4.46–4.47
overlap between ss 288 and 289 TCPA, 4.94–4.96
practice directions, 4.48–4.53
pre-action responses, 4.2–4.12
redetermination, 4.109
refusal of planning permission or listed building consent, as to, 4.76–4.84
standing, 5.43
summary grounds of defence, 4.54–4.57
time limit, 4.63–4.67
Part 52 claims, in
case management, 5.40–5.44
compromise, 4.107
consent to judgment, 4.108
costs, 6.29–6.30
evidence, 4.102–4.104
interim orders, 4.99–4.101
introduction, 4.85–4.87
overlap between ss 288 and 289 TCPA, 4.94–4.96

Statutory challenges – *contd*
Part 52 claims, in – *contd*
permission to proceed, 4.97–4.98
powers of court, 4.105–4.106
practice directions, 4.88–4.93
pre-action responses, 4.2–4.12
redetermination, 4.109
standing, 5.43
permission to proceed
appealing refusal, 3.128–3.129
generally, 5.44
hearing, 3.125–3.127
introduction, 3.123–3.124
planning statutory appeals
case management, 5.40–5.44
compromise, 4.107
consent to judgment, 4.108
costs, 6.29–6.30
evidence, 4.102–4.104
interim orders, 4.99–4.101
introduction, 4.85–4.87
overlap between ss 288 and 289 TCPA, 4.94–4.96
permission to proceed, 4.97–4.98
powers of court, 4.105–4.106
practice directions, 4.88–4.93
pre-action responses, 4.2–4.12
redetermination, 4.109
standing, 5.43
planning statutory reviews
case management, 5.36–5.38
compromise, 4.107
consent to judgment, 4.108
development plans, as to, 4.68–4.75
disclosure, 5.39
grant of planning permission or listed building consent, as to, 4.76–4.84
interim orders and relief, 4.58–4.62
introduction, 4.46–4.47
overlap between ss 288 and 289 TCPA, 4.94–4.96
practice directions, 4.48–4.53
pre-action responses, 4.2–4.12
redetermination, 4.109
refusal of planning permission or listed building consent, as to, 4.76–4.84
standing, 5.43
summary grounds of defence, 4.54–4.57
time limit, 4.63–4.67
practice directions
planning statutory appeals, 4.88–4.93
planning statutory reviews, 4.48–4.53
pre-action protocol, 4.2–4.12
redetermination, 4.109

Statutory challenges – *contd*
refusal of planning permission, as to
case management, 5.36–5.39
costs, 6.28
generally, 4.76–4.84
practice directions, 4.48
rejection of listed building consent, as to
case management, 5.36–5.39
generally, 4.76–4.84
practice directions, 4.48
relevant applications, 5.36
reviews
development plans, as to, 4.68–4.75
grant of planning permission or listed building consent, as to, 4.76–4.84
interim orders and relief, 4.58–4.62
introduction, 4.46–4.47
practice directions, 4.48–4.53
refusal of planning permission or listed building consent, as to, 4.76–4.84
summary grounds of defence, 4.54–4.57
time limit, 4.63–4.67
s 61N TCPA, under, 4.47
s 63 P(LBCA)A 1990, under
case management, 5.36–5.39
generally, 4.76–4.84
issuing claims, 3.97
practice directions, 4.48
s 65 P(LBCA)A 1990, under
calculation of time, 3.81
issuing claims, 3.105
permission hearing, 3.126
permission to proceed, 3.124
refusal of permission, 3.129
response to acknowledgement of service, 3.116
s 113 PCPA 2004, under
case management, 5.36–5.39
generally, 4.68–4.75
issuing claims, 3.97
practice directions, 4.48
s 287 TCPA, under
issuing claims, 3.97
practice directions, 4.48
s 288 TCPA, under
case management, 5.36–5.38
compromise, 4.107
consent to judgment, 4.108
development plans, as to, 4.68–4.75
disclosure, 5.39
grant of planning permission or listed building consent, as to, 4.76–4.84
interim orders and relief, 4.58–4.62
introduction, 4.46–4.47
issuing claims, 3.97

Statutory challenges – *contd*
s 288 TCPA, under – *contd*
overlap between ss 288 and 289 TCPA, 4.94–4.96
practice directions, 4.48–4.53
pre-action responses, 4.2–4.12
redetermination, 4.109
refusal of planning permission or listed building consent, as to, 4.76–4.84
standing, 5.43
summary grounds of defence, 4.54–4.57
time limit, 4.63–4.67
s 289 TCPA, under
case management, 5.40–5.44
compromise, 4.107
consent to judgment, 4.108
costs, 6.29–6.30
evidence, 4.102–4.104
interim orders, 4.99–4.101
introduction, 4.85–4.87
issuing claims, 3.97
overlap between ss 288 and 289 TCPA, 4.94–4.96
permission to proceed, 4.97–4.98
powers of court, 4.105–4.106
practice directions, 4.88–4.93
pre-action responses, 4.2–4.12
redetermination, 4.109
response to acknowledgement of service, 3.116
standing, 5.43
service, 3.101
simplified planning zone schemes, as to
practice directions, 4.48
standing
case management, 5.43
generally, 3.54–3.64
striking out
case management, 5.13
judicial review, 4.30
statutory reviews, 4.61
summary grounds of defence, 4.54–4.57
time limit, 4.63–4.67
Statutory reviews
See also **Statutory challenges**
case management, 5.36–5.38
compromise, 4.107
consent to judgment, 4.108
development plans, as to, 4.68–4.75
disclosure
case management, 5.39
interim orders, 4.62
grant of planning permission or listed building consent, as to, 4.76–4.84
interim orders and relief, 4.58–4.62
interim injunctions, 4.60
interim orders, 4.58–4.62

Statutory reviews – *contd*
interim relief
applications, 3.139–3.146
generally, 4.58–4.60
giving interim effect to enforcement notices, 5.60
powers of the court, 5.59–5.60
introduction, 4.46–4.47
overlap between ss 288 and 289 TCPA, 4.94–4.96
practice directions, 4.48–4.53
pre-action responses, 4.2–4.12
redetermination, 4.109
refusal of planning permission or listed building consent, as to, 4.76–4.84
standing, 5.43
summary grounds of defence, 4.54–4.57
time limit, 4.63–4.67
Strategic environmental assessment (SEA)
change in circumstances, 7.205
consultation, 7.208
future consent framework, 7.206–7.207
likely significant effects, 7.203–7.204
planning regulation, 1.35
reasonable alternatives, 7.201–7.202
Statement of community involvement
planning regulation, 1.22
Statements of common ground
jurisprudence, 7.210–7.211
Stay of proceedings
judicial review claims
case management, 5.4
interim relief, 5.54–5.56
Striking out
case management, 5.13
judicial review, 4.30
litigation procedure, 7.222
statutory reviews, 4.61
Structure plans
planning regulation, 1.20
Substitution of parties
case management, 5.12
Substantive hearings
appeals, 3.171–3.172
case preparation, 3.155–3.163
conduct, 3.164–3.165
costs, 3.169
judicial review, 4.44–4.45
permission to appeal, 3.170–3.171
relief, 3.166–3.168
Summary grounds of defence
judicial review, 4.16–4.27
statutory reviews, 4.54–4.57
Supply of housing
jurisprudence, 7.21
Supreme Court
resisting Planning Court claims, 4.112

T

Telephone hearings
case management, 5.4
Time limits
calculation of time for purposes of issue, 3.77–3.83
case management, 5.4
extension, 3.84–3.88
generally, 3.74–3.76
jurisprudence, 7.214–7.220
Timetabling
generally, 2.24–2.30
Totally without merit applications
judicial review claims, 4.31
litigation procedure, 7.235–7.236
Town and Country Planning Acts
central government's role, 1.17
change of use, 1.26–1.31
conservation area consent, 1.42
court's role, 1.52–1.59
current regime, 1.12–1.14
decision making
change of use, 1.26–1.31
deemed planning permission, 1.25
'development', 1.24
development management, 1.23
generally, 1.23
operational development, 1.25
deemed planning permission, 1.25
demise of 'exceptionalism', 1.44–1.51
'development', 1.24
development control, 1.23
development management, 1.23
development plans, 1.15–1.16
enforcement, 1.33
environmental regulation
EIA Directive, 1.35
general, 1.34–1.43
Habitats Directive, 1.36–1.39
impact assessment, 1.35
SEA Directive, 1.35
'exceptionalism', 1.44–1.51
forward planning, 1.15–1.22
general permitted development, 1.25
historical overview, 1.08–1.11
human rights, 1.40
land use, 1.17
listed building consent, 1.41
local planning authorities
decision-making, 1.23
development and use of land, 1.21
enforcement, 1.33
human rights, 1.40
land survey, 1.10
NPPF, 1.18
planning 'exceptionalism', 1.50
role of court, 1.53

Town and Country Planning Acts – *contd*
local plans, 1.21
material change of use, 1.26–1.31
National Planning Policy Framework, 1.17–1.18
National Planning Policy Guidance, 1.17
neighbourhood plans, 1.21
operational development, 1.25
planning permission
change of use, 1.26–1.31
deemed planning permission, 1.25
'development', 1.24
development management, 1.23
generally, 1.23
operational development, 1.25
Planning Policy Guidance Notes, 1.17
Planning Policy Statements, 1.17
regional development agencies, 1.20
regional planning, 1.20
role of the court, 1.52–1.59
statement of community involvement, 1.22
structure plans, 1.20
tree preservation, 1.43
use, 1.26–1.31
Transfer of proceedings
case management, 5.17
Planning Court claims, 2.3
Transport and Works Act 1992 applications
Planning Court claims, 2.3
Tree preservation
planning regulation, 1.43

U

Urgent claims
case management (judicial review claims), 5.30

V

Variation of orders
case management, 5.9
Venues
generally, 2.35–2.38
Very special circumstances
green belt, 7.155
Viability assessments
jurisprudence, 7.245–7.246
Village greens
legal principles, 7.169–7.170
Planning Court claims, 2.3

W

Waste control
Planning Court claims, 2.3
Wayleaves
Planning Court claims, 2.3
Whitley conditions
planning permissions, 7.139–7.140
Written evidence
case management, 5.20

www.ingramcontent.com/pod-product-compliance
Ingram Content Group UK Ltd.
Pitfield, Milton Keynes, MK11 3LW, UK
UKHW051416150926
475561UK00005B/199

9 781526 516725